Strength training is *the* most product
men *and* women. Here's why: It build
strengthens bones, improves overall f
caloric consumption, helps control bo
slows the effects of aging, increases re
transforms physical appearance.

No other single form of exercise can produce all these benefits. That's why strength training is the most important element of *The Program* of this book. And it's supplemented by other forms of exercise, to produce a *complete* program.

BUILD MUSCLE, LOSE FAT, LOOK GREAT

Why so much information?

The required know-how on fat loss is straight forward, but the required information on how to train, and build muscle, is extensive. To train safely and effectively, you must be expertly informed. This requires many pages of explanation. Thoroughness is essential.

Even if fat loss is your priority, building muscle is an indispensable part of the required strategy. Therefore, being thoroughly informed on physical training is still essential.

Beware of fads and gimmicks!

Some methods claim to produce maximum benefits from just 30 to 60 minutes of exercise per week. This is not supported by science, and usually ignores cardio training, and stretching. A greater investment is required to obtain the full benefits from training—but not the excessive time commitment that's common among trainees in almost all gyms.

Caution

Exercise produces great benefits *only* if it's done safely, and effectively. Done incorrectly, as is common in almost all gyms, exercise can do more harm than good. This book will teach you how to exercise safely, and effectively.

Two early reviews of this book

For over 20 years Stuart McRobert has been a voice of reason and honesty in a field usually devoid of both. Through hundreds of articles, HARDGAINER magazine, and his earlier books, Stuart has advocated sensible, safe training that produces good results for typical people. And Stuart has kept learning, and evolving his approach.

In **The Program** featured in his latest book—BUILD MUSCLE, LOSE FAT, LOOK GREAT—Stuart takes a person over a 12-month period of training in a highly systematic yet simple way. The overall approach is suitable for the novice and even the highly experienced trainee. The routines within **The Program** enable a person to gain appreciable strength and muscle mass without spending many hours per week in the gym.

And there's more to this book: An optimal program combines resistance training with cardiovascular training that's efficient and effective, and other healthy practices including nutrition, and physical activity outside of the gym. **The Program** provides the blueprint for a great overall approach to strength, physique, fitness, and health.

This book is likely the most complete, comprehensive guide to safe, effective, and healthy training. It surpasses McRobert's other books by representing his evolving and more scientifically based ideas about effective training, put together in a very readable and enjoyable package. In many respects, the book puts science into practice so that all readers can move toward optimizing their training and abilities.

The book is well-written, and easy to read. And it was written by someone who has paid his training dues. Stuart guides us through his own transformation from a person who was obsessed with the minute, inconsequential details of training, and whose life was utterly dominated by bodybuilding, to a person who seriously trains yet has a complete, balanced, and full life.

This wonderful book features lessons for effective training *and* for life.

Richard A. Winett, Ph.D. is the Heilig-Meyers Professor of Psychology at Virginia Tech in the USA, where he directs the Center for Research in Health Behavior and the Clinical Psychology program. Dr. Winett's primary interests are in disease prevention and health promotion. He has published almost 200 peer-reviewed articles and studies, and has received about 13 million dollars in funding for his research, primarily from the National Institutes of Health. An avid bodybuilder and lifter, Dr. Winett has been training for over 45 years. He publishes the MASTER TRAINER, available from www.ageless-athletes.com, which emphasizes health, fitness, and bodybuilding, combining science with practical applications.

BUILD MUSCLE, LOSE FAT, LOOK GREAT is for all trainees, both men and women. Stuart shares his extensive experience in an easy-to-understand way. His recommendations are thorough, practical, and easy to apply. And his emphasis on safe, effective yet time-efficient training allows you to maximize your progress while avoiding injuries.

This strength, muscle, and fitness book provides all the instructional tools you need in order to transform your body. **The Program** will take you month by month through all aspects of exercise, including strength training, cardiovascular work, and stretching.

Very importantly, Stuart explains how to modify **The Program** according to your training experience and any physical limitations or other special considerations you may have. And this is a drug-free, total fitness approach. By following his step-by-step guidelines you'll avoid common training mistakes, and see consistent, safe progress.

Conventional methods of training usually promote high-volume routines that commonly lead to overtraining and excessive time in the gym. And programs touted by elite bodybuilders and athletes don't take into consideration the concerns and limitations of most trainees. But Stuart's program is totally different.

Following McRobert's expert advice is like having your own personal trainer. For example, using detailed descriptions and hundreds of photographs he shows you correct lifting mechanics and superior technique—the cornerstones of any high-quality training program.

Be inspired to train correctly, make real progress, and see results fast!

And Stuart's highly effective, low-volume, low-risk program shows you that it's possible to achieve your fitness goals in a practical way *without* your training dominating your life.

Rachael E. Picone, MS, earned her Bachelor of Science degree in exercise science from Rutgers University, and her Master of Science degree in exercise physiology from The University of Massachusetts. She has two decades of diverse experience including cardiac rehabilitation, health education and promotion, sports and leisure management, and personal training. She has also worked as a strength coach, and has participated in competitive bodybuilding and mountain biking. Ms. Picone is a recognized speaker and author, and has contributed to MAXIMIZE YOUR TRAINING: INSIGHTS FROM LEADING STRENGTH AND FITNESS PROFESSIONALS (Masters Press, 1999) and THE FEMALE ATHLETE: TRAIN FOR SUCCESS (Wish Publishing, 2004). She resides in New Jersey, USA.

Abbreviated training works!

When done correctly, abbreviated training produces great results from much less gym time than most people believe is required. Abbreviated training is highly effective for strength training, muscle-building, body transformation, and fitness training in general.

The results you'll obtain from abbreviated training depend on your goals, your heredity, your age and gender, the form of abbreviated training you employ, and how well you apply yourself to your training and recuperation. Here are examples of the results:

"I've trained for about 25 years. For most of that time I've been a personal trainer, and I've worked with thousands of clients. I can summarize the formula for successful body transformation in four words: 'abbreviated training done correctly.'

"No one has written about 'abbreviated training done correctly' more thoroughly, carefully, and responsibly than Stuart. Follow the guidance given in this book, and forsake all the hype and bull that's rampant in the exercise world. Then you'll give yourself the best chance possible to achieve your goals for body transformation."

— Ian Duckett, *Body in Design Gym*, Leeds, England

"Since devouring the revelation of BRAWN, *Stuart's first book, I've trained in an abbreviated manner—for about 15 years. As a result I've made consistent progress but while still having the time to emphasize career and family pursuits. At 220 pounds bodyweight I've squatted well over 500 pounds, bench pressed nearly 400, and deadlifted 600, while competing drug-free and without support gear. These lifts are the result of my decision to paddle against the mainstream, while embracing the abbreviated training that Stuart promotes."*

— Chuck Miller, Nutter Fort, WV, USA

"I've been training for 26 years and I continue to be amazed at how effective abbreviated training can be when it's done correctly. I've long since reached my potential for building muscle mass. Even though I'm now busier than ever with my family and work, I was still able to lose a lot of bodyfat. I'm now strong, muscular, and lean, with sharp abs— a condition I couldn't achieve even when I was in my twenties. And I did this with very little time spent in the gym."

— Bill Piche, Marion, IA, USA

Why should you listen to me?

My qualifications for being able to help you include:

1. Over 30 years of personal experience of physical training.

2. A reputation for providing drug-free, non-commercialized, honest instruction free of any association with the food supplement and exercise equipment industries.

3. The experience of guiding countless people with their training.

4. A reputation for attention to detail, thoroughness, safety, and health that's rare in the training world.

5. Over 30 years of studying training.

6. Many years of conferring with colleagues who are strength trainers, coaches, chiropractors, and researchers. And this process is ongoing.

7. I edited a training magazine, HARDGAINER, for 15 years.

8. Since 1981 I've had over 400 articles on training published in newsstand magazines.

9. I've written four other books on training.

10. I have a degree in education.

11. I'm a qualified provider of Active Release Techniques®—a state-of-the-art, soft-tissue therapy for the treatment and prevention of injuries.

This book is my latest work, updating everything I've written previously, and including much information I've not written about before and that's not covered in any other book.

From just a few weeks of thorough study of this book you can learn what took me over 30 years to amass. The rewards will be great—the knowledge and wisdom you require to transform your body, improve your health, and enrich your life.

WOMEN . . .
"But we don't want big muscles."

The instruction in this book is for men *and* women, of all ages.

Many women are unwilling to strength train because they think it will develop big muscles. This concern is unfounded, and prevents them from obtaining the benefits that strength training produces.

Few women can develop big muscles even if they wanted to. Few women have the genetically determined characteristics required for strength training to yield big muscles.

Women are limited in strength and muscular size because of their hormones. They lack the large quantities of testosterone that produce many of the male characteristics. Furthermore, women generally have wider hips and narrower shoulders than men, have a higher bodyfat percentage, and carry most of their fat around their hips and thighs.

A tiny number of women have narrow hips, above-average testosterone production, longer muscle bellies than is typical for women, and little bodyfat. These women, when highly trained, and when enhanced by bodybuilding drugs, may obtain the extreme development of some competitive female bodybuilders. But for the huge majority of women, the development of big muscles is impossible.

If you're a woman with an unusual potential for developing muscle mass, but don't want to realize it, build the degree of muscle mass you're satisfied with, and then maintain it. Don't pursue greater mass. Focus on other components of overall physical fitness.

Women should train for strength and muscle. Even a little additional muscle can improve appearance greatly, and yield substantial health benefits. Aerobics alone won't do, and are overrated; and tinkering with bands and tiny dumbbells won't do. Serious strength training is needed for serious benefits.

This book will teach you how to realize as much of your potential for muscular development as you want.

BUILD MUSCLE
LOSE FAT
LOOK GREAT

Everything You Need to Know to Transform Your Body

First Edition

Stuart McRobert

CS PUBLISHING LTD
NICOSIA, CYPRUS

Cover design by Bright Ideas Graphics, copyright © 2006 by Stuart McRobert

CS Publishing Ltd., P.O. Box 20390, CY-2151 Nicosia, Cyprus
tel + 357-2233-3069   cspubltd@spidernet.com.cy
www.hardgainer.com

US office: CS Publishing Ltd., P.O. Box 1002, Connell, WA 99326
tel 509-234-0362   fax 509-234-0601   info@hardgainer.com
www.hardgainer.com

Printed and bound in the EU, by J.G. Cassoulides & Son Ltd., Nicosia, Cyprus
First printing 2006

Cataloging-in-Publication Data
McRobert, Stuart, 1958–
   Build muscle lose fat look great : everything you need
   to know to transform your body / Stuart McRobert. -- 1st ed.
      p. : photos. ; cm.
   Includes index.
   ISBN 9963-9163-0-9 (trade paper)
      1. Bodybuilding 2. Physical fitness 3. Exercise 4. Weight loss I. Title
613.7044 - dc22

CONTENTS

Introduction *1*
Four Preliminaries *4*

PART 1
The Foundation
1. Of first importance *13*
2. How to get training immediately *17*
3. The truth on age and exercise *71*
4. How to optimize your recuperative powers *75*
5. How to lose bodyfat *97*
6. Physical restrictions, and their correction or management *105*
7. Gym savvy, where to train, and gym conduct *123*

PART 2
How to Train
8. The essential terminology of training *137*
9. Cardio training *159*
10. How to avoid injuries *173*
11. Rep speed and control *189*
12. How to master exercise technique *193*
13. How to handle weights between exercises *403*
14. Seven extras for effective workouts *409*
15. How progressive resistance can help or hinder progress *417*
16. How to optimize your exercise selection from the gang of eight *423*
17. **The Program** *441*
18. Call to arms! *497*
19. Beyond **The Program** *501*

PART 3
Supplementary Material
20. Forewarned is forearmed *515*
21. What scientific studies really mean to you *523*
22. Burning issues *527*
23. A primer on anatomy *531*
24. The lexicon of muscle-building, and training *543*

About the author *611*
Resources *614*
Index *621*

Warning . . . SAFETY

Every effort was made in this book to stress the importance of correct technique, and safety measures, when using exercise programs. Regardless of your age, check with your physician to ensure that it's appropriate for you to follow such programs. Proceed with caution, and at your own risk.

Warning . . . DISCLAIMER

The purpose of this book is to provide information on bodybuilding, strength training, fitness training, fat loss, and related topics. It's sold with the understanding that neither the publisher nor author are engaged in providing legal, medical, or other professional services.

Every effort has been made to make this book as thorough and accurate as possible. Despite this, all information on the subject matter has not been included, and there may be mistakes in both content and typography.

CS Publishing, the author, and distributors of this book, shall have neither liability nor responsibility to any entity or person with respect to any injury, loss, or damage caused, or alleged to be caused, directly or indirectly, by the material in this book.

If you do not wish to be bound by the above, you may return your copy to the publisher for a full refund.

Before you start . . .

If you've never trained before, you're in a special position. By starting with a clean slate you can establish *only* good training habits. If you have some training experience you'll have adopted some bad habits. Clean your slate, and start afresh.

Especially if you're a beginner, you'll have little knowledge about training. This will make you vulnerable to being misled and scammed by fitness companies.

Forget the claims of fitness companies who promise near-effortless methods, and miraculous transformations. There's no effortless way to transform your body. Time and effort are needed, but not as much as you may think.

This book will teach you how to exercise safely and effectively, with minimal time investment.

Statement of intent

I am unequivocally against performance-enhancing drugs. I have no interest in drug-assisted training, but I'm not naive. I know much about the shambles of performance-enhancing drugs and dishonesty in the fields of muscle and might in particular, and in a lot of the sporting world in general.

Because I'm only interested in drug-free training, and primarily concerned with satisfying the needs of typical trainees, some of the methods and values promoted in this book are heretical relative to much of what's common in gyms today. There's no other approach to take if training methods that are safe, practical, and helpful for drug-free, typical people are to be promoted.

Acknowledgments

I would like to thank James Kiernan, DC, Dave Maurice, Gregory Steiner, DC, and Richard Winett, Ph.D., for providing input on sections of this book. Debts of appreciation are also owed to Carolyn Weaver for the index, and to J. G. Cassoulides & Son for the printing and binding.

A special debt of gratitude and appreciation is owed to Arty Conliffe. In his role as consultant and editor during the several years I required to write this book, Arty's rigorous input led me to a greater understanding of training, and writing style, to yield a much improved final product. Arty's contacts also led me to Active Release Techniques®, which helped to transform me physically, and also brought about a change of direction in my professional life.

A special debt of gratitude and appreciation is also owed to Dr. James Kiernan, a pre-eminent provider of Active Release Techniques. It was Jim's provision of ART® and other therapies—at his clinic in Rockaway Park, New York—that was responsible for healing my extensive, chronic injuries. The therapies will be explained in a chapter of this book.

Trademarks

All terms mentioned in this book that are known to be trademarks have been marked as such, but CS Publishing can't attest to the accuracy of this information. There may be unintentional omissions in acknowledging trademarks. The publication and use of this book doesn't affect the validity of any trademark or service mark.

Information boxes

There are information boxes throughout this book. The ones without shading mostly contain material unique to them, not excerpts from the general text. All the sidebars—the boxes with shading—contain material unique to them.

Both types of boxes contain information that's especially important.

Photography credits

I would like to thank the models, all of whom generously gave their time, and the gym owners, all of whom generously gave access to their premises. They were all wonderfully cooperative and patient.

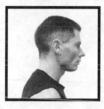

Left, Ian Duckett, owner of Body in Design Gym, in Leeds, England. Above, from the left, Claire Cotter, Helen Everson, Jenny Garside, and Robin Gorry. All photographs of these trainees were taken at Ian's gym.

Left, Con Demetriou. All photographs of Con were taken by Mike Christofides at what was then Gold's Gym in Nicosia, Cyprus. Con's photographs were first used in THE INSIDER'S TELL-ALL HANDBOOK ON WEIGHT-TRAINING TECHNIQUE.

Left, Eleni Papadopoulos. All photographs of Eleni were taken at Olympus Gym in Nicosia, Cyprus.

Here are the credits for the other models appearing in this book:

Brian Breech, pages 266 (top right), 267 (left), and 283 (top left, and bottom left); Brian Carlton, pages 393, and 395; Chip Kent, pages 272, 280, and 281; Brian Rayner, page 266 (top left, and top middle); Derek Wallace, page 372; Bill Windscheif, pages 56, 261, and 266 (bottom).

I'm just one of countless trainees who gave
their all to conventional training methods,
found them lacking, and THEN came across
alternative methods that work. This book
isn't based on one man's journey, but is a
distillation of the experiences and acquired
wisdom from generations of trainees.

As far as instruction goes, there's little that's new in the weight-training
world. Here's how I expressed this point in BRAWN: "Charles A. Smith,
over the time I knew him before his death in January 1991, used to
remind me that what we have today we owe to the past. How right he
was. As Chas used to put it, 'It's upon the pioneers' shoulders that we
have to stand in order to be as tall as they. We're merely the heirs of
those who have gone before us.'"

Charles Smith was a major figure working on Joe Weider's bodybuilding
magazines in the 1950s, and one of the final links with the pioneers of
muscle-building.

INTRODUCTION

Strength training, muscle-building, and fitness training in general, are exciting and satisfying because they can transform your body. But this is the case *only* if your training is working. If it's not working, training is hugely frustrating.

I started training in 1973, aged 15, when Arnold Schwarzenegger was in his prime as a bodybuilder. His training methods were promoted without caveats. The format was basically: "Here's how the champion does it. Train, eat, and take food supplements like the champion does, to become a champion yourself."

I was obsessed with trying to build a great physique. I trained as the famous bodybuilders of the time recommended. I became a recluse. All I wanted was to study physical training, train, and apply myself to recuperating between workouts.

I was gullible. I couldn't distinguish between good and poor instruction. If it was in print and supposedly written by a champion bodybuilder, I believed it.

I had no time for people who discussed realistic goals, overtraining, or the dangers of certain exercises and specific techniques.

Being young I could apparently get away with harmful training methods, but only temporarily. I paid for that recklessness and ignorance a few years later, when knee and back problems devastated my training. Had I listened to those people who urged a conservative approach to training, I probably wouldn't have caused the initial damage.

The need for caution, care, and education

Now, I promote a conservative approach to training. Experience from more than thirty years—from my own personal training, and from observing countless other trainees—has taught me that the conservative approach isn't only the safest way, it's the most effective over the long term.

The conservative approach isn't limited to exercise selection and technique. It also concerns exercise program design. Mainstream program design promotes an excessive volume and frequency of training, which is why most trainees overtrain.

In my youth I trained harder than anyone else at the gyms I attended, I ate well, I took lots of food supplements, and I got plenty of sleep. I epitomized dedication to bodybuilding. So I couldn't understand why I didn't make great progress. For a long time I didn't make any progress. It was only many years later that I understood why.

> *Only a minority of trainees aspire to the goals I did. Regardless of whether you want to build a lot of muscle, or only a little, the required know-how is the same.*
>
> *The mistakes I made as I tried to build a Mr. Universe physique, are made today by most gym members—whether bodybuilders, fitness trainees, or strength trainees.*

Firstly, I didn't have the genetic good fortune for muscle-building that bodybuilding's competitive elite have.

Secondly, I wasn't supplementing with anabolic steroids. I used to believe that the only supplements the bodybuilding elite took were vitamins, minerals, and protein shakes. (Anabolic steroids produce improved recuperation, greater muscle mass, and enable those who use them to tolerate high-volume training, *but at a cost to their health*.)

Thirdly, the training methods advocated by the elite bodybuilders retarded my development—they caused overtraining, injuries, and sickness. Countless other trainees have been similarly harmed. Elite bodybuilders have inspired millions, but they have also misled millions.

Countless others suffer in the same ways today because the instruction that misled me in the 1970s and 1980s is commonly rehashed (or reprinted) today.

When I learned about bodybuilding drugs, I was disciplined enough not to use them. I had enough sense to put my health first.

Train like a modern-day, elite bodybuilder and you'll never develop a terrific physique unless you're one of the minuscule few who have stellar genetic potential for bodybuilding.

Many trainees have suffered from the "train like a champion to become a champion" mentality, but eventually they learned the truth. Most trainees, however, don't know this truth. Consequently they will tread the same path of frustration that millions of others already have *unless* they are educated in an alternative way.

What not to do

Contrary to what conventional muscle-building and fitness-training methods would have you believe . . .

   1. You don't have to train with weights four, five, or six times a week.

2. You don't have to use high-volume training.

3. You don't have to take "bodybuilding supplements," although some food supplements may offer health benefits.

4. You don't have to use high-risk exercises or techniques, or apply the foolish "no pain, no gain" bravado.

5. And you don't have to use bodybuilding drugs.

But you do have to adopt a different approach to your training. There's a huge bonus on top of improved results—*reduced time spent in the gym*. You can achieve your exercise-related goals without sacrificing work or family life.

The RACE Method of Training

This book isn't written by a trainer of big-name bodybuilders, or by a big-name bodybuilder himself (or his ghostwriter). Such books are commonplace, and the lack of success they produce among typical trainees is also commonplace. A different approach is needed: the RACE Method of Training—*Responsible*, *Abbreviated*, *Conservative*, and *Effective*.

For training to be *responsible* and *effective* (and *safe*), it needs to be *abbreviated*, and *conservative*. This means training that's low in overall volume relative to gym norms, low-risk, cautious, and progressive in a gradual way. I define abbreviated training as brief strength-training workouts performed no more frequently than three times a week. The other components of a complete exercise program can also be abbreviated, and highly effective.

Abbreviated and conservative training methods are essential because only from careful progression on appropriate routines will you avoid injury and discouragement. To make excellent progress, you must train safely and consistently.

Properly done, the RACE Method of Training—through its sensible combination of strength training, cardiovascular work, and stretching—will transform your body externally and internally.

Read – Grasp – Apply – Persist . . . ACHIEVE!

FOUR PRELIMINARIES

I. Strength training, muscle-building, & bodybuilding

Some people use *strength training* synonymously with *bodybuilding*, while some others use strength training to refer to muscle-building *without* an association with the bodybuilding world. Some people also use strength training interchangeably with the terms *weight training*, *weight lifting*, *weightlifting*, and *resistance training*. Strictly, however, *weightlifting* is the specialized sport as performed in the Olympic Games. It consists of two events: the snatch, and the clean and jerk.

Training to increase strength is commonly part of bodybuilding, and muscle-building in general. This is especially the case for beginning and intermediate trainees. Advanced bodybuilders often focus on matters other than increasing their strength, including muscular hypertrophy without any strength gain, increased definition, overall muscular balance, and contest preparation.

Strength training is sometimes used for building strength when visible muscular hypertrophy is secondary, or even unwanted. In injury rehabilitation, for example, strength gain and functional improvement are the primary goals; and for some athletes, strength gain is desired but without significant muscular hypertrophy, because additional bodyweight may hinder their athletic performance, or alter their weight classes. There are, however, some footballers and rugby players, for example, who are dedicated to strength training but require hypertrophy and bodyweight gain, to help overpower opponents.

In this book, progressive resistance is a cornerstone of the weight-training routines. This is a form of strength training. At what pace, and to what degree it will produce strength improvements, or muscular hypertrophy, depends on the quality and consistency of training, how well the components of recuperation are satisfied, and the gender, age, and genetic potential for muscular growth of the individual. This form of strength training can also be called *bodybuilding*, and *muscle-building*.

The specific terminology used to describe the resistance training isn't important. What's important is that you train safely and effectively.

2. Genetic reality check

Genetics are the inherited instructions, or genes, that determine much of how you look and function, and how you respond to training. For training and physique improvement, know-how and dedication are essential, but how far you can go, at what pace, and what form the results will take, are determined by your genetics, or heredity.

As far as muscle-building goes, the phenomenally blessed—the genetic freaks, and I'm not using "freaks" in a pejorative sense—number fewer than 1% of the training population. The genetic freaks have a blend of body structure, muscle insertion points, neuromuscular efficiency, muscle belly length, muscle fiber type and number, tendency for leanness, recuperative powers, and resistance to injury that gives them *tremendously* responsive bodies, with potential for muscular development far in excess of that of the typical person.

Because of genetics, a few people are extremely responsive to cardiovascular training, a few have poor responsiveness, and most are somewhere in between. Only a few demonstrate phenomenal cardio fitness—such as Lance Armstrong, the seven-time winner of cycling's Tour of France. Most people have average cardio fitness potential.

Bodyfat storage patterns are genetically determined—for instance, it's possible to be lean overall and yet not have visible abdominal muscles.

It's true that many trainees get nowhere because they don't train well enough, long enough. But even had Woody Allen trained with greater dedication than Schwarzenegger, and taken more steroids, Schwarzenegger's physique would still have outclassed Allen's by far, such is their genetic disparity for bodybuilding.

Elite performers in the bodybuilding and fitness fields, and the world of athletics, usually minimize the role of genetics. For example, shortly after winning the 2003 London Marathon, in a world-record time, Paula Radcliffe was asked to what she owed her success: "Hard work, dedication, and the healing powers of emu oil." (Radcliffe had suffered injuries from a fall a few weeks prior to the race, and the emu oil was claimed to have helped her recovery.) Radcliffe is highly dedicated, and trains hard and consistently, but only together with phenomenal genetics for long-distance running can those

What can work well for the genetically gifted may be useless or even harmful for genetically typical trainees.

Goals

Set small, realistic, achievable goals.

If you're a beginner, you could, for example, set these initial targets: eat only healthy food, bring your bedtime forward half an hour, master the technique of the exercises in your program, train regularly, and lose half an inch around your waist.

If you're an experienced trainee, you could, for example, set these short-term targets: add 5% of extra resistance to each strength-training exercise in your program, increase the pace of your cardio exercise by 3%, and try a new, recommended strength-training exercise.

Achieve the small goals, set new ones, achieve them, set new goals, and so on . . . . Then your long-term success will be assured.

qualities yield stellar achievements. But Radcliffe made no reference to her genetic gifts.

The genetically gifted elite rarely acknowledge their inherited advantages, because to do so would make their achievements less impressive—their training know-how, hard work, and dedication would then be recognized as only *parts* of their success. Instead, the elite usually promote the view that it's their training know-how, hard work, and dedication that are *totally* responsible for their success. Furthermore, the elite tend to be in competition with other gifted individuals, and rarely notice ordinary trainees, let alone try to understand typical trainees' concerns and limitations.

Everyone can improve their bodies, and most people can improve enormously, but only a minuscule few have the genetic package required for superstar accomplishments. Genetics hold sway. *But genetic limitations shouldn't be used as excuses not to seek improvement.*

The best you can do, is the best you can do. Compete with *yourself*. Keep bettering yourself, again and again and again and again . . . .

There isn't an exercise-free method of exercising; there isn't an exercise-free method of building strength and muscle, and fitness in general; there isn't an exercise-free method of transforming your body externally and internally; and there isn't an exercise-free method of minimizing the effects of aging.

3. Fitness, and muscle-building

Fitness is relative to a given activity. For example, someone who's fit for playing as a goalkeeper in soccer may not be fit for playing as a forward, and fitness for running doesn't transfer to fitness for swimming. This book promotes total fitness, for a vigorous, healthy life. This total fitness is comprised of five components:

Strength and lean muscular development

Cardiovascular conditioning

Flexibility

General activity

Non-exercise factors, including healthy nutrition, not smoking, no drug abuse, sufficient quantity and quality of sleep, moderate exposure to sunlight (but don't get burned), good posture, healthy relationships, and satisfying work.

For sportsmen and women, the additional component of skills specific to a given sport would be necessary to be totally fit for that activity.

It's possible to be strong and well-developed, but physically unfit. Some strong, well-developed men may collapse if you make them run up just three flights of stairs.

It's also possible to be physically fit, but not healthy. Some marathon runners have died prematurely, because unbeknown to them they had heart disease and other problems. That they were fit enough to run marathons was no assurance that they were healthy internally. If your nutrition is poor, if you don't sleep well, if your relationships are full of conflict, if you smoke, if you take recreational or performance-enhancing drugs, if you misuse medical drugs, or if you hate your work, your overall physical fitness will be undermined.

Muscle-building, and strength training in general, focus on the strength and muscular development component of fitness, but, for most trainees, dietary control is also needed to produce a comparatively lean body.

Strength training doesn't produce only strength gains and aesthetic improvements. It produces many invisible physiological benefits. For example, it can improve blood test results, reduce resting blood pressure, increase resting energy

Low-intensity, general activity in moderation may help the body to hasten recovery from hard training. Total inactivity may delay recovery.

consumption (because of increased muscle mass), increase bone density, and improve cardiovascular efficiency. Strength training can also contribute to enhancing flexibility, provided that full ranges of motion are used in most exercises.

It isn't just cardio exercise that's good for one's health, provided it's done safely. Some scientists believe that safe, progressive, and consistent strength training may offer more health benefits than cardio exercise alone, or any other single exercise modality.

Cardiovascular conditioning is best provided through specialized, steady-state cardio work like that described later—"steady state" means maintaining a given elevated heart rate for a sustained period (usually predetermined).

General activity is an important component of total fitness, but neglected even by many ardent trainees. If you're already active, you may have the general activity component of total fitness covered. But if you're sedentary outside of your strength and cardio workouts, more general activity is needed. For example, hike or walk at a decent pace, or do garden work, for at least three hours total spread over the week—preferably about half an hour every day—to produce the minimum of general activity needed for some semblance of total physical fitness. Other ways of increasing general activity include walking to work, if practical. Alternatively, get off the train or bus early and walk the rest of the way to work, for example. And use stairs instead of elevators.

Two strength-training workouts per week, for example, may appear like a lot of exercise. Although strength training produces substantial physical benefits, it doesn't involve much exercise time, or caloric expenditure. More than half a typical workout is spent resting between sets and exercises, and most reps of a workout aren't demanding because it's only the final reps of a given set that are difficult. Consequently, not much time is spent on demanding training during a weights workout. That's why it's important to do cardio work, and general activity outside of the gym.

To look and feel better, to be stronger, fitter, and more resistant to injury, and to experience extensive internal health benefits, you must follow a good exercise program with regularity, and over the long term. Thirty minutes each week isn't enough, and neither is just an hour.

You've got to invest sufficient time and effort each week, but the RIGHT type of effort.

Make exercise a priority. Commit, and then you'll reap the rewards.

4. Too much exercise for you to handle?

Adopt a gradual approach.

If you're currently inactive, the prospect of strength training, stretching, cardio work, and general activity outside of the gym, may be overwhelming. While the introductory exercise program described in Chapter 2 is modest, the entirety of **The Program** described in Chapter 17 may appear to be too much at first investigation. If so, leave the cardio work and general activity of **The Program** until later. Focus on the strength training and a streamlined version of the flexibility routine. Then gradually work in the other components. Here's an illustration, with each phase lasting about two months:

Phase one

Strength training, and stretches 1, 2, 4, 5, and 7 (see Chapter 2).

Phase two

Strength training, full stretching routine, and walking for half an hour two times a week.

Phase three

Strength training, full stretching routine, adoption of the cardio program.

Phase four

Strength training, full stretching routine, cardio program, and general activity out of the gym for half an hour per day.

The Program in this book has been written as if you are adopting, right from the start, all three gym activities—strength training, stretching, and cardio work—and the general activity component outside of the gym. But this approach may not be for you. It's critical that you don't perform more exercise than you can presently handle. You may be best off adopting the gradual approach.

Take heart . . . as you adjust to an active lifestyle, and make physical training an important part of your life, you'll probably discover that a program that may have seemed overwhelming to begin with, is actually modest and manageable.

Part I

The Foundation

1. Of first importance 13
2. How to get training immediately 17
3. The truth on age and exercise 71
4. How to optimize your recuperative powers 75
5. How to lose bodyfat 97
6. Physical restrictions, and their correction or management 105
7. Gym savvy, where to train, and gym conduct 123

Here's what Charles A. Smith told me shortly before his death in 1991:

"You never know how important good health is, until you no longer have it."

Think about this. Dwell on it. Make it one with you.

Health is great wealth and should be revered, and preserved. Avoid all harmful habits, activities, and environments. Look after yourself!

Charles Smith was a major figure working on Joe Weider's bodybuilding magazines in the 1950s, and one of the final links with the pioneers of muscle-building.

Of first importance

Health

Train for health *and* physique, not just physique. Health comes first. You may not believe it now if you're young, but you *will* believe it later on when you're not-so-young.

Health is great wealth. When you're healthy, all problems and challenges can be tackled. Without your health, the problems and challenges of life are magnified.

Being well-developed, strong, and fit doesn't necessarily mean you're healthy, although it's better to be strong and fit, than weak and unfit. Many strong, well-developed bodybuilders and strength athletes neglected their health *because* they felt so strong and vigorous. The neglect eventually caught up with them, and they lost their strength and development. Exercise can't compensate for abuse and neglect in other areas.

Even exercise itself can be harmful to your health. Because of ignorance or foolishness, many trainees have damaged their bodies through exercise. This book will teach you how to train safely and effectively, *and* introduce you to other components of healthy living.

Dangerous bodybuilding drugs are endemic in the training world. *Train without bodybuilding drugs!* Some former, highly successful bodybuilders and strength athletes are testimonies to lives ruined by a drug-fueled obsession. Many have ruined their health as a result of taking performance-enhancing drugs, and some have died prematurely. When young and vigorous, and seemingly indestructible, they took big risks with their health with little or no consideration for future repercussions.

Physical care of your body isn't enough. If you live with resentment, anger, or other destructive emotions, you'll tear yourself apart from within. Happiness is an essential part of good health.

Appreciate what's going well in your life. Most people focus on what they *don't* have, rather than focus on what they *do* have.

While I was writing this book, a friend dropped dead from a heart attack, in front of his young children. He was 36 years old. This young man had neglected his health. His premature death robbed him of his most productive years, traumatized his family, and left a financial mess.

Never take good health for granted. It needs to be worked at. Take all possible actions to preserve good health— for your sake *and* those who depend on you.

Don't do anything that will undermine your health. Don't smoke; don't drink more than three glasses of wine or three half pints of beer a day for a man, or no more than two-thirds of that for a woman; don't take recreational drugs; don't take performance-enhancing drugs; don't misuse medical drugs; and don't exercise in an abusive manner. Do eat healthily, exercise regularly and safely, and sleep well. And find work and relationships that make you happy.

While I made many mistakes with my training and nutrition when I was young, I never got into drugs. While I injured myself repeatedly due to training ignorance and foolishness, I had enough sense to stay drug-free. Consequently, today I'm not dealing with drug-related health problems in my middle age, unlike many of my peers who *did* take performance-enhancing drugs—primarily anabolic steroids.

The greatest benefits from exercise

During my youth I sought muscle and strength primarily for aesthetic reasons, and I mistakenly thought that training was for young people only. Today, I still have aesthetic concerns, and I still love to train—I would continue to train for those reasons alone. But it's the health-related benefits of muscle and strength that are most important.

As well as building strength and developing muscle, strength training strengthens bones, improves overall fitness, increases the body's caloric consumption, helps control bodyfat, improves posture, slows the effects of aging, and increases resistance to injury. No other single form of exercise can produce all these benefits. That's why strength training is the most important element of **The Program** of this book. And it's supplemented by other forms of exercise, to produce a *complete* program and *further* health benefits.

The health benefits from *The Program* are extensive, and *additional* to the appearance benefits.

Time and effort put into *The Program* aren't expenditures. They are *investments* in your health and well-being. But for the fullest benefits, exercise must be a permanent part of your lifestyle.

Health tests

A regular, thorough physical examination that includes blood pressure, blood and urine tests, an electrocardiogram, and perhaps an exercise stress test, too, will help you to discover how you're doing *internally*. If you're under age 35, have the examination every three years. If you're over 35, have the examination annually. Consult your physician for the procedure to follow that's most appropriate for you.

Discuss with your doctor any predispositions for health problems that may exist in your family history, and the preventive lifestyle and dietary actions you should take.

An interesting project is to monitor changes in your test results following the implementation of **The Program**, and improvements in your nutrition.

The joy of exercise

Safe and effective exercise doesn't just produce great results. The training itself is enjoyable.

Train properly, and you'll experience the exercise high. Your workouts will become an essential part of your life— and they will make you look better, function better, and feel better.

Done properly, exercise isn't drudgery. It's a blessing, and a joy.

Start out *conservatively*. Your body has tremendous abilities of adaptation provided you start out comfortably, and increase the demands incrementally. This applies to all forms of physical training—resistance training, stretching, and cardio work.

2

How to get training immediately

Here's the quick-start information—the preparatory period of four weeks for beginners, and two weeks for other trainees. A gym is not needed for this period.

Before you start exercising, visit your doctor to get consent for starting an exercise program. Then visit a chiropractor—preferably one who is also trained in Active Release Techniques®—to see if you have one or more of common conditions such as scoliosis, tilted pelvis, limbs that may appear to be different in length, excessive lordosis or other postural problems, spondylosis, foot problems, and flexion imbalances between one side of your body and the other. Any of these conditions can influence your choice of exercises, because some movements may not be suited to you. You may not be aware that you have any of these conditions, so it's critical that you investigate the possibility. If you suffer from any of these conditions, perhaps they can be corrected, or at least minimized.

The preparatory month for beginners

I. Exercise

   a. Calisthenics

   b. Stretching

   c. Rehearsal of exercise technique for your first strength-training routine.

   d. Aerobic work

   Train at home, as described in this chapter.

2. Gym hunt

   Find a suitable gym by following the guidelines given in Chapter 7.

3. Study

   a. During the first two weeks of the preparatory period of training, study Chapters 1 through 8.

   b. By the end of the preparatory month, give priority to Chapters 9 through 11, and 13 through 16, and the early part of Chapter 17 (through to the first two weeks of training in a gym).

   c. Later on, study the rest of the book.

   Be patient. There's much to study if you're to become expertly informed.

4. Nutrition

   Establish good nutritional habits as outlined in this chapter.

5. Sleep

   If you need to be woken by an alarm clock, and if you regularly drink coffee, you're almost certainly not sleeping in enough quantity or quality. Take action to improve the quantity and quality of your sleep.

What if you already train in a gym?

1. If you've been training for only a few months, consider yourself still a beginner, and follow the preparatory month as written. Look for a gym only if you're not satisfied with where you train now.

2. If you've been training for more than about six months . . .

   a. Take a two-week break from training in the gym. You're probably in need of a rest, and may have accumulated some aches and pains as a result of incorrect exercise technique. Use the two weeks to get rested, healed, and re-educated on training. During this time, start on the stretching routine given in this chapter, establish good nutritional habits as outlined in this chapter, and improve the quantity and quality of your sleep. *And* study Chapters 1 through 11, and 13 through 16.

   b. Then start **The Program**, described in Chapter 17. Use the exercise technique instruction from the appropriate sections of Chapter 12. Follow the guidelines of **The Program** other than the starting weights. It's imperative that you learn correct exercise technique, apply it, and adhere to it steadfastly. Consequently you must start with no more than half of your usual weights for the exercises in **The Program** that you're familiar with. You probably need to *unlearn* faulty exercise technique. For exercises that are new to you, proceed as described in Chapter 17.

   c. Later on, study the rest of the book.

Be patient. There's much to study if you're to become expertly informed.

Technical accuracy

Throughout this book, strict anatomical definitions of arm, forearm, thigh, and leg are used. This means avoiding ambiguous terms such as *lower leg, upper leg, lower arm,* or *upper arm,* and not using *arm* and *leg* to encompass undetermined portions of the upper and lower extremities respectively. The leg is the portion between the foot and the knee, the thigh is the portion between the knee and the hip, the forearm is the portion between the hand and the elbow, and the arm is the portion between the elbow and the shoulder.

The word *flex* is used in this book only as the opposite of *extend*. Flex is commonly used to mean *make tense* but *without* flexion.

Exercise overview for beginners

1. Calisthenics

To introduce you to progressive resistance training, perform calisthenics. These are exercises that don't require a gym or any formal exercise equipment, although these same movements can also be done with gym equipment and progressive resistance in the form of weight plates. The five calisthenic exercises are crunches (sometimes called crunch sit-ups), floor back extensions, freehand squats, floor push-ups (often called press-ups), and chair chin-ups.

2. Stretching

Three times a week, immediately after the calisthenics, while your muscles are warm, perform the stretching routine. Chances are that you're insufficiently flexible, especially in your lower body. A careful, progressive stretching routine on alternate days is needed, to limber you up. Thereafter you'll be better able to adopt the correct technique in the exercises that demand suppleness. Although you may be flexible enough in some bodyparts, you may not be in others.

A limber body isn't required just for training. Insufficiently flexible muscles cause problems elsewhere. They are involved in faulty posture, and posture deterioration associated with aging. Insufficiently flexible muscles are also involved in other physical problems, such as chronic pain or discomfort in the knees and lower back.

3. Exercise technique rehearsal

After stretching, go through the technique rehearsal for the strength-training exercises you'll use during your first routine in the gym. The technique rehearsal instructions are given later in this chapter.

4. Aerobic work

After the technique rehearsal, go for a walk. This will introduce you to structured aerobic work during specific times.

Units of measurement

Imperial and metric units are used interchangeably in this book. An inch is about two and a half centimeters, four inches is about ten centimeters, and a foot is about 30 centimeters. A pound is about 0.45 kilogram, and about 2.2 pounds comprise one kilogram.

All exercises must be performed under CONTROL, *in a* DELIBERATE, SMOOTH *manner—two to three seconds for each descent, and a further two seconds for each ascent, with a brief pause between the phases. If in doubt, move slower not faster. Keep all movements* SMOOTH.

Photographs can't show all the details of exercise technique. Please study all the written instructions carefully, in order to learn how to master exercise technique.

Technique of the calisthenic exercises

1. Crunch (modified)

This exercise primarily works the abdominal muscles.

Get a chair, bench, or box. Lie on your back on the floor, with a folded towel under your hips and back, for padding. Bend your knees and place your calves on the elevation. Keep your knees bent at about a right angle. Don't cross your ankles.

Rest your hands on the floor by your sides. Keep your arms and forearms relaxed, and feet immobile, then lift the tip of your lower back (sacrum and coccyx) slightly off the floor and press the rest of your lower back against the floor, and then take two seconds to roll your upper torso off the floor. Hold the top position for a second, then unfurl over a further two seconds. Once your upper back returns to the floor, again press your lower back against the floor, and initiate the next repetition, or rep.

There are several forms of the crunch. Here are three of them, as described in the text.

Don't lift your entire torso off the floor—your lower back should retain contact with the floor throughout. Keep your chin off your chest during each rep, and keep your hands on the floor, and relaxed. Exhale during the ascent, and inhale during the descent; or, breathe freely and continuously throughout each rep. Keep your lips apart throughout each set (a sequence of reps).

Once you can perform 15 crunches, perform the exercise with your hands crossed on your chest, to increase the resistance. Once you can perform 15 reps that way, place your fingers on your cheeks, forehead, or temples.

2. Floor back extension

This exercise primarily works the lower back, mid back, buttocks, and rear thighs.

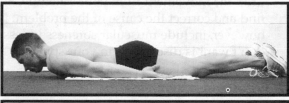

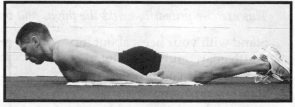

Lie face down on the floor. Lift your head so that your chin clears the floor. Rest the back of your hands on the floor by your sides, and keep your feet together. Without using your hands to assist you, slowly and smoothly lift your torso off the floor. Lift your torso until most of your rib cage just clears the floor. Hold the raised position for two seconds, then lower over a further two seconds. Repeat. Perform six reps, then rest a minute.

Now for the work set. While raising your torso, simultaneously lift your feet while keeping your knees straight, or almost straight, with your toes pointed. Smoothly and

Maintain a neutral neck position—neither flexed nor extended. The above photograph shows a somewhat extended neck. And the knees are flexed too much.

slowly lift your feet until your knees just clear the floor. At that point, most of your rib cage should also just clear the floor. At the top of each rep, hold for two seconds. Lower over a further two seconds. Exhale during the ascent, inhale during the descent; or, just breathe freely and continuously throughout each rep without holding your breath.

If this full technique is too difficult, for the moment, do the best you can, and gradually increase the range of motion from workout to workout, strength permitting.

Once you can perform 15 full reps, increase the resistance. Cross your forearms and keep them against your chest for the duration of each set. To further increase resistance, keep your arms straight out in front.

If you have a history of back problems, this exercise may irritate your spine. Provided the exercise is performed with smooth technique, without an exaggerated arch, and is introduced in a careful manner, it will be safe and effective for most trainees. If you experience any negative reaction to this exercise—during performance, or afterward—drop the movement from your schedule, and seek professional help to find and correct the cause of the problem. Negative reaction doesn't, however, include muscular soreness unless it's extreme. What you don't want is discomfort in your spine (or any other bony bodypart).

3. Freehand squat

This exercise primarily works the thighs and buttocks.

Stand with your heels about hip-width apart, and toes pointed out somewhat. If you imagine you're standing on a large clock face, with your feet being the outside ends of the hands of the clock, your feet would be positioned somewhere between "ten to two" and "five to one," according to what feels most comfortable. Raise your arms out in front, and keep them in that position during the set. Don't look down—keep your eyes looking forward.

Pull your shoulders back and stick your chest out, take a deep breath, then squat down slowly as if you were sitting down onto a chair. Take two to three seconds for the descent. Squat down as far as is comfortable for you, ideally to about where your upper thighs are parallel with the floor. Then immediately but slowly ascend. Take two to three seconds for the ascent, and exhale on the ascent. While standing, pull your shoulders back once more and stick your chest out, take a deep breath, and immediately but slowly descend into the next rep.

As you descend and ascend, don't allow your knees to buckle inward. Keep your knees pointing in the same direction as your feet.

If balance is a problem, you may find it impossible to keep your heels flat on the floor. Regular practice of the stretching routine will increase your flexibility, which in turn should help your squatting technique. At first, however, descend in the squat only as far as you can without your heels coming off the floor. Eventually, you should be able to descend deeper while keeping your heels on the floor.

4. Floor push-up

This exercise primarily works the chest, triceps, and shoulders.

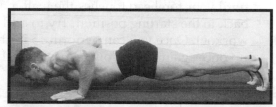

Lie on the floor, face down. Place your hands at the sides of your chest, palms flat on the floor, two to three inches (or five to eight centimeters) away from your rib cage. Spread your fingers and keep all the digits other than your thumbs pointing forward. Keep your elbows approximately above your wrists at all times. Keep your eyes directed at the floor below your face. Pull your toes as far as you can toward your knees then take your weight on your toes, hands, and chest. Your knees should be straight, and off the floor.

Keep a rigid, straight line between your shoulders and heels, and slowly push until your elbows are straight. Take two to three seconds for the ascent, and exhale during the ascent. At the top position, take a deep breath while sticking your chest out, and immediately yet slowly descend, over a further two to three seconds. Maintain the rigid, straight line between your shoulders and heels. Brush the floor with your chest, pause for a second without relaxing, then slowly push up and exhale on the ascent.

If that technique is difficult—as it will be for most women—and you can't do at least six reps, start out with the modified version. Perform the push-up with your hands placed on boxes or a low table.

If this is still too difficult, perform the exercise with your hands on the edge of a desk. Position your feet so that the edge of the desk touches your chest just below your nipples, at the bottom of each rep.

If the desk push-up is still too difficult, use the wall push-up. (The more you elevate your torso, the less stressful the push-up.) Stand on a non-slip floor two to three feet from a wall. Place your hands on the wall at about chest height, and a little wider than shoulder-width apart. Keep your back straight—don't sag—and bend at your elbows until your forehead touches the wall, pause for a second, then push back to the starting position. Try to add reps, from workout to workout. Once you can perform 15 in this manner, try the desk push-up once again. Once you've mastered the desk push-up, progress to the box push-up, and so on.

If you can perform 15 floor push-ups, elevate your feet on a low box, to increase resistance. This will reduce the reps. Then gradually build up the reps.

5. Chair chin-up

This exercise primarily works the upper back, and biceps.

Take a sturdy broom handle, and use it as your bar. Put two chairs side-by-side two to three feet apart, with the backs of the chairs facing in the same direction. Rest the bar across the chair seats, but put a folded towel over each seat under the bar, to help reduce bar movement. Alternatively, you could use two benches or boxes of sufficient height.

Sit on the floor and slide under the bar. While lying on the floor under the bar, grab it with your palms facing toward you, about shoulder-width apart, and your forearms perpendicular to the floor. Bend your knees fully, and draw your feet as close to your buttocks as possible. The starting position has your feet, buttocks, and back flat on the floor.

Your feet act as the pivot point. Take two to three seconds to pull until your chest touches the bar—or as near to the bar as possible. Hold for a second, then take two to three seconds to lower yourself. Once your back has touched the floor, pause for a second, then ascend again, over two to three seconds. Exhale during the ascent, inhale during the descent; or, breathe freely and continuously throughout each rep.

Starting position for the chair chin-up.

The range of motion will be determined by the height of the seats, your torso depth, and your arm and forearm lengths. By keeping your feet close to your buttocks, the exercise should be manageable for most trainees. Fine-tune the position of your feet to make the exercise comfortable. If, however, you can barely perform a few full reps, reduce the range of motion by putting some cushions beneath you. Even if you can only manage a range of motion of a few inches, that will suffice at first. Increase the range of motion later, as your strength increases.

Once you can perform 15 reps full reps, change the anchor point. Move your feet forward a little. This will increase the difficulty of the movement. Once you can perform 15 reps in this way, move your feet forward a little further, and so on. Alternatively, you could increase the range of motion by raising the height of the bar—for example, place an additional folded towel on each seat, beneath the bar.

Stretching routine, for ALL trainees

A flexible body is a requirement for the performance of correct exercise technique. If, for example, your hamstrings (rear of your thighs) are tight, that will proscribe correct squatting technique because it will lead to premature rounding of your lower back. A flexible body is also required for youthfulness, regardless of age.

Although flexibility is an important factor behind the ability to perform the major exercises correctly—for instance, the squat, and the deadlift—there are other important factors, including technique, practice, and inherited leverage factors.

Most people lack sufficient flexibility because of inactivity, or limited activity. Bodyweight and leverages also affect flexibility. A fat person, for example, may be inflexible because of the excess fat getting in the way.

While strength-training exercises can help improve flexibility where suppleness may be lacking, specific stretching is needed, too. Stretching is an important part of a complete exercise program.

Stretching elongates muscles, not tendons or ligaments. Tendons and ligaments are almost inelastic. Muscles need to be lengthened only a little to produce significant improvement in a joint's range of motion.

After a few months of regular use of a balanced program of stretches, you may increase your flexibility substantially. Thereafter you'll need to keep stretching in order to maintain your improved flexibility.

Introductory guidelines

Ideally, stretch immediately after you've done some resistance training, or immediately after a stint of aerobic exercise. Then your muscles will be warm, and many of your joints will be lubricated with synovial fluid. This will help to develop flexibility more quickly, reduce discomfort during the stretches, and decrease the chance of injury. When you stretch at another time, warm up first with five or more minutes of low-intensity work on, for example, an exercise bike, treadmill, or ski machine. Alternatively, go for a brisk walk, walk up and down a few flights of stairs, or do some easy calisthenic exercises for a few minutes. Stretch in a warm room, and keep yourself covered.

Sometimes it's necessary to stretch before you train with weights. This would follow the general warm-up work that should open every strength-training workout. If some muscles are tight, especially on one side of your body only, stretch to remove that tightness. If you don't get both sides equally pliable, you may promote asymmetrical exercise technique, which would increase the risk of injury. For example, assume that your right hamstring muscles are tighter than those on your left. When you squat, the less flexible right hamstrings may stop lengthening while the left ones keep lengthening. That would lead to asymmetrical exercise technique.

Especially prior to squatting and deadlifting, check for flexibility imbalances between the two sides of your body, and invest time in additional warming up and stretching to rectify imbalances. If you're equally stiff on both sides of your body, you may not set yourself up for asymmetrical technique, but you should still invest the time to get yourself loosened up to your normal state of flexibility. During the strength-training routines in this book, specific stretching is recommended immediately prior to squatting and deadlifting.

How to stretch

Stretching is dangerous if done incorrectly. If you try to rush your progress, you'll get hurt. Never force a stretch. Work progressively— within a given workout, and from week to week—until you reach the level of flexibility that you'll maintain. Never bounce while stretching. And avoid holding your breath—breathe rhythmically.

Don't move immediately into your usual level of flexibility for a given stretch. Work into that over several progressive stretches, each one taking you a little further than the previous one. You should feel only slight discomfort as you stretch.

Unless a different procedure is described for a specific stretch that follows, do the minimum of three reps of 20 to 45 seconds for each stretch. Be cautious—do more rather than fewer progressive stretches before getting to your current limit stretch.

As you hold each rep of a stretch, you should feel the muscular tension diminish. Depending on the stretch, and the individual, you may need to hold a stretch for up to 45 seconds (and perhaps even longer) before you feel this slackening. The easing of tension is the signal to relax for a few seconds, then move further into the stretch in order to make the muscle(s) feel tight again. If you don't feel the tension diminishing even after a hold of 45 to 60 seconds, let the stretch go for a few seconds, then slowly move into the next rep.

Never force yourself to feel pain, but you must feel tension during each stretch. Never have anyone force you into a stretch. And never be in a hurry.

Some days you'll be less flexible than on others, so don't expect to stretch equally well every session.

Stretching is a pleasure, if done properly. Enjoy it!

Here are essential stretches for preparing your body for the resistance training promoted in this book. Perform the stretches on three non-consecutive days per week.

Some stretches are performed on the floor. Be careful how you get up from lying supine, or you may irritate your lower back. Don't sit up with straight knees. While on your back, bend your knees and, with your knees held above your chest, briskly roll off your back into a sitting position. As an alternative, roll to one side and, using your hands for assistance, push into a sitting position.

Eye exercises

Eye muscles need exercise. Under-exercised, weak eye muscles hinder vision. Many people have reported an improvement in their eyesight following regular practice of eye exercises. I started performing eye exercises as a teenager, when I used to wear glasses. I've not worn glasses since then, and over 30 years later I still perform eye exercises regularly.

Prior to each session of stretching, spend a few minutes on these five eye exercises:

1. Keeping your head and neck still, eyes open, look up as high as possible, and then down as low as possible. Repeat at least ten times.

2. Keeping your head and neck still, eyes open, look as far to your right as possible, and then to your left. Repeat at least ten times.

3. Keeping your head and neck still, eyes open, move your eyes from upper left, to lower right. Repeat at least ten times. Then do the same from upper right, to lower left, for at least ten times.

4. Keeping your head and neck still, eyes open, simultaneously roll both of your eyes clockwise for at least ten circles. Then roll your eyes counter-clockwise for at least ten circles.

5. Keeping your head and neck still, eyes open, put your index finger 6 to 12 inches (15 to 30 cms) in front of your eyes. Focus on it until it's sharp; then, without moving your finger or head, focus on a distant object until that's sharp. Focus to and fro at least ten times. Vary the distances of your finger and objects from session to session.

Close and relax your eyes for about 30 seconds after each eye exercise.

1. Calves

Stand near a support such as a door frame, or a wall. Place the balls of your feet on a book, board, or side-by-side weight plates about half an inch or one centimeter thick, and your heels on the floor. Stand upright, with straight knees, and feel the tension in your calves. You may feel more tension in one calf than the other. After the tension has eased, lean forward until you again feel tension in your calves. After the tension has eased, lean forward a little more, until you feel tension once again. Keep your heels on the floor throughout this stretch.

The stretch may also be done one foot at a time, as illustrated.

Develop symmetrical flexibility.

As the weeks go by, you may need to increase the thickness of the board or plates, to produce the required tension in your calves. If you feel tension behind your knees, you're overstretching or rushing the stretch, and you should ease back.

If your calves are tight, you may not need any elevation to begin with. Work onto the elevation after a few weeks, as your calves increase in flexibility.

This stretch is for the calf muscle, not the Achilles tendon. As noted already, tendons are almost inelastic.

2. Groin muscles and thigh adductors

Sit with your torso vertical and
back resting against a wall. Bend
your knees while keeping your
feet on the floor. Put the soles of
your feet against each other at a
comfortable distance from your
hips, and rest their outside edges
on the floor. Your legs and thighs
should form a rhombus.

Let gravity gently pull your knees
toward the floor. You may feel
tension more in one thigh than
the other. Hold for about a minute, straighten your knees, adopt the
stretch again, and gravity will pull on a more supple lower body.

Keep your torso upright, with your back and head against the wall.
Don't round your back, lean forward, bounce, or push on your knees.
Haste or incorrect technique may produce a groin injury. You
shouldn't feel tension in the area in front of your pubic bone, because
that can lead to injury. If there is tension at your pubic bone, move
your feet outward, and progress at a slower pace.

Develop symmetrical flexibility.

After at least a month, rest your
hands on your knees for added
resistance, and after no less than
a further month, push downward
very gently. But don't force your
knees downward.

To progress in flexibility, bring
your heels gradually closer to
your hips. Progress will be slow,
however, so be patient. But
before you bring your heels
closer to your pelvis, you should be able to place your outer legs
flat on the floor at your current foot positioning. The trainee
demonstrating this stretch should increase her flexibility at the
illustrated foot positioning before moving her heels inward.

> *Breathe continuously as you stretch. Don't
> hold your breath.*

3. Hip flexors (over the front of the pelvis)

Stand next to a stable box or bench no more than a foot or 30 centimeters tall. Bend your left knee and place your left foot flat on the top surface, with the front of your right foot on the floor about 12 inches (30 cms) behind an imaginary line drawn through the heel of your left foot. Keep both feet pointing straight ahead. Gently and slowly move forward by bending more at your left knee, just enough to produce a slight stretch at the front of your right hip. Keep the heel of your right foot flat on the floor, and your right knee straight. Hold the stretch until the tension eases. Repeat on the other side, then return to the first side once more, and so on.

If you feel the stretch more in your calf than the front of hip, you probably have your rear foot too far back.

Develop symmetrical flexibility. Take great care, and progress slowly. This stretch will involve muscles you may never have stretched before, which may currently be tight. Don't arch your back during the stretch, or bend forward at your waist. Your torso must be straight, and upright, for the required effect on your hip flexors.

If your feet are turned outward, that will increase the involvement of your thigh adductors. Keep both feet pointing straight ahead. If the rear foot is turned inward a little, that may help focus the stretch on the hip flexors even more.

As your suppleness increases, you'll be able to bend more at your raised knee. Once you can comfortably bend your knee until its shin is vertical or slightly beyond vertical, increase the height of the elevation. Do this half an inch or a centimeter at a time—for example, put a weight plate on the box, or under it. Progress can also be made by gradually increasing the distance between the elevation and your rear foot, up to a maximum of about two feet or 60 centimeters.

Assisted stretch for the hip flexors

After at least a couple of months on the aforementioned hip-flexor stretch, add the following stretch:

Lie on a bench with your
hips approximately lined
up with the edge, and both
knees held toward your
chest. Lift your head and
shoulders off the bench,
and put both hands
around your left upper
shin. Press your lower
back onto the bench, and
move your right leg and
thigh forward so that they

hang loosely off the bench, with your right knee bent only slightly.
Let gravity pull on the limb until you feel the tension ease. Repeat for
the other side. Perform three stretches for each side. Keep your lower
back pressed onto the bench at all times. If your lower back comes off
the bench, you risk injuring your back.

You may need to elevate the bench as your flexibility increases, so
that you have a greater range of motion.

Develop symmetrical flexibility.

After two months of
letting gravity alone pull
on your hip flexors, get the
help of an assistant. On an
elevated bench—to make it
easier for the assistant, and
to provide sufficient range
of motion for you—get in
the same position as for
the unassisted version. The
assistant should hold your
ankle with one hand, and
your lower thigh with the
other hand, and your knee

should be only slightly bent. The assistant should apply just
sufficient, steady pressure to your thigh so that you feel tension in
your hip flexors. Wait until the tension eases, then work the other
side. Perform three stretches for each side.

Your assistant must be immediately responsive to your feedback.
Never force the stretch. And keep your lower back pressed onto the
bench at all times.

4. Hamstrings (rear thigh)

Lie on your back with both feet flat on the floor, and knees bent. Straighten your left knee, and lift that limb as far from the floor as is comfortable. Keep your right foot flat on the floor, and your right knee bent—this helps to reduce rotation of your pelvis. And keep your lower back pressed against the floor. Hold your left limb at the

rear of your thigh, or knee, with both hands, and pull gently. Hold this position until the tension in your hamstrings eases, then relax, and repeat. This time you should be able to pull a little further, but still keep your knee straight. Hold this position until, again, the tension eases, then relax, and repeat once more. Stretch your right hamstrings in the same manner.

There should be no tension behind your knee—there's no hamstring muscle behind the knee. If there is tension behind your knee, reduce the tension until it's felt in your hamstrings.

To progress in flexibility, incrementally bring your leg nearer to your face. To help with this, gradually move your hands toward your feet.

For another form of control, use a towel, strap, or belt, and loop it stirrup-like over the arch of your foot, and gently pull on it. Keep your toes above your heel. Don't pull on the ball of your foot, because that would cause your calf to tighten, and mar the stretch for the hamstrings. The calf muscle should be relaxed.

The knee nearest the floor should be bent, not straight as shown here, to reduce rotation of the pelvis. Note how the lower back and the hip bones are pressed against the floor, to prevent the lower back rounding and creating just an illusion of hamstring flexibility.

If this stretch is too difficult, start with the wall stretch. Lie on the floor with your heels against a wall, and knees bent a little. Position yourself close enough to the wall so that you feel slight tension in your hamstrings. Hold this position until the tension eases, then relax, and repeat. This time, straighten your knees to increase tension. To further increase tension, move your hips closer to the wall.

Develop symmetrical flexibility.

The wall stretch for the hamstrings.

Symmetrical flexibility

You may find that muscles of one limb, or on one side of your torso, are less flexible than those of the opposite side. If so, perform additional reps of each relevant stretch on the less flexible side in a one-sided stretch such as Stretch 3; or place greater emphasis on the less flexible side in a two-sided stretch such as Stretch 2. Be patient, and persistent. Over time this should yield symmetrical left-right flexibility unless there are physical restrictions that require treatment—see the box on the next page.

Kneeling—caution

Avoid compression on your kneecap during any activity. Kneecap compression can produce tendinitis, and damage to the underside of the kneecap and the articular cartilage of the thigh bone. This can lead to chondromalacia. When kneeling, don't apply pressure to the kneecap. Keep the pressure on the top part of the shinbone just beneath the kneecap, and even then, minimize the time spent in that position.

5. Buttocks

Lie on your back with your left knee bent. Put your hands over your shinbone just beneath your knee cap, or over your hamstrings just behind your knee if that's more comfortable. Pull your knee toward your chest until you feel slight tension in your left buttock. Hold that position until the tension eases. Next, without leaning to one side, pull your bent, left knee toward your right side until, again, you feel tension in your left buttock. Hold until the tension eases. Repeat on the other side, before returning to the first side. Press your lower back firmly against the floor at all times. Perform three stretches for each side. Develop symmetrical flexibility.

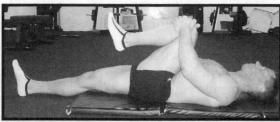
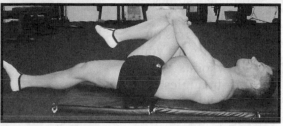

Especially to begin with—and this is not illustrated—you may prefer to keep your resting knee slightly bent.

Difficulty stretching?

If you have difficulties with these stretches, and don't progress in flexibility as the weeks go by, or don't progress symmetrically, you may have scar tissue, adhesions, or other restrictions in your muscles. These need to be treated so that your muscles can return to their normal, supple, efficient, discomfort-free operation.

As an illustration, I struggled with the quadriceps stretch—*Stretch 7*—for several years, and was never able to progress at it. Then following non-invasive, soft-tissue work to remove the restrictions in my thighs—including the removal of adhesions between my right vastus lateralis and right iliotibial band (thigh tissues)—the flexibility in my quadriceps increased instantly. Only *then* did the quadriceps stretch become effective. A few weeks after treatment I was able to sit on my ankles, which I hadn't been able to for many years.

Soft-tissue therapy will be explained later in this book.

6. Spine extension

Lie prone with your arms and forearms outstretched. Pull your arms back so that your hands are alongside your head. Raise your head and shoulders sufficiently so that you can rest your forearms on the floor with your elbow joints roughly at right angles. Hold for about 20 seconds, then return to the floor. Relax for a few seconds, then repeat and hold a little longer.

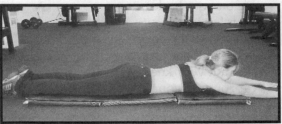

Next, while still on your front, put your hands alongside your chest, or shoulders, depending on your flexibility. Then slowly push yourself up so that your back arches and your elbows straighten. Don't force it. Relax your lower body so that it sags. Hold for only a few seconds to begin with, then return your torso to

The above photograph shows an extended neck AND an extended back. For most people, a NEUTRAL neck is the safest position during this stretch—neither flexed nor extended.

the floor. Do several reps. Over a few sessions, build up the duration of how long you hold the sag, the degree of sag, and the number of reps. *Work into this carefully and progressively.*

Spine extension can be great therapy for back discomfort. It can also help to prevent back pain. Doing this stretch daily can help maintain the natural curves of your spine, which tend to flatten with age.

7. Quadriceps (front thigh)

Stand with your right hand braced on a fixed object. Bend your left knee and lift your left foot behind you. With your left hand, grab your left ankle or leg, not your foot. If you hold your foot you'll load the tendons of your toes, and mar the stretch for your quadriceps. Keep your torso vertical.

Pull on your ankle until you feel tension in your quadriceps. And push your hips forward a little during the stretch. Hold the stretch until the tension eases, then relax. Repeat on the other side, and so on.

Develop symmetrical flexibility.

If you hold your left ankle with your right hand, the stretch is applied differently. The femur would be rotated, which would take the quadriceps out of their ideal functional alignment.

The quadriceps stretch can be done lying. Lie on your right side, with your legs, thighs, and torso in a straight line. Grab your left ankle with your left hand, and follow the same guidelines as for the standing version.

8. Shoulders and chest

Stand upright with your toes about three inches or eight centimeters from the center of a doorway. Place your hands flat against the wall or wooden frame around the doorway. Your palms should face forward, and your arms should be parallel with the floor. The elbow joint is maintained at an angle determined by the width of the doorway and the length of your arms. This is about a right angle for a typical doorway and an  average-size adult. Gently and slowly lean forward, and feel the stretch in your shoulders and pectorals. Don't overstretch. Don't force your shoulders forward. As your torso leans forward, your shoulders will move forward, too. Keep your heels on the floor, and don't allow your body to sag.

To progress in flexibility as the weeks go by, step back a little from the doorway, but maintain your hand placement. Then there'll be more tension in your shoulders when you lean forward.

Stretch #9, additional tips

For stability during this obliques and spinal musculature stretch, distribute the stress over your feet in a 50-50 split. And while you bend to the side you should take more of the stress on the inner sides of your feet than the outer.

9. Obliques (sides of your torso), and spinal musculature

Stand with your feet together, or almost together, and knees straight. With your hands resting on your hips, push your hips to your left and simultaneously lean your torso to your right. Lean to the point where you feel slight tension in your left side. Hold until the tension eases, then return to the upright position. On the return, lead with your *torso* and let your hips follow—don't bring your hips back first, because that could cause irritation or injury. Repeat on the other side. Perform three stretches for each side.

All movement should be lateral. Don't lean forward, or backward.

After a few sessions, perform the stretch with your forearms crossed on your chest. The raised hands will increase the resistance. After a few more sessions, or when you're ready, put your hands on your head, to increase resistance further. Later on still, perform the stretch with your arms straight overhead, hands together—reach out with your hands as far as possible while you lean to the side.

A wider stance may provide greater stability, but a less effective stretch. If stability is a problem, use a hip-width stance to start with, then after a few sessions, as you improve your stability, gradually reduce the width of your stance.

This isn't just a stretch. It will also strengthen your obliques, and some of your spinal musculature.

Develop symmetrical flexibility. But take great care—*progress slowly*. This stretch will involve muscles you may never have stretched before, and which may be tight currently.

The illustrations show the advanced form of this stretch. See the text for the less demanding versions.

10. Neck, back, and obliques

Sit sideways on a chair that doesn't have arms, as illustrated. (In a gym, you could use an adjustable bench that can be set at a high incline, to simulate a chair.) Keep your knees bent at about a right angle, and feet flat on the floor about shoulder-width apart. Rotate to your right and grab the back of the chair with both hands. This is the starting position.

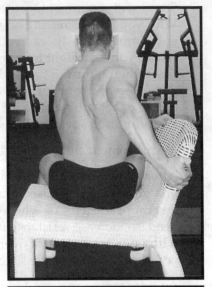

Rotate your torso and neck further to your right. Gently rotate your spine. Stay *upright*—don't slouch—and keep your buttocks and thighs on the seat. Rotate to the point where you feel slight tension in your back, obliques, and neck. Hold until the tension eases, then return to the starting position. Pause for a few seconds, and repeat. Perform three stretches for each side.

Develop symmetrical flexibility.

But take great care—progress slowly. This stretch will involve muscles you may never have stretched before, and which may currently be tight.

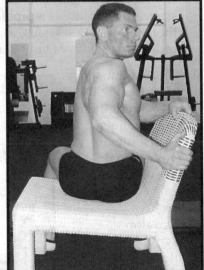

11. General knee flexibility test, and lower-body stretch

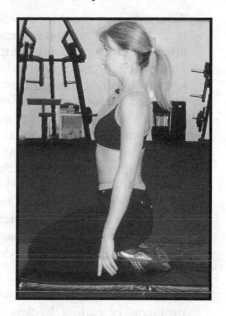

A general test of knee flexibility is the ability to sit on your heels while kneeling on the floor with your thighs and feet together. If you can't do this comfortably, you may not, yet, have the required flexibility or knee health to squat safely and effectively. Sit on your heels for 15 to 30 seconds, two or three times, as part of your stretching routine.

If you can't sit on your heels, perform the stretch with two or more stacked, thick books on the floor between your heels. (Your feet would have to be spaced accordingly.) Sit on the books. As your flexibility increases, incrementally reduce the height of the stack of books. It may require a few weeks of regular stretching, or longer, before you can sit on your heels. Make progress gradually.

A good preparatory exercise for this stretch, is *Stretch 7*.

12. Post-workout spine stretch

After every workout (once you're training in a gym), and especially after deadlifting and squatting, gently stretch your spine, to help keep it healthy. Hang from an overhead bar, or some other support, with a shoulder-width grip, and relax your lower body so that it gently pulls on your spine, to relieve compression from your vertebrae. Bend your knees a little, then raise them a few inches, or about ten centimeters, for a better stretch. Start with ten seconds per hang, and build up over a few weeks to 30 seconds per rep.

If you have shoulder or elbow problems, be careful, because the hanging could aggravate the problems. Don't relax your shoulders. Keep them tight.

Rather than perform this stretch with straight legs, as illustrated, bend your knees a little, then raise them a few inches, for a better stretch.

If you have purpose-built inversion-therapy equipment available (not illustrated), use it as an alternative to the overhead bar. But don't invert yourself for longer than one minute at a time, and work into that progressively over several weeks. Longer periods of inversion may irritate your spine rather than help it.

An alternative to purpose-built inversion-therapy equipment is the use of a back extension apparatus. You can use the 45-degree apparatus, or the traditional set-up.

Use of the traditional back extension apparatus for inversion therapy (left), and the 45-degree set-up (above).

Another possibility is to use bars designed for the parallel bar dip. Get in position with your elbows straight, and your shoulders tight (don't slouch), and then relax your lower body. Done correctly, you'll feel a gentle stretch in your spine. Start with ten seconds per stretch, and build up over a few weeks to 30 seconds per rep

As well as one of these three spine stretches, perform *Stretch 6* after each workout.

Implementing the stretching routine

This routine, with three reps for each stretch, can be completed in 15 to 30 minutes, depending on how long you hold each rep.

Don't consider the stretching as a burden on your time. It's an investment. When done properly, it's an injury-proofing, health-promoting, and enjoyable supplement to your training program.

Recommended reading

THE STARK REALITY OF STRETCHING (1997, The Stark Reality Corp.), fourth edition, by Dr. Steven D. Stark

More on stretching

Stretching increases the length of muscle fibers. The lengthening occurs through individual muscle fibers growing in length within a muscle because of the addition of sarcomeres—tiny contractile units. Additionally, the connective tissue in and around the muscle is expanded, including the fascia that surrounds the bundles of muscle fibers, and the wrappings of individual fibers. Fascia is a band or sheath of connective tissue, and it also supports, binds, covers, and separates muscles and groups of muscles, and organs, too.

Nerves also respond to stretching. Nerves don't take a straight course through the tissues that surround them. When stretched, the nerves are pulled straight somewhat. Beyond that lengthening, the meandering path of the individual fibers *within* a nerve can also be straightened in response to a stretch. Furthermore, the enveloping connective tissue has sufficient elasticity to accommodate some additional stretch without damaging the enclosed nerve fibers.

Strength training that uses full ranges of motion can help to promote flexibility, but there are some motions that strength training doesn't typically cover. Furthermore, some strength-training exercises can't be performed over the fullest possible ranges of motion because, under the load of progressive resistance, those exercises are dangerous for most trainees. A good stretching routine can, however, cover those ranges of motion safely.

A supple body isn't valuable merely to help enable correct performance of strength-training exercises. Without a supple body, movements in general become restricted, there's reduced resilience or give in the body to withstand sudden movements safely, dynamic balance is impaired, and the loose connective tissue of the body loses its lubricating properties. (Loose connective tissue fills the spaces between muscle, nervous, and epithelial tissue, and between bone and cartilage, tendons and ligaments, and joints and joint capsules.) Therefore, without a supple body, muscles lose some of their elasticity and ability to function smoothly, and tendons, ligaments, and joint capsules become brittle. Tissues in general become more susceptible to injury, and the body ages at an accelerated rate.

Should there ever be excessive flexibility, which is extraordinary, ease back on stretching. The muscles will get shorter, and the connective tissues will soon follow suit.

Hatha yoga

After about a year, once you've integrated **The Program** into your life, expand the stretching component. Then, hatha yoga postures are recommended. But if done incorrectly, these postures will produce injury. Employ warm-ups followed by a sequence of main postures intermingled with rest postures and compensation (or counter) postures, selected by an expert teacher. And make progress *slowly*.

Hatha yoga is one of the eight branches of yoga—the best known branch in the West. Hatha yoga is an ancient system of exercise that's revered by millions of people. The practice of hatha yoga develops flexibility, and promotes many other health benefits. Physical postures comprise the main part of hatha yoga.

Hatha yoga doesn't require freak-show flexibility, and doesn't have to have anything to do with chanting, gurus, or religion. You don't need to learn any strange jargon, Sanskrit names, or New Age philosophy. And hatha yoga is for women *and* men. Some top athletes in professional sports have discovered the benefits of hatha yoga.

For an introduction to hatha yoga, and to find out about how some star athletes use it as part of their program for peak performance, see John Capouya's book. See the other book for a deeper introduction to yoga.

REAL MEN DO YOGA (2003, Health Communications), by John Capouya
YOGA FOR DUMMIES (1999, Wiley), by Georg Feuerstein, and Larry Payne

Exercise technique rehearsal

For beginners, at home during the preparatory weeks, practice the technique of the exercises you'll use during your first strength-training routine at the gym:

1. Squat
2. Standing calf raise
3. Bench press
4. Deadlift
5. Seated dumbbell press
6. Pulldown
7. Dumbbell shrug
8. Seated dumbbell curl
9. Crunch

These exercises can be practiced at home without any formal gym equipment. Here are the tools you'll need: a broom handle to simulate an unloaded barbell, two cans from a kitchen shelf to simulate a pair of dumbbells, a bench, the technique instruction in this chapter, and a mirror and an assistant to help you with cues and feedback.

Slot the rehearsal time into your three-times-a-week training schedule, after stretching.

The squat and deadlift are the most technically demanding of the nine exercises, and the ones that will probably require the most work. You may have trouble with one or both of these exercises until you've limbered up from following the flexibility routine for a few weeks. If, for example, your lower back rounds in either exercise, or your heels come off the floor when you squat, don't despair. With improved flexibility, and technique adjustments as recommended in this book, your technique can improve greatly over just a few weeks.

Don't work merely on the bar pathways of the exercises. Also work on controlled rep speed—no faster than two seconds for the upward movement, and another two seconds for the downward phase.

Important note

What follows is a summary, for beginners, of the technique of the exercises in your first gym routine. First, you need to be familiar with the basics. Then, later on, when you go to a gym you'll know what to do with each exercise once you've found the right equipment. After two weeks of gym workouts you should be sufficiently familiar with the equipment for the *details* on exercise technique to make sense. Then you'll be able to put into practice the appropriate parts of Chapter 12, where exercise technique is described in detail.

1. Squat

Main muscles worked: quadriceps, thigh adductors, buttocks, hamstrings, and spinal erectors

A brief description of the squat, in its freehand form, has already been provided. There's much more to the *barbell* squat. It's one of the most technically demanding exercises.

Whereas the freehand squat doesn't involve resistance, the barbell squat necessitates use of a barbell resting across the upper back. A broom handle can substitute for a barbell. In a gym, the bar for the squat is kept on stands, or bar saddles in a power rack, when not in use. The bar is loaded to the required weight while resting at mid- to upper-chest height on the stands or saddles. Then you would get under it, position the bar in the right position on your upper back, grasp the bar securely, unrack it, and walk backward into position for the exercise. The required reps are performed, then you would return to the supports, rack the bar, and take your rest interval between sets.

At home, find a set-up that can mimic a pair of squat stands. The stands should be a few inches or eight to ten centimeters below your shoulder height. Place the broom handle across the stands. Grasp the bar using a grip wider than shoulder-width but less than the spacing between the stands. If this set-up isn't possible, hold the broom handle in front of you, at chest height.

In either case, dip under the bar, with your left foot a little in front of the bar, and right foot a little behind it. Pull your shoulders back and stick your chest out, and place the bar as far below the base of your neck as is comfortable. While looking straight ahead or upward, simultaneously straighten your knees, to raise the bar vertically off the stands. Keep your chest stuck out, and your lower back arched slightly. Shuffle backward so that you're about 20 inches or 45

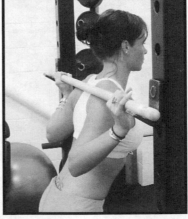

centimeters away from the center of the stands. When you have resistance over your back, don't lift your feet from the floor as you move from or to the squat stands. Sliding your feet over the floor gives you greater stability than if you lift your feet. Stability is critical, for safety, once you use weight on the bar.

Once in position about 20 inches or 45 centimeters from the stands, adopt a stance that has your heels about hip-width apart, and toes pointed out somewhat. If you imagine that you're standing on a large clock face, with your feet being the hands of the clock, your feet would be positioned somewhere between "ten to two" and "five to one," according to what feels comfortable and stable for you. Then while looking straight ahead or slightly upward, squat down as far as you comfortably can without your lower back rounding. Squat down slowly as if you were sitting down onto a chair, taking two to three seconds for the descent. Get the help of an assistant, or squat alongside a mirror, to see whether or not your lower back rounds. Back rounding is dangerous in the squat when you have weight over your back, because it greatly increases the stress on your vertebrae and surrounding structures, and the risk of injury.

Widening your stance, and flaring your toes a bit more, usually helps with keeping the required, slightly hollowed lower back during the descent; but widening your stance may require more flexibility than you have now. You may need to be patient for a few weeks until the benefits start to yield from the flexibility routine.

When you're at the lowest position you can reach without rounding your lower back, immediately yet slowly ascend—take two seconds for the ascent, and

This trainee doesn't have well-developed erector spinae muscles—alongside the vertebral column—that can fill the desired slight hollow in the lower spine to yield just the appearance of a flat lower back at the bottom position of the squat. The flat lower back shown here is because the hollow in her lower spine has flattened. With technique practice, strengthening of her back, and increased flexibility, this trainee should be able to improve her lower-back positioning.

exhale during it. While standing, pull your shoulders back once more, keep your chest stuck out, take a deep breath, and descend into the next squat, again taking two to three seconds.

As you descend, keep your knees pointed in the same direction as your flared feet; then on the ascent have your knees follow the same path as on the descent. Never allow your knees to buckle inward on the ascent or descent.

After your final rep, shuffle forward until the bar is directly above the stands. Then vertically lower the bar into the stands.

Your heels may come off the floor as you descend into the squat. With increased flexibility in your lower body, this tendency should reduce and, eventually, disappear. A slightly widened stance, and greater toe flare, may help reduce the tendency for your heels to raise.

You may lean forward excessively, and your lower back may round prematurely. These issues may result from insufficient back strength. As your back strength improves, so may your squatting ability.

2. Standing calf raise

Main muscles worked: gastrocnemius, and soleus

Stand on the bottom step of some stairs. Put the balls of both of your feet on the edge of the step, and hold the banister for balance. Alternatively, use a stable block instead of the step, and position it near a stable support you can hold, for balance. Lower your heels as far as is comfortable, pause for a second, then smoothly raise your heels as far as possible. Contract your calves as hard as possible in the top position, for two seconds. Then lower your heels once again, and repeat. Keep your knees straight, or almost straight.

Exhale during the ascent, and inhale during the descent; or, just breathe freely and continuously throughout each rep including during the pauses at the top and bottom positions.

When you can do over 20 reps of the two-legged calf raise, perform it one leg at a time, as illustrated.

3. Bench press

Main muscles worked: pectorals, deltoids, and triceps

The bench press is performed supine—while lying on your back. Lie on a horizontal bench, with a broom handle at arm's length above your chest. (In a gym, you would take the bar from vertical stands fixed to the bench. Your nose would be lined up with the stands, approximately. The bench press bar rests on the stands between sets.) A hand spacing of about 21 inches or 53 centimeters between index fingers is ideal for most men, and about four inches or ten centimeters closer for women, although this can vary according to shoulder width.

With your elbows still locked, inhale fully and raise your chest, then start the descent. Take two to three seconds to lower the bar to just below your nipples. Touch your chest with the bar, pause for a second without relaxing, then push it up until your elbows are straight again.

Take about two seconds for the ascent, and exhale during it. Push up vertically, or at a slight slope toward your head. Keep your elbows tucked in and directly below your hands—don't let your elbows flare out.

At the bottom position, your forearms should be vertical, as seen by an assistant from the side *and* the front. If they aren't, your grip spacing is amiss, or your bar pathway is wrong. With the correct grip, and lowering to just below your nipples, your forearms should be properly positioned at the bottom.

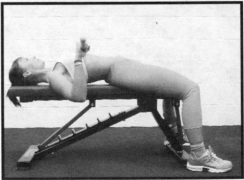

After completion of a set, the bar would normally be returned to the stands. Although you can't do this during the rehearsal at home, you will once you start working out in a gym.

For this trainee, her feet should be raised a few inches, to prevent excessive arching of her back. And her wrists should be extended slightly, to hold the bar securely, rather than flexed slightly as shown in the above photo.

4. Deadlift

Main muscles worked: spinal erectors, buttocks, quadriceps, hamstrings, latissimus dorsi, upper back, and forearms

In a gym the deadlift is usually started from the floor. Get two low boxes or stacks of books each about ten inches or 25 centimeters tall. Rest your broom handle across this elevation. The purpose of this set-up is to mimic the bar position as it would be if it was loaded with a pair of 45-pound or 20-kilo plates, which is the standard bottom-position bar height for most trainees when deadlifting. This isn't to imply that beginners should start deadlifting with a pair of full-diameter plates. It's a reference to the bar height when it's loaded with such plates.

Stand with your feet below the bar, bar touching your shins. Position your heels hip-width apart, toes slightly flared. Pull your shoulders back, look forward or slightly upward, and hollow your lower back a little. Maintain those positions, bend your knees, and squat down. Your torso will lean forward. Keep your entire feet flat on the floor. Your hips must be well below your shoulders, at all times. When your hands touch the bar, space them so that they are just to the sides of your legs, with your knuckles facing forward.

Preserving a slight hollow in your lower back, shoulders pulled back, and your head up and eyes looking forward or slightly upward, start the ascent. Your hips and shoulders should move simultaneously, as a unit. Lead with your shoulders. Your hips must not rise faster than your shoulders. And never round your back during the deadlift.

The bar should brush your lower limbs during the ascent. Don't allow the bar to travel forward.

Once in the standing position, keep your shoulders pulled back, chest stuck out, and lower back hollowed (but *without* exaggerating

Right: Excessive range of motion, neck extension, and forward lean. For this trainee, raising the height of the bar by three to four inches (eight to ten cms) would yield a better back position at the bottom. Furthermore, she should be closer to the bar.

In a gym setting, this powerlifter shows correct deadlifting technique. The range of motion isn't excessive, and neither is the degree of forward lean or extension of the neck. Adjust your home set-up so that you mimic the deadlifting technique illustrated above.

the arch), then descend into the deadlift by simultaneously bending your knees and leaning forward. As you descend, you'll naturally bend forward so that you can get the bar around your knees. Once again, your heels must not lift off the floor, and the bar should gently brush your lower limbs at all times.

Think of your hands as hooks, with the lifting done with your thighs, hips, and back—there should be no pulling by your hands or arms.

Descend to a count of three seconds, and ascend to a further count of three seconds. Inhale immediately before starting the descent, and exhale during the ascent.

If you perform this rehearsal sideways on to a full-length mirror, you can observe your technique and relative positions of your hips and shoulders. A mirror is useful for learning good deadlifting technique. Of course, for safety, never lift a weight with your head turned to the side to watch your reflection. Symmetrical technique is imperative in the deadlift, at least when lifting a weight.

5. Seated dumbbell press

Main muscles worked: deltoids, triceps, and trapezius

Get a pair of cans and sit on a chair with no arm rests, with your feet flat on the floor in front of and astride of the chair. Lean against the back of the chair. Keep your hips hard against the bottom of the back of the chair. Maintain a slight hollow in your lower back, with your shoulders pressed against the back of the chair.

Alternatively, sit on a box, as illustrated, and maintain correct but unsupported back positioning.

Hold the cans at the sides of your shoulders, and look straight forward. Press the cans overhead, pause for a moment, then lower the cans. Exhale as you ascend, inhale on the descent. Take about two seconds for each ascent, a further two seconds for each descent, and a pause for a second at the top and bottom positions.

6. Pulldown

Main muscles worked: latissimus dorsi, upper back, pectorals, biceps, brachialis, forearms

Sit on a stool or a box, with a broom handle in your lap as your bar. Hold it so that your knuckles face the floor, hands about shoulder-width apart. Raise the bar so that it's above and a little in front of your head. Look up so that you can see the bar. Imagine that the bar is suspended from a pulley attached to the ceiling.

Pull the bar until it touches your upper chest, just below your collar bones. As you pull the bar, arch your back slightly but don't lean back. At the bottom position, with the bar against your upper chest, crush your shoulder blades together for a second, and fully contract your upper back musculature. Exhale during the descent of the bar. Then straighten your elbows overhead, and simultaneously inhale. Pause for a second at the top position. Repeat for subsequent reps.

When you perform this exercise in a gym, using a pulldown apparatus, gravity will pull the bar overhead during the negative phase of each rep, and you'll need to resist it, to control its speed.

7. Dumbbell shrug

Main muscles worked: trapezius and entire upper back, deltoids, forearms

Stand upright with a pair of cans in your
hands, and your shoulders pulled back. Keep
your elbows straight, and lift your shoulders
vertically as high as possible. Try to touch
your shoulders to your ears. Pause in the top
position, then lower the cans to the bottom
position, pause again, and repeat. Breathe in
on the descent, and out on the ascent.

Although this is a short-range movement,
don't rush the reps. Take about two seconds
for each of the upward and downward
phases, and an additional second at the top
position of each rep, and another at the
bottom position.

8. Seated dumbbell curl

Main muscles worked: biceps, brachialis, and forearms

Get a pair of cans and sit on a chair with no arm rests, or a box, with your feet flat on the floor in front of you. Stay upright and maintain a slight hollow in your lower back. Hold the cans with your arms hanging vertically, and your hands parallel with each other. Look straight forward.

Lift the cans by flexing your elbows. Your elbows should stay fixed—don't allow them to move forward. As the cans are curled up, supinate your wrists, that is, turn your thumbs outward so that your palms face upward at the top position. Lift the cans as high as you can without your elbows moving forward. Fully contract your biceps at the top position as you fully supinate your wrists. As you lower the cans, pronate your wrists, that is, turn your thumbs inward, so that at the bottom position your palms are, again, parallel with each other.

Take about two seconds for the ascent, hold the contracted position for a second, take a further two seconds for the descent, and another pause for a second in the bottom position. Exhale on the ascent, inhale on the descent.

9. Crunch

Main muscles worked: the abdominal wall—rectus abdominis, external abdominal oblique, internal abdominal oblique, and transversus abdominis— and hip flexors

A brief description of this exercise has already been provided, because the crunch is part of the calisthenics of the preparatory routine. The crunch doesn't need additional work during the technique rehearsal periods.

Sets and reps

Perform three sets of ten reps per exercise during each workout—one group of ten reps, rest a minute, then another group of ten reps, rest a minute, then the final group of ten reps. The squat and deadlift are the most technically demanding of these exercises. If you need more rehearsal work to master them, perform additional sets.

Nutrition

Eat healthy food only, every three to four hours.

Cutting out junk food means eliminating food that has been distorted and corrupted by modern technology. Junk food isn't just what you can pick up from fast food restaurants. It's much of what's on the shelves of supermarkets. Generally, cutting out junk food means avoiding food that has been processed, refined, or distorted from its natural state, or contaminated with refined sugar and newfangled, processed oils. Making these changes may be difficult, but necessary if you want to improve your well-being and minimize your chances of succumbing to the health problems that are endemic in the western world largely because of the modern diet.

Here's a summary of what to avoid, adapted from "Dietary Dangers" published by The Weston A. Price Foundation, www.westonaprice.org:

1. Avoid commercially processed foods such as cookies, crackers, cakes, TV dinners, soft drinks, packaged sauce mixes, and so forth.

2. Avoid refined sweeteners such as sugar, dextrose, glucose, and high fructose corn syrup, and foods that contain them (*check labels*).

3. Avoid white flour, white flour products, and white rice.

4. Avoid all hydrogenated or partially hydrogenated fats and oils, including margarine and shortenings (*check labels*).

5. Avoid all vegetable oils made from soy, corn, safflower, canola, or cottonseed (*check labels*).

6. Avoid fried foods.

7. Avoid strict vegetarianism (veganism), because animal products provide vital nutrients not found in plant foods.

8. Avoid products that contain protein powders—get protein from foods that naturally contain it.

9. Avoid battery-produced eggs, and factory-farmed meats.

10. Avoid highly processed luncheon meats and sausage containing MSG and other additives.

11. Avoid canned, sprayed, waxed, bioengineered, or irradiated fruits and vegetables.

12. Avoid artificial food additives, especially MSG, hydrolyzed vegetable protein, and aspartame, which are neurotoxins. Most

soups, sauce and broth mixes, and commercial condiments, contain MSG, even if not so labeled.

13. Avoid caffeine-containing beverages such as coffee, tea, and soft drinks. Avoid chocolate.

A caveat is in order on the last point. If you have to drive when you may feel drowsy, this is a life-threatening situation for you, passengers, and fellow road users. Many accidents have occurred because drivers have fallen asleep. A cup of coffee or tea (not decaffeinated) can keep you alert and safe on the road. In future, however, get fully rested before you drive.

Check labels, *then* you'll see how much sugar, unhealthy fats, and additives there are in many common foods.

You'll be left with dairy products, meat (unless you're vegetarian), fish, eggs, wholegrain products (not refined, white ones), salads, legumes, nuts, seeds, and fresh fruit and vegetables, in quantities according to your caloric needs and digestive capabilities.

Here's a summary of what to eat, adapted from "Dietary Guidelines" published by The Weston A. Price Foundation:

1. Eat whole, natural foods.

2. Eat only foods that will spoil, but eat them before they do.

3. Eat naturally raised meat including fish, seafood, poultry, beef, lamb, game, organ meats, and eggs.

4. Eat whole, naturally produced milk products from pasture-fed cows, preferably raw and fermented, such as whole yogurt, cultured butter, whole cheeses, and fresh and sour cream.

5. Use only traditional fats and oils including butter and other animal fats, extra virgin olive oil, expeller-expressed sesame and flax oil, and coconut and palm oils.

6. Eat fresh fruits and vegetables, preferably organic, in salads and soups, or lightly steamed.

7. Use whole grains and nuts that have been prepared through soaking, sprouting, or sour leavening—to neutralize phytic acid and other anti-nutrients.

8. Make your own salad dressing using vinegar, extra virgin olive oil, and expeller-expressed flax oil.

9. Use natural sweeteners in moderation, such as raw honey, maple syrup, and molasses.

Healthy food should be tasty, and enjoyable to eat. Invest the time to prepare healthy food that you enjoy. Frying, however, is one of the worst ways of preparing food. It damages even good food.

Water

Consume enough water distributed over the course of each day to produce at least four clear urinations each day (in addition to colored urinations). Until you produce the minimum of four clear urinations a day, gradually increase your intake of plain water. Get a water filter if your tap water doesn't have a pleasant taste, or drink bottled water that tastes good. Replace most other drinks with plain water, or caffeine-free, herbal tea. Keep a bottle of water or herbal tea handy, and have a few mouthfuls every 15 to 30 minutes, and more often if it's hot or you're exercising. Large but infrequent drinks of water increase urination but don't necessarily produce adequate hydration. Little and often is a better strategy for water consumption.

Sleep, and recuperation

Recuperation from exercise requires adequate sleep. If you shortchange yourself of sleep, you'll hamper your training progress. Adequate sleep isn't important just for recovery between workouts. In order to feel enthusiastic for exercise, you need to be well rested. A sluggish body leads to sluggish desire for training.

If you need to be woken by an alarm clock, and if you regularly drink coffee, you're almost certainly not sleeping in sufficient quantity or quality. Recognize the importance of sleep—not just for your recuperation, and training ability, but for your overall health. Improve your sleeping habits, and sleep a little more each night.

Incremental changes

If you need to make substantial changes in your dietary and sleeping habits, make them gradually, step-by-step. Adapt to them incrementally. Spread them out over the preparatory month.

The preparatory month's training schedule for beginners

Progression caveat

Start out conservatively. Your body has tremendous abilities of adaptation provided you start out comfortably, and increase the demands incrementally. This applies to all forms of physical training—resistance training, stretching, and aerobic and cardio work.

Muscular soreness

Some muscular soreness, especially during the introductory period of an exercise program, is normal. And whenever you change exercises, some soreness is to be expected. Severe soreness can be debilitating and injurious, however, and should be avoided.

The foolish maxim "No pain, no gain"

A burning or aching sensation in the muscles being exercised is normal once you're training hard enough to produce it. Although this type of discomfort is fine, pain isn't. Pain comes from injury, or some other form of harm. Never work through pain. Pain means that something is wrong.

The "No pain, no gain" foolishness has been at the root of much pain, injury, frustration, and dissatisfaction with exercise programs.

The workouts

Choose three non-consecutive days each week—for instance, Tuesday, Thursday and Saturday, or whatever sequence of days is best for you. Other than if you're unwell, or there's an emergency, *train on schedule*. Consistency is essential.

For the illustration I've assumed you've previously been sedentary. If, however, you've been active for a number of years, then in the first week you may easily be able to perform more reps of the calisthenic movements, and you may start with brisk 20 to 30 minute walks rather than ease into them progressively. In some cases, however, fewer reps than in the illustration will be possible. *Do what you can, keep accurate records, and progress at your own pace.*

On Tuesday of the first week, perform one set of as many reps as you comfortably can of each calisthenic, without pushing to your limit. Keep a written note of how many reps you did of each exercise. Then on Thursday repeat what you did on Tuesday. On Saturday, duplicate the rep count you did for each exercise, but perform two sets of each exercise, with two minutes rest between sets. Over the subsequent weeks, add reps to each exercise as your strength and endurance improve, but maintain correct exercise technique as described in this chapter.

Week 1 *illustration*

TUESDAY
1. *Calisthenics*
   a. Crunch x 8 reps
   b. Floor back extension x 6
   c. Freehand squat x 15
   d. Floor push-up x 6
   e. Chair chin-up x 6
2. *Stretching*
3. *Technique rehearsal*
4. *Aerobic work*
   Walk for 10 minutes

THURSDAY
1. *Calisthenics*
   a. Crunch x 8
   b. Floor back extension x 6
   c. Freehand squat x 15
   d. Floor push-up x 6
   e. Chair chin-up x 6
2. *Stretching*
3. *Technique rehearsal*
4. *Aerobic work*
   Walk for 10 minutes

SATURDAY
1. *Calisthenics*
   a. Crunch: 2 x 8
   b. Floor back extension: 2 x 6
   c. Freehand squat: 2 x 15

d. Floor push-up: 2 x 6
e. Chair chin-up: 2 x 6
2. *Stretching*
3. *Technique rehearsal*
4. *Aerobic work*
   Walk for 10 minutes

Week 2 *illustration*

TUESDAY
1. *Calisthenics*
   a. Crunch: 2 x 10
   b. Floor back extension: 2 x 8
   c. Freehand squat: 2 x 20
   d. Floor push-up: 2 x 8
   e. Chair chin-up: 2 x 8
2. *Stretching*
3. *Technique rehearsal*
4. *Aerobic work*
   Walk for 15 minutes

THURSDAY
1. *Calisthenics*
   a. Crunch: 2 x 12
   b. Floor back extension: 2 x 10
   c. Freehand squat: 2 x 22
   d. Floor push-up: 2 x 9
   e. Chair chin-up: 2 x 9
2. *Stretching*
3. *Technique rehearsal*
4. *Aerobic work*
   Walk for 15 minutes

SATURDAY
1. *Calisthenics*
   a. Crunch: 2 x 14
   b. Floor back extension: 2 x 11
   c. Freehand squat: 2 x 25
   d. Floor push-up: 2 x 10
   e. Chair chin-up: 2 x 10
2. *Stretching*
3. *Technique rehearsal*
4. *Aerobic work*
   Walk for 15 minutes

Week 3 *illustration*

TUESDAY
1. *Calisthenics*
   a. Crunch: 2 x 15
   b. Floor back extension: 2 x 12
   c. Freehand squat: 2 x 28
   d. Floor push-up: 2 x 12
   e. Chair chin-up: 2 x 11
2. *Stretching*
3. *Technique rehearsal*
4. *Aerobic work*
   Walk for 20 minutes

Continue to make gradual progress during the rest of the preparatory period.

Motto for success

"No excuses, no procrastination."
DO WHAT NEEDS TO BE DONE, NOW!

Regardless of your age, or how out of condition you may be at present, it's never too late to start an exercise program. You can transform your fitness at any age, along with your appearance, and health.

3

The truth on age and exercise

The older you are, the more important it is that you exercise. You can add life to your years, and perhaps years to your life, but you must exercise safely and effectively, or otherwise the results will be injury, frustration, and failure.

The older you are, the more urgent it is *not* to make mistakes, and the more knowledgeable you need to be.

"Use it or lose it, but don't abuse it." This applies to all ages, but especially to older trainees.

The older you are, the greater the need for training consistency. A young person can lay off training for a couple of months, and then return to previous strength and fitness levels quickly; but it takes more time for an older trainee, and the chance of incurring problems along the way is usually greater. If you lay off too long, you'll never make it all the way back.

Older people often have some bodyparts that have restricted ranges of motion. Although ranges of motion can usually be improved, limitations will remain for some trainees. Some exercises may need to be modified, or even avoided.

Why strength train?

According to some reports there's typically a loss of about 1% of muscle mass per year from about age 50, unless strength training is employed to prevent or at least minimize the loss. From around age 60 there may be a slight escalation beyond 1% a year. By age 70 this may add up to a loss of over 25% of one's muscle mass relative to what it was at age 25, depending on the individual, and if there's been no strength-training intervention.

There can even be a substantial loss of muscle before middle age. If, for example, in your late teens you were very active, and involved in sports, but then became sedentary for two decades, you would lose a lot of muscle tissue. Even if your weight is the same at age 40 as it was at 20, you would have gained a lot of fat, and dramatically changed your body composition and appearance. Strength training is important for young people, too.

Many people get heavier as they age, while they lose muscle mass. Thus their overall gain of bodyfat is dramatic. They have more fat to lug around, and less muscle to employ to move their bodies. This is the major reason why most older people struggle physically.

Loss of muscle has many negative consequences, including strength decline, reduced caloric requirements, postural deterioration, reduced fitness, increased tendency to gain bodyfat, weakened resistance to injury, and deterioration in physical appearance.

Strength training is essential for building muscle, maintaining muscle, or minimizing muscle loss, depending on your age and how long and well you've been training. Strength training is one of the most important things you can do for your appearance and health.

Muscle is precious—build it, and then preserve it.

If you start strength training when you're in your late teens or early twenties, for example, and train effectively and consistently, you may reach your physical peak in your thirties. You should then continue to strength train. It would *maintain* your existing muscle mass for many years, and thereafter minimize its atrophy. But by starting from a higher base of muscle mass before the inevitable atrophy starts, the resulting muscle mass at, for instance, age 70, will be far greater than it would have been had you not strength trained. This will make a huge difference to your appearance, fitness, and general well-being, especially if you keep yourself lean.

If you start strength training in your middle or later years, you'll be able to build new muscle for a number of years, then maintain it for further years, and thereafter minimize its atrophy. The end result, again, will leave you with far more muscle than you would have had if you had not trained, and make a huge difference to your appearance, fitness, and general well-being, especially if you keep yourself lean.

Strength training also applies stress on the skeleton, which builds stronger, denser bones that are less likely to fracture during accidents. Strength training also builds or maintains the strong muscles required for dynamic balance, to help reduce the incidence of some accidents.

One of the functions of the muscular system is to maintain good posture. A steady contraction of the postural muscles—including the back, thighs, neck, shoulders, and abdominals—keeps the body in position. When these muscles lose strength, posture suffers. When the erector spinae weaken, for example, it causes rounding of the shoulders, gait change, reduced resistance to injury, and a decrease in height—common changes that start at about age 40 unless averted by strength training. Strong postural muscles are critical.

Strong muscles produce health benefits that reduce the impact of aging. Strength training helps you to stay young for your years.

But strength training alone isn't enough. Without a supple body, for example, muscles lose some of their elasticity and ability to function smoothly, and tendons, ligaments, and joint capsules become brittle. Tissues in general become more susceptible to injury, and the body ages at an accelerated rate.

The steadfast application of the *combination* of strength training, stretching, cardiovascular work, healthy nutrition, and a healthy lifestyle is the closest we can get to the fountain of youth, *but the exercise must be safe, and effective.*

Regardless of your age, you MUST *get a physician's clearance before starting an exercise program. Even minimal exercise may be harmful for someone in poor condition.*

Someone who's been exercising safely and effectively since he was a teenager can't be in the same condition at 65 as he was at 30. He can, however, maintain sufficient condition at 65 that will make him a phenomenon for his age.

A 40-year-old beginner to strength training who has kept herself fit from other activities can't be compared with a beginner of the same age who has neglected her health and fitness for many years.

Each individual is unique.

Training is essential, of course, but most trainees give it exaggerated importance compared with another pivotal component of success—*recuperation from training*. If you don't get your recuperative system in order, you won't make good progress with your training, and muscle-building.

4

How to optimize your recuperative powers

Training is the catalyst for stronger and bigger muscles. The breaking down of muscle tissue through training stimulates your body to repair it *and* build a little extra tissue. The "little extra tissue" is called *overcompensation,* and it accumulates to produce bigger muscles.

What you do in the gym provides only the stimulus for muscle growth. You must then avoid the gym for long enough to permit your body to repair the muscle damage, *and* overcompensate. Then return to the gym for another bout of growth stimulation. If you train too often you won't give your body enough time to repair the broken-down muscle tissue *and* build the overcompensation tissue.

Recovery time between workouts is only part of the anabolic environment. You must also provide a healthy, nutrient-rich diet—that's where the raw materials for muscle growth come from.

Sleep and rest

Without sufficient sleep on a consistent basis you'll never recover optimally from your training. If you don't recover optimally, you'll never progress optimally. Nothing can compensate for insufficient sleep.

> *Although you probably like the extra active hours you get from not sleeping sufficiently—to use for work, entertainment, or other purposes—you probably wouldn't be happy to trade lost gains in muscular development, and lost progress in the gym. But that's precisely the trade most trainees make.*

Sleeping well helps sustain a high level of desire for training, and gives you the ability to train well. If you're tired, you won't do justice to your training, and if you don't do justice to your training, you'll never reach your exercise-related goals.

If you exercise hard and consistently, sleeping well usually means getting at least eight hours of quality sleep each night. And not losing sleep in the first place is better than catching up on lost sleep.

Not only do you need to sleep well each night, you need to rest adequately during the daytime. It's good to be moderately active each day—walking and gardening, for instance—but outside of your training, minimize intensive exercise that competes for your limited recovery reserves.

Sleeping well doesn't just benefit your training. It's critical for your long-term health, and your day-to-day alertness, creativity, attentiveness, and capacity to learn. What many people consider fatigue, insufficient energy, boredom, and lack of attentiveness, are nothing other than the effects of sleep debt.

If my words aren't persuasive, read THE PROMISE OF SLEEP (1999, Delacorte Press), by William C. Dement, MD, Ph.D., one of the world's leading authorities on sleep, with more than 40 years of research experience. To quote from the book's dustjacket:

> "Healthy sleep has been empirically proven to be the single most important determinant in predicting longevity, *more influential than diet, exercise, or heredity,* but our modern culture has become an alarming study in sleep deprivation and ignorance . . . Sleep is sacrificed to meet the demands of our endless days. Unnoticed, deadly sleep disorders shorten countless lives . . . Doctors regard sleep deprivation as a fact of life and do little to promote sleep health or awareness. Meanwhile, the physical, emotional, and psychological costs of unhealthy sleep continue to mount."

As your first course of action to improve your sleep, apply these tips:

1. Establish regular sleeping habits. Going to sleep at 10:00 pm one night, and 1:00 am the next, isn't regularity. Instead, perhaps sleep from 10.30 pm to 7:00 am on a regular basis.

2. Avoid napping other than on occasional days when a special event such as a nighttime flight, or drive, may necessitate a daytime nap. Brief periods of sleep during the day usually disrupt nighttime sleeping patterns.

3. Sleep on a comfortable mattress. It's not necessarily true that a firm mattress is best, or a soft mattress is undesirable. It depends on the individual, the mattress concerned, the base of the bed, and the body position you sleep in. It pays to invest in a good bed. Consider an adjustable bed, as it allows you to elevate your head and legs to their most comfortable positions.

4. Put blocks of wood about four inches (10 centimeters) tall beneath the legs at the head of the bed. This slight elevation may enable gravity to help reduce brain congestion and pressure, and nasal congestion, which in turn may help reduce snoring, insomnia, sleep apnea (repeated, temporary cessation of breathing while sleeping), and headache upon waking. Flat sleeping may encourage brain congestion and pressure, and nasal congestion. This may lead to brain edema, which may be associated with a number of brain diseases. Waking during the night may, to some degree, be a reaction to brain congestion, to try to force sitting or standing, to reduce brain congestion. Don't elevate the bed more than four inches, because anything greater would lead to your sliding down the mattress, and risk pooling of blood in your legs.

5. The orientation of your bed may affect how well you sleep. Try different orientations.

6. If you usually sleep with someone, your bed should be large enough so that you don't bump into each other while sleeping. If it isn't large enough, consider getting a bigger bed, moving two beds together, or sleeping on separate beds.

7. Use a comfortable pillow. A pillow that's too thick or thin may impair sleep, and increase the risk of neck injury while sleeping. Experiment with various pillows to find one that suits you best. You may need to change it periodically, as it loses its shape.

8. Sleep in a dark room—fit shutters or black-out curtains.

9. Put a nightlight in your bathroom so that you don't have to turn a light on if you go to the toilet during the night.

10. Eliminate as much as possible all sources of noise that could disturb you. The hum from a fan or an air conditioning unit can mask external noise, as can a device that generates "white noise."

11. If you're too warm or too cool it could disturb your sleep even if you don't feel you're too warm or too cool. Although, for example, you may think you're warm enough, you may benefit from an extra blanket. Keeping your feet warm is important. Consider wearing socks while you sleep, especially in winter.

12. If you're a shift worker, the move from one shift to another is likely to ruin your sleep patterns. The only solution may be to get off changing shifts, to provide your body with the consistency of going to sleep at a regular hour.

13. Don't take sedatives or sleeping pills, as they tend to mask sleeping problems and make them worse over the long-term, and the medication can be addictive.

14. Don't smoke. Smoking increases the likelihood of snoring, the stimulative effect of nicotine can delay falling asleep, and the addictiveness of nicotine can trigger cravings that wake smokers up during the night. Because it mars sleep is just one of many serious reasons why you shouldn't smoke.

15. Don't have a computer in your bedroom, or anything else associated with work. Maintain a work-free environment there.

16. Don't drink coffee or any other stimulant for at least several hours before bedtime. Avoid stimulants such as caffeine other than for occasional, special use.

17. Don't weight train late in the day if it has a negative effect on your sleep—train earlier.

18. Low-intensity, aerobic work late in the day, or going for a walk, may help you to sleep.

19. To minimize the need to urinate during the night, finish your final meal two hours before retiring, avoid juicy fruit and vegetables at that meal, and minimize liquid consumption between then and bedtime. But have a small, high-protein, low-liquid snack just before retiring. Catch up with plenty of liquids during each morning and afternoon. If despite these actions you still have to

urinate more than once during the night—especially an *increased* need to urinate—see your doctor. In a man, for example, this may be a symptom of an enlarged prostate gland. Furthermore, you may actually be awakened by sleep apnea, snoring, or another disorder, and only *then* do you get up to urinate.

20. Don't have pets in your bedroom during the night. Pets will disturb your sleep if they are in the same room with you.

21. Have a cup of chamomile tea about two hours before bedtime. Chamomile tea has long been a traditional aid for sleep. A few people, however, are allergic to chamomile.

22. A warm bath an hour or so before going to bed may help prepare your body for sleep.

23. During the hour before bedtime, relax, de-stress, and calm yourself. Don't watch anything on TV or at a cinema that stirs up your emotions, don't deal with financial matters, don't check your email and voice mail, don't get into any arguments, and don't tackle any complex project.

24. Immediately before sleep, read something that relaxes you.

25. Learn to put problems and worries out of your mind when it's time to go to sleep. Concentrate on pleasant thoughts and memories. Recreate a pleasurable time or event in your life, and relive it in your mind. Learn a relaxation technique such as meditation, or the use of guided imagery.

26. Never use alcohol as a sleep aid. Alcohol is a sedative, and while it may help put you to sleep, it disrupts sleep patterns, and mars sleep quality. Avoid alcohol within three hours of bedtime.

Once you've caught up on your sleep debt—which may require an extra hour or two of sleep every night for a week or two, and could be timed during a vacation—just an extra 45 to 60 minutes of sleep each night relative to what you get now may be all you need to satisfy your sleep requirement. Although you'll be active for perhaps an hour less each day, you'll be more alert and energetic, you'll make better training progress, and you'll improve your health.

Sleep needs vary, to a degree. Once your sleep debt is cleared, keep a sleep log for at least a week. Wake naturally each morning, and calculate your average sleep per night. Eight hours may be sufficient

> *That many people depend on coffee to keep themselves alert is a clear sign of how a sleep deficit is commonly masked on a daily basis.*

under normal circumstances, but periods of intensified training or increased overall physical demands will increase your sleep needs.

Get the sleep you need, without any feeling of guilt for sleeping more than perhaps most of your friends do. It's a modern, social disease that some people feel proud for managing on as little sleep as possible each night. As Dr. Dement states in his book, "Sleep quotas are biologically fixed, and there is no more shame in needing ten hours a day of sleep than in needing a size ten shoe."

Getting more quality sleep may not be straightforward. For many people, going to bed earlier is all that's needed. For others, quality sleep doesn't come easily. Even the general rule of sleeping until you wake naturally each morning doesn't work for many people, especially those in and beyond middle age. If you nod off easily during the day, become drowsy while driving, or need to drink a stimulant such as coffee to remain alert, you're not sleeping enough or in sufficient quality, no matter how many hours you spend in bed.

Sleep disorders are common. If you snore, for example, you have a sleep disorder. Although snoring often causes amusement, it's a serious disorder. It's a symptom that indicates the creation of many health problems, some of the perceived effects of aging, and may even lead to premature death.

If you still have problems sleeping, such as snoring and sleep apnea, even after applying the tips given in this chapter, read GET IT UP (2000, ISCD Press), by Sydney Ross Singer and Soma Grismaijer (www.selfstudycenter.org), for possible solutions. A sleep clinic may be helpful, depending on the doctors there and their proposed solutions. Some doctors prescribe drug and surgical "solutions" that don't address the causes.

Improve your sleep and you'll improve your recovery ability, results from your training, *and* your health and quality of life. You may even add years to your life.

Further reading

THE PROMISE OF SLEEP (1999, Delacorte Press), by William C. Dement, MD, Ph.D.

SEVEN DAYS TO A PERFECT NIGHT'S SLEEP (2003, St. Martin's Griffin), by Debra L. Gordon

GET IT UP (2000, ISCD Press), by Sydney Ross Singer and Soma Grismaijer

Nutrition

During the first few months of training, consolidate the dietary changes implemented during the preparatory month, as explained in Chapter 2.

Your first few months of training shouldn't be intensive because during that period you focus on learning correct exercise technique and control. Noticeable muscle growth probably won't occur then. It's only from around the fifth month that you may need to boost your caloric and nutritional intake—*if* you don't need to lose bodyfat.

Once you're training hard, if you cut corners with your diet, your body will cut corners with its recuperation and building processes. No quantity of amino acid capsules, creatine, vitamins, or any other supplement will help you if you're deficient in sufficient healthy food.

Caloric intake

Calories come from the three major macronutrients—protein, fat, and carbohydrate. One gram of protein or carbohydrate yields four kilocalories, and one gram of fat yields nine kilocalories. Therefore, you need more than twice the weight of protein or carbohydrate to provide the same number of calories as pure fat or oil.

Your caloric requirements depend on your lean body mass, age, activity level, and goals. The basic rule for gaining muscle is to consume as many calories and nutrients as you can without increasing your bodyfat percentage, and to have meals frequently enough to avoid hunger.

Fast bodyweight gains are usually mostly if not totally fat gains. Measure your waist girth at least once every two weeks, first thing in the morning. Use a consistent procedure, with your abdominals tensed, not pulled in. Your waist girth can, however, increase without your bodyfat percentage increasing. Development of your lower back, obliques, and abdominals can add an inch or more of muscle to your waist girth, but that girth increase is desirable because it will produce a stronger, better-developed midsection.

For men, along with your waist girth, measure a fat pinch taken at the midpoint between your navel and hip bone. For women, along with your waist girth, take a fat pinch at a fixed spot on your hips. Either way, take the fat pinch in the

Even the best food will make you fat if you consume too much, and even the right quantity may make you fat if you're not training properly. You must provide the stimulus to grow before you can turn any nutrients into muscle.

Whether you can gain five, ten, or more pounds of muscle in a year depends on many factors, including your gender, age, genetic endowment, how underdeveloped you were before the period of assessment, how you train, how well you rest, and how dedicated you are. Do the best you can in and out of the gym, and let the results take care of themselves.

same way every two weeks, and measure its thickness. Use your thumb and index finger to dig in deep and pinch all the subcutaneous fat, and measure the thickness with a ruler. Better, however, is the use of fat calipers. Plastic calipers are available through mail order, or some stores.

To gain muscular weight, there are three fundamentals you must satisfy *before* increasing your caloric intake:

1. Consume a healthy diet of nutrient-rich food.

2. Know the baseline caloric intake that maintains your bodyweight, and then exceed it *slightly*.

3. Stimulate muscular growth without overtraining.

After your first six months on **The Program**, find a caloric intake that permits muscle building without bodyfat gain. Get a calorie ready-reckoner from a bookstore, a weighing scale, and a measuring jug. For at least four days of typical eating and drinking—perhaps two consecutive weekends—weigh all the food you eat, and measure the volume of all liquids you drink other than water. Calculate your total caloric intake each day, and produce an average over the number of test days. This would be your maintenance caloric intake provided that you didn't gain or lose weight over the testing period.

To get an estimate of your maintenance caloric needs, use 13 to 17 kilocalories per pound of bodyweight. Use 13 if you're inactive other than your gym work, 15 if you're moderately active, and 17 if you're very active. For example, if you weigh 154 pounds (70 kilos), and are moderately active, your maintenance caloric needs should be approximately 2,310 kilocalories daily (154 x 15).

After having done the recommended test, you'll have an idea of how you compare with the estimated maintenance intake for your bodyweight. The 13 to 17 figures are only estimates, but they work for many people and may be a starting point.

To gain muscle, you must increase your bodyweight (unless you're also losing bodyfat), and to do that you may need to increase your caloric intake. If you need to increase your caloric intake, do it *gradually* so that your digestive tract can adapt.

Add 200 kilocalories to your maintenance intake. Test this for a few weeks. In the aforementioned illustration, you would consume 2,500 kilocalories daily—2,310 plus 200, rounded to the nearest 100. Work out a schedule of five meals daily of 500 kilocalories each.

After four weeks, take your bodyweight, waist girth, and fat pinch. If you've gained a pound or so and your fat pinch has not increased, stick with that intake. If your fat pinch has increased, there are several possible explanations:

1. Perhaps you've consumed too many calories, and need to cut back.

2. Perhaps your caloric intake is fine, but you didn't stimulate any growth to convert the additional calories into muscle.

3. Perhaps you didn't provide sufficient rest and sleep to enable your body to convert the growth stimulus and additional nutritional intake into muscle.

If you didn't gain any weight, increase your daily caloric intake by a further 200 kilocalories—five meals of 540 kilocalories each, in this illustration. Test that for a few weeks. If that still doesn't increase your bodyweight, increase your caloric intake again, but only by 100 kilocalories this time. Thereafter make increases of just 100 kilocalories at a time.

Find the maximum caloric intake you can consume without adding bodyfat. Keep the testing process going until you find that your waist fat pinch has increased, then back off 100 to 200 kilocalories.

Each pound of new muscle needs up to about 20 additional kilocalories daily to maintain it. This is higher than the 13 to 17 estimation of kilocalories per pound of bodyweight referred to earlier. The latter is an average for bodyweight as a whole, including tissue that uses few or no calories, such as fat. New muscle has a higher per-pound caloric requirement. Following every five pounds of extra muscle, boost your daily intake by 100 kilocalories (*unless* you're trying to lose bodyfat).

Meal planning

Eat at three-and-a-half hour intervals, such as 7:00 am, 10:30 am, 2:00 pm, 5:30 pm, and 9:00 pm. Five small meals are commonly more easily digested than two or three bigger meals, and may provide a more even supply of nutrients.

When increasing your caloric intake, get the calories where you need them most. For example, if you currently eat little protein, get most of your extra calories from protein-rich food; and if you currently eat a low-fat diet, add some oil-rich natural foods to your daily fare.

If consuming additional calories is difficult for you, concentrate on calorie-dense foods. For example, eat bread rather than potatoes, dried fruit and bananas rather than juicy fruits, and foods high in healthy fats rather than low in fat. Furthermore, consume some liquid meals if you find getting extra calories through solid food to be a problem.

Stay at your gaining caloric level only if you're training hard. If you back off on the effort front, back off on your caloric intake, too, or the surplus calories will be stored as bodyfat.

As a starting point for individual fine-tuning, consume about 25% of your calories as fat; a sufficient percentage to supply about one gram of protein (mostly from animal sources) per pound of lean bodyweight when in intensive training, but just half of that may be enough at other times; and the balance of calories as carbohydrates. Too much protein is better than not enough—excess usually isn't a problem provided you're healthy. Within each macro-nutrient, get what you need from *healthy* food you can digest comfortably.

Compose lists of at least a dozen healthy meals (and some blender drinks, too), and compute their content in terms of calories, protein, fat, and carbohydrate. Refer to a book that provides listings of caloric and macronutrient contents of various foods.

The meals will reflect your tastes, religious and cultural background, food availability, powers of digestion, financial considerations, and any allergies or other health issues.

Some people have sensitive digestive systems, whereas others seem to be able to eat any mixture of foods without problems. Through experience, stick to the food combinations that work best for you.

Once you have a list of meals with caloric and macronutrient values, put together a selection to yield your food allocation for any given day.

Dietary fat

Not only are some fats not bad, they are essential for good health. Without them you can damage your health over the long-term. Some fats are harmful, however, and should be avoided, such as margarine, refined vegetable oils, and hydrogenated oil.

Essential fatty acids (EFAs) play a critical role in efficient digestion and joint health. An efficient digestive system and robust joints are vital for training success. Deficiencies in EFAs are linked with cancer, diabetes, cardiovascular disease, arthritis, weakened immune functions, and other health problems. Many people have taken the "fat is bad" opinion and applied it to all sources of fat and oil, even the good ones.

Getting most of your fat intake from fish high in essential fatty acids (such as herring, mackerel, salmon, and sardines), along with other healthy fat from avocados, olive oil, nuts and seeds, flaxseed oil and butter in moderation, and boiled or poached eggs (low-temperature preparation relative to frying and scrambling), is vastly different from getting the same total quantity of fat from fried food, margarine and shortenings (hydrogenated oils), refined vegetable oils, omelettes, and scrambled eggs. Over the long-term, the different effects on health from the two diets may be dramatic.

There are two major families of EFAs—the omega-6 fatty acids, and the omega-3s. Many common foods contain omega-6s in small quantities, and a few contain omega-6s in large quantities, such as corn oil, safflower oil, and sunflower oil, which many people use for cooking. Furthermore, lots of packaged and processed foods contain hidden omega-6s. Few foods in the typical diet contain omega-3s in anything other than small quantities. Therefore, the typical diet has few omega-3s, but lots of omega-6s, and usually poor omega-6s. This produces a serious imbalance between the EFAs.

Flaxseed oil is rich in the most important member of the omega-3 family—from which other omega-3s can be produced—and through consuming sufficient flaxseed oil you can correct an EFA imbalance. Oily fish doesn't contain the entire family of omega-3s. No matter what your consumption of oily fish, you may still be deficient in the primary member of the omega-3 family of fats unless you have a rich source of it in your diet. This is where flaxseed oil is helpful. Flax seeds themselves can be consumed, but they must be ground first, and eaten immediately. Consume oily fish, *and* flax seeds or oil, for the best all-round intake of omega-3s.

According to Drs. Udo Erasmus and Donald Rudin, two prominent researchers on fats,

Nuts

Nuts are nutritious, but can be hard to digest if consumed in anything other than tiny quantities, because of the enzyme inhibitors they contain. If the nuts are soaked overnight in water mixed with some salt, the enzyme inhibitors will be neutralized. This makes the nuts more digestible. The soaked nuts, removed from the brine and washed, should be kept in the refrigerator so that they don't spoil. If the soaked nuts aren't kept in a refrigerator, they should be dried first, in a warm oven.

Cod liver oil

This has long been a traditional remedy for joint pains and stiffness, and an aid for strong bones, good vision, healthy skin, and resistance to coughs and colds. Cod liver oil is rich in omega-3s, and fat-soluble vitamins A and D, which are commonly undersupplied. Cod liver oil is potent, and may be toxic in large amounts. Two teaspoons per day is sufficient for adults, and one is enough for children.

two or three tablespoons of flaxseed oil a day for a month or two or three may be needed to correct a deficiency of omega-3s, but much less is needed thereafter. A sustained high intake of flaxseed oil can produce an imbalance, and must be avoided.

An indication of balanced intake is skin condition. Dry hands, feet, elbows, and other bodyparts indicate insufficient consumption of omega-3s. Once your skin is smooth, supple, and no longer dry, consume just sufficient flaxseed oil to maintain that condition—perhaps one or two teaspoons a day. Keep flaxseed oil refrigerated once a container has been opened, and use it within a few weeks. If the oil tastes off, don't use it.

Use virgin olive oil daily: on salads and fish, and dip bread in it. Make your own salad dressing rather than buy inferior, ready-made ones that contain dubious ingredients, and poor oil. Mix olive oil and cider vinegar in proportions of about four to one, together with some herbs and mustard paste. Olive oil isn't a rich source of EFAs, but it is rich in healthy, monounsaturated fatty acids, and many nutrients and valuable substances unique to olives.

In moderation, saturated fats aren't harmful like some people make them out to be. Saturated fats were an important part of traditional diets that have kept many societies healthy for generations until the effects of modern farming, refining, and processing were felt, including the addition of refined sugar and oils (and products containing them), refined grain products, and the use of processed vegetable oils in place of natural oils and fats.

In the 1980s I was a vegan for four years, due in part to my believing at the time that a diet free of all animal products (especially saturated animal fat) was healthy. Paradoxically, my four years as a vegan damaged my health. Now, I know some of the reasons why veganism wasn't a success for me.

Although I still don't eat meat, meat isn't necessarily unhealthy. The type of meat, farming methods used to produce the meat, how the meat is cooked, and one's overall diet, are important in determining whether the meat is healthy or unhealthy.

It's a myth that a vegetarian diet is necessarily healthier than a mixed diet. Some vegetarian diets can be unhealthy. For instance, meat-free junk food is still junk food, and some meat-substitute products are unnatural and, in some cases, packed with poor oil, hydrogenated oil, and other harmful products.

A mixed diet can be unhealthy or healthy depending on how it's constructed, the specific food sources, farming methods, how the food is prepared, and one's lifestyle in general.

Dietary fiber

Many high-protein diets are low in dietary fiber, and wreak havoc on the elimination systems of those who follow them. To provide sufficient fiber along with many nutrients, eat these foods daily: porridge, whole-grain bread and cereals, vegetables, fruit (dates, figs, and prunes are rich in fiber), and perhaps legumes (soaked overnight before cooking).

If, however, you have a digestive tract problem such as irritable bowel syndrome (IBS), *insoluble* fiber in large quantities may irritate your colon. Rich sources of insoluble fiber include whole-grain bread and cereals, dates, seeds, and beans. If you have IBS, consume more *soluble* fiber—oats, white rice, barley bread, and corn bread are rich in it, for example—and reduced quantities of insoluble fiber. But for both types of fiber to do their important work, you must drink sufficient water.

The digestibility of grains is influenced by how they are prepared. Boxed breakfast cereals are usually refined and processed—to produce flakes, shapes, or even puffed grains—in a manner that mars their digestibility. They also have sugar added to them and, often, unhealthy oil. Check the labels of boxed cereals.

Breakfast

Substitute porridge for boxed cereals, but prepare it in the traditional way—for improved digestibility and nutrient availability. Soak the unrefined, rolled oats overnight in warm water acidulated with a little vinegar, or lemon juice. Use oats to water in a volume ratio of about 1:2.5. At breakfast time, add a little spice and unrefined sea salt, bring to a boil, and simmer for a few minutes. Then mix the porridge with butter and a natural sweetener, according to taste. The butter is important, not just for taste, but as a catalyst for mineral absorption. Never use margarine, because it's one of the worst forms of fat. As a natural sweetener, choose from pure date sugar, honey, maple syrup, or molasses.

Water

Adequate water intake is critical to health and well-being. Merely not being thirsty doesn't mean you're properly supplied with water. Coffee and tea, unless decaffeinated, and alcoholic beverages, don't count as water intake. Drinks containing caffeine or alcohol can increase your need for water, because of their diuretic effects.

Consume enough water distributed over the course of each day to produce at least four clear urinations a day (in addition to colored urinations). Until you produce the minimum of four clear urinations a day, gradually increase your intake of water. Get a water filter if your tap water doesn't have a pleasant taste, or drink bottled water that tastes good. Replace sodas, soft drinks, and caffeinated drinks with water. Keep a bottle of water handy, and have a few mouthfuls every 15 to 30 minutes, and more often if it's hot or you're exercising. Large but infrequent drinks of water increase urination but don't necessarily produce adequate hydration. Little and often is a better strategy for water consumption. Caffeine-free, herbal tea is a good source of water. Try aniseed, chamomile, fennel, ginger, mint, and peppermint. As an additional benefit, each of these herbal teas may help your digestion.

> *Products such as yogurt, kefir, and cheese may have advantages over milk* NOT JUST *because they are more easily tolerated by many people. The fermentation that milk goes through to produce these products may restore some of the enzymes destroyed during pasteurization. And kefir supplies beneficial bacteria, yeast, and lactic acid to the digestive tract.*
>
> *Regular consumption of kefir helps to create a healthier digestive system. Consume it alone, between meals, for easier digestion. If ready-made kefir isn't available, friendly bacteria are obtainable from specialized probiotic, yogurt-like drinks. Alternatively, make your own kefir once you have some starter culture—one source is www.kefir.net. There are also probiotic dietary supplements—these vary in quality and worth.*

Milk

Milk is a convenient nutriment, although pasteurized milk that comes from cows that aren't pasture-fed is a far cry from clean, unpasteurized milk from pasture-fed cows. Nutritional composition, nutrient availability, and digestibility of the latter is superior to the former.

If you suffer from gas, bloating, or diarrhea after drinking milk, you may be lactose intolerant—your small intestine doesn't produce enough lactase, the enzyme needed to digest lactose. Lactose is the natural sugar found in milk, and other dairy products. Lactose intolerance is common, but the extent of the intolerance varies.

Although some people don't produce enough lactase to handle even a couple of mouthfuls of milk, other people need to consume a couple of pints of milk before they exhaust their immediate production of lactase. Your tolerance of lactose may decrease as you age. But what some people may think is lactose intolerance may be a problem with digesting a milk protein called casein.

Dairy products including yogurt, kefir, and cheese come from a process of fermenting or souring milk that partially breaks down lactose, and predigests casein. The end products may be more easily tolerated by adults who can't digest fresh milk. Processed cheese, however, should be avoided, because it contains a number of unhealthy ingredients. Unfermented butter and cream contain little casein or lactose, and can usually be tolerated even by people who have problems with casein or lactose. Soured or fermented butter and cream may be even more digestible.

As convenient as milk is, you can manage well without it, especially if you can't find clean, unpasteurized milk from pasture-fed cows. You need to be more creative in your meal and drink design, and use fermented dairy products, and other food sources, instead of milk.

Convenient but healthy fast food

Use blender drinks for liquid food, especially if you have high caloric needs, or if you need nutritious, easily consumed food on the go. Rather than grab a bite to eat from somewhere out of convenience, drink a glass of a healthy, liquid meal from your flask. Make a thermos of a blender drink at night, ready for the following day. Blend ingredients that you like and can digest easily, in quantities that are appropriate for you. In addition, prepare some other food, such as healthy sandwiches.

Alcohol

Avoid anything more than moderate consumption of alcoholic drinks. Heavy alcohol consumption is harmful to the body in many ways, but *moderate* consumption may have some health benefits *except for people for whom alcohol is harmful*. People who shouldn't consume alcoholic drinks include pregnant women, anyone who has had an alcohol problem in the past, anyone with a condition that's irritated by alcohol, and anyone who takes medication that's incompatible with alcohol.

To quote Dr. Jeffrey Tobias—consultant specializing in cancer medicine at University College London Hospitals for over 20 years—from the

> *Never look to food supplements for answers to training problems. The answers are elsewhere, although prudent use of some supplements from reputable companies may help you once you have the fundamentals of training and recuperation in place.*

website of the British Broadcasting Corporation, "The present [maximum] recommendations for alcohol are 21 units weekly for men, and 14 for women (a unit is a standard pub measure of wine or spirits, or a half pint of beer)."

The units aren't cumulative. If a week's 21 units for a man are consumed over a weekend rather than seven days, that will be harmful.

To quote Prof. David J. Hanson, Ph.D., of the State University of New York, Potsdam (www2.potsdam.edu/alcohol-info/), "All of the many health benefits of drinking apply only to moderate consumption—never to heavy drinking. To the contrary, heavy drinking is associated with reduced longevity and increased risk of a diversity of diseases."

If you consume alcoholic drinks, have no more than three units per day if you're male, or two if you're female. Have them with meals or soon after eating (to slow the absorption of the alcohol into your system), not within three hours of bedtime (to avoid marring the quality of your sleep), and only when consumption does not put you or others at risk. Don't drink and operate complicated machinery, including motor vehicles.

The harm done by alcohol to your alertness and reflexes is exaggerated if you have a sleep debt. If you haven't slept well recently, you'll have a sleep debt. To quote Dr. William C. Dement from THE PROMISE OF SLEEP, page 68, "A fact little known by the public at large is that in nearly every accident linked to alcohol consumption, sleep debt almost certainly plays a major role." Even a small amount of alcohol can have a major sedating effect if it's consumed when there's a sleep debt.

Pre-workout nutrition

Don't wait too long after a meal before training, but don't train too soon either. Have a simple meal you can digest easily, and train about two hours afterward. Discover how much time you need for a meal to be processed enough so that you can train hard without any nausea or digestive tract discomfort.

The meal should be carbohydrate-rich, but not exclusively carbs, and the carbohydrates shouldn't be only the simple type. Complex carbs are needed to sustain your energy throughout a workout. Through trial and error, discover the food types and quantities that carry you through an intensive workout without any waning of energy.

Post-training nutrition

Within half an hour of your workout, have a liquid, easily digested, protein-rich, carbohydrate-rich meal. Consume 30 to 40 grams of protein, and 60 to 80 grams of carbohydrates, depending on your size. Within the next two hours or so, have a meal of solid food, or another liquid meal.

Food supplements

Nutrition is primarily about food, not supplements, yet when gym discussions touch on nutrition, it's food supplements that are often the focus. Some food supplement companies are guilty of dishonesty in several ways:

1. Making deceitful claims that their products can't deliver.

2. Listing fictitious ingredients and quantities.

3. Making up research studies, selecting research that has nothing to do with healthy, hard-training humans, and drawing on research that's based on methodology devoid of scientific credibility.

4. Paying people for fictitious endorsements.

Conditions to satisfy before trying "bodybuilding supplements"

You must have the fundamentals in place *before* you experiment with only possibly useful extras. No supplement will compensate for a diet deficient in a major component. Here are the essentials to get in place:

1. Daily satisfaction of your caloric needs.

2. Satisfaction of your caloric needs through five or six evenly spaced, easily digested meals.

3. Daily satisfaction of your sleep requirements.

4. Actual production of muscle and strength gains through the combination of 1 through 3, and training.

People who claim that food supplements work like steroids, are lying, possibly to try to persuade you to buy the supplements.

Vitamin and mineral supplements

Vitamin and mineral supplements, unless you're seriously deficient in nutrients, can't make an immediate impact on your training other than perhaps from a placebo effect. They may, however, benefit your health over the long-term, which may increase your training longevity.

I recommend cod liver oil, flaxseed oil, and a daily, balanced, vitamin-and-mineral formula. Furthermore, on top of what's in the latter, I recommend supplementary vitamins C and E, selenium, and some other antioxidants, because in moderately high quantities they may be helpful for long-term health.

Other possibly valuable supplements include glucosamine, chondroitin, and gelatin. These may help to maintain healthy joints, and aid the recovery of injured joints.

Weight-gain and protein supplements

Although weight-gain products may provide a big boost of calories, some of which come from protein, they can be difficult to digest. Some of these products are more accurately described as "fat-gain supplements," which also contain some unhealthy ingredients.

Even expensive, "engineered" protein supplements can cause digestive-tract distress. Despite the advertising hoopla, there's no guarantee that expensive, cross-filtered, lactose-free whey with digestive enzymes and whey peptides will be easily digested. These

---

Digestive tract problems

Digestive tract disorders are common, and mar digestion, health, well-being, and progress in physique and fitness. For example, irritable bowel syndrome (IBS)—also known as spastic colon, and sometimes improperly termed spastic colitis—may, to some degree, afflict about 20% of Americans, according to some reports. Digestive tract disorders affect food selection because certain foods irritate sufferers.

If you regularly have digestive tract discomfort, constipation, diarrhea, or a lot of gas, get checked out by a gastroenterologist. If you know you have a disorder, you can take action to correct it, or at least control it. This will involve dietary modifications. The result will be a better functioning digestive system, which will boost your health, improve your recuperation from training, and help you to make greater progress in physique and fitness.

items are unnatural, fractionated foods. You would be better off getting your calories and nutrients from healthy, natural, whole foods.

Growth hormone and testosterone elevating compounds

A number of "supplements" are claimed to produce significant elevations in growth hormone or testosterone production. A lot of the advertising claims are dishonest, and some are based on non-human studies. If any of the hormone elevations are substantial, the product concerned will soon become a prescription drug.

If you take hormone boosters for extended periods, it's likely that your natural production of the hormones concerned will be reduced, or impaired. And any substantial increase in hormone output beyond normal levels is potentially dangerous.

Are you what you eat?

What you digest and assimilate is what counts nutritionally, not just what you swallow. Your health is, however, the result of a composite of factors. Even if your nutrition is optimal, your health will be affected by your lifestyle, genetic factors, activity levels, working environment, relationships, emotions, and other factors. And what you *do* to eat—your gait and how that's affected by your posture—plays a major part in your health and well-being.

Further reading

NOURISHING TRADITIONS: THE COOKBOOK THAT CHALLENGES POLITICALLY CORRECT NUTRITION AND THE DIET DICTOCRATS (2001, New Trends Publishing, Inc.), revised second edition, by Sally Fallon, with Mary G. Enig, Ph.D.

THE FIRST YEAR—IBS (IRRITABLE BOWEL SYNDROME): AN ESSENTIAL GUIDE FOR THE NEWLY DIAGNOSED (2001, Marlowe & Company), by Heather Van Vorous
Van Vorous' book, and her website, may also offer help for people who suffer from digestive tract disorders other than IBS. Her website is at www.helpforibs.com

Preparation can be everything when it comes to healthy eating, especially if you're busy during the day and don't have time then to prepare food. Prepare your food the night before.

The importance of physical conditioning in recuperation

If you need to rest many days between workouts before you feel recovered, something is amiss. Typically, this means you're training too much, or you're not eating, resting or sleeping well, or you're in poor physical condition. Good physical conditioning through cardio work is important in general, and may improve recovery between workouts.

You can't cheat genetics

Very few people have the genetics required in order to have the potential to be able to build physiques to the standards of today's competitive bodybuilders. You can go only as far as your genetics will allow, regardless of how well you train and recuperate. But you won't know what your genetics will permit until you go as far as you can.

Assuming you're a physiologically mature adult, then after three to five years of training and recuperating consistently well, with no setbacks or wasted periods, even a change of approach may not make a significant difference for muscular development, although total fitness may be improved further. (I'm considering healthy, drug-free training only.) Although you may not be able to increase muscle mass further, if you become leaner and stronger, and fitter in your cardiovascular system, you'll still make progress in your physique and overall well-being.

Be the best you can. This can bring great satisfaction and health benefits. It will put you into a different world of physical conditioning and health relative to where you would be if you didn't train.

Tips for optimizing recuperation

There's no room for compromise on the components of recuperation if you want to make the fastest possible muscle-building progress.

1. Give sleep a high priority. If you exercise hard, sleeping well usually means at least eight hours of quality sleep every night.

2. Consume a slight surplus of calories unless you need to lose bodyfat.

3. Once you're training hard, consume about one gram of protein (mostly from animal sources) per pound of lean bodyweight.

4. Avoid a low-fat diet. Fat is imperative for your health and maintaining an anabolic metabolism, but avoid unhealthy fats.

5. Avoid junk food.

6. Consume meals that suit *you*. More important than what you eat and drink, is what you digest and assimilate.

7. Avoid getting hungry or going for long periods between meals (except when you're sleeping). In the evening, prepare meals such as sandwiches and blender drinks, ready for the following day. Preparation is vital.

8. Within half an hour of finishing a workout, have a liquid, easily digested meal that's rich in carbohydrates and protein. Then about two hours later have a solid-food meal.

9. Pay special attention to breakfast time. If you skip breakfast, you'll hurt your muscle-building progress.

10. Focus on food, not supplements.

11. Drink plenty of liquids. Even slight dehydration can affect your training performance, recuperative powers, and general well-being. Too much water is better than too little.

12. Conserve your energy. Reduce to a minimum all physically demanding activities outside of the gym—but walking and general activity are desirable.

13. Keep calm. Being highly strung or stressed out will impair your ability to recuperate. Whenever you feel agitated, take a few deep breaths, and calm down. And find solutions to problems. Anything that festers, harms your health *and* recuperation, which in turn mars the results you get from your training.

14. Stay healthy. Take your health seriously if you want to optimize your ability to recuperate.

The wrap-up

The components of successful muscle-building are simple, but putting them into consistent practice requires dedication. No one can provide the dedication for you. While in the gym, *you* have to stick with **The Program**, *you* have to use correct exercise technique, and *you* have to train hard once you're beyond the initial few months. When out of the gym, *you* have to eat every three hours or so (except when you're sleeping), *you* have to eat only healthy food in the required quantity, *you* have to rest well between workouts, and *you* have to go to bed early enough to get your required eight or more hours of quality sleep each night. All of this requires dedication.

These aren't my rules. I'm only the messenger.

If you need to lose fat, *build muscle*. Fat-loss plans that don't include strength training *rob* the body of muscle. Muscle loss reduces caloric requirements, makes fat loss more difficult, and creates increased obstacles to the maintenance of a lean body once the excess fat has been lost. And to help maintain a lean body, *build muscle*.

5
How to lose bodyfat

Bodyfat can't be melted away through plastic wraps, saunas, or steam baths; and it can't be rubbed away through massage, or vibrating and rubbing machines. Furthermore, fat can't be dissolved away through any food or dietary supplement.

Sweating—whether through saunas, or localized through special bands, belts, or wrappings—doesn't produce fat loss. Instead, it produces water loss, which is regained through fluid intake.

It's physiologically impossible to whittle away fat through working the muscle beneath the fat. Reduction of fat in a specific area of the body through exercise or diet—spot reduction—is impossible. The body sheds fat *overall*, but from some places more than others, *or not at all*. The only way to spot-reduce fat is through surgical intervention, which has perils and isn't a long-term cure.

There are no quick fixes for fat loss. It is possible to lose a lot of weight quickly, through dietary deprivation, but some of the loss will be muscle, which would be disastrous. Muscle is a major ally on multiple fronts, including external appearance, general well-being, overall fitness, the ability to lose fat, and the ability to keep excess fat off.

Weight-loss programs are usually driven by reductions in gross bodyweight. Fat loss is what's required, not just any weight loss.

Dieting alone isn't enough for successful fat loss and maintenance of the fat loss.

Why building muscle is important

If you need to lose fat, *build muscle*. Fat-loss plans that don't include strength training *rob* the body of muscle. Muscle loss reduces caloric requirements, makes fat loss more difficult, and creates increased obstacles to the maintenance of a lean body once the excess fat has been lost. To help maintain a lean body, *build muscle*.

Building muscle increases your metabolic rate—the speed at which your resting body uses calories to meet its basic survival requirements. Muscle is metabolically active, unlike fat, and requires calories to sustain it. While claims for each pound of new muscle burning 35 to 50 or more kilocalories daily are exaggerated, up to about 20 kilocalories per pound of new muscle may be realistic. If, for example, you build ten pounds of new muscle, you may increase your daily basic requirements by up to 200 kilocalories. Over time that adds up to a lot of food. The more food you can eat while losing fat, or while maintaining a lean body, the more likely you'll be satisfied by your food intake.

Beginners at strength training can lose fat while they build muscle, although probably more fat loss than muscle gain will occur. Once you've developed new muscle, you need to strength train to maintain the muscle.

The foundation of fat loss

There's nothing complicated about how to lose bodyfat. It's the implementation of the know-how that usually produces difficulty. The first requirements for fat loss are resolve, and self-control.

For background information on fat loss, here's some of what Rich Rydin and Dave Maurice wrote in their column in HARDGAINER magazine issue #66, in answer to "Why can't I lose weight?" The first paragraph quotes from a report issued by the US Department of Agriculture:

" 'In 1997, each American consumed, on average, 81 pounds more of commercially grown vegetables than in 1970; 65 pounds more of grain products; 57 pounds more of fruit; 32 pounds more of caloric sweeteners; 13 pounds more of total red meat, poultry, and fish (boneless, trimmed equivalent); 17 pounds more of cheese; 13 pounds more of added fats and oils; 3 gallons more of beer; 70 fewer eggs; 10 gallons less of coffee; and 7 gallons less of milk.'

"Thirteen more pounds of fats and oils. Yes, the percentage of calories from fat has decreased, but the total calories from fat has increased. And look at that additional caloric sweeteners intake (sugar, corn syrup). What do you think it would do to you if you were to consume 13 pounds less of fats and oils, and 32 pounds less of sweeteners each year than you do now? And what about those grain products? The average American takes in less than one serving of whole grains per day. That means they are taking in a whole lot more—60+ pounds more—of refined carbs. It's much harder to overeat with whole grains. Not because they taste bad, though if you've been eating the refined grains for years you may not like the whole grains at first. But because they are more filling and slower to digest. For all the bad things you may have read about carbs, we'll just respond with this—try to get fat on whole grains."

Over recent years, per-capita food intake has increased in the US and some other countries, but the average individual's activity level in those countries has decreased. This combination is the root of the increasing levels of bodyfat. It's simple arithmetic—increased energy input and reduced energy output produce a surplus of energy, which is stored as bodyfat.

There are many diets and exercise-diet plans that can produce the caloric deficit required for fat loss, but the end result is the same— living off fat stores in the body. A caloric deficit means consuming fewer calories than are used up through daily activity. Some diets and exercise-diet plans are better than others. Many are impractical over the long-term, some are unhealthy, and most don't include muscle-building. The best approach is the adoption of a healthy and practical diet-exercise strategy that can be sustained over the long-term.

There are three ways of producing a caloric deficit:

1. Reduce food intake sufficiently, and keep activity levels unchanged.

2. Keep food intake unchanged, but increase activity levels greatly.

3. Reduce food intake *and* increase activity levels.

If you depend exclusively on reducing your food intake, you would have to make a greater reduction than if you shared the job with an increase in activity. The dependency on food reduction alone could leave you hungry for much of the day. Furthermore, many people are so sedentary that their caloric requirements are below the norm. Therefore, if they cut their food intake significantly—for fat loss—they may consume insufficient nutrients, which can lead to health problems.

If you keep your food consumption unchanged, you would need to increase your activity levels greatly to produce a caloric deficit. For most people, such a strategy isn't practical.

The third option is usually the most practical, because there's a shared contribution to the caloric deficit—from reduced food intake, and boosted energy consumption through increased activity.

The required dietary and lifestyle changes shouldn't yield a spartan regimen, but a practical lifestyle that can be sustained over the long-term. The correct balance of energy intake and energy output is essential. Monitoring of your bodyfat level and caloric balance is required. If the former increases, you need to adjust the latter.

To monitor your bodyfat, follow the guideline given in Chapter 4:

"For men, along with your waist girth, measure a fat pinch taken at the midpoint between your navel and hip bone. For women, along with your waist girth, take a fat pinch at a fixed spot on your hips. Either way, take the fat pinch in the same way every two weeks, and measure its thickness. Use your thumb and index finger to dig in deep and pinch all the subcutaneous fat, and measure the thickness with a ruler. Better, however, is the use of fat calipers. Plastic calipers are available through mail order, or some stores."

Weight-loss scams

Weight-loss products—pills, potions, and programs—have produced a vast industry. The items are often marketed with exaggerated claims, and fictitious testimonials, and have yielded many ineffective products, and many effective products that have harmful side-effects.

The fat-loss program described in this chapter is safe, effective, and produces many benefits beyond the loss of bodyfat.

Based on findings that many if not most people who lose a lot of fat *gain it back*, keeping the fat off is a greater challenge than shedding it in the first place. To lose fat, you need attitudinal, dietary, and lifestyle changes. To keep the fat off, you need to continue with those changes other than slight modifications to avoid excessive weight loss.

Dedication, discipline, and self-control

Many people consider dedication, discipline, and self-control as drudgery. This is a mistake. These qualities are virtues. When properly applied, with perseverance, they lead to tremendous achievements.

Rid your house of foods you may have been addicted to. Stay clear of places that have those foods on view. Avoid gatherings where food is a focus. Eat only when you're hungry. Take satisfaction in being in charge of your food intake. Substitute some eating time with activity—go for a walk instead, for example.

A successful fat-loss program must include enjoyment of food. Learn to prepare tasty food that you enjoy—there are numerous cookbooks that can help. Take your time when you eat. Take smaller bites than you used to, and chew your food well. Savor your food.

In line with the guidelines given at the end of Chapter 2, devise healthy meals that satisfy your taste, budget, lifestyle, and possible religious proscriptions.

Your caloric requirements largely depend on your size, body composition, and activity levels. For example, a 130-pound, overfat, sedentary woman requires fewer calories than a 130-pound, lean, active woman, who in turn requires fewer calories than a lean, 200-pound lumberjack.

Fat-loss starting points
I. If your weight has been steady recently

Calculate your average, daily caloric intake, as described in Chapter 4:

"Get a calorie ready-reckoner from a bookstore, a weighing scale, and a measuring jug. For at least four days of typical eating and drinking—perhaps two consecutive weekends, if weekdays aren't convenient—weigh all the food you eat, and measure the volume of all liquids you drink other than water. Then calculate your total caloric intake each day and produce an average over the number of test days."

As a starting point for fat loss, cut 300 kilocalories from your daily average intake, and increase your energy output by walking for two miles every day in addition to your usual activity. This walking will use up an additional 200 kilocalories, approximately. With that and the reduction of 300 kilocalories from trimming your food intake, you'll have a shift of 500 kilocalories daily.

Maintain this strategy for a few weeks, and it should register a change on the scale of approximately one pound or half a kilogram a week. If it doesn't, trim your food intake a little more and increase your energy output by walking for an additional mile or two each day; or, trim your food intake alone sufficiently further until you achieve weight loss. Throughout this period, take your strength training seriously—build muscle if you're new to training, or maintain your muscle if you've already built substantial additional muscle.

2. If your weight has been increasing recently

Calculate your average, daily caloric intake, as already described, to discover how many calories adds bodyfat, then set your trial fat-loss caloric intake at two-thirds of that daily average. Additionally, increase your energy output by walking for two miles every day in addition to your usual activity. That, and the reduction of a third of your recent daily caloric intake, will yield a substantial caloric shift that will probably take you into caloric deficit.

Maintain this strategy for a few weeks. If it doesn't register a reduction on the scale, trim your food intake a little more and increase your energy output by walking for an additional mile or two each day; or, trim your food intake alone sufficiently further until you achieve weight loss. Throughout this period, take your strength training seriously—build muscle if you're new to training, or maintain your muscle if you've already built substantial additional muscle.

Pace of fat loss

Avoid rapid weight loss because that usually accompanies muscle loss. If you lose muscle, you'll reduce your metabolic rate. This will further reduce the caloric intake required to lose bodyfat, or increase the level of physical activity required to produce the necessary caloric deficit. Loss of muscle will also mar your appearance.

Don't fast to lose weight, don't go on an extreme diet, and don't go on a fad diet. When you make drastic changes to your caloric intake your body responds by slowing your metabolism, which makes fat loss increasingly difficult, and fat gain easier. Furthermore, you would probably lose muscle, too.

Target a loss of no more than one pound or half a kilogram a week, which could add up to 26 pounds or 13 kilograms over six months. It took time to put the fat on, and it will take time to shed it.

Body composition

The scale can be misleading because it tells you nothing about body composition. Monitor your waist girth, and a fat pinch taken at the midpoint between your navel and hip bone (for a man), or a fat pinch taken at a fixed point on your hips (for a woman). For most people, waist girth and a fat pinch at the waist or hips are barometers of overall bodyfat.

If you have a lot of fat to lose, you may shed, for example, 25 pounds over the next six to ten months. If you gain eight pounds of muscle over that period you would have a net bodyweight loss of 17 pounds. If this occurred, the change in your appearance, fitness, and well-being would be great.

Benefits from exercise for fat control

The muscle-building that results from strength training is beneficial for fat control because the additional muscle enables you to use up more energy even at rest. And the burning of energy by exercise, and activity in general, is another big help for fat control. But the benefits don't stop there.

If you're well-trained, there are improvements at the cellular level that reduce the tendency to store fat. Furthermore, the better condition you get into—the more muscle, and less fat you have—the easier it is to exercise and be active, the easier it is to burn more calories, and the easier it is to lose further fat or maintain a lean body once you've shed the excess fat.

Once you're lean

Once you're lean, and provided you want to build additional muscle, slightly increase your caloric intake, or reduce your energy output a little if you've been very active, to produce a slight caloric surplus. This will put you in anabolic or growth mode.

If you're to train safely and effectively, the information in this chapter is *essential* reading.

Many people mistakenly accept physical discomfort and restrictions as facts of life. Instead, they should investigate corrective treatment, and not just chiropractic or physical therapy, for example. Myofascial therapy such as Active Release Techniques® can work wonders.

Physical restrictions that don't receive appropriate treatment lead to training limitations, which in turn usually lead to *increased* restrictions and training limitations. Commonly, this eventually leads to "retirement" from the gym—"I'm too old" is the common refrain. Prevent this cycle of events, and you'll increase your training longevity.

6

Physical restrictions, and their correction or management

Get your doctor's consent before starting an exercise program. Then during the first month, visit a chiropractor—preferably one who is also trained in Active Release Techniques® (ART®)—to see if you have one or more of common physical anomalies such as scoliosis, tilted pelvis, limbs that may appear to be different in length, excessive lordosis or other postural problems, spondylosis, foot problems, and flexion imbalances between one side of your body and the other. You may not be aware that you have any of these conditions, so it's critical that you investigate the possibility.

Physical anomalies are common, and can influence whether or not certain exercises or specific variations of them are suited to you. What may be safe for most trainees may be unsafe for you. Physical irregularities can also have a negative effect on your general well-being. Many physical irregularities can, however, be corrected, or at least be treated so that their negative effects can be lessened.

If, for example, you have shortened hamstrings, a tilted pelvis, or calves with poor flexibility—all of which are common irregularities—you wouldn't be able to squat or deadlift correctly, or be able to run safely.

Many trainees go through life knowing little or nothing about their physical irregularities *until* they get injured. Get a thorough understanding of your physical structure and biomechanics.

Ideally, the professional you consult should also know the strength-training movements, or at least be willing to learn them from you. Recovering from injury isn't enough. You need to make the right decisions about exercise selection and technique, program design, and correcting or managing any physical anomalies you may have, to prevent injuries occurring in the first place.

To address the physical restrictions that may be limiting your training, and then to keep you free from restrictions, you need the help of more than chiropractic, osteopathy, physical therapy, and orthodox medicine. While those professions can provide valuable help, they don't address soft-tissue problems like some other therapies do. It took me almost 30 years of training, study, and personal experience before I learned this critical lesson.

Of GREAT importance

To benefit fully from an exercise program *you first need to be fit for exercise*. Without the prerequisite fitness, exercise may even be harmful.

Most people, of all ages, have some physical restrictions. While they have these physical restrictions they also have restrictions in how they can exercise. The physical restrictions need treating.

Many people give an illusion of being pain-free by avoiding the activities that produce discomfort. This has serious consequences. Inactivity, or only limited activity, encourages strength loss in general, weakened postural muscles, muscle atrophy (and a reduction in basal metabolic rate), weakened bones, reduced fitness, and decreased flexibility. This impaired physical well-being further diminishes the ability to exercise, which in turn further impairs physical well-being, and so on.

Physical restrictions usually increase in number and severity with age. Especially for middle-aged and older trainees, you need help to get you fit for exercise, and to *keep* you fit for exercise. And for younger trainees, you need help to keep you fit for exercise as you age.

Staying young for your years largely depends on maintaining a fit, strong, flexible body. And that largely depends on maintaining a body free of restrictions of the spine and soft tissues.

Common mistakes to avoid

I've made major mistakes that have blighted my training, physique, and health. Here are the seven biggest mistakes:

1. Using incorrect exercise technique.

2. Inappropriate exercise selection.

3. Application of the foolish "No pain, no gain" maxim.

4. Overtraining.

5. Harmful dietary practices.

6. Not getting expert help early on to discover my physical irregularities, and then take corrective action.

7. Not getting regular, soft-tissue therapy to prevent the build up of scar tissue, adhesions, or other restrictions in my muscles.

The same mistakes are made by most trainees.

All these mistakes could have been avoided had I been well informed. Although they denied me the opportunity to realize my full physical potential, and contributed to long-term limitations, they provided me with an education. Without making these mistakes I would never have understood the plight of typical trainees and how to train them, and how to treat and prevent injuries and other physical problems.

A near-miraculous intervention

An amazing healing experience, in Cyprus in 1998, illustrated the power of non-invasive therapy that has nothing to do with chiropractic, physical therapy, osteopathy, or conventional medicine. Without this experience I may never have had the confidence, in 2003, to risk a lot of money to visit New York City for the therapy that proved to be astonishingly successful, and career changing.

For more than 20 years my left shoulder had been about an inch or two centimeters higher than my right. Since discovering from x-rays in 1992 that I suffered from "borderline serious" scoliosis, I thought that the shoulder tilt was a side effect of my unusually curved spine. There was, however, more to it than that.

In 1998, HARDGAINER author Mike Thompson paid a visit to Cyprus, along with Kevin McGarey, a dentist with an interest in healing skills. Kevin had learned a technique from a therapist he had seen at work while treating his (Kevin's) wife for a tilted pelvis. Kevin noticed I had a laterally tilted pelvis—my right hip was higher than my left. As a consequence my body had compensated for that tilt by shifting my left shoulder higher than my right, in order to keep my eyes level.

Kevin had me lie on a table, and he performed no more than two minutes of gentle work on my lower back and the base of my sternum. What he did, I learned afterward, was to normalize the nerve flow to balance the musculature of my body, as well as normalize my chi. Chi is the vital life force in the body that's regulated, for example, by acupuncture.

Immediately after the treatment I stood and looked at the reflection in a glass door. I was stunned. For the first time I could remember, my shoulders were horizontal. Today, years later, my shoulders are still correctly aligned. Correcting the pelvic and shoulder tilts greatly reduced the degree of my scoliosis.

If I had had my pelvic tilt corrected when I was young, and other defects corrected or well managed, I would probably have had fewer injuries, fewer missed workouts, greater longevity of hard and heavy training, and a more successful training career.

The near-miraculous, pelvic tilt correction I had wasn't a chiropractic procedure. Some chiropractors may, however, use conventional thrusting techniques to try to correct hip tilts, but they are unlikely to produce the permanent correction that I experienced from the single use of a different technique.

I gambled on letting an unqualified man treat me. My gamble turned out well, but some amateur therapists have harmed trusting patients.

Beyond the near-miraculous intervention

As amazing as the benefits of the pelvic tilt correction were, I still had extensive soft-tissue restrictions throughout my body. Treatment of these restrictions didn't occur until five years later when I discovered further therapies beyond chiropractic, osteopathy, physical therapy, and orthodox medicine. *Then* I really started to get somewhere with my healing. In the interim period, trigger point therapy and chiropractic helped to slow the worsening of my physical restrictions, which were primarily in my knees and back.

An orthopedic surgeon believed the solution to my knee problems was arthroscopic cleaning out of my knee joints. That would have temporarily given me the feeling that all was well with my knees, but it wouldn't have addressed the cause of the incorrect tracking of my kneecaps that produced the skewed distribution of stress. The cause was in some of the soft tissue attached to my kneecaps. This tissue was jammed up with restrictions, and prevented the correct tracking of my kneecaps. Had I gone with the arthroscopic treatment, my knee problems would have recurred after some time, and I would have been left with less protective tissue in my knees.

Dramatic benefits from soft-tissue therapy

Soft-tissue or myofascial restrictions had hampered my training for many years. For example, these restrictions had impaired my quadriceps, which in turn caused knee problems and pain. Over that period I was never able to progress with stretching my quadriceps despite my consistent efforts. Then in August 2003, non-invasive, myofascial therapy by Dr. James Kiernan—Active Release Techniques—removed the restrictions in my thighs, including adhesions between my right vastus lateralis and right iliotibial band. The flexibility in my quadriceps increased *instantly*, and increased further over the following weeks. It was only *after* the restrictions had been released that the quadriceps stretching became effective. A few weeks after treatment I was able to sit on my ankles, which I hadn't been able to for many years.

After the treatment my kneecaps tracked correctly, and I was able to leg press without knee problems. My knees were transformed.

For many years I was unable to perform lateral flexion of my neck or lower back without discomfort. I had seriously impaired lateral flexion throughout my spine, which led to countless injuries. Myofascial therapy transformed my neck, and lower back.

I regained ranges of motion throughout my body that I'd not had for many years. I could now perform hatha yoga postures I'd been unable to since I was a teenager. I could now perform resistance exercises safely that I'd been unable to for several years. The benefits from the myofascial therapy were *dramatic*.

Similar benefits have been experienced by many other people. And these are just a few examples of what ART can do.

Of course, I shouldn't have accumulated the soft-tissue restrictions
in the first place. But I was ignorant of the implications of these
restrictions, and I didn't find a provider of Active Release
Techniques until 2003: Dr. James Kiernan, in Rockaway Park, New
York City. Dr. Kiernan is a full-body-certified provider of ART, with
many years of experience. He's also an instructor of ART.

Components of the healing

There was more to my treatment sessions from Dr. Kiernan than ART.
There were four components, in this order: electro pressure regeneration
therapy (EPRT), bio cranial (BC), ART, and chiropractic.

Electro pressure regeneration therapy

The EPRT devices, invented by Australian-born, Keith Wendell, Ph.D.,
are non-invasive, therapeutic devices that utilize ultra-low frequencies
for the treatment of pain, wound healing, and cellular regeneration.
These devices aren't like other electrical healing devices. They don't
work with crystals, they don't act as magnets, and nor do they act like
TENS devices. Dr. Kiernan uses a powerful, clinical EPRT device.

Bio cranial

The BC treatment protocol was discovered and developed in the 1970s
and 1980s by Robert Boyd, DO, a UK registered osteopath. The single
treatment procedure, as explained at www.biocranial.com, "utilizes the
pressure changes within the head to effect a specific objective in the
alignment of the cranial bones and status of the dural membrane."
The dural membrane is the tough, fibrous membrane that forms the
outermost of the three coverings of the brain and spinal cord.

Active Release Techniques

ART is a soft-tissue system that treats problems with muscles,
tendons, ligaments, fascia, and nerves. It's not chiropractic,
osteopathy, massage therapy, physiotherapy, or trigger point
therapy. And unlike some forms of myofascial therapy, ART
protocols don't use mechanical instruments. ART uses patient
motion and specific contact from the provider. The provider needs
to use tactile sensitivity, which isn't possible with mechanical
instruments. Mechanical instruments may even cause increased
inflammation and tissue damage.

As explained at www.activerelease.com, "ART has been developed, refined, and patented by P. Michael Leahy, DC, CCSP. Dr. Leahy noticed that his patients' symptoms seemed to be related to changes in their soft tissues that could be felt by hand. By observing how muscles, fascia, tendons, ligaments and nerves responded to different types of work, Dr. Leahy was able to consistently resolve over 90% of his patients' problems."

ART certification is in three parts: spine, lower extremities, and upper extremities. If you have a problem with a muscle connected to your spine, you would require an ART provider who is certified in *spine*. If, for example, you have a thigh, knee, or foot problem, you would require an ART provider who is certified in *lower extremities*. And if you have a shoulder, elbow, wrist, or hand problem, you would require an ART provider who is certified in *upper extremities*. Most ART providers, however, are certified in more than one part.

Treatment procedure

I visited New York City in August 2003 for nine treatment sessions spread over 12 days. The EPRT lasted at least 90 minutes per session, the BC lasted only about three minutes, and the ART required 30 minutes or longer in my case. (ART treatments are typically shorter than this, but because I was in New York City for only a limited time, I received longer treatments, for multiple areas each session.) The chiropractic was supplemental in my case—just two or three adjustments at the end of each session.

Dr. Kiernan used EPRT and BC primarily to prepare my body so that it responded better to the ART, to speed up the healing. Dr. Kiernan told me that it takes a combination of treatments to help difficult cases. Doctors Wendell and Boyd, however, claim far-reaching benefits from EPRT and BC as stand-alone treatment protocols.

Because Dr. Kiernan is a full-body provider of ART, chiropractor, and provider of EPRT and BC, and he has many years of experience of weight training, this combination may produce the ideal single therapist for strength and fitness trainees to consult. For instance, a problem with the vertebrae may, because of nerve compression, have contributed to the muscle imbalance that was behind at least some of the soft-tissue restrictions. That problem would need to be corrected. And knowledge of exercise selection and technique is required to help a trainee design an appropriate exercise program.

The right treatment can produce tremendous benefits, and may make you believe in miracles.

Hatha yoga

Upon Dr. Kiernan's advice I took up hatha yoga, to help maintain
the benefits of his treatment. Since August 2003 I've invested about
an hour per day, at least five days a week, to perform yoga postures.
I focus on my spine, and lower extremities. As a result I'm more
flexible now than I was in my youth. And there are benefits beyond
the increased flexibility. The postures invigorate me, and each
session leaves me feeling rejuvenated.

The blight of soft-tissue restrictions

Everyone knows of visible scar tissue on the surface of the skin.
There's also invisible scar tissue inside the soft tissues of the body,
including muscle, tendon, and fascia. Fascia is a band or sheath of
connective tissue that supports, or binds together, internal organs
and parts of the body, including the muscles.

Overused and abused soft tissues cause the body to produce scar tissue
and other abnormal changes in the affected areas. These restrictions
occur due, for example, to poor posture, acute injuries, accumulation
of micro injuries, poor lifting technique in and out of the gym, and
insufficient flexibility. People of all ages have soft-tissue restrictions,
regardless of whether they train.

These restrictions hamper the healthy, smooth, supple operation
of the soft tissues of the body. Muscles can become shorter and
weaker, and there can be adhesions between adjacent muscles and
other soft tissues. As a result, the muscles don't pull normally on
the skeletal system, and thus produce skewed stress on joints and
soft tissue, and cause discomfort or even pain during activity—or
even during inactivity, in some cases. The tension on tendons from
the restrictions can cause tendinitis. There may even be nerve
constriction. Ranges of motion can be reduced, and there can be
loss of strength. This affects everyday activities, and training, and
causes restrictions in both.

If, for example, the thigh muscles are blighted with restrictions,
they will pull in an abnormal, distorted way on the kneecap,
which will affect its tracking, and may lead to problems such as
chondromalacia patella, which causes discomfort, physical
limitation and, eventually, perhaps arthritis. If the thigh muscles
are treated so that they become smooth and supple, they will pull
correctly on the kneecap, and thus it will track properly, and not
sustain abnormal wear and tear.

Over the first few months of **The Program**, if you don't make steady progress in flexibility, and in adopting the correct techniques of the exercises, you probably have restrictions that are jamming up your soft tissues, and preventing them from functioning normally. Furthermore, if you have any range-of-motion problems, soft-tissue restrictions could be the cause there, too.

There are a number of non-invasive therapies, including ART, that can reduce or even remove the soft-tissue restrictions, and permit the body to return toward its normal, supple, efficient, discomfort-free operation. A broad term for these treatment techniques is *myofascial therapy*, or *soft-tissue therapy*. Skeletal muscles and their connective tissues are called *myofascia*.

As well as chiropractors, there are others who may have been trained in soft-tissue therapies, including physicians, osteopaths, physical and occupational therapists, exercise physiologists, and athletic trainers. Only let professionally accredited therapists treat you.

Rolfing®—another myofascial therapy, but not typically performed by chiropractors—can also remove soft-tissue restrictions. While there are many providers of ART in the USA and Canada, there are few elsewhere. In Europe, Rolfers may be more prevalent, albeit still rare.

The career-changing effect of ART

The success of Dr. Kiernan's treatments inspired me to become a provider of ART. In September 2003, at age 45, I returned to college to start preparatory study. In early 2004 I retired HARDGAINER magazine. This released the time I required to study for ART certification but while enabling me to continue with book production.

I got my first certification in ART—*spine*—in May 2004. In June 2005 I got my second certification—*lower extremity.*

As a provider I've witnessed repeated examples of the powerful benefits from ART even when it's the only form of therapy. Benefits can often be felt from the first treatment. Typically, however, three to eight treatments are required to yield the full benefits. The benefits from ART may, however, be realized quicker, and perhaps for longer, when supplemented with electro pressure regeneration therapy, and bio cranial.

How myofascial therapy works

When manual pressure is correctly applied to soft-tissue restrictions, they are released, and the normal functioning of the tissues returns. The restrictions usually require several treatments before they are released, but sometimes a single treatment produces immediate benefits. ART involves the *active* participation of the patient in many of the treatment protocols.

Chiropractic

If I was running a gym, every member would be examined by a chiropractor. Each member would receive a brief education in his or her physical structure and biomechanics. If the chiropractor wasn't also trained in soft-tissue therapy such as ART, a soft-tissue therapist would be employed, too. Then any action to correct or manage physical irregularities would be taken, and training programs would be designed considering the physical structure and biomechanics of each trainee.

Healthy nutrition, and a sensible exercise program, help to maintain healthy joints. Food supplements, including cod liver oil, glucosamine, chondroitin, and gelatin, may also help. And your body may be able to repair damage to cartilage, for example.

But if you have restrictions in your soft tissues, and postural problems, too, some of your joints won't track correctly, and they will continue to be damaged because your body's repair work will be undermined. As a result, you'll always have joint and muscle problems.

Get to the root of the restrictions and postural problems.

Don't wait until you get an injury before you look for a chiropractor's services. But check that he or she is registered with your country's appropriate national association.

The goal of traditional chiropractic is to find and correct vertebral subluxations. Vertebral subluxations are when a vertebra is misaligned from its normal position and causes (a) fixation, namely the inability of proper movement, and (b) pressure on a nerve, which causes pain, numbness, and weakness. There are various techniques to correct these subluxations, from soft to aggressive. The subluxations are caused by trauma (for example, sports, automobile, work) or improper posture and movements.

Chiropractic doesn't involve any medication, surgery, or other form of invasive treatment, but encompasses many techniques, and different chiropractors will probably select from different techniques.

If you experience one or more of the following symptoms, seek the attention of a chiropractor:

1. Pins and needles, or numbness, in a limb.

2. Pain that goes down the rear thigh along the path of the sciatic nerve (sciatica).

3. Pain that goes down the front thigh, to the knee (femoral neuralgia).

4. Any back pain or spasms.

5. Hip pain or spasms.

6. Neck pain.

7. Headaches or migraines.

And to treat the following problems, the chiropractor would need to be trained in soft-tissue therapy such as ART:

8. Shoulder pain.

9. Knee pain, and foot and ankle problems.

10. Elbow problems, and hand and wrist problems.

A chiropractor isn't a "fix it" person to treat symptoms of poor training methods. You must train sensibly, with correct technique. Many trainees, however, need the help of a chiropractor to enable them to train safely even when they use correct technique.

Permit only legitimate, fully trained and licensed professionals to work on you. Some people claim to be experts at spinal and other adjustments and manipulations, and "practice" freely, especially outside of North America. Many a chiropractor has had to correct the damage carried out by sham practitioners. Contact your country's appropriate professional association, or the international head office, for information on legitimate professionals in your area.

A number of medical doctors have taken brief courses in manipulation techniques (not chiropractic). The only type of chiropractor you should consult is one who holds the full degree qualification from an accredited chiropractic college.

> Some money-first chiropractors have given the profession a bad reputation—just as some individuals have in other professions—because they abused their responsibility and took advantage of patients. Finding a competent chiropractor may, however, be invaluable.

Limitations of chiropractic

Chiropractic can perform wonders with some problems, but additional therapies are required for comprehensive care, including soft-tissue therapy. Chiropractic doesn't focus on the treatment of soft-tissue problems. Instead, it focuses on the relationship between the spinal skeletal system, and the nervous system.

Podiatry

Consult a foot specialist such as a podiatrist (or chiropodist, as the practitioner is called in some countries). Foot problems can, for example, affect squatting and deadlifting technique. A foot specialist may be able to help you to reduce, if not eliminate, the negative effect of a foot problem on your exercise technique.

Feet are complex structures. Foot defects are common, and a defect affects how the stresses placed on the feet are borne by the feet and the rest of the body. When forces on the feet are exaggerated by high-load activities such as strength training, running, and any competitive sport, the defects are magnified.

While foot defects may not be the whole story behind foot, ankle, knee or back problems, they contribute.

Fundamental lesson

Investigate the possibility of your having physical irregularities and soft-tissue problems even if you're confident that you have none. Discover any defects and restrictions you may have, and get them corrected or at least managed so that they don't deteriorate.

The benefits may be extensive, over the short-term and long-term, and help to keep you young for your years, and minimize the effects of aging.

During training I recommend the use of orthopedic shoes with molded insoles (including arch support), to compensate for structural or postural instability in the feet, or, in the case of defect-free feet, to maintain existing good condition. Shoes with custom-made, molded insoles are ideal, but off-the-shelf shoes with molded insoles are usually superior to regular shoes. You can even get molded insoles that can be inserted inside regular footwear, but you may need to remove some of the existing insoles to make room.

Imagine, for example, you have arches in your feet that aren't as high and strong as they should be. During weight-bearing exercise while standing, your knees will endure skewed stress. This will apply an exaggerated load on a part of each knee, rather than apply it over the whole of each joint. This can lead to problems. Good arch support is essential while lifting weights, and not just for the sake of your knees.

A change in footwear, or the insertion of molded insoles into your existing footwear, may help you to train free of injuries. If you've been lifting weights for a long time already, use reduced weights when adapting to new footwear, and build back gradually. Your body needs time to adapt to the changes in how training load is applied.

Consult a podiatrist, preferably an ART-trained podiatrist, or an ART-trained chiropractor with training in orthotics. An orthotic—a shoe insert (not merely an arch support) designed to increase the mechanical efficiency of the whole foot—may be prescribed. An off-the-shelf, molded insole insert may, however, do a good job.

Footwear caveat

When there are foot defects, the use of orthopedic footwear, and orthotics, are especially important during exercise when the stresses on the feet are magnified. They may also be recommended for everyday activities *until you've addressed the causes of the foot defects.* Foot defects are commonly the result of postural problems.

The use of special footwear may, however, camouflage problems with the feet and posture, and hidden problems commonly get worse over time. Prudent use of special footwear is sensible, but correction of the foot or postural defects is vital. Excessive use of special footwear will make the body dependent on it, and the healthy musculoskeletal functions of the feet, ankles, knees, and hips, will further recede.

To help develop or maintain the healthy musculoskeletal functions of your feet, ankles, knees, and hips, spend time at home each day moving around without any footwear. Include standing on one foot at a time, barefoot. Stand on one foot for 30 seconds or so, then the other, and alternate for a few minutes. Furthermore, get your feet treated by a provider of ART because the problems that lead to the use of orthotics may be correctable, or at least considerably reduced.

How running may be harmful

Even if you run on a giving or soft surface, and in expensive shoes, it may still be harmful, depending on the individual. If you have foot problems, postural problems, or soft-tissue problems in general, your running gait will be impaired, which will put undue stress on your joints and soft tissues, and lead to injuries sooner or later.

Posture PRIORITY

Posture is the position or bearing of the body, and plays a major role in appearance, general health and well-being, and in determining whether or not specific exercises and athletic activities are safe for an individual. Good posture minimizes wear and tear on joints, and soft tissues. Faulty mechanical structure leads to faulty function.

While standing in a relaxed stance, and viewed from the side, the ideal posture is assumed to be when the earlobe, tip of the shoulder, hip joint, and outside bump of the ankle all line up vertically. From the front and rear views, the shoulders, hips, knees, and ankles should be horizontal, and imaginary lines drawn through all of them should be parallel to each other, and the ground. And the feet should point straight ahead. This arrangement indicates that an individual's overall structure is symmetrical, and in good mechanical balance.

Poor posture usually can't be immediately corrected because it's ingrained mentally and physically. Postural problems usually can't be corrected merely by pulling the shoulders back, for example. Asymmetrical strength and flexibility, and soft-tissue restrictions, are involved in most postural problems, and need to be addressed if there's to be meaningful improvement in posture.

The alignment of the spine that tolerates mechanical forces most efficiently, which can vary from person to person, is called the *neutral spine*. It means holding oneself in a natural, upright position with the spine retaining its natural curves.

For some exercises, however, there are specific techniques that modify the neutral spine. For example, when setting up to lift a weight from the floor, it's important to pull the shoulders back, and tense the spinal erectors. This naturally flattens the thoracic curve, to put the back in a more robust position.

If you have poor posture, seek help. Even if you think your posture is good, still have it checked out—what you may think is good posture, may actually be poor. Consult a chiropractor, or a full-body-certified practitioner of Active Release Techniques. Physical therapists, and practitioners of the Alexander technique and Feldenkrais method may also be able to help. And Pete Egoscue's books provide self-help guidance to try to deal with postural problems.

Exercise can be harmful if not done correctly in a manner that's appropriate for you. This is the reason why it's critical to get checked out by a podiatrist and a chiropractor, and a soft-tissue therapist, even if you think there's nothing amiss. Through taking appropriate action, restrictions can be discovered, and corrective action may be possible.

Treatment recommendations

I benefited tremendously from the treatment I received in New York City. The best recommendation I can give anyone seeking physical healing is to go through the same treatment I did. Perhaps combine it with a vacation, as I did. Alternatively, for a streamlined approach, but not necessarily the optimum one, seek an ART-trained chiropractor, or an ART-trained massage therapist, or an ART-trained athletic trainer, or an ART-trained physician, and so on. But only let professionally accredited therapists treat you. If it's an ART-trained therapist other than a chiropractor, then employ the services of a chiropractor, too. And employ a podiatrist's services, as well. If you can't find an ART-trained therapist, but can find a Rolfer, then try that therapist. For some guidance on how to find therapists, see *Resources* at the end of this chapter.

Following this recommendation will probably mean unexpected travelling, and expense, but if it means that you experience healing anything like I did, it will all be worthwhile. *The healing turned back the clock for me, and I wish I'd taken that action many years ago.*

Once you've had your soft-tissue restrictions treated, *employ regular treatment to maintain the improved condition*, and train without developing new restrictions. To help prevent recurrence of the problems, the areas concerned will probably need to be trained for increased flexibility, and increased strength, too, if weakness was present.

While having soft-tissue or any other physical problem treated, discuss with the therapist(s) the probable causes of the problems—inside and outside of the gym, postural, and lifestyle. The therapies *alone* won't yield a long-term solution. The causes of the problems need to be removed, or otherwise the problems will recur.

Independence of ART

Although the developer of ART—Dr. P. Michael Leahy—is a chiropractor, ART is independent of chiropractic. and isn't taught by chiropractic colleges. Dr. Leahy also has a background in engineering, and aviation.

Further reading

RELEASE YOUR PAIN (2003, Rowan Tree Books), by Brian Abelson, DC
Dr. Abelson's book is about Active Release Techniques.

THE TRIGGER POINT THERAPY WORKBOOK (2001, New Harbinger Publications), by Clair Davies
Trigger point therapy has helped me a lot over the years, but didn't get to the root of the restrictions like Active Release Techniques did.

THE EGOSCUE METHOD OF HEALTH THROUGH MOTION (2001, Quill), by Pete Egoscue, with Roger Gittines

PAIN FREE: A REVOLUTIONARY METHOD FOR STOPPING CHRONIC PAIN (2000, Bantam Books), by Pete Egoscue, with Roger Gittines

Resources

Active Release Techniques *www.activerelease.com*
Active Release Techniques, Printers Park Medical Plaza, 175 South Union Blvd. #230, Colorado Springs, CO 80910, USA, tel: 888-396-2727 *Visit www.activerelease.com for a listing of certified ART providers. There are, however, many ART providers who aren't listed at that website, so ask around among therapists in general in your search for an ART provider.*

Bio Cranial System *www.biocranial.com*
The Bio Cranial Institute, 43-44 Kissena Blvd., Suite # Lobby A, Comber, Flushing, NY 11355, USA, tel: 718-886-6056

The Bio Cranial Institute (Europe), 41-43 Castle Street, Co. Down BT23 5DY, UK, tel: +44 289-187-1334

Electro Pressure Regeneration Therapy *www.electroregenesis.com.au*
ElectroRegenesis Pty. Ltd., 54 Siganto St., Mt. Tamborine, Qld. 4272, AUSTRALIA, tel: 61 (0) 755-450-451

Rolfing Structural Integration *www.rolf.org,* and *www.rolfing.org*
The Rolf Institute of Structural Integration, 5055 Chaparral Ct. #103, Boulder, CO 80301, USA, tel: 800-530-8875

The Rolf Institute of Structural Integration, PO Box 14793, London SW1, ENGLAND, tel: +44 171-834-1493

Practitioner variation

As in all professions, there's great variation in the skills and competence of individual practitioners. If you're not satisfied with the work of a specific therapist, try someone else.

Recommended therapist

Dr. James Kiernan, DC
Kiernan Chiropractic and Sports Injuries Center, 115-06 Beach Channel Drive, Rockaway Park, NY 11694, USA, tel: 718-945-0406

Dr. Kiernan is a full-body provider of ART, chiropractor, and provider of electro pressure regeneration therapy, and bio cranial. He also has many years experience of weight training.

Gyms are usually terrible places for learning how to train. The standard instruction, and the examples provided by other trainees, are usually poor.

7

Gym savvy, where to train, and gym conduct

If you're a beginner, find a good gym. If you're not a beginner, but dissatisfied with where you train, find a better gym.

At least for your first year of training, a commercial or institutional gym is your best choice unless you know someone who has a good home gym you can use, or you know of a small multi-user facility you can train at. Institutional gyms include school, university, and YMCA weight rooms. After a year of consistent training you may want to invest in a home gym.

Commercial and institutional gyms vary greatly in their equipment, facilities, and quality of instruction. You're going to become your own personal trainer, so you won't need to depend on an instructor. You need adequate equipment to work with, but *adequate* doesn't necessitate an abundance of machines.

The strength-training routines in this book consist of free-weight exercises that can be performed in both super and basic gyms, and machine exercises that are available in most gyms.

Finding a gym

A gym can be an intimidating place for a beginner. But after a few workouts you should feel like one of the regulars. You just have to get over the initial feeling of discomfort—it's something all trainees have to deal with at some time.

Check the Yellow Pages for gyms nearby. If the gym isn't conveniently located, you immediately have an obstacle whenever it's workout time. Ideally, the gym should be in walking distance, or within a few minutes drive. Call each gym and get the basics on prices, hours, and equipment. Some gyms have websites for this information.

Your telephone conversations should give you an indication of how client-friendly each gym is. Perhaps some gyms won't provide a trial workout for free or a nominal charge, are excessively expensive, or don't have hours that suit you. This may reduce the number of possibilities. With what are left, pay non-training visits, look around, and discuss the possibility of training there.

It may be best to call the gym in advance, to see if there are specific times for guest tours. Ask to see all areas of the gym—on and off the training floor—and don't be pressured into signing up. Ideally, have your visit around the time of day you plan to train. A gym is a different place when it's quiet, compared with when it's busy.

Here are eight key points for gym assessment:

1. Tidiness

Is the gym neat and tidy? A gym isn't a showroom, but if it isn't neat and tidy, the general running of the gym is unlikely to be impressive.

2. Cleanliness

Are the toilets and locker room clean and well-maintained? If you plan to shower at the gym, are the facilities satisfactory?

3. Lockers

If you plan to go to work or a social event following some workouts, you'll require to rent a locker to put your possessions in. Are there lockers to rent, and are they adequate?

4. Condition of equipment

If there are frayed cables, torn upholstery, holes in carpets, or out-of-order equipment, you should probably look elsewhere.

5. Gym's machinery manufacturer(s)

Gyms often limit their machinery to one or two brands. If the machinery is from the better lines—for example, Body Masters, Cybex, Hammer Strength, MedX, and Nautilus—that's a good sign.

6. Equipment in general

Is there a good selection of free-weights (barbells and dumbbells) and benches, a power rack or cage, and squat stands or rack? Look for excellence in the free-weights department; resistance machines are a bonus. A gym that focuses on machines and throws in a small area for free-weights, may not be a good choice.

The advantage of a well-equipped gym is that it's likely to have the required essential items, and maybe some of the better pieces of high-tech machinery, too. A well-equipped gym will also have many cardio machines. This will give you a number of equipment options, and provide sufficient variety to keep cardio work interesting over time.

Some hardcore bodybuilding gyms have outstanding free-weights equipment, perhaps only minimal machinery, and barebones facilities beyond the gym floor. But the overall ambiance of the place, and the excellent free-weights facilities, could make that gym a pearl.

7. Instruction

If a gym insists that you follow its standard training routine, look for another place to train.

8. The money side

If you're looking for a gym for strength training and cardio work only, you don't need one that has features such as dance classes, aerobic classes, a pool, yoga, boxing, sauna, and a cafe. You'll pay for features you won't use unless you can get a limited membership that gives you access to the priority facilities only—weights and cardio machinery.

Ask questions to find out what you get for your money, compare that with what you require for your money, and look for value for money. It's worth paying a bit extra for a better gym.

The advantage of a well-equipped gym is that it's likely to have the required essential items, and maybe some of the better pieces of high-tech machinery, too. A well-equipped gym will also have many cardio machines. This will give you a number of equipment options, and provide sufficient variety to keep cardio work interesting over time.

When you think you've found what will work for you, go for a trial workout. If that goes well, you're ready to sign up.

Read the small print in any membership contract. Don't sign up for a year. Sign up for a single month, or at most three months. If that period goes well, sign up for longer—but no longer than a year, because you can't be sure about where you or the gym management will be in the future. If the short membership period doesn't work out, look for another gym.

Tips for your trial workout

A free-of-obligation, guest-pass workout, for free or only a nominal charge, is important. Arrange in advance in case there are specific times for such workouts. The workout may reveal qualities that a non-training visit didn't. Here are seven tips for your trial workout:

1. Preparedness

Be prepared to follow the first workout described in Chapter 17, using the exercise technique guidance described at the end of Chapter 2. For the trial workout, however, it will be simpler to exclude the deadlift because that requires more set-up work than the other exercises. Furthermore, because this is just a trial workout, omit any other exercise you have difficulty setting up.

2. Train with a friend

Go with a friend for the trial workout. If the friend already trains there, that would be ideal, as he or she could answer your questions regarding where each exercise should be done, where specific equipment is, and how it should be set up.

3. If you have to train alone

Be especially well prepared if you have to take the trial workout by yourself. Don't be shy to ask questions of the gym staff, to become familiar with the equipment. You're a prospective long-term client.

4. Workout timing

Go during a quiet time—typically late morning or early afternoon. If you can't go during a quiet time during the week, go during the weekend. Call the gym to find out the times that are quietest.

5. Dress appropriately

Dress modestly and appropriately—go for comfort and practicality. Don't take accessories like a belt or gloves—neither are necessary.

6. Be serious and focused

Be a serious trainee from the first workout, and make your mark as someone who's there to train, not to socialize.

7. Don't be self-conscious

Most trainees will be so busy with their own workouts that they won't pay you much if any attention. Most members will be friendly, and some will be keen to answer questions, but their answers may not be the ones you require.

Most of the aforementioned tips don't just apply to a trial workout.

Additional tips

Once you're satisfied with a gym, here's how to make it work well:

1. Become your own knowledgeable, personal trainer. Don't copy others in order to feel at ease through conformity.

2. Keep your mind focused on your own training, and stay clear of distractions, including discussions.

3. Never use equipment just because it's there. Use only what's appropriate for you.

4. Ignore anything and anyone that will hinder your progress.

5. Train during a quiet time, or at least not during peak time.

6. Take your own little discs if the gym has none—to permit gradual, progressive resistance of no more than a pound at a time. If the gym's management isn't willing to get a supply of small discs for all members to use, it may permit you to use your own.

7. After you've been there for a few months, try to persuade the gym's management to buy a shrug bar and power rack if it doesn't already have them. Both are cheap relative to machines, and will add to the gym's functional value for all members. If the management isn't interested, consider offering to buy the shrug bar in return for a discount on membership. Win the management over on the shrug bar, and then bring up the possibility of a power rack. Later, bring up the possibility of a cambered squat bar. This bar may help all members who squat.

Your first few workouts

If possible, time your first few workouts during a vacation from work, or take a morning off on each of the first few workout days. There's usually a world of difference between training before midday on a weekday, and after 6:00 pm. Especially when the gym is a strange place for you, the quieter the better, so you can familiarize yourself with the place and equipment without competing with others. Once you're comfortable, and know how to perform each exercise, then you'll be able to handle training during busy times if you need to.

Each rep and each set of each workout are chances for training perfection that can't be had again. Each workout is a one-off opportunity to improve. If you don't get everything right at a given workout, you'll miss a chance to maximize your progress. So, get every component right so that each workout IS another step forward.

Whenever you work out, focus on your training, and switch off from everything else.

If you have no option but to train during busy times during the week, consider scheduling one of your workouts during a quiet time on the weekend—quiet relative to peak evening time—for more efficient training, with fewer interruptions, delays, and distractions.

If you can train only during peak times, and the gym is too busy for you to train well, look for another gym that doesn't get so busy.

Gym decorum

Manners, consideration, and courtesy are important for the smooth running of a gym. Let a staff member know about problems. Here are 13 pointers on gym decorum:

1. Don't spread your sweat

Sweating is inevitable in a gym. Keep your sweat to yourself. Keep a towel handy, and wipe off any sweat you may leave on a bench, machine, bar, plate, floor, or mat. Leave all equipment as you would like to find it. If you forget to bring a towel, use paper towels the gym may provide, or some garment from your kit bag.

2. Don't hog equipment

In a public gym, exercise equipment is communal property. When you're not using it, release it for another user. Alternate sets with someone who wants to use the same piece of equipment as you—work in with each other. If, however, you're using a barbell on, say, the bench press, and your strength is at a different level to the other trainee's, it may be more convenient for you to finish all your sets before the other person starts—otherwise there would be a lot of plate changing.

3. Keep noise to a minimum

During intensive training, some grunting is normal, but that's no license to scream. Sudden, loud noises are distracting, and present the noise makers as braggarts.

4. Return weights to where they belong

Return dumbbells to their rack, unload any plates on machines, and return plates to their correct position on the plate holders. Strip a given adjustable barbell down to whatever is its starting weight, which may be the bare bar.

Leave equipment as you would like to find it. Furthermore, do the gym and its users a favor by putting away equipment that inconsiderate members didn't. But don't lift dumbbells, barbells, or plates that you can't comfortably handle, and use good lifting technique at all times. Many injuries have occurred while moving equipment around. Ask for help when you need it.

5. Turn off mobile telephones

Focus on your training, and leave the rest of your life outside the gym.

6. Don't obstruct the flow of traffic

Between sets and exercises, don't block the flow of gym traffic by standing in the isle between machines or other equipment, or in a lifting area. Keep out of the way of others. Furthermore, unless the gym is quiet, don't sit on a machine or bench that you're not using.

7. Don't give unsolicited advice

Gyms typically have trainees who assume they are experts when, in fact, they have minimal knowledge. Many people are unreceptive to unsolicited input, especially from those who don't have much experience. Avoid providing any input until you really know what you're doing, and even then you should be prudent.

8. Dress modestly and practically

Some trainees dress like exhibitionists, and distract other members.

9. Treat the locker room with respect

Leave these areas as you would like to find them before using them yourself. Tidy up after you've been in.

10. Queuing system

During peak time, some cardio machines may have sign-up sheets. Get your name down early if you want to get in line, and don't assume that if a given machine is vacated, it's available for anyone. Check if there's a queuing arrangement before you jump in. In some gyms, at least during peak time, there may be a time limit on specific cardio machines.

11. Don't hover

While waiting for a given machine or weights station, don't hover over the current user. Keep your distance, but ensure it's clear that you're next in line.

12. Don't talk while exercising

Don't talk to anyone while you exercise, other than to call for help if you need it. And don't talk to anyone who's exercising other than to provide encouragement, or if you need to confirm whether help is required—if you're in any doubt—prior to lending a hand. Conversing while exercising will mar your effort and exercise technique, and increase the risk of injury.

Between sets and exercises, conversations should be short and to the point. If something can wait until after the workout, so it should.

13. Flow with noise you can't influence

There'll be background noise in and out of the gym that you can't do anything about—for instance, traffic on the street, clanging of plates in the gym, phones ringing, and doors closing and opening. Live with it. Don't use noise as an excuse for not training well.

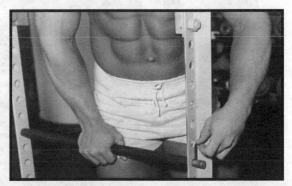

Power racks vary in how their safety bars are locked in position so that they can't move during use. Here's an example of a safety bar and its locking pin. Position safety bars about an inch (or two centimeters) below your bottom point of the bench press, or squat, as examples.

Safety equipment

There are several pieces of equipment that, if used properly, ensure you can never be pinned or crushed by a weight even if you train alone. They also make it easy to set up the barbell prior to use, and to unrack and rack the weight at the start and finish of an exercise. They are especially important for squats, barbell bench presses, barbell incline bench presses, and barbell presses, and have other uses, too.

A four-post power rack and its accessories: two adjustable barbell saddles (on the rear uprights), four pins or safety bars (on the floor), four small locking pins (on the base) for fixing the safety bars in the rack's uprights—see illustration on previous page—and two lengths of hose for putting over the safety bars to help prevent the barbell slipping when on the pins. A power rack is sometimes called a power cage.

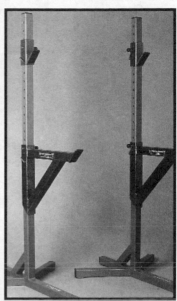

A squat rack (left), and an "open" rack. Squat racks are common in gyms, but many have fixed-height safety bars, whereas the one illustrated has safety bars that can be adjusted for height. The "open" rack is fully adjustable.

How to use a power rack

A power rack, correctly used, is perfect for self-spotting, and safety, and can be found in some gyms.

With a power rack, position the pins—or safety bars—about an inch (or two centimeters) below your bottom point of the bench press, or squat, as examples. Then if you can't perform a rep, lower the barbell under control to the safety bars, get out from under the barbell, remove the plates, and return the barbell to its holders.

The uprights of power racks typically have about two inches or five centimeters between successive holes. If one setting is too high, and the next too low, raise the floor. For example, to fine-tune for the bench press, put the pins in the "too high" position, and then raise the bench an inch or so, by putting rubbing matting underneath the bench's legs. For the squat, you would require non-slip rubber matting of the right thickness throughout the floor space within the rack, so there's no chance of tripping on the edge of the matting.

Part 2

How to Train

8. The essential terminology of training *137*
9. Cardio training *159*
10. How to avoid injuries *173*
11. Rep speed and control *189*
12. How to master exercise technique *193*
13. How to handle weights between exercises *403*
14. Seven extras for effective workouts *409*
15. How progressive resistance can help or hinder progress *417*
16. How to optimize your exercise selection from the gang of eight *423*
17. **The Program** *441*
18. Call to arms! *497*
19. Beyond **The Program** *501*

It's not just cardio exercise that's good for one's health, provided it's done safely. Some scientists believe that safe, progressive, and consistent strength training may offer more health benefits than cardio exercise alone, or any other single exercise modality.

8

The essential terminology of training

Please familiarize yourself with all of the following terminology:

A

Aerobic exercise

Aerobic literally means *with oxygen*. This is sustained, rhythmic, large-muscle activity at a level at which the heart and lungs can replenish oxygen in the working muscles, such as walking. Aerobic exercise yields many benefits, the two major ones being that it improves cardiorespiratory fitness (if the exercise is sufficiently demanding relative to the individual's current fitness level), and burns calories (which can contribute to bodyfat loss).

Age-adjusted maximum heart rate

An *estimation* of maximum safe heart rate commonly calculated through deducting one's age from 220. A 40-year old person will have an estimated maximum heart rate of 180, and a 20-year-old will have one of 200.

Anaerobic exercise

Anaerobic literally means *without oxygen*. This is activity in which oxygen is used up more quickly than the body can replenish it in the working muscles. For a given individual, anaerobic exercise is more demanding than aerobic exercise. Although aerobic exercise can be sustained for long periods, anaerobic exercise can be sustained only for short periods. Strength training and sprinting are examples of anaerobic exercise. Waste products and an oxygen debt are quickly built up during anaerobic exercise, terminating it quickly.

B

Barbell

A steel rod, typically between five and seven feet, on which plates of varying sizes and weights can be loaded, according to need. An adjustable barbell permits you to change the weight plates at will. Fixed-weight barbells have their plates locked in place. Some gyms have racks of fixed-weight barbells of varying weights (typically less than 100 pounds), ready for immediate use.

Basal metabolic rate (BMR)

The rate of energy use by the body under controlled resting conditions; the speed at which a resting body uses calories to meet its basic survival needs. The BMR is usually measured in calories per day. Through increasing your muscle mass, you'll also increase your BMR.

Basic exercises

The multi-joint movements are usually tagged *basic exercises*, although some trainees include a few single-joint exercises under that description.

Belts

Two main types: lifting belts, supposedly used for lumbar support; and weight belts used for attaching weight to the body for some exercises.

Benches

Long seats used for performing some exercises on: flat (horizontal) bench, incline bench, and decline bench. Fixed incline and decline benches are manufactured at various pre-set angles, whereas others are adjustable and can be set by the user to the desired angle. A bench may have uprights attached on its sides, for supporting a barbell.

Bodypart

Group of muscles in a specific area of the body. Exercises target specific bodyparts. In a simplified format, here are the main bodyparts:

1. abdominals (abs) and obliques of the front midsection

2. biceps and brachialis—front of the arm (above the elbow)

3. buttocks—gluteal muscles, or glutes

4. calves—gastrocnemius and soleus

5. chest—pectorals, or pecs (pectoralis *major*, not pectoralis minor)

6. forearms

7. latissimus dorsi, or lats—muscles on the back under the arms

8. neck

9. shoulders—deltoids, or delts

10. spinal erectors—columns of muscle on either side of the spine

11. thighs—quadriceps or quads on the front, hamstrings or hams on the rear, and thigh adductors on the inside

12. triceps—rear of the arm (above the elbow)

13. upper back—small muscles around the shoulder blades, and the large trapezius covering much of the upper back

C

Calories

Units of heat energy. Burning calories means converting food into energy, or converting stores of energy in the body, such as bodyfat, into energy for activity. *The calories referred to in nutrition are actually kilocalories (kcals).*

Cardiovascular training

Physical exercise that strengthens the heart and improves the efficiency of the whole system of heart, lungs, and blood vessels. Also called *cardiorespiratory training*, *cardio*, and *aerobic exercise*.

Cheating

Use of body English—sloppy exercise technique—to assist the target muscles with their work, or changing joint angles for greater leverage. Cheating is one of the major causes of injury, and should be avoided. Disciplined training maintains correct exercise technique free of cheating even under the stress of great effort.

Collars

Cylindrical metal clamps, and quick-release springs, used to hold weight plates securely in position on a barbell or dumbbell. Inside collars are usually fixed, to keep the plates from sliding inward. Outside collars keep the weight plates from sliding off the ends of the bar.

Compound exercises

Exercises come in two basic types: multi-joint movements, which are often called *compound* exercises, and single-joint ones, which are often called *isolation* exercises. The squat is a multi-joint exercise because it involves movement at more than one joint, and hence affects a lot of musculature—primarily the thighs, hips, and lower back. The leg extension—straightening your knee while seated—is a single-joint exercise, because it involves movement primarily at only one joint (the knee). It primarily targets the quadriceps (front thighs).

Single-joint exercises rarely involve only a single joint, as other joints (and bodyparts) get recruited to some degree. **The single-joint and multi-joint labels are used in this book to differentiate between the two basic groups of exercises but, strictly, they are inaccurate labels.**

Compound exercises are often called the *big, major,* or *core* movements, whereas single-joint exercises are often labeled as *small, little,* and *minor,* or *supplementary, auxiliary,* and *accessory* movements. This is, however, an oversimplification.

The Program of this book explains how to combine multi-joint and single-joint exercises in an effective manner.

Concentric contraction

The shortening of a muscle. For instance, when you raise your hand through bending your elbow, your biceps muscle contracts in a concentric way. The term is usually abbreviated to *a concentric.* Concentric contractions are also called *positives.*

A rep has two phases—the positive or concentric (pushing or pulling) part when the muscle performing the action *shortens*, and the negative or eccentric (lowering) part when the muscle *lengthens*. Standing up from a sitting position is the positive or concentric phase, while the descent to a sitting position is the negative or eccentric phase.

Cool down

A period of decreasing demands from exercise, to produce a gradual change from a state of intensive work, to one approaching a resting condition. After a hard cardiovascular workout, a period of two to three minutes working at a moderate pace, and then a further two to three minutes working at a gentle pace will wind your body down, and constitute a cool down. It enables your heart, breathing, and other functions to slow down gradually. End the cool down once your breathing has returned to normal.

Core exercises

The priority exercises in a routine—usually the big multiple-joint movements. In another definition, core movements refer to exercises that work the core of the body, that is, the trunk musculature of the abdomen, chest, and back.

Cycles

An abbreviation for *training cycles*. Cycles are periods of sustained training on a given program, for instance, a twelve-week cycle. Training intensity and training weights are typically varied over the course of a given cycle.

D

Double progression

The method of progressing in reps to a predetermined number, then adding weight to the bar and dropping reps a few, and then building back to the predetermined maximum number of reps prior to another weight increment. For example, 100 pounds for six reps this week, 100 for seven reps next week, and so forth, until 100 for ten can be performed; then the weight is increased to say 105 pounds, and the reps dropped to six once again. The *double* progression is in the reps *and* the weight, as distinct from *single* progression where only the weight *or* rep count is increased.

Dumbbell

A mini barbell, usually used with a single hand. Fixed-weight dumbbells have the plates locked in position, and are typically found in matching pairs, stored on racks at about thigh height. Adjustable dumbbells have collars that are easily released so that the weight can be adjusted to what's required, and then the collars are tightened.

E

Easy gainer

Opposite of *hard gainer*. Easy gainers are blessed with terrific heredity or genetics for muscle-building, and have highly responsive bodies. Genetic phenomena further enhanced by drug support are the ultimate easy gainers.

Eccentric action

The lengthening of a muscle. For instance, when you lower your hand through straightening your elbow, your biceps muscle is lengthened because of the eccentric action. Eccentric actions are often abbreviated to *eccentrics*. Eccentrics are also often called *negatives*.

Endurance

Ability of a muscle to work continually over a sustained period.

Equipment

Exercise equipment includes a variety of strength-training machinery, and free-weights (primarily long-bar barbells, and short-bar dumbbells), together with machines primarily used for cardiovascular work, such as treadmills (for walking, and running), ellipticals, and stairclimbers.

For strength training, exercises can be performed with free-weights, or machines. The former are the traditional and most versatile means of training. Machines reduce the need for instruction, and the chance of acute injury.

There are plate-loaded machines that require loading with the same plates that are used on barbells, and selectorized machines that have built-in weight stacks from which you select the required resistance using a selector pin. The built-in weight stacks make weight selection easy because you don't have to move plates around.

But because each section of metal on many weight stacks is substantial— ten pounds or more—the selectorized machines usually don't permit the gradual weight progression that plate-loaded machines do *unless* supplementary small plates are attached manually.

Machine quality varies greatly.

Exercise bar

Bar of about one-inch diameter, made to fit exercise weight plates. Exercise bars come in varying lengths, as opposed to the Olympic bar that has a standard length and requires plates with a hole in their center of about two inches diameter.

Exercise weight plates

Weight plates that have holes just large enough to fit onto an exercise bar, as opposed to Olympic plates that have larger holes in order to fit onto the thick ends of Olympic bars.

Exercises

The individual movements that work specific parts of the body. The words *exercises* and *movements* (and even *lifts,* in some cases), are used interchangeably. See *Compound exercises*, and *Isolation exercises*.

Extension

Opposite of flexion—movement that *increases* the angle between two bones, such as straightening out a bent elbow, and opening the fingers from a clenched fist.

F

Flexibility

Suppleness of muscle masses. Adequate flexibility is a requisite for being able to perform the major exercises with correct technique through a full or at least large range of motion. Tight muscles restrict joint movement, and general mobility.

Flexion

Opposite of *extension*—movement that *decreases* the angle between two bones, for example, raising your hand through bending at your elbow.

Form

Another term for *exercise technique*—the manner of exercise execution.

Freehand exercise

Calisthenic exercise that can be performed without equipment, such as the push-up.

Free-weights

Barbells, dumbbells, plates, and related easily movable equipment, as opposed to machines.

Full-body routine

Method of working the entire body in one routine that's performed at a single workout, as distinct from a split or divided program that targets particular bodyparts each session. Also called a *whole-body routine*.

G

Gear

Training clothing and equipment used for athletic training. *Gear* is also slang for bodybuilding drugs.

Four different grips: left, pronated grip (two views); middle, supinated grip (two views); top right, parallel grip; bottom right, mixed or reverse grip.

Genetics

The inherited instructions, or genes, that determine much of how you look and function in general, and how you respond to training.

Grips

There are four main grips: *pronated*, *supinated*, *parallel*, and *mixed*. See the photographs on this page, and the separate entries for each grip.

Gym

A location for exercising in. Although most people may think of gyms as specialist places such as a Gold's Gym, gyms can also be found at health clubs, YMCAs, some schools, colleges, universities, and leisure centers. There are also home gyms. Although gyms vary in their sizes and facilities, anywhere that houses exercise equipment can be considered a gym.

H

Hand off

Assistance in getting a weight to a starting position for an exercise. Also called a *lift off*.

Hard gainer

Opposite of *easy gainer*. A hard gainer is the genetically average or disadvantaged drug-free person, usually male, that typifies most trainees. Hard gainers are usually naturally thin, although there are fat hard gainers. Hard gainers respond poorly, or not at all, to conventional training methods, and vary in their degree of "hardgainingness." Because hard gainers are the majority, they are really *normal gainers*.

Home gym

A gym at one's home—perhaps in a garage—as against a commercial, or institutional gym. Institutional gyms are found in colleges and YMCAs, for example.

Hypertrophy

Increase in size of a tissue (usually muscle in our context), or organ. Opposite of atrophy

I

Intensity

In this book, intensity is the *relative* degree of effort put into training. High-intensity exercise is very hard training, whereas low-intensity exercise involves a much reduced effort level. Sufficient intensity of effort is required to stimulate muscular growth, although the precise degree of effort required is unknown.

Iron Game

Umbrella term to include all forms of activities that focus on strength training, weight training, or weight lifting in some form. The principle competitive activities, in alphabetical order, are bodybuilding, Olympic weightlifting, and powerlifting.

Isolation exercises

As noted earlier, exercises are commonly categorized into two basic types: isolation (*single*-joint), or compound (*multi*-joint). Isolation exercises are often tagged as being the *small*, *little*, and *minor* ones, or the *supplementary*, *auxiliary*, and *accessory* movements, whereas the compound exercises are often tagged as the *big*, *major*, or *core* movements. This is, however, an oversimplification.

Isometric exercise

Muscular contraction without movement—the muscles and joints don't move. Pushing against the jambs of a doorway is an example.

Isotonic exercise

Muscular action where the length of the muscle changes during the exercise, while the resistance or weight stays constant. Regular strength training is an example.

L

Lat machine

Exercise equipment that typically has one or two pulleys, and enables a bar to be pulled from overhead to the upper chest, with the resistance suspended from a cable that runs over the pulley(s). The older models are invariably plate-loaded, whereas the recent models may have built-in weight stacks. The major muscles worked by this machine include the latissimus dorsi, hence the name of the apparatus.

Little discs

Weight plates or discs lighter than the smallest ones that are typically available in most gyms. The little discs, or *microloads*, are plates that weigh, for example, 0.5 and 1.0 pound, and 0.1, 0.25, and 0.5 kilo.

Lockout

The final few inches of an exercise before the joints are fully extended or locked out.

Logbook

At the minimum, a written record of the weights, sets, and reps performed during each workout, to provide, among other things, a statement of what needs to be surpassed next time in order to register a progressive workout. A logbook is an essential training tool. It's also called a *training log* or *training diary*.

M

Maximum heart rate (MHR)

The MHR typically used in the exercise world is only an estimation, using the simple computation of (220 minus age). For example, if you're 35 years old, your estimated MHR would be 185 (220 minus 35). Although this computation may be accurate for some trainees, it's inaccurate for many, sometimes substantially so. Also called the *age-adjusted maximum heart rate.*

Metabolic rate

The amount of energy used by the body in a specific period of time.

Metabolism

The sum of the chemical and physical processes in the body by which its material substance is produced, maintained, and destroyed, and by which energy is made available.

Microloading

Use of small weight plates—microloads—to apply small weight increases to exercises.

Movement arm

The "arm" that extends from a machine, often with padding over or around the end part of it. It's against this movement arm that force from a trainee's limbs or other bodypart, depending on the machine, is applied, to produce movement. When the force is applied, the weight stack (or resistance) moves.

N

Negative rep

The lowering phase of a rep. Negatives are also called *eccentrics*.

O

Olympic plates

Weight plates with holes large enough to fit onto the ends of an Olympic bar, as opposed to exercise plates that have holes just large enough to fit onto an exercise bar that has a diameter of a little more than an inch throughout its length.

Olympic set

Barbell set with a revolving sleeve at each end of the bar, where the plates are placed, on a bar of total length of about seven feet. The sleeves are about two inches in diameter, and the central length of the bar is a little more than an inch in diameter. The plates for an Olympic set have holes large enough to fit onto the thick sleeves. Olympic sets are commonplace in gyms today. An Olympic barbell without outer collars weighs 45 pounds or 20 kilos.

Overcompensation

The response by the body to a given stimulus—not just training—that develops a little bit of reserve to cope with the possibility of increased demands. Muscle-building occurs from repeated overcompensation.

Overload

The principle of applying incrementally ever-greater resistance than normal, to stimulate an improvement in strength, muscular size, or other physical component.

Overtraining

Training beyond the body's current recuperative abilities.

P

Parallel grip

A grip that has the palms parallel with each other.

Plate-loaded

When individual plates are loaded onto a device used for resistance training. For example, modern barbells are plate-loaded, unlike the old-fashioned globe barbells. Some dumbbells are plate-loaded, whereas others are single-piece weights.

Plates

The weights that trainees slide onto the ends of barbells and dumbbells. They come in various sizes, including 45-pounders, 25-pounders, 10-pounders, and 5-pounders. For metric plates, they include 20-kilo plates, 15s, 10s, and 5s. There are also tiny discs, for making incremental changes in resistance.

The stacks of weights on certain machines are another form of plates.

Positive rep

A positive rep is when a muscle shortens. For example, when you raise your hand through bending your elbow, your biceps muscle contracts in a positive way. Also called *positives,* and *concentrics.*

Poundage

Another word for *weight,* the resistance used in a given exercise.

Power rack

Large four-post structure with cross members to hold the uprights in position. There's a series of holes in each post through which bars (called *pins*) can be placed, to provide range of motion limitations for any appropriate barbell exercise. Barbell exercises can be performed inside the rack. Properly used, a power rack ensures that you can never be pinned by a weight. A power rack is sometimes called a *power cage.*

Program

The total package of one or more training routines. It could, for example, be two different strength-training routines (which are alternated from workout to workout), a cardio routine, and a flexibility routine. Some trainees use *program* synonymously with *routine.*

Progressive resistance

System of training where the weight or resistance is incrementally increased as the muscles progress in strength and physical conditioning. Progressive resistance is at the heart of muscle-building, and strength training in general. The body is capable of tremendous achievement and adaptation provided that the resistance is increased in a *gradual* way, from an *easy* starting level. This adaptation applies to all sorts of physical and athletic stress, not just strength training.

Pronated grip

One of the most popular grips, used in many exercises. When your hands are at your sides, a pronated grip has your knuckles facing to the front, and palms facing to the rear. When your hands are overhead, the grip has your knuckles facing to the rear, and palms to the front.

R

Rack

Three meanings: A rack is used for storing barbells or dumbbells; a rack is an abbreviation for a power rack; and rack is a verb that means to return a bar to its holders in a rack or any sort of stand that holds a barbell—"rack the bar," the opposite of *unrack*.

Range of motion

The range of motion of an exercise, often abbreviated to *ROM*.

Recuperation

The process of recovering from exercise. The major components of recuperation are nutrition, rest (during the day), and sleep.

Rep

Abbreviation for *repetition*.

Repetition

One complete, up-and-down (positive and negative) movement of an exercise—a *single* unit of the sequence of reps that comprises a set. Usually abbreviated to *rep*. If you hang from an overhead bar using a pronated grip, and pull yourself up, and then lower yourself to the starting position, you would have done a single rep of the pull-up.

Rep out

Performance of as many reps as possible.

Resistance

The amount of resistance, which can include weight plates, that's used in an exercise. In manual resistance—for example, some neck work—weight plates aren't used for resistance. Instead, resistance is applied by another person, or by the trainee.

Rest interval

The rest period between sets—be it between sets of the same exercise, or between a set of one exercise and a set of another exercise. Rest intervals are also called *rest periods*.

Rest intervals can be almost non-existent (the few seconds it takes to move from one exercise to another, provided that the back-to-back exercises are set up beforehand), short (one minute maximum), moderate (two to five minutes), or long (more than five minutes). The rest interval varies according to the type of training, individual preference, and practicalities of training in a busy gym.

Sometimes a rest interval may refer to the brief pause between reps, although the between-*sets* rest period is the common definition.

Rest pause

The short pause between reps, usually for just a second, or a few seconds. Sometimes there's no rest pause between reps because they are performed in a continuous manner. In **The Program**, there's a brief pause between reps of each exercise, to set yourself for the next rep, and to help with bar control, and technique. This pause is often used to take a quick breath or two.

Reverse grip

A grip where a bar is held with one hand pronated and the other supinated. It's a specialized grip for a small number of exercises, such as the deadlift. It's also called an *alternating grip*, or *mixed grip*.

Routine

A list of exercises, sets, and reps used in one training session. There can be strength-training routines, cardio routines, and flexibility routines. A routine is also called a *schedule*, and sometimes a *program*.

S

Set

A sequence of reps. A set can consist of one rep (*a single*), low reps (2 to 4), medium reps (5 to 12), high reps (13 to 25), or very high reps (25+). These divisions are, however, subjective. Different trainees may have different definitions of rep counts.

Set system

The most common form of strength training. The system whereby a specific number of sets is performed for a given exercise before moving onto the next exercise.

Single progression

The method of maintaining a constant rep number for a given exercise, and progressively increasing resistance as the weeks and months go by. For example, 100 pounds for 8 reps this week, then 101 pounds for 8 reps next week, 102 for 8 reps the following week, and so forth. Another type of single progression is to maintain a fixed weight and keep adding reps.

Also see *Double progression*.

Spot

Assistance for someone performing an exercise—"I need a spot for my final set of bench presses."

Spotter

Someone who stands by and closely watches a trainee, to provide help—or a *spot*—when needed.

Sticking point

This has at least two meanings. It's the most difficult point in the range of motion of an exercise—the point at which the weight seems its heaviest. Most exercises have a point, often about halfway up, where the resistance seems to get heavier. This is the point where the resistance seems to stutter, or even get stuck if you're at your hilt of effort, hence the term *sticking point*. If you make it through the sticking point, the rest of the rep should be easy (but the sticking point could be at the end of the rep). A sticking point can also mean a *plateau* in overall progress.

Strength training

Training for the development of muscle and strength. Some people use *strength training* synonymously with *bodybuilding*, and some use it to refer to muscle-building *without* a connection to the world of competitive bodybuilding. Training for strength is an essential part of bodybuilding, and muscle-building in general.

Supinated grip

Another of the most popular grips, used in many exercises. When your hands are at your sides, a supinated grip has your knuckles facing to the rear, and palms facing to the front. When your hands are overhead, the supinated grip has your knuckles facing to the front, and your palms facing to the rear.

Systemic

Affecting the entire body, as contrasted with something that's localized.

T

Target heart rate (THR)

A percentage of your maximum heart rate to be sustained for a given period during cardio exercise. THR can typically be anywhere from 60% to 90% of your maximum heart rate (MHR).

Trainee

Anyone who lifts weights. Confusingly, some people use train*er* when they mean train*ee*. The coach is the trainer, as in *personal trainer*, for example, and the person being coached is the trainee. Trainees are commonly called *lifters*.

Training cycle

See *Cycles*.

Training diary

See *Logbook*.

Training frequency

How often you train. There's strength-training frequency, stretching frequency, and cardio work frequency. All three components may or may not be combined in a single training session.

Training partner

A person who works out along with you, largely if not wholly duplicating your routine, typically through alternating sets, albeit with different weights. A training partner also functions as a spotter.

U

Unrack

Verb that means removing a bar from the bar holders or saddles in a rack or any sort of stands that hold a barbell—the opposite of *rack*.

W

Warm-ups

A general warm-up for five to ten minutes—on a stationary cycle, ski machine, or rower, for example—should precede each weights workout, and should break you into a sweat before you touch a barbell. Thereafter, specific warm-up *sets* are performed for each strength-training exercise, to prime your muscles for the work sets that follow. Warm-up work should also precede other types of exercise.

Weight

Synonym for *poundage* and, often, for *resistance*, too.

Weights

Barbell plates. These are used for barbells, dumbbells, and plate-loaded machines. *Weights* may also be used, in a broader sense, to refer to plates *and* any equipment that employs weight plates.

Weight stack

Many machines—selectorized ones—have built-in plates in the form of a stack, akin to a vertical pile of thin bricks. This is a weight stack. A small pin is slotted in at the appropriate height to select the required weight. Weight stacks usually have increments such as 10 or 15 pounds per level. To produce a gradual progression, small plates may be fixed onto the weight stack by putting the loading pin through the small plates prior to the pin going into the stack.

Workout

A bodybuilding, strength-training, cardio, or flexibility session.

Work sets

The demanding sets of a given exercise, as distinct from warm-up sets. Work sets are the ones that have the potential to stimulate muscular growth and strength increase.

> *The first reading of this book will teach you a huge amount. A second reading will produce a further big leap in your understanding of how to train effectively. This will occur because the second reading will build on the first. It will deepen your grasp of each topic, and knit everything together.*

Follow the prescriptions given in this chapter and you may substantially decrease the risks of many serious problems including heart disease, diabetes, and some cancers, and greatly improve your health and well-being. This will add life to your years, and possibly years to your life.

9

Cardio training

The heart is a muscle. It can be trained for greater strength and endurance. The potential benefits are extensive—a more efficient and thus healthier cardiovascular system (heart, lungs, and blood vessels), and other internal health benefits.

The terms *cardio training*, *cardiorespiratory training*, and *cardiovascular training* are often used interchangeably with *aerobic exercise*. Aerobic exercise, however, may be insufficiently demanding to produce a cardiorespiratory training effect, depending on the intensity relative to the individual's fitness level. For example, a slow walk on the flat may produce a cardio training effect for a sedentary 50-year-old, but a fast-paced walk on an incline may be needed to produce a similar effect for a fit 25-year-old.

Cardio is used in this book to denote work of *sufficient* intensity to produce a training effect on the cardiorespiratory system.

Cardio work improves general conditioning so that you're in better shape for common demands—such as rushing up a couple of flights of stairs—*and* strength training. A better conditioned body may produce better strength-training performance, because you may recover from each set faster, and not fatigue so easily. A better conditioned body will probably recover quicker between workouts. At least part of why some trainees complain of being tired between workouts is that they lack good, general conditioning.

Unless you're already well conditioned because of regular endurance work, add cardio work to your overall exercise program. What follows is an incremental progression of cardio work for beginners. A *modest* start and *gradual* progression are imperative for previously sedentary people (or even weight-trained individuals not used to cardio work). *If, however, you're currently active physically, and already much better conditioned than the average person, you can progress at a much faster rate—for instance, start at week #7.*

Week-by-week cardio program

Perform the cardio work two times a week at the end of each gym workout, following strength training, and stretching. Then you'll already be warmed up. Performing all three types of exercise during each workout simplifies training, which is an excellent approach for beginners to adopt, and intermediate and advanced trainees, too. If you have convenient access to cardio equipment—at home, or at a gym close to work or home—you may prefer to do the cardio work on separate days. This will shorten the main workouts each week, but increase the overall number of workouts. But before the cardio work, first do some general warm-up work, and some careful stretching.

Aerobics

Ever since Dr. Kenneth Cooper popularized aerobic exercise, from around 1970, aerobics have evolved to include various methods of floor, gadget, or machine exercise, to elevate heart rate. These have had special appeal to women, supposedly as a means to improve the external appearance of their bodies.

The claim that aerobics is a complete system of exercise, is false. Aerobics produce minimal or no strengthening or development of the muscles. Aerobics comprise, at best, only a limited part of an exercise program. Some forms of aerobics, such as high-impact floor activities, are dangerous, and should be avoided. Many fanatical enthusiasts have developed serious overuse injuries.

Training for strength and muscular development is essential for aesthetic, functional, and health benefits, for men and women. Aerobics can't build strength and muscular development in a meaningful way. Exercise for the cardio system is essential for many internal benefits, but aerobics is only one possible way of delivering on this front, and not the most efficient.

Exercise at the given percentages of maximum heart rate (MHR). Choose a low-impact activity such as stationary cycling (with the seat positioned so that your knee is *almost* straight when the pedal is at its bottom position), or use a skiing, elliptical, climbing, or rowing machine, or walk on a treadmill (set at a slight incline as soon as brisk walking on the flat is too easy).

A well-equipped gym will have a good selection of cardio equipment. All you need is one piece of equipment you can use safely. You need to like it, too. You won't stick with anything you don't enjoy.

Week #	1	2	3	4	5	6	7	8
% of MHR*	65	65	65	65	65	65	70	70
duration in mins	10	12	14	16	18	20	16	17
total time**	15	17	19	21	23	25	21	22

* To find your estimated, age-adjusted maximum heart rate, subtract your age from 220. To find your target heart rate—a given percentage of maximum heart rate—multiply your estimated maximum heart rate by the given percentage. For example, if you're 30, your estimated maximum heart rate is 190 (220 minus 30). If your target heart rate is, for example, 75% of your estimated maximum heart rate, multiply 190 by 75%, which yields 142. Wearing an accurate heart monitor provides instant feedback of your heart rate. Alternatively, take your pulse over ten seconds. If your target heart rate is 142, that's means 23 or 24 beats per ten seconds (142 divided by six). The heart rate monitor is more accurate and convenient.

Your maximum heart rate is only an ESTIMATION. *Although it's a good guideline for beginners, it may have less value for fit trainees. Fit trainees can usually safely maintain a higher heart rate than unfit people. Fit trainees may need to work at a higher heart rate than the estimated maximum heart rate computes for them, to produce a training effect.*

** Open each cardio session with two to three minutes gradual progression from inactivity to the day's target heart rate. After the day's target heart rate work, taper off the rate of exercise over a final two to three minutes. The preliminary work, and final tapering off, add five minutes to the total duration of each session.

From the twelfth week onward, increase the warm-up and cooldown periods to five minutes *each*. This is for safety reasons, to allow the body a sufficient period to move gradually from resting, to the target heart rate, and then to readjust during the cooldown through a progressive decrease in the exercise-induced stress.

Don't treat the warm-up and cooldown casually. It may be harmful to rush to a highly elevated heart rate, and it may be harmful to come to an abrupt halt following exercise at a highly elevated heart rate. Take five minutes for a gradual warm-up; and five minutes for a gradual cooldown—at least until your breathing has returned to normal.

As long as you can cope with the above workload progression without being out of breath, you're on course. Although you should be breathing heavier than normal while exercising, you should be able to hold a conversation without spitting out your words. For the first eight weeks, should the prescribed work make you breathe heavily, ease back on the pace a little, and take additional weeks to build up your conditioning. *Proceed at your own pace according to your age, starting level, and individual rate of progression.*

Week #	9	10	11	12	13	14	15	16
% of MHR	70	70	70	75	75	75	75	75
duration in mins	18	19	20	16	17	18	19	20
total time	23	24	25	26	27	28	29	30

. . . thereafter maintain at least this minimum level of cardio work, twice weekly.

The ability to work at 75% of your maximum heart rate for 20 consecutive minutes—the target after four months of training for a previously sedentary individual, but quicker for an already active person—is no mean feat. Although it's far from the level of conditioning of an elite track athlete, it will probably take you into the top few percent of cardiorespiratory fitness for a random sample of the general population. This will improve your health and well-being. But the precise degree of fitness that the "75% of your maximum heart rate for 20 consecutive minutes" will yield for you in terms of your aerobic capacity—your maximal oxygen uptake, or VO_2 max—will depend on genetic factors and how long you've trained.

A 75% of estimated maximum heart rate is supposed to translate to 7.5 on a scale of one to ten, where ten is the limit—total exhaustion. Number 7.5 correlates with demanding exercise, but not very hard. After four months of training, if you find that 75% of maximum heart rate doesn't equate to 7.5 on the perceived exertion scale of one to ten, the 75% of maximum heart rate isn't accurate for you, and you need to adjust it to match your perception of the 75%.

To prevent monotony, and perhaps to increase the effectiveness of the cardio work, rotate two or three different types of low-impact cardio work from workout to workout. Furthermore, perhaps get out of the gym for some of your cardio work. Walk up flights of stairs in a tall building, two at a time if you're in good shape. Find a hill, and briskly walk up that. High-tech machinery isn't essential for effective cardio work.

The value of a treadmill

Millions of trainees have been injured from outdoor jogging, running, or cycling, in the quest for improved health and fitness. Some supposedly beneficial activities are dangerous. Don't use an activity that's likely to produce injury.

Provided the treadmill has a yielding belt (one that *gives*, to reduce impact forces), and provided there's an adjustable incline, it may be possible to achieve the required target heart rate safely from brisk walking (on an incline, when required). Depending on the individual and the set-up of the treadmill, it may be possible to achieve up to 80 to 85% of maximum heart rate without having to run.

What about jogging, on an incline or on the flat? As Dr. Steven Stark explains in THE STARK REALITY OF STRETCHING, slow jogging produces more stress on the joints than running (not sprinting), so you may be better off running on the flat on a treadmill, for example, than jogging on an incline, provided you're not overweight, and not suffering from back or lower-body joint problems. Although there's increased speed from running, the weight-bearing impact of running is less than from jogging—the impact forces from running are about three times those from walking, while those from jogging are about four times those from walking. If you're to run, walk briskly for five to ten minutes, to warm up, and then run. Don't jog.

Some of the apparent benefits of cardio training may, however, be from the muscle strengthening involved. For example, if untrained individuals add just stair climbing to their lives (on flights of stairs, or machines), the reduced challenge on their cardiorespiratory systems, over time, will primarily be because of the strengthening of their leg, thigh, and hip muscles, not any improvement in heart fitness. This general muscle strengthening would also make the everyday tasks of daily living easier. Once the muscles have been sufficiently strengthened, and provided that the cardio work is done correctly, THEN the cardio work will start to produce significant benefits for the cardio system.

Rate of progress caution

In each component of an exercise program, proceed at your own pace according to your age, starting level, and individual rate of progression.

Follow the manufacturer's safety recommendations. Falling off a treadmill could be extremely dangerous. Use the handrails in an emergency, for balance and safety. If you have to pull on the handrails to cope with the exercise, reduce the speed or incline setting so that you can cope unaided. If there's a wall behind the treadmill, there should be a well-padded surface affixed to it, in case you fall off the belt.

With a good treadmill you can control the incline and speed to meet your requirements, and control your rate of progress with precision. Some models have programs that vary speed and incline, to keep things varied once you're beyond the beginner stage. And because you're indoors you also have some degree of climate control.

Although many trainees can't run safely outdoors, and many trainees who do run outdoors end up suffering from chronic injuries, the use of a good treadmill may be safe, enjoyable, and effective.

Caveat on treadmills, and running

Running can be a harmful activity even when a good treadmill and footwear are used, and even if the running is low-volume and low-frequency. For example, if you're overweight, or if you have foot problems or defects, or anomalies elsewhere in your body, your running gait may be affected negatively, which will put undue stress on your body. This is why it's critical to act on the guidance given in Chapter 6. Any anomalies you may have can be discovered, and corrective action taken.

Jogging on an incline, although effective for elevating heart rate, may mask foot, leg, and knee problems, and perhaps even exacerbate them if done excessively. Slow running on an incline produces a shortened stride length, doesn't necessarily reduce impact forces relative to running on the flat, and encourages shortening of the hip flexors. If you use an incline, don't make it your only form of cardio work, and stretch your hip flexors several times each week.

Previously, you may not have been able to run safely on the flat. But following treatment to remove soft-tissue restrictions, and warming up and stretching adequately each time before you run (especially of your lower body), you may be able to run safely, in low volume, on the yielding belt of a good treadmill, while wearing good running shoes.

If, however, running on a regular basis isn't safe for you—even in the low volume required for harder but shorter cardio work—select alternative activities that are safe. Different pieces of cardio equipment apply stress to the body in different ways.

Harder but shorter cardio work

For increasing aerobic fitness, as Dr. Richard Winett of the Center for Research in Health Behavior at Virginia Tech, Blacksburg, USA, told me, ". . . there doesn't seem to be any relationship between duration of training and increasing fitness. Rather, intensity as defined by percent of oxygen consumption—more easily conveyed as a percentage of maximum heart rate—seems more important. Therefore, there's really no reason to start with longer duration, easier work *unless* you're a novice and/or in very poor aerobic condition."

Once you've been at the 75% of maximum heart rate level for a few weeks, and provided you have your doctor's consent for more demanding exercise, increase intensity to the 80% mark for four to five continuous minutes two times a week, for a few weeks. Then increase it to the 85% mark. There's no need to go higher—85% of actual maximum heart rate is hard. As your conditioning improves, incrementally increase your exercising pace or resistance in order to sustain the 85% of maximum heart rate. If you maintain a steady pace and resistance each workout, over time you won't be able to reach the 85% mark, because your body will have adapted to that load. The load will have a reduced demand on your body relative to earlier training.

The preliminary warm-up *must* be a full five minutes for this hard cardio work, and the cooldown *must* be for at least five minutes at the end of the session. In total, this sort of cardio work lasts just 14 to 15 minutes, which is about half of the total cardio time required for the moderate approach, and the hard cardio work need only be done two times a week for substantial benefits.

Don't rush the warm-up. It must be done incrementally and gradually, to allow your body to adapt aerobically. If you rush to the 85% mark, you'll move into anaerobic exercise, which will intensify the work, increase the perception of effort, and not yield the required benefits. If, for example, your heart rate is 80 before starting the warm-up work, and your target heart rate is 170, start gently and then increase the effort level so that your heart rate increases by about 20 a minute.

Risk factors caution

You must be free of any risk factors such as hypertension. Get the consent of your physician before doing any hard aerobics, in case you have risk factors you're not aware of that could preclude such demanding exercise. It's possible to be fit and yet have serious health risks. In such a case, it's dangerous to exercise at a high heart rate.

This prescriptive cardio work is called the *graded exercise protocol*, or GXP. Through intensifying the cardio work, the duration needed for cardiorespiratory benefits is reduced. The GXP was first developed by Dr. Robert Otto, and then adapted and studied by Drs. Ralph N. Carpinelli, Lesley D. Fox, Richard A. Winett, and Janet R. Wojcik.

Short but hard aerobic work produces benefits out of proportion to the limited duration of the work, because of the increased aerobic capacity or VO_2 max it produces. Improved aerobic capacity appears to be the key to substantial, cardiovascular health benefits. Aerobic capacity increase is more dependent on intensity of work than duration. If the cardio work isn't of sufficient intensity to cause adaptive changes in the cardiorespiratory system, an increase in aerobic capacity won't be produced. For a heavily referenced, peer-reviewed paper on this approach to cardio work, reviewed by some leading exercise scientists and epidemiologists, see "Examining the Validity of Exercise Guidelines for the Prevention of Morbidity and All-Cause Mortality," by Richard A. Winett, Ph.D., and Ralph N. Carpinelli, Ed.D., in the journal ANNALS OF BEHAVIORAL MEDICINE, reference 2000; 22:159–178.

The GXP is ideal for trainees who find lower-intensity, longer-duration aerobic work unchallenging, and motivation hard to sustain. It's also ideal for trainees who want to invest minimum time in cardio work, but without compromising on benefits.

Importance of accurate heart rate measurement

For the GXP's prescriptive 85% of maximum heart rate, it's pivotal that you know your *actual* maximum heart rate, or a close approximation, and not rely on the estimation of it as 220 minus your age.

If you *over*estimate your maximum heart rate, the 85% exercise level of it could work you too hard, which may be dangerous; and even if it was safe, it would be too uncomfortable for most trainees to do on a regular basis. If you *under*estimate your maximum heart rate, you're unlikely to train intensively enough to produce benefits from brief bouts of cardio work. Discover your maximum heart rate with the help of a cardiologist or other trained medical professional. Don't try to discover it by yourself! Alternatively, here are two methods of getting a close approximation of your actual 85% of maximum heart rate:

1. Perceived exertion

An 85% of maximum heart rate is supposed to translate to 8.5 on a perceived exertion scale of one to ten where ten is the limit—total exhaustion. Number 8.5 correlates with hard exercise, but not limit work. If you find that 85% of your estimated (220 minus age) maximum heart rate doesn't equate to 8.5 on the perceived exertion scale, the 85% of maximum heart rate isn't accurate for you and you need to adjust it to match the perception of *actual* 85% of your limit.

2. The talk test

In discussions, Dr. Winett explained that the 85% of actual maximum heart rate is roughly the anaerobic threshold, the point at which your body can't produce energy aerobically but shifts into anaerobic mode for a brief period, before fatigue and discomfort force you to terminate the exercise. The anaerobic threshold is roughly the point at which you can no longer converse, but where you can only spit out words as you struggle to breathe. For the GXP, you need to stay slightly below the anaerobic threshold. If, at the 85% of estimated maximum heart rate, you need only one or two breaths per average-length sentence, you're unlikely to be at your actual 85% of maximum heart rate, and would need to increase your work level. If, however, at the 85% of estimated maximum heart rate you can only spit out one or two words in between gasps for air, you'll have exceeded your actual 85% of maximum heart rate, and need to back off.

Your perceived exertion of 8.5 on the scale of one to ten should coincide with the talk test, give or take a few heart beats. Take the midpoint of the two, and use that as your 85% of actual maximum heart rate.

Don't exceed your target heart rate

You may find that once you've reached your 85% of maximum heart rate, even if you maintain a steady rate of exercising, your heart rate will continue to increase. This can be dangerous, so it's imperative that you continually monitor your heart rate. If you find that your heart rate increases more than two or three beats above your target

heart rate when working at 85% of actual maximum heart rate,
decrease the workload (resistance or speed) so that your heart rate
returns to where it should be. Be vigilant.

Training at 85% of MHR doesn't necessarily indicate fitness

Merely working at 85% of maximum heart rate, whether estimated
or actual, isn't a guide to an individual's fitness level. Take an
overweight, unfit, middle-age woman. Walking at a brisk pace may
quickly get her up to 85% of maximum heart rate (which may not be
safe, because of her poor condition), but clearly she's unfit. But if
she's trained well for a few months she'll then be able to work at a
greater speed or resistance in order to produce the 85% of maximum
heart rate, so by then she'll be fitter. Keep her at it for a few more
months, increase the speed or resistance further, and then she'll be
fitter still. Although the target heart rate is the same, the work
required to produce it will have changed substantially.

What matters is that you progress steadily in the level of work
required to produce the 85% of maximum heart rate, at the fixed
duration. Then you'll improve your level of cardio fitness. After
six to twelve months of gradual progression, you'll build to an
impressive fitness level for a non-competitive athlete—sufficient to
yield the many health benefits from cardio training. This would be
from a 15-minute workout two times a week—a tremendous reward
for a small investment of time and energy.

Heart rate monitor

For demanding cardio work, a reliable heart rate monitor is
essential. You need to know immediately if you're working too
hard or not hard enough, and respond accordingly. You can get a
heart rate monitor for about $50.00. This is inexpensive, and an
investment in your health that you'll use for many years. You don't
need a monitor with many features—a basic model will suffice.
Some cardio machines have built-in heart rate indicators that work
from special handles.

The heart rate monitor's sensor is worn around the chest, and the
special watch that shows the heart rate is typically worn around the
wrist. When I use a piece of cardio exercise equipment, I sometimes
strap the watch around part of the equipment that's in constant view
and sufficiently close to my chest that the signal from the sensor isn't
disrupted—then I can see what's happening to my heart rate
without having to look at my wrist.

The heart rate monitor isn't just for keeping tabs on your heart rate during the warm-up and the most taxing part of the cardio work. It's also important to keep an eye on what happens to your heart rate during the cooldown. Over the few minutes of the cooldown, your breathing should return to normal, or almost normal, and your heart rate be reduced greatly, but it may need another 15 to 45 minutes to return to normal resting levels (provided that you're no longer exercising during that period).

If you're so fatigued following the hard stage of the GXP that you can't perform any further exercise, and you want to flop on the floor, you've pushed too hard. Reduce the intensity of work next time. If, following the hard stage of the GXP you see that your heart rate doesn't drop steadily, with the biggest drop in the first minute of the cooldown, you were either pushing too hard during the intensive phase, or are pushing too hard in the cooldown phase.

Here's an example of what to do during the cooldown: For the first minute, reduce the speed of the exercise to no more than two thirds of what it was during the hard stage, then reduce it to about half for the next two minutes, and then cut back further on speed and resistance for the final two minutes. By then your breathing should be back to normal, or close to it.

Personal illustration of estimated and actual MHR

At the time of writing, I was 46 years old. My estimated maximum heart rate was 174—namely, 220 minus 46. The 85% computation of 174 was 148, but exercising at 148 beats per minute was comfortable for me—a perception of about 70% of my maximum. If I increased the work level to the point at which I couldn't speak more than four or five words without gasping for a breath, my heart rate was around the 170 mark. My perception of exertion at 170 was about 85%—8.5 on a scale of one to ten. The 170 beats per minute appeared to be my 85% of actual maximum heart rate, and a tad below my anaerobic threshold. That was what I used, give or take a few heart beats, during my GXP work. (I'd had a cardiologist give me a thorough check-up, and received his consent for performing hard cardio work.)

This level of work was hard, but not so hard that I was devastated after five minutes. Five minutes of it was sufficient to produce the required training effect, but any more than five minutes two times a week, would have converted an

Some pieces of cardio equipment have built-in heart rate monitoring devices, but usually they are not as accurate as using your own heart rate monitor.

The cardio work described here is primarily for cardiorespiratory conditioning, not calorie burning. If burning of calories is important for you, add low-intensity activity—for example, walk for an hour three times a week in addition to the cardio work.

enjoyable challenge into toil that I wouldn't maintain.

As Dr. Winett told me, maximum heart rate seems to be genetically based to some degree, and may not necessarily have much relationship to cardio fitness. It may be possible to have a high maximum heart rate but not a high level of cardio fitness, or a lower maximum heart rate but higher level of cardio fitness. Maximum heart rate may not increase with increased fitness. Again, it's important to find your *actual* maximum heart rate, and not rely on the estimated, age-adjusted maximum heart rate.

When to perform the GXP

When cardio work is of moderate intensity, it probably doesn't matter when it's done—same day as strength training, before or after resistance training, or on a different day to strength training. But when it's of high intensity—the GXP—it may be best to do it on two days each week that you also strength train. The GXP demands more from the recuperation system than moderate intensity cardio work does. If, for example, you strength train on three days a week and do the GXP on another two days, that would mean five days each week that you have a substantial demand on your recuperation system, which is too many for most people, and will lead to compromised results on both fronts. Limit to three the number of days each week you train hard, be it from strength training or from cardio work.

Do the GXP immediately after your strength training, or perform your stretching after your weights workout and *then* do the GXP. The break while stretching may help reduce the perceived exertion from the cardio work.

For simplicity and minimal time investment, perform the GXP after your weights work—either immediately following the stretching, or 10 to 15 minutes later, when you feel ready.

Cardio fitness manifestation

With a heart rate monitor you can see the improvements in your fitness. This is satisfying and will help spur you to greater achievements. On a treadmill, a workload (at a set incline and speed setting) that produces a heart rate of say 165 may, two months later, yield a heart rate of 158. That would be demonstration of improved fitness, and cardio efficiency. Furthermore, if your resting heart rate was 82 before you started the cardio program, but after four months it's 71, and then four further months later it's 64, that's evidence of substantial improvement in cardio fitness.

Individual responsiveness to cardio work

How cardiovascularly fit you'll become through following the guidelines given here, is influenced by genetic factors. Two individuals who can each complete workouts that produce 85% of actual maximum heart rate for each person, and for the same duration and frequency of training, won't necessarily have the same cardio fitness—one may be superior to the other. A similar point can be made for strength training. The same workouts, level of resistance, and training frequency, can produce differing effects in muscular development in different individuals, because of variations in genetics and other factors.

Comparing yourself with others isn't the best way to go. Compare yourself with yourself at different levels of training and conditioning. Never mind that you may not have the potential for great cardio fitness. What you do have the potential for is great improvement in your conditioning relative to what it would be if you didn't train.

Follow the prescriptions given in this chapter and you may substantially decrease the risks of many serious problems including heart disease, diabetes and some cancers, and greatly improve your health and well-being. This will add life to your years, and possibly years to your life. Furthermore, being able to exercise your body vigorously is a blessing, and a joy. Ponder on that for a moment.

Make the most of this blessing. Commit to cardio training.

Advanced cardio fitness

If you're interested in taking cardio fitness to a greater level than what's given in this chapter, the endurance training involved is likely to limit your muscle-building progress and expectations, as there would be competition for limited resources. Furthermore, although you'll be able to increase your fitness level further, there may not be additional health benefits. The increased fitness level would be for other reasons.

I promote a conservative approach to training. Experience from more than thirty years—from my own personal training, and from observing countless other trainees—has taught me that the conservative approach isn't only the safest way, *it's the most effective way over the long term.*

10

How to avoid injuries

To progress in strength and physique, you must train regularly, but you can't do that if you experience injuries. Barring freak accidents, training injuries have nothing to do with bad luck. They have everything to do with ignorance, following bad advice, and inattentiveness. Done properly, strength training *is* safe.

The building of strength itself, provided it's done safely, helps protect against injury. Most injuries are a result of an imposed force exceeding the structural strength of the involved bodypart. If structural strength is increased, resistance to injury will be increased, too.

To help you to avoid injuries, here are 38 recommendations:

1. Never apply the "No pain, no gain" maxim

Never do anything that hurts, don't train if you've hurt yourself, and never train through pain. Cumulative muscular discomfort, and systemic fatigue from an exercise done with effort and correct technique, are desirable, but pain isn't. Any sharp, stabbing, or sudden pain is a sign you've injured yourself.

Countless trainees have given up strength training because of having been hurt from following foolish advice. Those who live the "No pain, no gain" maxim usually regret it, sooner or later.

2. Know your physical anomalies

Modify your training according to any physical anomalies you may have. For example, if you've had back surgery, the barbell squat may be an unwise exercise selection; and if you have foot problems, running wouldn't be a wise choice of cardio exercise. Know your body before you go training it.

3. Seek correction of physical restrictions

With the right treatment you may be able to rid yourself of problems you may have accepted as permanent, or at least reduce them greatly. Investigate the possibility. You probably have restrictions in your muscles—soft-tissue restrictions are at the root of many physical problems and limitations. Seek expert therapists. You may need to look beyond your home area.

See Chapter 6 for details.

4. Don't neglect flexibility work

Generally, supple muscles are less likely to suffer injury than tight ones. Supple muscles have more give in them than tight muscles, and help protect against injury. Supple *and* strong muscles provide greater protection.

5. Adapt to exercises

Be patient when learning how to perform a new exercise. Use very light weights to begin with, and only once you've mastered exercise technique should you add weight, gradually, and pick up the effort level.

Once you've had a lot of experience with a particular exercise but haven't included it in your program for a few months, take a few weeks to refamiliarize yourself with it before you train it hard.

6. Apply training discipline

It's easier to use correct technique and controlled rep speed at the start of a set than during the final few reps when the required effort is higher. Hold correct technique and controlled rep speed even on the final "can just squeeze this out" rep. Never break correct technique to force out another rep. Perform correct reps only, or end the set.

If possible, train with a partner who can scrutinize your technique and rep speed, and, by oral cues, help you to keep your technique and rep speed correct.

7. Use a safe range of motion

Use the maximum safe range of motion for you for each exercise. For selectorized equipment, such as many leg curl machines, you can manually delimit the range of motion, if required. Remove the pin from the weight stack, then grip the cable that's attached to the guide rod that runs through the weight stack, and lift it. The top weight plate will rise alone, revealing the guide rod. Expose two holes on the rod, for example, and then use the pin to select the required weight. The gap between the first and second weight plates indicates the reduction in range of motion—two to three inches in this illustration. Fine-tune the reduction to what's required to produce the maximum safe range of motion for you. Make a note in your training logbook of the setting.

8. Maintain symmetrical lifting

Other than for one-side-at-a-time exercises such as the one-legged calf raise, and the L-fly, focus on symmetrical technique, to apply symmetrical stress to your body.

Don't let the bar slope to one side during barbell work. Keep it parallel with the floor at all times. Both hands must move in unison. For example, in barbell pressing, one hand should neither be above nor in front of the other.

A critical factor behind symmetrical lifting, is symmetrical hand and foot positioning. If one hand is placed further from the center of the bar than the other, or if one foot is positioned differently to the other, you won't be symmetrically positioned, and thus will be set up for asymmetrical lifting.

Load barbells carefully. If you loaded one end of the bar with more weight than the other, you'll lift asymmetrically. A substantial weight difference will be noticeable during the first rep of a set, whereupon the bar should be set down or racked, and the loading corrected. A bar that's slightly lopsided may not be detectable, but will nevertheless lead to asymmetrical lifting, and perhaps injury.

If you lift on a surface that's not horizontal, you'll lift asymmetrically. Train on a level floor. This is especially important for the big exercises, such as the squat, deadlift, overhead press, and bench press. Take a spirit level to the gym, and check out whether or not the lifting areas are level, and then use only the ones that are.

9. Use proper head and eye control

Key factors in maintaining symmetrical lifting are a fixed, face-forward, *neutral* head position, and keeping your eyes riveted on one spot during a set. (A neutral head position is neither extended nor flexed.) Except for neck exercises, avoid any lateral, forward, or rearward movement of your head when you train with weights.

10. Keep your eyes open

If you close your eyes while training, you'll risk some deterioration of balance. There may also be degradation of bar control, especially in exercises that use free-weights. Both can threaten your safety. Don't close your eyes while you train.

11. Use the right weight selection for you

Use weights you can handle in correct technique. Most trainees use more weight than they can handle correctly. This leads to cheating, and a loss of control.

12. Choose safe exercises

An exercise that's safe for some trainees may not be for others. As a beginner, with exercise intensity and weights being low, most trainees will be able to employ most exercises safely provided correct technique is used. But because of physical anomalies, accidents, or other injuries, specific exercises may be proscribed.

Don't use exercises that aren't suited to you. See Chapter 6 for how to find assistance to help guide you on which exercises may not be appropriate for you. If an exercise irritates a joint or causes sharp, stabbing, or sudden pain, don't persist with it. Fix the problem before returning to that exercise, or avoid the exercise if the cause of the problem can't be corrected.

13. Avoid high-risk lifting

All types of lifting weights can be dangerous if not done correctly, but some forms carry a higher risk than others. For example, rock lifting and other forms of handling awkwardly shaped objects carry a far higher risk of injury than barbell, dumbbell, and machine training.

14. Don't follow the examples of the genetic elite

A few trainees are so robust they can withstand training abuse that would cripple most trainees. But eventually even those robust trainees usually pay a heavy price. Don't take liberties in the gym. For each trainee who can apparently get away with training liberties, there are many who pay a high price for such abuse.

15. When using machines, follow the manufacturers' instructions

For some exercises, you may have to line up a specific joint with the pivot point of the machine. The right set-up position is critical. Changing the seat's position (and thus your position) by just one peg, for example, can make a difference in the comfort of a given machine exercise.

To line up with accuracy a given point on a machine with a given point on your body, your eyes need to be at the same level as the points being lined up. This usually isn't practical, so get an assistant to line you up. Once you have the right set-up for a specific exercise, make a note in your training logbook of the seat or other setting you require, for reference.

If you've used a machine as the manufacturer advises (often through instructions fixed to the equipment), have tweaked the set-up to suit you, and have used smooth rep speed, and yet the exercise still irritates a joint, substitute an alternative exercise.

16. Don't squeeze machine handles more than necessary

On some machine exercises, such as the leg curl and the leg press, you need to stabilize yourself through holding onto handles or other grip supports. Don't squeeze the handles more than necessary to stabilize yourself. Intensive squeezing increases blood pressure.

17. Be safety conscious with equipment

Never begin an exercise without having first checked safety considerations. Check that bolts are tight, cables aren't frayed, cable connections are secure, rack pins are securely in position, adjustable weight saddles are fixed in place, locking pin(s) for adjustable benches and seats are secure, and benches are stable and strong. Never use dumbbells without checking that the collars are securely fixed. A dumbbell coming apart while in use, especially overhead, could be calamitous.

Just one accident could stop you training for a long time. Be careful.

Put collars on a loaded barbell securely. Plates on one end of the bar that slide out of position can disturb your balance and symmetry. Get a pair of light-weight, quick-release collars, if where you train doesn't have them. Allow a few millimeters, or a small fraction of an inch, between a collar and the outermost plate, to permit the plates to play.

18. Avoid singles and low reps

Any exercise performed in any rep range will hurt you if you use poor technique. If you always use correct technique, all rep counts can be comparatively safe, at least in theory. Your body must, however, be accustomed to the rep count you're using before you start to push yourself hard. This especially applies to singles (one-rep sets), and low-rep work (sets of two to four reps).

Comparing the same degree of technique error, if you get out of the ideal groove during a maximum single, you're more likely to hurt yourself than if you get out of the groove during a set of medium or high reps. But this doesn't mean that high reps with reduced weights are guaranteed to be safe. Even with high reps and reduced weights, if you use poor technique, you would be asking for injury.

Beginners should avoid singles, and low-rep work. Stick with medium or higher reps.

19. Don't train when you're muscularly very sore

Sore and tight muscles are easily injured. A little local soreness, however, especially for beginners, shouldn't prohibit training. When you're training once again following severe soreness, reduce your effort level a little, and build it back over several workouts, to prevent a repeat of the excessive soreness.

When you're sore, you may be more prone to injury. Give yourself extra rest before you train the sore area hard again. To help speed the easing of soreness, do some additional low-intensity aerobic work. Massage may also help, as may a hot bath. Paradoxically, another bout of the exercises that made you very sore—but very light and easy this time—may help relieve the soreness.

Being sore doesn't necessarily indicate that you've stimulated growth. Good soreness comes from hard work on exercises done correctly, is purely muscular, and goes away after a few days. This is different from longer-lasting soreness because of abusive exercise technique, or having trained too heavily, too much, or too hard too soon.

Some muscle groups show soreness more readily than others. That your shoulders, for example, may never get sore, doesn't mean they aren't getting trained. And that another muscle may get sore easily, doesn't necessarily mean that it's going to grow faster than a muscle that's rarely if ever sore.

20. Don't train when you're fatigued from a previous workout

If you're systemically wiped out—which may or may not be accompanied by muscular soreness—rest for an extra day or two, until you're raring to go again. Then when you're back in the gym, reduce your training volume or intensity, and build it back over several workouts, to permit your body to adapt. If you get wiped out again, and provided the components of recuperation are in order, there's something amiss with your training program, and you need to modify it—abbreviate it.

21. Take heed of a sore back

If you regularly experience a sore back during or after training, investigate the cause, and rectify it. A sore back is a warning that a back injury may be nigh unless corrective action is taken. A back injury is among the most debilitating of injuries.

22. Increase resistance in small increments

Small increases in exercise weights permit gradual, progressive resistance, in manageable doses. This is easy to do with free-weights provided you have fractional plates. These small plates weigh less than the 1.25 kilos or 2.5 pounds that are commonly the smallest plates in most gyms. Fractional plates are typically quarter, half, and one-pound discs (and 100, 250, and 500 grams). Progressing from, say, 100 pounds to 110 in one jump, when 100 pounds was the most you could handle for 8 reps, is excessive. The 110 pounds—a 10% increase in resistance—would cause a substantial drop in reps and, in many cases, lead to a deterioration of exercise technique. Even an increase to 105 pounds may be excessive. An increase to 101 pounds may, however, be barely perceptible. Then the following week you may be able to increase to 102 pounds, and so on.

With weight-stack machines, incremental progressive resistance can be difficult to achieve, because the weight jumps between stacks are usually excessive—typically 10 to 15 pounds per unit on the stack. The solution is to attach small increments to the weight stack, provided the design of the weight stack permits it. Push the weight selector pin through a small weight plate and *then* into the weight stack. Alternatively, attach magnetic weight plates to the weight stack.

For example, let's say the weight stack units are 12 pounds, 24, 36, 48, and so on. Once you've mastered 36 pounds, to move immediately to 48 pounds is too much—an increase of a third, which isn't incremental, progressive resistance. But attach two pounds to the 36-pound level, and you have an incremental increase to 38 pounds. Master that, and then move to 40 pounds, and so on. The precise increments will be determined by the available little plates.

Get your own set of fractional plates if where you train doesn't have them. Take them with you when you train.

23. Use accurate weights

Unless you're using calibrated plates you can't be sure you're getting what each plate is supposed to weigh. A bar loaded to 100 pounds may, for example, really be 103 or 97 pounds. Then if you strip that bar down and reload it to 100 pounds using different plates, you're likely to get a different weight than before. Furthermore, the weight excess or discrepancy may be just on one side of the bar, producing an unbalanced barbell.

This is an especially serious matter when you're moving your best weights, and once you're no longer a beginner. An unbalanced or overweight bar may ruin a set and perhaps cause injury, and an underweight bar will give a false sense of progress. When you're using small discs to increase the weight by a pound a week, for example, if your big plates aren't what they seem, you can't be sure you're getting a small overall weight increase relative to the previous workout.

If you have calibrated plates available, use them exclusively. If there are no calibrated plates, at least weigh the big plates so that their actual weights can be discovered. If this is impossible, manage as best you can—try to discover the plates that are the worst offenders and avoid using them, or find the brand that's the most accurate and stick to that one, or use the same plates and bars every time you train.

24. Never make big changes in training intensity

Make the changes gradually. Sensible, progressive resistance training means increasing training intensity progressively, too.

25. Always warm up well before training hard

The purpose of the general warm-up (for five to ten minutes) that every workout should start with, is to elevate your core temperature, get synovial fluids moving in most of your joints (for lubrication), and probably break you into a sweat (depending on the temperature of the gym). This isn't the same as sweating while being in a hot environment but without exercising.

Following the general warm-up, immediately start strength training. Don't have a break and cool down. Additionally, perform one or more warm-up sets prior to the work set(s) for each exercise—it's better to do too many warm-ups than not enough.

26. Keep your muscles warm

Don't rest excessively between sets and exercises. Warm up properly, and then train at a pace that keeps your muscles warm. A cool environment but a warm body is what you want. Ideally, the gym temperature should be no higher than 70 degrees Fahrenheit, or 22 degrees Celsius.

27. Develop balanced musculature

If, for example, you work your chest and shoulders hard, but neglect your upper back, or if you train your quadriceps hard but neglect your hamstrings, the imbalanced musculature will increase the risk of injury in the involved muscles and joints.

28. Prepare fully for each set

Check that the weight you've loaded is what you want—consult your training logbook. Add up the total weight of the plates and bar, to check. It's easy to load a barbell, dumbbell, or machine incorrectly.

When you get in position for a set, take the right grip, stance, and body position. Don't rush into a set, grab the bar and then realize after the first rep that you took an imbalanced grip, wrong stance, or are lopsided while on a bench.

29. Use reliable spotters

Spotting—help from one or more assistants—can come from a training partner, or anyone who's in the gym at the time and willing and able to spot you. Good spotting helps in three ways:

a. To assist you with lifting the weight when you can lift it no further, such as when the bar stalls during a bench press ascent.

b. To provide the minimum assistance to ensure that the last rep of a set is done in correct technique. In this case, you probably could get the rep out under your own power, but your technique may break down. A spotter can make the difference between safety or injury.

The first two ways shouldn't apply to beginners, because beginners don't need to train this hard.

c. During a set, you may forget to apply a key point of exercise technique. A knowledgeable spotter could correct this.

30. Train on an appropriate surface

Lifting on a wooden or a rubber surface (a level surface, as noted earlier), preferably one that doesn't have concrete directly underneath, is better than training directly on concrete. Wood and rubber are giving, whereas concrete isn't. Wood and rubber reduce the amount of giving that your joints and connective tissues have to tolerate.

Before a set, plant your feet securely, on a non-slip surface.

31. Don't hold your breath

The common tendency, especially when training hard, is to hold your breath during the hard stage of a rep, clench your teeth, and jam your lips together. All of this should be avoided because it increases blood pressure, and may cause blackouts and dizziness. Even if it's for just a split second, a loss of consciousness during training could be disastrous. Although you may not suffer blackouts or dizziness, headaches are a common, immediate result of breath holding during training. And over the long term, breath holding during training encourages varicose veins, and hemorrhoids, because of the damage to vein walls and valves caused by the elevated blood pressure.

A common general rule, while exercising, is to inhale during the brief pause between reps *or* during the negative phase of the movement, and exhale during the positive phase (especially the sticking point). For exercises where there may be a pause for a couple of seconds between reps, inhalation and exhalation may occur during the pause, with the final inhalation taken immediately prior to the start of the next rep.

It's this general rule that's referred to in the technique instruction in this book, but it's not the only way to breathe while strength training. Here's an alternative: Never hold your breath, but focus on the given exercise and muscles being trained, not on your breathing. As long as you're not holding your breath, you'll automatically breathe sufficiently. After some practice you'll find the points during your reps where it's easier to breathe in or out.

Six tips for being a good spotter

1. Be honest with yourself, and respect your limitations. If you can't spot adequately by yourself, get help.

2. Be alert, especially when the trainee begins to struggle.

3. Focus on what the trainee's doing.

4. Don't injure yourself! While spotting, don't round your back; keep your feet planted—immobile—in a symmetrical way; and stand as close as possible to the bar or dumbbells.

5. Know the trainee's intentions prior to each set. For example, does he or she need help getting into the starting position?

6. Keep your hands close to the bar but without interfering with the exercise. When needed, apply assistance with both hands in a symmetrical way. For example, spotting through putting one hand under the center of the bar commonly leads to the bar tipping, as will using two hands asymmetrically on the bar.

When reps are performed slower than about four seconds for each positive or negative phase, it's necessary to breathe *continuously* throughout the reps, and more than once during each phase of a rep.

Not holding your breath also applies out of the gym. Whenever you put forth effort, *exhale*, to avoid elevated blood pressure.

During demanding exercise you won't be able to get enough air through your nose alone. Breathe through your mouth.

To prevent breath holding, *don't close your mouth*. Keep your mouth open—just slightly open will suffice—and your upper and lower teeth apart. It's usually when the lips are jammed together that problems with breath holding occur.

32. Avoid using knee or any other joint wraps

Tight bandages around joints can mask injury problems that are aggravated through training.

33. Avoid pain killers

Don't use pain killers before, during, or after training, as they usually mask problems. Solve problems, don't cover them up and incubate serious injury.

34. Don't wear a lifting belt

Many trainees wear a lifting belt—especially while deadlifting, and squatting—under the misconception that it will protect them from back injuries. And some trainees wear a loose lifting belt throughout their workouts as if it's an item of general clothing.

A loose belt doesn't provide any support. And a tight belt is uncomfortable, can restrict exercise technique, can lead to increased blood pressure, and can only be tolerated for short-duration sets. Powerlifters use lifting belts for singles and low-rep work.

Even if a lifting belt is worn tightly, correct exercise technique is still a necessity for safe training. Wearing a lifting belt can create a false sense of security that encourages the use of incorrect exercise technique. And a tight belt can be harmful in another way because it may permit more weight to be used than would otherwise, which will cause greater injury if exercise technique isn't correct.

Build your own natural belt through a strong corset of muscle. Not wearing a belt *helps* your body to strengthen its core musculature. A lifting belt is a crutch—train without it.

35. Don't be foolish

Many injuries occur because a trainee has given in to bravado. Don't try something you know you're not ready for, and don't try another rep when you know you can't hold correct technique. Never go heavy in an exercise you're not familiar with, or haven't done for a few weeks. Ignore people who encourage you to try something you know is risky. They won't have to live with the consequences of a moment of foolishness, but you will.

For exercises where the weight could pin you, especially the squat and the bench press, *always* use safety bars such as those of a power rack, and ideally a spotter as well. Squat, bench press, and incline bench press stations should incorporate safety bars that the barbell can rest on if you fail on a rep.

36. Keep your wits about you

Don't just be concerned about what you're doing in the gym. Be aware of what's happening around you, and stay clear of danger.

37. Wear appropriate footwear

Shoes with thick, spongy soles and heels may be fine for some activities, but not for strength training. A spongy base won't keep your feet solidly in position. Especially when you're squatting, deadlifting, or overhead pressing, if your feet move just a little, the rest of your body will move, too. It doesn't have to be much movement to throw you out of the correct exercise groove. But don't train barefoot. Your feet need support while you're training, but it needs to be support of the right kind.

Function comes first in the gym. Get yourself a sturdy pair of shoes with good grip to the floor, arch support, no more than the standard height of heel (and preferably no height difference between the sole and heel), and which minimizes deformation when you're lifting heavy weights. No heel elevation relative to the balls of your feet is especially important when squatting, deadlifting, and leg pressing, because heel elevation increases stress on the knees in those exercises.

Worn shoes can lead to deviations in exercise technique. Discard shoes that have unevenly or excessively worn soles or heels. Ideally, have a pair of shoes solely for gym work that isn't used for other purposes, so that the shoes keep their shape and condition for years. Furthermore, when you train, keep your laces tied tightly.

Even a small change in the size of the heel, or the relative difference between the heel and sole thicknesses of your shoes, can mar your training. This especially applies to the squat and the deadlift, although a change in balance factors can have a negative effect on some other exercises, too.

As noted in Chapter 6, I recommend the use of orthopedic shoes with molded insoles (including arch support) while training, to compensate for structural or postural instability in the feet, or, in the case of defect-free feet, to maintain existing good condition. Although shoes with custom-made molded insoles are ideal, off-the-shelf shoes with molded insoles are, in most cases, superior to regular shoes. You can even get molded insoles that can be inserted inside your regular footwear, but you may need to remove some of the existing insoles to make room.

38. Concentrate!

Be 100% focused while you train. Never be casual. Furthermore, never turn your head or talk during a set, or pay attention to what anyone's saying other than a spotter who may be giving you technique reminders, or encouragement. Even a slight loss of focus leads to a loss of correct exercise technique, and an increased risk of injury.

All the aforementioned recommendations should be heeded. In addition, there are three *paramount* components of safe, effective strength training:

Controlled rep speed.

Correct exercise technique.

Correct lifting technique when moving equipment.

Because of their paramountcy, each of these three topics merits its own chapter.

Rep speed caution

Some elite bodybuilders, lifters, and athletes can tolerate and even prosper on explosive training because they have the required robustness of joints, and connective tissue. But even they often pay a heavy price in terms of injuries, eventually. There's no need to take any risk with explosive training. A slower and controlled rep speed—as promoted in this book—is much safer, and by far the best option for typical trainees. Why risk pushing your body beyond its structural limits, and possibly suffering permanent injuries, when there are safer ways to train that are highly effective?

For safe training, a smooth, controlled rep speed must be combined with correct exercise technique. Exercise technique is concerned with equipment set-up, grip, stance, body positioning, and bar pathways.

Although rep speed and exercise technique are two separate issues, they are integral parts of safe training.

Rep speed and control

Lift the weight, don't throw it; and lower the weight, don't drop it. Most trainees perform their reps too fast—typically taking only about one second for each phase of a rep. When doing the exercises described in this book, you should be able to stop each rep at any point, hold the weight briefly, and then *continue*. In an intensive set you may not be able to pause *and* get your target reps, depending on which rep you paused, but the idea is that you *could* pause as a demonstration of control.

Let rep *smoothness* be your guide. If your reps are smooth—including during the transition or turnaround between the positive and negative phases of each rep—you're using the control required for safety and applying stress on the involved musculature. In practice, smooth reps typically take no faster than two to three seconds for the positive phase, and no faster than another two to three seconds for the negative phase. For the positive phase of the final rep of a tough set, when you almost grind to a halt, you may need more than five seconds.

Some exercises have longer strokes or ranges of motion than others, and thus need more seconds to show comparable control. For example, the pulldown has a greater range of motion than the press, the press has a greater range of motion than the bench press, and the bench press has a greater range of motion than the shrug.

It's not necessary to perform reps extremely slowly. Some outlandish claims are sometimes made on behalf of extremely slow training. It's not the best, safest, or "only" way to train. Alone, it can't deliver all the benefits possible from exercise. Extremely slow reps aren't even a guaranteed way to train safely. One of the most persistent injuries I've ever had was sustained while performing extremely slow reps. But I've sustained many injuries while performing reps quickly. Avoid fast reps, but there's no need to move to the other extreme.

The first few reps of a work set don't require the degree of effort that the final reps do. As you fatigue, you need to increase your effort level. If you apply your full effort at the start of a set, the weight will move explosively and without the smooth control required for safe training. But toward the end of a set, once you're training hard, you'll *need* to apply your full effort in order to complete the reps. Apply *only* as much effort as you need to complete each rep with the required control.

The use of smooth, controlled rep speed is essential for safe training. Never use fast or jerky movements.

Smooth, controlled reps can, however, be performed with correct *or* incorrect exercise technique. Even if a smooth, controlled rep speed is used, if it's combined with incorrect exercise technique it will produce high-risk training.

For safe training, a smooth, controlled rep speed must be *combined* with correct exercise technique. Exercise technique is concerned with equipment set-up, grip, stance, body positioning, and bar pathways. Although rep speed and exercise technique are two separate issues, they are integral parts of safe training.

Correct exercise technique is the subject of the next chapter.

Let rep SMOOTHNESS *be your guide. If your reps are smooth—including during the transition or turn-around between the positive and negative phases of each rep— you're using the control required for safety, and for applying stress on the involved musculature.*

An illustration of the importance of heredity

In 1978 I went to college in Liverpool, England, where my single-minded dedication to bodybuilding continued. This included working out at a bodybuilding gym where one of Europe's leading physiques trained. We often worked out at the same time.

This man helped me to learn a major lesson. He was on bodybuilding drugs and, generally, was a genetic phenomenon for bodybuilding. But I had better calf development even though I was drug-free and had been training for far fewer years. He even asked me for advice on how he could improve his calves. *The explanation for the difference in our calf development was solely in our heredity.* I had better genetics for calf development, but he was much better off in all other bodyparts. *I trained my calves like I trained my arms, chest, and shoulders, but my calves were much more responsive than those other muscle groups.* And he hadn't neglected his calves. He knew they were his weakness.

To achieve your training-related goals, you *must* train over the long-term. To do that, you must train *safely*.

The consistent use of correct exercise technique is essential.

Become a MASTER of exercise technique.

12

How to master exercise technique

This long chapter is a totally revised version of most of the content of THE INSIDER'S TELL-ALL HANDBOOK ON WEIGHT-TRAINING TECHNIQUE. A few of the exercises described in that book have been excluded from this book, but additional exercises and many more photographs have been included here.

Properly done, weight-lifting is safe, but the use of correct exercise technique is the exception in nearly all gyms. Gyms are usually terrible places for learning correct exercise technique. Few trainees practice correct technique because hardly anyone knows what it is, and this includes most gym instructors, and personal trainers. Exercise technique isn't secondary to program design, and training intensity. Technique comes first!

Exercise technique isn't simple. It requires detailed instruction, and serious study, if you're to master it. Make *correct exercise technique* your number one training motto. Make no compromises, *ever*.

For the first two of weeks of **The Program**, if you're a beginner, follow the exercise technique guidance from Chapter 2, in the section "Exercise technique rehearsal." Once you've trained in a gym for two weeks, you should be sufficiently familiar with the equipment to benefit from the detailed instruction given in this chapter.

If you're not a beginner, apply the instruction in this chapter from the start of **The Program**.

All the exercises used in **The Program** are detailed in this chapter. All strength-training exercises aren't included, for three reasons:

1. The most effective exercises are limited in number.

2. Many of the excluded exercises are inferior to the selected ones.

3. Effective strength training for typical trainees is built around short routines.

Some exercises don't produce acute injury but an accumulation of damage that, over time, causes chronic injury. Just because an exercise doesn't hurt you today, next week, or next month, doesn't mean that it won't hurt you later.

When I was a beginner I had little or no time for anyone who talked or wrote about the possible dangers of training. Being a teenager I could, at first, get away with foolish training methods without much immediate discomfort. Therefore I continued with harmful practices that included squatting with my heels raised on a board and the barbell too high on my shoulders, hack machine squatting, Smith machine squatting, bench pressing with a wide grip and to my upper chest, round-back deadlifting, explosive lifting, and specific cheating movements. A few years later I was plagued with serious injuries, especially to my knees and back. Countless trainees have experienced similar problems.

I sustained most of my training injuries because I used incorrect exercise technique. All of these injuries were avoidable.

Exercise technique MASTERY

Once you've studied the sections in this chapter on the exercises in the first routine of **The Program**, start studying the rest of the chapter. You need to be knowledgeable on all the exercises. Although you won't employ all the exercises immediately, you will employ many of them during the course of **The Program**. You may also need to make some exercise substitutions because of equipment considerations, or some physical limitations you may have that could proscribe certain exercises.

The ESSENTIAL factor of individuality

Even if exercise technique is correct, rep speed is controlled, and the handling of weights is faultless while setting up equipment, an exercise can still cause problems if, for a given individual, training is excessive in terms of frequency or volume, or if the adding of weight to the bar is rushed.

For instance, perhaps you're not a beginner, and you're squatting and deadlifting two times per week, your exercise technique is correct, rep speed is controlled, and your training volume is low, yet your lower back and knees still don't feel right. But when you were a beginner, there was no problem with this training frequency. Now, because of the increased training load, the situation has changed. A change to deadlifting and squatting just once a week each, on the same day, will give more recovery time, and your knees and lower back may start to feel fine again. You may still be able to train your lower back two times a week, but make it the back extension at the second session. And you may still be able to train your thighs two times a week, but make it the leg press at the second session, for example.

With exercise technique, what's "safe" can be an individual matter. Age, body structure and proportions, and any past injuries, among other factors, may turn what's generally a safe exercise into a potentially harmful one.

Study this chapter to learn about correct exercise technique, and then apply it *consistently*. If, however, despite using *correct technique*, along with a *controlled* rep speed, *gradual* increases in progressive resistance, *abbreviated* training routines, and *adequate* recovery time between workouts, you *still* experience joint or soft tissue irritation from a given exercise, substitute it with a comparable exercise. (How to modify training routines to accommodate individual variation in exercise tolerance, and recovery ability, is explained in **The Program**.)

Apply the first imperative of exercise: "Do no harm."

Personal coaching

Don't assume that anyone who claims to be a qualified personal trainer knows what he's doing. Strings of letters that indicate certifications of various organizations, or degrees obtained, don't necessarily signify competence as a coach. Be on your guard.

To determine whether someone can help you to improve your technique, watch the trainer at work. Although the following checklist isn't entirely to do with exercise technique, the non-technique components reflect on overall ability as a trainer.

1. Is the technique taught like that described in this chapter?

2. Does the trainer remind his charge of key technique points before an exercise, and in the course of it?

3. Has the trainer modified his client's exercise selection and technique according to any physical limitations the trainee may have?

4. Does the trainer keep accurate records of weight and reps for every work set?

5. Does the trainer consult his client's training log before each set, to ensure that the correct weight is loaded?

6. Is the trainer attentive, supportive, and respectful?

7. Does the trainer keep his charge's mind focused on the work at hand?

If the trainer doesn't score well on all these points, look elsewhere. If the trainer scores well on these points but the deadlift, squat, and other major movements weren't done in the workout you inspected, ask the trainer to demonstrate how he teaches those movements. Compare his instruction with what's described in this chapter. If the differences are more than minor, look elsewhere.

Joining a local powerlifting club, or attending occasionally, may help. A savvy coach from the club should be able to provide technique tips.

Once you know about correct exercise technique, teach an observer what to look for to provide feedback to help you improve your technique. Alternatively, use a video camera and record your technique, for analysis later. A video camera can be an outstanding tool to help you to improve your exercise technique.

Free-weights, and machines

With a barbell and dumbbell set you can do the same exercises anywhere in the world. Free-weights are almost universal in gyms, but good machinery isn't. The technique instruction for exercises that use free-weights is the same for all brands of that gear, but not so for machinery where, for example, the instructions for one brand's squat machine are different from another's. As a result of these factors, and others, free-weights are given priority in this book.

If, however, you have access to the generally good machinery—for example, Body Masters, Cybex, Hammer Strength, MedX, and Nautilus—you could substitute it for the comparable free-weights exercises; but tread carefully because even some of the generally good machines can cause irritations and injuries for some trainees even when those machines are used correctly. And most machines can't accommodate all body sizes. Of course, exercises that use free-weights can also cause problems, especially if they aren't performed correctly.

A machine exercise may cause irritation, but the comparable free-weights exercise may not, and vice versa, depending on the individual and the exercise concerned.

Features of good machinery include smoothness of motion, ease of entry and exit, and the ability to accommodate a variety of body types (through adjustment of seats, back pads, and movement arms).

Although high-tech machinery can be useful, it's not essential. Free-weights alone, properly used, have proven to be tremendously effective.

General note regarding machines

Various manufacturers produce variations on the same basic machine designs. One manufacturer's pullover machine, for example, may produce an effective upper-body exercise, whereas another version may be a source of joint irritation.

Whenever you use a machine, follow the manufacturer's guidelines—which are often fixed to the machines themselves. The correct set-up position is essential. For instance, on a shoulder machine, you may need to line up your shoulder joints with the pivot points.

Fine-tune your set-up until you find what feels most comfortable. You may need several workouts. A set-up that initially felt awkward may, after some adjustment, feel fine. Never push hard on a machine until after you've found a set-up that's proven safe for several workouts, without producing any negative reaction.

The exercises

Here are the exercises from which the strength-training routines of **The Program** are composed. Only a limited number of the exercises are used in a single routine.

1. Back extension *202*
   basic back extension 203
   45-degree back extension 205
   spinal extension 205
   machine back extension 206
2. Bench press *208*
   barbell bench press 208
   dumbbell bench press 216
   close-grip bench press 220
   incline barbell bench press 224
   incline dumbbell bench press 228
3. Calf raise *230*
   standing two-legged calf raise 232
   standing one-legged calf raise 234
4. Chin-up (and pull-up) *236*
5. Crunch *240*
   basic crunch 242
   modified basic crunch 244
   machine crunch 245
   reverse crunch 246
   twisting crunch 248
6. Curl *250*
   seated dumbbell curl 252
   incline dumbbell curl 253
   barbell curl 254
   hammer curl 255
7. Deadlift *256*
   deadlift (basic, or conventional deadlift) 260
   parallel-grip deadlift 270
   partial deadlift 278
   sumo deadlift 282
8. Finger extension *284*
9. Hand-gripper work *286*
   torsion-spring gripper 287
   Ivanko super gripper 289
10. Lateral raise *292*
   dumbbell lateral raise 292
   machine lateral raise 293
11. Leg curl *294*
12. Leg press *298*

13. L-fly   *304*
14. Neck work   *308*
     manual resistance neck work   309
     four-way neck machine   310
15. Parallel bar dip   *312*
16. Press   *316*
     seated barbell press   316
     seated dumbbell press   320
17. Pulldown   *324*
18. Pullover   *328*
     machine pullover   328
     breathing pullover   332
19. Pushdown   *334*
20. Rotary torso   *336*
21. Row   *338*
     one-arm dumbbell row   338
     cable row   340
     seated machine row   344
     prone low-incline dumbbell row   345
22. Shrug   *346*
23. Side bend   *350*
     dumbbell side bend   351
     pulley side bend   353
24. Squat   *356*
     squat (conventional or back squat)   360
     front squat   378
     ball squat   388
     hip-belt squat   392
25. Timed hold   *398*

> *The main muscle involvement in each exercise is noted in the sections that follow. See Chapter 23 if you require background anatomy.*

Technical accuracy

Throughout this book, strict anatomical definitions of arm, forearm, thigh, and leg are used. This means avoiding ambiguous terms such as *lower leg*, *upper leg*, *lower arm*, or *upper arm*, and not using *arm* and *leg* to encompass undetermined portions of the upper and lower extremities respectively. The leg is the portion between the foot and the knee, the thigh is the portion between the knee and the hip, the forearm is the portion between the hand and the elbow, and the arm is the portion between the elbow and the shoulder.

The word *flex* is used in this book only as the opposite of *extend*. Flex is commonly used to mean *make tense* but *without* flexion.

Important breathing guidelines

A common general rule while exercising is to inhale during the pause between reps, or during the negative phase of the movement, and exhale during the positive phase. For exercises where there may be a pause between reps, inhalation *and* exhalation may occur during the pause, with the final inhalation taken immediately prior to the start of the next rep. It's this guideline that's usually referred to in the technique instruction in this chapter, but it's not the only way to breathe while strength training.

Here's an alternative guideline: While never holding your breath, focus on the given exercise and muscles being trained, *not* your breathing. As long as you're not holding your breath, you'll automatically breathe sufficiently. To prevent breath holding, *don't close your mouth.*

When reps are performed very slowly—slower than about four seconds for each positive or negative phase—it's necessary to breathe continuously throughout each rep, perhaps with more than one inhalation-exhalation cycle during each phase of a rep.

Exercise technique checklists

When learning a new exercise, or correcting a familiar exercise, there are many points to remember. Use a checklist for each exercise, to remind you of the key points.

Write a brief checklist for each exercise that requires it, on a separate card for each. Use bold, clear writing. Prior to performing a given exercise, review the relevant checklist.

As valuable as technique checklists are, they are no substitute for serious study of the details given in this chapter. Even after you've studied this chapter you'll need to review parts of it regularly. Review the technique of the exercises in each routine you undertake. Everyone benefits from review work.

Dumbbell training

Some trainees prefer dumbbells to barbells in upper-body exercises because the dumbbells allow more flexibility with wrist positioning, and thus permit more comfortable training.

Units of measurement

Imperial and metric units are used interchangeably in this book. An inch is about two and a half centimeters, four inches is about ten centimeters, and a foot is about 30 centimeters. A pound is about 0.45 kilogram, and about 2.2 pounds comprise one kilogram.

Chapters 10 and 11 cover many essential general components of safe exercising, which should be applied together with the guidance of this chapter.

Books on strength training and bodybuilding usually provide skimpy descriptions of exercise technique. But exercise technique isn't a simple matter. The exercises need to be described in detail.

Photographs alone can't show all the details of exercise technique. Please study all of the written instructions.

The photographs are for illustration purposes only. In some cases, the models didn't wear shirts so that the involved musculature or back positioning could be seen clearly. And spotters and safety set-up considerations aren't illustrated other than in a few specific photographs. When YOU train, wear a shirt, and fully attend to all safety considerations, as described in the text.

I. BACK EXTENSION

Main muscles worked

lower back, quadratus lumborum, multifidii, buttocks, hamstrings (the latter two muscle groups are especially heavily worked in back extensions that use conventional apparatus)

The multifidus muscle group is deep to the erector spinae, from the sacrum to the neck, and extends and rotates the vertebral column.

Capsule description

flex and extend your torso while keeping your legs fixed

The basic or conventional back extension, often called a *hyperextension*, has your legs fixed and your torso moves into line with them. In the *reverse* back extension, your torso is fixed and your legs move into line with it. The reverse back extension is a valuable exercise but it doesn't provide the spinal flexion and extension of the conventional back extension, and the special apparatus required isn't commonly available. Therefore, the reverse back extension isn't included in this book.

Done correctly, back extensions involve safe flexion (or rounding) of the spine, and extension (or straightening) of the spine, whereas deadlifts, done correctly, primarily involve static contraction of the spinal erectors. For safety, deadlifts should *never* be performed with a rounded back.

The back extension strengthens the lower back in a way that deadlifts may not, because of the spinal *extension* of the former. The back extension may even strengthen some muscles of the lower back that deadlifts can't. Back extensions aren't, however, a substitute for deadlifts unless you're unable to do any form of deadlift safely. When compared, deadlifts are whole-body exercises, whereas back extensions affect limited musculature.

For most trainees, back extensions and deadlifts are complementary, and correct use of both will produce the best overall results.

Basic back extension

A purpose-built apparatus is available in many gyms for the basic back extension.

Rest your upper thighs on the support pad, and your heels or calves against the rearmost support. With your hands on the floor, find the position so that the front edge of the support pad doesn't hurt your groin. You may need additional padding over that edge. If the apparatus has adjustable components, fine-tune them for thigh and groin comfort.

Keep your knees slightly bent, to avoid exaggerated stress on them.

With your head and torso hanging vertically, cross your forearms on your chest. Raise your torso in a

The top photograph shows a partially extended neck. In this exercise, maintain a neutral neck—neither extended, nor flexed.

slow, smooth, controlled, symmetrical fashion until your torso is parallel with the floor, or just above parallel. Hold the top position for two seconds.

As you return to the starting position, gradually round (flex) your spine. Pause for a second at the bottom, then slowly and smoothly start the next rep. Rounding the spine on the descent, and then extending or straightening it on the ascent, are required for the best effect.

This exercise is commonly done with the hands behind the head, or with a plate held behind the head. Both place unnecessary strain on the neck and cervical vertebrae. Keep your forearms crossed on your chest, and hold a plate or dumbbell to your chest when extra resistance is needed.

Inhale at the bottom position or during the descent, and exhale during the ascent; or, just breathe freely—*don't* hold your breath. You may need multiple breaths per rep.

Apparatus improvisation

If you don't have
access to a purpose-
built apparatus for
the back extension,
or a machine, try an
old-fashioned way.
Elevate a horizontal
bench on crates or
boxes. Place your
thighs on the
bench, face down,
and put your hands
on the floor. Find
the precise position
on the bench that's
comfortable. Have
an assistant hold
you down, at your
calves. You may
need a folded towel
under your knees,
and over the edge
of the bench, for
padding. Then
perform the basic
back extension.

Alternatively, position a bench or board over the pins in a power
rack, set at the appropriate height to permit a full range of motion
at the bottom of the exercise. The bench or board must be secured
in position so that it can't slide off the pins during use. Furthermore,
jam the rear of the bench or board between a pair of pins, so that it
can't come out of position during a set. Use a belt to strap your legs
to the bench.

In both cases, experiment to find the position to be held or strapped
to the bench that's comfortable for your knees. Avoid compression
of your kneecaps.

The 45-degree back extension

This is an alternative to the basic back extension. Exercise the same control, flexion, and extension as in the basic back extension, and the same method of holding resistance. To bring your torso into line with your legs in the 45-degree back extension, your back has to come up to above parallel with the floor.

Generally, the 45-degree back extension provides greater muscular loading at the bottom of the movement, while the basic version provides greater loading at the top.

Spinal extension

Using the set-ups for the basic and 45-degree back extensions, spinal extension *alone* is possible if technique is modified as illustrated on the right. This yields a shortened overall range of motion relative to traditional back extensions, but focuses the work on the spinal musculature. In traditional back extensions there's back *and* hip extension. For back or spinal extension *alone*, keep your lower vertebrae fixed throughout, and move only your middle and upper vertebrae. Practice is required before this technique can be mastered.

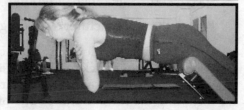

Machine back extension

Back extension machines are also called *lower-back* or *lumbar-extension* machines. Different brands have different designs, and the effectiveness for the lumbar musculature varies. The MedX lumbar-extension machine is probably the premier one. Because of their design and use, some back extension machines provide little or no meaningful exercise for the lumbar musculature.

To be maximally effective for working the lumbar musculature, a back extension machine *must* fully restrain the body in four locations: feet, knees, thighs, and pelvis. The feet are restrained by a foot board. The knees are restrained by a belt or bar. The thighs are restrained by a belt strapped tightly over the upper thighs. The pelvis is restrained by a pad that's positioned against the rear of the hips. (Some machines may have head rests, too.)

If any of these four restraints are absent, or not correctly employed, you'll increase the involvement of your hamstrings and muscles of your hips, but reduce the involvement of your lumbar-extension muscles. For best effect on your lumbar musculature, there must be no movement of your legs, thighs, or pelvis. The muscles of your legs, thighs, and hips contract, but the restraints prevent these muscles contributing substantial force to the movement.

It's also essential that you don't involve your hands. Cross your hands on your chest. Furthermore, it's critical that you use a controlled rep speed, and a safe range of motion.

Follow the manufacturer's set-up guidelines, and fine-tune to suit you.

In the starting position, flex (round) your back moderately. Then as you extend your back, gradually straighten and then slightly arch your back. Don't exaggerate the arch. Move smoothly at all times, including the turnaround points of each rep.

Take at least three seconds for the positive phase of the rep; pause for a second at the extended, fully contracted position, with your scapulae fully retracted; and then take at least a further three seconds for the negative phase, while gradually rounding your back. Pause for a second in the starting position, then smoothly move into the next rep.

Use as full a range of motion as is safe for you. At first, don't try the maximum degree of (forward) flexion or (rearward) extension.

Start with minimal resistance, and very low intensity of effort. Only after you know the maximum safe range of motion for you—after perhaps a couple of weeks use—should you start to increase resistance and effort levels *gradually*. You may find that your flexibility increases during the first few weeks of use, and permits a greater safe range of motion. *But even when you've fully adapted to the machine back extension, don't work it until muscular exhaustion because that may cause injury.* Train each work set hard, but *not* until your limit.

Be especially careful if you have had any back injuries.

Don't try to maintain a flat back in the back extension. It's important that the spine flexes and extends, that is, rounds and arches moderately. Without this flexion and extension, the lumbar musculature won't be fully stimulated.

Progression in back extensions

The 45-degree back extension may be a good introduction to back extensions if you don't have sufficient strength to perform the basic version for the required reps, and don't have access to a back extension machine. (A back extension machine can be used with little or no resistance, but the basic and 45-degree back extensions have the minimum resistance of the weight of your torso.) Graduate to the basic back extension after two to three months on the 45-degree version. If the 45-degree back extension is currently too difficult, use the floor back extension as described in Chapter 2. Once you can perform 20 floor back extensions with your arms extended, elbows straight, and a pause at the top of each rep, progress to another form of the back extension. Try the 45-degree back extension, or, if the set-up for that exercise isn't available, try the basic back extension.

The Program *lists two work sets for the back extension each week, as from the fourth month. If you have access to the basic and 45-degree back extensions, do a single work set of each rather than two sets of only one of them. Alternatively, use the machine back extension.*

2. BENCH PRESS

Five forms of the bench press will be described:
barbell bench press
dumbbell bench press
close-grip bench press
incline barbell bench press
incline dumbbell bench press

Barbell bench press

Main muscles worked

pectorals, deltoids, triceps

Capsule description

lie on your back, bar in your hands, arms vertical, elbows locked; lower the bar to your chest, then push it up

Set-up

This exercise is done supine, lying on your back on a horizontal bench. Use a straight barbell, not one with bends or cambers in it. Bench press inside a four-post power rack with pins and saddles correctly positioned, and securely in place.

Alternatively, bench press between sturdy squat stands together with spotter (or safety) bars or racks, or use a half rack, or use a combination bench-and-weight-stands unit together with spotter bars. Some bench-and-stands units have built-in, adjustable spotter bars. Set the safety bars at the appropriate height, and position yourself on the bench so you won't miss the safety bars if you need to set the barbell on them.

See *Safety equipment* in Chapter 7.

If there are no spotter or safety bars to stop the bar getting stuck on your chest if you fail on a rep, you must have an alert and strong spotter in attendance.

Center a sturdy, stable bench between the weight supports. In a power rack, if possible, mark where the bench should be, to be centered. Use a tape measure to ensure correct centering. The rack and bench should be level—have them checked, and corrected if necessary.

Depending on the bench press unit you use, the bar saddles may be adjustable. Position them neither too high, nor too low.

A combination bench-and-weight-stands unit, but without spotter bars. An assistant must be used as a spotter with this type of unit. There's a raised platform here for the spotter to stand on, for easier handling of the barbell by the spotter. An unloaded barbell is shown resting across the unit's upper bar saddles.

Positioning on the bench

Position yourself on the bench so that you won't hit the uprights of the rack or stands with the bar during the bench press ascent, but also so that you minimize the horizontal movement of the bar during the unracking and racking of the bar. The bar, when racked, may, for example, be directly above your nose. The set-up varies according to individual body structure, height of the bar holders, and depth of the saddles. Experiment with a bare bar, to find what works best for you. Make a note of where your eyes are, relative to the bar, when you're on the bench with the bar in the saddles, ready to unrack the bar to start a set.

Lie on the bench with your feet, hips, back, and head all in position. Your heels should be on an imaginary vertical line drawn from your knees, or slightly in front of it. If your heels are behind this line (that is, pulled toward your pelvis) that will lead to exaggerated arching of your lower back. Avoid that. Although some arching in the lower back is normal, don't exaggerate it. Some trainees exaggerate the arch, to raise their chests as much as possible in order to reduce the distance the bar has to move before it touches their chests, to increase the weights they use. This technique has injured many trainees.

Establish a strong base, with your feet flat on the floor wider than shoulder width. Don't place your feet close together on the floor, and don't place them on the bench in any manner—both placements would reduce your stability. Never lift your heels off the floor during the bench press. If you have short lower limbs and can't keep your feet flat on the floor, raise your feet a few inches using low blocks, or plates stacked smooth side up.

Set the rack's pins, or whatever safety bars you use, an inch below the height of your inflated chest when you're in position on the bench. A length of hose or tubing may be put over each safety bar, to soften contact

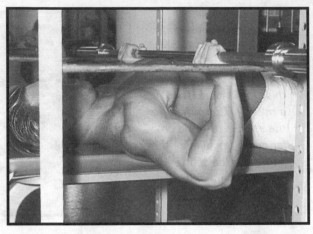

with the barbell. If you fail on a rep, lower the bar to your chest, exhale, and set the bar on the supports.

Grip

While the bar is at the line of your lower pecs, your hand spacing should put your forearms in a vertical position when viewed (by an assistant) from the side and from your feet. Your elbows should be directly under your wrists. Adult men should use a grip with 21 inches or 53 centimeters between their index fingers as a starting point. Women should use a grip four inches or ten centimeters narrower. Fine-tune from there to find the grip that gives you the proper forearm and elbow positioning. Once you find your optimum grip, have someone measure the distance between your index fingers, and make a written note of it.

Don't use a thumbless grip, because it reduces your control over the bar. Wrap your thumbs under and around the bar.

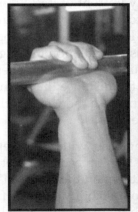
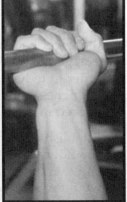

The thumbless or false grip on the left, and the correct grip on the right.

Grip with your hands equidistant from the bar's center. Be sure you're not even a fraction of an inch off center. Before a set, know precisely where your hands should be—use a tape measure if necessary.

If the back of your hands, wrists and forearms is in a straight line during the bench press, or any pressing movement, the bar will fall out of your hands. Your hands must move rearward sufficiently so that you can grip the bar securely. But don't allow the bar to extend your hands to the maximum, because that can mar your lifting technique, and injure your wrists. (The bar should be gripped firmly, because the slacker the grip, the less the actions of the flexors on the palm side of the forearm, which translates to less muscular counteraction to the rearward bending.) Once the bar is in a secure position in your hands, keep your wrists rigid for the duration of each set.

Performance

Get in position on the bench, hands in place on the bar, with a spotter or training partner standing directly behind you. Have the spotter or training partner give you a hand-off as you fully straighten and lock out your elbows. Pause until the bar is steady above your chest, inhale fully to fill your chest, pull your shoulders back, then immediately lower the bar under control. The full inhalation, and pulling back of the shoulders, help to produce the required tight, full torso. Take at least two to three seconds for the descent.

Lower the bar to a point below your nipples, at about the bottom line of your pectoral muscles. Find the precise point that's best for you. When the bar is on your chest, your forearms should be vertical when viewed from the side *and* the front (or rear, depending on where the viewer is). If they aren't, your hand spacing is incorrect.

Never bounce the bar off your chest. Touch your chest with the bar, pause there for one second, then push it up. Stay tight at the bottom with a full chest and firm grip—don't relax.

The ascent of the bar should be vertical, or slightly diagonal if that feels more natural—with just three or four inches of horizontal movement toward your head. Try both, and see which works best for you. Keep your forearms as vertical as possible during the ascent. Do this through keeping your elbows directly beneath your wrists. Exhale during the ascent.

Check yourself on a video recording, or have someone watch you from the side. What you may think, for example, is a vertical movement, may be angled slightly toward your feet. Practice until you can keep the bar moving correctly.

The ascent, just like the descent, should be symmetrical. The bar shouldn't tip to one side, both hands should move in unison, and you shouldn't take more weight on one side of your body than the other.

After locking out the bar, pause for a second or until the bar is stationary, inhale fully, pull your shoulders back, then again lower the bar slowly to the correct position on your lower chest.

The hand-off to start a bench press set (top), the top position prior to the descent of a rep (middle), and the bottom position at the lower pectoral line (above).

Common errors—DANGER

 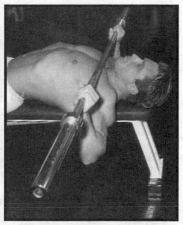

Two of the most common bench pressing errors. Left, exaggeration of the arch in the lower back—from having the feet behind the knees, and from not keeping the feet flat on the floor. NEVER DO THAT. It has injured the lower backs of many trainees. Right, bench pressing to the upper chest. NEVER DO THAT. It has injured the shoulders of many trainees.

Other tips

Keep your head flat on the bench. Never turn your head while you're lifting or lowering the bar. If you do, the bar may tip, and then your groove would be marred, and you could injure yourself.

Don't drive your head back into the bench, or otherwise you'll risk injury to your neck.

Use chalk or rosin on your hands to improve your grip on the bar, but keep the knurling clean.

When applying chalk, cover each hand, including the area on the inside of your thumb and index finger.

Once you've learned correct technique in the bench press, drill yourself on a fixed set-up and approach-to-the-bar procedure.

Once you've mastered bench pressing technique, give 100% attention to ensure that you deliver correct technique on every rep. Even a slight slip of concentration can lead to lowering the bar slightly out of position, or having one hand out of step with the other. Either of these will ruin your groove. This will make the weight feel heavier, make your reps harder, and risk injury.

Spotting

A hand-off to get the bar out of the saddles to start the set, is the first function of a spotter. During a set, as soon as the bar stalls or tips, or one hand gets forward of the other, the spotter must act to prevent the rep deteriorating further and causing injury.

The spotter must use both hands and provide sufficient assistance to keep the bar horizontal and moving correctly, centered above the lifter.

Even if the spotter doesn't need to assist during a rep, he should guide the bar back into the weight saddles after the final rep. At the end of a hard set of bench presses, you'll be tired. Without a guiding pair of hands on the bar from a spotter, you may miss getting the bar into the weight saddles. Throughout spotting, the spotter must not round his back, to protect *his* back.

How a single assistant should spot the bench press. This bench press unit has a platform for the spotter to stand on, for more efficient spotting.

Two pectoralis muscles

"Pectorals" and "pecs" refer to the pectoralis MAJOR—*the large, flat muscle on each side of the upper rib cage. There's also the pectoralis* MINOR, *a much smaller muscle that's* BENEATH *the pectoralis major.*

The pec minor protracts the scapula forward, as when a person reaches for something. The pec major is a prime mover of the humerus, as when a person bench presses, for example.

The pec minor isn't the upper pec, and doesn't make any significant contribution to chest development. What's considered to be the upper pec is the clavicular portion of the pectoralis major.

Technique recordings

Periodically, use a video camera and record your exercise technique, for analysis later. A video camera can be an outstanding tool to help you to improve your exercise technique.

Dumbbell bench press

Main muscles worked

pectorals, deltoids, triceps

Capsule description

lie on your back, dumbbells in your hands, arms vertical, elbows locked; lower the dumbbells to your chest, then push them up

The bench press can also be done with dumbbells, again from a supine position on a horizontal bench. Once the 'bells are in pressing position, the technique is similar to the barbell version.

There are some advantages of the dumbbell version. First, provided there are suitable dumbbells available, you can probably dumbbell bench press whenever you want, and avoid having to wait your turn at the barbell bench press stations. Second, the dumbbell bench press doesn't require a power rack or other safety set-up, but a spotter is still required. Third, the 'bells provide more potential than a barbell does for optimizing hand and wrist positioning—a barbell fixes the hands into a pronated position.

The disadvantages of the dumbbell bench press are several. First, getting two heavy dumbbells into and out of position is difficult— and potentially dangerous—unless you have at least one competent assistant. Second, there's a greater chance of overstretching on the lowering phase than with a barbell. Third, balance is tricky, and if control is lost over one or both dumbbells during a set, you could sustain serious injury. In addition, the floor and equipment could be damaged if the dumbbells are dropped. Of course, the barbell bench press can be dangerous unless done correctly, inside a power rack with pins properly positioned.

Performance

To get into position for dumbbell bench pressing, have a spotter hand you the 'bells one at a time while you're in position on a bench (as you would be for the barbell bench press).

Alternatively, get the dumbbells into position by yourself. Sit on the end of a bench with the 'bells held vertically on your thighs. Center your hands on the handles. Keep your elbows bent, chin on your chest, *back rounded*, and, with a thrust on the 'bells from your thighs, *roll* back on the bench and position your feet properly, like for the barbell bench press. With your forearms vertical, and hands lined up with your lower pecs, inhale fully to fill your chest, pull your shoulders back, and immediately begin pressing.

Press in a similar pathway as in the barbell version. Keep the 'bells moving in tandem, as if they were linked. Don't let them drift outward from your torso, or let one get ahead of the other.

Clockwise, from the bottom left, how to get into position, without assistance, for the dumbbell bench press, and the first ascent of the set.

With dumbbells you don't have to hold your hands as if holding a barbell. Use a parallel grip, or one somewhere in between that and the barbell-style pronated grip. You can change your wrist positioning during the course of each rep.

If the back of your hands, wrists and forearms is in a straight line during the dumbbell bench press, or *any* pressing movement, the dumbbells will fall out of your hands. Your hands must extend rearward sufficiently so that you can grip the dumbbells securely. But don't allow the dumbbells to extend your hands to the maximum, because that can mar your lifting technique, and injure your wrists. (The dumbbells should be gripped firmly, because the slacker the grip, the less the actions of the flexors on the palm side of the forearm, which translates to less of a muscular counteraction to the rearward bending.) Once the dumbbells are in a secure position in your hands, keep your wrists rigid for the duration of each set.

Don't seek an exaggerated range of motion. Keep your hands near to the spacing that was recommended for the barbell bench press. Don't use a wider grip so that you can get your hands lower at the bottom of the exercise. Descend to a point no deeper than you would on a barbell bench press. Pause at the bottom for a second, then ascend smoothly, under control. Pause for a second at the top, or until the dumbbells are stationary, then smoothly perform the next rep.

From the top, the last descent of a set of dumbbell bench presses, and the return to the seated position.

Your control may be poor at first, but with practice you'll develop control over the dumbbells.

Adding weight

Fixed-weight dumbbells usually increase in increments of 5 pounds (or 2.5 kilos). Going up in dumbbells usually means a total increase of 10 pounds, which is large. Stick with a pair of dumbbells until you can comfortably do several reps more than your target count, before going up in weight the next time you dumbbell bench press.

If you use adjustable dumbbells, you can use smaller increments than 5 pounds provided you have small discs. Even if you use fixed-weight dumbbells, you can attach two small discs to each dumbbell. Use strong adhesive tape and ensure that the discs are securely attached. Over time, build up to the weight of the next pair of fixed-weight dumbbells. To ensure proper balance, attach the small discs in pairs to each dumbbell, one at each end. A better choice is to use magnetic small plates.

Spotting

A spotter should crouch behind your head, ready to provide assistance. One hand should apply force under each elbow. But this is strictly for assisting a lifter to get a tough rep up in correct technique. A single person can't simultaneously take a pair of 'bells from someone who fails on a rep. Two spotters are needed, then.

Don't push this exercise to failure. Even when you're training hard, stop this exercise one rep short of failure, so you don't risk losing control. Losing control could cost you an injury. Even an alert spotter may not be able to prevent loss of control of both dumbbells.

A spotter, or better still two spotters, can take the dumbbells off you at the end of a set. Alternatively, get off the bench while holding the dumbbells. Here's how, as illustrated on the left: Lower the 'bells to your lower torso, keep your forearms, arms, shoulders and chest tight, and lift your bent knees as high as you can. With the 'bells touching your thighs, and your chin on your chest, immediately throw your feet forward and roll into a seated position. This is especially easy to do if a spotter places his hands under your shoulders and helps you to roll up.

A spotter should be careful not to round his back while spotting you, to protect *his* back.

Close-grip bench press

Main muscles worked

triceps, pectorals, deltoids

Capsule description

lie on your back, bar in your hands with a shoulder-width grip, arms vertical, elbows locked; lower the bar to your chest, then push it up

This exercise is similar to the standard barbell bench press. The principal difference is the grip spacing. The closer grip increases the involvement of the triceps. The section on the barbell bench press should be studied together with this one.

Set-up and positioning

The commonly seen close-grip bench press has the hands touching, or very close together. This is harmful for the wrists, and the elbows. The safe close-grip bench press is not very close. Make it about five inches or 13 centimeters closer than your regular-grip bench press. Depending on torso girth, and forearm and arm lengths, about 16 inches or 41 centimeters between index fingers will probably be fine for most men, and about 12 inches or 30 centimeters for women. Find what feels most comfortable for you. If in doubt, go wider rather than narrower. Apply the bench press rule of keeping your forearms vertical—vertical as seen from the front *and* from the sides.

Position yourself on the bench like in the standard bench press, and don't use a thumbless grip.

Performance

Take your grip on the bar and get a hand-off to help you to get the bar out of the saddles. Keep your elbows straight, move the bar into the starting position above your lower chest, and pause briefly. Inhale fully and fill your chest, pull your shoulders back, keep a tight torso, and start the descent. Bring your elbows in a little as you lower the bar, to keep your elbows beneath your wrists.

The bar should touch your chest at the line of your lower pecs, or a little lower. Never bounce the bar off your chest. Touch your chest and pause there for one second, then push the bar up. Stay tight at the bottom, with a full chest and firm grip—don't relax. Exhale during the ascent.

The hand spacing of the standard bench press (left) and a safe close-grip bench press (right). In this case the difference is only about five inches or 13 centimeters. The bar is at the lower pectoral line in both cases. The elbows should be directly beneath the wrists. In the illustration on the right, the hands could be brought in a little further provided the elbows follow. A shoulder-width grip is ideal.

The ascent of the bar should be vertical, or *slightly* diagonal if that feels more natural—with just a few inches of horizontal movement toward your head. Try both, and see which works best for you.

During the ascent of the bar it may be natural for your elbows to move outward a little, prior to their return to a line directly beneath your wrists as you near the top position. This especially applies if there's any horizontal movement during the ascent.

Hand positioning this close is dangerous, especially for the wrists and elbows.

Other tips

The narrowed grip relative to the standard bench press can cause excessive extension of the shoulders, especially in long-limbed, lanky trainees. If the close-grip bench press bothers your shoulders, and you're doing the exercise as described here, modify the movement.

Do the exercise in a power rack with pins set so that you reduce the range of motion by a few inches. That will reduce the extension of your shoulders, and make the exercise safer.

Fatigue occurs suddenly in the close-grip bench press. Use a set-up that will safely catch the bar if you have to dump it—see the set-up guidelines for the standard barbell bench press. Terminate a set as soon as your elbows start to drift out of position despite your best efforts to keep them in position.

Spotting

See the guidelines for the standard barbell bench press. Similar guidelines for spotting apply here. But because fatigue occurs more suddenly in the close-grip bench press, your spotter must be especially alert. He must be ready to help you when the bar stalls, or when your elbows start to drift out of position.

> *Even if exercise technique is correct, rep speed is controlled, and the handling of weights is faultless while setting up equipment, an exercise can still cause problems if, for a given individual, training is excessive in terms of frequency or volume, or if the adding of weight to the bar is rushed.*

Incline barbell bench press

Main muscles worked

pectorals, deltoids, triceps

the incline bench press may place more stress on the upper pectorals (clavicular head) than does the horizontal, supine version

Capsule description

lie on your back on an incline bench, bar overhead; lower bar to your chest, then push it up

Set-up

Use a heavy-duty, adjustable bench, preferably one that has an adjustment for tilting the seat—to prevent the user slipping out of position. Use a low-incline bench that has an angle no greater than 30 degrees with the horizontal. Most incline benches are set too upright for this exercise.

Ideally, do the exercise in a power rack, with pins properly positioned for safety. Alternatively, do the exercise in a purpose-built, incline bench press unit. If you do the exercise outside the safety of a power rack, have a spotter standing by in case you get stuck on a rep. The spotter is also needed to help you to get the bar out of the saddles safely, and return it to the saddles after the set is over.

An incline bench press unit, with built-in (black) adjustable safety bars. An unloaded barbell is shown resting across the unit's bar saddles.

Grip, and bar placement

Start with the same grip as in the standard bench press, and fine-tune if necessary. Don't use a thumbless grip, but wrap your thumbs around the bar properly. Furthermore, as in the bench press, your hands must extend rearward sufficiently so that you can grip the bar securely. But don't allow the bar to extend your hands to the maximum, because that can mar your lifting technique, and injure your wrists. Grip the bar firmly, to help keep your wrists in the right position. Once the bar is in a secure position in your hands, keep your wrists rigid for the duration of each set.

Don't lower the bar as low on your chest as in the regular bench press. Because of the inclination of the bench, a low position of the bar on your chest would lead to excessive and unsafe extension of your shoulders. Nor should you lower the bar to your neck or clavicles— that positioning is also dangerous for your shoulders.

Rather than wonder where to place the bar on your chest at the bottom of the incline press, look at it in terms of your forearms and arms. Your forearms should be vertical at the bottom—vertical when viewed from the side *and* from the front. (Get the help of an assistant.) At that position your

Top, hand spacing a little too wide. Bottom, better hand spacing, elbows directly beneath the wrists.

arms should be at
about a 45 to 60
degree angle to
your rib cage. The
precise angle will
vary from individual
to individual, largely
because of forearm
and arm lengths,
and torso girth
variations. Get your
forearms in the right
position, and you
should automatically
find the ideal
placement of the bar
on your chest.

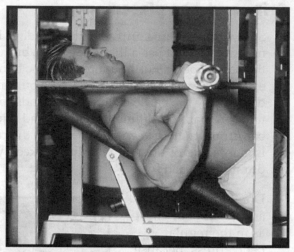

Performance

Position yourself on
the incline bench,
and plant your feet
solidly on the floor,
or on a foot brace if
one is provided.
Keep your feet fixed
in position. Don't lift
or shuffle them. Your
feet should be flat
on the floor, wider
than shoulder width.
Feet positioned
close together
reduce stability.

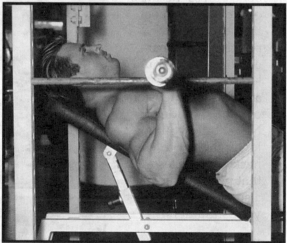

*Your forearms should be vertical when viewed from
the side. Top photograph, bar too low on the chest,
which produces excessive shoulder extension.
Above, correct positioning.*

With a hand-off, take the barbell out of the stands. Straighten your
elbows, pause for a second, then lower the bar under control. Touch
your chest at the position explained earlier, and pause for a second.
Keep yourself tight during the pause, with your abdominal muscles,
buttocks, and lats contracted. Then smoothly press up and slightly
back. After straightening your elbows, pause for a second, or until
the bar is stationary, then lower it for the next rep.

Use the same breathing pattern as in the regular bench press.

Spotting

See *Bench press*. The same guidelines apply to spotting the incline barbell press. In addition, the spotter needs to be elevated, to apply assistance with least difficulty. For the spotter to avoid injury, he must maintain a slightly hollowed lower back, and get as close to the trainee as possible.

Caution

When you incline press, don't exaggerate the hollow in your lower back. With your feet flat on the floor, keep your heels directly beneath or slightly in front of an imaginary vertical line drawn through the middle of your knees. If your feet are behind your knees, the arch will probably be exaggerated, and the risk of injury increased.

But, if the seat of the bench is too high and can't be adjusted, or if you have short lower limbs, this strategy won't work well. A non-slip, low block or platform under each foot will be required. A wide single platform would also do the job. The wider your feet, the greater your stability.

When preparing to unrack the bar from behind your head to get ready for the first rep of a set of the incline barbell bench press, don't draw your elbows behind your wrists, or even in line with your wrists. If your elbows are drawn back, then as you unrack the bar the stress on your shoulders will be increased greatly, and unnecessarily. Keep your elbows in front of your wrists while you unrack the bar. But provided you use a spotter, you won't have to take much of the strain from unracking the bar while getting set up for the first rep.

Incline dumbbell bench press

Main muscles worked

pectorals, deltoids, triceps

the incline bench press may place more stress on the upper pectorals (clavicular head) than does the horizontal, supine version

Capsule description

lie on your back on an incline bench, with the dumbbells overhead; lower the dumbbells to your chest, then push them up

The incline bench press can also be done with dumbbells. Once the dumbbells are in position for pressing, the technique is basically the same as in the barbell version.

A big advantage of dumbbells is that you can use whatever wrist positioning is most comfortable, rather than have your wrists fixed by a barbell into a pronated position. But there are handling difficulties getting the 'bells into position. See *Dumbbell bench press* for the main pros and cons of dumbbell bench pressing.

As in other pressing movements, your hands must extend rearward sufficiently so that you can grip the dumbbells securely. But don't allow the dumbbells to extend your hands to the maximum, because that can mar your lifting technique, and injure your wrists. Grip the bar firmly, to help keep your wrists in the right position. Once the dumbbells are in a secure position in your hands, keep your wrists rigid for the duration of each set.

To perform the dumbbell incline bench press, you require a method for getting the dumbbells into position ready for pressing. See *Dumbbell bench press* for how to do this.

During the pressing, pay special attention to keeping the dumbbells from drifting out to the sides, go no deeper than in the barbell version, and keep the 'bells moving in tandem. You'll probably need a few workouts to get the feel for the exercise, and to find the wrist positioning that best suits you.

See *Dumbbell bench press* for tips on how to progress gradually from one pair of fixed-weight dumbbells, to the next.

Spotting

See *Dumbbell bench press*. The same guidelines apply to spotting the incline dumbbell bench press, but in the latter there's no need for the spotter to crouch.

With any type of dumbbell pressing, key markers of technique deterioration are the 'bells drifting out to the sides, and one hand getting above, in front of, or to the rear of the other. Don't push this exercise to failure. Stop a rep short of failure, so that you don't risk losing control of the 'bells.

Caution

Don't exaggerate the hollow in your lower back. See *Incline barbell bench press*.

3. CALF RAISE

Main muscles worked

gastrocnemius, soleus

Capsule description

stand with the balls of your feet fixed, then raise and lower your heels

The soleus is underneath the gastrocnemius, so most of the soleus isn't visible, but it still contributes significantly to calf girth. The soleus crosses the ankle joint only, but the gastrocnemius crosses the ankle *and* knee joints. Both muscles plantar flex the foot—namely, point the toes—but the gastrocnemius also assists with flexion of the knee.

The calf raise is often called a *heel raise*. Confusingly, it's also sometimes called a *toe raise* even though the toes don't rise.

There are several types of calf raises: standing using both legs, standing using one leg at a time, seated (usually with both legs working simultaneously), and donkey style (where an assistant sits on the bent-over trainee's hips, for added resistance). Avoid the leg press machine for calf work. This offers nothing that other calf exercises don't, but can be dangerous if your feet slip out of position.

Keeping your knees straight in calf work, or just slightly bent, fully recruits the gastrocnemius *and* the soleus. Bent-knee calf work—especially the seated calf raise—reduces gastrocnemius involvement according to the extent of knee flexion.

The standing two-legged calf raise, and the one-legged variation, are the calf exercises used in the routines in this book. Both of these exercises fully involve the gastrocnemius and soleus simultaneously.

Set-up and positioning

In all calf work, place the balls of your feet on a stable block, to enable your heels to descend below the level of the balls of your feet. If the block is free standing—not attached to a calf machine—fix it to a board that has a larger area. This will prevent the block from flipping over. For example, get a 4 x 4 x 20 inch piece of wood and nail it to the center of a 1 x 10 x 22 inch board. Round one of the top two long edges of the block, for the side where you'll place your feet. As an alternative, at least for the dumbbell one-legged calf raise, use an immovable object such as a step.

Depending on the soles of your shoes and the surface you stand on, your feet may slip out of position during the course of a set of calf raises. If this happens, quickly reposition your feet, but next time try different shoes or a different platform or block (perhaps one with rubber fixed on top of it) to help prevent your feet from slipping. Slipping can, however, be caused by incorrect foot positioning, and excessive range of motion at the bottom of the exercise.

If the full range of motion produces foot problems, cut your range of motion a little. Find the maximum range of motion that's safe for you, and which doesn't lead to your feet slipping off the elevation.

Your calves may be tight at present. The calf stretch described in Chapter 2 should help you to increase the flexibility of your calves. Then as your flexibility improves you may be able to increase your depth of descent in the calf raise.

As well as the aesthetic benefits of calf development, there are health benefits from regular calf exercise. With age, the return of blood to the heart through the veins decreases in efficiency. This is prominent below the knees, and may lead to varicose veins because of blood pooling, and damage to the venous valves. The venous blood is moved upward through muscle contraction. Inactivity of the calves increases the difficulty of getting the venous blood to the heart. Keep your calves strong and trained.

Standing two-legged calf raise

A machine is needed for this exercise. If one isn't available, stick with the one-legged calf raise.

Compression of the spine may occur in the standing two-legged calf raise *if* your heels touch the floor *before* the resistance reaches its resting position. Set up the machine so that the resistance rests on a support *before* your heels touch the floor. Alternatively, use a block high enough so that it's impossible to touch your heels to the floor even at full stretch. If you can't ensure you don't risk compressing your spine, change to the dumbbell one-legged calf raise.

When you get positioned for the first rep of any machine standing calf raise, distribute the weight symmetrically over your back and lower limbs, but don't round your upper back. Put the pads in position on your shoulders, pull your shoulder blades back, bend your knees, and place your feet in position on the foot support. Put the entire balls of your feet on the support, not just your toes. Use a hip-width foot placement rather than a close stance, to help you to keep your balance. Keep your big toes pointing directly forward or slightly outward. None of the stress of the weight should be taken on your shoulders yet. Now, hollow your lower back slightly, lock your torso, and straighten your knees. Then you'll safely be in the starting position for the first rep, with the resistance bearing down on you.

Don't take the full load of the resistance on your shoulders and then shuffle into position on the foot support or block. Get correctly in position *before* you take on the resistance.

Hold the calf machine during the exercise, to help keep your balance and maintain a rigid torso. During the course of each set, never allow your back to round, torso to relax, or knees to bend anything more than just slightly, to remove tension from your knees.

Perform your reps smoothly. Go as high as possible at the top of each rep, and contract your calves hard for two to three seconds. Descend under control, reach your safe, bottom position, pause for a second without relaxing, then smoothly push out of it. Never bounce at the bottom of a rep.

Left, correct technique for the standing calf raise—note the proper curvature of the spine. Right, don't round your back while performing any machine standing calf raise.

Some squat machines, with the addition of a block under the balls of the feet, can double as calf machines. Keep your knees straight or just slightly bent.

Standing one-legged calf raise

The one-legged calf raise is done while holding a dumbbell on the same side as your working calf, using a standing calf machine, or with resistance hanging from a belt. With a dumbbell, hold with your free hand something sturdy and stable at about shoulder height, to keep your balance—for example, a bar set at the right height in a power rack.

Put the entire ball of your foot on the elevation, not just your toes. Keep the knee of your working leg straight or just slightly bent during each set, and your big toe pointing directly forward or slightly outward. Bend your non-working limb and keep it out of the way—for example, rest it on the heel of your working limb.

Perform your reps smoothly. Go as high as possible at the top of each rep, and contract your calves hard for two to three seconds. Descend under control, reach your safe, bottom position, pause for a second without relaxing, then smoothly push out of it. Never bounce at the bottom of a rep.

Left, one-legged dumbbell calf raise, holding a horizontal bar for balance. Right, one-legged calf raise using a calf machine.

In all calf work, avoid an exaggerated range of motion at the bottom of the exercise. If you overstretch, you'll lose your foot positioning, and have to re-set, which would mar the set. Descend as far as is comfortable for you without it leading to your feet slipping. Calf stretching should be done during a flexibility routine, not while strength training.

4. CHIN-UP (AND PULL-UP)

Main muscles worked

latissimus dorsi, biceps, brachialis, pectorals, upper back, abdominal wall, forearms

Capsule description

holding a fixed overhead bar, pull yourself up to the bar

There's confusion with the names *chin-up* and *pull-up*. In this book, the chin-up refers to pulling yourself up on an overhead bar using a supinated grip, and the pull-up refers to the same movement but with a pronated grip. Many trainees, however, use the two names interchangeably, regardless of the grip used.

Your ability to pull yourself overhead is influenced by your bodyfat percentage, and your bodyweight in general. The more bodyfat you have, and the heavier you are, the harder this exercise will be.

Set-up and positioning

If your overhead bar is adjustable—for example, if you use an Olympic bar on saddles in a power rack—set the height so you can just grab the bar when standing on your toes. The knurling on an Olympic bar will help your grip, especially if you have chalk or rosin on your hands.

If you use a fixed, high, overhead bar, arrange a box or platform of the appropriate height so that you only have to stand on your toes to grab the bar. During the exercise, bend your knees, or keep them straight.

Initially, hold the overhead bar with a supinated grip. Start with a shoulder-width grip, and fine-tune to find the spacing that feels best for your wrists and elbows. A hand spacing a little closer than shoulder-width may work best.

If you can't find a workable supinated grip, try a pronated one. Take a pronated grip that's two to three inches wider on each side than your shoulder-width grip, so that your forearms are vertical at the contracted position. Regardless of the grip you choose, never use a very wide spacing, and don't pull to the rear of your head. Pulling to the front is safer for your shoulders and neck, and more effective.

A Smith machine has a bar that's adjustable for height, and may be well-knurled. It may be ideal for chin-ups and pull-ups.

Some chinning units provide the option of using a parallel grip. This may be more comfortable than a supinated or a pronated grip on a single bar. The parallel handles may, however, be too close to produce a good training effect.

A possibility for chinning with a parallel grip is to use a power rack. If its uprights are appropriately spaced for you, position a bar on saddles on the front uprights, and another bar across the rear uprights at the same height. Set the height of the bars so that when your elbows are straight, your feet *just* touch the floor.

Performance

Pull until you touch the bar to your collar bones, or lower on your chest. Comparing the same resistance and degree of effort, you'll be able to pull your hands to a lower point on your chest with a supinated or pronated grip than with a parallel one. Fully contract your lats by pulling your shoulder blades *down*.

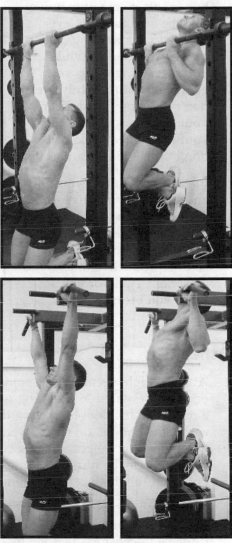

Top, chin-up (supinated grip). Above, pull-up (pronated grip).

Your top position will depend, in part, on your grip spacing, forearm and arm lengths, and your strength and bodyweight. Don't pull beyond what's comfortable for your shoulders and elbows. Your back should be slightly arched at the top of the exercise. If you have to hump your back in order to finish a rep, the set is finished, you're using too much resistance, or you're not ready, yet, for this exercise.

Pause for a second at the top position, then smoothly lower yourself to an inch short of the bottommost position. Pause for a second at the bottom, then smoothly move into the next ascent. Never drop into the bottom position, or relax and stretch while you're hanging. Keep your eyes looking up slightly, and don't turn your head. Keep your shoulders tight, and your head tilted back, but don't throw your head back.

Inhale as you lower yourself, and exhale during the ascent. Trying to catch your breath during a momentary pause at the bottom position is usually counterproductive unless you can briefly stand or kneel while you breathe.

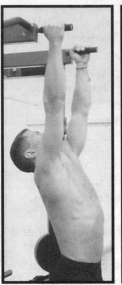

Use of a parallel grip.

Other tips

Attach weight securely and comfortably. Use a shoulder harness or a belt designed for hanging weight from, wear a belt and put a dumbbell inside it by having the dumbbell vertical and the belt across the handle, or, use a strong piece of rope or chain to attach a dumbbell or weight plates securely to a belt. For the latter, the resistance can be hung from the front or the rear of the belt. Try both to find which is most comfortable for you.

Add weight slowly, in small increments. To work from one fixed-weight dumbbell to the next, gradually attach weight to the lighter dumbbell—most easily done by using small magnetic plates. Alternatively, use an adjustable dumbbell, or weight plates only.

Spotting

Though not essential, use a spotter if possible. When you grind to a halt short of completing a rep, get a spotter to assist. Enough pressure should be evenly applied to your back. The assistant should push you up in your regular groove, not push you forward and mar the pathway.

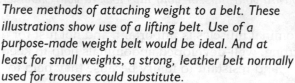

Three methods of attaching weight to a belt. These illustrations show use of a lifting belt. Use of a purpose-made weight belt would be ideal. And at least for small weights, a strong, leather belt normally used for trousers could substitute.

5. CRUNCH

Five forms of the crunch will be described:
>   basic crunch
>   modified basic crunch
>   machine crunch
>   reverse crunch
>   twisting crunch

Main muscles worked

*rectus abdominis, external and internal abdominal obliques, transversus
abdominis, hip flexors, (and the twisting crunch also works the multifidii)*

Capsule description

curl your shoulders toward your hips, or your hips toward your shoulders

Exercise for the abdominal muscles is important, and not just for
aesthetic reasons. Strong, well-developed abdominals help to keep
the lower back strong and resistant to injury because they help to
stabilize the spine during many exercises.

Crunches come in two basic types: The basic crunch curls the
shoulders toward the hips, and the reverse crunch curls the hips
toward the chest. Each works both functions of the rectus abdominis
and transversus abdominis—compression of the abdomen, and
flexion of the trunk—but only two of the functions of the obliques:
compression of the abdomen, and flexion of the trunk. A third
function of the obliques—trunk rotation—isn't worked by most
crunches. The *twisting* crunch employs rotation.

The rectus abdominis ("six-pack") is one long, flat, continuous
muscle that runs from the lower ribs to the groin. While it's not
possible to isolate the upper or lower abdominals, the two sections
may respond differently to flexion exercises that require the
shoulders to move toward the hips, than to flexion exercises that
require the hips to move toward the shoulders.

Trainees commonly get poor results from crunches for two main
reasons: many perform excessive reps with little or no added resistance,
and most use incorrect technique regardless of their rep count. With
correct technique, moderate reps, and progressive resistance, good
results will come. *But whether you'll see your abdominal development will
depend on how much fat you have covering your midsection.*

Preparatory movement

Before every rep
of any crunch, tilt
your hips so that
your lumbar
vertebrae are
pushed into the
floor or mat.

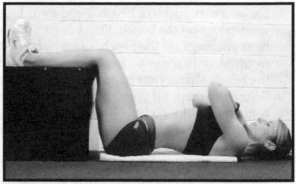

*In Chapter 2, during descriptions of
the modified crunch, the breathing
guidance is to exhale during the
ascent. But in this chapter, the
guidance is to exhale fully before
the ascent. The former method is
less demanding on the abdominal
musculature than the latter. Most
beginners will be best starting off
with the less demanding variation.*

Basic crunch

Lie on a mat next to a bench. Bend your knees at a right angle and rest your calves on the bench. Don't cross your legs. Get an assistant to hold your legs on the bench, use a purpose-built bench with a leg restraint, or brace your feet in some way so that your legs stay fixed to the bench. Cross your hands and rest them on your chest or shoulders. Before each rep, tilt your pelvis so that while your coccyx and sacrum come off the floor a little (that is, your buttocks rise slightly), your lumbar vertebrae are pushed into the floor. Smoothly curl your torso off the floor until your forearms touch your thighs. Pause for a second at the top position, and contract your abdominals hard. Then take about three seconds to smoothly unfurl onto the floor. Maintain the pelvic tilt during the ascent and descent. Once your shoulders are on

the floor, pause for a second, again push your lumbar vertebrae into the floor (that is, tilt your pelvis), and repeat.

Don't hold your breath. Exhale fully before the concentric or lifting phase, and inhale during the descent.

Keep your head and neck in one fixed position throughout each rep, with your chin slightly off your chest.

A common mistake is putting the hands behind the head. This leads to pulling on the head, causing neck irritation. When you require resistance, hold a dumbbell across your chest, with the handle parallel with your shoulders. You could hold small plates on your chest, but large plates will obstruct the proper movement. Once you've progressed beyond using small plates, move to a dumbbell. Be consistent with where you place the dumbbell on your mid to upper chest, so that you apply resistance in the same way each time. If you vary the position of the dumbbell, you'll change the perceived weight of the resistance.

Loading and unloading the resistance can be a problem—because asymmetrical movement is involved in taking a dumbbell from the floor at one side, for example. Have an assistant put the dumbbell directly on your chest, and remove it for you at the end of the set.

The basic crunch with a
dumbbell held horizontally
on the chest.

Hip flexors, and abdominal work

The hip flexors are involved in most forms of abdominal work, including crunches. (The iliopsoas hip flexors—iliacus, psoas major, and psoas minor—are located deep in the pelvis, and are hidden from view. The other major hip flexor, the rectus femoris, is visible—it's part of the quadriceps.) The degree of involvement of the hip flexors depends on the technique used. Abdominal work with straight knees may employ the hip flexors to a greater extent than the abs, and should be avoided. By keeping the knees bent, the involvement of the hip flexors is reduced, and the relative involvement of the abs is increased. Substantial hip flexor involvement can produce lower-back problems for many trainees—typically those whose lower backs aren't strong enough, and who lack sufficient flexibility. Generally, the greater the hip flexor involvement in abdominal work, the greater the possibility of lower-back irritation.

If you've had any back problems, use the *modified* basic crunch for a few months before you consider progressing to the full-range basic crunch. The modified crunch has a reduced range of motion relative to the basic crunch, and involves the hip flexors to a lesser extent. This reduced hip flexor involvement means reduced stress on the lower back. In the meantime, get checked out by a chiropractor (see Chapter 6), strengthen your abs with the modified basic crunch, strengthen your lower back with back extensions, and work on the flexibility routine.

The hip flexor involvement in the basic crunch is desirable *provided* the exercise can be done safely. The hip flexors need to be strengthened, too, once the lower back and abs have been sufficiently strengthened. What's required is balanced strength across the three areas.

Modified basic crunch

Adopt the same set-up as for the basic crunch, although it may not be necessary to have your calves held against the bench. The modified crunch is a short-range exercise. Only about half your spine should come off the floor. Your lumbar vertebrae must retain contact with the floor throughout each rep.

Use a slow ascent and forcible crunch of your abdominal muscles. Hold the top position for a second. Slowly lower your upper back to the floor. Move smoothly at all times.

Don't hold your breath. Exhale fully before the concentric or lifting phase, and inhale during the descent.

Why sit-ups with straight knees are dangerous

Especially in days gone by, school students and youngsters elsewhere were urged by instructors to perform quick-fire sit-ups with their knees straight, and hands interlocked behind their heads or necks. That technique can be harmful even for youngsters, and is potentially harmful for most adults. Avoid it.

Crunches are safe, relative to sit-ups, because the knees are bent, the hips are flexed, and the lower back is rounded to the *rear*. As a result, the abdominal muscles pull you up and forward, and the hip flexors help

Machine crunch

Follow the manufacturer's guidelines for the set-up.

Smoothly flex the upper half of your spine. Crunch your torso forward, hold the intense contraction for a second, then smoothly return to the starting position. Pause for a second, then smoothly begin the next rep.

Don't hold your breath. Exhale fully before the flexion phase, and inhale during the extension.

Compare the effect from the machine on your abdominals with that from the non-machine crunches. The latter may be better, because many crunch machines aren't well designed.

The crunch machine shown on the left has the resistance arms above the chest. The other one has a resistance pad applied against the chest.

as synergists (not prime movers) to keep the pelvis stabilized at the crucial moment the crunch is initiated by the rectus abdominis muscles.

But in sit-ups with straight knees, the hip flexors are the prime movers as they first pull the lower back into a more arched position (curved to the *front*), and *then* they pull the torso up and forward. It's this initial pull on the lumbar arch that feels uncomfortable, and commonly creates problems.

Perform crunches, not sit-ups with straight knees.

Reverse crunch

Lie on your back on a horizontal bench. Hold the bench behind your head. With straight knees, lift your legs so that they are perpendicular to the bench. Keep your feet directly above your hips, and bend your knees so that they are above your lower chest. Tilt your pelvis so that while your coccyx and sacrum come off the floor a little, your lumbar vertebrae are pushed into the bench. Initiate every rep in this manner. Then roll your lower back off the bench. Hold the top position for a second, then slowly return to the starting position. Pause for a second, tilt your pelvis again, and smoothly move into the next rep.

This is a short-range movement. Maintain the pelvic tilt throughout each rep. At no point should you arch or hollow your lower back.

Don't hold your breath. Exhale fully before the concentric or lifting phase, and inhale during the descent.

Performing the reverse crunch on a horizontal bench with your feet above your hips and knees bent above your lower chest, provides low resistance. To increase the resistance, straighten your knees but keep your feet above your hips. To further increase the resistance, keep your thighs perpendicular to the bench, and knees bent so that your feet are in front of your hips. Progress until you can perform your target reps with your knees bent at a right angle and thighs vertical. For increased resistance thereafter, perform the reverse crunch on an incline bench, with your head higher than your hips in the starting position.

Remember to tilt your pelvis so that your lower back (other than your coccyx and sacrum) is flattened against the bench prior to each rep—for safety, and to focus the stress on your abdominal muscles.

In all variations of the reverse crunch, don't jam your head onto the bench, because that could cause neck injury. Maintain a relaxed neck, and keep the strain of the exercise on your abdominals.

The topmost photographs show the least demanding of these three forms of the reverse crunch. If required, the resistance can be further reduced by bringing the knees closer to the chest.

The bottommost photographs show the most demanding of these three forms of the reverse crunch. To make it even more taxing, perform the reverse crunch on an inclined bench, with your head above your hips in the starting position—the photograph on the left page shows the top position. Start with little inclination, and increase the degree of slope gradually.

Twisting crunch

This crunch variation increases the involvement of both obliques, because it involves rotation of the trunk. The rest of the abdominal wall is involved, too. *Because it involves rotation of the trunk, this crunch also works the multifidii.* This muscle group is deep to the erector spinae, from the sacrum to the neck, and extends and rotates the vertebral column.

Adopt the same set-up for the basic crunch, and perform the movement in the same way except add a slight twist during the ascent. As you ascend—following a hip tilt, and full exhalation—point your left elbow toward your right inner thigh. Hold the top, slightly twisted position for a second, then as you descend, return to the symmetrical position. On the next rep, point your right elbow toward your left inner thigh, and so on. Just a slight twist is enough to increase greatly the involvement of the obliques. Although there's asymmetry in this exercise, it's safe, and necessary.

When you twist to your right, you use your right external oblique, and your *left* internal oblique. When you twist to your left, you use your left external oblique, and your *right* internal oblique.

A purpose-built bench with leg restraints, suitable for the basic crunch (illustrated), modified crunch, and twisting crunch.

Prior to each rep of any form of the crunch, remember to tilt your pelvis so that your lower back (other than your coccyx and sacrum) is flattened against the bench, floor, or mat—for safety, and to focus the stress on your abdominal muscles.

6. CURL

Main muscles worked

biceps, brachialis, brachioradialis, forearms

Capsule description

standing or seated, arms and forearms hanging straight, lift the weight through bending at your elbows

The curl can be done with dumbbells or a barbell, standing or seated. If done seated, use dumbbells in order to extend your forearms fully. There are also cable and machine variations of the curl.

The biceps flex the elbows *and* supinate the hands. To supinate your hands fully, rotate them from a palms-down to a palms-up position. You can't do this with a barbell. The biceps isn't the only elbow flexor. There are the brachialis (beneath the biceps) and the brachioradialis (from just above the elbow, to the wrist), too, which are also worked by the curl. The latter two muscles flex the elbow only, they don't supinate the hand.

While permitting supination and a full range of motion even while seated, the dumbbell curl produces another advantage over the barbell curl—the ability for the wrists and elbows to adopt the most comfortable positioning. Because of these advantages, dumbbell curling is used in **The Program**. In case dumbbells aren't available, the barbell curl will be described, too.

In all curls, keep your wrists and hands in a straight line—the neutral position. If you don't maintain the neutral position, you may develop wrist and elbow problems.

Spotting

Technique deterioration is shown through leaning back (unless you use back support) and bringing the elbows too far forward. As soon as your torso goes back even a whisker beyond the vertical, your spotter should urge you to straighten up. If you perform another rep, a little assistance may be needed if you're to complete the rep in correct technique. Assistance should be applied with two hands, in a symmetrical way. Just enough help should be given to keep your torso and arms vertical.

The correct, straight, or neutral position of hands and wrists (top), and the incorrect position (above).

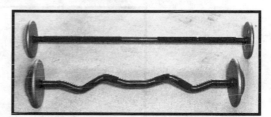

Comparison of a straight bar and an EZ-curl bar. The EZ-curl bar may be more comfortable to use for the barbell curl than a straight bar.

Seated dumbbell curl

Sit at the end of a bench, with your knees together, and feet on the floor. Hold a dumbbell in each hand, with straight elbows, hands parallel with each other, an upright torso, and your shoulders retracted.

Curl the dumbbells, don't swing them—move smoothly. As the dumbbells ascend, supinate your hands as much as possible—rotate your thumbs outward. On the descent, pronate your hands so that, in the starting position, they are parallel with each other once again.

Start with your elbows at your sides so that your arms are vertical when viewed from the side and from the front. As you curl, your elbows may come forward only *slightly*. At the top position, your hands should be several inches short of where they would be to make your forearms vertical. Your hands may come to shoulder height, but no higher.

Pause for a second in the top position. Contract your biceps hard at the top position as you fully supinate your wrists. It's not possible to rest at the top of a properly performed curl. Lower the resistance under control, pause for a second at the bottom position, then smoothly perform the next rep. Exhale during the ascent, and inhale during the descent.

Incline dumbbell curl

Perform the dumbbell curl with your hips, back, and shoulders against an incline bench set at about 45 degrees. For comfort, your head doesn't have to rest against the bench. To make it easy to pick up the dumbbells from the floor, use the lowest seat setting, if it's adjustable. And because of the incline bench, your arms may not be perfectly vertical. Otherwise, the technique is the same as for the *Seated dumbbell curl*.

Barbell curl

Stand with your feet about hip-width apart. Keep your knees slightly unlocked, and your buttocks tensed, to help support your spine. Use a supinated (palms-up) grip on the barbell, with hands spaced a little wider than hip-width. Fine-tune this to find the hand spacing that's most comfortable for your wrists and elbows. Other than there being no wrist rotation in the barbell curl, the rest of the technique is the same as for the *Seated dumbbell curl*.

If the straight bar irritates your elbows or wrists, try a closer or wider grip. If that doesn't correct the problem, try the EZ-curl bar. If that doesn't produce a comfortable curl, use dumbbells. An EZ-curl bar is a short barbell that has a number of bends or cambers in it, to enable the user to try to find the grip that feels the most comfortable.

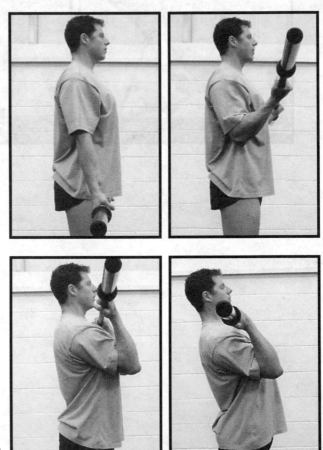

Correct starting and finishing positions (above). Incorrect finishing positions (right).

Hammer curl

Different wrist positions produce different effects on the elbow flexors, and apply stress differently to the elbow joints. One alternative is to keep your thumbs *up* all the time—the *hammer curl*. If you've had wrist, elbow, or shoulder problems, the hammer curl may be the variation that feels the most comfortable. The hammer curl may be performed standing (illustrated), seated at the end of a horizontal bench, or seated on an incline bench.

7. DEADLIFT

Four forms of the deadlift will be described:
  basic or conventional deadlift
  parallel-grip deadlift
  partial deadlift
  sumo deadlift

The basic, or conventional deadlift, is what's usually meant by *the deadlift.* Any specification of *basic,* or *conventional,* for example, isn't usually used. This can, however, lead to confusion, because there are several forms of deadlifting.

Properly done, variations of the deadlift are among the most effective strength-training exercises. But use poor technique, abuse low reps, overtrain, or try to lift weights that are too heavy for you, and you'll hurt yourself with any form of the deadlift.

Before you can deadlift with correct technique, you need to be flexible enough to adopt the necessary positioning. You especially need to have supple calves, hamstrings, thigh adductors, and buttocks.

If you've had a serious back injury, don't deadlift without the clearance of a chiropractor. If you've had any minor back injuries, *still* get a chiropractor's clearance. See Chapter 6.

"Flat back" confusion

The spine is curved when seen from the side. This curvature is the natural, strong structure for absorbing and distributing stress efficiently. When the curves are lost, the strong, load-bearing capability is diminished.

"Keep a flat back" is a common admonition when lifting a weight, and one that I used in my earlier writing. It's not, however, an accurate one. What it really means, is, "Don't round your lower back." Although it may look like the lower back is flat at the bottom of a correctly performed deadlift or squat, as examples, this is an illusion. When contracted, the spinal erectors, if sufficiently developed, may fill the required slight hollow in the lower back's profile at those bottom positions, giving an impression that the lower back is flat, but the actual *lower spine* should be slightly concave, or hollow.

It's the strong contraction of the lumbar musculature that produces the desired, concave lower back, to create a bracing effect. The strong contraction of the muscles on both sides of the spine not only prevents the forward rounding of the back, but helps prevent sideways, asymmetrical bending as well.

If the lower spine is truly flat, the upper back will be rounded, which is a dangerous position when lifting a challenging weight (or even a light one in many cases). A spine that's intentionally straightened while under heavy load bearing is a weakened one that's exposed to an increased risk of injury. A spine that's naturally straight suggests pathology.

When lifting a weight, inside or outside of the gym, keep your shoulders retracted, hips pushed back (extended), and lower back slightly hollowed. There are exceptions, however. For example, during the back extension the back *should* round, and during crunches the lower back shouldn't be hollow—keep it flat against the floor.

How to improve your ability to deadlift

To be able to deadlift competently in any of the four variations described in this chapter, you need to work at deadlifting technique *and* the essential supportive work. (For most trainees, the conventional deadlift is the most technically demanding of the four variations, and the partial deadlift the least.) There are three major components of good deadlifting ability:

1. The flexibility to be able to *adopt* the correct body positioning.

2. The back strength to be able to *maintain* the correct back positioning.

3. Correct exercise technique.

You need sufficient flexibility in the major musculature of your lower body. Follow the flexibility program in Chapter 2. If any of the muscles have anything less than at least a normal, healthy level of flexibility, deadlifting technique will probably be compromised, with a reduction in safety and productivity. Deadlift correctly, or not at all.

You need sufficient strength throughout your back—lower, middle, and upper—to be able to hold your lower back in the required slightly hollowed position during the deadlift. This is critical for safety. The back must not round while deadlifting. Four key back exercises—deadlift itself, back extension, row, and shrug—will help build the required back strength *if* they are worked with correct form, and progressive resistance.

It may take several months before correct deadlifting technique can be implemented, even with minimal weight. Don't be frustrated to begin with. As your flexibility and back strength improve, and your ability to *use* them, so will your deadlifting ability. Until you can adopt the correct technique, keep the resistance very light.

As your deadlifting weight grows, so should your strength in the back extension, row, and shrug, to help you maintain correct back positioning.

Footwear reminder

Especially for deadlifts, squats, and overhead presses, you should not wear shoes with thick or spongy soles and heels.

Get yourself a sturdy pair of shoes with good grip to the floor, arch support, and which minimizes deformation when you're lifting heavy weights. No heel elevation relative to the balls of your feet is especially important for deadlifts and squats.

See pages 185 and 186 for details.

CRITICAL note for ALL forms of deadlifting

The greater the extent of the forward lean, the greater the risk to the back because of the increased chance of losing the concave lower spine that's essential for safe deadlifting. To try to minimize the risk from deadlifting, keep your maximum forward lean to about 45 degrees from an imaginary vertical line. There has to be forward lean in order to heavily involve the back musculature, but excessive forward lean must be avoided. *A concave lower spine must be maintained.*

Basic or conventional deadlift

Main muscles worked

spinal erectors, multifidii, buttocks, quadriceps, hamstrings, latissimus dorsi, upper back, forearms

Capsule description

with knees well bent and positioned between your hands, and a slightly hollowed lower back, lift the resistance from the floor

Set-up

Once you have the required strength, deadlift using a bar with a 45-pound or 20-kilo plate on each end. Until you have this strength, or if you have to use smaller-diameter plates, set the plates on blocks of wood so that the height of the bar from the floor is the same as it would be *if* it was loaded with full-size plates. Alternatively, use a power rack and set it up so that the bar, when set across the pins, is at the height it would be if it was loaded with full-size plates on the floor or platform.

For best control of the bar, don't train on a slick surface or bare concrete, or the bar will move around when set down, and there's also the chance that your feet will slip. Deadlift on non-slip rubber matting, or construct a simple deadlifting surface through affixing hard-wearing, non-slip carpet to the top side of a 7-foot x 3-foot x 1-inch piece of wood.

Stance

Place your feet about hip-width apart, with toes turned out somewhat. Your hands should just touch the outside of your legs at the bottom of the exercise. Fine-tune the heel spacing and degree of toe flare to find the stance that helps your lifting technique the most. A slightly different stance may help you to deliver more efficient deadlifting technique, because of improved leverage.

Find a foot placement that spreads the stress of the deadlift over your thighs, buttocks, and back. Don't try to focus most of the stress on a single body structure. You must deadlift without your lower back rounding, or your torso leaning forward excessively. Your feet should be firmly planted to the floor, with your heels flat against it. You should feel stable at all times, with no tendency to topple forward or rearward. And push largely through your heels, not the front of your

Start, midpoint, and finish of a correctly performed basic or conventional deadlift.

feet. Furthermore, your knees should point in the same direction as your feet. Don't let your knees buckle inward as you ascend.

Neither stand too far from the bar, nor too close. If you pull the bar into your shins on the ascent, you probably started too close to it. If you're too far from the bar, it will travel away from your shins and you'll place excessive strain on your lower back, risk losing the rep and, perhaps, injure yourself. Position yourself so that the bar brushes against your legs and thighs throughout the ascent. Find the foot positioning that has the bar touching your shins when your knees are bent at the bottom position. But when you're standing erect before descending to get set for the first rep, your shins may be a little away from the bar.

Closely related to how near you stand to the bar, is your arm positioning. Your arms and forearms should hang in a vertical line, and there should be no bending at your elbows. Your arms and forearms should be vertical or near vertical throughout the lift—they link your torso to the bar.

For symmetrical technique you must have symmetrical foot positioning. Each foot must be exactly the same distance from the bar. Even if one foot is just slightly ahead or behind the other, relative to the bar, this will produce an asymmetrical drive and a slight twisting action.

The bar must be parallel with a line drawn across the toes of your shoes. If the bar torques slightly and touches one lower limb but is an inch or two in front of the other, the stress on one side of your body increases substantially, as does the risk of injury.

Grip

A secure grip is especially important for all forms of the deadlift. To aid your grip, use bars with knurling. Smooth bars hinder the grip.

A reverse grip produces asymmetrical distribution of stress, and torque. A correct pronated grip produces symmetrical stress, but isn't as secure as a reverse grip. A bar slipping out of one hand, regardless of the grip used, can result in a lot of torque. If you can't hold onto a bar, don't try to lift it.

As a beginner, a pronated grip should be fine. Use of chalk or rosin on your hands, when required, will help strengthen your grip. If, despite this action, your grip still isn't adequate, use a reverse grip and continue to use chalk or rosin. Use a reverse grip only for your work sets, and alternate from set to set which way around you have your hands. For one set, have your left hand under and right hand over, and the next set have your right hand under and your left hand over. In this way you'll avoid applying the asymmetrical stress in the same way, so that both sides of your body get their turns.

The start

With your feet and the bar in the correct positions, stand and get ready for the first rep. Straighten your elbows and place your hands at your sides ready to drop down into position on the bar. Pull your shoulders back, take your final breath, hold it, and lock your back. Descend with a synchronized bend of your knees *and* forward lean of your torso. Sit down *and* back, and push your hips to the rear. Maintain a slightly hollowed back. Descend until your hands touch the bar (on the knurled area). Keep your bodyweight primarily over your heels, but don't rock back and lose your balance.

If you have to fiddle to get your grip spacing right on the bar, you risk losing the rigid torso and slightly hollowed lower back required for a safe pull. Learn to get your grip right without fiddling around. To help here, get two pieces of garden hose about an inch long each. Slice them open and tape one in the correct position on each side of the bar so that when your hands brush against them, your hands are in the right position. In this way you won't need to look down and then have to re-set your back before the ascent. Instead, descend, keep your head up and torso rigid, immediately place your hands into position, stay tight, then start the ascent.

At the bottom position, your knees should be bent, hips much lower than your shoulders, bar against your shins, head up, and

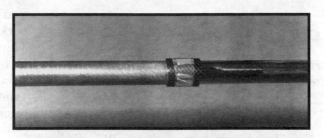

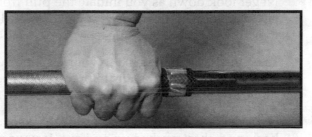

Two pieces of hose appropriately placed on a deadlift bar enable each hand to be positioned without having to look down to check. See text. Here's one of those pieces of hose. For clear viewing, the legs were kept out of the photographs.

your bodyweight felt mostly through your heels. The deadlift is done by the thighs and back *together*.

If you start the deadlift primarily with your thighs, your knees will straighten too quickly and your back will then bear the brunt of the load. If you start the deadlift with little thigh involvement, you won't get far unless it's a light weight for you.

Hold the relative positions of your head, shoulders, and hips during the lift—keep your back slightly hollowed throughout, and shoulder blades retracted. *Never* round your back. Leading with your head and shoulders helps to maintain the proper back positioning.

Ascent

The first part of the ascent is to shrug your shoulders vertically against the bar. Although you won't lift the bar unless it's light, this shrug helps to lock your back into the right position for the pull. Stick your chest out, too. Then squeeze the bar off the floor through simultaneously pushing with your thighs—mostly through your heels—and pulling with your back. When you pull, make it smooth and slow. Don't yank at the bar.

Yanking at the bar leads to bending your elbows, moving you forward, raising your hips too quickly, and increasing stress on your back. Your hips must not rise faster than your shoulders.

Once the bar is off the floor and moving, accelerate its speed a little. Push through both your feet with equal force. If you favor one limb, you'll produce a dangerous corkscrew-like motion. Think of pushing your feet through the floor. *Keep your shoulders pulled back, scapulae retracted, and chest pushed up and out.*

Never look down as you initiate the pull from the floor. Keep your jaw parallel with the floor, and look forward or slightly up. Don't look down during the course of a rep.

Keep the bar moving next to your legs, or thighs. If necessary, wear something over your shins to prevent abrasions. Never let the bar move away from you—*this is critical*.

Over the final few inches of the ascent, keep your shoulders pulled back, and chest pushed up and out. If your shoulders slump, your back will round, stress on your spine and its musculature will increase greatly, and you'll set yourself up for a serious injury. Part of the reason why the shrug has been included in each routine in **The Program** is to help you to develop the strength required to keep your shoulders pulled back even under stress.

Remain *vertical* at the top of the lift. If you lean back at the top of the deadlift, that would cause dangerous compression of your intervertebral discs.

As you stand, keep your scapulae retracted, lower back hollowed slightly, weight felt mostly through your heels, and your shoulders, hips, and ankles lined up. Pause for a second, then start the descent.

Exhale on the ascent, and inhale at the top or during the descent.

Descent with the bar

Lowering a straight bar can be awkward, depending on your body structure. Keep your shoulder blades retracted, and chest pushed up and out, as you lower the bar slowly and symmetrically, with a synchronized bend of your knees *and* forward lean of your torso. Sit down *and* back, and push your hips to the rear. Always maintain a slightly hollowed back.

For the descent with a straight bar, slide the bar down your thighs to your knees, through bending at your knees *and* leaning forward. Lean forward the minimum required to get the bar around your knees. Then bend further at your knees and lower the bar to the floor. As soon as the bar is below your knees, keep it as close to your shins as possible, to reduce stress on your lower back. Descend slowly, to keep correct control over the bar—take three to four seconds for the descent.

Once the weight gently touches the floor or platform, immediately start the next rep through shrugging hard on the bar just prior to trying to push your feet into the floor.

Once you've built up the weight so that it's challenging, take a pause for a couple of seconds at the bottom of each rep. But keep your hands in position, torso tensed and tight, lower back slightly hollowed, and eyes looking forward. Breathe as required, then begin the next rep.

Other tips

While experimenting to find your optimum stance, and while using a very light weight, stand on cardboard when you deadlift. When you've settled on your stance, draw around your feet with a marker. Then next session, stand on your footprints and you'll know where you were positioned last time. If you revise your positioning, draw a new pair of footprints. Eventually, you'll settle on a stance that works best for you. Mark that position on cardboard, and refer to it when required.

For work sets once the weight becomes demanding, use chalk or rosin on your hands to improve your grip on the bar, and use a bar with deep knurling. Then through combining specialized grip work and gradual weight increases in the deadlift, you should be able to hold securely any weight you can deadlift. Wrist straps are crutches that promote a weak grip—avoid them.

Always deadlift with collars on the bar. This is critical for keeping the plates in position, and a balanced bar.

Don't bounce the weights on the floor. Gently set the weights on the floor or platform. If you rush the reps, you'll risk banging the floor with the plates on one or both sides. This will disrupt your balance, produce asymmetrical pulling, and stress your body unevenly. This is dangerous.

Never turn your head while you lift or lower the bar, or otherwise the bar will tip somewhat, your lifting groove will be marred, and you could hurt yourself.

If you can't complete a rep without your shoulders slumping, dump the weight. End the set of your own volition before you get hurt.

Common errors—DANGER

Hips too low in the set-up position.

Hips too high, excessive forward lean, loss of correct back set.

Hips have moved too fast in the ascent, and the degree of forward lean has been exaggerated.

Loss of back set during the lockout.

Leaning back during the lockout.

Warning

The photographs on these two pages illustrate common errors that turn the deadlift from one of the most effective exercises, to one of the most dangerous. Deadlift correctly, or not at all.

| Loss of back set, and rounding of the back. | More exaggerated rounding of the back. | Legs have locked out too fast, and the bar has drifted away from the legs. |

Never drop the weight, even if you have to dump it because you feel your back about to start rounding. Protecting the equipment and floor is only part of the reason for lowering the bar with control. A bar slamming on the floor or platform, or rack pins, can injure your back, shoulders, elbows, or wrists. Lowering the weight too quickly can also lead to rounding the back and losing the important slightly arched lower back.

Once you're training hard, never work the deadlift to failure. Keep the "do or die" rep in you.

Don't deadlift while your lower back is still sore from an earlier workout, or heavy manual labor. Rest a day or two longer, until the soreness has gone.

As seen from the side view, get feedback from an assistant, or record yourself with a video camera. Discover your actual hip, shoulder and head positions. The technique you think you use may not be what you actually use.

Once you've mastered deadlifting technique, don't become overconfident. Just a slight slip of concentration can lead to lowering the bar slightly out of position, for example This will mar your groove, make the weight feel heavier, make the reps harder, and risk injury.

Deadlifts cause callus buildup on your hands. If this is excessive, your skin may become vulnerable to cracks and tears. Both may temporarily restrict your training. Avoid excessive build-up of calluses. Once a week, after you've showered or bathed, use a pumice stone or callus file and gently rub the calluses on your hands. Don't cut the calluses with a blade or scissors. Keep the calluses under control so that they don't cause loss of elasticity on the skin under and around them. To help maintain the elasticity of the skin of your palms and fingers, consume enough essential fatty acids—see Chapter 4.

Spotting

Spotting isn't required in the deadlift—*never* perform assisted or forced reps in this exercise, or negative-only reps. An alert and knowledgeable assistant can, however, critique your technique, and help keep it correct.

Use of a belt

Two of the men shown in this section are powerlifters, and wear lifting belts out of habit because they use them when they compete in meets. A lifting belt isn't required for training, however, and some powerlifting competitions don't allow belts or any other support gear.

Build your own natural belt through a strong corset of muscle. Train without a belt. Not wearing a belt HELPS your body to strengthen its core musculature. See point #34, on page 184.

Critical tip

It may take time for the deadlift to feel natural. Don't lose heart if you find that deadlifting with the bare bar feels awkward, and you wobble a lot. But don't go adding a lot of weight prematurely. Build up gradually as described in **The Program**, *and be confident that the exercise will feel better later than it does at first.*

Parallel-grip deadlift

Main muscles worked

spinal erectors, multifidii, buttocks, quadriceps, thigh adductors, hamstrings, latissimus dorsi, upper back, forearms

Capsule description

with knees well bent, and a slightly hollowed lower back, lift the resistance from the floor

Properly done, the parallel-grip deadlift is one of the most effective exercises—a big, multi-joint exercise that works most of the musculature in the body, namely the thighs, buttocks, and back. There are a number of pieces of equipment used for performing parallel-grip deadlifts, primarily the trap bar, shrug bar, and dumbbells. The dumbbells are the trickiest to use—they get in the way of the lower limbs, constrain stance width and flare more than the one-piece bars, may prohibit ideal foot positioning, and thus hamper technique. Furthermore, many gyms don't have dumbbells heavy enough for trainees other than beginners. Consequently it's the technique of deadlifting with a one-piece, parallel-grip bar that's described in this section.

Before you can parallel-grip deadlift with correct technique, you need to be flexible enough to adopt the necessary positioning. You especially need flexible calves, hamstrings, thigh adductors, and buttocks.

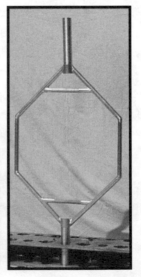

Two examples of parallel-grip bars: the trap bar (left), and the shrug bar.

The parallel-grip deadlift. At the bottom position the inward curvature of the model's lower spine is filled with contracted erector spinae muscle, presenting the appearance of a flat back. The trap bar is tipping here, but should be horizontal to the floor.

Set-up

With the parallel-grip deadlift you can involve more knee flexion than in the regular deadlift, hand spacing is determined by the bar's gripping sites (about 22 to 24 inches apart, or 56 to 61 centimeters, depending on the manufacturer), and the bar doesn't drag against your thighs. The pathway of an imaginary straight line joining the ends of the parallel-grip bar can run through your body, rather than in front of it like with a straight bar.

Stance

As a starting point, use a hip-width heel spacing, with your toes turned out about 20 degrees on each side. Fine-tune this to suit you—a little wider, or a little closer. Your legs must fit inside your hands when your hands are on the handles, but without your knees moving inward. Your knees must be in the same plane as your feet. If your feet are too wide, your knees will travel inward to make room for your hands and forearms during the lower part of each rep.

If you can't use this constrained stance safely, the parallel-grip deadlift isn't suited to you. The more roomy inside area of the shrug bar, compared with the trap bar, may provide greater stance options.

The ability to adopt the correct back set is determined primarily by flexibility, back strength, and technique. These take time to develop, for all variations of the deadlift. Progress gradually, as explained in the text. With time, you may be able to adopt a greater range of motion WITHOUT losing the correct back set. It's not necessary to extend the head as much as is shown in this illustration.

With the spacing of your heels determined, place your feet inside the bar in the best position for you. As a starting point, place your feet so that the center of the ends of the bar runs through the bony prominence in the center of the outside of each of your ankles, as you stand with your knees straight.

Although this foot positioning will suit some trainees, for others it may not be ideal. Try it with a light weight, and see. Then, for example, move your feet back an inch, and see how that works. And try an inch forward of the original positioning, too.

Optimal foot positioning is affected by your body structure, and degree of knee flexion. You may need several workouts of practice, and trial and error, before you settle on the optimum foot positioning for you. If you're positioned too far to the rear, you'll probably be bent forward too much and the bar may swing as you lift it off the floor. If you're positioned too far to the front, the bar will probably also swing as you lift it off the floor. There should be no swinging of the bar.

Once you know the foot positioning that works best for you, use a reference point so that you can adopt the right set-up each time. With the trap bar, for example, you could use ankle position relative to an imaginary line running through the ends of the bar. Or, you could use the position of the front rim of your shoes relative to the front of the rhombus. Your eyes must, however, view from the same point each time. For example, as you stand upright, cast your eyes down and perhaps the front rim of your shoes is directly below the inside edge of the front of the rhombus. Perhaps it's an inch inside.

A piece of garden hose of the right size, and appropriately positioned, permits hand centering on a parallel-grip bar's handle without having to look down to check. See text. The legs were kept out of the photographs so as not to obstruct viewing.

Grip

Use a parallel-grip bar with knurling. A smooth bar hinders the grip.

If your hands are off center on the handles, the parallel-grip bar will tip. If only one hand is off center, dangerous rotational stress may result. Keep both hands correctly centered, and the bar parallel with the floor.

Here's how to center your hands on the handles without having to look down and lose the tensed torso and correct get-set position: Slice open two pieces of garden hose, and slip them over each handle, flush against the front bar. Cut the length so that when you feel your hand touching the edge of the hose, your hand is centered. Slip the lengths in position prior to when you parallel-grip deadlift.

Performance

Most of the performance guidelines in the *Basic or conventional deadlift* section apply to the parallel-grip deadlift, including the "Other tips." Please review that material before parallel-grip deadlifting.

Common errors

Left, hips are too high for the starting position, producing excessive forward lean, and loss of the correct back set. Right, following a correct start (not illustrated here) the hips have moved too fast, producing loss of back set, and rounding of the back. The errors illustrated in the previous section, for the conventional deadlift, also apply to the parallel-grip deadlift except for hip depth in the starting position. For the parallel-grip deadlift the hips can safely start at a lower position, provided the back is correctly set, and the range of motion is safe for the knees.

With the conventional deadlift, the problem of getting a straight bar around the knees is what produces the increased forward lean and reduced knee flexion compared with the parallel-grip deadlift. With the latter, you're inside the bar as against behind it with the straight-bar deadlift. This is what permits the reduced forward lean and increased knee flexion in the parallel-grip deadlift, and potentially makes it a safer exercise.

Here's the torso set you need to fight to maintain throughout the parallel-grip deadlift: While standing, take a big breath, keep a high chest, tense your upper-back muscles, and rotate your shoulders back into a military posture. This will tend to push your arms out away from your body, as your lats will be hard. Your lower back will be slightly hollowed, or concave.

Start the descent with a synchronized bending of your knees *and* forward lean of your torso. Sit down *and* back, and push your hips to the rear. Always maintain a slightly hollowed lower back, and keep your shoulder blades retracted.

Guide the bar, don't just lower it. With a straight-bar deadlift, the bar should brush your shins or thighs throughout the movement, but in the parallel-grip deadlift, here's the general guideline: Your hands should follow a line along the center of your femurs and, further down, along the center of the sides of your calves. When your hands are at knee height, they should also be in line with your knees. If your hands get behind that line, you risk being too upright. Your hands may, however, be a little forward of that line.

At the bottom of each rep, rather than pull on the bar, focus on trying to push your feet into the floor while maintaining the correct torso set.

The parallel-grip deadlift can increase thigh involvement further if it's done from a raised surface. The two critical provisos are that your lower back can be kept slightly hollow in this extended range of motion, and you have no knee limitations. To try a raised surface, start with no more than one inch. If, after a few weeks, all is well—correct technique maintained, with no knee or back problems—perhaps try a further half inch, and so on, up to a maximum of two to three inches.

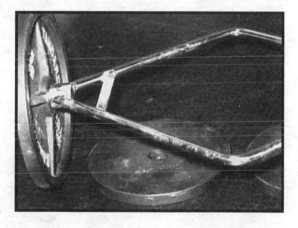

Two 15-kilo plates, smooth sides up, can be placed side-by-side under a parallel-grip bar, to produce a raised, stable surface from which to deadlift for increased quadriceps involvement provided that the correct back set is maintained, and the increased range of motion is safe for the trainee.

Use of dumbbells for the parallel-grip deadlift can work provided you have access to dumbbells heavy enough to provide adequate resistance. But if the dumbbells are touched to the floor or platform on each rep, there's a potential problem because of the small-diameter plates—increased range of motion relative to that with a trap bar or shrug bar with 45-pound or 20-kilo plates on it. Elevate the dumbbells on strong boxes or crates so that the range of motion isn't excessive for you. Never descend beyond the point where your lower back loses the required slightly hollowed position.

Performing the parallel-grip deadlift in an exaggeratedly upright manner, to further increase stress on the quadriceps, should be

This home-gym trainee is using plates of smaller diameter than the usual 20-kilo or 45-pound ones. Such plates lead to an exaggerated range of motion that's unsafe for many trainees. By using a pair of platforms—for example, as illustrated—the range of motion can be reduced as required.

avoided, because of the overly limited back involvement and increased knee stress, which may lead to knee problems. A natural spread of work between the thighs and back produces a balanced division of the stress.

Elevated handles

Some parallel-grip deadlift bars have raised handles, which reduce the range of deadlifting motion when compared with a bar with regular handles (like in the illustrations) and if both bars are loaded with the same diameter plates. The elevated handles may suit you if you can't safely use the full range of motion with 45-pound plates on a regular parallel-grip bar. If you can safely use the full range of motion, but only have access to a bar with raised handles, elevate yourself on a sturdy, non-slip surface the same height as the elevation of the handles, or use smaller-diameter plates.

Partial deadlift

Main muscles worked

spinal erectors, multifidii, buttocks, hamstrings, latissimus dorsi, upper back, forearms

Capsule description

with a slightly hollowed lower back, straight elbows, and slightly bent knees, lift a bar from knee height

The partial deadlift described here is a variation of what's commonly called a *stiff-legged deadlift*. Importantly, the variation is done with a *reduced* range of motion. Some people may call it a *Romanian deadlift*.

The partial deadlift is often used as a substitute for the conventional deadlift for trainees who have safety concerns for their backs because of the greater range of motion of the regular deadlift. Substantial back, buttock, hamstring, and grip involvement remain, but quadriceps involvement is minimized.

Performance

In a power rack find the pin setting that puts the bar at just below your kneecaps when your knees are slightly bent. That's the bottom position. Alternatively, set a loaded bar on boxes at the height so that the bar's starting position is the same as in the rack set-up.

Stand with your feet under the bar, heels about hip-width apart, and feet parallel with each other, or flared a little. Take a shoulder-width or slightly wider overhand grip. For just the first rep, bend your knees more than slightly, to help ensure correct back positioning. Hollow your lower back slightly and, with straight elbows, shrug against the bar and pull your shoulders back, and push your chest up and out. The bar won't move unless the weight is light, but the shrug will lock your lower back into the required, hollowed position. Now, while looking forward or upward, *simultaneously* pull with your back *and* straighten your knees, to move the bar.

During subsequent reps, bend your knees only slightly. Your knees should straighten as you complete the lift, and bend slightly once again during the descent. Keep your head up at all times, shoulder blades retracted, and chest pushed up and out. During the descent, push your hips rearward, to help keep your lower back in the correct hollowed position. The bar should brush your knees or thighs. Don't

lean back at the top. Stand straight, pause for a second, keep your scapulae retracted and lower back hollowed (without exaggeration), then lower the bar to the pins through bending your knees slightly and simultaneously leaning forward.

Don't rest the bar on the pins or boxes at the bottom position. Instead, pause for a second just above the pins. Maintain a locked, hollowed lower back, with your shoulders pulled back. Smoothly move into the next rep.

Exhale during the ascent, or at the top. Either inhale and make the descent, or inhale as you descend.

Lift and lower symmetrically, and don't turn your head. Furthermore, don't let your shoulders round. If your shoulders start to slump, and you can't pull them back, dump the bar instantly but with control.

The exercise can be done with a straight bar, or a parallel-grip bar such as a shrug bar. With a parallel-grip bar, it has to be done from boxes, because the bar isn't long enough for use inside a power rack unless the bar has elongated ends.

Even with chalk or rosin on your hands, and a well-knurled, straight bar, you may eventually be forced to use a reverse grip. If so, alternate which way around you have your hands from set to set.

A lower position for the bottom of the partial deadlift, illustrated outside of a power rack. This trainee—because of his flexibility, strength, and technique—can maintain the correct back set even at this degree of forward lean, and range of motion. But most trainees can't, and thus for safety should use a lesser range of motion like that shown on the previous page. Individual leverages—torso and limb lengths, and their relative proportions—affect performance in deadlift variations, and other exercises. Some trainees are better constucted to perform a given exercse than are other trainees.

It's not necessary to extend the head as much as is shown in this photo.

FULL-RANGE, stiff-legged deadlift—*DANGER*

The full-range, stiff-legged deadlift isn't included in **The Program** because it's too hazardous. Instead, less risky but effective exercises are employed for the hamstrings, buttocks, and back, which are the primary areas worked by the full-range, stiff-legged deadlift. The recommended exercises employed for these areas are the conventional deadlift, parallel-grip deadlift, partial deadlift, sumo deadlift, leg curl, and back extension. Of course, these exercises must be performed correctly if they are to be safe.

The further the torso leans forward, the more difficult it is to maintain the proper set position of the back, where the lower back is slightly hollowed. The full-range, stiff-legged deadlift takes the forward lean to an extreme, where the lower back rounds. This massively increases the stress on the various structures of the back, and greatly increases the risk of injury. Back rounding is important for working the spinal musculature, but it should take place in back extensions, *not* in any form of the deadlift, whether with bent knees or straight knees.

The stiff-legged deadlift to the floor, and the stiff-legged deadlift while standing on a box. The former is the most common form of the full-range, stiff-legged deadlift, but it's sometimes done on an elevated surface for an even greater range of motion. For safety, BOTH SHOULD BE AVOIDED. *Notice the back rounding, and severe loss of back set. But the partial, stiff-legged deadlift described on the previous pages is a safe, effective exercise if performed correctly.*

Sumo deadlift

Main muscles worked

spinal erectors, multifidii, buttocks, quadriceps, thigh adductors, hamstrings, latissimus dorsi, upper back, forearms

Capsule description

with knees well bent and positioned outside your hands, and a slightly hollowed lower back, lift the resistance from the floor

The sumo deadlift uses a straight bar, but because of the widened stance relative to that used in the regular deadlift, and the hands positioned *between* the legs, the back may be more upright in the sumo deadlift when comparing the two styles on the *same* trainee. There'll probably be more knee flexion to balance the more upright torso. Although the back is heavily involved in the sumo deadlift, the buttocks *and* thighs take relatively more stress.

The sumo and conventional deadlifts are similar in performance and pathway of the bar. It's the different stance that distinguishes the sumo deadlift. The grip used in the sumo deadlift may be a little closer.

Your knees may be less of an obstacle to get around in the sumo deadlift, which is why you'll probably bend forward to a lesser degree in the sumo deadlift than in the conventional style.

Sumo-style powerlifters may benefit from an extreme width of stance that has their feet almost touching the plates. This reduces the range of motion to the minimum. But for general training, an extreme stance isn't desirable. Use a moderately wide stance.

For example, if you're about 5-10 tall, use a stance with about 22 to 24 inches or 56 to 61 centimeters between your heels as the starting point, with your toes turned out at about 45 degrees. Fine-tune from there. Try the same flare but a slightly wider stance. Then try a little less flare but the same stance. Keep fine-tuning until you find what helps your technique the most. After a few weeks of experience you may want to fine-tune your stance further.

Find the foot positioning relative to the bar that, when your knees are bent at the bottom position, has the bar touching your shins. But when you're standing erect prior to descending to take the bar for the first rep, your shins may be a little away from the bar.

For the first descent, follow the same format as given for the conventional deadlift. Descend until your hands touch the bar, then take your grip. Don't grip the bar so closely that your hands are on

Bottom and midpoint of the sumo deadlift (left), and bottom and top position of the sumo deadlift (right). The former shows a wider stance than the latter.

the smooth part of the bar. Use a hip-width grip as a starting point, with your hands on the knurling, and fine-tune from there. If your grip is too close, you'll find it difficult to control the bar's balance.

For the drive from the floor, ascent, lockout, descent, and breathing, follow the same guidelines as in the conventional deadlift.

Don't immediately introduce intensive, wide-stance deadlifting, because that would be a road to injury. Take several weeks to progressively work into the wide stance, using a weight that doesn't tax you. Stretching for your thigh adductors, hamstrings, and buttocks may be needed, to give you the flexibility to adopt your optimum stance. Once you've mastered the technique, *then* progressively add resistance.

8. FINGER EXTENSION

Main muscles worked

finger extensors

Capsule description

against resistance, open all the digits of the hand

The finger extension is an important exercise. It strengthens the muscles that extend the fingers, whereas exercises that involve the grip work the muscles that flex the fingers. A strength imbalance between these opposing muscles can cause elbow problems.

Manual resistance

Put the digits of your right hand together. Put the tips of the fingers (and thumb) of your left hand on the outside ends of the corresponding digits of the other hand. Open your right hand against resistance provided by your left hand. Allow the finger joints to bend sufficiently to produce a full range of movement.

Once you're working the exercise hard, following a period of gradual adaptation, perform a warm-up set for each hand with minimal resistance. Then perform the work sets with enough resistance to make each rep taxing. Apply resistance against the fingers as they open *and* close—positive phase and negative phase, respectively. Provide more resistance during the negative phase. Perform each rep smoothly, over a full range of motion.

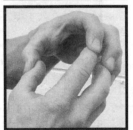

Another method, while seated, is to place the tips of your right hand together, and put your hand between your lower thighs, with your wrist turned so that your right thumb is against your right inner thigh. Keep all your digits straight, and spread the load evenly over all of them. Find the precise positioning of your hand that permits this. Perform each rep smoothly, over a full range of motion, with enough resistance from your thighs to make each rep taxing on the positive and negative phases.

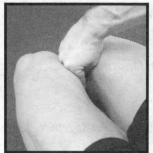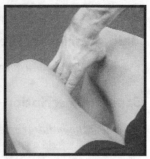

Thigh-assisted, manual finger extension. Try with feet together, and feet hip-width apart. The latter may enable you to apply resistance with greater control.

The manual finger extension doesn't permit measurable resistance. Over time, however, gradually increase the manual resistance.

Band resistance

For measurable resistance, get some elastic bands that are about three inches or eight centimeters long when not stretched. Take just one of them, to learn the exercise. Put all five digits of your right hand inside the elastic band so that the band rests approximately on the joints nearest your finger nails. Smoothly stretch out your fingers as far as you can without the elastic band slipping down. Find the degree of curvature in your fingers needed to keep the elastic band in place throughout the exercise.

Find elastic bands of various strengths so that you can add gradual resistance. Regularly replace the bands because, with use, they lose strength and elasticity.

To help keep the bands in position, twist them around your middle finger before putting your other digits inside the bands. This will increase the tension on the bands and reduce the number of them you can use, unless you switch to longer bands.

The Metolius "GripSaver Plus" is a ready-made device for finger extension, designed specifically for rehab or prevention of climbing-related finger, wrist, and elbow injuries. It's an alternative to elastic bands, although it doesn't provide variable resistance.

www.metoliusclimbing.com

9. HAND-GRIPPER WORK

Main muscles worked

finger flexion muscles, forearms

Capsule description

crush the hand gripper's handles together

Hand-gripper work is an optional element of **The Program**, as from the eighth month. Grip work is already in **The Program**—especially from the deadlift, shrug, and timed hold—but gripper training will further strengthen your grip, and hands, and perhaps build forearm musculature, too. And many trainees find gripper training especially enjoyable. It can be done at home, with your own grippers.

Grippers are inexpensive—see *Resources*. The ones with knurled, metal handles—torsion-spring grippers—start at under 100 pounds closing strength, and go up to over 300 pounds. The ability to close a gripper of 200 pounds rating is rare. The ability to close a gripper of 300 pounds is phenomenal. Ideally, initially get a gripper under 100 pounds, and two or three with the smallest increments in resistance thereafter. You may need to use more than one manufacturer, to obtain a gradual progression in resistance.

Although different manufacturers produce torsion-spring grippers that are claimed to have the same closing strengths, the actual strength ratings may be different, because of variations in construction, and the springs. And the same manufacturer's grippers may vary in strength from batch to batch. For example, a gripper with a rating of 140 pounds may be more like 150 pounds, for example, whereas another with a 140-pound rating may be more like 130 pounds.

Get grippers that have handles spaced no more than ten centimeters or four inches between the bottom, outside edges. Some grippers are significantly wider than this, which makes them difficult to handle, especially if you have small hands.

You may need to start with a gripper that has plastic grips, which sporting goods stores sell. This has a rating of no more than about 50 pounds. When you can do at least 20 full closes with it, with a pause on each crush, move to the lowest-strength torsion-spring gripper.

With the Ivanko super gripper, however, just one is required to produce resistances from about 50 pounds closing strength, to over 300, and the resistance can be adjusted in small, gradual increments.

Torsion-spring gripper

Look at the
spring or wire of
a torsion-spring
gripper. There
are two sides,
where each goes
into a handle.
One side of
the spring
is perfectly
curved. The
other side has a
slight ridge in

The dogleg is shown on the right side of the left torsion-spring gripper. For the right photograph, another gripper has been turned over to show the non-dogleg side on the right.

it—this is the "dogleg." Always put the dogleg side into the thumb
side of your hand, for consistency. The gripper may also be a little
less difficult to close that way around.

With the gripper in your right palm, dogleg side nearest your
thumb, thrust your thumb forward and position the dogleg handle
at or just in front of the fold in your palm that marks the start of
your thumb mound. Then set the gripper by using your left index
finger and thumb to pinch the handles of the gripper just sufficiently
so that you can wrap the finger tips of your right three longer
fingers around the handle, with your right little finger lined up to
be about half off the bottom edge of the handle. This set-up position
maximizes leverage. Remove your left hand from the gripper, and
put your right little finger in position. Keep all four parallel fingers
touching one another—don't spread them. The little finger isn't long
enough to go around the handle in the starting position, but will
move around during the crush, and contribute then.

How much you need to pinch the handles to get into the starting
position depends on the spacing of the handles, and your hand size.
Avoid excessively spaced handles.

Using a gripper you can close fully, experiment to find your strongest
starting position. A small change in where the gripper rests in your
palm, and in how your fingers are placed on the handle, can make a
significant difference in your ability to close the gripper.

Once properly set in the starting position, crush the handles together.
As you crush, thrust your thumb forward, to increase its involvement.
Hold the crushed position for a second or two, then return to the
starting position.

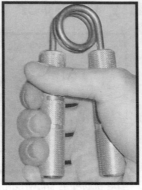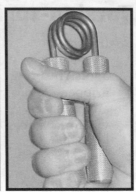

When back in the starting position, pause for a moment without losing the correct set—this means not opening the gripper fully, because that would take you beyond the correct starting position—and then perform the next rep. Complete the set, and change hands. If you're doing singles, perform just one rep, then change hands. Take a brief rest, perform another single for each hand, and so on.

If you can shut the gripper fully, you'll hear the handles click together. During the brief pause at full closure, grind the handles together.

You may not be able to close the gripper fully, depending on its strength relative to yours. If you can't shut the gripper, briefly hold the maximum degree of closure, then let the gripper open to the starting position. Work on increasing the degree of closure, as the weeks and months go by.

Negative reps can be helpful in gripper training, especially using a gripper that you can't close without assistance. Push the handles together with the assistance of your other hand (and your torso), or push the gripper against your thigh as you squeeze. With the gripper shut, or as near shut as you can manage, try to crush it as the gripper opens. Don't merely try to slow the gripper's opening. Month to month, increase the duration of the negatives, and the degree of closure if you can't fully close it now, even with assistance.

During all forms of gripper work, breathe freely. *Don't hold your breath.*

Take it easy for the first few weeks, to condition your hands to the rigors of gripper work. If you try to rush your progress, you'll risk injury to your finger muscles and joints, and damage to your skin.

If your hands slip on the handles, use chalk or rosin. If the knurling is overly sharp and cuts into your skin, wrap some tape around the handles, or use some emery cloth to take the edge off the knurling. Periodically, use a wire brush to clean the knurling.

Ivanko super gripper

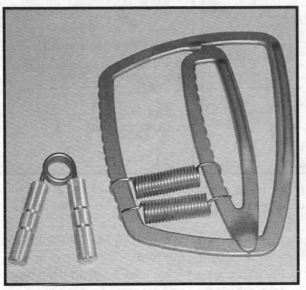

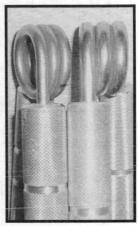

Comparison of a torsion-spring hand gripper, and the Ivanko super gripper. The springs on the Ivanko unit are set in the slots of least resistance for two springs: 1 and 3—the springs can't fit in adjacent slots.

Comparison of the springs of 70-pound and 300-pound strength torsion-spring grippers.

The Ivanko super gripper has twelve slots for positioning two springs. This yields over 100 different possible resistance settings, to cater for all levels of gripping strength, and to permit progress in small increments.

Furthermore, it has a large handle that permits you to use two hands to position the gripper while setting up for negative reps, and for sustained, single holds.

The large handle is also helpful for fine-tuning resistance. The lower your hand is on the handle—the closer your hand is to the pivot point—the harder it is to close the gripper. If, for example, you can close the gripper at one setting with your hand at the outermost position on the handle, but are unable to close it at the next setting, you can stay at the lower setting for a while longer but increase its resistance a little (but not as much as it would be at the next setting) by using a lower hand position on the handle. Build your strength a bit further at the lower setting, and then move to the next setting but with your hand in the outermost position.

You may experience slippage on the Ivanko handle, because it has a smooth finish. Slippage can be prevented by wrapping some tape with high friction around the handle.

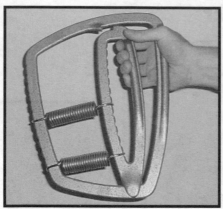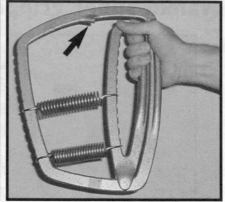

Note the protrusion on the inside, upper rim of the Ivanko super gripper, which prevents the handle opening excessively and the springs losing their tension.

Position the outer part of the unit at or just in front of the fold in your palm that marks the start of your thumb mound. Wrap the tips of your fingers around the moving part. You may need to use your disengaged hand to help get set for the first rep of a set. Smoothly close the handle until the moving unit strikes the fixed outermost structure, hold the contact for a moment, and then smoothly release. Breathe freely. Don't hold your breath.

When back in the starting position, pause without losing the correct set—this means not opening the gripper fully, because that would take you beyond the correct starting position—and then perform the next rep. If you're doing singles, perform one rep, then change hands.

Release the handle gradually and smoothly after each close—for the best training effect, and to maintain the set-up of the springs. If the release is fast, the moving unit may miss the stop protrusion on the gripper that limits the range of motion. If that happens, the springs will loosen and slip out of position, and need to be re-positioned.

Take it easy for the first few weeks, to condition your hands to the rigors of gripper work. If you try to rush your progress, you'll risk injury to your finger muscles and joints. The Ivanko unit isn't knurled, so it doesn't cause the skin friction that the torsion-spring grippers do.

Between training sessions, keep tension off the springs by slipping the moveable part off the stop protrusion. If the gripper is stored under tension, the springs will slacken with time.

For all hand-gripper work, keep your elbow flexed. This reduces the strain in and around the elbow compared to doing the grip work with a fully extended elbow.

Here are 40 of the possible settings of the Ivanko super gripper, arranged in order of the force required to close the gripper at those settings. Use this so that you can increase resistance in small, gradual increments. These settings and poundages are given by S. Stamp, at www.ivanko.com/products/html_stuff/gripper_info.html

The exact poundages at these settings may vary across different batches of the super gripper, and according to the condition of the springs, but the sequence will still produce the required gradual progression.

The first two numbers show the slots that the springs are positioned in to produce the resistance shown in the third number. For example, 3-1-45 means that when the springs are positioned in the third and first pairs of slots, about 45 pounds of force is required to close the handle.

3	1	45 pounds	9	5	182 pounds
4	1	56 pounds	11	1	185 pounds
4	2	64 pounds	4	10	191 pounds
5	1	70 pounds	9	6	197 pounds
5	2	77 pounds	3	11	203 pounds
6	1	85 pounds	12	1	211 pounds
6	2	92 pounds	9	7	214 pounds
7	1	101 pounds	2	12	219 pounds
7	2	109 pounds	5	11	228 pounds
6	4	113 pounds	7	10	235 pounds
8	1	120 pounds	6	11	242 pounds
8	2	128 pounds	5	12	253 pounds
8	3	137 pounds	7	11	259 pounds
9	1	140 pounds	6	12	268 pounds
7	5	143 pounds	8	11	278 pounds
8	4	149 pounds	7	12	285 pounds
9	3	157 pounds	9	11	298 pounds
1	10	162 pounds	8	12	303 pounds
9	4	169 pounds	9	12	323 pounds
8	6	177 pounds	12	10	345 pounds

Keep accurate records of the spring settings you use.

It may take months of consistent training to progress from one entry-level, torsion-spring gripper to the next, provided there's a gradual progression of resistance across the grippers. If the jump between grippers is large, it may take over a year, or forever, to progress from one gripper to the next. With a single, inexpensive Ivanko super gripper you can progress in small increments, from little resistance, to a great deal.

IO. LATERAL RAISE

Main muscles worked

deltoids, especially the medial or side head, trapezius

Capsule description

with a vertical torso, lift the resistance to your sides until your elbows are just above your shoulders

The lateral raise is a valuable exercise because, in addition to working the deltoids and trapezius, it works a number of small muscles around the shoulders that are involved in abduction of the humerus. Strengthening these muscles helps to keep the shoulders healthy.

Dumbbell lateral raise

Stand with your feet about hip-width apart, a dumbbell in each hand at the side of your thighs, palms facing your thighs. With your scapulae pulled back, head up, and elbows slightly bent for comfort, raise your hands to about chin height. Pause, then lower the dumbbells under control. Keep your palms facing the floor in a neutral position—don't turn your wrists so that your thumbs move forward or rearward. Furthermore, keep your wrists neutral—don't flex or extend them.

Take about three seconds for the ascent, pause for a second at the top, take a further three seconds to lower the dumbbells, pause for another second, then move into the next rep. Keep your torso and head upright at all times—don't lean forward or rearward. Don't crane your head, or move it to the rear or one side— keep your head in a neutral position. Keep your weight evenly distributed over your feet. Furthermore, don't let the dumbbells drift forward. Exhale on the ascent, inhale on the descent.

The lateral raise may be performed one side at a time. Brace your non-working hand on a stable object, and keep your torso upright. Reverse the set-up to work the other side.

There are three variations that aren't illustrated. The

lateral raise may be performed seated—for example, on the end of a bench, with feet on the floor. It may also be done while sitting against an incline bench set at about 75 degrees, facing *into* the bench.

Although not illustrated, the lateral raise may be done one arm at a time while lying *sideways* against an incline bench set no higher than at about 45 degrees. Raise your arm to just above head height. This variation heavily stresses the deltoids at the bottom of the exercise, whereas the other lateral raises heavily stress the deltoids at the top.

Machine lateral raise

Follow the manufacturer's guidelines for the set-up. This may mean setting the height of the seat so that your shoulders line up with the pivot points. The correct set-up position is important, for joint care and the desired effect on the deltoids.

Perform the exercise with a controlled movement—about three seconds for the ascent, pause for a second at the top, another three seconds for the descent, a further pause for a second at the bottom, and so on. Keep your torso upright, shoulders retracted, chest out, and head in a neutral position. And apply the force through the pads alongside your elbows, not through the handles. Applying force through your hands may cause shoulder irritation. Grip the handles *lightly*.

II. LEG CURL

Main muscles worked

hamstrings, lower back

Capsule description

with resistance against your heels, lift your heels toward your hips

The leg curl provides direct exercise for the hamstrings—the three muscles of the rear thighs. This is important for developing healthy, balanced musculature around the knees and hips. There are also aesthetic benefits—a curve to the rear thigh, which in turn helps offset the protrusion of the buttocks.

Set-up

Lie face-down on a leg curl bench. The bench shouldn't be flat, but have a hump where your hips are placed. Place your heels beneath the resistance pad. It's essential that you line your knees up correctly— center of your knees in line with the center of the pivot point of the machine. The correct set-up will have your kneecaps positioned *just* over the edge of the bench—not on the bench itself.

Where the resistance pads are positioned is adjustable on some machines. If you use an adjustable machine, set the resistance pads so that they are flush with your ankles when your knees are straight and in the correct position.

If you use a machine with a range-of-motion limitation control, set it at the fullest safe setting for you. You would need to experiment, with minimal resistance, to find what this range of motion is for you. If there's no range-of-motion control, do it yourself—don't lower your heels all the way down to the position of straight knees if that's excessive for your knees. Instead, maintain a slight degree of flexion even at the bottom (starting) position—an inch or two short of your knees being straight.

If you use a selectorized leg curl machine you may be able to delimit the range of motion manually. Remove the pin from the weight stack, then grip the cable that's attached to the guide rod that runs through the weight stack, and lift it. The top weight plate will rise alone, revealing the guide rod. Expose two holes on the rod, for example, then use the pin to select the required weight. The gap between the

first and second
weight plates
indicates the
reduction in range of
motion. Fine-tune the
extent of the reduction
according to what's
required to produce
the maximum safe
range of motion for
you. Make a note in
your training log of
the setting.

How to manually delimit the range of motion using a selectorized weight stack. See text.

The procedure for delimiting the range of motion in the leg curl can
be used for other selectorized machines, when excessive stretching
needs to be avoided, such as the machine pullover.

Performance

Grasp the handles or other gripping sites in a symmetrical manner,
and hold them lightly—just sufficiently to stabilize yourself. Don't
involve your upper body in the leg curl. Keep your hips firmly

against the bench, and lift your head and shoulders slightly off the bench. Face forward or to the floor—don't turn your head to the side. Pull your toes toward your shins—opposite of pointing your toes—and keep them in that position throughout the set.

Slowly and smoothly lift your heels as far toward your hips as is comfortable. Hold the position of fullest contraction for a second, then smoothly lower your heels to the starting position. Pause for a second, then repeat. There must be no sudden or jerky movements. Move smoothly up, and smoothly down, about three seconds for each phase, plus a second for the pause at the top, and another second for the pause at the starting position. Exhale on the ascent, inhale on the descent.

During the ascent of your feet, your hips should come off the bench slightly, to permit full contraction of the hamstrings. Your hips should rise no more than one inch. Any more than that will overstress your lower back through excessive extension of your spine, which can cause injury. Excessive lifting of the hips also reduces the work done by your hamstrings.

The start of the rep must be done with great care—ease into it, don't heave the weight. After the final rep, when lowering the weight to its resting place, place it gently.

Options for leg curl machines

Some manufacturers produce leg curl machines for seated or standing work, one leg at a time in some cases. Some provide work for both limbs simultaneously, but each thigh may have independent resistance so each would perform its full share of the work.

The standing leg curl is a unilateral movement that usually leads to technique flaws, including a torso twist, and uneven stresses on the spine and torso from the asymmetrical loading.

If there's more than one leg curl machine where you train, find the one that feels best for you. For trainees with back problems, the prone and standing leg curls may irritate the back even when done with correct technique. Try the seated version instead. Generally, the seated leg curl is the pick of the machines—for comfort, maintenance of correct technique, and isolation of

Chapters 10 and 11 cover many essential general components of safe exercising, which should be applied together with the guidance of this chapter.

Seated leg curl.

the hamstrings. During the seated leg curl, however, never press down on your thighs—there should be no exaggerated compression of your hamstrings.

Adding weight

Selectorized cable units, and selectorized machines in general, commonly have weight increments of 10 pounds or 5 kilos, and larger in some cases. This is too much weight to progress by in a single jump. Where you train may have special weights of 5 pounds or 2.5 kilos—and perhaps smaller ones, too—designed to fit on the top of a weight stack. If it doesn't, you may be able to get your own from an exercise equipment store. Use them to help you to work from one pin setting to the next.

Alternatively, place the weight selection pin through a small barbell weight plate before the pin goes into the weight stack. Although a pin that holds a plate won't go fully into the weight stack, it should go through enough to hold the plate securely and select the resistance, too.

Magnetic small plates are another option for adding small increments of weight to a stack.

Whichever option you choose, check that the set-up is secure before you perform a set.

Origin of "hamstrings"

The three thigh muscles of the posterior or rear thigh are usually referred to as the "hamstring" group. This is because tendons of those muscles are used by butchers to attach curing hams to meat hooks.

12. LEG PRESS

Main muscles worked

quadriceps, buttocks, thigh adductors, hamstrings

Capsule description

with your feet against the foot plate, bend and straighten your knees

The leg press can be done seated or lying, depending on the model of machine. Some leg presses, especially the models where the resistance is pushed vertically, are dangerous for many trainees.

For most trainees, the leg press of choice will be of the leverage style—for example, the models produced by Hammer Strength, and the Nautilus XP LOAD Leg Press. If such a machine isn't available, use a 45-degree leg press, which can be found in most well-equipped gyms. The 45-degree leg presses vary according to their design and adjustability. Ideally, they should be adjustable in small increments for knee flexion, and inclination of the back support.

Some leg presses have the foot plate near or at the bottom position when not in use, while other leg presses have the foot plate near or at the top position when not in use.

The involvement of the thigh adductors can be substantial in the leg press. Careful stretching of the adductors—*Stretch 2* (see Chapter 2)—is recommended prior to leg pressing.

Set-up and positioning

Center yourself, side to side, on the seat or bench. Place your feet on the middle or, better yet, on the higher part of the foot plate. The lower your feet, the greater the knee stress. Some leg presses have insufficiently sized foot plates. Depending on the model, you may need to position your toes off the top edge of the foot plate, to produce a safe set-up for your knees. But the balls of your feet, and your heels, must be in full contact with the foot plate throughout each set.

A small change of foot spacing or flare can improve knee comfort. Without any plates on the leg press, try a hip-width heel placement, with the inside edges of your feet parallel with each other. Then try turning your toes out a little. Next, try a bit more flare. Then try different heel positioning in the different positions of toe flare. Find the heel spacing and angle of flare that feel the most comfortable for

A type of leverage leg press.

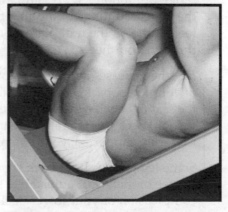

The 45-degree leg press. Above, a good set-up of the feet. Above right, wrong set-up, feet too low and too close, which produces exaggerated stress on the knees. Right, excessive range of motion, resulting in the lower back coming off the back support. The lower back must be supported.

you. The foot positioning must help to keep your knees pointing in the same direction as your toes. Don't let your knees buckle in.

Some leg press machines have foot plates that can be adjusted to find the best angle of fit for the user, but most have a fixed position. If you use an adjustable machine, set the angle of the foot plate so that you can push mostly through your heels throughout each rep. If you don't push mostly through your heels, knee problems may result.

Avoid excessive forward travel of your knees, to minimize stress on those joints. To begin with, keep your knees behind the line of your toes. To judge the position of your knees, view them from the bottom position of a leg press rep. If your knees are ahead of the line of your toes, reduce the forward travel of your knees—move your feet up on the footplate (if there's room), or reduce the depth of motion.

Some leg presses don't have adjustable seat positioning to set the depth of motion, but have an adjustable, delimiting arrangement instead. If the machine isn't adjustable for depth of motion by a built-in means, use some marker of your own to indicate when the carriage is at your safe maximum depth. Place a restraint block in the appropriate place.

If, after two months of building up the resistance there's no negative reaction in your knees, lower back, hips, or anywhere else, finish off each leg press session with one set of a greater range of motion, with a much reduced weight. For that set, increase the depth of motion by about two inches. This will mean that there's more knee flexion, and probably more forward travel of your knees. This may be safe for you, and beneficial.

Provided there's no negative reaction to the increased range of motion, build up the resistance gradually over at least two months until you're using the same weight in the increased range of motion as you were in the lesser range. During that process, drop the lesser-range-of-motion leg pressing. If there's still no negative reaction to the increased range of motion, try a further increase by lowering your feet a little on the foot plate *provided* you can still push mostly through your heels.

But, the increases in range of motion may be limited by the positioning of your lower back. Your lower back must always be fully supported by the seat or bench—there must be no rounding of your lower spine, even if your knees will tolerate a greater range of motion. If your lower back isn't fully supported, your risk of injury will increase greatly.

Some leg presses have back supports that can be adjusted for their degree of incline. If adjustable, select a setting that minimizes compression of your lower back. Try all the settings, with minimal resistance, to discover which setting appears to suit you best. As you progress in the leg press, if you experience discomfort because of compression of your lower back, experiment with a different inclination of back support—perhaps more upright than less upright.

Performance

Keep your head stationary, in a neutral position, and fixed against the head support if one is built into the machine, and it's comfortable to rest against. Hold the machine's hand grips. If there aren't any hand grips, hold rigid parts of the machine clear of the moving carriage.

With your feet flat on the foot plate, correctly positioned for you, push mostly through your heels. Unless the footplate is already at the top position, smoothly and slowly extend your legs to get into the top position ready for the first rep. Never slam into the locked out position. Brake before your knees lock out, and stop the movement half an inch short of the point where your knees are straight. Pause for a second, then start the descent.

For leg presses that start from or just below the top position, carefully lock out your knees and then release the machine's top stops, so that you can perform the descent without obstruction, down to the bottom stops that have been pre-set to suit you. (At the end of a set, with your knees locked out, put the top stops back in position, and gently set the carriage down.)

Lower under control—take about three seconds to make the descent. As you reach the maximum safe depth for you, stay tight, pause for a second, and press out of it. Don't bounce. Do the turnaround slowly and smoothly, without relaxing. And take about three seconds for the extension of your legs—the positive phase of the rep.

Apply force symmetrically, with your legs working in unison. Distribute the stress of the exercise symmetrically over your thighs, hips, and back.

Inhale at the top of each rep, or during the descent, and exhale during the ascent. *Don't hold your breath.*

Other tip

Don't work your lower back intensively immediately before you leg press, because that would reduce your lower back's potential as a stabilizer.

Unilateral leg press

A few leg presses, such as one of the models produced by Hammer Strength, have independent foot plates, one for each foot. These *isolateral* or *unilateral* machines can be used one limb at a time, as against the usual *bilateral* machines that have a single foot plate for *both* feet. A unilateral leg press also gives you the option of working both limbs bilaterally, although each will have its own resistance to deal with. It may, for example, be especially valuable if you have one limb shorter than the other.

If you exercise one limb at a time, keep your non-working limb extended and braced, while your other one completes a set. But a unilateral leg press machine applies asymmetrical and rotational stress to your lower back, because both limbs don't push at the same time *unless the machine is used bilaterally.* Asymmetrical stress in the leg press is best avoided, because it increases the risk of injury.

Hammer Strength Iso-Lateral Leg Press, used unilaterally. This is risky. Instead, train both legs simultaneously.

Because the unilateral leg press can be used bilaterally, be conservative and use it in bilateral mode only.

The leg press produces compression of the lower back. If you start with minimal weight, use correct technique, smooth rep speed, and build up resistance gradually, your body should adapt to the compression, be strengthened by it, and may suffer no negative consequences. Some trainees, however, will be unable to leg press safely because of the compression.

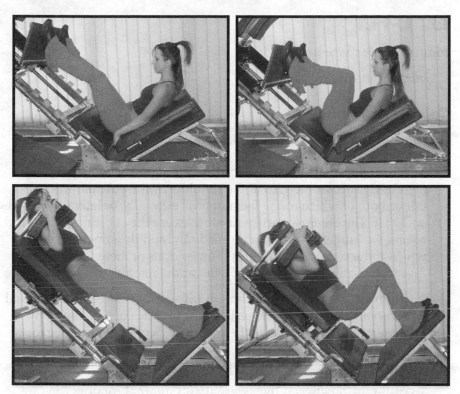

Some leg press machines have constructional problems. The foot plate of the one illustrated in the top photographs, for example, isn't big enough, which precludes correct foot positioning, especially for larger trainees. And the hand supports aren't positioned well. Because the model shown here is diminutive, the shortcomings of this machine aren't as pronounced as they would be for a large trainee.

This leg press doubles as a hack squat machine—see above photographs. Modern hack squat machines are more like reverse leg presses than machine versions of the barbell hack squat. The latter is an awkward exercise. Machine designers have tried to improve the hack squat.

The variety of hack squat machines is considerable, and the quality varies across the brands. There's a variety of leg press machines, too, but the extent of variation isn't so extensive, and most public gyms have a decent leg press. Therefore, the leg press is used in **The Program**.

Hack squat machines aren't recommended in this book because of the extent of their variation. If used properly—correct foot positioning (like in the barbell squat), concave lower spine, safe range of motion, controlled rep speed, and gradual building up of resistance—some of these machines are good. But some of them are constructed in such a way that they will harm most users if used regularly.

13. L-FLY

Main muscles worked

infraspinatus, teres minor

Capsule description

with a bent, fixed elbow, move its hand outward against resistance

This is an important exercise because it strengthens two commonly neglected articular muscles of the shoulder: infraspinatus, and teres minor, both of which rotate the humerus *externally*, or laterally, and also adduct it. The other two articular muscles are the subscapularis, which rotates the humerus *internally*, or medially; and the supraspinatus, which abducts the humerus only. The tendons of these four muscles fuse with tissues of the shoulder joint, at the rotator cuff.

The L-fly acts to reduce the strength imbalance between the external (weaker) and internal (stronger) rotator muscles of the shoulder. The internal rotators include the powerful pecs and lats. An excessive strength imbalance between the opposing external and internal rotators is a major contributing factor to shoulder problems.

To distinguish between the external and internal rotators of your humerus, imagine you're shaking someone's hand with your right hand. Keep your right elbow bent at a right angle, and your elbow fixed at your side. Moving your right hand to the right is *external* rotation, while moving your right hand to the left is *internal* rotation.

The L-fly has a small weight potential. A male novice may need a year or more to build up to using just ten pounds, and a female novice may need a year or more to build up to using just four or five pounds.

The use of small discs is critical, to ensure that progressive resistance is applied *gradually*.

Performance

Lie on your left side on a bench, and place your left hand on the floor, for stability. With a small plate or very light dumbbell in your right hand, form a 90-degree angle at your elbow—the L shape. Put your right elbow on your right oblique muscles, or hip, depending on your body structure. A folded towel placed in the hollow between your hip and rib cage may help you to maintain the correct elbow positioning. Lower the weight until your right forearm rests against your abs, then raise your right forearm as far as possible. Keep your right elbow fixed

Lying L-fly. Lift your forearm as near to vertical as possible.

against your side throughout the set. Inhale on the descent, and exhale on the ascent. Finish the set, turn around, then work your left side.

Do the exercise slowly—three seconds for the lifting phase, a pause for a second at the top, a further three seconds for the lowering phase, a pause for a second at the bottom, then smoothly move into the next ascent.

Never train the L-fly to failure, never raise your elbow, and never roll backward even a little.

Variations

The L-fly can be performed while standing, using a cable or band that runs horizontally to the floor at about waist height. Stand sideways to the cable, right foot nearest the cable, your feet about hip-width apart, a single cable handle in your left hand, left elbow near your left side and bent at a right angle, and left forearm across your abdomen. Rest your right hand on your right hip or thigh. That's the starting position. Slowly and smoothly move your left hand outward. Keep your left humerus vertical, left elbow near your left side, and left forearm parallel with the floor. Pause for a second at the point of fullest rotation, and smoothly and slowly return to the starting position. Pause for a second, then repeat.

Alternatively, use the cable from a floor pulley. Kneel on your heels on the floor, sideways to the pulley, and the midpoint of your thighs in line with the pulley. Space your knees for stability, keep your torso vertical, and perform the L-fly as described for the standing cable version. You may, however, need to keep the elbow of your working arm a little further away from your body, for better alignment with

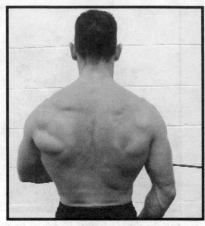

Cable L-fly, standing.

the direction of the cable, because the cable may not be horizontal to the floor, depending on the apparatus, and your size. Set your elbow position for the cable pathway that feels the most comfortable, and keep it fixed there throughout the set.

Take special care with any variation of the cable or pulley L-fly. The muscular tension arising from these forms of the L-fly is such that when your muscles tire, near the end of a set, it's especially easy to lose the groove of a rep, and get injured. The dumbbell lying L-fly can be controlled better, and is safer.

Furthermore, depending on the minimum resistance of the cable or pulley arrangement, you may first need to build sufficient strength by using the lying L-fly, which can start from a tiny plate or other item. And incremental resistance isn't possible with the type of cables that come in bands—to progress from one band to two, for example, is a huge jump. Incremental resistance *can* be applied to the lying L-fly, and the pulley L-fly.

Pulley L-fly, kneeling. If, when the pulley is lined up with the midpoint of your thighs, the resistance is too great at the minimum setting, you may be able to reduce it if you sit further back, depending on the design of the apparatus. If so, then as your strength increases, gradually move forward until the midpoint of your thighs is lined up with the pulley. Then increase the resistance with a tiny increment.

The L-fly acts to reduce the strength imbalance between the external (weaker) and internal (stronger) rotator muscles of the shoulders. An excessive strength imbalance between these opposing muscles is a major contributing factor to shoulder problems.

14. NECK WORK

Main muscles worked

sternocleidomastoid, upper trapezius
deeper muscles, over and between the cervical vertebrae, are also involved

Capsule description

seated or lying, move your head against resistance

The neck may be the most responsive bodypart, probably because it receives so little exercise during the course of regular living. Neck work must, however, be done with special care, because the neck is easily injured. As well as improving your physique, neck work—when done correctly—will increase your resistance to neck injuries from training, accidents, and during sleep.

There are six functions of the neck: extension (to the rear), forward flexion, flexion to the right, flexion to the left, rotation to the right, and rotation to the left. The entire musculature of the neck is worked through extension and forward flexion alone—the upper trapezius through extension, and the sternocleidomastoid through forward flexion. These two movements are also perhaps the simplest neck exercises, and the only ones recommended in this book. Lateral flexion, and rotation, may also carry a greater risk of injury than extension, and forward flexion.

Neck caution

In all neck work—non-machine, and machine—the speed of movement must be smooth and slow at all times, including the turnaround points of each rep. Keep the rep speed no faster than four seconds for each phase, plus a pause for a second at the position of fullest contraction, and another second in the starting position, for at least ten seconds total per rep.

Manual resistance neck work

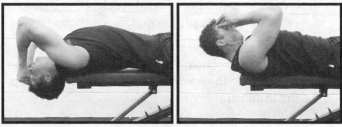

For forward flexion, lie on your back on a bench, with your head and neck off the end. Don't extend your head in an exaggerated way. Extend only to a degree that feels comfortable. Place your fingers on your forehead and gently push down for resistance. Slowly raise and lower your head, and apply manual resistance during both phases of each rep.

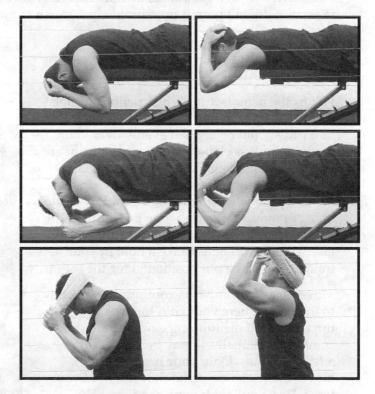

For extension against resistance, turn around, face down, and place your hands on the rear of your head. Alternatively, apply resistance using a small towel held between your hands and across the rear of your head. Slowly raise and lower your head, and apply manual resistance during both phases of each rep. The extension can also be done seated.

Before doing the work sets of extension, or flexion, perform a warm-up set without any manual resistance. For the work sets, after an introductory period of several weeks of progressive adaptation from a very easy start, apply enough resistance to make each rep taxing.

Don't use an exaggerated range of motion, a*lways* use a *slow* rep speed, and *never* use jerky movements. Do each rep *smoothly,* and use resistance that permits moderate to high reps—consider 10 reps as the minimum.

Four-way neck machine

A four-way neck machine is the first choice for neck work. Used correctly, it provides comfortable, controlled, direct, full-range, and safe exercise with measurable, incremental resistance. Manual resistance doesn't permit measurable, progressive resistance.

Forward flexion

Follow the manufacturer's instructions for the correct set-up position. The force against the face pad should be applied evenly over your forehead and cheek bones, and perhaps upper jaw, too, but not your lower jaw. And there should be no pressure on your eyes. Grip the handles just sufficiently to hold position. Using little or no resistance, fine-tune the set-up until you find what works best for you—this may take several workouts. Make a note in your training log of the pin position(s) for the set-up.

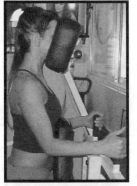

Move as far forward as is comfortable—ideally to the point where your chin touches your upper chest. If the full range of motion isn't comfortable initially, it may become so after a few workouts. Only your head and neck move—there should be no movement of your torso. Don't pull with your hands to help complete the neck flexion. Hold the position of full forward flexion for a second.

On the return to the starting position, never go beyond the vertical-neck, starting position; and *ease* into the starting position. A loss of control, and thrusting into the starting position, will jar your neck and may lead to a whiplash-like effect, and injury.

Following completion of the final rep, exit the machine with control so that you avoid jolting—don't suddenly unload your neck.

Extension

Follow the manufacturer's instructions for the correct set-up position. You'll probably need a seat position two to four inches *lower* for neck extension than what you use for forward flexion. Keep your back against the bench, and start each rep from where your chin touches your chest (ideally), or from where it's near your chest, according to comfort. If you have to lean forward, or slouch, to adopt the correct starting position, you have the seat positioned too high. Keep your chest high, not sunken or deflated—don't slump—to avoid excessive forward range of motion. Position the head pad so that it doesn't move during the exercise. If the full range of motion isn't comfortable initially, it may become so after

a few workouts. Grip the handles just sufficiently to hold position. Place your feet out in front, with your knees only slightly bent, to brace yourself. Then you may not need to hold the handles. Instead, keep your hands on your chest, and exercise your neck without any assistance from your hands.

Using little or no resistance, fine-tune the set-up until you find what works best for you. It may take several workouts before you find the set-up that suits you best. Make a note in your training log of the pin position(s) for the set-up.

Extend your head—move it rearward—while maintaining a fixed torso. Only move your head and neck. Extend as far as is comfortable—don't force an exaggerated range of motion. And don't push with your hands to help complete the neck extension. Pause for a second in the position of full extension, then smoothly and slowly return to the starting position while keeping your chest in a fixed, high position. Pause for a second, then move into the next rep.

Following completion of the final rep, with your chin on or near your chest, under perfect control, exit the machine without jolting your neck.

15. PARALLEL BAR DIP

Main muscles worked

pectorals, triceps, deltoids, latissimus dorsi

Capsule description

while on parallel bars, lower and raise yourself through bending at your elbows

Most trainees can dip safely *if* they use correct, controlled technique. If you've had shoulder problems in the past, and the dip bothers you no matter how careful you are, you may still be able to use the machine version safely.

Men who have the most difficulty with dips are frequently heavy. Other factors that lead to difficulty with dips are rounded shoulders, and shortened pectoral muscles. If you're tight in those areas, work for a few weeks on gradually increasing your shoulder and pectoral flexibility before you start dipping.

Female beginners usually have difficulty with the dip, but can prosper on the machine version. The orthodox dip has bodyweight as the minimum resistance; but with the machine dip, resistance starts from almost nothing.

Set-up

If there are multiple pairs of parallel bars, or an adjustable pair, try various width positions. About 22 inches or 56 centimeters between the centers of the bars is a good starting point for most men. Women and slender or small men will be more comfortable with closer bars. Big men may prefer wider bars. Try v-shaped bars to find the optimum hand spacing for you. Face the part of the unit where the v-shaped bars come together, not where they fan out. Another option is to use a power rack. If its uprights are suitably spaced, position a bar on saddles on the front uprights, and another bar on the rear uprights. Set the height of the bars at what's ideal for you.

Some v-shaped bars have thick handles, which enable the load to be spread over a bigger area of the hands, and produce greater comfort than regular-thickness bars. The thick handles also permit fine-tuning of hand positioning, for greater comfort.

Regardless of the type of set-up, the bars must be securely fixed so that they can't wobble as you dip.

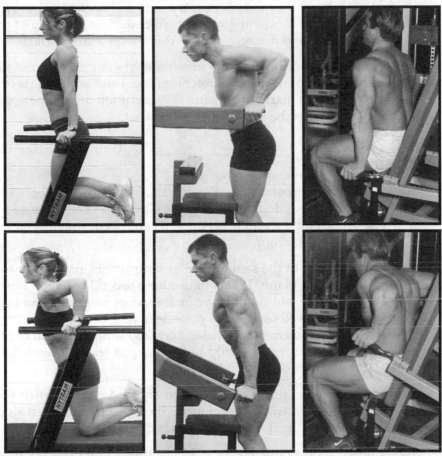

Three set-ups for the parallel bar dip: unit with v-shaped bars (left), standing machine, seated machine.

Positioning

Find the strongest, most comfortable, and natural dipping position for you. Distribute the stress from the dip over all the involved muscles. Don't try to focus the stress on any one particular area.

Stand on a box or bench of the right height so that you can easily get into the elbows-locked-out position. When you bend your knees and descend into the dip, your tibias just below your kneecaps should graze the box or bench when you're at your maximum safe depth. For most trainees, this is where the rear arm is parallel with the floor, or a little beneath that point. Some trainees can safely dip below the parallel position, whereas others need to stop a little above parallel.

To find a depth marker to suit you, try various benches or boxes. To fine-tune, place something of the correct thickness on top of the best-fit bench or box, preferably something with a soft surface.

Dipping so that your tibias graze something at your maximum safe depth isn't just to prevent overstretching. It ensures accurate record keeping. Without a marker to ensure consistent rep depth, there's a tendency to shorten the reps at the end of a set.

Performance

Never bounce (or *pre-stretch* as it's sometimes called) at the bottom of the dip, and avoid doing reps rapidly. Go down slowly, pause for a second at the bottom, and push up in a controlled, smooth manner. Never relax at the bottom.

Keep your elbows in the same plane as your wrists, or slightly to the outside of that plane. Take a pause for a second between reps at the top position, but don't let your shoulders slump as you hold yourself on locked elbows. Keep your head and shoulders up high, and stay tight. Women in particular may find it uncomfortable to lock out fully. In such cases, stop the ascent just short of the fully locked out position.

Don't let your lower limbs swing as you dip, and neither thrust your head forward nor throw it back. Furthermore, keep your chest stuck out to help keep your shoulders pulled back and safe.

Never descend on a deflated chest. Inhale before you descend, then exhale during the ascent. Going into the bottom position of the dip on a deflated chest increases the risk of injury, so keep your chest full during the descent and early part of the ascent.

Other tips

To warm up for the dip, start with floor push-ups. Then from the upright position of the dip, perform partial reps as you gradually work into your bottom position. Then you would be ready for a work set. If you use a dip machine, matters are simpler, because you have full control over resistance.

For the non-machine dip, find a method of attaching weights comfortably and securely. Use of a purpose-made weight belt for the parallel bar dip would be ideal. An alternative, at least for attaching small weights, is to wear any strong, leather belt normally used for trousers, and put a dumbbell inside it through having the 'bell vertical and the belt across the handle. Another option is to use a piece of strong rope to attach a dumbbell or plates to your belt. Let the resistance hang at the front of your thighs—see page 239. If that's uncomfortable, try suspending it from the rear. The resistance must not hang so low that it touches your depth marker before you reach your bottom position.

Strength permitting, add weight slowly and in small increments. To work from one fixed-weight dumbbell to the next, attach one or more small discs, or use an adjustable dumbbell. Alternatively, use individual weight plates, with a belt fitted through them before being buckled.

With the machine dip, a slight change in torso or wrist position can produce significant improvement in comfort, and the range of movement can be easily controlled. In addition, because resistance starts at little or nothing, the machine unit can be used by trainees who don't yet have the strength to do regular parallel bar dips.

Spotting

The main markers of technique deterioration are swinging lower limbs, throwing the head back, back arching, elbows wobbling, and stalling. The spotter should stand behind you. If you dip on bars attached to a wall, dip facing the wall so that your spotter has plenty of room. The spotter should place his hands under your shins—with your knees bent—and apply the minimum of assistance that's necessary if you require help to complete a rep.

Purpose-made weight belt with attachments, for the parallel bar dip.

The parallel bar dip has been corrupted by extreme interpretations. An excessively wide grip, turning the hands in rather than using the correct knuckles-OUT grip, keeping the elbows out as wide as possible, maintaining a concave chest, descending on a deflated chest, and going for maximum depth, are dangerous practices.

16. PRESS

The overhead press is usually called the *press*, without the *overhead* qualifier. When done standing, it's called the *military press*. The press can be done seated, to reduce the tendency to lean back. It can also be done seated against a high-incline bench, to remove much of the stress from the lower back—this is the most conservative form of the press, and the one used in **The Program**.

Seated barbell press

Main muscles worked

deltoids, triceps, trapezius

Capsule description

seated, push resistance from your shoulders to overhead

Set-up

Don't use a vertical bench. Use one set at about 75 to 80 degrees. Tilt the seat a little, if it's adjustable, to help prevent your slipping off the bench while pressing. Ensure any adjustable bench you use is sturdy, heavy, and stable.

Many gyms have purpose-built units for the seated barbell press, with fixed back support, and built-in uprights to hold the bar. Some can be good, but most have problems. The back support may be too upright, or too tall. Because the uprights that support the bar are usually behind the trainee, a spotter is essential for unracking and racking the bar. Taking the bar unassisted from behind your head is bad for your shoulders, and pressing from behind your neck can be harmful, too. The press behind neck is an unnatural movement that causes neck, shoulder, and rotator cuff problems for many trainees, and is best avoided.

The seated press can be done in a power rack. Position the bench inside the rack so that you can't hit the uprights with the bar during a rep. Load the bar on pins set at the height from which you press.

You can also do the seated press close to squat stands. Position yourself and the stands so that you have minimum handling problems getting the barbell out of the stands to start a set, and returning it to the stands at the end of a set. Spotters should be used here so that you don't have to wrestle with the bar.

Don't use a machine that forces you to use a vertical bar pathway, such as a Smith machine. That will lock you into an unnatural groove that commonly leads to shoulder problems.

Positioning

When you're sat on the bench ready to press, your feet should be wider than shoulder width. Flare your feet for greater stability, and keep your heels directly beneath or slightly in front of an imaginary vertical line drawn through the middle of your knees.

The bottom position from where you press is typically at about the height of your clavicles (when you're in your pressing position), or a little higher (at, or just below chin height). For shoulder comfort, long-limbed trainees will need a slightly higher starting position than will short-limbed trainees. Starting too low will put excessive stress on the shoulder joints.

Take a pronated grip on the barbell. Start with a hand spacing two inches wider on each side than your shoulder width, and fine-tune from there. Don't use a thumbless grip. Your forearms should be vertical at the bottom position of the press, when viewed from the front or rear.

Note the two flaws in this starting position for the seated press from the pins of a power rack. The elbows need to be moved forward to produce forearms nearer to vertical. And the lower back shows exaggerated arching, largely because the heels are behind the knees.

Performance

Push the bar up vertically, and keep the rest of your body braced. Don't let the bar move forward. Push it up near your face, but be careful not to strike your face. Apply force evenly with both arms and shoulders. Don't let one hand get ahead of or in front of the other. Once the bar is above your head, allow it to travel two to three inches to the rear as it ascends, for a more natural pathway than a perfectly vertical one. Lock out your elbows smoothly, without jolting. Pause for a second at the top position.

Lower the bar under control, don't lower it beyond your safe point, and don't bounce at the bottom. Pause momentarily at the bottom before pushing the bar up, but don't relax at the bottom. Keep yourself tight, like a coiled spring.

Inhale at the top during the brief pause, or during the descent; and exhale during the ascent.

Keep a rigid wrist position during the press. Don't allow the weight to bend your hands backward more than just a little, because that can mar your lifting technique, and injure your wrists, too. Grip the bar firmly, to help keep your wrists in the right position.

Keep all your body's musculature tensed as you press and lower the bar, especially your legs, thighs, abdominals, buttocks, and back.

Back support height

If the back support from the bench is too tall, it won't allow your head to go back a little, out of the way of the barbell's ideal pathway. This would put the bar forward of the ideal pathway—to prevent striking your face—mar the exercise, and could produce injury because of poor distribution of stress. A shortened back support would be required. Alternatively, use dumbbells.

Spotting

At the end of a set of the press, the groove can easily be lost. The spotter should look out for the barbell tipping, one hand getting forward of the other, or the bar being pressed off center. The moment that one of those markers occurs, the spotter should provide assistance to prevent more serious technique deterioration.

The spotter should stand as close as possible behind the presser, to be able to apply assistance easily. The spotter must use both hands, apply help in a balanced way, and maintain a slightly arched back.

Caution

To help prevent back injuries while pressing, preserve a non-exaggerated hollow in your lower back. This is the natural weight-bearing formation.

To avoid exaggerating the hollow in your lower back while performing the seated press, keep your feet flat on the floor, with your heels directly beneath your knees, or a little in front of them.

> *The press behind neck is an unnatural movement that causes neck, shoulder, and rotator cuff problems for many trainees, and is best avoided. The press from the FRONT is safer. If you find the barbell press awkward, use the dumbbell press instead.*

Seated dumbbell press

Main muscles worked

deltoids, triceps, trapezius

Capsule description

seated, push resistance from your shoulders to overhead

Dumbbell pressing can be done simultaneously, or by alternating hands. For the alternating dumbbell press, press with one hand as you lower with the other, or press and lower one dumbbell while the other waits at its shoulder. This produces asymmetrical stress and encourages leaning from side to side. Simultaneous pressing is safer.

Getting dumbbells into position

Set up a bench with an incline of 75 to 80 degrees, and tilt its seat if it's adjustable. Then get the help of an assistant or, better yet, two assistants to hand you the dumbbells, or use the following method.

Stand immediately in front of a bench, feet about hip-width apart. Each dumbbell should touch the outside of its corresponding foot, with the two handles parallel with each other. Bend your knees and take the 'bells from the floor with a parallel grip and correct deadlifting technique. Because of the small-diameter plates on the dumbbells, the range of motion when lifting them from the floor is considerable. Taking the 'bells from off a rack or boxes is safer than lifting them directly off the floor, provided that good lifting technique is used.

While standing, center the rear end of each dumbbell on its corresponding thigh just above the knee. If you use dumbbells with protruding ends or collars—probably adjustable 'bells—place just the inside part of the bottom plate of a given dumbbell on the outside of its corresponding lower thigh. This will work if the radius of the dumbbell plate concerned is sufficient so that you can have the 'bell positioned vertically on your thigh while you're seated. The collars must be securely in place—a 'bell that falls apart during use could be disastrous.

Keep the dumbbells against your thighs, and sit on the bench, with your hips against the bottom of the back support. The 'bells will move into a vertical position as you sit down. The dumbbells must remain against your thighs, just above your knees.

Clockwise, from the bottom left, how to get into position for the seated dumbbell press without assistance, and the first ascent of the set.

Once you're sat on the bench, pause for a moment and then thrust your left knee up and simultaneously pull vigorously with your left arm. This will get the dumbbell to your left shoulder. Do the same for your right side.

Once you have the dumbbells at your shoulders, *roll* your back onto the back support—don't keep an arched back as you lean backward. Now, you'll be in position for pressing, with your back supported.

When you've finished a set of dumbbell presses, move your feet and knees together, and lower the 'bells directly to the floor, quickly but under control. Keep the dumbbells well away from your legs and thighs. Alternatively, return the 'bells to your thighs using a reverse of the handling that got them to your shoulders. Control the dumbbells—don't let them crash onto your thighs. Then stand and return the dumbbells to their rack.

Before you do any dumbbell pressing, practice handling the 'bells.

The use of competent spotters will resolve the handling issue.

Performance

The dumbbell press allows you to find the wrist positioning and pressing groove that feel most comfortable for you. Your hands can be parallel with each other, pronated, or somewhere in between. Try each variation, and find the dumbbell pathway that feels the strongest and most comfortable for you. For example, start with your hands parallel with each other at shoulder height and, during the top half of the movement, move your hands to or toward a pronated position.

Keep a rigid wrist position, and don't allow the weights to bend your hands backward more than just a little, because that can mar your lifting technique, and injure your wrists, too.

By permitting the natural positioning of your hands at the sides of your head, your head doesn't get in the way, unlike with a barbell.

Keep the dumbbells directly over your shoulders. Don't let them drift out to the sides, and don't overstretch at the bottom.

Push up smoothly from the bottom position, pause for a second at the top position, lower under control, pause momentarily at the bottom while keeping your entire body tight and tensed, then push smoothly into the next rep.

Pressing from a parallel grip at the bottom, to a pronated one at the top.

Spotting

Spotting someone who's pressing dumbbells can be awkward. One hand should apply force under each elbow. This is strictly for assisting the trainee to get a tough rep up in correct technique. A single person can't simultaneously take a pair of dumbbells from a presser who fails on a rep—two spotters are needed. With dumbbell pressing, the key markers of technique regression to look out for are the 'bells drifting out to the sides, and one hand getting above, in front of, or to the rear of the other.

Caution

To help prevent back injuries while pressing, preserve a non-exaggerated hollow in your lower back. This is the natural weight-bearing formation.

To avoid exaggerating the hollow in your lower back while performing the seated dumbbell press, keep your feet flat on the floor, with your heels directly beneath your knees, or a little in front of them. If your feet are behind your knees, the arch will probably be exaggerated, and the risk of injury increased.

17. PULLDOWN

Main muscles worked

latissimus dorsi, upper back, pectorals, biceps, brachialis, forearms

Capsule description

sit beneath an overhead pulley, pull the bar to your chest

Set-up

Sit in the pulldown apparatus so that the cable runs vertically during the exercise, or sloped slightly toward you. A common mistake is to sit too far in the apparatus. Brace your thighs under the T-shaped restraint that has been set at the correct height for you.

Grip

There are several bar and grip options. Use the one that lets you use the most resistance over the fullest but safe range of motion.

With a straight bar, start with a supinated and shoulder-width grip, and fine-tune your hand spacing for wrist and elbow comfort. A hand spacing a little closer than shoulder-width may work best for the supinated grip.

For the parallel grip, a shoulder-width spacing produces a better effect than a close grip. Grip each handle in the center.

For the parallel and supinated grips, use a hand spacing that keeps your forearms vertical during the exercise, provided that's safe for you.

The parallel grip results in a smaller weight potential than a supinated grip. Comparing the same range of motion, you'll need about 15% less weight with a parallel grip than a supinated one.

If a supinated grip is uncomfortable, even after having tried different hand spacings, and the bar for a shoulder-width, parallel grip is unavailable, try a pronated grip using a straight bar. Take it two to three inches wider on each side than your shoulder-width grip, so that your forearms are vertical at the contracted position of the exercise.

Regardless of the bar you choose, avoid a wide grip, and don't pull to the rear of your head. Pulling to the rear is an unnatural action that puts unnecessary stress on the neck, cervical vertebrae, and shoulders.

Correct top and bottom positions of the pulldown, using a supinated grip.

Pulling to the rear doesn't improve the muscle- and strength-building values of the pulldown, but increases the risk of injury.

Performance

Look forward or upward, and smoothly pull the bar until your hands are at your upper chest or a little lower, according to wrist and shoulder comfort.

During the descent, lean back only a little and arch your back slightly. Never round your back. If you have to round your back or crunch your abdominal muscles to help, the weight is too heavy. If you round your shoulders, you'll be unable to pull your shoulder blades down, and will rob yourself of working the target musculature properly.

If you can't pull your hands to below your clavicles, the weight is too heavy and you'll be unable to pull your shoulder blades down fully. Make a special effort to pull your shoulder blades down, but don't pull beyond what feels comfortable for your shoulders and elbows.

Pause for a second in the contracted position (at your chest), then let your elbows straighten smoothly and under control. The weight stack must not yank on any structure. Keep your shoulders tight when

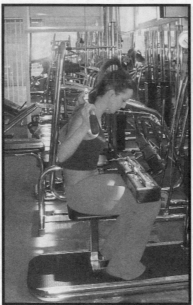 

Common errors in the pulldown.

your arms are extended. Never relax in order to get extra stretch. Pause for a second at the top, then smoothly move into the next rep.

Look forward or slightly upward at all times, and keep your head in a neutral position—don't turn, crane, or extend your head. Exhale as you pull the bar down, and inhale as you straighten your elbows.

Use chalk or rosin on your hands when you need grip support. If the bar is smooth, the chalk or rosin won't help you as much as they will with a bar that has knurling. To help your grip on a slick bar, put a palm-size piece of neoprene between each hand and the bar. Neoprene is a synthetic rubber with many uses. Get some small pieces from a scuba gear shop, an engineering storeroom on campus, or a hardware store.

Spotting

Spotting isn't essential here, because the weight can't come down on you. But spotting is desirable for ensuring that the final rep of a demanding set is done correctly. Technique starts to become ragged when your shoulders start to round. A spotter can push on the bar or pull on the weight stack.

Adding weight

Selectorized cable units, and selectorized machines in general, commonly have weight increments of 10 pounds or 5 kilos, and larger in some cases. This is too much weight to progress by in a single jump. Where you train may have special weights of 5 pounds or 2.5 kilos—and perhaps smaller ones, too—designed to fit on the top of a weight stack. If it doesn't, you may be able to get your own from an exercise equipment store. Use them to help you to work from one pin setting to the next.

Alternatively, place the weight selection pin through a small barbell weight plate before the pin goes into the weight stack. Although a pin that holds a plate won't go fully into the weight stack, it should go through enough to hold the plate securely and select the resistance, too.

Magnetic small plates are another option for adding small increments of weight to a stack.

Whichever option you choose, check that the set-up is secure before you perform a set.

> For the pulldown, regardless of the bar you choose, avoid a wide grip, and don't pull to the rear of your head. Pulling to the rear is an unnatural action that puts unnecessary stress on the neck, cervical vertebrae, and shoulders. Pulling to the rear doesn't improve the muscle- and strength-building values of the pulldown, but increases the risk of injury.

18. PULLOVER

There are two types of pullover used in **The Program**—the muscle-building one that requires a machine, and the type that may have potential for enlarging the rib cage. Both involve moving resistance from behind your head. The former has your elbows bent, whereas the other keeps your elbows straight or almost straight.

Machine pullover

Main muscles worked

latissimus dorsi, pectorals, triceps, abdominal wall

Capsule description

move resistance from behind your head, with bent elbows

Use a machine, not a barbell, single dumbbell, or pair of dumbbells. Some pullover machines are better than others. If you find a machine that suits you, exploit it. It will enable you to train your lats without your elbow flexors, and grip, limiting you. Most other exercises for the lats require substantial involvement of the elbow flexors, and grip.

Some pullover machines have the user apply force through the elbows or rear arms, which are positioned against pads. Other machines require the user to apply force solely against a bar that's held by the hands. The former is the pick of the two machines. If only the other type is available, use the pulldown, chin-up, or pull-up instead.

Some pullover machines, like the one shown in the photographs, have pads for the arms and a bar for the hands. Here, focus on applying force through the arms against the pads.

Set-up and positioning

Find the best set-up for you according to your torso and arm lengths. Follow the manufacturer's set-up guidance, and fine-tune the adjustments to find the body and arm positioning that enables you to work hard without producing any joint soreness. Depending on the machine, you may have to adjust the height of the seat, and the range-of-motion limiter. The machine must have a belt, to restrain your pelvis.

Your shoulder joints should line up with the pivot points of the machine, or perhaps be an inch or so below the pivot points. Sit with your hips and back firmly against the back support, and have an assistant view the pivot points from the height of your shoulders, to determine the correct positioning. Move the seat height accordingly.

Some pullover machines have a foot pedal or bar that's used to assist with proper set-up, and to transfer the resistance to and from the user. Once the resistance has been selected, and the trainee is seated and belted into position, the pedal must be depressed so that the elbows can be positioned on the pads of the movement arm. Removing the feet from the pedal transfers the resistance to the trainee, for the first rep. After the set is finished, the foot pedal is depressed again, to unload the resistance so that the elbows can be removed from the movement arm.

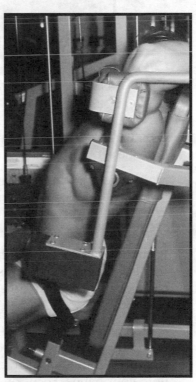

The danger in the pullover primarily comes from an excessive range of motion for the shoulders in the top, stretched position. Set the seat at the right height for you, push your hips as far back on the seat as possible, and strap yourself in tightly. Then with a very light weight on the machine, discover how far back you can take your arms before your back starts to come off the back support. Your starting position should be about an inch short of the point where your back starts to come off the back support. Set up the machine accordingly. Then keep your back against the machine's back support.

If even this less-than-full-range of motion irritates your shoulders, reduce it until there's no irritation. Over the first few weeks of use, however, your shoulder flexibility may increase, and thus you may be able to increase your range of motion a little.

A dangerous starting position for the pullover. Note the exaggerated arch in the lower back.

If the machine you use doesn't have a built-in range-of-motion control to delimit the top, stretched position, you can do it manually if it has a weight stack. See *Leg curl* for details.

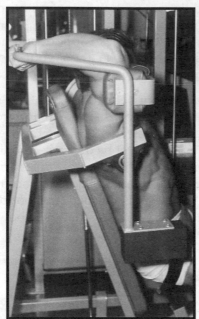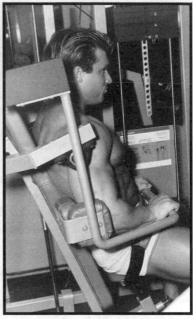

A reduced and safer range of motion in the machine pullover.

Over the first few times you use the pullover, you may need to fine-tune the set-up to find the one that feels the most comfortable for you.

Make a note in your training log of the settings you use.

Performance

Focus the exercise on your back musculature, not your arms. Mentally connect with your back musculature and direct the work there, consciously maximizing the contraction and involvement of your back.

Move out of the stretched position slowly. Move smoothly and under control at all times. Allow (but don't force) your neck to flex as you move into the contracted position. Keep your back against the back support throughout each rep. Only lightly hold the bar or handles with your hands. Focus on trying to crush the pads with your arms. Hold the fully contracted, bottom position for a second, and contract your lats hard.

As you return to the stretched, starting position, slow down. Pause in the starting position for a second, then smoothly move into the next rep. To protect your shoulders, don't relax them in the stretched, starting position. Keep your shoulders tensed.

This exercise has a large range of motion. You should take three to four seconds for each phase, plus the additional second for the hold in the contracted position, and another second for the pause at the starting position. Inhale as your arms move back, and exhale during the positive (or contraction) phase.

Although not essential, use a spotter once you're training hard. As soon as a rep grinds to a halt, the spotter should apply a tad of help. This will keep the rep moving, and help ensure correct technique.

Adding weight

Selectorized cable units, and selectorized machines in general, commonly have weight increments of 10 pounds or 5 kilos, and larger in some cases. This is too much weight to progress by in a single jump. Where you train may have special weights of 5 pounds or 2.5 kilos—and perhaps smaller ones, too—designed to fit on the top of a weight stack. If it doesn't, you may be able to get your own from an exercise equipment store. Use them to help you to work from one pin setting to the next.

Alternatively, place the weight selection pin through a small barbell weight plate before the pin goes into the weight stack. Although a pin that holds a plate won't go fully into the weight stack, it should go through enough to hold the plate securely and select the resistance, too.

Magnetic small plates are another option for adding small increments of weight to a stack.

Whichever option you choose, check that the set-up is secure before you perform a set.

> *Books on strength training and bodybuilding usually provide skimpy descriptions of exercise technique. But exercise technique isn't a simple matter. The exercises need to be described in detail. Please take the time to study the exercise descriptions. In order to train safely and effectively, it's critical that you MASTER exercise technique.*

Breathing pullover

Main structure worked

rib cage

Capsule description

move resistance to and from behind your head, with straight elbows

This is a stretching and forced breathing exercise that may enlarge your rib cage, deepen your chest, and help to improve your posture. It may be especially effective for teenagers, and trainees in their early twenties, but is worth a try at any age. There's no science to confirm this, however. I believe the breathing pullover helped me, and other people have reported benefits, too.

Use no more than 10 pounds to begin with—a short and unloaded bar, a pair of small dumbbells, a single dumbbell, or a barbell plate. (The pullover machine shouldn't be used for the breathing pullover.) After a few months you may increase to 15 pounds, and later on to 20 pounds if you're a large man, but no more. Don't use progressive resistance in this exercise. The use of heavy weights will defeat the purpose of the exercise, as well as risk harm to your shoulders. If in doubt over which weight to use here, select the lighter one.

Hold the resistance and lie lengthwise on a bench, not across it. Keep your feet on the bench. This will prevent excessive arching of your back, and excessive stretching of your abdominal wall. Hold the resistance above your upper chest, with straight elbows. Take a shoulder-width grip, or closer if you're using a single dumbbell, or weight plate. Keep your elbows stiff and straight throughout, slowly lower the bar and simultaneously inhale as deeply as possible. Don't inhale in one gulp, but in a steady stream. Spread your ribs as much as possible. Lower your arms until they are parallel or only slightly below parallel with the floor. Don't go down as deep as possible. At the bottom position, take an extra gulp of air. Pause for a second, then return to the starting position, simultaneously exhaling. Repeat for at least 15 slow reps. Focus on stretching your rib cage.

Experiment with a different positioning. Do the exercise with your head just off the end of the bench, as illustrated. This may produce a better effect on your rib cage.

Keeping your elbows completely straight may irritate them. If so, bend your elbows slightly. Keep this to the minimum, however, or you'll reduce the potential expansion effect on your rib cage.

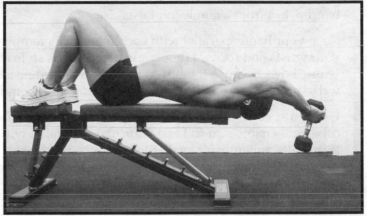

Elbow irritation may come from using more weight than has been recommended, or from not introducing the exercise into your program carefully enough. Elbow irritation may also come from using a straight bar, whereas a parallel grip on a weight plate, or dumbbell(s), may be safe.

The breathing pullover is traditionally done immediately after an exercise that gets you heavily winded, such as the squat, especially when the latter's done for higher reps.

Go easy at the beginning. The forced and exaggerated breathing may make you feel dizzy unless you work into it progressively over a few weeks. Your chest may get sore, too, if you don't work into the exercise *gradually*.

19. PUSHDOWN

Main muscles worked

triceps

Capsule description

using resistance from an overhead pulley, press down with fixed elbows

The pushdown is sometimes called the *pressdown*, and is a form of the *triceps extension*. If you can't do the parallel bar dip, include the pushdown in your program. The parallel bar dip provides a degree of triceps extension that the bench press, close-grip bench press, incline bench press, and overhead presses don't. The pushdown provides a similar degree of triceps extension to that of the parallel bar dip, but from a single-joint exercise.

Keep your hands parallel with each other. This removes stress from your wrists and focuses it on your triceps. This style also protects your elbows because it helps to prevent wrist extension. Keep your wrists stiff and immobile throughout—don't let them flex or extend.

Use of a special, purpose-made rope attachment connected to the cable will enable you to keep your hands parallel with each other. If that attachment isn't available, securely attach your own sturdy but flexible strap or rope to the cable's connection. A bathrobe's belt can work well if you put a knot at the bottom of each end to prevent your hands slipping.

Push down under control until your elbows are straight, hold the contraction for a second, let the bar back up under control, pause in the top position for a second, and repeat. Keep your wrists rigid, your elbows fixed at the sides of your ribs, and your torso and lower limbs rigid. Focus on elbow extension and flexion. Exhale as you push down, and inhale as you let the resistance return to its starting position.

Don't use a range of motion that causes your forearms and biceps to crush together in the top position. Stop the ascent of your hands just before your forearms and biceps meet. And don't relax at the top of the pushdown. Keep tight control.

A homemade attachment for the pushdown—a bathrobe belt threaded through a carabiner, and knotted at both ends.

20. ROTARY TORSO

Main muscles worked

most of the abdominal wall, especially the external and internal obliques, and the multifidii

Capsule description

with your feet and hips fixed, rotate your torso to one side, and then the other

Although not a commonly available machine, the rotary torso may be available where you train. As well as training most of the abdominal wall, the rotary torso works some of the small, intervertebral muscles, but it provides only secondary involvement of the quadratus lumborum. It's an alternative to the side bend if the latter can't be performed safely.

The rotary torso is commonly performed in a dangerous manner—with an excessive range of motion, and a rep speed that's too fast.

Follow the manufacturer's set-up guidelines, and fix the range of motion at what feels comfortable for you. After a few weeks your flexibility may improve, and then you may be able to increase your range of motion.

Smoothly move into each rep, take three to four second to rotate into the fully contracted position, hold it for a second, then smoothly return to the starting position over a further three to four seconds. Pause for a second, then repeat. Complete the set for one side, pause for a minute and set up the machine for the other side of your body, then complete the set for that side.

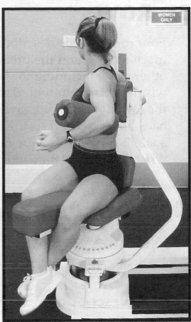

Starting (left) and finishing positions for rotation to the trainee's right on the rotary torso machine.

Reminder

Study this chapter to learn about correct exercise technique, and then apply it *consistently*. If, however, despite using *correct technique*, along with a *controlled* rep speed, *gradual* increases in progressive resistance, *abbreviated* training routines, and *adequate* recovery time between workouts, you *still* experience joint or soft tissue irritation from a given exercise, substitute it with a comparable exercise. (How to modify training routines to accommodate individual variation in exercise tolerance, and recovery ability, is explained in **The Program**.)

Apply the first imperative of exercise: "Do no harm."

21. ROW

Four rows will be described: one-arm dumbbell row, cable row, machine row, and the prone low-incline dumbbell row. There are other rows, including the barbell row, and the T-bar row, both of which are fraught with danger. They don't have the body supported, the lower back is excessively involved, it's difficult to keep the lower back hollowed and secure once the weight becomes substantial—just a slight slip in technique can produce lower-back injury—and the wrist positioning they impose isn't ideal.

One-arm dumbbell row

Main muscles worked

latissimus dorsi, upper back, biceps, brachialis, rear deltoid, forearms

Capsule description

with one hand braced on a bench, take a dumbbell and pull it to your obliques

Stand next to a bench (or something stable of a similar height), with a dumbbell on the floor at your left side. Bend over and brace your right hand on the bench. Your right knee should be bent and your right foot well ahead of your left. Alternatively, your right knee could be placed on the bench. Either way, your left knee should be almost straight, and your torso inclined somewhat, as illustrated. Keep your lower back slightly hollowed throughout the exercise.

With your left hand, grab the dumbbell from the floor, with the handle parallel with your spine. Keep your elbow in, and smoothly pull the dumbbell as high as possible at your left oblique, or hip (depending on your body structure, and what feels comfortable for you). Pull in an arc, not a straight line. Don't yank the dumbbell up, don't rotate about your spine, and don't twist your torso. Only move your hand, forearm, arm, and shoulder.

Hold the top position for a second, and crush your shoulder blades together. At the top position, your elbow should be several inches above the height of your spine.

On the descent, smoothly retrace the arc of the ascent. At the bottom, pause for a second without relaxing or putting the dumbbell on the floor, then smoothly move into the next rep. Your forearm should be vertical or almost-vertical throughout the exercise. Inhale during the descent or while your elbow is straight, and exhale on the ascent.

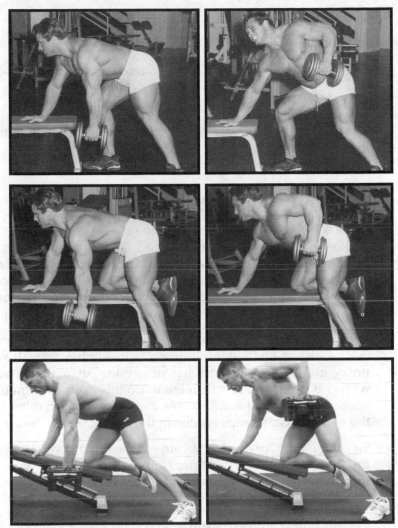

Top left, correct starting position. Top right, incorrect finish. Middle, correct technique. Above, alternative set-up using a low-incline bench—probably the pick of the three variations—and correct technique.

This method works your left side. To train your right side, reverse the procedure.

To reduce the size of the weight jumps between fixed-weight dumbbells, use the same approach described for the *Dumbbell bench press*. But in the dumbbell row, use of wrist weights (obtainable from a sporting goods store) may be a good option for progressively working from one fixed-weight 'bell to the next. The wrist weights shouldn't spoil your balance in the dumbbell row, unlike in pressing movements.

Cable row

Main muscles worked

latissimus dorsi, upper back, biceps, brachialis, rear deltoid, forearms

Capsule description

while seated, pull to your waist or lower chest a bar fixed to a cable running from a low pulley

Set-up and positioning

Use a shoulder-width supinated grip on a straight bar, a shoulder-width (or slightly wider) pronated grip on a straight bar or, better still, use a shoulder-width *parallel grip* on a special bar. One of the most common mistakes in this exercise is doing it with hands too close. A shoulder-width grip produces a better effect than a narrow grip, because it keeps the forearms parallel and in a more natural position.

For the parallel grip, encourage the management where you train to get a shoulder-width bar if it doesn't already have one. If you're unsuccessful, buy your own bar, or get one custom made and take it with you when you're scheduled to do this exercise. Aim for a grip spacing that keeps your forearms parallel with each other throughout the exercise. Grasp each handle in the center.

Sit on the floor, or on the built-in low seat, with your feet against the foot restraint. If where you train doesn't have a foot restraint, improvise so that you have a solid foot brace that lets you space your feet as required.

The starting position has you seated with your torso vertical, lower back slightly hollowed, elbows pulled out straight by the resistance, knees slightly bent. To get into that position, bend your knees sufficiently so that you can take the handle with your back in the correct starting position. Then maintain the correct back positioning and straighten your knees sufficiently so that you won't bang them with the bar during the exercise. Keep your knees bent to some degree, to help you maintain the right back positioning.

Some cable row set-ups have cables that are too short, and it's difficult to get into the starting position. There's even the risk of injury while getting into position. To correct this, add a piece of chain between the bar and the cable, so that the bar is precisely where you want it for the starting position.

If you use a selectorized pulldown apparatus, you may be able to set up the weight stack so that the bar is where you want it for the starting position. See *Leg curl* for how to use the weight stack selector pin as a delimiter. But for a large adjustment, extra chain between the bar and cable may be required.

The top two photographs show correct technique, using a pronated, shoulder-width grip on a straight bar. The next one shows incorrect technique—raised elbows, and rounded back—but using the especially recommended PARALLEL, shoulder-width grip. The right photograph shows improved technique, but there's still some rearward lean that should be avoided.

Performance

Smoothly pull the bar into your upper abdomen or lower chest, according to what feels most natural for you according to the lengths of your torso, forearms, and arms. Keep your forearms parallel with the floor, and don't let your elbows drift out to the sides. Your elbows should be equally spaced throughout each rep. Arch your back slightly as you crush your shoulder blades together, but don't lean back. Your elbows must not rise when you're in the contracted position—keep your forearms parallel with the floor. Hold the contraction for a second, then let the resistance pull your elbows straight in a controlled manner. Pause for a second in the starting position, don't relax your shoulders, then smoothly move into the next rep.

Keep your torso upright and rigid throughout each rep. Imagine that your torso is supported, and can't move.

Each phase of a rep should take two to three seconds, plus an additional second for holding the contracted position, and another second at the starting position.

Other tips

If you lean back beyond the vertical, at least with a demanding weight, you'll round your shoulders, be unable to crush your shoulder blades together, and rob yourself of working the target muscles.

Don't relax your shoulders between reps, to permit a full stretch. A full stretch puts great stress on the rotator cuff muscles at the back of your shoulders, and will set you up for an injury. Keep your shoulders tight.

Look forward or slightly upward at all times, and keep your head in a neutral position—don't turn, crane, or extend your head.

Use chalk or rosin on your hands when you need grip support. If the bar is smooth, the chalk or rosin won't help you as much as they will with a bar that has knurling. To help your grip on a slick bar, put a palm-size piece of neoprene between each hand and the bar. Neoprene is a synthetic rubber with many uses. Get some small pieces from a scuba gear shop, an engineering storeroom on campus, or a hardware store.

Spotting

Spotting isn't essential here, because the resistance can't come down on you. Technique becomes ragged when your shoulders start to

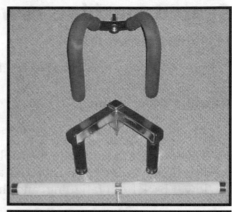

Close-parallel-grip bars are commonly used in the cable row, but such a grip is inferior to a shoulder-width one. A shoulder-width PARALLEL grip is the ideal. The bottommost photograph shows an adjustable, parallel-grip bar—a single-width grip won't suit all users.

Use a shoulder-width pronated grip, or a shoulder-width supinated grip, as the alternative to the ideal of the shoulder-width parallel grip. Try both, to find which feels the most comfortable.

slump. Immediately, a spotter should pull on the weight stack cable just enough to enable you to get the rep out in correct technique.

Adding weight

Selectorized cable units, and selectorized machines in general, commonly have weight increments of 10 pounds or 5 kilos, and larger in some cases. This is too much weight to progress by in a single jump. Where you train may have special weights of 5 pounds or 2.5 kilos—and perhaps smaller ones, too—designed to fit on the top of a weight stack. If it doesn't, you may be able to get your own from an exercise equipment store. Use them to help you to work from one pin setting to the next.

Alternatively, place the weight selection pin through a small barbell weight plate before the pin goes into the weight stack. Although a pin that holds a plate won't go fully into the weight stack, it should go through enough to hold the plate securely and select the resistance, too.

Magnetic small plates are another option for adding small increments of weight to a stack.

Whichever option you choose, check that the set-up is secure before you perform a set.

Seated machine row

Main muscles worked

latissimus dorsi, upper back, biceps, brachialis, rear deltoid, forearms

Capsule description

sit and pull the handles to your waist or lower chest

This exercise is similar to the cable row, but with a simpler set-up. Furthermore, the chest is braced against a pad, which prevents the lower back from fatiguing, and thus increases stability and safety.

There may also be a foot bar, to help increase stability further. If there isn't, place your feet on the floor in front of you, wider than hip-width.

Depending on the machine, you may have the choice between a pronated grip, supinated grip, and a parallel grip. A parallel grip of shoulder-width is ideal.

If the parallel-grip handles are a lot closer than shoulder-width, use a pronated grip (palms down, in this case) of shoulder-width or a little wider, depending on comfort. A supinated grip (palms up, in this case) may feel comfortable, or it may irritate your wrists and elbows, depending on the positioning of the handles.

Adjust the seat's height to find the position that permits you to have your forearms parallel with the floor when you're in the contracted position. Pull your elbows as far behind you as possible, but keep your chest on the pad. Crush your shoulder blades together, hold the contraction, then let the resistance pull your elbows straight in a controlled manner. Pause in the starting position, don't relax your shoulders, then smoothly move into the next rep.

Keep your torso against the chest pad throughout each set, and your back slightly arched.

Take two to three seconds to pull the handles to your torso (the positive phase), pause for a second in the contracted position with your scapulae fully retracted, take two to three seconds for the negative phase, and a further second in the starting position.

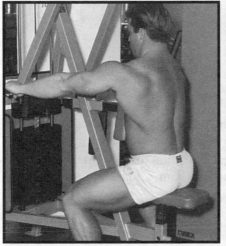

Seated machine row.

Prone low-incline dumbbell row

This two-arm dumbbell row is an alternative to the one-arm variation described earlier in this section. It's also an alternative to the cable row, and the machine row. Illustrated is the starting position. You may need to move your knees further to the rear, so that they aren't struck by the dumbbells during the ascent. Follow the same pathway and control guidelines as for the one-arm dumbbell row.

22. SHRUG

Main muscles worked

trapezius, deltoids, forearms

Capsule description

while holding resistance, with straight elbows, shrug your shoulders

There are several types of shrugs, including upright, incline, and prone. The upright shrug is used in **The Program**. Other shrugs may be used beyond your first year of training.

Set-up, and performance

Stand, with your elbows straight, and hold a bar as if you were in the top position of a deadlift. Without bending your elbows, smoothly shrug as high as possible—try to raise your shoulders to your ears—and pause for a second. Lower under control, pause for a second without relaxing, and repeat.

As an alternative to taking equipment from the floor for each set, place a barbell over pins set in a power rack at your bottom position, or, place a loaded barbell, parallel-grip bar, or dumbbells on boxes of the appropriate height. Position the dumbbells one at a time. You may need an assistant to help you set up the equipment.

Keep your body tight, a slight arch in your lower back (don't round your back), don't shuffle your feet around, and don't take more of the stress on one side of your body than the other. Keep the stress distributed symmetrically.

Dumbbells and a parallel-grip bar are ideal for the upright shrug. They aren't obstructed by your thighs or hips, unlike a straight bar. Use a parallel grip in the dumbbell shrug, with your hands by the sides of your thighs, or hips.

The barbell shrug and parallel-grip-bar shrug are performed standing only. The dumbbell shrug can be done seated, too, at the end of a bench.

Grip

Keep your elbows straight. Use your bench press grip or slightly wider. A close grip, or moving quickly, will prompt your elbows to bend. With a pronated grip, keep your elbows rotated inward, to lock your elbows.

Three standing shrugs: barbell (left), dumbbell (middle), parallel-grip-bar (right). The parallel-grip-bar shrug illustrations show bending of the elbows. The elbows should be straight.

Use a pronated grip on a straight bar with deep knurling, and chalk or rosin on your hands when you need grip support. Only when you need further grip support should you use a reverse grip. From set to set, alternate which hand is supinated.

With a parallel-grip bar, or dumbbells, deep knurling is also required. Use chalk or rosin, too, when you need additional grip support.

Caution

Don't use a circular action when shrugging, because it places unnecessary wear on the shoulder joints. Furthermore, keep your shoulders tight at the bottom of each rep—don't let the weight yank your shoulders.

A common error is to stretch the head forward during the ascent. This can lead to neck and trapezius injuries. Keep your head in an upright, neutral position.

The seated incline dumbbell shrug is an alternative to the regular shrug, although some trainees may find the compression of the chest uncomfortable.

Position an adjustable bench at the lowest setting that, when you're face down, allows you to keep your elbows straight and take dumbbells off the floor without forcing a stretch.

While in position on the bench, shrug your shoulders *and* pull them back. Crush your shoulder blades together, then lower the dumbbells under control to the floor, pause for a second, and then start the next rep.

Don't jam your chin onto the bench.

Calf machine shrug—DANGER

For this form of the standing shrug, the resistance rests against the actual musculature that's primarily worked by the exercise. When the musculature contracts, it's distorted because of the compression from the weight. This produces a skewed effect on the musculature, and leads to possible tissue damage. The musculature being worked should be free of compressive impediment to its contraction and relaxation.

The negative effect of the calf machine shrug on the trapezius depends on the design of the calf machine, and the body structure of the individual trainee. There'll probably be a severe pull at the base of the skull regardless of the size of the user or design of the machine. Avoid the calf machine shrug. Use another type of shrug.

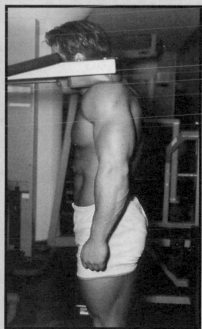

Calf machine shrug—don't use this exercise.

23. SIDE BEND

Main muscles worked

abdominal wall including the quadratus lumborum, erector spinae

Capsule description

hold resistance against a thigh, bend to that side, and return upright

The side bend also provides direct work for some of the small, intervertebral muscles. The side bend works most of the body's core musculature.

The side bend is an asymmetrical exercise. Provided you have a healthy spine free of restrictions—see Chapter 6—the side bend, when correctly performed, will strengthen your body's core muscles, and increase their robustness, and resistance to injury. If, however, your spinal musculature has restrictions, the side bend will probably be a harmful exercise, and should be avoided.

Perform the side bend with a dumbbell, or a cable from a low pulley.

Dumbbell standing side bend. The range of motion shown here could have been increased had the model moved his hips to his left during the descent to his right side.

A stance a little wider than what's shown here may give greater stability.

Dumbbell side bend

Space your feet about hip-width apart, but fine-tune this to best suit you. If you have a tendency toward groin strains, a close stance with your feet touching may be better. Balance may be harder to maintain with a close stance than a wider one. Keep your buttocks contracted.

A simpler way of doing the dumbbell side bend is while seated at the end of a bench, across the middle of a bench with one foot on each side, or on a box. With a wide enough foot placement to maintain balance, the seated side bend can work well. There'll be no problem with the plates striking your thighs and obstructing performance.

Performance

Take the weight in your right hand. Rest your left hand on your left hip, or external oblique. Bend to your right side as far as feels comfortable, pause for a second, then return to the vertical position. Pause for a second, then repeat. In the standing side bend, as you bend to your right, push your hips to your left. This may help improve stability, and increase the range of motion, too. As you

Dumbbell seated side bend. A wider spacing of the feet than what's illustrated here would give increased stability.

return to the vertical position, move your torso first, then your hips. Do all your reps to your right side without interruption. To exercise the other side of your body, reverse the procedure.

Face forward throughout each set. There should only be lateral movement. Don't lean forward, don't lean back, and don't overstretch.

For stability, distribute the stress over your feet in a 50-50 split. To that end, while you perform the standing side bend, as you descend you should take more of the stress on the inner sides of your feet than the outer.

Do the reps carefully—about three seconds up, and three seconds down, plus a pause for a second at the top, and another at the bottom. Use smooth, controlled movements. Inhale on the descent, and exhale on the ascent, or just breathe freely.

After an intensive set of side bends, take two to three minutes rest before working your other side, so that your performance on the latter doesn't suffer. From workout to workout, alternate the side you work first.

Pulley side bend, standing. The lowest position, left, could be increased if the trainee's hips were pushed out to her left during the descent to her right. The middle photograph shows the usual completion point of a rep—the hips should be symmetrical at this point. Each rep of the side bend can be continued by bending over toward the other side, for further range of motion (right photo).

Pulley side bend

Use a cable that arises from a low pulley. Stand sideways to the apparatus, with the handle in your hand that's nearest to the apparatus. Stand a sufficient distance away from the apparatus so that the plates can't come to rest at the bottom position. And line up the pulley with your ankle, and the direction of the cable with the center of the side of your hips, to keep the resistance in the same vertical plane as your body.

Then follow the guidelines for the dumbbell standing side bend.

General tips for the side bend

Carefully adapt to side bend if you've not done it before, or if you've not done it for a long time. For two weeks, do it two times a week without added resistance. Do a couple of sets of high reps each time. Keep your hands by your sides, then progress to placing them on top of your head. Focus on smooth, controlled reps. Go down to a depth that feels comfortable. If your flexibility increases, you may be able to increase the depth a little during the first few weeks.

To learn the movement, do the exercise sideways to a mirror. Keep your head turned to the side, scrutinize your technique, and ensure lateral movement only. Don't, however, do any intensive side bends with your head turned. You must have your head facing forward when you side bend intensively.

In your third week of side bends, use a light weight and thereafter add poundage slowly and gradually, using small increments.

When you take the resistance to get set up for the side bend—whether a dumbbell, or from a low pulley—keep the stress as symmetrical as possible. Bend your knees, keep your shoulders pulled back, lower back slightly hollowed, and brace your disengaged hand against the thigh on the same side, while the engaged hand takes the resistance from the other side. And reverse the procedure at the end of a set, when you return the resistance to the floor.

Ideally, for the dumbbell side bend, take the 'bell from a dumbbell rack, and set it on a bench rather than the floor. Consequently you would need to bend your knees only slightly in order to take the dumbbell with one hand. Then adopt your stance ready to start the set. At the end of the set, put the dumbbell back on the bench while you rest prior to the next set.

Technique recordings

Periodically, use a video camera and record your exercise technique, for analysis later. A video camera can be an outstanding tool to help improve your exercise technique.

To demonstrate exercise technique clearly, the models sometimes didn't wear shirts, and weight stands and safety bars were often not used. This was for illustration purposes only. When you train, wear a shirt, and take proper safety measures.

24. SQUAT

Two forms of the *barbell* squat will be described. The front squat has the bar held at the front of the shoulders, whereas the back squat has the bar held at the back of the shoulders. The front squat always has the *front* qualifier, whereas the back squat is usually called *the squat* without the *back* qualifier.

Properly done, by trainees without physical limitations or restrictions, the barbell squat is safe and highly effective. But use poor technique, abuse low reps, overtrain, or try to lift a too-heavy weight, and you'll hurt yourself. Learn to squat correctly before you concern yourself with weight, then add weight slowly while maintaining correct technique.

Before you can barbell squat with correct technique, you need to be flexible enough to *adopt* the necessary positioning, and have sufficient back strength to be able to *maintain* the correct back positioning. You especially need flexible calves, hamstrings, thigh adductors, and buttocks. Women who usually wear shoes with high heels are likely to have tight calves. You also need flexible shoulders and pectorals in order to hold the bar in the right position with ease.

If you've had a major back injury, get the clearance of a chiropractor before you barbell squat. If you've had any minor back injuries, still get a chiropractor's clearance.

Two non-barbell forms of the squat will be described: the ball squat, and the hip-belt squat. Neither use a barbell, or resistance on the shoulders.

How to use a power rack

A power rack, correctly used, is perfect for self-spotting, and safety, and can be found in some gyms. A power rack is especially useful for barbell squats, barbell bench press and its variations, deadlifts, and barbell presses. For example, position the pins—or safety bars—an inch or two centimeters below your bottom point of the squat. Then if you can't perform a rep, lower the bar under control to the pins, get out from under the bar, remove the plates, and return the bar to its holders.

The uprights of power racks typically have about two inches or five centimeters between successive holes. If one setting is too high, and the next too low, raise the floor. For the squat, place non-slip rubber matting of the right thickness throughout the floor space within the rack (so that there's no chance of tripping on the edge of the matting).

"Flat back" confusion

The spine is naturally curved when seen from the side. This curvature is the natural, strong structure for absorbing and distributing stress efficiently. When the curves are lost, the strong, load-bearing capability is diminished.

"Keep a flat back" is a common admonition when lifting a weight, and one that I've used in my earlier writing. It's not, however, an accurate one. What it really means, is, "Don't round your lower back." Although it may look like the lower back is flat at the bottom of a correctly performed squat or deadlift, as examples, this is an illusion. When contracted, the spinal erectors, if sufficiently developed, may fill the required slight hollow in the lower back's profile at those bottom positions, giving an impression that the lower back is flat, but the actual *lower spine* should be slightly concave, or hollow.

It's the strong contraction of the lumbar musculature that produces the desired, concave lower back, to create a bracing effect. The strong contraction of the muscles on both sides of the spine not only prevents the forward rounding of the back, but also helps prevent sideways, asymmetrical bending.

If the lower spine is truly flat, the upper back will be rounded, which is a dangerous position when lifting a challenging weight (or even a light one in many cases). A spine that's intentionally straightened while under heavy load bearing, is a weakened one that's exposed to an increased risk of injury. A spine that's naturally straight, suggests pathology.

When lifting a weight, inside or outside of the gym, keep your shoulders retracted, hips pushed back (extended), and lower back slightly hollowed. There are exceptions, however. For example, in the back extension, the back *should* round during the course of this flexion-extension exercise; and during crunches, the lower back shouldn't be hollow—keep it flat against the floor.

Squats, knees, and lower back

Forward travel of the knees is inevitable in squatting, but should be minimized, to reduce stress on the knees. A common guideline for squatting is, during the descent, to avoid the knees traveling forward beyond an imaginary vertical line drawn from the toes. I, too, have recommended this guideline, but few people can follow it for barbell squatting unless they perform partial squats only. The fullest, safe range of motion—safe for the lower back, and the knees—is recommended, and this usually means that the knees will travel forward of the toe line during the barbell squat. Some competitive powerlifters squat with almost vertical shins. They can do this because they have favorable leverages for the squat, use a wide stance, and exaggerate the involvement of their lower backs, and hips. Their goal is to increase their one-rep maximum performances.

The general rule recommended in this book for barbell squatting is to descend until about two inches or five centimeters above the point at which your lower back would start to round. Your back must never round while squatting. For most trainees, provided that controlled rep speed and correct technique are used, this range of motion is safe for the lower back and the knees. For some trainees, this range of motion will mean that the upper thighs will descend to below parallel with the floor, while for most trainees the thighs will descend to parallel with the floor, or a little above parallel.

While learning to use this safe range of motion, it may mean, initially, using a reduced depth of descent. With practice, improved flexibility, and increased strength of your back, you may be able to increase your safe range of motion. Start with just the bare bar when learning how to squat correctly, and progress in resistance gradually.

Footwear reminder

Especially for squats, deadlifts, and overhead presses, you should not wear shoes with thick or spongy soles and heels.

Get yourself a sturdy pair of shoes with good grip to the floor, arch support, and which minimizes deformation when you're lifting heavy weights. No heel elevation relative to the balls of your feet is especially important for squats and deadlifts.

See pages 185 and 186 for details.

Correct technique to minimize forward travel of the knees while squatting, includes:

1. Wearing a pair of shoes with no heel, or only minimal heel.

2. Not elevating your heels on plates, or a board.

3. Using a medium-width or wider stance—not a close stance.

4. Turning the toes of each foot out at least 20 degrees from the feet-parallel-to-each-other position.

5. Keeping the stress of the weight mostly over your heels—not the balls of your feet.

While applying these guidelines, maintain a slight hollow in your lower back, and minimize forward lean of your torso. Some forward lean of your torso is, however, necessary while barbell squatting.

To minimize forward travel of the knees while squatting, and to keep the back vertical or near vertical, the ball squat, or the hip-belt squat, can be employed. They may be safer forms of the squat for trainees who have knee or back problems when barbell squatting. Properly performed, the ball squat and the hip-belt squat involve little or no loading of the spine.

Knee or lower-back problems may, however, be correctable, with the right therapy. Please see Chapter 6.

Squat (back squat)

Main muscles worked

quadriceps, thigh adductors, buttocks, hamstrings, spinal erectors, multifidii

Capsule description

hold a bar over your shoulders, squat, then stand erect

Set-up

Always squat inside a four-post power rack with pins and saddles correctly and securely in place. Alternatively, use a half rack, sturdy and stable squat stands together with spotter racks or bars, or squat rack unit that combines stands and safety bars. Should you fail on a squat, you must be able to descend to the bottom position and safely set the bar down on supports. Make no compromises—*safety comes first*. Ideally, you should have spotters standing by in addition to the aforementioned safety set-up.

See *Safety equipment*, in Chapter 7, for illustrations.

There have been terrible injuries among trainees who squatted without a safety set-up, or spotters standing by. When they failed on a rep, they got crushed by the weight before they dumped it, or they toppled forward and severely injured their backs.

A straight bar is fine for squatting, but most trainees may find that a cambered squat bar is better. A cambered bar is bent like that of a yoke. Relative to a straight bar, the bent bar is easier to hold in position, sits better on the upper back, and is less likely to roll out of position. Encourage the management of where you train to get a cambered squat bar. (A skilled metal worker can put a camber in a straight bar.) Straight or cambered, the bar you use for the squat should have knurling around its center, to help you keep it in position during a set.

Cambered squat bar (top), and a straight barbell.

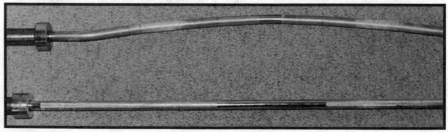

The above right photograph shows the error of shifting stress from over the rear two thirds of the feet (but mostly over the heels), to mostly over the balls of the feet. This has resulted in heel lifting, reduced stability, and exaggerated load on the knees. The model is wearing shoes with thick heels, which has contributed to the technique error.

Safety bars/pins

The safety pins (horizontal bars) have been positioned just above where the barbell is lowered to at the safe, bottom position of the squat for this trainee. Thus, should he fail on a rep—usually during a tough work set—he would lower the barbell to the safety pins, and escape.

From the bottom left, the sequence for the first rep of a set of squats. The final two photographs (bottom right) show the return of the bar to the rack's saddles at the end of the set.

If you can't squat well with a straight bar, a bent bar will probably not make enough difference to warrant the investment. But if you can squat well with a straight bar, you may be able to squat even better with a cambered bar.

Set the bar on its saddles at mid- to upper-chest height. If the bar is too low, you'll waste energy getting it out. If it's too high, you'll need to rise on your toes to get the bar out. The too-high setting is especially dangerous when you return the bar after finishing a hard set of squats.

If you're used to squatting with a straight bar, and move to a cambered bar, you must lower the position of the saddles, and that of the pins or safety bars set at the bottom position of the squat. The ends of a cambered bar are about three inches or eight centimeters lower than the central part that rests on your upper back.

Use little or preferably no padding on the bar. If you're a training novice you'll probably have little visible muscle over and above your shoulder blades. After a few months of progressive training that includes deadlifts and shrugs, you'll start developing the muscular padding required on your upper back. Then the bar can be held in position more comfortably.

The more padding that's around a bar, the more likely that the bar will be incorrectly positioned, or that it will move during a set. Wear a thick sweatshirt rather than a thin T-shirt, to provide acceptable padding to cushion the bar. If more padding is needed, wear a T-shirt and a sweatshirt.

Bar positioning

Before you center the bar on your upper back you must hold the bar properly, with your shoulder blades crushed together. This creates a layer of tensed muscle on your upper back over and above your shoulder blades. Position the bar on the muscle just above the center of the top ridge of your shoulder blades. This is lower than what's typically used by most trainees.

This bar position is essential—to avoid metal to spine contact, and to provide a greater area of contact than that from a higher position. This yields greater bar control.

Practice correct bar positioning until you can do it automatically. What will initially feel awkward, will become relatively comfortable after a few weeks of practice.

Good bar placement for the squat (left). Bar too high and hands not holding it properly (right). A cambered bar may not drape over your shoulders properly (left) unless there's weight pulling on it.

Grip

Hold the bar securely in your hands, not loosely in the tips of your fingers. Don't drape your wrists over the bar, or hands over the plates. Furthermore, each hand must be the same distance from the center of the bar.

The width of grip depends on your torso size, forearm and arm lengths, and shoulder and pectoral flexibility. For the best control over the bar, use the closest grip that feels comfortable. But if your grip is too close, it will be hard on your shoulders and elbows.

If your grip is too wide, you'll risk trapping your fingers between the bar and the safety supports or rack pins at the bottom of the squat. Place your hands so that there's no chance of your fingers getting trapped.

Stance

Following experimentation using a *bare* bar, find *your* optimum width of heel placement, and degree of toe flare. As a starting point, place your feet hip-width apart and parallel with each other, then turn out the toes on *each* foot about 30 degrees. Perform some squats. Then try a bit more flare and the same heel spacing. Next, try a slightly wider stance, and the initial toe flare. Then try the wider stance with more flare.

The combination of a moderate stance and well-flared toes usually gives plenty of room to squat into, helps to prevent excessive forward lean, and lets you squat deeper without your lower back

Left, feet too close. Middle, feet well spaced but with insufficient flare. Right, this stance for the squat, or something close to it, will work well for most trainees. The bar is positioned too high in these photos, and the back isn't properly set.

rounding. But too-wide a stance will restrict your descent. Experiment until you find the stance that best suits you. Individual variation in leg and thigh lengths, torso length, hip girth, and relative lengths of legs and thighs, contribute to determining the squat stance that's ideal for you. Tall trainees usually need a wider stance than trainees of average height.

Find a foot placement that spreads the stress of the squat over your thighs, buttocks, and back. Squat without your lower back rounding, your torso leaning forward excessively, or your heels coming off the floor. There should be no tendency to topple forward. Keep forward movement of your knees to a minimum, and keep your knees pointing in the *same* direction as your feet. Don't let your knees buckle inward.

If you have a stance that's too close, or has insufficient toe flare, then buckling of your knees may be inevitable when you squat intensively.

It may take a few workouts before you find the best stance for you. With just a bare bar over your upper back, stand on some cardboard, adopt your squat stance, and check it out. After tinkering with your stance, once you're sure it's correct, and while keeping your feet in position, get someone to draw the outline of your feet on the card. Then you'll have a record of your stance for when you want to refer to it. Practice repeatedly until you can adopt your squat stance automatically.

The right-side pair of photographs shows the correct stance—heels well spaced, and toes flared. The far-right photographs show an incorrect stance—feet close together, and parallel with each other. Notice how the incorrect, cramped stance increases forward travel of the knees, and forward lean of the torso.

The bar is positioned too high in these four photographs.

Initial performance

Face the bar so that you have to walk *backward* from the saddles before taking your squatting stance. Take your grip on the bar, and get under it as it rests on the weight saddles or stands. Don't lean over to get under the bar. Bend your knees, and get your torso and hips underneath the bar. Your feet can either be hip-width apart under the bar, or split. If split, one foot will be a little in front of the bar, and the other will be a little behind the bar. Pull your scapulae together, tense the musculature of your back, and position the bar correctly.

Your lower back should be slightly hollowed, and your hips directly under the bar. Look forward, tense your entire torso, then straighten your knees. The bar should move *vertically* out of the saddles or stands.

Stand still for a few seconds. Check that the bar feels correctly centered. If it feels heavier on one side than the other, put it back on the saddles. If it felt a little unbalanced, stay under the bar as it rests on the saddles, reposition the bar, and try again. If, however, it felt considerably lopsided, get out from under the bar, check that you loaded the bar correctly, and make any necessary corrections. Then get under the bar again, position it properly, and unrack it.

Never walk out of squat stands with a bar that doesn't feel properly centered on your upper back.

Step back the minimum distance so that you don't hit the uprights of the rack or squat stands during the ascent. Don't step forward after you've taken the bar out of its supports. If you do, you'll have to walk backward and look to the rear to return the bar to its supports. This is more hazardous than returning the bar forward to its supports.

Slide your feet over the floor as you walk with the bar. This keeps both of your feet in constant contact with the floor. Put your feet in the stance you've drilled yourself to adopt. Don't look down. At all times while standing with the bar, whether stationary or moving into your stance, maintain a natural degree of lower-back inward curve. Never slouch. Maintenance of the natural strong curves of your spine is critical for back health, when bearing weight.

Keep your jaw parallel with the floor—during and between reps. Your eyes should look straight ahead or slightly up, but not down. Fix your eyes on one spot throughout a set.

The weight should be felt mostly through your heels, not the front of your feet, but don't rock back on your heels and lose your balance.

Descent

With the bar, center of your hips, and heels in a vertical line, weight felt mostly through your heels, unlock your knees and sit down and back. The knee and hip breaks should be simultaneous. Maintain a tight, tensed back, with your shoulder blades retracted, and make a deliberate effort to tense your back further as you descend. Push your chest out as you descend, and push your hips to the rear. Doing all of this will help to maintain the slightly hollowed lower back, which is essential for safe, effective squatting.

Descend symmetrically, under control, with the weight felt mostly through your heels. Take about three seconds to descend to your bottom position.

Left, squat to a depth where the upper thighs are parallel with the floor. The lower spine is still slightly hollowed, albeit the hollow is filled with muscle. This is the maximum safe depth for this trainee. Middle, the increased depth has caused the lower back to round. Right, severe rounding or flexion of the lower spine. DANGER: never allow your back to round in the squat. The right photograph also illustrates the incorrect shift of the stress from the exercise to mostly over the balls of the feet, and exaggerated forward travel of the knees, whereas the left-most photograph illustrates stress mostly over the heels.

Some forward movement of your knees and shins is necessary, but keep it to the minimum. Keeping the weight felt mostly through your heels helps to maintain correct leg positioning. Provided that correct technique is used, how much forward movement there is of your knees largely depends on your body structure and how deep you squat.

Depth of descent

With poor squatting technique, your lower back will round earlier in the descent than it would had you used correct technique. With correct set-up and technique, as described here, and just a bare bar, find the depth of descent at which your lower back just starts to round. An assistant must watch you from the side, with his eyes level with your hips at your bottom position.

Set your squatting depth at two inches or five centimeters above the point where your lower back just starts to round. Position the safety bars of the power rack, or squat stands, at that depth.

When the hips rise faster than the shoulders, the torso tips forward excessively, and stress is greatly exaggerated on the lower back—DANGER. Your hips must not rise faster than your shoulders.

Ideally, descend until your upper thighs are parallel with or just below parallel with the floor. If your lower back starts to round before you reach the parallel position, you mustn't squat to parallel. Most trainees who are flexible enough, and who use correct technique, can squat to parallel without their lower backs rounding. Don't reduce your squatting depth except for safety reasons. The deeper you squat, the less weight you'll need to exhaust the involved musculature.

Although some trainees can squat safely to well below parallel, they belong to a minority. You may belong to that minority. Squatting to below parallel is called the *full squat*.

Ascent

Don't pause at the bottom position. Immediately start the ascent. Ascend while pushing mostly through your heels. Push with equal force through both feet. If you favor one side, you may produce asymmetrical motion in your ascent, which is dangerous. Take two to three seconds for each ascent.

During the ascent, the bar as seen from the side should move vertically. It mustn't move forward before it moves upward. If you tip forward at the bottom of the squat, the bar will go forward before it starts to go up. This is a common mistake, and has produced many lower-back injuries.

Your hips must not rise faster than your shoulders.

Knees coming in on the ascent is a common symptom of set-up flaws in the squat. Insufficient toe flare, and heels too close, are common flaws responsible for buckling of the knees. Tight thigh adductors may also contribute.

Heel elevation—DANGER

Squatting with the heels elevated is a mistake. Some trainees elevate their heels under the belief that they will isolate certain areas of their quadriceps. Others do it to maintain their balance, to compensate for insufficient flexibility, or poor squatting technique.

Safe squatting involves distributing the weight over the rear two thirds of each foot, and pushing primarily through the heels on the ascent. When the heels are elevated, the balls of the feet take more of the weight, forward travel of the knees is increased unnecessarily, and the hips and knees shift forward, which corrupts the balanced spread of stress over the thighs, buttocks, and back. The result is unnecessarily increased knee stress, with potentially harmful consequences.

The flexibility work recommended in this book will help address the insufficient flexibility that's often at the root of trainees' desire for heel elevation while squatting. When adequate flexibility is combined with good squatting technique—including the right width of stance, and degree of toe flare—the heels will stay where they belong: on the floor.

Never squat with a board, plate, or block under your heels. Raising your heels produces a more upright torso, but distorts the balanced spread of stress over the thighs, hips, and back. The result is unnecessarily increased knee stress, with potentially harmful consequences.

Focus on pushing mostly through your heels. This will help you maintain the proper ascent. Pushing through the front part of your feet will almost inevitably tip you forward, and ruin your ascent. Make a special effort to keep your shoulder blades pulled back, your chest pushed out, and hips pushed to the rear, to help you keep your ascent in the right groove.

The ascent, like the descent, should be symmetrical. The bar shouldn't tip to one side, and you shouldn't take more weight on one side of your body than the other.

While standing

Pause briefly to take one or more deep breaths, then move into the next rep. While standing between reps, don't sway at your hips, don't rock the bar on your shoulders, don't take more of the weight on one foot than the other, and don't rotate your hips. Stay rigid, with the weight distributed symmetrically, and maintain the natural inward curve in your lower spine. If you move your hips forward during the pause between reps, you'll flatten the curve at the bottom of your spine and greatly weaken your back.

While standing between reps, preserve the natural curves of your spine (left). Don't round your back (right).

Racking the bar

At the end of a set, rack the bar. While sliding your feet so that you always have both feet in contact with the floor, shuffle forward until the bar is directly above the saddles or stands. Check that you're not going to miss the bar holders with the bar, and ensure that your fingers aren't lined up to be trapped between the bar and its holders. Then bend your knees and set the bar down.

The bar should be returned to its holders in a vertical motion. A common error is to stop short of the saddles or stands and lower the bar through leaning forward while keeping the knees straight. This is dangerous. It leads to reduced control over the bar, and excessive stress on a tired back.

Other tips

Don't squat in a sweaty shirt. Change your shirt before you squat, if need be. Don't squat with a bare torso, because it reduces the stability of the bar on your back.

Before you get under the bar for a work set, put chalk or rosin on your hands, and perhaps get someone to put chalk or rosin on your shirt where the bar will rest. This may help the bar to stay in position.

Increasing your shoulder and pectoral flexibility will help you to hold the bar in position with less difficulty.

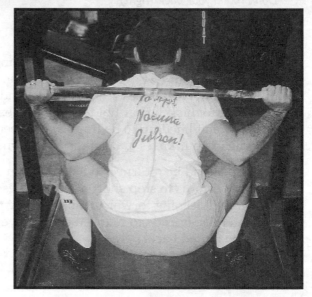

Good squatting form—down to parallel while maintaining good back positioning, and minimal forward travel of the knees.

Practice, practice, and practice again, with just a bare bar, until you can get into your correct squatting stance without having to look down or fiddle around to get your feet in the right position.

Never turn your head while you're squatting. If you do, the bar will tip slightly, your groove will be spoiled, and you could hurt yourself.

The orthodox breathing pattern when squatting is to take one or more deep breaths while standing, descend, and then exhale during the ascent. If you're squatting for 10 or fewer reps, then one or two deep breaths before each rep should suffice. For longer-duration sets, take three deep breaths before reps 11 through 15, and three or four deep breaths before reps 16 through 20.

Don't squat to a bench, box, or chair, as that would cause compression of your spine because your vertebrae would get squeezed between the weight up top and the hard surface down below. You could, however, squat to a soft object of the right height for you, such as a large piece of soft packing foam. When you feel the foam brushing against your buttocks or hamstrings, depending on where the foam is placed, you'll have reached your maximum safe depth but without risk of spinal compression.

To help you to improve your squatting technique, record yourself with a video camera, from the side view. Watching yourself in a mirror isn't adequate alone.

Once you've mastered the technique, give 100% attention to ensure that you deliver correct technique on every rep. Just a slight slip of concentration can lead to lowering the bar out of position, one hand getting ahead or in front of the other, or one thigh taking more load than the other.

Don't squat if your lower back is sore from an earlier workout, or heavy manual labor. Wait until you've recovered. Furthermore, don't perform any form of deadlift before you squat. Don't fatigue your lower back and reduce its potential as a major stabilizer for the squat.

Don't use a lifting belt. It's not required. See point #34, on page 184.

Spotting

As soon as the bar stalls, moves laterally, tips, or the squatter starts to twist to one side, the spotter or spotters must act to prevent the rep deteriorating further. If there are no spotters, set the bar down immediately (under control) on the safety bars. Don't try to complete a squat unassisted when your technique has started to break down.

If two spotters are involved, there must be excellent communication and synchronized action. If one spotter shouts "Take it!" the other must respond even if the latter thinks the assistance could have been delayed. Assistance needs to be applied equally to each side, to maintain a horizontal bar.

If one spotter is involved, he should stand directly behind the trainee. Assistance is given by the spotter standing astride the trainee, grabbing him or her around the lower rib cage, maintaining bent

Spotting for the squat.

knees and a slightly arched back, and applying upward pressure. This will work only if a little help is needed to get the trainee through the sticking point. It's no way of providing a lot of assistance when the trainee is exhausted. It is, however, a quick way of injuring the spotter because he'll end up leaning forward and heavily stressing his lower back. A single spotter shouldn't even try to help you up if substantial assistance is needed. Instead, the spotter should help you to lower the bar safely to the rack pins or safety bars.

Even if the spotter doesn't need to assist during a rep, he should be alert to help guide the bar back into the weight saddles after the final rep. At the end of a hard set of squats, you'll be tired. Without a pair of guiding hands on the bar from a spotter you may miss getting the bar into the weight saddles.

Patience

It may take time for the squat to feel natural. Don't lose heart if you find that squatting with the bare bar feels awkward, and you wobble a lot. But don't go adding a lot of weight prematurely. Build up gradually as described in **The Program**, and be confident that the exercise will feel better later than it does at first.

How to improve your ability to squat

Only a small proportion of trainees are naturally gifted for back squatting and front squatting, largely because of their body proportions and leverages. Most trainees need to work at squatting technique *and* the essential supportive work, to make themselves into competent squatters.

There are three major components of good squatting ability:

1. The flexibility to be able to *adopt* the correct body positioning.

2. The back strength to be able to *maintain* the correct back positioning.

3. Correct exercise technique.

You need sufficient flexibility in the major musculature of your lower body, along with the required shoulder flexibility to hold the bar in position correctly. Follow the flexibility program in Chapter 2. If any of the muscles have anything less than at least a normal, healthy level of flexibility, squatting technique will probably be compromised, with a reduction in safety and productivity. Squat correctly, or not at all.

You need sufficient strength throughout your back—lower, middle, and upper—to be able to hold your lower back in the required slightly hollowed position during the squat. This is critical for safety. Your back must not round while squatting—there must be no back flexion. Four key back exercises—deadlift, back extension, row, and shrug—will help build the required back strength provided that they are worked with correct technique, and progressive resistance.

Having the required flexibility and back strength is one thing, but learning to *use* the flexibility and strength during the squat is something else.

It may take several months before correct squatting technique can be implemented, even with minimal weight. Don't be frustrated to begin with. As your flexibility and back strength improve, and your ability to use them, so will your squatting ability. Until you can adopt the correct squatting technique, keep the resistance very light—perhaps just the bare bare. Thereafter, as your squatting weight grows, so should your strength in the deadlift, back extension, row, and shrug, to help you to maintain the correct back positioning.

The Smith machine

Smith machine squats give only an illusion of safety relative to the barbell squat. With the Smith machine, the bar is locked into a fixed pathway so you don't have to be concerned with balance; and you don't have to take a barbell from stands, step back to perform your set, and step forward at the end of a set in order to return the bar to the stands. But when you look further into the Smith machine squat, there are perils.

Don't squat in the Smith machine. Its use is loaded with dangerous compromises. It forces you to follow the bar path dictated by the machine, but the bar path should be dictated by your body.

If you put your feet forward in the Smith machine squat, to prevent your knees travelling too far forward at the bottom of the movement relative to your feet, you would put your lower back at risk. If your feet are well forward, you would lose the natural, required slight hollow in your lower back—including at the bottom of the movement—because your hips would be forward of their ideal position. Although your knees may be spared some stress, it would be at the cost of a back injury, sooner or later.

If you bring your feet back so that they are directly beneath your shoulders, all may look well until you descend. Then your knees would travel forward excessively, the load would shift more to over the balls of your feet, the stress on your knees would be exaggerated, and the risk of injury would increase.

When used for full-range movements such as the squat, bench press, incline bench press, and overhead press, correct exercise technique is corrupted by the vertical bar pathway that the Smith machine enforces. This will set you up for injuries.

Used correctly, free-weights provide the freedom required to move through pathways that are natural for your body.

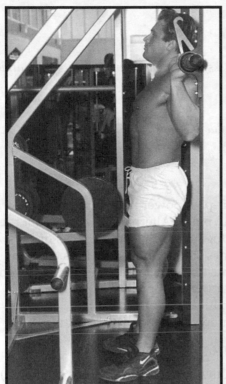

Don't squat in the Smith machine because the rigid, vertical pathway corrupts natural squatting technique. This is hostile to the back and the knees.

Front squat

Main muscles worked

quadriceps, thigh adductors, buttocks, hamstrings, spinal erectors, multifidii

Capsule description

hold a bar at the front of your shoulders, squat, then stand erect

Set-up

Always front squat inside a four-post power rack with pins and saddles correctly and securely in place. Alternatively, use a half rack, sturdy and stable squat stands together with spotter racks or bars, or a squat rack unit that combines stands and safety bars. Should you fail on a front squat, you must be able to descend to the bottom position and safely set the bar down on supports. Make no compromises—*safety comes first.* Ideally, you should have spotters standing by in addition to the aforementioned safety set-up.

See *Safety equipment*, in Chapter 7, for illustrations.

Position the bar saddles so that the barbell (straight, not cambered) is set at mid- to upper-chest height. If the bar is too low, you'll waste energy getting it out. If it's too high, you'll need to rise on your toes to get the bar out. The too-high setting is especially dangerous when you return the bar after finishing a hard set of front squats.

Wear a thick sweatshirt rather than a thin T-shirt, to provide padding to cushion the bar where it rests on your deltoids next to your clavicles. Some of the weight will end up on your clavicles, but not all— minimize it, to prevent excessive discomfort. If more padding is needed, wear a T-shirt and a sweatshirt.

Bar positioning

To find where the bar should sit during the front squat, lift your left arm out in front so that your left elbow is higher than your left shoulder. Then with your right hand find the groove where your left front deltoid meets your left collar bone. That's the groove where the bar should sit—mostly on the deltoid, not the clavicle. Place a bare bar there, to get the feel for it.

To keep the bar in position, cross your hands on the bar—left hand over the bar on your right side, and right hand over the bar on your

left side. The bar should be just in front of your windpipe. Keep your hands firmly on the bar, and elbows higher than your shoulders. This elbow positioning is critical, to maintain a sufficiently upright torso to prevent the bar falling forward and out of position. If your elbows drop, your technique will crumble.

Because of the use of a closer hand spacing in the front squat than the back squat, a shorter bar than an Olympic one may be easier to handle. If you have a shorter bar available, and the stands to support it between sets (or assistants to help you), try that for the front squat.

Stance

Following experimentation using a bare bar, find your optimum width of heel placement, and degree of toe flare. As a starting point, place your feet hip-width apart and parallel with each other, then turn out the toes on each foot about 30 degrees. Perform some front squats. Then try a bit more flare and the same heel spacing. Next, try a slightly wider stance, and the initial toe flare. Then try the wider stance with more flare.

Too close a stance will hamper stability, and too wide a stance will restrict your descent. Experiment until you find the stance that best suits you. Individual variation in leg and thigh lengths, torso length, hip girth, and relative lengths of your legs and thighs, contribute to determining the front squat stance that's ideal for you. The stance you settle on may be a little closer than what you would use in the back squat.

Find a foot placement that provides stability, the fullest *safe* range of motion, no rounding of your lower back, and minimal forward lean. Your heels must remain fixed to the floor. You need to be stable, with no tendency to topple forward. Never put a board or plates under your heels.

Keep your knees pointing in the same direction as your feet. Don't let your knees buckle inward.

If your stance is too close, or has insufficient flare, then buckling of your knees may be inevitable when you front squat intensively.

Fine-tune your stance, and keep working on your buttock, hamstring, and calf flexibility. As you loosen up over a few weeks, along with fine-tuning your stance, your front squatting technique will improve. Don't lose heart if it's difficult to begin with.

It may take a few workouts before you find the best stance for you. When you've got it, stand on some cardboard, and adopt your front squat stance. Get someone to draw the outline of your feet on the card. Then you'll have a record of your stance for when you want to refer to it. Practice repeatedly until you can adopt your front squat stance automatically, without having to look down to check where your feet are.

Initial performance

Face the bar so that you have to walk backward from the saddles before taking your squatting stance. Get under the bar as it rests on the weight saddles or stands. Don't lean over to get under the bar. Bend your knees and get your hips underneath the bar. Place your feet directly beneath the bar, side-by-side a bit wider than shoulder-width apart. Pull your scapulae together, tense the musculature of your back, keep your lower back slightly hollowed, then position the bar. Remember, the bar should sit mostly on your deltoids, not your clavicles.

Cross your hands on the bar—left hand over the bar on your right side, and right hand over the bar on your left side. Hold your head and neck upright, to prevent the bar jamming into your windpipe. This will take time to adapt to, and require a number of workouts. At all times, keep your hands firmly on the bar, and elbows higher than your shoulders. Fight to do it. Then your control will be good.

With the bar in position, your lower back slightly hollowed, scapulae pulled together, and your hips directly under the bar, look forward, tense your torso, then straighten your knees. The bar should move vertically out of the saddles or stands. Don't unrack the bar in an inclined pathway. Stand still for a few seconds, without moving your feet. Check that the bar feels correctly centered. If it feels heavier on one side than the other, put it back on the saddles, reposition it, and try again. If it felt considerably lopsided, get out from under the bar, check that you have loaded the bar correctly, and make any necessary corrections. Then get under the bar again, position it correctly, and unrack it.

Step back the minimum distance so that you don't hit the uprights of the rack or squat stands during the ascent. Don't step forward after you've taken the bar out of its supports. If you do, you'll have to walk backward to return the bar to its supports. This is more hazardous than returning the bar forward into the rack saddles or squat stands.

Slide your feet over the floor as you walk with the bar. This keeps both your feet in constant contact with the floor. Then put your feet in the stance you've drilled yourself to adopt. Don't look down.

At all times, keep your hands firmly on the bar, and elbows higher than your shoulders. Fight to do it. Then your control of the bar should be good.

Keep your jaw parallel with the floor—during and between reps. Your eyes should look straight ahead or slightly up, but not down. Fix your eyes on a spot throughout the set.

The weight should be felt mostly through your heels, but don't rock back on your heels and lose your balance.

Caution—bar tipping

Because the hands are closer in the front squat than the back squat, and because the bar may rest on a narrower area in the former, the bar tips more readily in the front squat than the back squat. Although the bar should be horizontal for every exercise—for symmetrical distribution of stress—special care is required to maintain it in the front squat.

Descent

With the bar, center of your hips, and heels in a vertical line, weight felt mostly through your heels, unlock your knees and sit down and back. The knee and hip breaks should be simultaneous.

Maintain a tight, tensed back, with your shoulder blades retracted, and make a deliberate effort to tense your back further as you descend. Stick your chest out as you descend, and push your hips to the rear. Doing all of this will help to maintain the slightly hollowed lower back, which is critical for safe, effective front squatting.

At all times, keep your hands firmly on the bar, and elbows higher than your shoulders. Fight to do it. Then your control of the bar should be good.

Descend symmetrically, under control, and with the weight felt mostly through your heels. Take about three seconds to descend to your full, safe, front squatting depth.

Some forward movement of your knees is a necessity, but keep it to the minimum. Provided that correct technique is used, how much forward movement there is of your knees largely depends on your body structure, and how deep you squat.

Depth of descent

With poor front squatting technique, your lower back will round earlier in the descent than it would had you used correct technique. With correct set-up and technique, as described in this section, and just a bare bar, find the depth of descent at which your lower back just starts to round. An assistant must watch you from the side, with his eyes level with your hips at your bottom position.

Set your depth at two inches or five centimeters above the point where rounding of your lower back just starts. Position the safety bars of the power rack, or squat stands, at that depth.

Ideally, descend until your upper thighs are parallel with or just below parallel with the floor. Most trainees who are flexible enough can front squat to parallel or a bit below without their lower backs rounding.

Don't reduce your front squatting depth except for safety reasons. The deeper you front squat, the less weight you'll need to exhaust the involved musculature. Most trainees can front squat deeper than they back squat before their lower backs start to round.

Comparison of the back squat (right) and front squat (far right) with the identical stance—heels well spaced, and toes flared. Notice how the back is more vertical in the front squat, but the knees travel forward more.

The increased forward travel of the shins in the front squat should be safe for healthy knees provided the stress from the exercise is felt mostly through the heels, not the balls of the feet.

Ascent

As soon as you reach your bottom position, push up in a controlled manner, with equal force through the heels of both feet. If you favor one side, you may produce an asymmetrical ascent, which is dangerous. Take two to three seconds for each ascent.

At all times, keep your hands firmly on the bar, and elbows higher than your shoulders. Fight to do it. Then your control of the bar should be good.

During the ascent, the bar, as seen from the side, should move vertically. It mustn't move forward before it moves upward. If you tip forward at the bottom of the front squat, the bar will go forward before it starts to go up. This is a common mistake that causes loss of bar control, which produces lower-back injuries, and other problems.

Your hips must not rise faster than your shoulders. Lead with your head and shoulders.

Focus on pushing mostly through your heels. This will help you to maintain the proper ascent. Pushing through the front part of your feet will almost inevitably tip you forward, and ruin your ascent. Make a special effort to keep your shoulder blades pulled back, chest stuck out, and hips pushed to the rear, to help you keep your ascent in the right groove.

The ascent, like the descent, should be symmetrical. The bar shouldn't tip to one side, and you shouldn't take more weight on one side of your body than the other.

While standing

Pause briefly to take one or more deep breaths, then move into the next rep. While standing between reps, don't sway at your hips, don't rock the bar on your shoulders, don't take more of the weight on one foot than the other, and don't rotate your hips. Stay rigid, with the weight distributed symmetrically, and maintain the natural inward curve in your lower spine. If you move your hips forward during the pause between reps, you'll flatten the curve at the bottom of your spine, and greatly weaken your back.

Once again . . . *keep your hands firmly on the bar, and elbows higher than your shoulders. Fight to do it. Then your control of the bar should be good.*

Racking the bar

At the end of a set, rack the bar. While sliding your feet so that you always have both feet in contact with the floor, shuffle forward until the bar is directly above the saddles or stands. Check that you're not going to miss the bar holders with the bar, and ensure that your fingers aren't lined up to be trapped between the bar and its holders. Then bend your knees and set the bar down.

The bar should be returned to its holders in a vertical motion. A common error is to stop short of the saddles or stands and lower the bar through leaning forward while keeping the knees straight. This is dangerous. It leads to reduced control over the bar, and excessive stress on a tired back.

Other tips

Never turn your head while you're lifting or lowering the bar. If you do, the bar will tip slightly, your groove will be spoiled, and you could hurt yourself.

The orthodox breathing pattern when front squatting is to take one or more deep breaths while standing, descend, and then exhale during the ascent. Alternatively, breathe freely.

Consolidating front squatting technique takes time and patience. With a bare bar, practice on alternate days for as many sessions as it takes until you master the technique. Then build up the resistance slowly and carefully.

Expect awkwardness with the positioning of the bar. You must persist with the front squat. Don't give up after a brief trial. With a bit of practice you *will* adjust—you'll find the precise position for the bar that will work for you. A small adjustment in bar position can make a big difference. What may have felt impossible to begin with may, a few weeks later, feel fine.

If, however, after six weeks of persistence, holding the bar in position still feels too uncomfortable, use a little padding between the bar and your deltoids additional to what you get from your clothing. Tightly wrap a small towel around the bar before putting the bar in place on your shoulders or, better yet, slip a thin strip of compressed foam tubing over the center of the bar. Don't use a large towel or thick piece of foam (whether soft or compressed), as both lead to incorrect bar positioning, and bar movement on your shoulders during a set, which will ruin your technique.

One last time: *Keep your hands firmly on the bar, and elbows higher than your shoulders. Fight to do it. Then your control of the bar should be good.*

As observed from the side view of the front squat, get feedback from a training partner. Alternatively, record yourself with a video camera. Watching your reflection in a mirror isn't adequate for analyzing your front squatting technique.

Once you've mastered the technique, give 100% attention to ensure that you deliver correct technique during every rep. Just a slight slip of concentration can lead to lowering the bar out of position, the elbows dropping beneath shoulder height, or one foot taking more load than the other. Any of these will spoil the pathway of the bar, make the weight feel heavier, make your reps harder, cause frustration, and risk injury.

Don't front squat to a bench, box, or chair, as that would cause compression of your spine because your vertebrae would get squeezed between the weight up top and the hard surface down below.

Don't front squat if your lower back is sore from an earlier workout, or heavy manual labor. Wait until you've recovered. Furthermore, don't perform any form of deadlift before you front squat. Don't fatigue your lower back and reduce its potential as a major stabilizer for the front squat.

Don't use a lifting belt. It's not required. See point #34, on page 184.

Safety reminders

Always back and front squat inside a four-post power rack with pins and saddles correctly and securely in place. Alternatively, use a half rack, sturdy and stable squat stands together with spotter racks or bars, or a squat rack unit that combines stands and safety bars. Use a set-up so that should you fail on a squat, you can descend to the bottom position and safely set the bar down on the supports. There must be no compromise here—*safety comes first*. Ideally, you should have spotters standing by in addition to the aforementioned safety set-up.

To demonstrate exercise technique clearly, the models sometimes didn't wear shirts, and weight stands and safety bars were often not used. This was for illustration purposes only. When you train, wear a shirt, and take proper safety measures.

Ball squat

Main muscles worked

quadriceps, thigh adductors, buttocks, hamstrings

Capsule description

stand with a ball between your hips and a wall, squat, then stand erect

The ball squat, also called the *wall squat*, is an alternative to the barbell squat that doesn't heavily involve the lower back. It's technically easier than the back squat and front squat, and requires minimal equipment.

Set-up and positioning

Obtain a soft, exercise or stability ball 12 to 16 inches (or 30 to 40 centimeters) in diameter. Stand on a non-slip surface, parallel with an area of a smooth wall that has no objects mounted on it, facing away from the wall. Position the center of the ball between your hips and the wall. Stand upright, with the ball snugly in place, and your heels about hip-width apart. Next, move your feet forward four to five inches, and turn your toes out about 30 degrees on each side.

You may need to try several exercise balls to find one that works best for you. The ideal size of the ball varies according to the size of the individual. A large person will require a larger ball. The degree of preferred softness may vary, too.

Performance

Keep your torso vertical, head up, eyes forward, shoulders retracted, and lower back slightly hollowed, and take about three seconds to sit down to the point where your upper thighs are approximately parallel with the floor. Pause for a second, then smoothly ascend to the starting position, pushing only through your heels. Pushing only through your heels minimizes the stress on the knee joints. Again, keep your torso vertical, head up, eyes forward, shoulders retracted, and lower back slightly hollowed. And keep your shoulders directly above your hips throughout each rep. Take two to three seconds for each ascent. At the top of each rep, either gently fully straighten your knees, or keep them slightly bent. Pause for a second at the top, then descend into the next rep.

Your knees should point in the same direction as your toes. Don't allow your knees to move inward.

As you descend and ascend, the ball will move up and down your back. Keep the ball centered on your back. And keep your body moving symmetrically. Lean against the ball the minimum amount—just enough to maintain balance and correct positioning.

Fine-tune the set-up position so that during each descent your shins remain vertical, or close to vertical, and your knees and hips feel comfortable. Minimize forward travel of your knees. Depending on your height and body proportions, you may need to move your feet forward a little further, widen your stance a little more, and turn out your toes a little further. You may also benefit from fine-tuning the ball position—probably by lowering its starting position. And remember to push through your heels on the ascent.

Make one change at a time, and perform a few reps following each change. Perform one or two sets, ten reps per set, each rep to approximately parallel with the floor.

If, the following day, you have no negative reaction in your knees or hips, try a greater range of motion the next workout—descend to below the parallel position, but not so low that your lower back rounds. Find the maximum range of motion for you that keeps your lower back slightly hollowed, and is comfortable for your knees and hips. This range of motion will probably be greater in the ball squat than in the back squat or front squat.

If, however, you had a negative reaction in your hips or knees, don't increase your range of motion. Instead, once your joints feel fine, test the exercise again, but adjust your foot positioning to try to find a safer set-up.

Once you've found a safe set-up, and maximum range of motion for you, gradually increase your performance. When you can perform three sets of 15 reps, start to use additional resistance. Hold a dumbbell in each hand as you perform the ball squat, with your palms parallel with each other. Keep your forearms and arms straight and vertical—consider them as links to the dumbbells.

The ball may ride up your back during the set, and need to be lowered. If so, and if you're holding additional resistance, get an assistant to lower the ball quickly while you stand upright.

Lean the minimum amount against the ball—just enough to maintain balance and correct positioning. Excessive leaning into the ball changes the dynamics of the exercise, and may increases stress on your knees.

The orthodox breathing pattern when squatting is to take one or more deep breaths while standing, descend, and then exhale during the ascent. Alternatively, breathe freely.

Other tips

Take the dumbbells from the floor at the bottom of the first ball squat, or from low bases. Thereafter keep hold of the dumbbells until the bottom position of the final rep, when you would return them to their starting positions. When you're at your maximum, safe, bottom position of each rep, the dumbbells should just brush the floor or elevation. Whether you'll need bases will depend on your limb and torso lengths, and their relative proportions, depth of squatting, and size of the dumbbells. If the dumbbells would be too low for you when on the floor, elevate each of them on one or more plates, smooth sides up.

In some cases, the dumbbells may strike the floor before the trainee has reached the bottom position. In this case, the lifter needs to be elevated sufficiently—for instance, on a side-by-side pair of large weight plates turned smooth sides up—so that the dumbbells are in the correct position on the floor for taking at the bottom of the first rep.

Don't lean to one side to pick up a dumbbell. Keep yourself symmetrical. Furthermore, don't descend deeper than your usual depth to get the dumbbells on your first rep.

With weighty dumbbells, use chalk or rosin on your hands. If the dumbbell handles have sharp knurling, that will help your grip greatly, especially if you have chalk or rosin on your hands, too.

An alternative to using a pair of dumbbells is to suspend securely a single dumbbell, or weight plates, from a chain or rope attached to a belt around your hips. The belt could be the same one used for parallel bar dips—a purpose-made weight belt. You'd probably need to stand on two stable platforms so that the suspended dumbbell or weight plates don't hit the floor before you reach your bottom position.

The squat with suspended resistance but without use of a ball for support, is called a *hip-belt squat*, and is described next.

Hip-belt squat

Main muscles worked

quadriceps, thigh adductors, buttocks, hamstrings

Capsule description

stand with resistance suspended from your hips and between your legs, hold a support, squat, then stand erect

The hip-belt squat is another alternative to the barbell squat that doesn't heavily involve the lower back if done correctly. It provides tremendous work for the thighs and buttocks. It usually permits a deeper squat than can be safely tolerated in the barbell squat because with the hip-belt squat there's rearward movement of the torso, little or no forward lean of the torso, minimal involvement of the lower back, and reduced forward travel of the knees.

Set-up and positioning

Find or make two sturdy, broad, *non-slip* platforms, to stand on. If there's any wobble of the platforms, wedge shims under one or more of the corners. The platforms should be at least 15 inches tall, preferably over 20. The lower the resistance hangs from your body, the more comfortable the set-up may feel, but the more easily the weight will swing. Use a rep speed slow enough to prevent the weight swinging.

Until you're using about 125 to 150 pounds (57 to 68 kilos), a belt for attaching weight for the parallel bar dip can substitute for a hip belt. But beyond that weight, or earlier in some cases, a proper hip belt—a heavy-duty weight belt with special attachments—is recommended, for comfort and safety. A supplier of such a hip belt is www.ironmind.com.

With a hip belt the weight stack may be attached by straps or chain to the front *and* rear of the belt, and there may be reduced friction between your body, belt, and attachments compared with other belts. If front *and* rear attachments are used, the length of the one between the rear of the belt and the loading pin will be longer than that of the front one, maybe by three to four inches. Some trainees may prefer to attach the loading pin to the front of the hip belt only, rather than the front *and* the rear.

Some trainees may fix the attachments to the hip belt using carabiners (spring clips), but others may fix them directly to the hip belt, and use a carabiner only to make the connection with the loading pin. Multiple carabiners, perhaps of different sizes, could be linked to fine tune the total length of an attachment. If chains are used as attachments, and they are loose near the belt, use an additional carabiner to pull them together.

A safety-first, heavy-duty set-up for the hip-belt squat.

Safety is paramount. Whatever belt and attachments you use, they must not fail you. They must be strong enough to hold the weight. And all carabiners must be heavy duty, and secure. There must be no risk of them opening during a set.

Rest the belt on your hip bones and upper buttocks. Don't cinch it around your waist. Experiment to find the most comfortable position for you. Depending on the belt, and the attachments, you may need to use padding such as a folded towel between the belt and your hips, and perhaps between the chains or straps and your body, too.

Place the platforms next to a power rack, or a stable, stationary object that's secured to the floor. Space the platforms so that there's just room for a 35-pound or 15-kilo plate on a loading pin to travel up and down without striking the platforms. To accommodate a larger plate you would need to use a wider stance—perhaps too wide. This wouldn't be necessary unless you had a full stack of 35-pounders and needed to use 45-pounders. Another alternative would be continued use of the smaller plates but with a taller loading pin, and taller platforms.

As an alternative to the loading pin, at least to begin with, you could suspend plates or a dumbbell directly from your belt.

You'll be tethered to the rack or other stationary object, so it must be steadfast. If the rack isn't fixed to the floor, load it with sufficient weight on the opposite side to you, so that it can't topple when pulled. Alternatively, have someone pull on the opposite side to you, for counterbalance. There must be *no chance* of the rack (or other stationary object) moving while you hip-belt squat, *or* of your feet slipping.

A simple, introductory set-up for the hip-belt squat, using a belt designed for applying resistance for the parallel bar dip (see page 315 for a close-up), and a strong band. The band should be looped around the hands before being grasped in the hands. A slight hollow should be maintained in the lower back at all times. The far right photograph shows some rounding of the lower back—avoid this.

Loop a strong length of towing strap or rope securely around the rack or other stable object, at about the height of your hips when you're standing on the platforms, or lower if the attachment point on the rack is further than about four feet or one meter from the platforms. There must be no risk of the strap snapping, or slipping out of position.

If the strap is fixed on the support at chest height or higher, it will probably lead to your torso leaning forward during the descent.

Strap may be preferable to rope, because the latter may cut into your skin. Alternatively, use rope and wear gloves. You'll need about five meters if you loop the strap around the posts of a rack. The ends of the strap must be within easy reach when you're on the platforms.

Wrap the ends of the strap or rope snugly around your hands next to your thumbs rather than around the knuckles at the base of your fingers. Grip the ends securely, so that when you stand on the platforms your elbows are almost straight, and the strap is taut. There must be no chance of losing your grip.

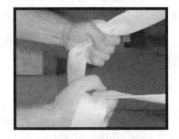

The loading pin should be placed on a sturdy crate or box that's temporarily positioned on the floor between your feet. The pin is loaded while on the crate or box. The loading pin needs to be elevated so that you don't have to squat down far to attach your belt to the loading pin.

Performance

Without a belt or weight, familiarize yourself with the exercise. Stand with the towing strap around your hands and pulled taut, elbows

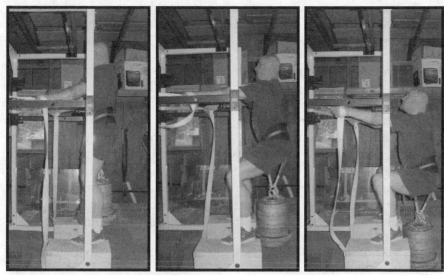

The heavy-duty set-up for the hip-belt squat. Regardless of the type of belt used, note the position of the torso with respect to the rack uprights. The torso must move down and back, not merely down.

straight or slightly bent, heels hip-width or a little wider, and each foot flared about 30 degrees. Reposition the platforms if need be.

Keep your torso vertical, head up, eyes forward, shoulders retracted, and lower back slightly hollowed. As you descend, *move your torso and hips to the rear*, allow but minimize forward travel of your knees, and keep your back vertical.

If the strap is too short, or the platforms are too far from the rack, you'll lean forward as you descend. If you lean forward, your lower back will round earlier than it would otherwise, which would reduce the safe range of motion for your thighs. Keep your torso vertical. Configure the set-up accordingly.

Take about three seconds for the descent. Descend as low as is safe for your knees and back—ideally to below the point where your upper thighs are parallel with the floor. Pause for a moment, stay tight, then smoothly ascend to the starting position—push only through your heels. Pushing only through your heels minimizes the stress on your knees. Take about three seconds for each ascent. At the top of each rep, either gently straighten your knees fully, or keep them slightly bent. Pause for a second at the top, then descend into the next rep.

During each rep, don't tug on the towing strap, or bend your elbows more than just slightly. The purpose of the strap is to help you to avoid forward lean of your torso, and minimize forward lean of your shins.

Perform several reps, then try a slightly wider stance, and different degrees of toe flare, to find what feels most comfortable for you. And experiment with the length of the strap, to find what works best.

When you're familiar with the exercise, try it with a belt and one plate on the loading pin. Load the pin while it's on the crate. Then grab the towing strap and stand in position on the platforms. Dip the short distance required to connect the attachment(s) from your belt to the loading pin, using a carabiner. Now, pull your shoulders back, slightly hollow your lower back, and stand. When the weight is significant, push your hands on your thighs to help you safely into the starting, upright position. Then get an assistant to move the crate away. While standing upright on the platforms, loop the strap around your hands until it's taut, and get set for your first rep.

As you descend, the plates should move down *and* to the rear, as should your hips and torso.

Although there's no compression on your back from the hip-belt squat, still keep your back slightly hollowed, for safety. *Never round your back, flatten your back, or slump forward.* If you can't maintain the right positioning, you may be holding a strap that's too short, and you may be descending too far. Adjust the length of attachment between your belt and the loading pin so that at your bottom position the resistance is about an inch above the floor, and you're about two inches above the point at which your lower back would start to round.

Get the feedback from an assistant, who should assess you from the side view, to help you to find the right set-up configuration, and to master the performance of the exercise.

Finish each set in the standing, upright position. Then get an assistant to reposition the crate. Set the weight on the crate, release the belt, stand and then rest in order to get ready for any subsequent set.

Don't set the resistance on the floor between reps. If, however, you get stuck on the ascent, descend further than normal, set the weight on the floor, and release the belt. For the next set, reposition the crate under the weight. Strip the loading pin before repositioning it on the crate, and reloading it. But, as much as possible, avoid failing on a rep like this, because releasing the belt is awkward when you're in a full squat, as is getting off the platforms. Both may irritate your knees.

The orthodox breathing pattern when squatting is to take one or more deep breaths while standing, descend, and then exhale during the ascent. Alternatively, breathe freely.

Once you know your set-up configuration, be consistent. Always put the platforms the same distance from the rack and same space apart, place the belt around your hips in the same position, use the same attachments between the belt and loading pin, use the same tethering strap and fasten it to the rack at the same height, grip the strap the same distance from the rack, loop it the same number of times around your hands, and so on.

If you've tried the technique as described, started very light with low intensity, and built up the poundage and intensity gradually, but *still* experienced knee irritation, try modifications. Wait until the knee irritation has healed, then reduce the range of motion so that your upper thighs don't descend further than where they are parallel with the floor. If that doesn't correct the problem, adjust the technique further while still not descending beyond the parallel position. When your shins are vertical, or almost vertical, there may be excessive stress on your knees. If a little more forward lean of your shins is allowed, that may increase involvement of your hip musculature, and hamstrings, and perhaps reduce stress on your knees. Try it with a reduced poundage to see if it's safe for you. If it is, try it with a greater range of motion, too.

Find the greatest, safe range of motion for you, and then gradually build up the poundage.

Especially for men, wear elasticated, giving briefs and shorts (or tracksuit bottoms) while performing the hip-belt squat, or otherwise the tension of the attachments against the clothing around your groin area may produce excessive discomfort.

It may require several workouts of experimentation before you find the hip-belt squat set-up and performance that works best for you. And initially you may find that your lower-back and hip musculature tires quickly once resistance is loaded. Be patient but persistent while you familiarize yourself with the exercise, and adapt to it. The hip-belt squat has the potential to be a safe, highly effective exercise, and especially valuable if you can't safely back squat, front squat, parallel-grip deadlift, or leg press. It's worth the time investment required to master it.

The hip-belt squat described here is based on that reported in the article "Safe and Heavy Hip-Belt Squats," by Nathan Harvey, published in HARDGAINER *issue #89. Nathan reported the methods of Ed Komoszewski. Photographs from that article have been reprinted here.*

25. TIMED HOLD

Main muscles worked

finger flexion muscles, forearms

Capsule description

hold a bar next to your thighs while you stand with straight knees

For best effect, use a bar that's thicker than usual. A standard bar of an inch, or slightly thicker, will work your grip hard and do a good job, but a thick bar will do a better job. A small increase in diameter produces a substantial change in girth, and a big increase in the difficulty of handling the bar.

If there's no thick bar where you train, improvise. At the minimum, wrap something around a bar to mimic a thick bar. Use the same modification each time you do the exercise.

Encourage the management of where you train to buy a ready-made thick bar. Alternatively, a local metal worker could make one to order. It will be a terrific addition to the gym and won't be expensive unless it's a solid, chromed bar.

Comparison of a regular-diameter barbell, and a two-inch diameter one.

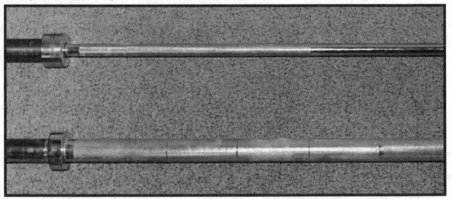

Set-up and positioning

Load a bar on boxes, or set it on the pins in a power rack, or across the safety bars in a squat rack, so that you have only to pull it up two inches before holding it in a standing position. You'll need to lower it only two inches once your grip has given out at the end of the hold. In effect, you hold the lockout position of the deadlift.

In a power rack getting into position for the timed hold, using a thick bar. The pin position should be higher than shown here, to make it easier to get the bar into the starting position.

Performance

Start with clean, dry hands and bar, and apply chalk or rosin to your fingers, palms, and the inside area of your thumbs and index fingers. Take a pronated grip on the bar a little wider than hip width, and keep the back of each hand in a straight line with its forearm. Then bend your knees a little, pull your shoulders back, hollow your lower back slightly, and stand upright.

While standing, keep your knees straight, shoulders retracted, and torso vertical or tilted forward slightly. Never round your back. The bar can be pressed against your thighs, but don't bend your knees or lean backward or otherwise you'll cheat through taking some of the weight on your thighs. Furthermore, leaning backward while supporting a load is harmful for the spine.

During the second half of each timed hold, don't merely grasp the bar. Try to crush it. Just holding the bar isn't the way to get the most staying power out of your grip. Squeeze the bar as hard as possible. Then when your grip is close to failing, try to bend the bar. Although you can't bend it, attempting to can extend the life of your grip. Shrugging your shoulders a little, and keeping your elbows slightly bent, may also help you to get more mileage out of your grip.

Don't be concerned about when to breathe during thick-bar holds—breathe freely. Don't hold your breath.

Select a duration for the holds. Between 30 and 60 seconds will probably suit most trainees. Settle on a specific number of seconds. Once you can hold the bar for that time, add a little weight next session.

Chapters 10 and 11 cover essential general
components of safe exercising, which should
be applied together with the guidance of
this chapter.

Exercise technique checklists

When learning a new exercise, or correcting a familiar exercise, there
are many points to remember. Use a checklist for each exercise, to
remind you of the key points.

Write a brief checklist for each exercise that needs it, on a separate
card for each. Use bold, clear writing. Review the relevant card prior
to doing an exercise.

As valuable as technique checklists are, they are no substitute for
serious study of the details given in this chapter. Even after you've
studied this chapter, you'll need to review parts of it regularly. Review
the technique of the exercises in each routine you undertake. Everyone
benefits from review work.

REMINDERS . . .
Fundamentals of correct exercise technique

1. Before you can apply correct exercise technique, you first need to know what correct exercise technique is. Study this chapter carefully.

2. Before a set, review the correct exercise technique.

3. Never rush into a set, grab the bar and then realize after the first rep that you took an imbalanced grip, the wrong stance, or are lopsided while on a bench. Get correctly positioned for every set.

4. Be 100% focused and attentive while you train.

5. Lift the weight, don't throw it; and lower it, don't drop it. Use control at all times. Move the resistance *smoothly*, without any sudden, or explosive movements.

6. Most trainees use more weight than they can handle correctly. This leads to cheating, loss of control, and produces injury sooner or later.

Whenever you lift something—including setting up or putting away equipment in the gym, or lifting objects at home or work—*lift as if you're lifting to exercise.* Never compromise on correct lifting technique.

13

How to handle weights between exercises

Correct lifting technique isn't restricted to exercises. It's also needed while setting up an exercise, or putting equipment away. Many trainees have been injured through improper weight handling *between* exercises.

Plate handling

With a large plate, carry it by itself in two hands, held tightly to your abdomen or chest. When putting the plate on a bar, plate stand, or rack, or when taking it from a bar, plate stand, or rack, get as close as possible, feet side-by-side, plate close to and centered on your torso, head up, shoulders pulled back, and your lower back slightly hollowed. Never round your shoulders as you handle any load.

If you return a heavy plate to a plate stand using one hand only—perhaps in a confined place—keep the plate close to you, and brace your other hand on the stand.

Don't carry two or more stacked plates. When carrying two plates, hold one in each hand, for symmetrical distribution of load. Never struggle with multiple large plates—carry them one at a time. The additional time you need to make multiple visits to a bar, stand, or rack is a small price to pay for safety.

Weight plates with a deep, outer ridge, or lip (left), permit easier handling than plates with a shallow outer ridge (right).

If there's a selection of plates, choose those that have a deep, outer ridge or lip. That construction is easier to hold than that of smooth-sided plates, or ones with only a shallow outer ridge.

If you ever drop a plate, immediately get your feet out of the way. Feet have been broken by dropped plates.

Barbell handling

Strip a bar of any plates, before moving it. The bar may, however, be a fixed-weight one, which you can't strip down. The heavier the weight, the greater the care required. But even light weights need care. When taking a bar from or returning it to stands, or anywhere else, keep it close to your body, get your feet as close as possible to it, bend at your knees, keep your head up, and lower back slightly hollowed.

Dumbbell handling

When lifting dumbbells from a rack, get as close as possible to them. Bend your knees, keep your head up, and your lower back slightly hollowed. Lift two dumbbells simultaneously and symmetrically, or one at a time (with both hands on the handle) but symmetrically. With two dumbbells, the load will be symmetrical provided the 'bells are lifted at the same time, your feet are side-by-side, and the weights are equidistant from your midline. If one foot is in front of the other, for example, stress will be applied asymmetrically, and the risk of injury will be increased.

An alternative way of handling a single dumbbell is to get close to the rack, with knees bent and lower back slightly hollowed, grab the dumbbell with one hand, and brace the other hand on the rack or another dumbbell. As you lift the dumbbell, simultaneously push hard with your bracing hand, to maintain symmetrical distribution of stress. Once you're standing, hold the dumbbell symmetrically in front of your thighs, with both hands, and then carry it to position. Return for the second dumbbell, if required.

When taking a dumbbell off the floor, take special care. This involves a greater range of motion than taking the weight from an elevated surface, and easily leads to rounding of the back. With your feet side-by-side about shoulder-width apart, and astride the dumbbell, bend at your knees, keep your head up, and your lower back slightly hollowed. Grab the dumbbell with your left hand, for example, and place your right hand on your right thigh. As you lift the dumbbell, simultaneously push hard with your right hand, for symmetrical distribution of stress. Once you're standing, hold the dumbbell symmetrically in front of your thighs, with both hands, and then carry it away. Return for the second dumbbell, if required.

Between sets, to reduce dumbbell handling awkwardness, set the 'bells on a bench, box, or other elevated surface, rather than the floor.

Plate handling on a loading pin

The hip-belt squat is the only exercise recommended in this book that requires use of a loading pin.

The longer the loading pin, the more space there is for stacking plates. When plates of the same size are loaded consecutively, especially large ones, it's easy to trap your fingers, and tricky to remove the plates. To make loading safer and easier, place a small plate between each pair of large plates. This will, however, use up more of the loading pin than

A loading pin with one 15-kilo and four 20-kilo plates stacked on it, with a single 1-1/4 kilo plate between each pair of large plates, to produce a gap between the big discs. See text. The loading pin here is attached to a carabiner, which in turn is attached to the front strap of an IronMind® Enterprises' hip belt.

would stacking the same number of large plates directly on top of each other, and thus a taller loading pin may be required sooner. For the hip-belt squat, taller platforms may be required for standing on, to compensate for a taller loading pin, so that the range of motion of the exercise isn't reduced.

Respect your limitations

Don't try to lift something you know is beyond you. Get help.

Exercise-related products and programs are favorites of infomercials. The combination of pseudo science, exaggerated claims, lies, dishonest testimonials, and celebrity endorsements, produce powerful advertising packages that deceive millions of people.

14

Seven extras for effective workouts

1. Timing of training

Some trainees work out first thing in the morning, but most don't feel comfortable training so early. Some like to work out in the evening, others have trouble sleeping if they train late at night. Find the time of day that's practical and agreeable to you, physically and mentally. By scheduling one training day on the weekend, you may have at least one workout a week at the optimum time of the day for you.

If you train at 7:00 pm, for example, you may have time for only one meal before you sleep, unless you go to bed late, which isn't recommended. If, however, you can train at 4:00 pm, you'll have time for a post-workout liquid meal followed about two hours later by a solid-food meal. The few hours after working out may be especially important nutritionally. Therefore, having sufficient time after training for more than one meal before you go to sleep, may be beneficial.

It may be advisable to avoid anything unusual in the 24 hours before a workout. If you usually sleep eight hours a night, but only get five the night before a workout, your training may suffer. If you had an extraordinarily tiring day yesterday, that may spoil your workout today—better to train tomorrow instead, readjust your training days for the week, and get back on track the following week.

2. Adaptation

It's normal to feel tired the day after a workout, at least when you first start to train. The body has tremendous abilities to adapt, provided that the demands on it are progressive in an incremental way, and start from a reasonable base point. As the months go by, and as your physical conditioning improves, you'll cope with greater effort and load, and possibly with less fatigue than when you began working out.

3. Grip aids

Chalk

The chalk that's commonly used in gyms is magnesium carbonate. Chalk is a form of support gear that's recommended for training safety. Belts, straps, wraps, squat suits, bench press shirts, and other forms of durable support gear aren't recommended.

During your first six or more months of training you may never feel the need for chalk on your hands, because your grip can comfortably cope with the demands you place on it. Once you feel your grip struggling to cope, use chalk on your hands. Use it only where you need the help, especially in back exercises and upper-body pressing movements. In the latter, your grip isn't going to give out like it may in the deadlift, for example, but during the reps of the bench press, for instance, your hands may slip outward a little unless you apply chalk.

Experiment to find the right amount of chalk. Use too little and you won't feel much if any benefit, use too much and your grip may slip, but use enough and your grip will be strengthened. Rub a piece on your fingers and palms, including the area between your thumb and index finger. Rub your hands together, and blow off any excess chalk. Keep it away from your face or else the dust may impair your breathing or get in your eyes.

Don't get chalk on the floor or any other surface for feet, because chalk can act as a lubricant there, and lead to foot slippage.

Chalk isn't only for hands. For the squat, to help prevent the bar from slipping out of position, get someone to chalk your shirt where the bar is going to rest. If you're sweating heavily, and are going to do some pressing with your back on a bench, get someone to chalk your upper back. This may help prevent your torso from sliding on the bench during the exercise.

Get some chalk from an outdoor goods store that sells mountaineering gear, or from a general sporting goods store.

The knurled parts of bars should be scrubbed with a stiff brush periodically, to prevent clogging of the knurling.

Rosin

Rosin powder is a possible alternative to chalk. Rosin may be less messy, which may make it acceptable in gyms that proscribe chalk. It's used by baseball players, specifically pitchers. Rosin may also be put on the undersides of footwear, to help prevent foot slippage on smooth surfaces. You can get a rosin bag from a sporting goods store.

4. Grip staying power

If you take a number of preventive measures, your grip may never seriously limit your training. First, don't use a thick bar for general training—use a regular-diameter bar. Second, use a bar with deep, sharp knurling. If a bar has no knurling, or barely any, it has no use for heavy deadlifting, for instance. Third, the knurling must not be clogged with chalk, rosin, or dirt. Use a stiff brush to remove clogging. Fourth, use lifter's chalk, or rosin. Fifth, use a reverse or mixed grip for the deadlift and barbell shrug (but not for other exercises)—one hand supinated, the other pronated—and alternate which way you have your hands from set to set. Sixth, hold the bar in your palms, not your fingers—wrap your hands around the bar.

A seventh measure doesn't produce benefits immediately—specific grip training, which can incorporate the use of a thick bar in order to increase the stress on the grip. Grip work needs time before it pays dividends. Grip work is included in **The Program** in the form of timed holds, and hand-gripper work is an additional possibility.

Few trainees get even close to achieving the strength potential of their hands, often because they use grip crutches and fail to train their hands properly. Don't use wrist straps, or hooks that attach you to a bar. If you use grip supports, you may end up with underdeveloped hands on a well-developed body. As your grip strength increases, so will the muscle and connective tissue of your hands.

Gloves aren't necessary, and the hands can slide within them because of sweating.

If you get excessive build-up of calluses on your hands, control it by weekly use of a pumice stone after a shower or bath.

> *Appreciate the skin-on-metal contact of strength training, and the mental focus it can provide. And use chalk or rosin as your only grip aid.*

5. How to cope with sickness

Minor sickness, such as a cold, shouldn't mess up your training. Stay out of the gym until two or three days after when you started feeling well again, then re-start training. As long as no more than about 10 to 14 days have passed since you last trained, and as long as you've felt 100% for a few days, you should be able to repeat your previous workout.

If you return to the gym when you know you've not fully recovered, then not only may you be unable to repeat your previous workout, you may injure yourself in the attempt.

If sickness kept you out of the gym for a protracted period, start back with reduced weights and effort, and take two or three weeks to build back to where you were before you became ill. Then return to the progression scheme you were following before you got sick.

Never train if you're sick. Even a minor cold or sore throat, if trained through, could develop into something serious. The older you are, the more strictly you need to follow this advice, and the more heavily you'll probably feel the consequences if you don't.

6. Don't be scammed by infomercials

Exercise-related products and programs are favorites of infomercials. The combination of pseudo science, exaggerated claims, lies, dishonest testimonials, and celebrity endorsements, produce powerful advertising packages that deceive millions of people. Often, the people providing the endorsements had never touched the product *until* the filming of the infomercial, and they are often well paid for their bogus testimonials.

7. Don't fall victim to myths of abdominal training

Many myths of training the abdominal muscles are perpetuated by fitness companies and individuals who prey on ignorance. Here are nine:

Myth #1

Twisting movements will pare fat from the sides of your waist.

Go to most gyms, and at some point you'll find trainees with a light bar across their shoulders, vigorously twisting from side to side. They do this under the mistaken belief that they will whittle away the fat on their waists. Some trainees have been doing this for years, without success. The twisting may, however, cause back problems.

Myth #2

Lots of ab work will pare fat from the front of your waist.

As with Myth #1, muscle and fat are different types of tissue. It's physiologically impossible to whittle away fat through working the muscle beneath the fat. Fat reduction in a specific spot of the body, through exercise, is impossible. The only way to spot-reduce fat is through surgical intervention, which has perils and isn't a long-term cure. The other way to reduce bodyfat is to reduce your food intake and increase your activity level so that you're in overall caloric deficit; *then* your body will turn to its fat reserves to provide for the balance of its energy needs. See Chapter 5.

You could build a great set of abdominal muscles, but whether you could see the lines of your abdominals depends on how much fat covers your waist. Well-developed abdominals can, however, show a six-pack to some extent without a low level of bodyfat, because the abdominals will protrude more. It's also possible to have visible but weak and undeveloped abdominals, if you don't exercise but have a low level of bodyfat.

You could do three hours of abdominal work daily, but if your food intake and activity level don't combine to yield an overall energy deficit, you'll never reduce the fat around your waist. On the other hand, you could do no abdominal work, but if you're in sustained caloric deficit you'll draw on your energy stores and thus reduce your bodyfat. Whether you do abdominal work is irrelevant in determining the amount of fat around your waist. But to build strong, well-developed abdominals, ab work is essential.

Myth #3

The abs need high reps.

To strengthen and develop the abdominals—which is all that ab work can do—keep the reps moderate and effort levels high, use sufficient resistance to keep the reps down, and keep adding resistance as you develop strength. Treat your abdominals like any other muscle.

A benefit of doing extreme amounts of abdominal work is that it consumes sufficient calories to make a contribution to energy output over the long haul. This, however, is an inefficient way of burning calories. For efficient calorie burning, perform an activity that's easier, involves more musculature, and can be sustained for long periods, such as walking.

No matter how many calories you burn through activity, if you eat excessively, you won't be in caloric deficit, and unless you're in caloric deficit, you'll never reduce your bodyfat.

Myth #4

The abs need daily work.

Although the abdominal muscles may tolerate more frequent work than most other bodyparts, they can be overtrained, too. Excessive training frequency for these muscles is connected to the mistaken belief that a lot of exercise for them will help reduce waist fat levels. Train your abdominals only two, or, at most, three times a week.

Myth #5

Everyone can develop a six-pack if they train and diet correctly.

Some people are genetically more likely to lay down fat on their waists than others. A few people may be lean throughout their bodies yet still have a layer of fat on their waists, whereas some others may achieve six-packs but have a thick layer of fat elsewhere on their bodies. The near-perfect bodies you see in advertising belong to genetically gifted specimens who have the natural ability to achieve lean waists.

Myth #6

The abs have two separate muscles—upper abs and lower abs.

The six-pack or washboard is the rectus abdominis muscle, and is the visible, frontal part of the abdominal wall *provided* there's minimal fat covering it. In addition, the abdominal wall includes the external abdominal oblique, and internal abdominal oblique—the sides of the waist—and the transversus abdominis beneath the rectus abdominis.

The rectus abdominis is one long, flat, continuous muscle that runs from the lower ribs to the groin. While it's not possible to isolate the upper or lower abdominals, the two sections may respond differently to flexion that requires the shoulders to move toward the hips than to flexion that requires the hips to move toward the shoulders.

Myth #7

Gadgets are needed to train the abs.

Some gadgets, properly used, *do* target the abdominals. There's nothing, however, a gadget can help you do that crunches can't, provided the crunches are done correctly. But many of the gadgets are ineffective and poorly made, and some are dangerous. Don't be misled by hype. Stick to crunches, which don't require special equipment, and do them well.

Myth #8

Electronic muscle stimulation is the easy way to great abs.

Electronic stimulation of muscles is a way to make people think they can exercise effectively without moving. There's some legitimate use for electro-muscle stimulation in physical therapy, but for healthy trainees it's a joke compared with proper resistance training. You have to move, sweat, and push yourself, progressively, if you're going to change the form of your body.

Even if the electronic gadgets stimulated muscle like regular progressive resistance training does, you would still need to lose the fat to see your abdominals. No electronic stimulation will remove the fat that covers muscle.

Myth #9

Development of the abdominal obliques is undesirable.

The external abdominal oblique, and the internal abdominal oblique are parts of the abdominal wall. Many trainees avoid direct work for their obliques under the misunderstanding that development of their obliques would thicken their waists, and be unaesthetic.

Strong obliques are desirable for torso stability during many exercises, and to increase resistance to injury. Even if well-developed, the obliques add little muscle. Rather than be unaesthetic, this muscle adds an attractive sweep to the waist if it isn't covered with a thick layer of fat.

> *It's not possible to whittle away fat through working the muscle beneath the fat. Fat reduction in a specific spot of the body, through exercise, is impossible.*

The body is capable of tremendous achievement and adaptation provided that resistance is increased in a *gradual* way, from an *easy* starting level. This adaptation applies to all forms of physical stress.

Inch by inch, training's a cinch.

If you try to rush your progress, your body will protest through excessive soreness, severe fatigue, or injury. Being in a hurry is one of the biggest mistakes in physical training.

15

How progressive resistance can help or hinder progress

Progressive resistance training is a system whereby the weight or resistance used in a given exercise is incrementally increased as the involved muscles progress in strength and conditioning. It's at the heart of strength training, muscle-building, and weight lifting in general, because it's a simple, quantifiable and incremental approach that's easy to track. It's the primary method of progression promoted in this book. Progressive resistance can, however, take other forms.

It's not the weight added to a given exercise that causes strength gain and possibly tissue growth. The ability to handle additional weight on a given exercise comes about only *after* the body has adapted to stimulation from previous workouts, which may include a tiny increase in muscle mass. But the caveat is that correct technique and rep speed are used for all reps, of all sets, in all workouts.

If you rush your reps, or loosen your exercise technique to permit extra weight to be added to a given movement—such as a slight thrust, heave, or jerk—that wouldn't be a weight increase you've earned through adaptation. It would be false progress, and the sort

> *If possible, train with a partner who can scrutinize your technique, and rep speed. His or her verbal cues can help you to keep your technique and rep speed correct and consistent from workout to workout. A good training partner is invaluable. Of course, the training partner needs to know what correct technique and rep speed are, in order to enforce them.*

of "progress" that leads to growth stagnation, and injury. This is *dirty* training. Some of these cheats are slight, and rarely noticed by most trainees. But now that you're aware, be alert.

An exaggerated focus on progressive weights is detrimental because it leads to degradation of exercise technique and rep speed control. Never should exercise technique or rep speed control be compromised to enable more weight to be added to an exercise.

The cardinal watchwords are correct technique and rep speed control, *correct technique and rep speed control*, CORRECT TECHNIQUE AND REP SPEED CONTROL . . . even at the end of a set when the reps are hardest.

Hardly anyone has an expert trainer to ensure that correct technique and rep speed are used. You must discipline yourself. Start with correct technique and rep speed, and then *continue* with correct technique and rep speed. That's the bedrock for safe and effective strength training.

If you find yourself guilty of dirty training in a given exercise, take corrective action immediately. Reduce the weight used, and use correct technique. Pause the early reps of a set—hold each rep for a second during some point of the positive phase, and again at the midpoint of the negative phase. This will quickly cleanse your training. Complete the rest of the set without the pauses, but with correct technique, and control. Then over the next two or three months gradually build the weight back while maintaining clean technique.

Compromising on exercise technique or rep speed control aren't the only ways to create an illusion of progress. Reducing the range of motion of an exercise, and increasing the rest intervals between reps and sets, are other ways of making an exercise appear easier in order to allow increased weight to be used. Don't reduce the range of motion, and be consistent with rest intervals between reps and sets. The rest interval between sets changes during the early months of **The Program**, then becomes consistent as from Month #4.

Combine correct technique, rep speed control, range of motion, and inter-rep and set intervals, with brief, hard training and the satisfaction of the components of recuperation from training. This will provide the best opportunity for the adaptations that produce increased strength—the extra weight or reps that are *properly* earned—and possible growth.

Make progressive weights a vital part of your training, but be a model for correct technique, *and* consistency with rep speed, range of motion, and inter-rep and inter-set rest intervals. Add weight only in line with your body's adaptation to your prior training. *Then* the progressive weights may have the best effect on your muscular development, but *will* minimize the risk of injury.

Stronger muscles aren't necessarily bigger muscles

Although the precise mechanisms for how muscle is built aren't fully understood, there's a correlation between added strength and increased muscle mass. The correlation is often not linear, however, and it's possible to become considerably stronger without developing significantly bigger muscles. Stronger muscles may mean bigger muscles, but not always, just like bigger muscles may mean stronger muscles, but not always. The biggest muscles aren't the strongest, and the strongest muscles aren't the biggest. Some lightweight powerlifters and Olympic weightlifters, for example, are fantastically strong—far stronger than bodybuilders who are much larger.

Powerlifting, and other tests of absolute strength, are about lifting weight. The competitor who lifts the most weight wins, regardless of appearance or lifting technique, so long as no rules are broken. Any skill, technique, or aid such as joint wraps and special suits (permitted in many powerlifting contests) that enable more weight to be raised, are used. This weight-first approach is high-risk training that's suited to only a physically highly robust minority, and even then it commonly produces injuries. This is different from the safety-first, healthy training promoted in this book. There are, however, some long-term successful powerlifters who use good technique and don't take the liberties that many of their fellow competitors do.

There are specific training techniques that may promote big gains in strength but little or no gains in muscular size. These aren't relevant to novices and most other trainees, and aren't covered in this book.

How much progress?

How much muscle growth you'll achieve depends heavily on your gender, age, and genetic propensity for growth. It may also be affected by the specific manner of training you use to produce the progressive resistance, whether or not you're in caloric surplus, how long you've been training, your starting level of development, and how close you are to your maximum potential for muscular size.

No amount of obsessing, fretting, or worrying can change how the genetic chips have fallen. Follow *The Program* of this book, and you'll make substantial and perhaps even tremendous improvement in your strength, development, appearance, cardio fitness, flexibility, health, and overall well-being, although the precise degree of improvement will vary from individual to individual.

Hardly anyone has an expert trainer to ensure that correct technique and rep speed are used. You must discipline yourself. Start with correct technique and rep speed, and then CONTINUE with correct technique and rep speed. That's the bedrock for safe and effective strength training.

When will you see muscle growth?

Especially during your early years of strength training, incremental strength gains should be seen as the principle means by which you make progress. To begin with, however, you're likely to make substantial strength gains but with minimal or no muscle growth. For the first few months of training, you'll increase your strength with the muscle you already have. Your nervous system will adapt by improving its ability to recruit additional muscle fibers, and thus generate more muscular force. There are other invisible adaptations, too. Furthermore, improvement in the skill needed to perform each exercise also contributes to your ability to lift more weight. You'll become more efficient at lifting weights using your existing muscle mass.

Only after the first few months of training, especially after about six months, may hypertrophy become clearly apparent. A rare few trainees will grow in the first month or two of training. Others may take longer than six months to show hypertrophy. A few trainees may only ever make minimal size gains despite considerable strength gain. For most beginners, muscular growth follows a few months after getting started.

For the most effective training of the musculature of your thighs and hips, and the most effective overall program, you need to employ at least one multi-joint thigh-and-hip exercise. The squat and deadlift are such exercises, but because not everyone can perform them safely, this chapter will cover the most important alternatives.

16

How to optimize your exercise selection from the gang of eight

The squat, deadlift, parallel-grip deadlift, sumo deadlift, leg press, front squat, ball squat, and hip-belt squat are grouped together because they are major exercises for the thigh (front *and* rear) and hip musculature; and other than for the leg press, ball squat, and hip-belt squat, they heavily involve the lower back, too. Each of the gang of eight works over half of the total musculature of the body. The thigh, hip, and lower back unit is the foundation of muscle-building, *and* mobility. To try to optimize your progress, it's essential that you include one or two of the gang of eight in any training program. Finding at least one of the gang of eight that's safe and effective *for you*, is critical.

No matter how effective an exercise may be for someone, if it doesn't suit *you*, it will do you no good, and perhaps do you harm. When considering the preferences of a trainer, coach, or author, consider *your* limitations and technical proficiency. "First cause no harm" is the medical prime directive that's equally applicable to training.

Throughout **The Program** I've assumed that you can safely and progressively use all the listed exercises. Most beginners will be able to, but some won't; and some experienced trainees won't be able to, either. The problem exercises are usually the squat, and the deadlift. These two are technically demanding, and their performance is powerfully affected by body structure, flexibility, and any past injuries.

Most trainees who feel that they can't do some specific exercises safely, haven't been performing those exercises correctly. Through improving their technique, and using weights that permit correct technique, and correct rep speed control, most of these trainees will be able to train safely on formerly unsafe exercises.

Priorities for beginners

The squat and deadlift are potentially highly valuable—each works about two thirds of the body's total musculature. I recommend that all beginners use the squat and the deadlift *provided* that correct technique is used and all safety measures are taken as described in Chapter 12, and a sensible progression schedule is applied like that promoted in **The Program**. Used properly, few beginners will have serious problems with these exercises.

Although some people have better mechanics for squatting than others, most trainees can squat well enough to obtain considerable benefits from the exercise if they master the technique of squatting.

Even if you think you don't squat well, don't give up on the exercise because of initial difficulties. Once you've mastered squatting technique, you may be able to squat more effectively.

If, however, you have followed up on all the recommendations in Chapter 6, have applied correct squatting and deadlifting technique as described in Chapter 12, have used a controlled rep speed, have followed **The Program** to the letter, and yet still have joint or back problems, you must use alternative exercises. Some trainees can't squat well. For example, a tall man with, proportionately speaking, long legs and thighs, and a short torso, will always struggle in the squat. It could be to such a degree that he may never obtain benefits from the exercise, but he will run a high risk of injury.

Leverages, the squat, and the deadlift

How well you squat or deadlift is heavily affected by your leverages—your relative torso, thigh, and leg lengths, and relative femur (thighbone) and tibia (shinbone) lengths. And there are other important structural factors, including muscle insertion points (that vary from person to person, to some degree), which influence squatting and deadlifting efficiency.

Although they may train both exercises with equal dedication, some trainees will squat more than they deadlift, others will deadlift more than they squat, while others will lift similar weights in both.

Trainees who are built well for the squat tend to have legs and thighs of average or shorter-than-average length relative to their height. But trainees who are built well for the squat often struggle in the deadlift, relatively speaking, especially if they have short arms and forearms.

Short legs and thighs together with a long torso may not be well suited to conventional deadlifting. But long legs and thighs can inhibit deadlifting because, when the knees are bent, the knees can get in the way of a straight barbell, and compromise technique. Short legs and thighs may be fine for the deadlift, however, depending on the lengths of the torso, forearms, and arms, and other structural factors. And forearm and arm lengths by themselves are also influential in the deadlift—long ones favor the exercise.

The relative lengths of legs, thighs, torso, forearms, and arms affect leverages, which in turn affect deadlifting ability.

Don't obsess over your structure as it affects the squat, and the deadlift, but be aware of the general relationship. Provided you can squat and deadlift safely, train the exercises hard and progressively.

A few trainees have ideal physical structures for the squat, and the potential to build up to using astonishing weights relative to their bodyweight. But in some cases they don't have the potential for building big muscles, thus they develop great squatting strength but at a low bodyweight.

Some others, too, have excellent physical structures for the squat, but they also have the potential for building big muscles, so their squatting produces great muscular gains. Similar comments can be made for the deadlift, too.

Most trainees, however, have average leverages, and average potential for muscular growth.

> *It may be that any difficulty you have with a particular exercise is related to physical anomalies or soft-tissue scarring, which are correctable or at least can be minimized, with the appropriate, treatment. Follow up on the recommendations given in Chapter 6. The content of that chapter is of tremendous importance. The right treatment can produce wonders.*

The parallel-grip deadlift

This is an excellent substitute for the squat, an outstanding exercise in its own right, and potentially one of the most effective exercises.

For a number of years, the parallel-grip deadlift was called the *trap-bar deadlift*, because the trap bar was the device often used for this form of deadlifting. The rhombus-shaped trap bar was developed by Al Gerard, in a successful effort to enable him to deadlift without the back problems he was experiencing from the straight-bar deadlift. Over recent years, the shrug bar has provided a variation on the trap bar that permits more foot room because of the hexagonal shape of the shrug bar. Furthermore, there are other ways of performing the parallel-grip deadlift—rectangular and square bars, some specially bent bars that don't enclose the trainee, and even a Hammer Strength machine. And a pair of dumbbells can mimic a trap bar or shrug bar, if they are held at the sides of the thighs using a parallel grip.

The trap-bar deadlift isn't an adequate name, because a number of bars and devices can be used to produce the same movement. A general-purpose name was needed, to prevent confusion and to accommodate all the involved bars and devices. The *parallel-grip deadlift* reflects the deadlift-like movement *and* the parallel grip that the gripping sites of the trap bar, shrug bar, and other related bars and devices permit.

The dumbbell deadlift has been around longer than the trap bar and other parallel-grip devices; therefore, the trap bar and other devices are simulations of the dumbbells, for the purposes of deadlifting and shrugging. Eventually, for many male trainees, large dumbbells will be required for the parallel-grip dumbbell deadlift, and most gyms don't have such dumbbells.

Large dumbbells are also unwieldy to use, and even small 'bells can get in the way of the legs and thighs. Dumbbells may limit stance width and flare more than the one-piece bars do, and thus hamper optimum technique. Furthermore, dumbbells, because of the smaller circumference of their plates relative to the full-size barbell plates used on a parallel-grip bar, produce an increased range of motion that will produce dangerous rounding of the lower back for most trainees. If you use dumbbells, restrict the range of motion by deadlifting from sturdy crates or platforms. Find the right height of crates or platforms for you that permits the fullest safe range of motion without any rounding of your lower back.

Although it's a form of the deadlift, the parallel-grip deadlift can involve the thighs to a greater extent than the regular straight-bar deadlift, because of the increased knee flexion. This has led to the parallel-grip deadlift being used as an alternative to the squat.

Both the parallel-grip deadlift and the squat can be highly effective, depending on the individual user, and the technique used. Squat aficionados need to understand that the squat isn't as effective for everyone as it may be for them, and parallel-grip deadlift aficionados need to understand that the exercise isn't as effective for everyone as it may be for them.

You can't change your body structure—limb lengths, the relative proportions of femur length to tibia length, and relative proportions of torso length to limb lengths, and upper limbs to lower limbs. All these factors have substantial influence on deadlifting, parallel-grip deadlifting, and squatting efficiency. Through adjusting your technique and exercise selection you can modify the effects of your body structure on your training and physique.

Some trainees who are structurally well built for the squat get tremendous thigh development from the squat. Some others, with different structures, are ungainly squatters who can't avoid leaning over heavily. This turns the movement into more of a lower-back exercise than a thigh one, and greatly increases the risk of injury. Of those who can't squat well no matter what flexibility, technique, training program, or weight progression adjustments they make, and of those who can't squat safely because of knee or back limitations because of injury or accident, some have found the parallel-grip deadlift (with bent knees) to be a godsend—it has enabled them to train their thighs safely and effectively like the squat never could.

In the parallel-grip deadlift there are advantages relative to the squat:

1. The parallel-grip deadlift is less technically challenging than the squat.

2. The bar is held beneath the body rather than precariously near the top of the spine as in the squat, and thus there's no bar bearing down on you.

> The biggest disadvantage of the parallel-grip deadlift is the lack of universal supply of the required purpose-built equipment. Conversely, almost all gyms are set up for the squat. Considering the whole strength-training population, few trainees have tried the parallel-grip deadlift as compared with the squat. But out of the relatively few users of the parallel-grip deadlift, there has been much success, often from trainees who previously didn't do well on the squat.

3. No squat stands, power rack, or safety bars are needed for the parallel-grip deadlift.

4. It's easier to dump a failed parallel-grip deadlift than a failed squat.

5. Spotters aren't needed for the parallel-grip deadlift.

6. The parallel-grip deadlift is easily done from a dead stop at the bottom position.

The parallel-grip deadlift is tailor-made for many trainees who don't squat well. The parallel-grip bar will, however, benefit any type of trainee. Encourage the management of where you train to get a parallel-grip deadlift bar. It's not expensive. It should be a required piece of equipment for all gyms. It's more valuable and less costly than many pieces of equipment that most gyms consider essential, but which are harmful or only marginally useful.

Generally speaking, the parallel-grip deadlift carries a lower level of risk than the squat because the former is technically simpler. That's not to say the parallel-grip deadlift is inherently safe, and the squat is inherently dangerous.

It's easy to injure yourself in the parallel-grip deadlift if you don't use correct technique, just as it's easy to injure yourself with any incorrectly performed exercise. Correct technique in the parallel-grip deadlift includes keeping a naturally concave lower spine at all times, minimizing forward travel of the knees, and avoiding extremes of torso positioning—neither leaning forward greatly, nor exaggeratedly upright. Perform the parallel-grip deadlift correctly, or not at all. See Chapter 12.

How much lower-back stress the parallel-grip deadlift provides varies according to the degree of forward lean, which is related to body structure, stance, and technique. If you parallel-grip deadlift with substantial knee flexion, hands never forward of your legs or thighs, and only a little forward lean, the exercise would stress your quadriceps more, and your lower back, upper back, and hamstrings proportionately less than if you were to parallel-grip deadlift with less knee flexion, hands forward of your legs or thighs, and substantial forward lean. But parallel-grip deadlifting with exaggerated forward lean, and reduced knee flexion, isn't the form I recommend.

Parallel-grip bar design—specifically the spacing between the gripping sites, and room inside the bar—affect stance, and stance affects technique. There isn't the same stance width freedom as in the squat, because the gripping sites' placement sets the limit on stance width. If you plan to get a parallel-grip bar, check with the manufacturer that the gripping sites will be spaced adequately for you—according to your physical size—to permit you to take at least a medium-width stance, or otherwise you could be so constrained that you may not be able to parallel-grip deadlift safely.

The parallel-grip deadlift is the equal of the squat for many trainees. For some trainees, it can be a more effective exercise. It has the potential to be the number one effective exercise for many trainees.

Leg press

In my youth I had a blind devotion to the squat that deflected me from serious pursuit of the leg press, and variations of the deadlift. On hindsight, I should have exploited the potential of the squat, deadlift, parallel-grip deadlift, and leg press. I urge you to do the same.

There are at least four possible ways of using the leg press:

1. As one of the major, multi-joint exercises in its own right, regardless of whether or not you squat well.

2. An alternative to the squat when a break from squatting is desired.

3. A squat alternative for trainees who have leverages that make the squat only a marginally effective if not dangerous exercise.

4. A substitute for the squat if the latter can't be performed because of lower-back or knee limitations.

The critical caveat is that the leg press is performed safely and effectively on a machine that suits you.

The leg press is technically simpler than the squat and the parallel-grip deadlift. It's easier to maintain correct technique while leg pressing intensively than it is while squatting or parallel-grip deadlifting.

Assuming you use correct technique, the leg press enables you to work your thighs and hips hard without your lower back coming into the picture other than as a stabilizer. This is great for trainees who have lower-back problems, or lower backs that fail before their thighs, when squatting. With some machines, because of the control over pressing depth and foot placement, knee stress may be lessened in the leg press relative to the squat. This may still enable trainees with knee limitations to work their thighs and hips hard and heavily.

Leg press machines

The major problem with the leg press is the need for a safe machine.
There are several types of leg presses. Each can stress the thighs and
hips differently, because of the different angles of body positioning.

Some leg presses, because of their design and insufficient adjustability,
produce more compression of the lower back than others. Excessive
compression must be avoided, as it can lead to injury.

There are vertical leg presses, including the Smith machine. This
type puts great stress on the knees and lower back, and isn't
recommended. Although these leg presses may not harm young,
injury-free trainees, they can cause havoc for others.

There are 45-degree leg press machines. Some may reduce the knee
and lower back stress relative to the vertical models. If used with
caution and correct technique, by trainees with no injury limitations,
the 45-degree leg presses can yield good results.

For most trainees, the leg press of choice will be from another
category—the near-horizontal-movement type, such as the leverage-
style models from Hammer Strength, and the Nautilus XP LOAD Leg
Press, which are plate-loaded. Some other companies, such as Cybex
and MedX, have selectorized models. These are convenient because
they don't require any plate handling—leg presses typically require
loading with many plates once the user is beyond the beginner stage.

A few leg press machines can be used one limb at a time, or
alternately—the isolateral or unilateral models. These contrast with
the usual bilateral machines that each have a single platform, which
is moved by both feet together. The unilateral leg press machine gives
you the option of working both limbs bilaterally, too, although each
limb will have its own resistance to overcome.

A unilateral leg press applies asymmetrical and rotational stress
to your lower back, because both limbs aren't pushing at the same
time unless the machine is used bilaterally. Asymmetrical stress in
the leg press is best avoided, because it increases the risk of injury.
Because the unilateral model can be used bilaterally, be conservative
and stick with using it in bilateral mode.

Front squat

If you can't back squat safely, don't have access to a parallel-grip
deadlift bar or good leg press, try the front squat.

Here are some advantages the front squat has over the back squat:

1. It produces a more upright torso, and thus less forward lean.

2. Comparing the same trainee, the lower back usually rounds at a greater depth in the front squat than the back squat. A deeper but still safe squat is usually possible in the front squat. Rounding of the lower back must be avoided in any type of squat, but the greater the range of motion without rounding of the lower back, the better the effect on the muscles, theoretically. This produces greater muscular involvement, and requires less weight to do the job, which may enhance safety.

3. The greater range of motion may be beneficial for the knees, depending on the individual. In the back squat, generally speaking, the descent is stopped at around where the upper thighs are parallel to the floor, to avoid losing the concave lower spine. Some trainees, however, can go below parallel in the back squat without rounding their lower backs. The front squat permits many trainees to go below parallel without rounding their lower backs.

4. The bar is kept off the upper back and away from the spine. This is important for trainees who have spinal limitations that proscribe putting a bar on the upper back. But the technique of the front squat must be correct. If technique is compromised, and the back rounded, or bar tilted, exaggerated stress will be placed on the back, and the risk of injury will be greatly increased.

It's necessary to perform the front squat with some weight—perhaps just a bare bar—to involve the upper back musculature sufficiently to pull the torso more upright, to prevent the bar falling forward.

The downside of the front squat is that there are difficulties keeping the bar in position across the front of the shoulders. And, because the hands are close together on the bar, it can tilt easily. Although the bar can also tilt in the back squat if correct technique isn't used, the potential for tilting is greater in the front squat. Maintenance of a horizontal bar is critical.

Most gyms have a set-up for the back or conventional squat (where the bar is positioned on the upper back), and for the front squat (where the bar is positioned at the front of the shoulders). Only a minority of gyms, however, have the recommended set-up of a power rack, or squat stands with safety bars or racks. Most large gyms have leg press machines, but not necessarily the type recommended in this book. Few gyms have parallel-grip deadlift bars. As a result of this situation, the back and front squats are the most-universally practical, multi-joint thigh-and-hip exercises.

These difficulties with the front squat are manageable for many trainees *if* correct technique and persistent practice are employed— see Chapter 12. If you can't master the front squat, and can't back squat safely, get a parallel-grip deadlift bar and master the parallel-grip deadlift. If that's not possible, leg press instead, provided you have access to a good leg press machine.

Because the maintenance of correct bar positioning is demanding in the front squat—to prevent the bar slipping forward, and tipping laterally—keep the reps fewer than ten. Alternatively, rather than continually add weight, spend a few months building to a weight you can maintain correct technique with, then gradually increase your range of motion as much as possible—while always maintaining the correct back positioning—and thereafter focus on increasing reps.

Ball squat

The ball squat, also called the *wall squat*, is another alternative to the barbell squat. The muscle involvement of the ball squat is similar to that of the leg press. Both involve the back only as a stabilizer. The ball squat, however, has three major advantages over the leg press:

1. A machine isn't required.

2. The ball squat can be done almost anywhere.

3. There's no compression of the back.

Although there's flexibility over foot positioning with the leg press, there may be more flexibility with the ball squat, to find the best set-up.

The ball squat is technically easier than the back squat, parallel-grip deadlift, and front squat. Furthermore, the thighs and hips can receive stimulation with much reduced weights relative to those required for the back squat, parallel-grip deadlift, leg press, and front squat. The ball squat is a safe and practical alternative if you're unable to perform safely any of the other multi-joint, lower-body exercises.

Hip-belt squat

The hip-belt squat shares the same advantages of the ball squat, relative to the barbell squat, and the leg press, but doesn't involve a ball or wall, the movement isn't so constrained and contrived, and the resistance is applied only around the hips and doesn't need to be held. Large weights can be handled with this arrangement. Some trainees may use the ball squat as the introductory movement that leads to the hip-belt squat once substantial resistance is required.

The hip-belt squat can be a highly effective exercise, even for trainees who can perform the other multi-joint, lower-body exercises safely, but it's especially valuable for trainees who can't back squat, front squat, or parallel-grip deadlift safely, and who don't have access to a good leg press machine, or who can't leg press safely.

The hip-belt squat is preferred to the ball squat in the exercise combinations that are listed in this chapter.

Sumo deadlift

The sumo deadlift provides another alternative to the regular, straight-bar deadlift. For some trainees, the sumo deadlift may be a good choice as the primary, multi-joint, lower-body exercise.

The sumo deadlift uses a straight bar, but because of the widened stance relative to that used in the regular deadlift, and the hands positioned *between* the legs or thighs, the back may be more upright in the sumo deadlift when comparing the two styles on the same trainee. Although the back is heavily involved in the sumo deadlift, the hips and thighs take relatively more stress.

The knee flexion in the sumo deadlift is usually greater than in the regular deadlift, but less than is typically used in squat variations.

Some trainees have body structures that are better suited to the sumo deadlift than the conventional style. Trainees who prefer a wide stance in the squat, and who have good leverages for the squat but not so favorable ones for the deadlift, may prefer the sumo style. Tall people who have poor leverages for the squat, and the conventional deadlift, may be able to sumo deadlift efficiently. The key factor is being able to maintain correct positioning with the lower spine slightly hollowed. The sumo style may enable some trainees to keep the proper back set at a lower position than they can in the conventional deadlift, and hold it with less difficulty throughout the exercise.

If you can't deadlift

Some trainees experience problems maintaining correct technique while straight-bar deadlifting from the floor, usually because the knees get in the way of the bar. If this applies to you, and you've followed the guidance in Chapter 12, substitute the *partial* deadlift for the regular deadlift, from pins set at knee height inside a power rack. In the partial deadlift, the knees are bent only slightly, and there's no heavy involvement of the quadriceps. The partial deadlift is really a partial *stiff-legged* deadlift.

> Some influential writers and coaches in the field of training never "get it." They will never admit they have superior heredity. And they may think that just because they aren't elite competitive bodybuilders, they must be genetically typical. Furthermore, many of these influential people don't have typical family lives, have near optimal training conditions, and often have a background in drugs. Their training advice often has little or no connection with the practical reality for typical, drug-free people.

The full-range, stiff-legged deadlift isn't included in *The Program* because it's too hazardous. Instead, less risky but effective exercises are employed for the hamstrings, hips, and back, which are the primary areas worked by the full-range, stiff-legged deadlift. The exercises employed for these areas are the conventional deadlift (and the recommended variations of it), leg curl, and back extension. Of course, these exercises must be performed correctly if they are to be safe.

The partial deadlift fixes the problems of many trainees who can't deadlift safely in the regular manner, but at the expense of some range of motion, and the loss of any meaningful involvement of the quadriceps. But the involvement of the back, hips, hamstrings, and grip aren't reduced. Reduced range of motion usually leads to greater loads being employed, which places even greater importance on correct technique.

Back extensions produce some of the benefits that deadlifts provide (and some benefits that deadlifts don't provide). Shrugs would need to be included, too, to cover some of the benefits the deadlift provides but that back extensions don't.

The back extension and the shrug are already incorporated in **The Program**. If the deadlift can't be performed safely in any form, perhaps perform a second bout of back extensions each week, instead. But do your best to master either the regular deadlift, or the partial deadlift.

The parallel-grip deadlift can replace the straight-bar deadlift, as the former is technically easier for most trainees, because you stand inside the bar and have no bar to get around your knees.

The parallel-grip deadlift is, however, potentially more of a substitute for the squat than the straight-bar deadlift, because of the increased knee flexion that's possible in the parallel-grip deadlift.

The parallel-grip deadlift reduces spine stress relative to the straight-bar deadlift, and puts the arms, forearms, and hands into a position that feels more comfortable.

Risk rating

The squat, deadlift, parallel-grip deadlift, sumo deadlift, leg press, front squat, ball squat, and hip-belt squat are multi-joint thigh-and-hip movements. Of these, the deadlift (conventional style) usually provides the least range of motion for the thighs, but greater involvement of the back musculature. The ball squat, hip-belt squat, and leg press are principally thigh-and-hip exercises, whereas the other five involve the back substantially, too.

All eight exercises can be dangerous, or safe, depending on the trainee's suitability, and the technique used, but some have greater potential risk than others. Comparing the same trainee across all eight exercises, using comparable exercise intensity, and correct technique, here's how they can be rated, mostly in groups, from lowest risk to highest risk:

> *hip-belt squat, ball squat, leg press*
> *parallel-grip deadlift, sumo deadlift*
> *deadlift*
> *front squat, back squat*

Barbell squats probably have the highest risk because of the movement involved in getting set up for the first rep, the movement involved in returning the bar to the weight saddles at the end of each set, the downward bearing of the weight on the body, and the difficulty in dumping the load. All of these concerns can be minimized if correct technique and set-up are used, but substantial risk will always remain.

But, even the hip-belt squat can be dangerous if not done correctly. If, for example, you lose your grip, or an attachment to the belt breaks, there could be serious consequences.

For safety, you must use correct technique for any exercise, and fully attend to all safety concerns.

Select the exercises that are most appropriate for you, according to equipment availability, and your suitability to the exercises (which may change as you age).

Thigh, hip, and lower-back development

The back squat, parallel-grip deadlift, leg press, front squat, ball squat, hip-belt squat, deadlift, and sumo deadlift, singly or together, don't train the entire thigh, hip, and lower-back area *fully*. Here are combinations of those exercises and others that do fully cover that entire area:

1. back squat, leg curl, and back extension
2. back squat, leg curl, deadlift, and back extension
3. back squat, leg curl, partial deadlift, and back extension
4. back squat, leg curl, sumo deadlift, and back extension
5. parallel-grip deadlift, leg curl, and back extension
6. parallel-grip deadlift, leg curl, partial deadlift, and back extension
7. leg press, leg curl, and back extension
8. leg press, leg curl, deadlift, and back extension
9. leg press, leg curl, partial deadlift, and back extension
10. leg press, leg curl, sumo deadlift, and back extension
11. front squat, leg curl, and back extension
12. front squat, leg curl, deadlift, and back extension
13. front squat, leg curl, partial deadlift, and back extension
14. front squat, leg curl, sumo deadlift, and back extension
15. sumo deadlift, leg curl, and back extension
16. hip-belt squat, leg curl, and back extension
17. hip-belt squat, leg curl, deadlift, and back extension
18. hip-belt squat, leg curl, partial deadlift, and back extension
19. hip-belt squat, leg curl, sumo deadlift, and back extension

The ball squat could replace the other squats, but I prefer the hip-belt squat.

Critical note

Combinations (7) and (16) are probably the safest, assuming correct technique is used. The exercises in (7) and (16) aren't as technically demanding as squat and deadlift variations. Combinations (7) and (16) may not, however, be the most effective for overall progress *if* squats or deadlifts can be performed safely and effectively.

If the partial deadlift is included with combinations (7) and (16), to yield (9) and (18), that adds a major, barbell, hip-and-back exercise but without the fuller-range, higher-risk qualities of the back squat, front squat, deadlift, parallel-grip deadlift, or sumo deadlift. Combinations (9) and (18) may be ideal for many trainees, especially those who can't barbell squat safely, or deadlift safely over a full range of motion.

When comparing the hip-belt squat and the leg press, the former may be safer for some trainees because of the compression on the back during the leg press. Furthermore, the hip-belt squat doesn't require a machine. But for some other trainees, the hip-belt squat may provide excessive stress on the knees, and the leg press may be preferable provided the compression on the back isn't a problem.

In **The Program**, the back squat is a mainstay because, as already noted, I recommend all trainees experiment with the back squat other than those who have insufficient equipment to permit safe squatting, or those who have unusual physical limitations. Unless you back squat for a sufficient period you'll never know whether or not it's suited to you.

The deadlift—or partial deadlift, for trainees who can't perform the regular deadlift safely—is another mainstay in **The Program**.

The leg curl is a mainstay in **The Program** from the fourth month. The leg press is also employed as from the fourth month, in addition to the squat, to work the thighs hard on non-squatting days. The back extension, too, is employed as from the fourth month.

The parallel-grip deadlift isn't included in **The Program**, because the required bar isn't commonly available. The parallel-grip deadlift should, however, be experimented with by all trainees.

Individuality reminder

With exercise technique, what's "safe" can be an individual matter. Age, body structure and proportions, and any past injuries, among other factors, can turn what's generally a safe exercise into a potentially harmful one. Study Chapter 12 to learn about correct exercise technique, and then apply it *consistently*. If, however, despite using *correct technique*, along with a *controlled rep speed*, *gradual* increases in progressive resistance, abbreviated training routines, and *adequate* recovery time between workouts, you *still* experience joint or soft tissue irritation from a given exercise, substitute it with a comparable exercise. Apply the first imperative of exercise: "Do no harm."

No matter how effective an exercise may be for someone, if it doesn't suit you, it will do you no good, and perhaps do you harm. When considering the preferences of a trainer, coach, or author, consider *your* limitations and technical proficiency.

From the fourth month, the parallel-grip deadlift could be employed instead of the leg press *and* regular deadlift, on the non-squatting day.

If you can't back squat, or don't want to back squat, you could parallel-grip deadlift *or* sumo deadlift once a week, and leg press *or* front squat *or* hip-belt squat once a week, at different workouts.

If it's impossible to back squat, parallel-grip deadlift, or sumo deadlift, you could, for example, leg press two times a week, front squat two times a week, hip-belt squat two times a week, *or* perform two of the latter three exercises once a week each.

Some trainees, especially advanced ones, train their quadriceps just once a week. That may be insufficient for other trainees for optimal progress, but two times a week may be too frequent, at least once beyond the beginner level. An alternative is to train the quadriceps three times every *two* weeks—once every four or five days.

Lower-back, and thigh recovery times

Even if you can barbell squat safely, and can perform deadlift variations safely, too, you may find that your lower back needs more recovery time from those exercises than your thighs, especially once you've been training consistently for at least a year. Then, to barbell squat *or* parallel-grip deadlift at one workout (and perhaps barbell deadlift, *or* partial deadlift, *or* sumo deadlift at that workout, too), and hip-belt squat *or* leg press at the other workout each week, may be better. You'll need to experiment, at the time. The hip-belt squat, and leg press, work the thighs hard, but don't heavily involve the lower back. Either way, include the leg curl, and back extension, once a week each, to balance your thigh, hip, and lower-back work.

Some trainees may prefer to do a form of deadlifting once each week but train their quadriceps three times every *two* weeks. And some advanced trainees deadlift hard only once every *two* weeks, and do light, technique work at one or two workouts between the major ones.

Hack machine squats, and machine squats in general

There are many types of hack squat machines, which primarily train the quadriceps, hips, and hamstrings. They derive from the *barbell* hack squat, named after its most famous proponent, George Hackenschmidt (1878–1968), a legendary wrestler and strongman. In the barbell hack squat, the bar is held in the hands behind the legs or thighs, elbows straight. This is an awkward exercise and never became as popular as regular barbell squats. The initial hack squat machines were developed to try to make the exercise feel more comfortable, and to greatly reduce stress on the lower back. They had a small, angled platform to stand on, still had the resistance held in the hands behind the legs or thighs (which remained a problem), but the back was guided by a support. These simple machines were cramped, and produced severe knee stress for most users.

Recent hack squat machines apply the resistance differently—typically through two pads resting on the shoulders, rather than a single bar as in the barbell squat. And the foot platforms are much larger (to permit foot positioning that's safer for the knees), typically still at an angle, and with the exerciser positioned on the machine at an angle. There's an improved back support, and sometimes a head support, too. These machines come with a weighted sled that rolls up and down on tracks, or slides on bearings, and the weight plates are placed on bars extending on either side.

With the resistance being applied to the shoulders, the hack squat machines aren't true hack squat devices. Squat machines and hack squat machines have merged. And some leg press machines are designed to double as hack squat machines. Modern hack squat machines can be considered more like reverse leg presses than machine versions of the barbell hack squat.

Leg presses and most hack squat machines fix the hips, unlike in barbell squats where the hips are free to move. A few hack squat machines have the user facing *into* the machine, which gives some freedom of hip movement. Most hack squat machines have the user facing *out* of the machine.

The variety of hack squat machines, and squat machines as a whole, is considerable, and the quality varies across the brands. There's a variety of leg press machines, too, but the extent of variation isn't so extensive, and most public gyms have a decent leg press. Therefore, the leg press is used in **The Program**.

Hack squat machines, and squat machines in general, have not been recommended in this book because of the extent of their variation. If used properly—correct foot positioning (like in the barbell squat), safe back positioning (concave lower back), safe range of motion, controlled rep speed, and gradual building up of resistance—some of these machines are good. But many of them are constructed in such a way that they constrain the users so much that they will cause harm if used regularly.

The Program, if implemented as described, will establish training consistency, ingrain correct exercise technique, embed controlled and smooth rep speed, apply progressive resistance, and develop the ability to train hard. The visible results will be substantial strength development, and significant muscular size. Furthermore, you'll greatly improve your flexibility, and cardiorespiratory fitness.

You'll transform yourself externally and internally, and set yourself up for many years of success *provided* you continue to follow the tenets of abbreviated, safe, consistent, progressive training.

17

The Program

The previous chapters provide information that's pivotal to successful implementation of _The Program_. If you skipped any of them, please turn back and study them in the order they are presented. If you're a beginner, however, Chapter 12 is best left until after you've had two weeks of gym work to familiarize yourself with the equipment required for the first routine.

Successful muscle-building arises from satisfying a package of components. Even if the training is perfect, it won't deliver good results unless all the supporting components are in order.

Before you start **The Program**, _complete the preparatory work described in Chapter 2._

Beyond your first year of training, your program will be shaped by your long-term goals—for example, whether you want to develop your muscular size to its maximum, or whether you prefer to develop and then maintain moderate development. But for your first year, the fundamentals must be covered. Learning the exercises, establishing workout regularity, training safely and progressively, limbering up, developing a foundation of muscle and strength, and building all-round conditioning, are required by all beginning trainees regardless of their long-term goals. These fundamentals are covered by **The Program**.

Be patient, follow **The Program**, and master your training. Most trainees try to rush their progress, which usually leads to poor results, setbacks, and failure.

The Program has been designed in a painstaking manner. It will produce consistent progress provided it's followed as described. Variety is built into it through carefully planned changes to the routines. Any further changes—including increases in training volume or frequency—would undermine the productivity of **The Program** for most trainees.

The RACE Method of Training

Most books on muscle-building start beginners on simple, basic routines, and after a few months move to "advanced," split routines that have multiple exercises per bodypart, and more strength-training days than non-strength-training days. It's no surprise that trainees typically make noticeable progress over their early months, partly because of the novelty of training, but then make only minimal progress, stagnate, or even regress when the training is increased in volume and frequency. Insufficient time is allowed for recuperation. Eventually, many trainees who could have made good progress for many years, quit training because of excessive workload, or because of injuries produced by that workload or the use of incorrect exercise technique. This book promotes the *RACE Method of Training* (Responsible, Abbreviated, Conservative, and Effective) not merely as an approach for beginners, *but as the best choice for all of one's training years.*

What if you're not a beginner?

If you've been training for a few weeks or months, consider yourself a beginner, and follow **The Program** as written.

If you're an experienced trainee, follow **The Program** as written except for the suggested exercise weights. Start out with 50% of your current weights in the exercises you regularly use. With the exercises that are new for you, start out very light as explained in **The Program**. For both categories of exercises, progress in weights gradually, as explained.

If you're not a beginner, you'll almost certainly have errors in your exercise technique to correct. That's why it's necessary to cut back your weights severely. Correct exercise technique must be learned first, and then the weights should be built back gradually.

RACE Training is the approach of choice because it's more practical and time efficient than conventional or supposedly "advanced" methods that require a greater time and energy commitment. *One of the biggest problems in the muscle-building world is the belief that brief training routines are for beginners only.*

RACE Training is built on correct exercise technique, short routines, and hard work, combined with sufficient nutrition and recovery time. This combination produces progress in strength, physique, and fitness, and applies to beginners, intermediates, *and* **advanced trainees, although the specific interpretations of training can vary.**

The Program implements *The Seven-Point Plan*—the set of interrelated fundamentals required for muscle-building success.

The Seven-Point Plan

1. Passion and desire for physique improvement and training—training regularity is essential.

2. Appropriate training routines, employing exercises that suit *you*.

3. Correct exercise technique, and smooth, controlled rep speed.

4. Hard, serious training.

5. Full satisfaction, every day, of the components of recuperation from training—nutrition, rest in general, and sleep—and the adoption of a healthy lifestyle. Staying healthy is imperative. Without your health you can't train hard and consistently.

6. Consistent Progression—the ability to add weight to your exercises without any perceived increase in effort required to achieve the target reps and sets, and without any compromise on correct exercise technique, and smooth, controlled rep speed. For example, if you add some weight to a given exercise every week or two, and each time you perceive an increase in the effort required to achieve your reps and sets, you'll soon grind to a halt because you won't be able to add further weight. But if you're able to add a tad of weight on a consistent basis to each exercise without a perceived increase in effort required to achieve your reps and sets, and while maintaining correct exercise technique and rep control, you'll be able to add

weight at that gradual rate for months on end, and perhaps even for year after year during your first few years of training (should that be desired). This is *Consistent Progression*.

7. Apply points two through six with *persistence* and *patience*.

The pivotal truth

The Seven-Point Plan is "all" you need. Get today right, and then tomorrow, then the following day, then the next, and so on. Regardless of whether or not it's a training day, each day contributes to your progress. Each day is another potential step toward your goals. Knock off one day at a time, again and again and again . . . .

The learning curve

Progress in training isn't linear, and has several aspects. Part of progress, for example, is exerting greater effort in order to maintain weight progression. You'll learn to train harder, and tolerate a greater degree of exercise-induced discomfort, provided you set about it properly, as described in this chapter.

One of the major characteristics that distinguishes advanced trainees from novices is that the former are able to exert a greater degree of effort.

CRITICAL SECTION
Key principles of program design

How much training is required?

The Program employs two or three workouts per week, with the strength-training portion of each being no longer than an hour. This is a more time-efficient way to train than four or more workouts per week. Furthermore, the fewer workouts usually encourage improved recuperation, heightened enthusiasm for training, a lesser chance of injury to the body through excessive repetitive stress, and a greater potential to train safely, consistently, and effectively.

Some methods claim to produce maximum benefits from just 30 to 60 minutes of training *per week*. This is not supported by science, and usually ignores cardio training, and stretching. A greater investment is required to obtain the full benefits from training—but not the excessive time commitment that's common among trainees in almost all gyms.

For trainees who can progress on conventional programs and four or more workouts per week, they may make the same progress, or perhaps greater progress, if they trained according to the principles promoted in this book. And they would have more time for life outside of the gym.

The strength-training routines

The Program is designed to develop balanced musculature and strength throughout the body. **The Program** is comprised of a series of different routines. Full-body routines are the mainstay, but a special split-routine format is provided, too. Full-body routines aren't just for beginners. Full-body routines are time-efficient for all trainees because fewer workouts are required compared with a typical split routine that trains half the body on, for example, Mondays and Thursdays, and the other half on Tuesdays and Fridays. Some split routines require five or six workouts each week. Full-body routines provide more days of recovery.

The greater number of workouts required on a split routine isn't practical for many trainees. Although only part of the body is trained each workout, there's still a systemic demand on the body, and thus a high risk of insufficient recuperation.

The special split routine option in **The Program** involves only three workouts a week, which gives four recovery days. This may be effective. Most split routines have more training days than off days.

The exercises in the routines have been carefully sequenced. For example, the arms aren't trained before the upper back is worked, because if they were you wouldn't be able to do justice to your upper-back work; and the lower back isn't trained before the squat, because you shouldn't tire your lower back before you squat.

Number and variety of exercises

Alternating two different routines, for example, permits more exercises to be employed compared with using the same routine each workout. It also prevents the repetition of the same set of exercises each workout. For many trainees this variety helps to maintain training enthusiasm, but excessive variety is counterproductive.

Some of the exercises in **The Program** work only small areas of muscle—for instance, L-fly, lateral raise, and neck work—but they still have big potential benefits, including strengthening of important muscles that would otherwise be neglected. This helps to protect against injuries from training and from out-of-the-gym activities. And performance in the exercises that work big areas of musculature may be improved, too.

Frequent changes of routines and exercises usually hinder progress because insufficient time is provided for initial familiarization with a given exercise (or *re*-familiarization, for an exercise reintroduced after a period off it) *and* a sustained period of improving at it.

The Program is an illustration of sufficient variety but with the consistency required for progress in building muscle and strength. The variety is within each week's training, and from one stage of **The Program** to another. Sufficient consistency is also required for developing and then maintaining the skills of exercise performance.

How many sets?

For beginners it's necessary to do multiple work sets, in order to learn correct exercise technique, and the skills involved in exercising. Training intensity should be low to moderate at this stage. Practice is needed before single work sets—one per exercise—can be used to best effect.

Based on an extensive review of comparative resistance training studies, by R. N. Carpinelli and R. M. Otto [Strength Training: Single Versus Multiple Sets; in SPORTS MEDICINE. 26 (2):73–84, 1998], there appears to be little or no difference in the results of hypertrophy, muscular strength, endurance, and power arising from one work set per exercise, and multiple work sets. But numerous work sets per exercise lead to a reduction in intensity, overtraining through excessive volume, and perhaps injury because of overuse. Intensity is the key behind effective training, not volume. But while hard training is required—at the appropriate stage, as described in **The Program**—extremely hard training may be counter-productive. The primary goal of **The Program** is progress in muscular development and strength through gradual increases in the resistance used in each exercise. This can be achieved without "killer" workouts.

A benefit of low-volume training is that it's practical for busy people who don't have a lot of time for working out.

From the second week of **The Program**—as it's written for *beginners*—there are three work sets per exercise, of low intensity. Thereafter the intensity increases gradually over time. Warm-up sets are added as the weights are built up, and the work sets are reduced to two. Single work sets could be progressed to later on, once you've developed the ability to train with the required intensity but while maintaining correct exercise technique.

If you're not a beginner at the outset of using *The Program*, and provided you have the discipline to train hard but with correct technique as described in this book, you may immediately be able to use single work sets effectively. But adequate warm-up work must precede each work set.

The ability to train hard is a learned skill. With experience of proper training you'll train harder, and tolerate more exercise-induced discomfort. What you may now consider to be hard training, may, for example, be two reps short of what you would do if you could, today, use your ability of a year from now.

The harder the training, the less training that's possible. Although some increase of volume or frequency of training may compensate, to some extent, for reduced intensity, the details are uncertain, and it's easy to overtrain through excessive volume of work.

There's no single, best interpretation of training intensity, volume, and frequency that's appropriate to all trainees. Individual variation, goals, preferences, lifestyle, age, health, ability to train hard and tolerate exercise-induced discomfort, and other factors, influence training program design, especially when beyond the beginner stage. Then one, two or, at most, three work sets per exercise is the general rule. If you can do more than three work sets per exercise, you may not be exercising hard enough to stimulate growth, but you will be spending more time in the gym than is required.

Single-work-set training is effective at building strength and muscle, when done correctly. But periods of two or three work sets for some exercises may help to maintain enthusiasm for some trainees, and produce varied stimulus, which in combination may help to sustain progress.

How many reps?

The Program employs sets of between 6 and 12 reps for most exercises. At times, higher reps are used for some lower-body exercises.

Training tradition and many publications claim that low-rep sets—sets of under five reps—build strength but not much muscular size, whereas medium reps (and sometimes higher) build more size for a comparable degree of strength. Powerlifters and Olympic weightlifters, who focus on strength, usually favor low-rep sets. The differences in the effects of the different reps may not, however, be as pronounced as tradition suggests, and may vary among different trainees and different exercises.

More important than the specific rep counts used, are these factors: training safety, training consistency, and progress in muscular development and strength through gradual increases in the resistance used in each exercise. These elements are the linchpins of **The Program**.

Rest intervals

Taking a short rest interval between sets produces training that feels more uncomfortable than that of the same effort level but performed with a longer rest interval between sets. Consequently, short rest intervals are the least practical for most trainees even though workout duration is minimized. Short rest intervals can also mar the performance of individual sets. For example, if you're fatigued from one set (whether of the same exercise or a different one), and start another almost immediately, the weight used in the latter will be compromised, and effort and technique may be marred, too. Furthermore, it's difficult to train in this manner in a busy gym.

Relative to shorter rest intervals, moderate ones provide systemic and localized recovery that can enable work sets to be performed with greater effort and weight, and permit focus on correct technique without the burden of severe general fatigue. But long rest intervals produce long workouts that are impractical for many trainees. Long rest intervals can also lead to muscles cooling down, which can increase the risk of injury.

Moderate rest intervals are used in **The Program** other than during the first few months for beginners, where rest intervals are shorter because the effort level is low to moderate. The use of moderate rest intervals is usually the most practical way to train because it enables individual set performance to be high, but the overall workout to feel comfortable. Moderate rest intervals also permit better demonstration of strength than shorter rest intervals, and may permit easier progression in strength.

THE PROGRAM

Choose two well-spaced training days, such as Tuesday and Saturday, or Wednesday and Sunday. By having one workout on the weekend you may have the chance, at least one day a week, to train at a time that's optimal for you.

The Program has three major gym components: strength training, stretching, and cardiorespiratory work. Doing all three components during each workout simplifies training, and may be an especially useful approach for beginners. If you have convenient access to cardio equipment—at home, or at a gym close to work or home—you may prefer to do the cardio work on separate days. This will shorten the main workout days, and spread the overall training over the week.

Although stretching was performed three times a week during the preparatory month, two times per week may suffice now. You may, however, do a third session of stretching, at home.

Here's the five-part structure of exercise in the gym:

1. General warm-up of five to ten minutes
2. Calisthenics
3. Weights work (strength training)
4. Stretching
5. Cardio work

The general warm-up should be a constant before every weights workout. This applies even if it's warm when you train. Spend five to ten minutes on a zero-impact piece of cardio equipment such as a rower, stationary cycle, or ski machine. A full-body exerciser—rower or ski machine, from the aforementioned examples—is preferable to a lower-body-only piece, to warm up the entire body. Start out slowly, and increase the pace sufficiently so that within five minutes you've broken into a sweat. The aim is to elevate your core temperature a little.

The older you are, or the colder it is, the more time and care you should devote to the general warming up.

Here are three crucial benefits from an adequate general warm-up:

1. Muscles are made more elastic, and less susceptible to injury.

> *Baring emergency, or if you're not feeling well, follow* **The Program***. An irregular schedule is usually a death sentence for consistency.*

2. Heart irregularities that may be associated with sudden, intensive exercise, are reduced.

3. The nervous system is primed, and mental preparedness for rigorous training is heightened.

Immediately following the general warm-up, and before using the weights, perform a single set of each of the calisthenics used in the preparatory month. Aim to add at least one rep to each movement per week. The calisthenics will take only a few minutes. Because you won't start training hard with the weights until the fifth month of **The Program**, keep the calisthenics in your program until at least the end of the third month.

The stretching component of **The Program** is another constant. See Chapter 2. The progression here isn't in terms of resistance or volume of work. It's in the form of gradually increased flexibility. Eventually, however, once you're limber enough, you'll need only to maintain that level of flexibility. But this assumes that your flexibility isn't limited by restrictions in your muscles and other soft tissues. See Chapter 6.

Some of the stretches should be performed immediately before the squat and deadlift, rather than at the end of the weights workout. This will help limber you up for the squat and deadlift, to help you to use correct technique in those two exercises.

This leaves two components of **The Program** that will vary over each month, and from month to month—cardio work, and strength training.

General activity

If you're sedentary outside of your strength and cardio workouts, more general activity is needed. For example, hike or walk at a decent pace, or do garden work, for at least three hours total spread over the week—preferably about half an hour each day—to produce the minimum of general activity needed for some semblance of total physical fitness.

For your general activity on a training day, you could incorporate it into your workout. At the end of the workout, use a treadmill or elliptical machine, for example, for 30 minutes at moderate intensity.

Too much exercise for you to handle?

A reminder: Adopt a gradual approach

If you're currently inactive, the prospect of strength training, stretching, cardio work, and general activity outside of the gym, may be overwhelming. If so, leave the cardio work and general activity of **The Program** until later. Focus on the strength training and a streamlined version of the flexibility routine. Then gradually work in the other components. Here's an illustration, with each phase lasting about two months:

Phase one

Strength training, and stretches 1, 2, 4, 5, and 7 (see Chapter 2).

Phase two

Strength training, full stretching routine, and walking for half an hour two times a week.

Phase three

Strength training, full stretching routine, adoption of the cardio program.

Phase four

Strength training, full stretching routine, cardio program, and general activity out of the gym for half an hour per day.

The Program has been written as if you are adopting, right from the start, all three gym activities—strength training, stretching, and cardio work—and the general activity component outside of the gym. But this approach may not be for you. It's critical that you don't perform more exercise than you can presently handle. You may be best off adopting the gradual approach.

Take heart . . . as you adjust to an active lifestyle, and make physical training an important part of your life, you'll probably discover that a program that may have seemed overwhelming to begin with, is actually modest and manageable.

Progression caveat reminder

Start out conservatively with any type of exercise program, or with any change in a program. Your body has tremendous abilities of adaptation provided that you start out comfortably, and gradually increase the demands. This applies to all forms of physical training—resistance training, stretching, and cardio work.

Rope jumping

Rope jumping, or skipping, is sometimes considered a warm-up activity. But for most trainees, rope jumping isn't a warm-up exercise. If you want to do it, work into it gradually from a modest start. Rope jumping can be demanding.

Although you don't need to bounce more than an inch off the floor, rope jumping is still an impact activity, albeit low-level provided you do it correctly. If you choose to jump rope as part of your main cardio work, take it easy to begin with, as just one minute of it can produce severe foot, leg, and knee soreness the following day, for trainees with little or no conditioning. Use a giving surface such as rubber, not concrete; and wear shoes that absorb some of the impact. Try just 30 seconds of skipping the first time out, and add half a minute each workout provided you had no negative reaction from the previous session. Progress slowly.

Skipping is potentially a good, general conditioning and coordination exercise, which is why it's popular among boxers; but if it's not suited to you, find an alternative. If you haven't jumped rope since you were a child, you may find it difficult, and require a number of sessions of practice before you master the skill. The length of the rope is important. If the rope is too long or too short, it will snag easily. Adjust the length of the rope until you find the best length for you.

Cardio work

See Chapter 9.

The previous chapters provide information that's pivotal to successful implementation of **The Program**. *If you skipped any of them, please turn back and study them.*

Strength-training program
Exercise technique guidelines

For the first two weeks of training in a gym, if you're a beginner, follow the exercise technique guidance given at the end of Chapter 2. Thereafter you should be sufficiently familiar with exercise equipment to be able to understand the details of exercise technique. Then you'll be able to apply the information in Chapter 12, where the details on exercise technique are provided. But if you're not a beginner, apply the instruction from Chapter 12 immediately.

Haste makes waste

Most trainees don't invest the necessary time to learn and ingrain correct exercise technique prior to training hard. Without knowing it they learn poor exercise technique at best, and awful technique at worst. Then using poor technique they add weight to the bar too fast, and build up to intensive training over just a few weeks.

The combination of poor technique and intensive training produces injury, missed workouts, recovery, reinjury, missed workouts, recovery, reinjury, and so on. And that's on top of overly long and frequent workouts that are typical of most trainees' programs. The combination produces frustration and disillusionment, and loss of passion for training. It's no surprise that so many people give up training within twelve months of starting.

The conservative approach leads to consistent progress without setbacks, not only during the first twelve months of training, but thereafter. Therefore, use abbreviated routines, focus on learning and ingraining correct exercise technique over the early months, incrementally build up exercise weights and intensity (without compromising on correct technique), avoid injury, and doggedly apply patience and persistence. *That* is the approach promoted in **The Program**. *Make haste slowly.*

Equipment shortcomings

All well-equipped, and even most modestly equipped gyms, will have all that's needed to perform the exercises listed in the routines in this chapter. The pieces of equipment perhaps most likely to be unavailable in minimally equipped gyms, are the pulldown apparatus, calf machine and, for later routines, the pullover machine, leg curl, leg press, and four-way neck machine. If necessary, for the first routine, substitute a dumbbell row for the pulldown, and the one-legged calf raise for the calf machine version.

MONTH #1
Week 1

Same full-body routine, two times a week

p. 356   1. Squat: bare Olympic bar (45 pounds, or 20 kilos), 2 sets of 8 reps
          *Immediately prior to squatting, to help with flexibility, perform the
          calf, groin and thigh adductor, hip flexor, hamstring, buttock, and
          quadricep stretches—numbers 1, 2, 3, 4, 5, and 7, from Chapter 2.*

p. 232   2. Standing calf raise: 40 pounds or 20 kilos, 2 x 15

p. 208   3. Bench press: bare Olympic bar (45 pounds, or 20 kilos), 2 x 8

p. 256   4. Deadlift: bare Olympic bar (45 pounds, or 20 kilos), 2 x 8

p. 320   5. Seated back-supported dumbbell press: 10-pound or 5-kilo
          dumbbells, 2 x 8

p. 324   6. Pulldown: 40 pounds or 20 kilos, 2 x 8

p. 346   7. Dumbbell shrug: 20-pound or 10-kilo dumbbells, 2 x 8

p. 252   8. Seated dumbbell curl: 10-pound or 5-kilo dumbbells, 2 x 8

p. 242   9. Basic crunch: no weight, 2 x 12

*Rest 60 seconds between sets of exercises 2 and 5 through 9. Rest 90 seconds
between sets of the other exercises.*

*The basic crunch is included in both the calisthenics and strength-training
routines. In the former, the progression is through increasing the reps; in the
latter, weight progression will shortly come into play.*

The suggested starting weights are for typical, adult males. Females
should use half these weights. The weights may, however, need
adjusting for you. They must feel very light. If any particular weight
feels anything other than very light, reduce it.

Very light weights are required to enable you to concentrate on
correct exercise technique, and a controlled, smooth rep speed,
and to enable your body to start the adaptation process from a
very easy start.

Strength training is *progressive* resistance training—start very light,
and add a *little* weight as you can.

Stretches for the squat and deadlift

Tight lower-body muscles will hamper squatting and deadlifting
technique. Throughout **The Program**, these muscles should be
stretched prior to each bout of squatting or deadlifting: stretches 1, 2,
3, 4, 5, and 7, from Chapter 2. Perform the remaining stretches after
completing the weights workout.

Special notes

This full-body routine of nine exercises mixes multi-joint movements with important single-joint moves. The possibly unusual inclusion for a first routine, is the shrug. This exercise, together with the deadlift, builds the trapezius muscle. This is important in its own right, and because it builds muscle where the bar rests for the squat. The squat is potentially a very valuable exercise, and having enough natural padding for the bar to rest on is essential for successful, long-term squatting.

I've assumed that all the listed movements can be performed safely. The weight for each exercise should be minimal, because the emphasis over the initial months is upon technique, *technique,* and TECHNIQUE. You must not strain at this stage, because pushing too intensively, too early, is a death sentence for correct exercise technique. And you can't ingrain correct technique from just a few workouts.

Focus 100% on your workout, and leave chit chat and socializing until after you've finished. Never talk while you lift weights, unless you need to call for assistance. When you talk during a workout—and probably only home trainees can realistically train in silence—keep it brief and between sets. But before each set spend a few seconds in silence, to focus on the job at hand, and *then* perform the set.

Much can be done at home to practice correct exercise technique, and controlled, smooth rep speed. But putting it into practice in a gym— especially if it's during a busy time—may be another matter. Don't be rushed or intimidated by others. At least for your first few months of training, it would be ideal if you worked out at quiet times so that you don't feel self-conscious or pressured by others.

For the deadlift, make the mid-shin point the lowest that the bar should descend to—limit the bar there, or a little higher, depending on individual bodily proportions. See Chapter 12 for details on deadlifting technique. Set up your equipment so that the bar doesn't descend beyond the mid-shin position. Here are two ways of doing this:

1. Use a power rack. Set the pins of the rack so that when the barbell rests on them, it's at the mid-shin point, or slightly higher.

2. Use two stable blocks or stacks of plates on the floor or lifting platform, arranged so that when your loaded barbell rests on the blocks or stacks, the bar is at mid-shin height, or slightly higher. This is a clumsy method, however. The other method is superior.

Written records

Start a training logbook. Buy a purpose-designed one, or get a notebook and design your own workout logbook. Record precisely what you do in each workout, especially the weight used and reps performed for each set. An accurate training logbook is essential, so you know exactly what you did last time around, and what you need to do next time to notch up progress. You also need a record of equipment set-up details.

The 60-minute guideline

The guideline for the maximum duration of the strength-training portion of each workout is 60 minutes. This may, however, be exceeded during the early stages of **The Program***. But as* **The Program** *develops, as you gain experience, and as you become more efficient at setting up equipment, the 60-minute guideline can be met provided that you don't get distracted during workout time.*

Don't hold your breath

Breath holding during training—or during any type of physical exertion—increases blood pressure. This can lead to headaches, dizziness, and even blackouts. Over the long term, breath holding during exertion encourages varicose veins, and hemorrhoids, because of the damage to vein walls and valves caused by the elevated blood pressure.

To prevent breath holding, don't close your mouth. Keep your mouth open—just slightly open will suffice—and your upper and lower teeth apart. It's usually when the lips are jammed together that problems with breath holding occur.

Sample page from a workout logbook

Here's an illustration for an advanced, male trainee. It tracks four workouts of one routine. The sample program alternates two different, full-body routines, on a two-times-a week training schedule.

NOV THROUGH FEB PROGRAM Workout #1, every Wednesday			Nov 8 5:00pm	Nov 15 6:00pm	Nov 22 4:00pm	Nov 29 11:00am
Deadlift	stretch lower body first, alternate reverse grips	135×6 225×6 315×6 360×2	400×6 400×4	400×6 400×5	400×6	402×6
One-legged calf raise	standing calf machine, one leg at a time	0×15 60×15	100×15	100×15 100×14	100×15 100×15	101×15 101×14
Leg press	groin stretch, depth pin #3, inclination #2	90×12 180×12 270×8	345×12 345×10	345×12	347×12 347×12	348×12
Leg curl	rom limitation of two weight stack levels	50×8 90×8	118×8 118×6	118×8 118×7	118×8	119×7 119×6
Parallel bar dip	bench raised on 45-lb plates, to set max descent	bw×6 60×6	123×6 123×5	123×6	124×6 124×5	124×6 124×5
Pulldown	knee restraint #3, supinated grip	125×8 175×8	221×8	221×8 221×7	221×8 221×8	222×8 222×6
Seated barbell press	rack pin hole 22	100×6 160×6	193×6	193×6 193×5	193×6 193×6	194×6
Lying L-fly		5×8	15×8	15×8	15×8	16×6
Neck flexion & extension	height setting #1 for forw. flexion, #3 for extension	fl 60×10 ex 80×10	fl 111×10 e 133×9	fl 111×10 e 133×10	fl 112×8 e 133×10	fl 112×9 e 134×9
Twisting crunch	ankles restrained, dumbbell held on chest	0×8 60×8	122×8	122×8 122×7	122×8 122×8	123×8
General warm-up to precede each workout, until break into a sweat.			trimmed four work sets today, to reduce overall load	deadlifts felt especially heavy	dropped second dead work set, to try to help recovery	deads great today, just one work set feels better than two

The Haven

Treat your training time as inviolable—*The Haven*. Make each set *perfect*—perfect technique, perfect control, and perfect concentration. This is possible on a long-term basis as long as you keep your mind on one set at a time.

The instant you're in the gym, switch off from non-training matters. Turn off your phone. Cut yourself off from the hoopla that may be taking place where you train. Ideally, train during a quiet time when there are few if any distractions. Furthermore, don't squeeze your training between two demanding out-of-the-gym activities.

Protect and respect your privacy while you train. Then make each rep a journey into *The Haven*, where you're master. Without such a single-minded application, you'll fall short of your best performance.

Mental preparation

You can't enter the gym with your mind full of problems and concerns, and expect to put in a good workout. Transform yourself from your working and family persona, to your training persona.

Before you start your pre-workout, general warm-up, sit down somewhere out of the way, switch off from what's happening around you, and switch on to your training. For a few minutes, mentally go through each exercise that's planned for the workout. Close your eyes and imagine performing two or three slow reps for each exercise. Feel your muscles working. See the weights moving with control. *Become* each rep.

The first few times you do this you'll probably find that your mind wanders. Keep pulling it back to the focus you need. With practice it will become easier. Continue to keep your mind on your workout as you do your general warm-up work. Don't allow people or events to disrupt your focus. Then maintain your focus throughout the workout.

MONTH #1
Week 2

Same full-body routine, two times a week

P. 356   1. Squat: 3 x 8
            Immediately prior to squatting, to help with flexibility, perform the calf, groin and thigh adductor, hip flexor, hamstring, buttock, and quadricep stretches—numbers 1, 2, 3, 4, 5, and 7, from Chapter 2.
P. 232   2. Standing calf raise: 3 x 15
P. 208   3. Bench press: 3 x 8
P. 256   4. Deadlift: 3 x 8
P. 320   5. Seated back-supported dumbbell press: 3 x 8
P. 324   6. Pulldown: 3 x 8
P. 346   7. Dumbbell shrug: 3 x 8
P. 252   8. Seated dumbbell curl: 3 x 8
P. 242   9. Basic crunch: 3 x 12

Use the same weights, reps, and rest intervals as in Week 1. The only change is to perform three sets per exercise, rather than two.

Keep accurate workout records.

Remember the watchwords of correct exercise technique, and a controlled, smooth rep speed no faster than two to three seconds up per rep, and no faster than another two to three seconds down—no exceptions. Never mind if you're the only one in the gym who trains with correct technique and control.

After Week 2 you should be sufficiently familiar with the gym equipment to put into practice all the details on exercise technique. If you haven't already, study the parts of Chapter 12 that cover the exercises in your current routine, and put what you learn into practice.

Workout tape

Get someone to video tape your entire workout. Then study the recording at home. Examine your exercise technique, rep control, lifting technique while setting up equipment, concentration level during each set, effort level, and use of time between sets. Look for areas to improve, and then address them at your next workout.

MONTH #I
Week 3

Same full-body routine, two times a week

First workout

Same exercises, sets, and reps as in Week 2.

Provided the weights used in Weeks 1 and 2 were very light for you, add weight increments in Week 3. (If the weights didn't feel very light in Week 2 in any specific exercise or exercises, wait another week or two before adding weight there.) Hold a small plate on your chest for the basic crunch, add 5 pounds or 2.5 kilos per 'bell in the dumbbell exercises, and 10 pounds or 5 kilos for the other exercises. Women should add half these weight increases. But NEVER should you add weight to an exercise if, during the previous workout, you struggled to get your target reps. Should any exercise be a struggle, REDUCE the weight.

Second workout

Same exercises, sets, and reps as in the previous workout.

Relative to the previous workout, add 10 pounds or 5 kilos for exercises 1 through 4, 6, and 7. Women should add half these weight increases. If, however, the weights used in the previous workout didn't feel very light, DON'T add the weight increments.

If you're a beginner, by your sixth workout you should be able to perform every exercise without any wobbling or obvious control problems. If you're still having control problems, put in extra rehearsal time at home, and add no further weight increments for a week, or even a few weeks—until you have no control difficulties in the gym.

Please re-read Chapter 10. The guidance on how to avoid injuries will make even greater sense once you've had a few weeks of experience in a gym.

The next nine weeks

Until the end of the third month of strength training, **The Program** remains unchanged other than for the resistance used on each exercise. The rate at which you add weight is critical. If you add it too quickly—which is usual—your exercise technique will degrade, and you'll start training intensively too soon (with poor technique), which is a recipe for injury and frustration. If, however, you add weight too slowly, you'll delay your progress.

After three weeks of **The Program** you'll perceive a variation of effort across the nine exercises—all nine won't require the same degree of effort. Over the next nine weeks or so, even out the perception of effort so that it's comparable across all nine exercises. This is achieved through incremental weight progression appropriate to each exercise—different exercises progress at different rates.

The target, at the end of your first three months of strength training, is that all exercises involve *nearly hard* work of a comparable level of exertion. "Nearly hard" training means working until about two reps short of what would be your limit on the final work set on a given exercise if you were pushed to the maximum, and a rep or two more of slack on the other work sets (where you're fresher).

A set of a single-joint exercise such as the dumbbell curl can't match a set of a big, multi-joint exercise such as the squat, for overall demands on the body. But if you perform sets of eight reps in both exercises, for example, and in each case you could, if pushed to your limit, just squeeze out ten reps, then the relative effort level on both is comparable.

Even after three months of **The Program** it's too early to move into hard training where you perform every rep possible in each work set. Exercise technique is still being consolidated, and the discipline to hold correct technique during intensive work has yet to be fully developed. Furthermore, for beginners, it's unnecessary to train hard at such an early stage.

Weight progression

Over weeks four through twelve, add weight at a gradual, incremental rate. Some exercises have greater weight progression potential than others—for most trainees, the deadlift has the largest potential. Here's the basic rule of progression to apply during these early weeks:

For men, provided that at your previous workout you made your target reps and sets for a given exercise with reps to spare (that is, you could do several reps more on each set if you pushed hard), add five pounds to each of exercises 1, 2, 3, 4, 6 and 7, and add just two pounds to each of the other exercises. For dumbbell movements, a total increase of two pounds means a single pound on each 'bell, while a total increase of five pounds means half of that on each 'bell. Women should increase their weights by half of these numbers.

Progress at this rate won't continue for all exercises for long. As soon as you can't make your target reps and sets with room to spare, for a given exercise, slow the frequency of weight increments on that particular exercise, or reduce the size of the increments. In this way the varying perception of difficulty of the exercises will get evened out. The exercises where you're furthest away from using your current maximum weights, for the given reps, will continue at the given weight progression longer than will those exercises where you're getting close to your current maximum weights.

To recap, you initially started in the gym with training that felt very comfortable, with many spare capacity reps on each exercise. Then you progressed gradually, through weight increments on each exercise, to the stage, at three months, where you're training "nearly hard," with about two spare reps at the end of the final set of each exercise.

Important note on progressive weights

The progression schedule given here is a guideline only, primarily for beginners. It will apply to some trainees, but will need adjusting for others. To repeat a critical point, *if you don't manage to complete your target reps and sets very comfortably, you haven't qualified for a weight increase next workout.* Wait until you've built the required spare capacity *before* increasing the weight on a given exercise. Intermediate and advanced trainees can qualify for weight progression without so much spare capacity.

The variation among beginners is vast. As examples, a stocky 25-year-old man used to manual labor has a far greater starting strength, and perhaps progression potential too, than a tall, lanky, sedentary 18-year-old male student who, in turn, has a far greater starting strength and progression potential than a 50-year-old, female beginner.

Not training hard enough?

Hard training will come later in **The Program**, when it's appropriate. Correct exercise technique, and smooth rep speed, must be entrenched first. This takes at least two months of consistent training. Then the discipline needed to *maintain* correct exercise technique and smooth rep speed under maximum exertion in an exercise takes more time. If technique breaks down during hard training, injury is almost inevitable. *Hard training must be worked into progressively.*

How to add small weight increments

Small weight increments require the use of small discs, or microloads. Few gyms have them. If your gym won't get its own stock of small discs, get your own, perhaps have them engraved with your initials or name, and take them to the gym with you. But keep a watchful eye on them, so they don't get stolen.

With adjustable dumbbells, remove the collars and add, for example, a pound disc or two half-pound discs on each 'bell. If the dumbbells are fixed—the collars can't be removed—use small magnetic discs or attach a little disc with strong tape, or perhaps use wrist weights, thus applying the increment to your wrists rather than to the dumbbells. See *Resources* for suppliers of small discs and magnetic plates.

On the far right are the smallest plates usually found in gyms—1.25 kilos (or the 2.5-pound equivalents). On the far left are spring collars, which weigh about half a pound each, and can be used as an alternative to small discs. The other plates are true small discs: 0.1 kilo, 0.25 kilo, 0.5 kilo, 0.125 pound, and 0.25 pound.

Magnetic PlateMate® weight plates come in several sizes, including 1.25-pound and 0.625-pound. These are especially useful for applying microloads to selectorized weight stacks, and fixed-weight dumbbells and barbells.

Large washers and industrial magnets, available from some hardware stores or ironmongers, are a reduced-cost alternative to specially made small discs and magnetic plates. Find how many washers are needed to produce one pound or half a kilo, then slip them on a barbell when you need an increment of just one pound or half a kilo. Another alternative, also available from some hardware stores, is chain. Have lengths of chain cut to the weight you want—for instance, half a pound or a quarter kilo per length. The chains can be jammed between plates on a barbell, or hung from a weight belt for some exercises. Finally, spring collars are available in most gyms, and can be used in pairs to add approximately one pound or half a kilogram per increment.

Achieving progressive resistance in small increments is a problem on most weight-stack machines. Some of these machines are designed so that you can pin on a small increment to produce a transition between two adjacent weight levels. Put the weight-selection pin through a small disc and then slot it into the weight stack. You could even loop pieces of chain around the top of the weight stack. Some of these machines have purpose-made small weight pieces for slotting on top of the weight stacks.

 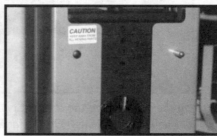

Left, a weight designed to fit on top of a selectorized weight stack. Right, a little plate pinned to the weight stack, for a small increase in resistance—a microload.

A few machines, such as the Nautilus Four-Way Neck, have a supplementary weight stack attached to the main stack, to add weight in small increments, perhaps pound by pound.

Main and supplementary weight stacks on the Nautilus Four-Way Neck.

Plate-loaded machines permit smaller resistance increments than most weight-stack machines, because you can add as little as half a pound to the former provided you have small discs, or an alternative.

What if you can't use little plates?

The use of little plates for making small increases in exercise weights is a tremendous help for making gradual, steady, safe, long-term progress. Most gyms don't have little plates. Although most gyms may allow individual members to bring in their own small discs, for the members' personal use, some gyms won't. What do you do if where you train doesn't have little discs, and won't allow you to bring your own? The gym may have a selection of lightweight collars, including spring collars, which can be used to progress pound by pound from one multiple of five pounds on a barbell, to the next. If even the lightweight collars aren't available, it may be time to find a better gym. In the meantime, apply the principle of *double progression*.

Let's say you can manage to dumbbell press a pair of 20-pound 'bells, for three sets of eight reps. The next pair of 'bells is likely to be 25-pounders, which is a 25% increase in weight. This is too much for a single jump when the 3 x 8 with the 20-pounders was tough. The ideal progression would be to tack a half- or one-pound disc, or a small magnetic plate, on each of the 20-pounders. This would enable you to keep the reps up while making an increase in weight. As an alternative, however, stay with the 20-pounders and build up the reps until you can get three sets of twelve reps. Then you should be able to handle the 25-pounders for perhaps 3 x 6, and be in reach of 3 x 8.

Below is an illustration of how the progression could go without small discs, using the double progression scheme of building up the reps before adding weight and dropping reps, and building up the reps again, and so on. Each listing (for instance, 3 x 8) signifies the work for a given workout. If the dumbbell press is trained two times a week, keep both workouts in a given week the same, so as not to rush progress and risk marring it. Make the rep progress weekly.

20-pounders
> 3 x 8 (three sets of eight reps)
> 3 x 9
> 3 x 10
> 2 x 11, 1 x 10
> 3 x 11
> 3 x 12 . . . *at the next workout, move to the next pair of dumbbells*

25-pounders
> 8, 8, 6 (two sets of eight, and one of six)
> 3 x 8
> 3 x 9
> 10, 10, 9

> 3 x 10
> 11, 11, 10
> 3 x 11
> 12, 11, 11
> 12, 12, 11
> 3 x 12
> 3 x 12 again, and perhaps a further time the following workout, to
>   ensure mastery of the weight for the target sets and reps . . .
>   *then move to the 30-pounders at the following workout.*

Progress in reps varies among individuals according to starting
strength, training experience, age, gender, and the specific exercise
concerned. The key point is to make *gradual* progress from week to
week in line with *your* strength development, while maintaining
correct exercise technique and rep control. For beginners, there must
still be spare capacity on each set, even on the final set of an exercise.

Apply the same principle of double progression to barbell and
machine exercises, if it's not possible to use microloads. The bigger
the minimum weight increment for a given exercise, the more you
need to build up the reps before making the weight increase.

This can be a particular concern with weight-stack machines because
some of them have a minimum increase of 15 pounds or more. Ten
pounds is common as the minimum increase on weight-stack machines,
and even that's excessive because it's enough to cut your reps in half, or
worse, relative to what you could do at the previous weight.

For example, rather than make a weight increase at say 3 x 8 in such a
machine exercise, build up to 3 x 12 first (like with the illustration of the
dumbbell press), which may take you two or three months, or longer,
depending on the individual and exercise concerned. By then, when the
extra 10 or 15 pounds go on, you should get your reps close to eight,
from where you would build up once again. But had you added weight
when you were at the 3 x 8 point, you would struggle, and perhaps
only make 5, 4, 3 the following workout, which is a recipe for
frustration at best, and technique breakdown, and injury, at worst.

There is, however, a problem with double progression. Especially
beyond your first six months or so of training, you may find you have
a rep ceiling in some if not most of your exercises, but not necessarily
the same ceiling for the different exercises. For example, no matter how
much you try, you may find it difficult to do more than eight reps in
work sets of the bench press. But if you have small increments, and
add just a pound at a time, you may be able to keep getting your eight
reps even with the gradually increasing weight.

Reminders

Before training, check your logbook. Find out what you need to do—for weights, and reps—to make today's workout progressive.

Double check that the weight you've loaded is correct. It's easy to load a bar incorrectly.

When in position for a set, adopt the correct grip, stance, and body position. Don't charge into a set, grab the bar, and then realize after the first rep that you took an imbalanced grip, wrong stance, or are lopsided while on a bench.

Dehydration mars training intensity and focus. Be sure you're not dehydrated *before* you train. Then regularly hydrate yourself during the workout. Drink at least one full glass over every fifteen minutes of training. Drink water between some sets, but keep your mind fixed on your training. Drinking from your own water bottle is usually more convenient than repeatedly going to the water fountain. Aim to drink enough water to produce at least one clear (color-free) urination after training.

Warm-up sets

After around six weeks of **The Program**—for each of the squat, bench press, and deadlift—add a single warm-up set of eight reps with about two-thirds of your work sets' weight. Perform the warm-up set, rest about 90 seconds, then perform the first work set for the given exercise. For example, it may be 60 pounds for the warm-up set in the squat, followed by 3 x 8 with 90 pounds.

There are at least three important reasons for warming up properly for each exercise:

1. To get synovial fluids moving in most of your joints (for lubrication), and get your joints, tendons, and muscles ready for demanding exercise.

2. To rehearse the technique and rep control of each exercise. Take all warm-up reps and sets seriously. Do each one carefully. Only once you're *sure* you have the correct groove and rep control entrenched, should you proceed to your work

> Do your utmost to add weight in SMALL INCREMENTS to all your exercises. If the gym you use doesn't have small discs already, its management should be willing to get some, or at least let you use your own. Otherwise, it may be time to look for another gym.

sets. Add extra warm-up work if you feel you would
benefit from more physical rehearsal. This especially
applies to the more complicated exercises such as the
deadlift, and the squat.

3. To prime the mind, muscles, and body as a whole, for
   demanding work.

For the early months of strength training, the weights are light, and there
isn't the need for the specific warm-up work that there will be later.

Between-sets rest intervals

For the first two months, the recommended rest intervals were 60
seconds between sets of single-joint exercises, and 90 seconds between
sets of multi-joint exercises. For the third month, take 90 seconds before
each set of single-joint exercises, and two minutes before each set of
multi-joint exercises.

If this change makes your workouts too long, perform two work sets
for each exercise rather than three.

The bench press may be the most popular
exercise in most gyms, at least among
bodybuilders. Although the bench press, done
correctly, is a valuable exercise, it's given
exaggerated importance by many trainees.
The bench press is employed in the routines
in **The Program**, *but in a balanced context*
relative to other exercises.

Technique recordings

Periodically use a video camera and record your
exercise technique, for analysis later. A video
camera can be an outstanding tool to help
improve your exercise technique.

Progress report for the first three months

Following the progression schedule outlined so far, for an adult male, the squat would have moved along as follows, monitoring the second workout of each week:

Week #	Weight
1	45 pounds
2	45
3	65
4	75
5	85
6	95
7	105

five pounds increment at each workout over weeks four through seven

8	110

now, five pounds increment at only the first workout each week

9	115
10	120
11	125
12	130
13	135

Here's an illustrative progression schedule for the dumbbell press:

Week #	Weight per dumbbell
1	10 pounds
2	10
3	15
4	20
5	21

one pound increment once a week per 'bell, two pounds total for the pair

6	22
7	23
8	24

spare capacity not sufficient to have earned an increment next week

9	24
10	25
11	26

spare capacity not sufficient to have earned an increment next week

12	26
13	27

These are illustrations only. You may or may not be able to maintain this rate of progression, depending on your age, gender, starting strength and condition, and responsiveness to training. The illustrations show the incremental and progressive approach to take.

Remember, at this stage of your training (three months), you still must train sub-maximally on all your sets. For example, on a final eight-rep work set, if you have the correct weight, you should be able to complete the eight reps with enough strength left so that you could, if pushed to your limit, complete another two reps. If you're struggling to get your target reps out on a given exercise, the rate of weight progression is too great for you.

If you don't have spare capacity of two reps on the final set of each exercise, slow the rate of weight progression—either add less weight each increment, or add the given increment less often.

The plan is to set up Consistent Progression for your first twelve months of strength training, and add a tad of weight every week in the big exercises, and every other week or so in the smaller exercises. This is possible provided you use tiny increments, and provided you don't add the increments at a faster pace than you can adapt to.

A classic mistake most trainees make is that they rush to their best current working weights, and in the meantime degrade their exercise technique, degrade their control of the weights (by rushing the reps), degrade their training discipline, and produce premature weight stagnation at best, and injury at worst.

Don't, however, go to extremes and add weight overly slowly during your first few months of strength training. Follow the spare capacity guideline given here, but "room to spare of two reps" on your final work set means exactly that, not five reps of slack.

Progressive weights caveat . . . a reminder

Never should exercise technique be compromised to enable more weight to be added to the exercise. A slight compromise on technique—a slight thrust, heave, or jerk—makes an exercise appear easier in order to enable increased weight to be used. This dirty training produces only an illusion of progress.

Start with correct exercise technique, and *continue* with correct exercise technique. Be consistent, even at the end of a set when the reps are demanding. This is the bedrock for safe and effective strength training.

Compromising on exercise technique or rep speed control aren't the only ways to create an illusion of progress. Reducing the range of motion of an exercise, and increasing the rest periods between reps and sets, are other ways of making an exercise appear easier in order to allow increased weight to be used. Don't reduce the range of motion, and be consistent with rest intervals between reps and sets. The rest interval between sets changes during the early months of **The Program**, then becomes consistent as from Month #4.

Make progressive weights a vital part of your training, but be a model of consistent, correct performance—*then* the progressive weights will have the best effect on your muscular development.

Technique review

After three months of **The Program**, re-read the sections of Chapter 12 that cover the exercises in your current routine. There'll probably be some details of exercise technique you've been omitting, and other details that are clearer now that you've had significant experience of the exercises. Put the improved knowledge into practice. *Become an exercise technique perfectionist.*

Status report

At the end of your first twelve weeks, if the weight progression has been correct, the effort level of each exercise should be nearly hard—but not hard. Importantly, you'll have learned to adapt to an increasing degree of effort while ingraining correct exercise technique, and

Perform the mental preparation prior to each workout, as described earlier in this chapter, to transform yourself from your working and family persona, to your training persona.

controlled rep speed. You'll have established a gaining momentum, and learned how to train with increasing effort and discipline.

At this nearly hard level of effort, the weights required to produce it will vary among trainees. Using the three illustrations of novices given earlier—the stocky 25-year-old man, lanky 18-year-old student, and 50-year-old woman—the weights across the various exercises will vary greatly. The stocky 25-year-old may have incrementally worked to 180 pounds for 3 x 8 in the squat, the lanky teenager to 110 pounds, and the 50-year-old woman to just 35 pounds, *but they should all be working at a comparable level of effort.* The 25-year-old, and the teenager, may have started with the same 45-pound bar, but the former would have progressed at a faster pace while *still* having a comparable number of reps to spare at each workout. The woman may have started with a broom handle, and added just a few pounds each week.

The stretching routine continues as before. The cardio work continues as before, too, with a small weekly change, as described in Chapter 9, to ensure progression toward increasing fitness.

Calisthenics update

After your third month of strength training, you can drop the calisthenics you had been performing prior to each weights session.

Poundage progression vs. rep progression

The Program focuses on poundage progression. Another form of progression is adding reps: for example, 100 pounds x 6 reps for a given exercise at one workout, 100 x 7 at the next workout, 100 x 8 later on, and so on. When training is hard, however, to add an extra rep is a big accomplishment, and may take several workouts to achieve, or longer. For instance, if today you can *just* make 8 reps with 180 pounds in the squat, to add a ninth rep will be more difficult than to do 8 reps with 181 pounds, 182 pounds, or perhaps even a tad more. It may take a few weeks to achieve the extra rep with 180 pounds. In the meantime, if you had stayed with 8 reps, you may have been able to add one pound or half a pound at each squat workout over that period. Small poundage increments permit more gradual, regular progression than adding reps. This is why poundage progression is favored over rep progression. With both methods, use of consistent, correct exercise technique is essential.

Years ago I called small weight plates "little gems." They are that valuable.

Final workout of Month #3

Take this workout off, to give yourself a rest from training of seven days prior to the upcoming program changes.

Training partner

While not essential, having a serious, like-minded training partner is usually an advantage. A good training partner promotes training consistency, encourages you to do your best on each set, alerts you to technique imperfections (which must be eliminated), and spots you. A dependable spotter will give you the confidence and security to push on when the reps get tough.

Alternate sets with your training partner, but without rushing between sets, or without taking excessive rest. Between the sets you perform, still take the rest intervals that are recommended in **The Program**. Training with a partner is especially convenient if you're of similar strength levels, and use the same program or similar programs. What matters most, however, is that you share the same training philosophy and commitment, get along with each other, and are both punctual for workouts. You also need similar recovery abilities so that you can agree on a common training frequency.

As you get to know gym members you may find someone you could work with. Publicize your search for a training partner using the gym's notice board, or newsletter if there is one. If possible, also put up a notice in other gyms in your town. You could even extend your search to any colleges that may be in your area. Some couples work well as training partners, when they are like-minded in their goals.

Don't train before you've fully recovered from your previous workout, don't perform exercises in ways that don't suit you, don't add unplanned exercises to your program, and don't abuse forced reps. If you allow a training partner to encourage you to do any of these things, he or she will mar your progress, and possibly injure you. Work together in an intelligent way, and do what's best for *both* of you.

During your workouts, focus on your training. Leave chitchat until after your training is done.

But don't become dependent on a training partner. Always be able to train well by yourself. Have spells when you train alone.

MONTH #4

It's time for changes, to move to two different full-body routines, each to be performed once a week. All the exercises from the first routine of **The Program** remain, but divided over the two different workouts. New exercises have been brought in, to produce the potential for developing balanced musculature. Prudent changes to **The Program** every few months also help to maintain interest and enthusiasm.

Always remember the watchwords of correct exercise technique, and a controlled, smooth rep speed no faster than two to three seconds up per rep, and no faster than another two to three seconds down.

First workout (for example, Tuesday)

P. 356   1. Squat: warm-up set, plus 2 x 8
          Immediately prior to squatting, to help with flexibility, perform the calf, groin and thigh adductor, hip flexor, hamstring, buttock, and quadricep stretches—numbers 1, 2, 3, 4, 5, and 7, from Chapter 2.

P. 234   2. Standing one-legged calf raise: 2 x 15 for each leg

P. 208   3. Bench press: warm-up, plus 2 x 8

P. 338   4. Seated cable *or* machine row, *or* one-arm dumbbell row, *or* prone low-incline dumbbell row: warm-up plus 2 x 8

P. 320   5. Seated back-supported dumbbell press: warm-up, plus 2 x 8

P. 292   6. Lateral raise: 2 x 10

P. 346   7. Dumbbell shrug: warm-up, plus 2 x 8

P. 252   8. Seated dumbbell curl: warm-up, plus 2 x 8

P. 246   9. Reverse crunch: 2 x 10

P. 202   10. Back extension: warm-up, plus 2 x 8
          Provided you have a healthy back, perform the side bend, or rotary torso, instead of the reverse crunch, for 2 x 12 (P. 350, or P. 336).

Keep accurate workout records.

Use no extra resistance for the one-legged calf raise, two thirds of your pulldown weight for the cable row, a pair of small plates for the lateral raise, and perform the reverse crunch on a horizontal bench with your knees bent toward your chest to permit easy completion of the reps. For the side bend, start without any weight; or, for the rotary torso, start with minimal resistance. For the new exercises, take four to six weeks to work from an easy starting level, to the nearly hard level of effort.

The intensity of work for the familiar exercises should gradually increase over the next four weeks or so, through weight increases, to the point where you perform every rep possible in each work set, while maintaining correct exercise technique, and controlled rep speed. This will take you to the level of *hard* training.

Back extension

If there's a back extension machine, try that first, because it has little or no starting resistance. If a machine isn't available, try the basic back extension, which has the weight of your torso as the starting resistance. If you can't perform the required reps on the basic back extension, try the 45-degree back extension, which may be less demanding than the basic version, depending on the apparatus. If that's too difficult, or unavailable, use the floor back extension as described in Chapter 2. Once you can perform 20 floor back extensions with your arms extended, and a pause at the top of each rep, try the basic back extension once again, or the 45-degree back extension.

Second workout (for example, Saturday)

P. 256   1. Deadlift: warm-up set, plus 2 x 8
   Immediately prior to deadlifting, to help with flexibility, perform the calf, groin and thigh adductor, hip flexor, hamstring, buttock, and quadricep stretches—numbers 1, 2, 3, 4, 5, and 7, from Chapter 2.

P. 232   2. Standing two-legged calf raise: warm-up, plus 2 x 10

P. 298   3. Leg press: warm-up, plus 2 x 12
   If the parallel-grip deadlift is used instead of the straight-bar deadlift, for exercise #1, the leg press will be unnecessary because the quads will already have been thoroughly worked at this workout. Perform the groin stretch, again, immediately prior to leg pressing.

P. 294   4. Leg curl: warm-up, plus 2 x 10

P. 312   5. Parallel bar dip: warm-up, plus 2 x 8
   If the ability to dip isn't present yet, or the right equipment to permit comfortable dipping, substitute the floor push-up—see the technique guidelines in Chapter 2—or use the close-grip bench press (P. 220).

P. 324/328 6. Pulldown, *or* machine pullover: warm-up, plus 2 x 8

P. 316   7. Seated back-supported barbell press: warm-up, plus 2 x 8

P. 304   8. Lying L-fly: 2 x 10 each side

P. 242   9. Basic crunch: warm-up with no weight, plus 2 x 10

Keep accurate workout records.

For the leg press and the leg curl, start with weights that feel very comfortable. Because of differences across different brands of leg press and leg curl machines, it's not possible to provide suggested starting weights.

Technique practice

During the two or three weeks immediately following the introduction of a new exercise, perform an extra (low-intensity) set for it at each workout. This will help to hasten mastery of technique.

If you have access to a dipping machine, try that for the parallel bar dip, because you can adjust the starting resistance to permit the 2 x 8 *with reps to spare* requirement. With the conventional dip, the minimum starting resistance is bodyweight. Especially for women, and heavy men, the conventional parallel bar dip will be too difficult at this stage of training.

If you can perform dips for 2 x 8 with reps to spare, using conventional equipment or a machine, keep the dip. If not, or if the equipment to permit dipping isn't available, perform floor push-ups with your feet elevated sufficiently on a platform or bench so that you can perform 2 x 8 with just a few reps to spare. (Women may not need to elevate their feet.) As the weeks go by, gradually elevate your feet further—to make the exercise harder. A month later, try the parallel bar dip again, and stay with it if you can perform 2 x 8 with reps to spare. Thereafter add resistance to a belt around your waist—a special belt for dips includes a chain, for attaching to plates or a dumbbell. As your warm-up for the dip, do a set of floor push-ups. As an alternative to the parallel bar dip, or the push-up, use the *close-grip* bench press.

In the seated barbell press, start with 10 pounds under your total weight of the two 'bells in the dumbbell press. In the lying L-fly, start with just two pounds, or one kilo—hold a plate, or plates.

For the new exercises, take four to six weeks to work from an easy starting level, up to the nearly hard level of effort.

The intensity of work for the familiar exercises should gradually increase over the next four weeks, through weight increases, to the point where you perform every rep possible in each work set, while maintaining correct exercise technique, and controlled rep speed. This will take you to the level of *hard* training.

Warm-up sets

Nearly all exercises now have a warm-up set. For a given exercise's warm-up set, employ about two-thirds of the weight you'll use for the work-sets, for the same rep count as for the work sets.

Between-sets rest intervals

At the start of the fourth month, increase the rest interval between sets. Take two minutes before each set of single-joint exercises, and three minutes before each set of multi-joint exercises. This increase will help to sustain the required steady progress in strength. Maintain these rest intervals for the remainder of **The Program**.

Rib cage work

From month #4, include the breathing pullover immediately after each work set of the squat and the deadlift, while you're still panting. Do at least 12 reps for each set of the pullover. This pullover may enlarge your rib cage, deepen your chest, and help to improve your posture. This rib cage work may be especially effective for teenagers, and trainees in their early twenties, but is worth a try at any age. There's no science to confirm this, however. I believe the breathing pullover helped me, and other people have reported benefits, too.

The breathing pullover is safe if done sensibly, takes little time and effort, and won't demand anything of your recovery ability.

Workouts too long?

Especially now that the rest interval before each set has increased, and the number of warm-up sets has increased, too, your workouts may be unduly long. Here are possible responses, to shorten your workouts:

1. Train at a quiet time. This usually leads to shorter workouts because less waiting time is usually required, and distractions may be fewer.

2. Do cardio work and stretching on different days to your weights workouts. This would, however, mean more visits to the gym unless you have cardio equipment at home. But the GXP is probably best done on two days each week that you also strength train.

3. From each routine, pair up exercises that work *different* groups of muscles, then alternate sets—one group of muscles gets recovery time while the other group is trained. This reduces inactive time between sets, and is a way to shorten workouts. For example, pair the bench press with the row. Perform a set of the bench press, rest a minute or so while you move to the row, then perform a set of the row. Rest about two minutes, and repeat. You may need to rest only one minute if the second exercise of the pair was a single-joint one.

   Don't rush between exercises or otherwise your performance will probably suffer greatly. Don't take less than a minute between sets even when alternating sets of exercises that work different groups of muscles. But exclude squats and deadlifts from the alternated exercises because they are so demanding that they require focus one at a time.

   It may be difficult to have access to two specific exercises at one time if the gym is busy. And some trainees may lose focus by alternating sets, and thus prefer to perform their sets in the regular manner.

MONTH #5

Continue with the current routines. Make progress as already explained.

Consistent Progression

By the start of the fifth month you should reach the level of hard training in the exercises you've used since your first routine. You should be at the weights that, for you, produce no spare reps on the work sets. This exercise intensity now becomes your mainstay. *There should be no perceived increase in intensity of work for the rest of* **The Program**, *but there should be consistent increases in exercise weights.*

This ongoing increase in exercise weights *without* a perceived increase in exercise intensity, is *Consistent Progression*. It means increasing your weights in line with your progression in strength.

For the average male trainee who's recovering well, this should translate to approximately two pounds a week in the squat, deadlift, shrug, and calf raise, one to two pounds a week in the bench press and pulldown, and a half or one pound a week in the other movements other than the L-fly, which has a much lower progression potential. The rate of progress should be slowed for trainees who are less responsive than the average male trainee.

At the point where the exercises you've used right from your first routine have moved into Consistent Progression mode, the other movements—the ones introduced during the fourth month of **The Program**—should have moved into nearly hard mode. Over the next few weeks the latter exercises should gradually move into hard mode, too.

Warm-up sets update

From now on, following the general warm-up for every workout, do 20 freehand squats (with no extra weight). And from now on do two warm-up sets each for the squat, bench press, and deadlift. Use 50% of the work-set weight for the first warm-up set, for the full target rep count, and 80% for the second warm-up set but only for half the target rep count of the work sets. For example, if your first work set of the deadlift is with 160 pounds for eight reps, the 50% warm-up set would be with 80 pounds for eight reps, and the 80% one would be with 130 pounds for four reps. Perform a single warm-up set for each of the other exercises, with about two-thirds of the work-set weight.

Arm development

Some trainees have developed their arm muscles—primarily the biceps and brachialis (flexors), and triceps (extensor)—with minimal or no single-joint arm exercises. The use of many single-joint arm exercises is common in gyms, but usually leads to overwork. For trainees who overwork so, the elimination of single-joint arm exercises may improve results in their arm development. The bench press, close-grip bench press, incline bench press, overhead presses, pulldown, chin-up, pull-up, and rows provide substantial training for the arm muscles. But the best strategy for arm development employs some of the aforementioned multi-joint exercises *together with* judicious single-joint work.

The parallel bar dip may be a more effective triceps developer than the above pressing exercises. The dip involves greater triceps extension provided the range of motion is sufficient. *If you can't safely perform the parallel bar dip, or there isn't the equipment for it (or for the machine dip), include the pushdown (*P. 334*) in the routines that the dip is listed in, for a warm-up set plus one or two work sets.* The pushdown is also called the pressdown, and is a form of the *triceps extension*.

For the arm flexors, single-joint exercises are included in **The Program**.

Heredity determines the potential for muscle growth in any bodypart. But to realize your potential for muscle growth you must train and recuperate correctly for a period of years.

"No pain, no gain"?

Some people have been led to believe that they must do certain exercises or specific techniques even if those exercises and techniques hurt. The "No pain, no gain" maxim has done untold damage. But if it's poor exercise technique that's responsible for the pain, and it usually is, then learn about correct technique, apply it, and there should be no further pain.

Over the years, countless trainees have given up strength training because of having been hurt from following the prescriptions of macho writers and coaches. But you don't hear from these trainees. You may, however, hear success stories from trainees who can break the rules and get away with it, at least over the short term. But even these trainees are usually forced to improve their habits *eventually*.

MONTH #6

Continue with the current routines. Make progress as already explained.

Second work sets

Now, or soon, you may not be able to perform your full target reps on the second work set of each exercise. If, for example, you just manage eight reps on your first work set of the bench press, then even after three minutes rest you may not be able to get another eight reps. Once this happens, reduce the weight for the second work set by about 10%, to keep your reps up.

Keep accurate records of both sets. Provided you make your target rep counts on both sets, then next time you perform that exercise, increase the weight for each work set by the same small amount.

Intensity and progression update

By now, all exercises should be in Consistent Progression mode, where you're training hard on all movements.

Final workout of Month #6

Take this workout off, to give yourself a rest from training of seven days prior to the upcoming program changes.

More on exercise variety

Different exercises can stimulate muscles differently. But the claim that certain exercises or variations of them affect specific muscles of a given bodypart in clearly defined ways, is exaggerated. And the claim that many exercises are needed to train each bodypart fully, is exaggerated, too. How a muscle group responds often has more to do with genetics than the specific exercises used.

Not progressing well?

Have you stuck rigidly to **The Program**?

Have you been uncompromising in your adherence to correct exercise technique, and rep control?

Have you eaten well, consuming five or six similarly spaced meals each day that, in total, satisfy your caloric needs?

Have you made training your main if not sole physically demanding activity?

Are you sleeping well for at least eight hours each night?

Have you focused on gradually increasing your exercise weights?

If you've done all of this you'll have made steady but substantial progress in strength, and your muscles will have filled out noticeably. But if you've given in to a temptation to expand your workouts, to train more often, to eat only two or three times per day, to give more attention to food supplements than food, to shortchange yourself of sleep, and to play a lot of physically demanding sports, your progress will have slowed, or halted.

Some trainees may find that the volume of work per workout is excessive. If you're fully satisfying all the components of recuperation from training, and yet are still not making progress, *cut back to just warm-up work plus a single work set of each exercise.*

Caution

Never should exercise technique or rep control be compromised in order to sustain a weight increment. Weight progression is important, but correct technique is MORE important. Be disciplined at all times.

You started with correct technique, now continue with correct technique. This is the bedrock for safe and effective strength training.

MONTH #7

The format of two different, full-body routines remains, each to be performed once a week, but there are exercise changes.

First workout

P. 356   1. Squat: two warm-up sets, plus 2 x 12
         Immediately prior to squatting, to help with flexibility, perform the calf, groin and thigh adductor, hip flexor, hamstring, buttock, and quadricep stretches—numbers 1, 2, 3, 4, 5, and 7, from Chapter 2.
P. 232   2. Standing two-legged calf raise: warm-up, plus 2 x 10
P. 208   3. Bench press: two warm-up sets, plus 2 x 6
P. 338   4. Seated row, *or a dumbbell row*: warm-up, plus 2 x 8
P. 292   5. Lateral raise: warm-up, plus 2 x 10
P. 346   6. Shrug (parallel-grip bar, dumbbell, *or* barbell): warm-up, 2 x 8
P. 253   7. Incline dumbbell curl: warm-up, plus 2 x 6
P. 398   8. Timed hold: one set of 60 seconds
P. 246   9. Reverse crunch: warm-up, plus 2 x 8
P. 202   10. Back extension: warm-up, plus 2 x 8
P. 284   11. Finger extension: 1 x 8–12 for each hand

Second workout

P. 256   1. Deadlift: two warm-up sets, plus 2 x 6
         Immediately prior to deadlifting, to help with flexibility, perform the calf, groin and thigh adductor, hip flexor, hamstring, buttock, and quadricep stretches—numbers 1, 2, 3, 4, 5, and 7, from Chapter 2.
P. 234   2. Standing one-legged calf raise: warm-up, plus 2 x 15 each leg
P. 298   3. Leg press: warm-up, plus 2 x 12
         If the parallel-grip deadlift is used instead of the straight-bar deadlift, for exercise #1, the leg press will be unnecessary because the quads will already have been thoroughly worked at this workout. Perform the groin stretch, again, immediately prior to leg pressing.
P. 294   4. Leg curl: warm-up, plus 2 x 8
P. 312   5. Parallel bar dip, *or machine dip, or elevated push-up, or close-grip bench press* (P. 220): warm-up, plus 2 x 6
P. 324/328 6. Pulldown*, *or machine pullover*: warm-up, plus 2 x 8
P. 316   7. Seated barbell *or* dumbbell supported press: warm-up, 2 x 6
P. 304   8. Lying L-fly: warm-up, plus 1 x 8 each side
P. 308   9. Neck forward flexion, and extension: warm-up, plus 2 x 10 each
P. 248   10. Twisting crunch: warm-up, plus 2 x 8
P. 284   11. Finger extension: 1 x 8–12 for each hand
P. 350/336 *Provided you have a healthy back, perform the side bend, or rotary torso, instead of the twisting crunch, for warm-up, plus 2 x 12.*

> ** Graduate from the pulldown to the chin-up or pull-up (P. 236), especially if you don't have a good pullover machine available. If you can perform at least six consecutive chin-ups or pull-ups, substitute one of them for the pulldown. Perform an easy set of pulldowns as a warm-up, rest for about 90 seconds, perform your first set of chin-ups or pull-ups, rest three minutes, then perform a second set. When you can perform two sets of six reps, add a pound next workout to a belt around your waist. Once you can perform two sets of six reps with that weight, add a further pound, and so on. If you're unable to perform six reps, try again after a couple of months of further increasing your strength on the pulldown.*

Keep accurate workout records.

The incline dumbbell curl, timed hold, finger extension, neck work, and twisting crunch are the new exercises. All the other exercises should continue in Consistent Progression mode—a tad of extra weight every week or two in most of them, but without any perceived increase in intensity of effort. Progress should still be straightforward provided you fully satisfy the components of recuperation from training.

For the incline dumbbell curl, start with two-thirds of your regular seated dumbbell curl, and take a few weeks to acclimatize to it before you train hard on it.

For the timed hold, experiment until you find a weight you can just hold onto for 75 seconds. Try your bench press weight, and adjust it until you find the right starting weight. Once a week thereafter, perform a single hold of 60 seconds. For the first few weeks, add five pounds a week. When you barely have any spare capacity seconds left, reduce to just two pounds a week as you move into Consistent Progression mode.

For your neck, take it easy to begin with, and build up so that after four weeks you're working nearly hard, and then after four further weeks you're working hard, performing every rep possible under your own efforts. If a four-way neck machine is available, use that. For neck work, use a rep speed no faster than four seconds for each phase of each rep.

The rep count has been changed on some exercises, to give you experience of different counts. The rep count in the squat has been boosted to 12. Don't try to handle your usual 8-rep weight for the 12 reps. Reduce the weight by about 15%. Then add two pounds a week provided there's the capacity for it.

Finger extension

The gripping muscles are worked by the timed hold and all exercises that involve the grip. Without finger *extension* work, the imbalanced development in the forearms often leads to elbow problems.

Not progressing?

If you're fully satisfying all the components of recuperation— see "Not progressing well?" under Month #6—and yet are still not making progress, *cut back to just warm-up work plus a single work set of each exercise.*

Squat and deadlift

Once the intensity of these exercises is high, your performance on the movements that follow immediately afterward, may suffer. If so, rest a few extra minutes after squatting or deadlifting.

Again . . . workouts too long?

Now that you've had seven months on **The Program**, here are two further possible actions to take to shorten your workouts. Keep the strength-training portion of each workout to no more than one hour.

1. Do warm-up work plus just a single work set for each exercise rather than the two work sets that are usually listed in the routines.

2. Use a special split routine. See the next page.

If you use the special split routine *and* single-work sets, that would reduce the length of each workout greatly, although you would have three short gym workouts each week rather than two longer ones.

If you have cardio equipment at home, you could do your cardio work there and further reduce the time for each gym workout. Stretching could be done at home, too. This will, however, yield many bouts of exercise each week. You may prefer the special split routine, with single work sets, and doing your entire exercise program at the gym.

Try the options and see what works best for you. You can return to a prior set-up later on, and even alternate approaches based on what's going on in your life, and which regimen is most convenient at the time.

MONTH #8

No program changes. Add a small weight increment on each exercise when possible. If your reps drop following a weight increment, you've added too much weight, or added it too soon. Cut back a little, and add a smaller increment next time, or wait longer before adding anything. You may need to improve your satisfaction of the components of recuperation, to enable your body to progress between workouts.

Second work sets

When you can't get your target rep count on the second work set of a given exercise, reduce the weight by about 10% for the second work set next time you perform that exercise, to keep your reps up.

Keep accurate records of both sets. Provided you make your target rep counts on both sets, then next time you perform that exercise, increase the weight for each work set by the same small amount.

THE SPLIT-ROUTINE POSSIBILITY

From the eighth month of **The Program** you may try a special split routine, to reduce the duration of your strength-training sessions. There would be an extra workout each week, but the total time spent in the gym would be reduced. Instead of two workouts of eleven exercises, there would be three of just five to seven exercises. In general there would be an increase in recovery time between workouts for the same bodypart—from two times a week, to three times every two weeks. But a bodypart that may have been trained directly only once a week on the other format, could now be worked three times every two weeks.

Divide each full-body routine into two parts. Put exercises that primarily work your lower body in one group, and those that almost exclusively work your upper body in another group. This is one way to divide the exercises so that there's only minimal overlap between each pair of resulting sub-routines. Then rotate the four workouts over the three-times-a-week training schedule, as follows:

Week one
TUESDAY
First workout

P. 356   1. Squat: two warm-up sets, plus 2 x 12
   Immediately prior to squatting, to help with flexibility, perform the calf, groin and thigh adductor, hip flexor, hamstring, buttock, and quadricep stretches—numbers 1, 2, 3, 4, 5, and 7, from Chapter 2.

P. 232　　2. Standing two-legged calf raise: warm-up, plus 2 x 10

P. 246　　3. Reverse crunch: warm-up, plus 2 x 8

P. 202　　4. Back extension: warm-up, plus 2 x 8

P. 284　　5. Finger extension: warm-up, plus 1 x 8–12 for each hand

Week one

THURSDAY
Second workout

P. 208　　1. Bench press: two warm-up sets, plus 2 x 6

P. 338　　2. Seated row, *or* a dumbbell row: warm-up, plus 2 x 8

P. 292　　3. Lateral raise: warm-up, plus 2 x 10

P. 346　　4. Shrug (parallel-grip bar, dumbbell, *or* barbell): warm-up, 2 x 8

P. 253　　5. Incline dumbbell curl: warm-up, plus 2 x 6

P. 398　　6. Timed hold: one set of 60 seconds

Week one

SATURDAY
Third workout

P. 256　　1. Deadlift: two warm-up sets, plus 2 x 6
Immediately prior to deadlifting, to help with flexibility, perform the calf, groin and thigh adductor, hip flexor, hamstring, buttock, and quadricep stretches—numbers 1, 2, 3, 4, 5, and 7, from Chapter 2.

P. 234　　2. Standing one-legged calf raise: warm-up, plus 2 x 15 each leg

P. 298　　3. Leg press: warm-up, plus 2 x 12
If the parallel-grip deadlift is used instead of the straight-bar deadlift, for exercise #1, the leg press will be unnecessary because the quads will already have been thoroughly worked at this workout. Perform the groin stretch, again, immediately prior to leg pressing.

P. 294　　4. Leg curl: warm-up, plus 2 x 8

P. 248/350　5. Twisting crunch, *or* side bend, *or* rotary torso: warm-up, 2 x 10

P. 284　　6. Finger extension: warm-up, plus 1 x 8–12 for each hand

Week two

TUESDAY
Fourth workout

P. 312　　1. Parallel bar dip, *or* machine dip, *or* elevated push-up, *or* close-grip bench press (P. 220): warm-up, plus 2 x 6

P. 324/328　2. Pulldown*, *or* machine pullover: warm-up, plus 2 x 8

P. 316　　3. Seated barbell *or* dumbbell supported press: warm-up, plus 2 x 6

P. 255　　4. Seated hammer curl: warm-up, plus 2 x 6

P. 308　　5. Neck forward flexion, and extension: warm-up, plus 2 x 10 for each movement

P. 304   6. Lying L-fly: warm-up, plus 1 x 8 each side
           * *Graduate from the pulldown to the chin-up or pull-up* (P. 236),
             especially if you don't have a good pullover machine available. If you
             can perform at least six consecutive chin-ups or pull-ups, substitute
             one of them for the pulldown.

Keep accurate workout records.

Thereafter rotate the four routines in the same order over the same three training days. General warm-up work, and stretching, should be done at each workout, but cardio work need only be done two times a week—Tuesday and Saturday in this illustration.

SECOND SPLIT-ROUTINE POSSIBILITY

A simpler interpretation of three-sessions-per-week training is to take one full-body routine and split it like previously. Alternate the two workouts from session to session while training three times per week. This produces the same general bodypart training frequency as in the other interpretation, but greater frequency of each exercise because fewer exercises are involved. Here's an example:

First workout
P. 256	1. Deadlift
P. 234	2. Standing one-legged calf raise
P. 298	3. Leg press
P. 294	4. Leg curl
P. 232	5. Basic crunch
P. 202	6. Back extension

Second workout
P. 312/208	1. Parallel bar dip, *or* bench press
P. 324/328	2. Pulldown, *or* machine pullover
P. 316	3. Seated barbell *or* dumbbell supported press
P. 253	4. Incline dumbbell curl
P. 308	5. Neck forward flexion, and extension
P. 304	6. Lying L-fly
P. 284	7. Finger extension

Perform the first workout on Tuesday, the second on Thursday, the first on Saturday, the second on Tuesday, the first on Thursday, and so on.

Try one of these three-sessions-per-week schedules for three months, to see if it works better for you than a two-times-a-week schedule.

Hand grippers . . . *optional* extra training

To supplement the grip work already in **The Program**—mostly from the deadlift, shrug,, and timed hold—add work on hand grippers, at home. Gripper training will further strengthen your grip and hands, and perhaps build forearm musculature, too. And many trainees find gripper training especially enjoyable. See pages 286 through 290 for technique.

Grippers are inexpensive. The ones with knurled, metal handles—torsion spring grippers—start at under 100 pounds closing strength, and go up to over 300 pounds. The ability to close a gripper of 200 pounds rating is rare. The ability to close a gripper of 300 pounds is phenomenal. Ideally, initially get a gripper under 100 pounds, and two or three with the smallest increments in resistance thereafter—see *Resources*. You may need to use more than one manufacturer, to obtain the required *gradual* progression in resistance.

You may need to start with a gripper that has plastic grips, which sporting goods stores sell. This has a rating of no more than about 50 pounds. When you can do at least 20 full closes with it, with a pause on each crush, move to the lowest-strength torsion spring gripper.

Train with grippers two times a week, say Monday and Friday. Start by repeatedly squeezing a small, soft ball for half a minute for each hand. Warm up the muscles and joints of your hands. Then take the weakest gripper you have and do half a dozen, slow, easy, partial reps with each hand. Then after two minutes rest perform a few full reps with the same gripper. Hold each crush for two seconds. If you can't fully close the gripper, do partial reps but get the handles as close as possible.

Take it easy for the first few weeks, to condition your hands (including your skin) to the rigors of gripper work. If you rush the progression, you risk injury to your finger muscles or joints, or damage to your skin.

The Ivanko super gripper

Rather than use one or more fixed-resistance, torsion-spring grippers, you could use a single, adjustable Ivanko super gripper. Follow the same basic guidelines as for the torsion-spring gripper training, but add small increases in resistance in line with your increasing grip strength—see page 291 for a table of resistance settings for the super gripper.

MONTH #9

No program changes. Add a small weight increment on each exercise when possible. Apply Consistent Progression to all exercises.

Final workout of Month #9

Take this workout off, to give yourself a rest from training of seven days prior to the upcoming program changes.

Program evolution relative to training frequency

There are three types of strength-training frequency:

1. Overall frequency, that is, the number of visits to the gym.

2. Frequency of training a given exercise.

3. Frequency of training a given bodypart

Even if the overall training frequency doesn't change, how a program is put together will affect the second and third types of frequency.

The first workout schedule in **The Program** repeats each exercise two times a week because each workout is the same full-body one, thus each bodypart is trained two times a week. As correct exercise technique and rep speed are established, and the intensity of work increases, new exercises are introduced. As from the fourth month of **The Program**, two different full-body routines are alternated each week. Thus while each *exercise* is usually worked only once a week, most *bodyparts* are still trained two times a week albeit it with different groups of exercises.

"The split-routine possibility" described in Month #8 increases workouts per week to three, but reduces the volume of work per session, and reduces the number of times each *bodypart* is trained to three times every two weeks—that is, once every four or five days.

MONTH #10

The new exercises are the one-arm, side-on, incline lateral raise, and the low-incline barbell bench press. The former heavily loads the deltoids at the bottom of the exercise rather than at the top as with other lateral raises, and the incline bench press may involve the upper pectorals more than the regular bench press does. From the bench press and parallel bar dip (or close-grip bench press), choose the one you feel better suited to, and keep that one in your program. Instead of the other exercise, substitute the low-incline, barbell bench press. A low-incline bench is one set at no more than 30 degrees. Use an adjustable incline bench that you can set at the required incline.

Take the new exercises easy to begin with. Build up so that after four weeks you're training hard on them.

In the squat, change to 1 x 15 using your previous week's 2 x 12 weight. By performing just a single work set of squats you should be able to continue with your usual poundage, and the usual weekly increment of two pounds (for the average male trainee).

Always remember the watchwords of correct exercise technique, and a smooth rep speed no faster than two to three seconds up per rep, and no faster than another two to three seconds down (and much slower for neck work).

For the other exercises, which continue as in the previous three months other than for a few changes with where the exercises are positioned in the routines, continue to add a tad of extra weight on each exercise when possible.

First workout

P. 356   1. Squat: two warm-up sets, plus 1 x 15
                 Immediately prior to squatting, to help with flexibility, perform the
                 calf, groin and thigh adductor, hip flexor, hamstring, buttock, and
                 quadricep stretches—numbers 1, 2, 3, 4, 5, and 7, from Chapter 2.
P. 232   2. Standing one-legged calf raise: warm-up, plus 2 x 15 each leg
P. 224   3. Low-incline barbell bench press: warm-up, plus 2 x 6
P. 338   4. Seated row, *or* a dumbbell row: warm-up, plus 2 x 6
P. 292   5. One-arm, side-on, incline lateral raise: warm-up, plus 2 x 8
P. 346   6. Shrug (parallel-grip bar, dumbbell, *or* barbell): warm-up, 2 x 6
P. 253   7. Incline dumbbell curl: warm-up, plus 2 x 6
P. 398   8. Timed hold: one set of 60 seconds
P. 248/350   9. Twisting crunch, *or* side bend, *or* rotary torso: warm-up, 2 x 10
P. 202   10. Back extension: warm-up, plus 2 x 8
P. 284   11. Finger extension: warm-up, plus 1 x 8–12 for each hand

Keep accurate workout records.

Second workout

P. 256 1. Deadlift: two warm-up sets, plus 2 x 6
Immediately prior to deadlifting, to help with flexibility, perform the calf, groin and thigh adductor, hip flexor, hamstring, buttock, and quadricep stretches—numbers 1, 2, 3, 4, 5, and 7, from Chapter 2.

P. 232 2. Standing two-legged calf raise: warm-up, plus 2 x 10

P. 298 3. Leg press: two warm-up sets, plus 2 x 8
If the parallel-grip deadlift is used instead of the straight-bar deadlift, for exercise #1, the leg press will be unnecessary because the quads will already have been thoroughly worked at this workout. Perform the groin stretch, again, immediately prior to leg pressing.

P. 294 4. Leg curl: warm-up, plus 2 x 8

P. 208/312 5. Bench press, *or* parallel bar dip: two warm-up sets, plus 2 x 6

P. 324/328 6. Pulldown*, *or* machine pullover: warm-up, plus 2 x 6

P. 316 7. Seated barbell *or* dumbbell supported press: warm-up, plus 2 x 6

P. 308 8. Neck forward flexion, and extension: warm-up, plus 1 x 10 for each movement

P. 304 9. Lying L-fly, *or* cable variation: warm-up, plus 1 x 8 each side

P. 246 10. Reverse crunch: warm-up, plus 2 x 8

P. 284 11. Finger extension: warm-up, plus 1 x 8–12 for each hand
  * *If you haven't already, graduate from the pulldown to the chin-up or pull-up, especially if you don't have a good pullover machine available. See Month #7.*

Keep accurate workout records.

These routines may be divided into four sub-routines and rotated over three workouts per week, using the same format described in "The split-routine possibility," in Month #8.

Warm-up sets update

Now do two warm-up sets for the leg press, like for the deadlift, squat, and bench press.

No more than two warm-up sets are specified in **The Program** for any given exercise. But advanced trainees may require more than two warm-up sets for each of the biggest exercises, and two warm-up sets for some of the other exercises. The heavier the weights you use, the more warm-up sets you require, for safety *and* performance level.

Once you start using demanding work-set weights, in order to rehearse the groove of each exercise prior to the work set(s) you probably can't do a good job if you use weights that feel light. For your final warm-up set, use at least 80% of your work-set weight, for just a few reps.

Workout tape

Again, get someone to video tape your entire workout. Then study the recording at home. Examine your exercise technique, rep control, lifting technique while setting up equipment, concentration level during each set, effort level, and use of time between sets. Look for areas to improve, and then address them at your next workout.

Dropping hurriedly into your heaviest sets, under the assumption that you're saving energy, can backfire. It can make the work sets harder than they would have been had you warmed up thoroughly.

More on hand-gripper training

Gradually increase the number of full reps you perform, or increase how far you crush the handles if you can't close the torsion-spring gripper, and build up to performing full reps. Alternatively, use an Ivanko super gripper for full reps, and increase the resistance in small increments as required. You could even use both types of gripper.

After two months of gripper training, add a set of singles at the end of each gripper workout, using a unit you can perform only a few consecutive full reps with. Alternatively, use the Ivanko super gripper set at a comparable resistance. Crush it with your right hand, and hold the closure for two seconds. Then do the same with your left hand. Rest a minute, and repeat. Start with six singles for each hand. Build up the number of singles by one each workout, until you get to 12. Work thereafter to increase the length of pause on each single, or increase the resistance if you use an Ivanko super gripper.

Continue to progress gradually, to condition your hands to gripper work. Again, if you rush the progression, you risk injuring your hands.

MONTH #11

No program changes. Add a small weight increment on each exercise when possible. Apply Consistent Progression to all exercises.

AGAIN, *NOT PROGRESSING WELL?*

Have you stuck rigidly to **The Program**?

Have you been uncompromising in your adherence to correct exercise technique, and rep control?

Have you eaten well, consuming five or six similarly spaced meals each day that, in total, satisfy your caloric needs?

Have you made training your main if not sole physically demanding activity?

Are you sleeping well for at least eight hours each night?

Have you focused on gradually increasing your exercise weights?

If everything is well in all these areas, and you're still not progressing steadily, the volume of work per workout may be excessive for you. Cut back to just warm-up work plus a single work set of each exercise.

If that change doesn't produce progress after a few weeks, shorten the routines further. Alternate the following routines while training every third, fourth, or fifth day, according to your recovery rate. For example, first workout on Monday, second on Friday, first on Wednesday of the following week, second on Monday of the next week, first on Friday, and so on.

First workout

P. 356　　1. Squat
P. 234　　2. Standing one-legged calf raise
P. 224/312　3. Low-incline barbell bench press, *or* parallel bar dip
P. 338　　4. Seated row, *or* a dumbbell row
P. 242/246　5. Basic crunch, *or* reverse crunch
P. 202　　6. Back extension
P. 284　　7. Finger extension

Second workout

P. 256　　1. Deadlift
P. 294　　2. Leg curl

P. 298   3. Leg press
P. 316   4. Seated barbell *or* dumbbell supported press
P. 253   5. Incline dumbbell curl
P. 308   6. Neck forward flexion, and extension
P. 304   7. L-fly

For both workouts, perform warm-up work and a single, hard work set for each exercise. Use the same rep counts as in the original routines.

Yet more on hand-gripper training

After three months of gripper work, try it three times a week but make the extra session a moderate one where you use reduced volume and intensity. The grip may benefit from a greater training frequency than other bodyparts can profit from. But only train the grippers (or the single Ivanko super gripper) hard two times a week—for example, Monday and Friday. The moderate day would then be Wednesday. If the extra frequency helps your progress, continue with it. If it doesn't help, return to gripper work two times a week. Don't do gripper work if your hands haven't recovered from the previous session.

To try to aid recovery between gripper workouts, gently squeeze a soft, spongy ball on your off days. Alternate your hands, for spells of about 15 seconds for each, until you total about a minute for each hand. Keep the work light—don't exhaust your grip.

Once every few weeks, test your strength on the gripper you perform the singles with. Once you can perform ten full, consecutive closes with a pause on each crush, include the next-strength gripper in your workout. You'll only be able to do partial reps to begin with, with the harder gripper. Perform singles with it, following the preliminary work as before. Gradually increase the degree of closure of the handles.

Perform negatives at the end of one workout each week, using a torsion-spring gripper you can't quite close, yet, without assistance, or using the Ivanko super gripper set at a comparable resistance. Push the handles together with the assistance of your other hand. With the gripper shut, or as near shut as you can manage, try to crush it as it opens. *Don't try merely to slow its opening.* Do the same with your other hand, rest a minute, and repeat, for five reps with each hand. Month to month, increase the range of motion and duration of the negatives.

It may take months of consistent training to progress from one torsion-spring gripper to the next, assuming a gradual progression of resistance across the grippers. If the jump between grippers is large, it may take over a year (or forever) to progress from one gripper to the next.

MONTH #12

No program changes. Add a small weight increment on each exercise when possible. Apply Consistent Progression to all exercises.

Take charge!

The Program, if implemented as described, will establish training consistency, ingrain correct exercise technique, embed controlled and smooth rep speed, apply progressive resistance, and develop the ability to train hard. The visible results will be substantial strength development, and significant muscular size. Furthermore, you'll greatly improve your flexibility, and level of cardiorespiratory fitness.

You'll transform yourself externally and internally, and set yourself up for many years of success *provided* you continue to follow the tenets of abbreviated, safe, consistent, progressive training.

This book promotes the RACE Method of Training (Responsible, Abbreviated, Conservative, and Effective) not merely as an approach for beginners, *but as the best choice for all of one's training years.*

RACE Training is the approach of choice because it's more practical and time efficient than conventional (or supposedly "advanced") methods that require a much greater time and energy investment. One of the biggest problems in the muscle-building world is the belief that brief training routines are for beginners only.

RACE Training is built on correct exercise technique, short routines, and hard work, combined with sufficient nutrition and recovery time. This combination produces progress in strength, physique, and fitness, and applies to beginners, intermediates, *and* advanced trainees, although the specific interpretations of training can vary.

Keep accurate workout records.

The components of successful training are straight forward, but putting them into practice requires *dedication*.

When in the gym, *you* have to stick with *The Program*, *you* have to use good technique, and *you* have to train hard once you're beyond the initial few months of training. When out of the gym, *you* have to eat well, and get sufficient sleep each night.

Rise to the challenge . . . *then reap the rewards.*

18

Call to arms!

Did you deliver?

Did you follow **The Program** as written? Did you train consistently? Did you use correct technique in every set? Did you train progressively? *Did you deliver the training goods?*

Did you sleep enough each night? Did you avoid distractions that would reduce your sleeping hours? *Did you deliver the goods as far as sleep is concerned?*

Did you eat well each day? Did you meet your caloric requirements each day? Did you avoid junk food? Did you concentrate on food, not supplements? *Did you deliver the nutritional goods?*

Make each day count, and make each week a perfect example of training, sleep, and nutrition. You *can* do this—week in and week out.

Dedication

Even the best training know-how is worthless unless fused with dedication to consistent action. But even dedication in abundance will be wasted if it's combined with a poor training and recovery program.

Many people consider dedication as drudgery. This is a mistake. *Dedication is a virtue.*

Dedication includes discipline. Discipline means doing what needs to be done with consistency and perseverance. If it's time to train, then train you must regardless of the weather, what's on TV, or whatever other potential distraction there may be. This is dedication, and essential for training and muscle-building success. Make exercise a *priority*.

Never bemoan the discipline that must accompany serious training. And never bemoan the discipline that must be applied to your nutrition, and other components of recuperation. To have the opportunity to apply this discipline is a *blessing*.

The greatness of *real* bodybuilding

Muscle-building isn't just for competitive bodybuilders. It's for everyone who wants to take charge of their physical appearance and conditioning, regardless of age, gender, or background.

With the required determination of purpose, know-how, dedication, and perseverance, you can transform your body.

The benefits aren't merely cosmetic. The training and recuperative program promoted in this book, if implemented as described, will produce extensive health benefits. By improving your health and vigor you'll add life to your years, and possibly years to your life.

Real bodybuilding is worth your best effort!

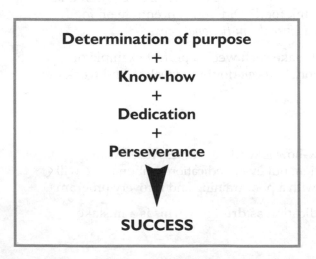

Determination of purpose
+
Know-how
+
Dedication
+
Perseverance

▼

SUCCESS

You won't be able to train forever. Make the most of the present—commit to unwavering dedication to your training, recuperation, and health.

How to train hard but with discipline

Some trainees find visualizations helpful, others find them a distraction. Try some, and see if they help. Either way, the essence of training effectively is to work intensively and progressively, without rushing, and while holding correct exercise technique and smooth, controlled rep speed. Theoretically this is easy, but executing it demands great discipline.

1. With the bar loaded for a work set, switch to *training mode.* Switch off from your life. *Become* your training. Nothing else matters now. Visualize bigger muscles and power to spare to complete your set.

2. Perform the set one rep at a time. Look no further than the current rep. Don't rush. *Use correct exercise technique.*

3. When the discomfort intensifies, dissociate yourself from it. Imagine you're watching yourself on film. Push on. Don't rush. *Use correct exercise technique.*

4. Remind yourself of how much you want a stronger, better physique. Keep the reps coming. Don't rush. *Use correct exercise technique.*

5. To be able to train hard is a privilege. Don't quit prematurely. Forge on. *Use correct exercise technique.*

Intensity *together* with correct technique and rep control is what successful training is about, not merely banging out as many reps as possible. *Never* cheat, *never* use more weight than you can handle correctly, and never use explosive lifting. Use a smooth, controlled rep speed no faster than two to three seconds up per rep, and no faster than another two to three seconds down per rep. No exceptions!

Many trainees look for a "better" program when they haven't fully realized the potential of what they are currently doing.

19

Beyond **The Program**

Please don't concern yourself with this chapter until *after* you've applied *The Program* exactly as written.

If you only partially apply *The Program*, including not fully satisfying the components of recuperation, don't look elsewhere for the solution to your lack of progress. What you would need to do is implement *The Program* properly.

Especially for trainees who were beginners at the start, the routines of **The Program** over the final few months could be extended, in cycles of three to four months. Start each cycle with a layoff for a week, and then make a few changes in exercise selection, and perhaps in set-rep format, too. This approach may yield years of gradual progress in strength and muscular development.

Experienced trainees will also progress in strength and muscular development from applying **The Program**. The extent depends on how much progress they made from their prior training, and on their genetic potential for continued progress in strength and muscular development.

At some point, growth stagnation will set in, although strength gains may still occur. It's at that point, if you want additional muscular growth, that you should try increased variation but *within* the confines of safe, brief, progressive training.

This increased variation isn't for physiological change alone, but for mental change, too. Keeping training varied is important for many trainees in order to sustain a high level of training enthusiasm, which is required for training consistency. But training variation for the sake of variation is counterproductive.

Many trainees, however, look for a "better" program when they haven't fully realized the potential of what they are currently doing.

A case study

A consultation client asked me to design his training schedule for the next 12 months. His recent training hadn't produced any progress in strength or muscular development. He wanted to know which routines to follow, how long for each cycle, how many sets and reps, and so on. He sent me a video recording of his current training. It was a revelation. He didn't need a new program per se. He needed to implement his current program properly. He was performing too many exercises, some of the exercises were inappropriate for him, and his energies were spread thinly. His exercise technique was incorrect, he was using more weight than he could handle correctly, and he was using forced reps on many sets. Furthermore, after questioning him, I discovered that he wasn't eating well most days, and he wasn't sleeping well most nights.

If he corrected all those errors, his progress would recommence.

Don't ignore errors in your own training and recuperation. Unless the errors are corrected, they will remain with any new program, and undermine it.

You can't cheat genetics

As noted in Chapter 4, very few people have the genetics required in order to have the potential to be able to build physiques to the standards of today's competitive bodybuilders. You can go only as far as your heredity will allow, regardless of how well you train and recuperate. But you won't know what your genetics will permit until you go as far as you can.

Some people are more responsive to the same training than other people, and some people have bodyparts that are more responsive than others even when all their bodyparts are trained similarly.

Assuming you're a physiologically mature adult, then after three to five years of training and recuperating *consistently well*, with *no setbacks or wasted periods*, even a change of approach may not make a significant difference for muscular development, although total fitness may be improved further. (I'm considering healthy, drug-free training only.) Although you may not be able to increase muscle mass further, if you become leaner and stronger, and fitter in your cardiovascular system, you'll still make progress in your physique and overall well-being.

But because most trainees rarely if ever train well, and they invariably compromise on the components of recuperation, they will never accumulate the three to five years of good workouts and adequate recuperation required to approach or reach their potential for muscular development.

Be the best you can. This can bring great satisfaction and health benefits. It will put you into a different world of physical conditioning and health relative to where you would be if you didn't train.

How to vary your training
I. Vary your exercises

Different exercises can stimulate muscles differently. But the claim that certain exercises or variations of them affect specific muscles of a given bodypart in clearly defined ways, is exaggerated. And the claim that many exercises are needed to train each bodypart fully, is exaggerated, too. How a muscle group responds to the exercise stimulus often has more to do with genetics than the specific exercises used.

Multiple exercises per bodypart, for most bodyparts, have already been used in **The Program**, especially from the fourth month. For example, the hamstrings are trained by the leg curl, deadlift, squat, and leg press; and the quadriceps are trained by the squat, leg press, and deadlift. Provided that single work sets are used, it's possible to employ multiple exercises per bodypart and yet still keep each workout brief—the strength-training portion should be kept to no more than one hour.

Change some exercises in your program every three to four months. There are many exercises described in Chapter 12 that weren't used in **The Program**. But

> **Most important lesson**
>
> *Keep your training safe, brief, hard, and progressive. These elements are the linchpins of* **The Program**, *and should be the linchpins of all programs. Many interpretations of this basic format can be similarly effective, but to what degree depends on your satisfaction of the components of recuperation and, especially, on your genetics.*

if the changes are too frequent, there won't be the consistency required for progress in strength on each exercise, or mastery of the technique of each exercise through repeated practice.

2. Vary your bodypart training frequency

Here are the three main options for training a particular bodypart: two times a week, three times every two weeks, and once a week. Rather than stick with one exclusively, try each of them, during different periods.

Two times a week

Perform the same full-body routine two times a week, or alternate two different full-body routines while training two times a week.

Three times every two weeks

This means training each bodypart every four or five days, and has two interpretations:

1. The use of a split routine and three training days each week, like that described in Month #8 of **The Program**.

2. The use of a single full-body routine, while training three times every two weeks, for example, Monday, Friday, Wednesday, Monday, and so on.

Once a week

There are two interpretations:

1. Divide your exercises into two groups—upper-body exercises, and lower-body exercises, for example. Perform each group or routine once a week. You would train two times a week in total.

2. Perform a single full-body routine once a week.

Mixed training frequency

You can train some bodyparts two times a week, and the others once a week, within the same program of three training days each week. For example, perform the squat, deadlift, and back extension on Wednesday, and the rest of your body on Monday *and* Friday. Use a different set of exercises for each of the Monday and Friday workouts. During different training cycles, vary which bodyparts get trained two times a week, and which get trained one time.

3. Vary your reps

Periodically using different rep counts in some exercises is another way of keeping your training varied. Perhaps a rep range of six to eight is your standard for most upper-body exercises, but you may want to try, for example, periods of using 10 to 12 reps. For lower-body work, the range of reps that may be helpful may be greater than that for upper-body work. But other than for specialized training for advanced trainees at specific times—primarily competitive powerlifters and Olympic weightlifters—singles and low reps are best avoided in all exercises, as explained on page 178.

But as I noted in Chapter 17, "Especially beyond your first six months or so of training, you may find you have a rep ceiling in some if not most of your exercises, but not necessarily the same ceiling for the different exercises. For example, no matter how much you try, you may find it difficult to do more than eight reps in work sets of the bench press. But if you have small increments,

Ultra-abbreviated training

During periods when you have very little time available for training,, you can still make progress in strength and muscular development. An ultra-abbreviated strength-training routine requires only about half an hour. Just three major exercises can work most of your body, either directly or indirectly. Here's an example of an ultra-abbreviated routine: squat *or* parallel-grip deadlift, parallel bar dip, and chin-up *or* pulldown. Perform this routine either three times every two weeks or, if training time is extremely limited, once a week.

Ultra-abbreviated routines help to maximize training effort and focus, minimize training volume, and minimize the risk of exceeding your abilities to recuperate. They are worth trying at any time, but are especially valuable when time to train is in very short supply.

The fewer exercises a program has, the greater likelihood that some bodyparts will be neglected. That isn't a problem over the short term, but it may be over the long term. Therefore, during at least some of each year, employ routines like those used in **The Program**.

and add just a pound at a time, you may be able to keep getting your eight reps even with the gradually increasing weight."

What about exercise intensifiers?

Exercise intensifiers are methods of intensifying a set beyond the point at which you've completed the maximum number of reps under your own efforts with a constant weight. The intensifiers include drop sets, forced or assisted reps, negative-only reps, and partial reps.

Intensifiers have no place in a beginner's program. Other trainees may find intensifiers helpful but only if they are used very sparingly. Exercise intensifiers are commonly misused, with negative consequences. Exaggerated claims are often made for them.

Here are the two major problems with exercise intensifiers:

1. When you know, for example, you have forced reps to perform at the end of an eight-rep set of bench presses, you're likely to consciously or unconsciously conserve some energy from the normal part of the set so that you can complete the forced reps. Rather than grind out an eighth rep, for example, you stop after the seventh rep and then do the forced reps. And forced reps are often not done with full effort, so the set would be extended but not intensified. It would have been better to have completed the set properly and got all eight reps, and ended it there rather than to cut the main set short in order to tack on some less-than-100%-effort forced reps.

2. For trainees who have the zeal to perform a full set of reps and then give their all to an intensifier, they risk overtraining through training too hard. Hard training is necessary for progress, but extremely hard training can be counterproductive. Provided you're already training at a sufficient intensity, the use of an intensifier may hinder your progress.

During my youth I was fanatically motivated, and trained extremely hard. I would perform a set to failure, then an assistant would help me to perform several forced reps, and then I would finish with a few negative-only reps. But I made no progress in strength or muscular development from using this approach. Many other trainees have had the same experience.

For safety, forced reps or other intensifiers shouldn't be performed in the back extension, L-fly, neck work, side bend, or any squat or deadlift.

4. Vary your exercise volume

You may want a variation on single-work-set training. Periods of two or three work sets for some exercises provide that variation. If you do multiple work sets for some exercises, reduce the number of exercises in your program in order to keep your workouts brief.

If you're already doing multiple work sets, then do single sets—perhaps of more exercises—to supply variation.

Once you've trained well for a few years, all the aforementioned options may produce similar results. But perhaps one alternative is more doable and efficient for you during a given period.

The more variation you adopt at any one time in your strength training, the more difficult it will be to account for any change in the results you get.

5. Vary your cardio training, and your stretching

Keep these varied, to help sustain your enthusiasm. See Chapter 9 for cardio training. If you haven't already introduced hatha yoga into your overall training program, consider doing so now. It's an excellent way of developing and maintaining flexibility, and it produces many additional benefits regardless of your age or how long you've trained. See page 47.

6. Vary where you train

Training variation can be produced by changing where you work out, provided there are several adequately equipped gyms within easy reach. You could, for example, change gyms every 12 months.

Now that you're no longer a beginner, you may want to invest in a home gym. Even if you've always thought a home gym to be out of the question, reconsider.

A home gym

Although an initial investment is involved, consider the gym fees you won't pay, and the traveling time and expenses you won't have if you train at home. You can use the equipment for the rest of your life. A home gym may even pay for itself after a few years, depending on how much you invest, and on the cost of where you currently train.

If you pool your resources with those of a few other trainees, you can all have access to a training den with little money outlay from any one of you. Put the gym in a basement, or garage, so there's no rent.

You don't need a whole room for a home gym—a portion of a room you use for something else can be adequate. I've trained in a seven-foot by ten-foot space and managed to include a full-size power rack, an Olympic bar, a bench, plenty of plates, a weight tree, and a few small accessories. Two people could train in such a space, alternating sets, and three could fit in although it would be cramped.

Here's the minimum equipment investment:

1. A barbell or a pair of dumbbells, and plates including little discs. Dumbbells may be more convenient than a barbell, because less space is required.

2. A reliable method of self-spotting and securely setting up a barbell in some sort of stands—for example, a four-post power rack, a half rack, or sturdy and stable squat stands together with spotter/safety racks or bars.

3. A sturdy, stable bench.

You can train effectively even without a rack, safety bars, straight bar, or bench, if you don't squat or bench press. Parallel-grip deadlifts, plus parallel bar dips, and chin-ups or pull-ups, cover most of the body's musculature. Overhead presses with the parallel-grip bar could be done, too. A method of getting the bar into the starting position would be necessary, though.

This equipment bare minimum could be a starting point for a home gym where economy is the priority, and space is at a premium.

Later on, space and money permitting, you may want to add a parallel-grip bar, an overhead pulley, an overhead bar for chin-ups, parallel bars for dips, a heavy-duty adjustable bench, perhaps a two-inch-thick bar and a few items for grip work, and possibly a hip belt. If you initially got a barbell, you could get a pair of dumbbells, or vice versa.

Your own gym will be a source of pride and pleasure. It may become a sanctuary from the trials and tribulations of life. The convenience will be terrific, and no longer will you have to put up with aspects that may have bothered you in a commercial gym.

With a home gym you're set for getting family members involved in training. This may be the best way to win people over to your interest in exercise—get them training, too. With the convenience of a home gym there's little or none of the self-consciousness an untrained person often feels in a commercial setting.

A home gym keeps you at home for your training, eliminates travelling time, and gives you more time for family matters. While you must avoid being disturbed while you train other than for emergencies, your family will probably appreciate having you home more of the time.

For details on setting up a home gym, see Chapter 6 of BEYOND BRAWN, one of my earlier books.

Specialization routines

If balanced routines are used—like in **The Program**—and each exercise is trained with comparable effort, all bodyparts will develop as well as they can according to individual genetic potential. But if some areas are neglected, they may lag behind other areas, comparatively speaking.

One of your bodyparts may be more responsive to training than the rest of your physique, because of a greater genetic potential in the former. There may be a big difference. For example, a few people have huge calves even though they have never done any exercise for them other than everyday activities. Some people have potential in *several* bodyparts that's out of proportion to that of the rest of their physiques.

If you have a lagging bodypart because of neglect, you may be able to bring it up to the level of the rest of your physique if you train it progressively for long enough. But if the imbalance is genetically determined, and substantial, it may not be correctable no matter how much specialization is done *unless* the strong areas are allowed to atrophy sufficiently. This may not be acceptable, especially for men.

A specialization routine may help to correct or minimize a lagging bodypart: a short-term focus on a specific exercise, muscle, or muscle group, typically with increased training volume, intensity, and perhaps frequency. If, however, the specialization work is overdone, it will hinder progress, not help it.

Twenty-rep squats

Especially in the pre-steroids era, the 20-rep squat program was popular. It still has the potential to be effective. There's nothing special about the number 20. It could have been 21 reps, 19, or 17, as examples. But 20 is a round number, and what was initially championed. What makes the 20-rep squat program effective is the *single* work set of squats incorporated in an *abbreviated* training routine. Done correctly, that combination yields brief training, hard work, plenty of recovery time, progressive poundages, and progress in strength and muscular development.

If you can't squat safely, the same principles that make the 20-rep squat program effective can be applied to programs with a different linchpin exercise: 20 reps in the deadlift, parallel-grip deadlift, or leg press, for example.

The 20-rep squats are done in rest-pause manner—one rep at a time, with a short pause before each. Keep the bar over your upper back, stand upright between reps, and breathe deeply. The breathing sequence could be one breath before each of the first five reps, two breaths before each of the second group of five reps, three breaths before each of the third group of five reps, and four or more breaths before each rep of the fourth group of five reps.

A set of intensive 20-rep squats is a workout in itself—a test of the body and spirit. You must, however, take your time to adapt to the rigors involved. The demands aren't just muscular. Your heart and lungs need to adapt, as does your entire supporting structure including your shoulder girdle, vertebral column, and even the arches of your feet.

There's a tradition attached to 20-rep squatting that exaggerates the severity of the exercise: "Take a weight you can squat only 10 reps with, and then force yourself to get 20 reps!" While unnecessarily exaggerating the severity of the exercise, this approach also increases the chances of failure, and injury.

Adopt a conservative approach. Start by using a weight with which you could do over 30 reps if you were to go to your limit, but stop at 20. Add no more than a few pounds each workout until you get to the point where you could just get 25 reps if you were to go to your limit, although you still stop at 20. Then drop to a weekly increment of no more than two pounds, or one kilo. Later on, reduce the increment further. Target a long cycle of at least six months from start to finish.

Never try to progress at a rate that you risk failing to get your full 20 reps. Train hard, but don't go over the edge and lose your gaining momentum. Take the extra months to progress slowly and steadily, rather than try to pack all the progress into six to eight weeks, and then burn out after four weeks, for example, or get injured.

Train each exercise of the 20-rep squat routine three times every two weeks during the early stage, then drop to squatting just once a week thereafter if you need more recovery time. The other exercises could still be trained three times every two weeks.

You could start your routine with the 20-rep squat, when your energy should be at its highest. Do at least two progressive warm-up sets before the single work set. You could, however, do the 20-rep squat at the end of the workout, because after that set you may not have enough energy left to do justice to much else. Either way, keep your workouts *brief*—no more than one hour for all the strength training.

Part 3

Supplementary Material

20. Forewarned is forearmed *515*
21. What scientific studies really mean to you *523*
22. Burning issues *527*
23. A primer on anatomy *531*
24. The lexicon of muscle-building, and training *543*

About the author *611*
Resources *614*
Index *621*

You can build bigger muscles.
You can develop greater strength.
You can develop a tremendously
improved physique. And you
can greatly improve your overall
level of fitness.

*But the extent to which you can
do all of these things has been
determined by your heredity.*

20

Forewarned is forearmed

I'm going to be up-front with you, as I wish someone had been with me early on in my training. Then I could have side-stepped the poor instruction that caused me enormous frustration, and disappointment.

Conventional training methods

Conventional methods of muscle-building are promoted by many authors, publishers, books, magazines, websites, organizations, and gyms. Typically, they involve four, five, or six weight-training workouts a week, for about two hours per session. And then, in addition, there's cardio work, and stretching.

1. Conventional training methods promote workout volume and frequency that are impractical for busy people and no more than minimally effective for most trainees, if effective at all.

2. Conventional training methods promote high-risk exercises and dangerous techniques that have injured countless trainees.

3. Conventional training methods promote exaggerated expectations, and invariably use drug-fed genetic freaks as gurus and role models.

4. Conventional training methods aren't personalized to meet individual needs and goals.

5. Conventional training methods encourage drug assistance because without drug use those methods don't work well for most trainees.

What *really* makes champion bodybuilders

From around the mid-to-late 1960s the bodybuilding world has been infested with drugs, and not just anabolic steroids. Anabolic steroids have, however, been around since the 1950s, within limited circles. Drugs have led to widespread dishonesty in the training world. They have also led to widespread health problems—the conversion of supermen into sick men, and premature deaths in some cases.

But there's much more than drug use to explain extreme bodybuilding achievements. The current big-name bodybuilders have great genetic advantages that *alone* make them specially responsive to training. And, of course, these bodybuilders are highly dedicated to their training.

An illustration of genetic inequality

Because of their genetic good fortune for bodybuilding, the big-name bodybuilders have a blend of body structure, muscle insertion points, muscle belly length, muscle fiber type and number, tendency for leanness, recuperative powers, and resistance to injury that produce a potential for muscular development *far* in excess of the typical person's.

As an illustration of the effect genetic factors have on potential ultimate muscular size, consider the arms. Men who find it difficult to build arm size, even when using a good training program, usually have . . .

1. Arms that are longer than those of a man of about the same height but who has muscularly large arms.

2. Bone structure on the small side—under seven-inch wrists. Most big-armed men have wrists an inch or more larger. This translates to a bigger skeleton, which is usually an advantage when building muscle.

3. Muscle bellies on the short side. This means that the tendons are long compared with the meaty part of the muscle. Big-armed trainees are blessed with long meaty parts, and apparently short tendons. This produces greatly increased muscle growth potential.

Men with big muscular arms usually don't have long arms, but do have medium or larger skeletons, and long muscle bellies. This combination gives their arm girth a drug-free size potential of perhaps 18 inches. With the assistance of bodybuilding drugs, the girth potential may increase to over 20 inches. Men with longer arms, lighter bone structures, and shorter muscle bellies, usually have a drug-free, maximum girth potential of no more than 16 inches.

Whether you realize your genetic potential depends on how you train and attend to the components of recuperation, but muscular size potential is genetically determined.

Few people *fully* appreciate the importance of genetics, or heredity, in muscle-building, strength, and fitness. People who play down the importance of genetics are either ill-informed, genetically gifted themselves, or have something to sell and it's commercially advantageous to make light of the role of heredity.

But genetic limitations should never be used as excuses not to seek improvement.

Don't train like the champions

"Train like a champion, to become a champion" has been trumpeted by almost all bodybuilding and strength magazines, and by most trainers and gyms, too. It sells magazines, books, courses, food supplements, and gym equipment. Although it's been a commercial success in some respects, it's been disastrous for the training masses.

The most influential books on muscle-building come from famous bodybuilders (or their ghostwriters), or from people who have been directly involved with big-name physiques.

Some of the genetic phenomena are highly dedicated to bodybuilding. It's that dedication together with their natural talent that makes them extraordinary. But they live in another world relative to typical trainees, and what works for the phenomena is often harmful to others.

The legacy of modern physique superstars

When sizing up the contribution to bodybuilding of modern-day physique superstars, consider the following:

1. They are presented as role models for others to follow, with the implicit or explicit mantra of "train like a champion, to be like a champion." Millions of typical trainees tried exactly that, in good faith, but without success.

2. Food supplements are often claimed to make a major contribution to training success. Millions of dollars have been made through selling overpriced food supplements that couldn't deliver what the hyped-up claims promoted. Drug-fed genetic supermen often

endorse food supplements. Many if not most trainees believe that food supplements play a major role in the success of the men who provide the endorsements. That drugs are *the* big "supplement," and food supplements themselves are insignificant, is kept quiet.

3. Many trainees have discovered that the champions' training methods do work to a degree *if* steroids are taken. Consequently the failure of those training methods to yield results for the masses indirectly promotes drug abuse.

4. The drug abuse has caused deaths, countless health problems, crime, jail terms, ruined relationships, and devastated families.

But there wasn't a golden age of training instruction in the pre-steroids era. I have a library of training publications going back over a hundred years. Training volume inappropriate for most trainees, exercise techniques that cause problems for most trainees, high-risk exercises, non-individualized training, and deceitful advertising, have been promoted to the masses for a century. Modern-day big business, and the drugs problem, have made matters worse.

The real champions

The biggest champions of the bodybuilding world aren't the drug-enhanced, genetically blessed, famous physiques. The biggest champions are the unsung heroes who applied years of dogged effort to build themselves up without using drugs, without seeking or finding publicity, and without divorcing themselves from the responsibilities of work, and family life.

Food supplements

Food supplements are mass produced, consumed quickly, and need to be replenished often. They provide a huge potential for repeat sales, and the profit margin is large. A barbell set can last a lifetime, as can a book on training instruction, but a can of protein powder, for example, may last only a week or two.

Exaggerated claims, dishonest reporting, abuse of editorial responsibility, nonsense, and shameless lies, are used to produce demand for food supplements. Some food supplement companies publish bodybuilding magazines, or are intertwined with the publishers, and use those magazines to promote the supplements.

Ask gym members who have no vested interest in the sales of food supplements, or ask any of the genetic elite who are similarly unbiased, and you won't find many who will tell you that they experienced much if any increase in their progress as a result of using food supplements. But many will tell you that the most obvious results they experienced were digestive tract discomfort, and hefty financial costs.

Deception

Conning the training masses takes many forms. Here are six of them:

1. Some trainees who have never used a given trainer's workout and dietary program, endorse it and claim to have used it.

2. Some trainees who have taken steroids for many years claim to be drug-free examples of what a certain coach's training and food supplement regimen can do.

3. "Research" referred to by some people in the training world is fictitious, or factual but *misrepresented*.

4. Some people who have never used the touted food supplements, endorse them.

5. The benefits of bodybuilding food supplements are usually exaggerated, or made up.

6. Many advertisements are deceptive, especially before-and-after comparisons. Perhaps the featured individual was coming back after a long layoff, perhaps he's genetically highly gifted (but detrained in the "before" shot), perhaps he was on steroids, perhaps the time period involved was much longer than reported, or perhaps there's been extensive digital retouching of the photos.

Be on your guard.

Physique changes, and drugs

To illustrate how physiques have changed, compare bodybuilding magazines from before and after the steroid era started.

Come the late 1950s and early 1960s there was a jump in the standard of competitive bodybuilders—larger and harder-looking musculature. During the 1960s the change became pronounced, as drug use moved out of limited circles. Thereafter the caliber of physiques increased as bodybuilding drugs became more widespread and potent.

> *Modern-day bodybuilding isn't, however, overrun with drugs. Most gym members and non-competitive bodybuilders are drug-free; and there are drug-free bodybuilders who compete in drug-tested competitions, although the effectiveness of the testing may be questionable. The caliber of physiques in legitimate, drug-free competition is, however, different from that in the top-level contests that have no testing for drugs.*

Some of today's drug-enhanced women, who are also genetically highly gifted for bodybuilding, have more muscle than some of the pre-steroids elite male bodybuilders had. The effects of the androgenic drugs on women go beyond muscular development, and include deepening of the voice, acne, hirsutism, and hypertrophy of the clitoris.

Along with the de-feminizing outward effects are internal changes that cause serious health problems, and affect mortality.

In the new millennium the caliber of physiques will become even more extreme—bigger, harder, more ripped, more vascular. This will result from the use of more potent drugs, and the involvement of a greater number of men and women with fantastic genetics for bodybuilding. But because steroids and other performance-enhancing drugs are illegal in many countries, including the USA, users can't admit they take them, so a pretense is made that they are drug-free.

Bodybuilding drugs and related problems have done enormous damage—not only to individual users and their families, but to the public perception of muscle-building. Most people find modern, elite competitive bodybuilding grotesque, and repulsive.

Furthermore, there's the problem of drug-assisted training methods being presented as appropriate for drug-free trainees. *Sham training instruction has produced muscle-building failure on an enormous scale.*

The view that bodybuilding drugs are safe if used "properly," is untrue. Bodybuilding drugs have dramatic effects on physiology, and produce serious negative side effects.

Some famous bodybuilders, and some drug "experts," suffered premature deaths or serious health problems largely if not wholly because of their use of bodybuilding drugs. There'll be further high-profile premature deaths with strong suspicions of drug involvement, but for each of them there are many no-profile premature deaths related to drug use, and extensive health, relationship, family, financial, or crime-related problems about which the public never hears.

Beyond appearances

At the gym recently there was a young man with genetic potential for bodybuilding much greater than average, and thus much greater than mine. He had a large muscular torso, with excellent arms. Upon talking with the man I discovered that a few years ago he had his colon removed. More recently he had a hip replacement. The operations were unrelated to bodybuilding.

His genetic advantages for bodybuilding were suddenly irrelevant to me. My intactness was much more important.

Reality check

Despite what some publications and individuals state or imply, not everyone can build big muscles, a perfectly balanced physique, or super-human strength.

Many trainees who could have transformed their bodies, strength, and fitness levels *had* they trained appropriately, ended up quitting training because they followed inappropriate methods promoted by people who promised more than what's realistic.

You can build bigger muscles. You can develop greater strength. You can develop a tremendously improved physique. You can greatly improve your overall fitness. *But the extent to which you can do all of these things has been determined by your heredity.*

The best you can do, is the best you can do. Compete with *yourself*. Keep bettering yourself, again and again and again and again . . . .

Especially if you're a beginner, you'll have little knowledge about training. This will make you particularly vulnerable to being misled and scammed by fitness companies.

The more you learn, the more discerning and critical you'll become of your sources of information. Education is critical.

21

What scientific studies really mean to you

Training magazines have many advertisements for food supplements. Scientific studies are often referred to, to try to add credibility to the advertisements. Advertising copy sometimes includes statements along the lines of "Proven to add 26% more muscle!" "Studies show 58% increased fat loss!" "Proven to boost testosterone production by 212%!"

What the advertisements don't tell you is that the studies may have been carried out on mice, geriatric women, convalescents, or other population samples that have nothing to do with healthy trainees engaged in vigorous exercise; and perhaps the population samples were tiny, and there was no control group. In some cases the "research" is fictitious, or real but *misrepresented*.

Similar comments apply to training methods. Studies without peer review (evaluation of a person's work by a group of people in the same profession), or without publication in reputable journals, are sometimes selected to support a given method of training. Pseudo scientists, and even some holders of Ph.D. degrees, distort test results to "prove" what they or their sponsors want.

A line can be pulled out of a study or its abstract, and taken out of context to produce a conclusion that's at odds with what the study really indicates. Some quoted studies may not exist, and even legitimate studies may be interpreted incorrectly. Writers of advertising copy—including advertorials—know that hardly anyone will follow up on a quoted study.

When reading a study, or seeing a reference to one, what isn't known is the number of studies that refute the one being focused on. The whole of the area of research needs to be seen, not an isolated study.

The foregoing concerns the misuse of science, but there is good science. Good science has a valuable contribution to make toward understanding resistance training, cardiovascular exercise, nutrition, and recuperation in general. Here's how to find good science and help protect yourself from those who abuse science:

1. Be suspicious when you hear or read of "incredible" results and claims, whether or not they are backed by science. Anything that seems too good to be true, is usually precisely that. The word "prove" shouldn't be used. Science doesn't "prove" anything, although it can "disprove" much.

2. Be skeptical of advertisements that cite science. Some writers of articles and books are also guilty of citing pseudo science, or citing good science in a distorted manner. Follow up yourself, or find someone who can follow up on your behalf, and see if the reality matches with what was cited in the advertisement, article, or book.

3. Check that the studies are published in reputable journals. Studies that are unpublished, or not published in a reputable journal, haven't been through the process of rigorous peer review that usually sifts out the unreliable material. Although being published in a reputable journal isn't a guarantee of good science, it's a good sign; but not being published in a reputable journal is almost always a mark of poor science.

4. Look beyond a single study. Although one selected study may support whatever it is that's being promoted, the consensus of studies in that area may support a counter view. Science is a continuous process, with lots of checks and balances. The existence of many studies with good methodology in an area accumulates a web of evidence about certain mechanisms, associations, and relationships. One study doesn't change the entire field.

5. When possible, read a study in its entirety. Summaries and abstracts don't give the whole story. Sometimes the data in a study is at odds with the abstract or summary, possibly because

the researcher didn't like the outcome, and preferred to present a different opinion. The different opinion may be reflected in the summary or abstract more than the actual results of the data. It's also possible that the researcher made a genuine mistake with the interpretation of the data. Check that the data agrees with the results claimed for the study. This takes discipline and experience.

6. The internet provides free tools for research. Visit www.acsm-msse.org/ and www.ncbi.nlm.nih.gov/PubMed/ for resources to hunt down specific studies, or to find what science has to say, for example, on some of the training world's ever-changing crop of food supplements.

Even if you have a perfectly designed training program, and have fully attended to all the components of recovery, if you don't have the passion to train in a disciplined, consistent way using correct technique, then everything else will be wasted. Successful training is the result of getting the whole package in good order.

For most women, there are many qualities in a man that, collectively, are far more attractive than muscle size. They include—in no particular order—thoughtfulness, affection, humor, compassion, honesty, understanding, tolerance, financial good sense, and friendship. Physical attraction is important to most women, but big muscles usually aren't part of it.

22

Burning issues

This chapter is based on three of my Editorials in HARDGAINER. *It addresses psychological and emotional issues related to physique improvement.*

Self shame

For many years I hated my physique because of shame and dissatisfaction, although I was much better built than most men, and healthy, strong, vigorous, and young. I sought an imaginary view of physical perfection, and nothing less than "perfection" would make me happy, or at least so I thought.

Through experience and observation I learned truths that shocked me. Many people who attained what most trainees would consider to be physical perfection, or something close to it, were miserable, a few took their own lives, many propped themselves up with drug abuse, and because most of them focused on what they *didn't* have, they failed to appreciate what they *did* have (including their outstanding physiques).

No matter how much physique improvement I could have made in my youth, I would still have wanted a bit more, a bit more again, and then a bit more still. I would never have been satisfied.

My heredity prohibited the physique I craved, but even if I had been able to build the physique I hankered after, it would have led to the discovery that even physical "perfection" doesn't produce happiness.

I'm not saying I should have accepted mediocrity. I should have striven just as hard for improved physique, strength, and fitness, but not with the anticipation that, someday, it would yield happiness.

Delaying happiness until the attainment of a specific goal meant that I failed to enjoy the process of living and training. That I was able to train hard and regularly was great wealth, and should have been a source of joy. But I failed to see that, and appreciate it, because of my fixation on an unattainable final result.

Although I don't regret taking up bodybuilding, I regret having had a perspective that caused me years of emotional pain.

Striving for the unattainable

For many years I was critical of anyone who didn't comply with my standards for a satisfactory physique. I was unable to see people without passing judgement (in my mind) on their bodies. This came from years of being mesmerized by famous physiques in bodybuilding publications, and applying those standards to myself and other people. I even found fault with famous competitive bodybuilders.

My standards made me unhappy, and for many years I failed to appreciate what I and others *had* achieved, much of which was impressive and worthy of respect.

Although competitive bodybuilding was my ideal, different trainees have different standards for what's ideal, but the end result of self shame and continual dissatisfaction is common.

Because I live in Cyprus I see many people in minimal clothing at pools, and beaches. Never have I seen a physique that would meet the standards I used to have. But I see many people—all untrained—who, apparently, feel more comfortable with their bodies than I used to be with mine, even though I was well-trained. This isn't to say that all the aforementioned people are happy with their bodies. Either way, I no longer look at untrained people with scorn for revealing their bodies.

While seeking self-improvement and building a leaner, fitter, and better-developed physique is desirable, seeking "perfection" and making comparisons with physique champions is usually destructive.

I'm now more at ease with myself and others. I'm better able to live with the reality of my own heredity, and the lack of interest in serious training shown by most people. I no longer compare myself and others with absurd ideals. I'm no longer tormented with the discrepancy between reality and the fanciful.

Myth busting

There's a long-standing belief in the bodybuilding world that women are attracted to men with big muscles. Advertising sometimes shows women fawning over men with big muscles.

I used to believe that big muscles were attractive to women. It was many years before I accepted the truth. All the closest females in my life—wife, daughters, mother, and sisters—don't give a hoot about big muscles. In fact, they all dislike them. I haven't met any woman who likes very big muscles. Only very few women like them.

In my experience, most women do like well-trained, lean men with moderate muscular development, but big muscles are usually a turn off, and huge muscles are repulsive.

For most women there are many qualities in a man that, collectively, are far more attractive than muscle size. They include—in no particular order—thoughtfulness, affection, humor, compassion, honesty, tolerance, financial good sense, and friendship. Physical attraction is important to most women, but big muscles usually aren't part of it.

But having big muscles doesn't preclude the qualities that women really find attractive. It's possible to have those qualities *and* big muscles.

I also used to believe the hokum that very big muscles are desired by most men. In truth, most men aren't interested in very big muscles.

I'm not denigrating muscle-building and strength training. Done properly, building bigger and stronger muscles is enjoyable, healthy, and tremendously rewarding. I'm all for it provided it's not taken to extreme levels such as drug-fueled excesses.

Part of the reason why I strove to get big and strong was to impress or perhaps even intimidate *men*. Why I was motivated so raises questions about my self-image at the time.

Mostly, however, I trained for my own satisfaction and well-being. These are the only reasons why I train today. They are the only reasons that really matter over the long term.

Training, along with dietary control, can transform your outward appearance; but they are highly unlikely to make any improvements in your relationships, work, financial circumstances, and home, or in how caring and compassionate you are, or in your level of satisfaction with your overall life. Other changes are needed to affect those big issues.

As far as instruction goes, there's
little that's new in the weight-
training world. Here's how I
expressed this point in BRAWN:

"Charles A. Smith, over the
time I knew him before his
death in January 1991, used
to remind me that what we
have today we owe to the
past. How right he was. As
Chas used to put it, 'It's upon
the pioneers' shoulders that
we have to stand in order
to be as tall as they. We're
merely the heirs of those
who have gone before us.'"

23

A primer on anatomy

To understand the muscle involvement in each exercise you need at least a rudimentary knowledge of the names and functions of the main muscles of the human body, as outlined in this chapter. Most of the deep, hidden muscles have been excluded, however, because of the complexity of the entire system. For example, there are many deep muscles in the back, between and around the vertebrae.

But first you need to know the basics of the skeleton.

The skeletal system

The bones comprise the framework to which the muscles are attached. There are 206 bones in the human body, including 28 in the skull. These are arranged into a cranial group (eight bones), facial group (14 bones), and the three tiny bones in each ear (the auditory ossicles).

The skeleton is divided into two regions: The axial skeleton consists of 80 bones and is comprised of the skull, spine, and thorax (ribs and sternum). The appendicular skeleton consists of 126 bones and is comprised of the shoulder girdle, pelvis, and limbs.

Most of the bones of the skeleton are joined to one another by movable joints, or articulations.

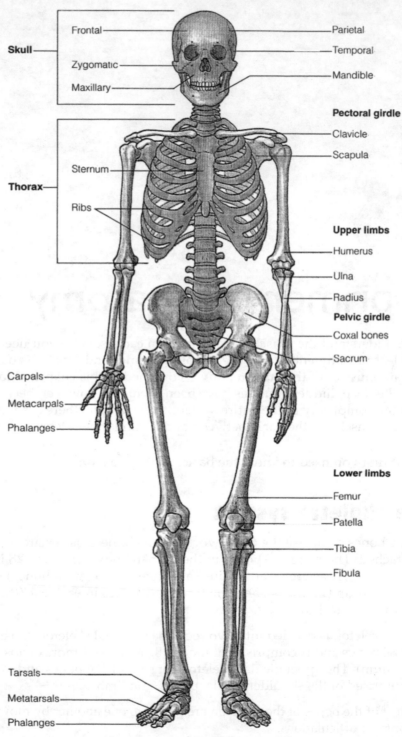

Anterior

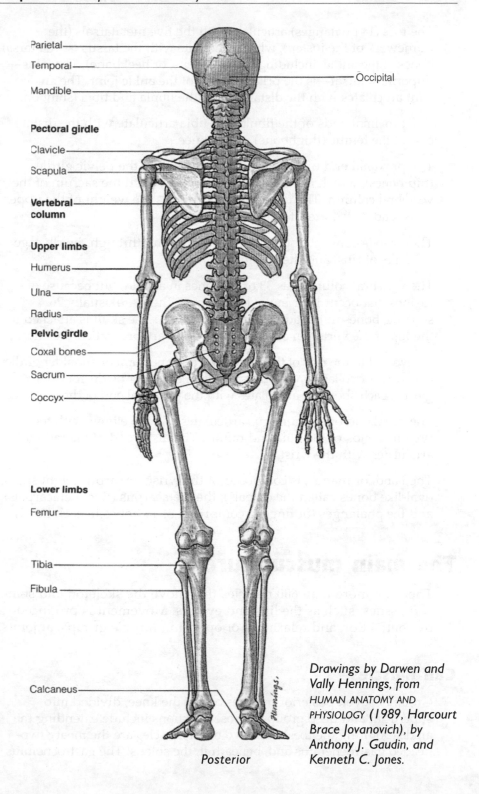

Parietal

Temporal

Mandible

Occipital

Pectoral girdle

Clavicle

Scapula

Vertebral column

Upper limbs

Humerus

Ulna

Radius

Pelvic girdle

Coxal bones

Sacrum

Coccyx

Lower limbs

Femur

Tibia

Fibula

Calcaneus

Posterior

Drawings by Darwen and Vally Hennings, from HUMAN ANATOMY AND PHYSIOLOGY *(1989, Harcourt Brace Jovanovich), by Anthony J. Gaudin, and Kenneth C. Jones.*

The toes (14 phalanges) articulate with the five metatarsals (the framework of the instep), which articulate with the tarsus (seven tarsal bones of the ankle, including the calcaneus, or heel bone). The talus—uppermost tarsal—is the primary bone of the ankle joint. The ankle joint articulates with the distal ends of the fibula and tibia (shinbone).

The proximal ends of the fibula and tibia articulate with the distal end of the femur (thighbone), at the knee.

The proximal end of the femur articulates with the pelvic girdle (hip bones), which in turn articulates solidly with the sacrum of the vertebral column. The pelvic girdle supports the weight of the upper body, and distributes it to the lower limbs.

The torso is connected to the vertebral column through the rib cage (12 pairs of ribs, and the sternum).

The vertebral column has 33 or 34 bones in a child, but because of fusions that occur later in the lower spine, there are usually 26 separate bones in the adult vertebral column. The skull is attached to the top of the vertebral column at the first vertebra, called the atlas.

Above and to the rear of the rib cage, are the pectoral or shoulder girdles (a clavicle or collar bone, and a scapula or shoulder blade, for each girdle). Each shoulder articulates with the proximal end of the humerus.

The distal end of the humerus articulates, via the elbow, with the proximal ends of the ulna and radius. The distal end of the radius articulates with the wrist.

The hand, or manus, is composed of the wrist, or carpus (eight small, oval-like bones called the carpals), the metacarpus (five metacarpals), and the phalanges (or fingers, comprised of 14 bones in each hand).

The main musculature

There are more than 600 muscles that move the skeleton and some soft tissues, such as the lips and eyelids. Movement is produced by contraction and relaxation of opposing muscle groups, at joints.

Calf muscles

Group of seven posterior muscles below the knee, divided into superficial and deep groups, whose functions include extending the ankle (pointing the toes). The two main muscles are the meaty two-headed gastrocnemius and, beneath it, the soleus. The gastrocnemius connects the heel to the femur, and the soleus connects the heel to the tibia and fibula—the gastrocnemius crosses the ankle *and* knee joints, while the soleus crosses the ankle joint only. The tendons of these two muscles, together with the plantaris, fuse to form the Achilles tendon.

Exercises that train the calves are calf raises.

Other muscles below the knee

There are four anterior muscles, which move the toes and foot–the largest is the tibialis anterior, which runs alongside the tibia. And two muscles extend along the lateral surface of the fibula—peroneus longus, and peroneus brevis, which lower and evert the foot.

Hamstrings

The three muscles of the rear thigh: biceps femoris (two-headed muscle), semitendinosus, and semimembranosus. They flex the knees, and contribute to hip extension (rearward movement of the femur). The hamstrings are abbreviated to *hams*.

The primary exercise that trains the hamstrings is the leg curl. Deadlifts, squats, leg press, and back extensions also work the hamstrings.

Quadriceps femoris

Group of four muscles of the frontal thigh: rectus femoris, vastus lateralis, vastus medialis, and vastus intermedius. The tendons of insertion of the four quadriceps muscles form the patella tendon.

The rectus femoris connects the tibia (through the patella) to the pelvis, whereas the other three connect the tibia (through the patella) to the femur. The rectus femoris flexes the femur (raises it) at the hip joint *and* extends the leg at the knee joint; the other three quadriceps muscles extend the leg only. The quadriceps are abbreviated to *quads*.

Exercises that train the quadriceps include squats, parallel-grip deadlift, and leg press.

Sartorius

The longest muscle in the body, which runs diagonally across the frontal thigh, from the proximal end of the tibia, to the outer edge of the pelvic girdle. The sartorius flexes the femur, and rotates the femur laterally.

Some of the musculature shown on the right side of each anatomy chart is different from that shown on the left. This occurs where the outer layer of muscle has been omitted in order to show some of the deeper musculature.

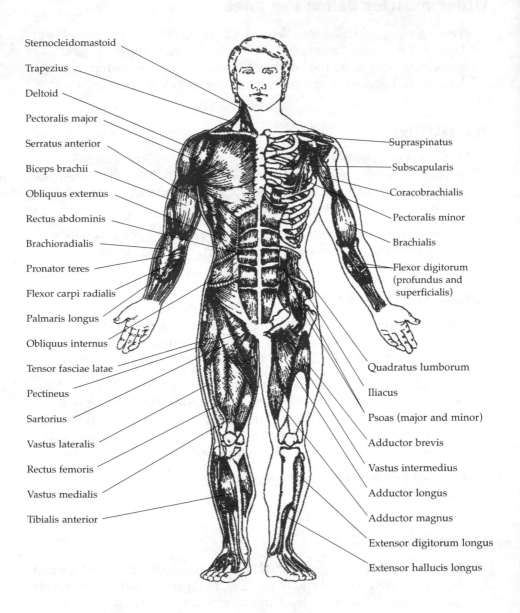

Sternocleidomastoid
Trapezius
Deltoid
Pectoralis major
Serratus anterior
Biceps brachii
Obliquus externus
Rectus abdominis
Brachioradialis
Pronator teres
Flexor carpi radialis
Palmaris longus
Obliquus internus
Tensor fasciae latae
Pectineus
Sartorius
Vastus lateralis
Rectus femoris
Vastus medialis
Tibialis anterior

Supraspinatus
Subscapularis
Coracobrachialis
Pectoralis minor
Brachialis
Flexor digitorum (profundus and superficialis)
Quadratus lumborum
Iliacus
Psoas (major and minor)
Adductor brevis
Vastus intermedius
Adductor longus
Adductor magnus
Extensor digitorum longus
Extensor hallucis longus

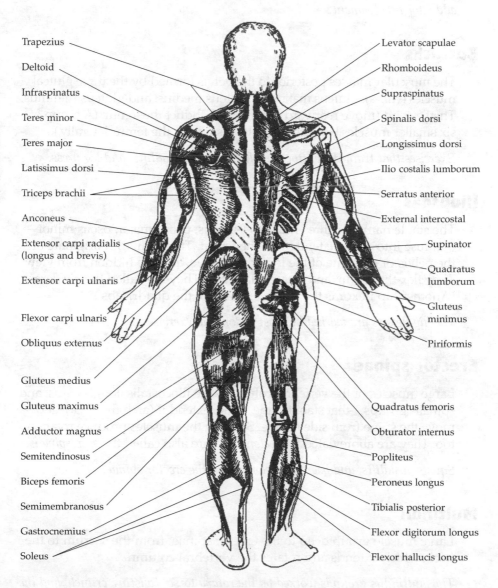

Trapezius

Deltoid

Infraspinatus

Teres minor

Teres major

Latissimus dorsi

Triceps brachii

Anconeus

Extensor carpi radialis
(longus and brevis)

Extensor carpi ulnaris

Flexor carpi ulnaris

Obliquus externus

Gluteus medius

Gluteus maximus

Adductor magnus

Semitendinosus

Biceps femoris

Semimembranosus

Gastrocnemius

Soleus

Levator scapulae

Rhomboideus

Supraspinatus

Spinalis dorsi

Longissimus dorsi

Ilio costalis lumborum

Serratus anterior

External intercostal

Supinator

Quadratus
lumborum

Gluteus
minimus

Piriformis

Quadratus femoris

Obturator internus

Popliteus

Peroneus longus

Tibialis posterior

Flexor digitorum longus

Flexor hallucis longus

Drawings by Eleni Lambrou, based on those of Chartex Products, England.

Adductors, thigh

There are five major adductors of the femur, in the inner thigh: pectineus, adductor longus, adductor brevis, adductor magnus, and gracilis. They connect the pelvis to the femur, except for the gracilis that connects the pelvis to the tibia. They are responsible for adduction, flexion, and lateral rotation of the femur.

Squats, and the leg press, work the thigh adductors. A wider stance increases adductor involvement.

Buttocks

The muscular masses posterior to the pelvis formed by the three gluteal muscles (*glutes*): gluteus maximus, gluteus medius, and gluteus minimus. They extend (move rearward), rotate, and abduct the femur. (A group of six smaller muscles beneath the buttocks rotates the femur laterally.)

Exercises that train the buttocks include squats, deadlifts, and leg press.

Iliopsoas

The single name for three muscles—iliacus, psoas major, psoas minor— that fuse into a single tendon on the femur. These muscles originate on the pelvis or on some of the lower vertebrae, and are hidden from view. They flex the femur, and rotate it laterally. They are called the *hip flexors*. (Another hip flexor is the rectus femoris, of the quadriceps.)

The hip flexors are worked by most abdominal exercises.

Erector spinae

Large muscles of the vertebral column—the iliocostalis, longissimus, and spinalis groups—that stabilize the spine, extend it (arch the back), and move the spine from side to side. Some of the muscles produce rotation, too. They are abbreviated to *erectors*, and are also called the *sacrospinalis*.

Squats, deadlifts, and back extensions train the erector spinae.

Multifidii

Large muscle group deep to the erector spinae, from the sacrum to the neck, which extends and rotates the vertebral column.

The multifidus group is worked by the rotary torso, twisting crunch, and the same exercises that train the erector spinae.

Rectus abdominis

The frontal, "six-pack" muscle of the abdominal wall, connecting the pelvis to the lower ribs. It compresses the abdomen, and flexes the trunk. The rectus abdominis is abbreviated to *abs*.

Exercises that train the rectus abdominis include variations of the crunch.

Obliques

The two muscles at the sides of the abdominal wall—external abdominal oblique, and internal abdominal oblique—connecting the ribs with the pelvis. They compress the abdomen, and flex and rotate the trunk.

Exercises that train this muscle include side bends, and crunches.

Transversus abdominis

Deep muscle of the abdominal wall, beneath the rectus abdominis, and obliques. It compresses the abdomen, and flexes the trunk.

Exercises that train this muscle include variations of the crunch.

Quadratus lumborum

Deep muscle either side of the lower spine that helps form the rear of the abdominal wall. Unlike the other muscles of the abdominal wall, the quadratus lumborum doesn't compress the abdomen; instead, it depresses the ribs. When one side acts alone, it bends the spine to the side; when the two sides act together, they extend the spine.

Exercises that train this muscle include side bends, and back extensions.

Serratus anterior

The muscle on the rib cage underneath and slightly forward of the armpit, which gives a ridged appearance on a lean body. It protracts and rotates the scapula.

Pectoralis major

The large muscle of the chest connecting the chest and clavicle to the humerus. It adducts, flexes, and medially rotates the humerus. The pectorals are abbreviated to *pecs*.

Exercises that train the pecs include bench presses, and parallel bar dips.

Pectoralis minor

The muscle beneath the pectoralis major, connecting some ribs to the scapula. It protracts the scapula, and elevates the ribs.

Latissimus dorsi

The large, wing-like back muscle that connects the humerus to the lower vertebrae and pelvic girdle. It adducts, extends, and medially rotates the humerus. These muscles are abbreviated to *lats*.

Exercises that train the latissimus dorsi include the machine pullover, pulldown, and rows.

Rhomboids

The rhomboideus major and rhomboideus minor, which connect some of the upper vertebrae to the scapula. They retract and rotate the scapula.

Exercises that train the rhomboids include the pulldown, and rows.

Rotator cuff muscles

The rotator cuff is where the tendons of four small muscles in the upper back and shoulder area—supraspinatus, infraspinatus, teres minor, and subscapularis—fuse with the tissues of the shoulder joint. The rotator cuff muscles—or *articular* muscles of the shoulder—are involved in abduction, adduction, and rotation of the humerus.

The external rotators are usually neglected, and are trained by the L-fly.

Trapezius

The large, kite-shaped muscle that connects the skull, scapulae, clavicles, and some upper vertebrae. It retracts, elevates, depresses and rotates the scapula, and extends the head (moves it rearward). The trapezius is abbreviated to *traps*.

Exercises that train the trapezius include shrugs, rows, and the deadlift and its variations. The neck extension works the upper traps.

Sternocleidomastoid

The muscle at the sides of the neck, connecting the sternum and clavicles to the skull. Acting together, both sides of the sternocleidomastoid flex the head and neck; when acting separately, each muscle produces rotation and lateral flexion.

The four-way neck machine is the preferred exercise for this muscle.

Deltoid

The shoulder cap muscle, and a prime mover of the humerus—it abducts, flexes, extends, and rotates the humerus. It has three heads: anterior, medial, and posterior. The deltoids are abbreviated to *delts*.

Exercises that train the deltoids include the dumbbell press, barbell press, and lateral raise.

Biceps brachii

The two-headed muscle (long, and short heads) of the front or anterior surface of the arm, which connects the upper scapula to the radius and forearm muscle, and flexes the forearm and thus the elbow joint, and supinates the forearm. The biceps are abbreviated to *bis*.

Exercises that train the biceps include curls, pulldown, and rows.

Brachialis

The muscle of the front of the arm beneath the biceps, which connects the humerus to the ulna, and flexes the forearm and elbow joint.

Exercises that train the brachialis include curls, pulldown, and rows.

Triceps brachii

The three-headed muscle (long, medial, and lateral heads) on the rear or posterior surface of the arm, which connects the humerus and scapula to the ulna, and extends the forearm (and the elbow joint). Just the long head of the triceps adducts the arm. The triceps are abbreviated to *tris*.

Exercises that train the triceps include bench presses, presses, parallel bar dips, and the pushdown.

Forearms

The anterior surface (palm side) has eight muscles spread over three layers, most of which are involved in flexing the wrist and fingers. The posterior surface has ten muscles spread over two layers, involved in extending the wrist and moving the fingers.

Timed hold, deadlifts, shrugs, grippers, rows, pulldown, and finger extension train the forearms, along with all exercises that work the grip.

Whenever you think that it's tough to deliver on all the components for training success, remind yourself that having the good fortune to be able to dedicate yourself to training and everything that should go with it, is a *privilege*. Eventually, you won't be able to train hard, or dedicate yourself to anything, so make the most of the present—*no* slacking, *no* corner cutting, and *no* excuses.

Get to work! Make the most of your opportunity to train and achieve physical improvement.

24

The lexicon of muscle-building, and training

Here's an extensive glossary-like listing of terminology of and related to muscle-building, and training in general, to broaden and deepen your knowledge. Some of the terms are listed in this chapter precisely as they are in Chapter 8—where the essential terms are covered—but most of them are either unique to this chapter, or presented here in greater detail. Some terms have multiple interpretations, and lack definitions that have universal acceptance.

Descriptions of exercises, and the muscles of the body, aren't included in this chapter. They are covered in Chapters 12 and 23 respectively.

Throughout this book, strict anatomical definitions of arm, forearm, thigh, and leg are used. This means avoiding ambiguous terms such as *lower leg, upper leg, lower arm,* or *upper arm,* and not using *arm* and *leg* to encompass undetermined portions of the upper and lower extremities respectively. The leg is the portion between the foot and the knee, the thigh is the portion between the knee and the hip, the forearm is the portion between the hand and the elbow, and the arm is the portion between the elbow and the shoulder.

The word *flex* is used in this book only as the opposite of *extend. Flex* is commonly used to mean *make tense* but *without* flexion.

I RM

One-rep maximum, or *a single*. The most weight that can be used in a given exercise for a single repetition.

A

Abdomen

The portion of the body between the pelvis and the thoracic or chest cavity.

Abduction

The movement of a bodypart *away from* the midline, such as lifting of a leg to the side. The midline is the vertical plane that divides the body into symmetrical halves.

Abductor

A muscle whose contraction results in abduction.

Abs

Abbreviation for the abdominal muscles.

Achilles tendon

Tendon that attaches three posterior calf muscles to the heel bone (calcaneus).

Active Release Techniques®

ART® is a patented, state-of-the-art, soft-tissue system that treats problems with muscles, tendons, ligaments, fascia, and nerves—developed, refined, and patented by P. Michael Leahy, DC, CCSP.

Acute

Something that occurs quickly, and may be sharp or severe in effect.

Adduction

The movement of a bodypart *toward* the midline, such as lowering an outstretched arm.

Adductor

A muscle whose contraction results in adduction.

Adenosine triphosphate (ATP)

Source of cellular energy for physiological reactions, especially muscle contraction.

Adhesion

An abnormal joining together of parts of the body, by fibrous tissue.

Adipose tissue

Fat (bodyfat).

Aerobic exercise

Aerobic literally means *with oxygen*. This is sustained, rhythmic, large-muscle activity at a level at which the heart and lungs can replenish oxygen in the working muscles, such as walking. Aerobic exercise yields many benefits, the two major ones being that it may improve cardiorespiratory fitness (if the exercise is sufficiently demanding relative to the individual's current fitness level); and secondly, it burns calories (which can contribute to bodyfat loss).

Whether or not a given activity is aerobic is relative to the individual's fitness. Walking is aerobic for a young, fit person, and could be sustained for hours, but the same speed of walking may be anaerobic for an old, sedentary person, and could be sustained for only a minute or two.

Aerobics

A *category* of aerobic exercise that has various styles, such as step aerobics and aerobic dancing, but *not* aerobic exercise in general.

Age-adjusted maximum heart rate

An estimation of maximum safe heart rate commonly calculated through deducting one's age from 220. A 40-year-old will have an estimated maximum heart rate of 180 (220 minus 40), and a 20-year-old will have one of 200 (220 minus 20). Also see *Maximum heart rate.*

Agonist

Muscle directly engaged in contraction—the one primarily responsible for the movement of a given bodypart.

Alimentary canal

The digestive tube from the mouth to the anus.

All-round lifting

An organized form of lifting, including competitions, that has more than 100 official lifts, including some bizarre, potentially high-risk ones.

AMDR

Adult minimum daily requirement of certain nutrients as established by the United States Food and Drug Administration (FDA).

Aminos

Abbreviation for amino acids, the building blocks of protein.

Anabolic steroids

Synthetic hormones that stimulate anabolism.

Anabolism

Constructive metabolism—the synthesis or building up in the body (or any living organism) of more complex substances, including muscle tissue, from simpler substances. Anabolism is the opposite of catabolism.

Anaerobic exercise

Anaerobic literally means *without oxygen*. This is activity in which oxygen is used up more quickly than the body can replenish it in the working muscles. For a given individual, anaerobic exercise is much more intensive than aerobic exercise. Although aerobic exercise can be sustained for long periods, anaerobic exercise can be sustained only for short periods. Strength training and sprinting are examples of anaerobic exercise. Waste products and an oxygen debt are quickly built up during anaerobic exercise, terminating it quickly.

Anaerobic threshold

The level above which exercise brings about strong accumulation of lactic acid in the muscle cells, from anaerobic work.

Anatomy

The study of the structure of the body.

Androgen

Any substance that stimulates the development of male characteristics, such as testosterone.

Antagonist

Muscle that counteracts the agonist. The antagonist is lengthened as the agonist contracts. For example, as the elbow is bent, the biceps (muscle on the front of the arm) is the agonist, and the triceps (muscle on the rear of the arm) is the antagonist.

Anterior

Directional term referring to the front or ventral surface of the body, or referring to something located in front of an organ or structure.

Anthropometry

Measurement of the human body and its parts.

Anticatabolic

A substance that prevents or lessens catabolism.

ART®

See *Active Release Techniques®*.

Artery

A blood vessel that carries blood *away from* the heart.

Arthritis

A group of conditions that arise from inflammation of the joints.

Articular

   Of or pertaining to a joint—for example, articular cartilage.

Articulation

   Any joint, including the freely movable synovial joints such as the elbow, knee, and fingers joints, and the cartilaginous joints between vertebrae, which have only limited movement.

Assisted reps

   Repetitions of an exercise that are performed with assistance, typically from a spotter or a training partner.

Asymmetry

   Not identical on both sides of a central line; lacking symmetry.

ATP

   See *Adenosine triphosphate.*

Atrophy

   Decrease in size or functional ability of a tissue (especially muscle) or organ, resulting from lack of use or disease—the opposite of *hypertrophy.*

Axial

   Located in or related to the axis of an organ or other structure.

Axis

   The line about which a structure is symmetrical.

B

Backdown set

   A final set for special use for a given exercise, in which the weight (relative to the previous set) is reduced sufficiently to permit more reps to be performed relative to the previous set. For example, the series of sets for a given exercise could be 100 pounds x 8 and 130 x 8 as progressive warm-ups, followed by 150 x 8 and then 150 x 8 again as the first two work sets, succeeded by a backdown set of 100 x 15 or more reps, as the third work set.

Ball-and-socket joint

   A joint in which the rounded head of one bone moves in a concave socket of another bone—for example, the hip joint.

Ballistic movement

   A sudden, jerking movement.

Barbell

A steel rod, typically between five and seven feet, on which plates of varying sizes and weights can be loaded, according to need. An adjustable barbell permits you to change the weight plates at will. Fixed-weight barbells have their plates locked in place. Some gyms have racks of fixed-weight barbells of varying weights (typically under 100 pounds), ready for immediate use.

Basal metabolic rate (BMR)

The rate of energy use by the body under controlled resting conditions; the speed at which a resting body uses calories to meet its basic survival needs. The BMR is usually measured in calories per day. Through increasing your muscle mass, you'll also increase your BMR.

Basic exercises

The multi-joint movements—for instance, the squat, deadlift, bench press, overhead press, pulldown, parallel bar dip—are usually tagged *basic exercises*, although some trainees include a few single-joint exercises such as the barbell curl, and standing heel raise, under that description.

Belts

Two main types: lifting belts, supposedly used for lumbar support; and weight belts used for attaching weight to the body for some exercises.
See *Dipping belt*, and *Lifting belt*.

Benches

Long seats used for performing some exercises on. There's the flat (horizontal) bench, the incline bench, and the decline bench. Fixed incline and fixed decline benches are manufactured at various pre-set angles, whereas other benches are adjustable and can be set by the user to the desired angle. A bench may have uprights attached on its sides, for supporting a barbell.

Bench shirt

A tight, strong shirt worn by powerlifters to artificially increase the weight lifted in the bench press.

Biofeedback

A learned response or function to stimuli; a conditioned response.

Biomechanics

The science concerned with the forces acting on a living body, and the effects produced by those forces, especially to do with the locomotor system.

Blood

Fluid that circulates through the capillaries, veins, arteries, and heart, which carries nutrients, oxygen, cellular products, and waste materials.

Blood pressure

The force exerted by the blood on the walls of the blood vessels.
Also see *Diastolic blood pressure,* and *Systolic blood pressure.*

BMR

See *Basal metabolic rate*.

Bodybuilding

An athletic hobby and competitive sport. The development of the musculature in a proportionate manner, with appearance and aesthetics being more important than performance and function. Only a tiny percentage of bodybuilders take part in competitions. Strength is secondary to muscular size for a bodybuilder, although building strength is an important part of building size, especially for beginning and intermediate bodybuilders.

Here's most of the entry on *Body building* in the ENCYCLOPAEDIA BRITANNICA:

Also spelled "bodybuilding," a regimen of exercises designed to enhance the human body's muscular development. As a competitive activity, body building aims at displaying pronounced muscle tone and exaggerated muscle mass and definition for overall aesthetic effect. Barbells and dumbbells and other devices are used in the exercises. For the use of similar exercises for sports training and conditioning, general conditioning, and rehabilitation therapy, see *Weight training*.

Body building was practiced from the time of the ancient Babylonians, but the modern competitive form grew largely out of European strong-man theatrical and circus acts of the 19th century. The first American physique contest, staged by physical culturist Bernarr Macfadden (1868-1955), took place in 1903 in New York City, with the winner named "the most perfectly developed man in America." Thereafter many promoters staged body-building competitions, the most important annual events becoming the International Federation of Body Builders' Mr. Universe contest (founded in 1947) and its later and more prestigious Mr. Olympia contest. From the 1920s through the '60s, Charles Atlas, the 1922 Macfadden title winner, vigorously promoted the activity through a program of mail-order lessons advertised around the world.

Bodyfat

The subcutaneous fat (fat under the skin), and fat around some internal organs (the deeper fat in the body). An average, young adult male has a bodyfat of approximately 16% to 18%, and a female around 26% to 28%. This changes with age. Females have a higher bodyfat percentage because of the genetics and hormones that distinguish their gender.

To be lean means having a bodyfat level of no more than 10% to 12% for a male, and 15% to 17% for a female. To be extremely lean—*ripped* in bodybuilding lingo—would mean reducing bodyfat to no more than half of those percentages.

Bodyfat storage patterns are genetically determined. For example, it's possible to be lean overall and yet not have visible abs.

Bodyfat can be measured, or at least approximated, using skinfold thicknesses at specific sites over the body, along with a computation formula.

Bodyfat percentage changes can be shown by monitoring the waist girth using the same conditions, and the thickness of a single pinch of fat at the same point on the waist (for a man) or hips (for a woman). If the waist girth and fat pinch increase, bodyfat percentage has increased. If the waist girth and fat pinch decrease, bodyfat percentage has decreased. Bodyweight change alone isn't an indication of bodyfat percentage change.

Bodypart

Group of muscles in a specific area of the body. Exercises target specific bodyparts. In a simplified format, here are the main bodyparts:

1. abdominals (abs) and obliques of the front midsection
2. biceps and brachialis—front of the arm (above the elbow)
3. buttocks—gluteal muscles, or glutes
4. calves—gastrocnemius and soleus
5. chest—pectorals, or pecs (pectoralis *major*, not pectoralis minor)
6. forearms
7. latissimus dorsi, or lats—muscles on the back under the arms
8. neck
9. shoulders—deltoids, or delts
10. spinal erectors—columns of muscle on either side of the spine
11. thighs—quadriceps or quads on the front, hamstrings or hams on the rear, and thigh adductors on the inside
12. triceps—rear of the arm (above the elbow)
13. upper back—small muscles around the shoulder blades, and the large trapezius covering much of the upper back

Bodytype

Bodytyping or somatyping was originally an attempt to model temperament based on physical traits, as described by the theories of Dr. William H. Sheldon. It was discredited in the field of psychology, but the vestiges of somatyping linger on in areas related to exercise and fitness, and involve trying to classify people into categories of bodytype: ectomorphic (naturally thin), mesomorphic (naturally muscular), and endomorphic (naturally fat and rounded).

Breakdowns

See *Descending sets*.

Buffed

Looking good through muscle size and definition.

Bulking up

The adding of bulk—gaining bodyweight through adding muscle, bodyfat, or (usually) both.

Bumper plate

A weight plate with a rubber outer rim to reduce damage to the floor and plate when the plate is dropped. These are most commonly used in Olympic weightlifting, where heavy weights are often dropped from overhead.

Burn

The hot or burning feeling in the working muscles produced by some forms of strength training, and endurance work, because of the build up of fatigue toxins including lactic acid.

Burns

A training technique whereby short partial reps are performed immediately after a full set of complete reps has been completed, producing an intensive burning feeling.

Bursa

A small, fluid-filled pouch or sac, usually found near joints, which reduces friction between structures that rub against one another, such as between a tendon and a bone.

Bursitis

Inflammation of a bursa.

C

Cables

The older meaning of cables is another term for *chest expanders*—springs or elastic cables attached to a pair of handles. They can be used for a variety of exercises, and through changing the number or type of springs or cables, the resistance can be changed. Because of their portability, chest expanders or cables can be used at home and on the road. But resistance usually can't be added in small increments, and the most effective cable exercises are for the upper body only.

A more recent meaning of cables refers to machine exercises that use cables.

Calcaneus

The heel bone.

Calibrated weights

Weight plates that have been calibrated for accuracy. Cheap weight plates are likely to be inaccurate—a 45-pound plate may weigh 46 pounds, or only 43 pounds, as examples, with greater discrepancies in some cases. What you may think is, say, 200 pounds on the bar, may be 203 or perhaps only 198, unless you're using calibrated plates.

Calipers

An instrument consisting of two hinged legs used to measure dimensions. Bodyfat calipers are used to measure thicknesses of subcutaneous bodyfat. Specific thicknesses at a certain sites can be used to indicate bodyfat percentage.

Calisthenics

Exercises that require no formal equipment, such as push-ups, and sit-ups.

Calories

Units of heat energy. Burning calories means converting food into energy, or converting stores of energy in the body, such as bodyfat, into energy for activity. One gram of protein or carbohydrate yields four calories, and one gram of fat yields nine calories. The calories referred to in nutrition are actually kilocalories (kcals). Also see *Kilocalories*.

Cambered bench press bar

A bar that has four near-right-angle bends in its middle area, to produce a wide protrusion. This bar increases the range of motion for the bench press, but simultaneously increases the stress on the shoulder joints.

Cambered squat bar

A bar bent like a yoke, to make it better suited to the squat. The cambered squat bar has more gradual bends than a cambered bench press bar.

Capillary

Microscopic blood vessel through which exchange of materials takes place between the blood and surrounding tissues.

Carbs

Abbreviation for carbohydrates.

Cardiac output

The volume of blood that's pumped from the left ventricle of the heart in one minute. (The heart has four chambers—two atria on top, side-by-side, and two ventricles at the bottom, side-by-side.) Cardiac output is measured through multiplying stroke volume (the volume of blood pumped from a ventricle as it contracts) by the heart rate.

Cardiac reserve

The capacity of the heart to increase cardiac output over the resting value; the difference between maximum heart output and resting heart output.

Cardiorespiratory training

Cardiorespiratory training is often used interchangeably with *cardiovascular training*, *aerobic exercise*, and *cardio*. Aerobic work may, however, be insufficiently demanding to produce a cardiorespiratory training effect, depending on the intensity relative to the individual's level of fitness. A slow walk on the flat may produce a cardiorespiratory training effect for a sedentary 50-year-old, but a fast walk up an incline may be needed to produce a cardiorespiratory effect for a fit 25-year-old.

Cardiovascular training
Physical exercise that strengthens the heart and improves the efficiency of the whole system of heart, lungs, and blood vessels.

Carotene
Any of three yellow or orange, fat-soluble pigments found in many plants, especially carrots, and transformed to vitamin A in the liver.

Cartilage
Dense connective tissue that consists of cells embedded in a tough but flexible base. Cartilage functions as support structure in the skeletal system.

Cartilaginous joint
A joint without a cavity or synovial fluid, held together by fibrous cartilage. It has only limited movement. The joint between two vertebrae is cartilaginous.

Catabolism
Destructive metabolism—the breaking down in the body (or any living organism) of more complex substances into simpler ones.

Central nervous system
The brain and spinal cord.

Certification
Attempt to provide qualifications for personal trainers, through a variety of unregulated organizations that provide a diversity of courses, examinations, and certificates. Certification may or may not be an indication of competence. There are competent exercise coaches who have no formal certification, and there are competent exercise coaches who do have formal certification. There are, however, incompetent coaches who have acquired some certification and thus can present an impression of competence. Even having a degree in physical education isn't an indicator of competence, as some courses include no study of strength training; and of the degree courses that do include strength training, it's usually rudimentary.

Many certified personal trainers are deficient in even basic training information, which makes a mockery of the course material covered for the certification, and also makes a mockery of the accrediting organization. With or without certification, a good trainer should have many years of personal experience and study of training additional to any certification course material. There's much to learn. A good trainer also needs to have the ability to teach—knowing about something is one thing, being able to teach it is another thing.

Cervical vertebrae

Vertebrae in the neck, numbered C1 through C7. The first cervical vertebra (C1) is called the *atlas*, which supports the head, and the second cervical vertebra (C2) is called the *axis*. The seventh cervical vertebra (C7) is called the *vertebra prominens*.

Chalk

The chalk that's used in the gym is magnesium carbonate. Chalk is most commonly used for grip support, especially in back exercises, upper-body pressing movements, and grip work.

Cheating

Use of body English—sloppy exercise technique—to assist the target muscles with their work, or change joint angles for greater leverage. Cheating is one of the major causes of injury, and should be avoided. Disciplined training maintains correct exercise technique free of cheating even under the stress of great effort.

Chest expanders

See *Cables*.

Chinning bar

An overhead bar from which a number of exercises can be performed, including chin-ups (whereby the bar is held in the hands and the body is pulled up until the chin is above the bar).

Chiropractic

A system of non-invasive medicine based primarily on the interactions of the spine and nervous system; the method of treatment that adjusts the segments of the spinal column. One who legitimately practices chiropractic, is a doctor of chiropractic. Many chiropractors have training beyond the standard chiropractic course, and are able to treat physical problems that may not have direct involvement with the spine.

Cholesterol

A substance that occurs in all animal tissues, especially in the brain, spinal cord, and fat tissue. It functions chiefly as a protective agent in the skin and myelin sheaths of nerve cells, a detoxifier in the bloodstream, and as a precursor in the synthesis of many steroidal hormones.

Chondromalacia

Softening or degeneration of cartilage in a joint, especially of the kneecap.

Chronic

Something of long duration—for example, a chronic injury or disease.

Circuit training

Moving quickly from exercise to exercise in a circuit, to maintain a sustained high heart rate in order to promote overall fitness, but while also building or maintaining some muscular size and strength. Although neither optimal for muscle-building nor cardiorespiratory conditioning, circuit training provides a mix of both from a time-efficient system. There are no rest intervals between exercises, or only short ones. A rest interval is taken between circuits.

The balance of muscle-building, strength, and cardiorespiratory conditioning produced from circuit training depends on how the weights, rep counts, sets, rest intervals, and progression scheme are arranged.

CKD

Cyclical ketogenic diet. Although the CKD is primarily about percentages (approximately 25% to 35% protein, 5% carbohydrates, and 60% to 70% fat), and typically includes a one- or two-day, high-carb phase each week, there's more to it than that. How you produce the percentages plays a huge role in the effect of the diet on your body and health. If you get most of your fat from fried food, over-cooked meat, cured and processed food, scrambled and fried eggs, margarine, refined vegetable oils, and junk food, the effect on your health will be different from if you got your fat from healthy sources, even though the overall percentages of macronutrients may be the same in both cases.

Two further potential problems of a CKD schedule are insufficient micronutrient and fiber intake. Generally, a CKD is more suited to fat loss than it is for overall gaining, and is a short-term regimen only.

Clavicle

The collar bone.

Clean

The lifting of a weight from the floor to the shoulders in one continuous, rapid manner. It requires skilled, coordinated strength of the legs, thighs, back, arms, and shoulders.

Clean and jerk

One of the two Olympic weightlifting events, where the weight is lifted from the floor to the shoulders, and then from the shoulders overhead—a two-part, highly skilled lift. The other Olympic lift is the *snatch*.

Coccyx

The small, triangular bone that forms the lower extremity of the spinal column in humans. It's formed from the fusion of three, four, or five (usually four) rudimentary coccygeal vertebrae.

Collagen

The primary protein in connective tissue, cartilage, bones, tendons, and skin.

Collars

Cylindrical metal clamps, and quick-release springs, used to hold weight plates securely in position on a barbell or dumbbell. Inside collars are usually fixed, to keep the plates from sliding inward. Outside collars keep the weight plates from sliding off the ends of the bar, and are usually adjustable.

Compound exercises

Exercises come in two basic types: *multi*-joint movements, which are often called *compound* exercises, and *single*-joint ones, which are often called *isolation* exercises. The squat is a multi-joint exercise because it involves movement at more than one joint, and hence affects a lot of musculature—primarily the thighs, buttocks, and lower back. The leg extension—straightening your knee while seated—is a single-joint exercise, because it involves movement primarily at only one joint (the knee). The leg extension primarily targets the quadriceps. Compound exercises are often called *big*, *major,* or *core* movements, whereas the single-joint exercises are often labeled *small, little,* and *minor,* or *supplementary, auxiliary*, and *accessory* movements. In practice, a prudent mixture of single- and multi-joint exercises is usually employed, to produce balanced development.

This is a simplification of exercise categories. Some single-joint exercises work much larger areas of musculature than others, and it's not accurate to call all of them *small* exercises. And some multi-joint exercises work far greater areas of musculature than others—some of the *big* exercises aren't so big. Furthermore, single-joint exercises rarely involve only a single joint, as other joints (and bodyparts) get recruited to some degree.

The single-joint and multi-joint labels are used in this book to differentiate between the two groups but, strictly, they are inaccurate labels.

There's a further pair of labels for the two simplified categories—muscle *builders,* and muscle *refiners*. The multi-joint exercises are said to be the *builders*, and the single-joint exercises the *refiners*. This, too, is a simplification. Both groups of exercises are potential builders, although a given multi-joint exercise typically works more muscle mass than a given single-joint exercise, so the former has the potential to build more overall mass than the latter. Depending on the exercises being compared, a given multi-joint exercise may not build as much muscle as a single-joint exercise in the particular muscle(s) that both train, because the work of the former is dispersed, but the latter is focused.

A multi-joint exercise works multiple muscles simultaneously, through spreading the load and effect over them. The involved muscles share the load and benefits. The body can be trained to good effect using only a handful of compound movements. This has particular value if a trainee is pressed for time, or limited in equipment. Furthermore, when beyond the beginner stage—for specific individual cases and particular periods—there are times when it may be desirable to give exclusive or nearly exclusive priority to multi-joint exercises. For trainees interested in competitive lifting, multi-joint exercises must be used.

Only single-joint exercises can provide meaningful work for some muscles. Single-joint exercises are sometimes essential for direct, specific, and controlled exercise for a particular muscle or muscle group when highly controlled, safe work is needed, such as in rehabilitation. It's impractical, however, to train the entire body using single-joint exercises only, because of the number of exercises that would be required.

Generally, the multi-joint exercises are more demanding than the single-joint ones, because the former usually involve greater muscle mass and exact a heavier toll on the whole body. This combination is positive, because hard work on multi-joint exercises produces a lot of growth stimulation, both for the muscles directly involved in the exercises and, to a degree, in muscles that are involved indirectly. Most single-joint exercises don't have much indirect effect. Done in excess, however, single-joint exercises will still rob the recuperative system (the recovery "machinery") of a lot of its reserves, thus restraining if not preventing progress in all exercises. An excess of multi-joint exercises would have the same negative effect. The key point is to avoid an excess of exercise *in total*.

Regardless of the lack of precision with the categorization of exercises, treat both groups seriously. Regardless of the category a given exercise belongs to, perform it properly—correct technique, control, and discipline, and, once beyond your first six months or so of training, with effort.

The Program in this book explains how to combine multi- and single-joint exercises in an effective manner.

Compound training

Performance of two or more exercises, one after the other with minimal rest in between—usually exercises for different bodyparts rather than the same bodypart.

Concentric contraction

The shortening of a muscle. For instance, when you raise your hand through bending your elbow, your biceps muscle contracts in a concentric way. The term is usually abbreviated to *a concentric*. Concentric contractions are also called *positives*.

A rep has two phases: the positive or concentric (pushing or pulling) part when the muscle performing the action *shortens*, and the negative or eccentric (lowering) part when the same muscle *lengthens*. Standing up from a sitting position is the positive or concentric phase, while the descent to a sitting position is the negative or eccentric phase.

Connective tissue

The type of tissue used to connect and support organs, fibrous tissue, cartilage, and bone.

Continuous tension

The performance of reps in a continuous manner without any pauses, to maintain constant tension of the involved musculature.

Contraction

When applied to muscle, contraction means the development of tension, and expenditure of energy, whether the muscle is elongating, shortening, or maintaining constant length.

Conversion tables

Tables that attempt to convert maximal effort achievements of one given rep count into another rep count. For instance, a known ten-rep achievement can be used to project a one-rep maximum, and a known five-rep achievement can be used to project what could be lifted for 20 reps.

Upper-body exercises

Desired ⇨	1	2	3	4	5	6	7	8	9	10	12	15
⇩ Current												
1	1.00	0.97	0.94	0.91	0.89	0.86	0.83	0.81	0.78	0.76	0.72	0.65
2	1.03	1.00	0.97	0.94	0.91	0.89	0.86	0.83	0.81	0.78	0.74	0.67
3	1.06	1.03	1.00	0.97	0.94	0.91	0.89	0.86	0.83	0.81	0.76	0.69
4	1.10	1.06	1.03	1.00	0.97	0.94	0.91	0.89	0.86	0.83	0.78	0.72
5	1.13	1.10	1.06	1.03	1.00	0.97	0.94	0.91	0.89	0.86	0.81	0.74
6	1.16	1.12	1.10	1.06	1.03	1.00	0.97	0.94	0.91	0.89	0.83	0.76
7	**1.20**	**1.16**	**1.13**	**1.10**	**1.06**	**1.03**	**1.00**	**0.97**	**0.94**	**0.91**	**0.86**	**0.78**
8	1.24	1.20	1.16	1.13	1.10	1.06	1.03	1.00	0.97	0.94	0.89	0.81
9	1.28	1.24	1.20	1.16	1.13	1.10	1.06	1.03	1.00	0.97	0.91	0.83
10	1.32	1.28	1.24	1.20	1.16	1.13	1.10	1.06	1.03	1.00	0.94	0.86
12	1.40	1.36	1.32	1.28	1.24	1.20	1.16	1.13	1.10	1.06	1.00	0.91
15	1.53	1.49	1.44	1.40	1.36	1.32	1.28	1.24	1.20	1.16	1.10	1.00

Lower-body exercises

Desired ⇨	1	2	3	4	5	6	7	8	9	10	12	15	20
⇩ Current													
1	1.00	0.99	0.97	0.96	0.94	0.93	0.91	0.90	0.89	0.87	0.85	0.81	0.75
2	1.02	1.00	0.99	0.97	0.96	0.94	0.93	0.91	0.90	0.89	0.86	0.82	0.76
3	1.03	1.02	1.00	0.99	0.97	0.96	0.94	0.93	0.91	0.90	0.87	0.83	0.77
4	1.05	1.03	1.02	1.00	0.99	0.97	0.96	0.94	0.93	0.91	0.89	0.85	0.79
5	1.06	1.05	1.03	1.02	1.00	0.99	0.97	0.96	0.94	0.93	0.90	0.86	0.80
6	1.08	1.06	1.05	1.03	1.02	1.00	0.99	0.97	0.96	0.94	0.91	0.87	0.81
7	**1.09**	**1.08**	**1.06**	**1.05**	**1.03**	**1.02**	**1.00**	**0.99**	**0.97**	**0.96**	**0.93**	**0.89**	**0.82**
8	1.11	1.09	1.08	1.06	1.05	1.03	1.02	1.00	0.99	0.97	0.94	0.90	0.83
9	1.13	1.11	1.09	1.08	1.06	1.05	1.03	1.02	1.00	0.99	0.96	0.91	0.85
10	1.15	1.13	1.11	1.09	1.08	1.06	1.05	1.03	1.02	1.00	0.97	0.93	0.86
12	1.18	1.16	1.15	1.13	1.11	1.09	1.08	1.06	1.05	1.03	1.00	0.96	0.89
15	1.24	1.22	1.20	1.18	1.16	1.15	1.13	1.11	1.09	1.08	1.05	1.00	0.93
20	1.33	1.31	1.29	1.27	1.25	1.24	1.22	1.20	1.18	1.16	1.13	1.08	1.00

Repetition-conversion tables, based on the formulae of Dave Maurice and Rich Rydin, from HARDGAINER *issue #20.*

For example, if you've been pressing for ten reps (upper-body exercise), and want to convert it to a five-rep weight, you would multiply your best ten-rep poundage by 1.16. If you have been squatting for eight reps (lower-body exercise), and want to convert it to a 20-rep weight, you would multiply your best eight-rep poundage by 0.83.

Cool down

After a hard bout of cardiovascular work, a period of two to three minutes working at a moderate pace, and then a further two to three minutes working at a gentle pace, constitutes a cool down. It enables your heart, breathing, and other functions to slow down gradually. End the cool down once your breathing has returned to normal. A cool down is also recommended following intensive strength training that involves little rest between sets and exercises. Strength training at a slower pace, however, doesn't require a formal cool down, because heart rate, breathing, and other functions aren't sustained at elevated levels during such training.

Core exercises

The priority exercises in a routine—usually the big, multiple-joint movements. In another definition, core exercises refer to those that work the *core* of the body—the muscles of the abdomen, back, and deep in the torso.

Cortisol

A hormone stimulated by stress. Its effect is to produce an increase in available carbohydrate to be used as an energy source for combating trauma and shock, for example.

Cramp (muscle cramp)

A sudden, involuntary, spasmodic contraction of a muscle or group of muscles, sometimes with severe pain.

Creatine

A naturally occurring amino acid that's a constituent of the muscles of vertebrates—a store of energy used for muscular contraction.

Cross-training

The combination of two or more types of exercise to produce a more comprehensive total training program than can be had from just a single form of exercise. Strength training along with cardio work such as stationary cycling, is an example of cross-training.

There's also cross-training within a single type of exercise. For example, in cardio exercise you can use a variety of machines, for example, a treadmill and an elliptical, rather than just one machine.

Cutting up

Reducing bodyfat and water retention in order to increase muscular definition.

Cycles

An abbreviation for *training cycles*. Cycles are periods of sustained training on a given program, for instance, a twelve-week cycle. Training intensity and training weights are typically varied over the course of a given cycle.

Cycling

This term has multiple interpretations. Using a bicycle or a stationary cycle is one interpretation. For muscle-building training, cycling refers to the varying of exercise intensity in a structured way over a period of time. Cycling may also refer to performance-enhancing drugs—the varying of dosages and specific drugs, over time.

D

Decelerate

To slow down.

Definition

The condition whereby the muscles are covered with little fat, so that the lines of the muscles show. Extreme definition is often described as *ripped*.

Degeneration

Deterioration, change from a higher form to a lower form, especially a change of tissue to a less functionally active form.

Dehydration

Abnormally low body fluid volume, because of excessive loss of water.

Delts

Abbreviation for the deltoid muscles (sides of the shoulders).

Density

Muscle *hardness*, the product of well-developed *and* defined muscle.

Descending sets

Specialized form of training in which decreasing weights are used for the same set of a given exercise. For example, 150 pounds may permit just four reps, then through using 120 pounds a further three reps may be performed straight away, followed by another immediate reduction to 90 pounds to permit a final three reps to be performed, for a single set that totals ten reps. Descending sets are also called *multi-poundage sets*, *breakdowns*, *drop sets*, and *strip sets*, although there are variants on this form of training, and different trainees may interpret the method and specific terms differently.

Diaphragm

Muscular partition that separates the thoracic (or chest) cavity from the abdominal cavity that, through its contraction, contributes to the filling and emptying of the lungs.

Diastolic blood pressure

The blood pressure that results from relaxation of the lower chambers of the heart. The diastolic blood pressure is the second and lower of the two numbers that indicate blood pressure, such as 120/80.

Digestion

The chemical and mechanical processes involved in the breakdown of food into component molecules that can be absorbed.

Dipping belt

A *weight belt* as distinct from a *lifting belt*. A dipping belt is worn around the waist or hips from which plates or a dumbbell can be suspended, to provide additional resistance for the parallel bar dip, and a few other exercises. A purpose-made weight belt usually doesn't have a buckle, but has a chain or other method for attaching a weight. Weight can also be suspended from a lifting belt that has a buckle, although that isn't its primary function, and its potential for holding resistance may be smaller than that of a weight belt.

Distal

Directional term referring to portions of limbs or bones relatively *away from* their point of origin or attachment. For instance, the elbow is distal to the shoulder, and the knee is distal to the pelvis. Distal is opposite of *proximal*.

Divided program

The division of a full-body program of exercises into two or three different routines, as distinct from a full- or whole-body routine that's performed in its entirety at a single workout. A divided program is a form of a *split routine*.

DOMS

Delayed-onset muscle soreness. This is the type of soreness that takes a day or two to be felt following exercise, but when it comes it can be severe. It's usually caused by sudden, severe demands in an exercise program. Careful, progressive introduction of changes to an exercise program should prevent severe DOMS.

Dorsal

Pertaining to the posterior or back part of an organ or body.

Dorsiflexion

Movement of a bodypart in the direction of its rear aspect—for example, dorsiflexion of the foot means bringing the foot toward its shin.

Double progression

The method of progressing in reps to a predetermined number, then adding weight to the bar and dropping reps a few, and then building back to the predetermined maximum number of reps prior to another weight increment. For example, 100 pounds for six reps this week, 100 for seven reps next week, and so forth, until 100 for ten can be performed; then the weight is increased to say 105 pounds, and the reps dropped to six once again. The *double* progression is in the reps *and* the weight, as distinct from *single* progression where only the weight *or* rep count is increased.

Double-split routine

Working out two times a day, rotating different routines over two or three days, then repeating the sequence. It was popularized by famous bodybuilders who had fantastic genetics for bodybuilding, and drug assistance.

Drop sets

See *Descending sets*.

Dumbbell

A mini barbell, usually used with a single hand. Fixed-weight dumbbells have the plates locked in position, and are typically found in matching pairs, stored on racks. Adjustable dumbbells have collars that can be released so that the weight can be adjusted, and then the collars are re-tightened.

E

Easy gainer

Opposite of *hard gainer*. Easy gainers are blessed with terrific heredity or genetics for muscle-building, and have highly responsive bodies. Genetic phenomena further enhanced by drug support are the ultimate easy gainers.

Some potential easy gainers are obvious by their appearance before starting muscle-building, because they are already muscular, strong, and lean; but, for others, their "easygainingness" isn't apparent until they start lifting weights, whereupon they grow quickly almost regardless of how they train. It's the ability of easy gainers to respond to training methods that typical trainees get nowhere on that makes easy gainers poor role models.

As easy gainers close in on their drug-free potential for bodybuilding, they may find gains hard to make, but until that point they found gains easy.

Eccentric action

The lengthening of a muscle. For instance, when you lower your hand through extending your elbow, your biceps muscle is lengthened because of the eccentric action. Eccentric actions are often abbreviated to *eccentrics*. Eccentrics are also often called *negatives*.

Ectomorph

See *Bodytype*.

Edema

Swelling, an accumulation of fluid in the body.

EFAs

Essential fatty acids, required for a healthy diet.

Electrocardiogram (ECG or EKG)

Recording of the electrical activity of the heart, used to investigate heart function.

Electrolytes

Any of certain inorganic compounds—mainly sodium, potassium, magnesium, calcium, chloride, and bicarbonate—that dissociate in biological fluids into ions capable of conducting electrical currents, and constituting a major force in controlling fluid balance within the body.

Elliptical machine

Also called an *elliptical, elliptical cross trainer, elliptical exerciser, elliptical fitness machine,* and *elliptical glider.* It's a machine that simulates a blend of walking, cycling, and skiing, through a single action.

Endocrine system

The glands and tissues responsible for production and secretion of hormones.

Endomorph

See *Bodytype.*

Endorphin

Substance used by the nervous system, composed of amino acids. Endorphins are made by the pituitary gland and aid the body's management of pain and emotions. Two endorphin-like compounds produce enkephalins that are thought to be responsible for the high that some runners experience.

Endurance

Ability of a muscle to work continually over a sustained period.

Enzyme

A catalyst of metabolic reactions, that is, a substance that speeds up reactions. For example, many enzymes are involved in digestion.

Epithelium

One of the four primary types of tissue, the other three being muscle tissue, nervous tissue, and connective tissue. Epithelium covers surfaces, lines cavities, and forms glands.

Equipment

Exercise equipment includes a variety of strength-training machinery, and free-weights (primarily long-bar barbells, and short-bar dumbbells), together with machines primarily used for cardiovascular work, such as treadmills (for walking, and running), stairclimbers (also called *stairsteppers* and *steppers*), arm-and-leg-action climbers, rowers, ski machines, cycles (upright, and recumbent), and ellipticals (see *Elliptical machine*). Indoor machines have advantages over their comparable outdoor activities, including climate control.

For strength training, exercises can be performed with free-weights, or machines. The former are the traditional, most versatile means of training. Machines reduce the need for instruction, and the chance of acute injury, which are perhaps the two main reasons why they are popular in gyms. (Another reason for their popularity is visual impressiveness, especially to novices, which is necessary for attracting new clientele. Furthermore, machines are harder to steal than free-weights equipment.) It's harder to lose control with a machine than free-weights. Free-weights *are* safe when used properly, but they require more expertise and skill.

There are plate-loaded machines that require loading with the same plates that are used on barbells, and selectorized machines that have built-in weight stacks from which you select the required resistance using a selector pin. The built-in weight stacks make weight selection easy because you don't have to move plates around. But because each section of metal on many weight stacks is substantial—ten pounds or more—the selectorized machines usually don't permit the gradual weight progression that plate-loaded machines do *unless* supplementary small plates are attached manually.

Machine quality varies greatly. Some machines are valuable if used properly, and a few are outstanding. Some are poor, however, and even dangerous, because they lock the user into a movement pattern that may not fit individual variables such as height and limb lengths. Although the risk of acute injury is usually reduced in machine exercises, there's still considerable chance of chronic injuries and irritations.

Even if a given machine has potential benefits over other machinery and the free-weights equivalent, the benefits won't be realized unless the machine is used well. Machines aren't elixirs, but the good machines can be useful. Being able to distinguish the good machines from the bad ones is difficult, and the quality of machinery can vary even within the same brand name. For instance, while a lower-back machine may be excellent, perhaps the shoulder press machine in the same line isn't.

With a barbell set you can perform the same exercises anywhere in the world, with consistency, and minimal financial cost to the gym. Free-weights are almost universal, but good machinery isn't. The technique instruction for exercises that use free-weights is the same for all brands of that gear, but not so for machinery, where the instructions for one brand's squat machine are different from another's. As a result of these factors, and others, free-weights are given priority in this book. If, however, you have access to the *generally* good machinery—for example, Body Masters, Cybex, Hammer Strength, MedX, and Nautilus—substitute it for the comparable free-weights exercises; but tread carefully because even some of the generally good machines can cause irritations and injuries for some trainees even when those machines are used correctly. Of course, exercises that use free-weights can also cause problems, especially if they aren't performed correctly.

Although the theoretical advantages of some features of some machines seem impressive, the practical application often produces little evidence to support the theory. Some machines have been touted as being vastly superior to free-weights, but in practice have not delivered the hyped "superiority." For example, while altering how force is exerted against the muscles, to try to improve on how free-weights exercises apply it, may seem positive in theory, perhaps in practice it makes little or no positive difference, and the unnatural application of force may even be a step backward in practice. Furthermore, some machines are sticky during use, some don't accommodate trainees of varying sizes, and some have mechanical and maintenance problems.

Features of good machinery include the accurate tracing of the intended muscular function of a given exercise, smoothness of motion, ease of entry and exit, and the ability to accommodate varying sizes of individuals through being able to adjust seats, back pads, and movement arms. Good machines enable trainees who are incapable of performing many free-weights exercises, to exercise safely and well.

The original Nautilus machinery was designed by Arthur Jones, and Hammer Strength machinery was designed by Jones' eldest son, Gary. After Arthur Jones sold Nautilus Sports/Medical Industries, Inc., in 1986, he founded MedX Corporation and designed the equipment there—primarily clinical evaluation and rehabilitation equipment. In 1991, MedX entered the non-medical exercise equipment field, with less costly machines based on the design of the medical units. Jones has since sold MedX Corporation. The Joneses are the brains behind three of the best brands of exercise machinery.

Also see *Nautilus*.

Erectors

Abbreviation for the erector spinae muscles, on either side of the spine.

Ergogenic aid

A product that improves physical or athletic performance, such as a performance-enhancing drug.

Ergometer

Apparatus on which exercise tests are done—for instance, a bicycle ergometer.

Estrogen

Any of several steroidal hormones produced chiefly by the ovary, responsible for the development and maintenance of female sex characteristics.

Exercise balls

Medicine balls are hard and come in different weights. Stability balls are soft and light, and come in different sizes—for instance, Swiss balls. Stability balls can be valuable for a limited number of exercises, such as the ball squat, and some abdominal exercises. Because of their instability,

stability balls should never be used for pressing or bench pressing from, or for standing on while performing any exercise.

Exercise bar

Bar of about one-inch diameter, to fit *exercise* weight plates. Exercise bars come in varying lengths, as opposed to the Olympic bar that has a standard length and requires plates with a hole of about two inches diameter.

Exercise overlap

Different exercises that work at least some of the same muscles produce exercise overlap if used in the same program.

Exercises

The individual movements that work specific parts of the body. The words *exercises* and *movements* (and even *lifts*, in some cases), are used interchangeably. See *Compound exercises*, and *Isolation exercises*.

There are many exercises. Some of them are more valuable than others, but only a limited number can be used effectively in any given program. If an excessive number is used, results will be minimal or non-existent. Employing enough but not too many exercises, a balanced selection of them, and choosing ones appropriate to a given individual, or avoiding movements that are inappropriate to a given individual, is what good program design is about.

Exercise weight plates

Weight plates that have holes just large enough to fit onto an exercise bar, as opposed to Olympic plates that have larger holes in order to fit onto the thick ends of Olympic bars.

Extension

Movement that *increases* the angle between two bones, such as straightening out a bent elbow, and opening the fingers from a clenched fist. Extension is the opposite of *flexion*.

Extensor

A muscle that extends or stretches a limb or other bodypart.

EZ-curl bar

Short barbell that has a number of bends or cambers in it, to enable the user to try to find the grip that feels the most comfortable. Although this bar is commonly used for the curl, it has other applications.

F

Failure (training to)

Method of training whereby a set is taken to the point at which you can't move the bar any further against gravity. This is also called *training to momentary failure,* or *training to positive failure.* At the point of failure, you either lower the resistance to a safe resting place, or a training partner helps you to complete the rep. In practice, most trainees could extend their "to-failure" sets by a rep or two or three if they were well supervised and motivated.

False grip

A grip commonly used in the barbell bench press and overhead press, where the thumb stays *alongside* the index finger. This is best avoided. A false grip is often called a *thumbless grip.* Wrapping the thumb fully around the bar and on top of one or more finger tips, produces a more secure grip.

Fascia

Band or sheath of connective tissue that supports, binds, covers, and separates muscles and groups of muscles, and organs, too.

Fast-twitch fibers

Muscle fibers that fire quickly and are used in intensive anaerobic activities.

FDA

The United States Food and Drug Administration.

Femur

Thighbone.

Fiber

An indigestible component of food found in unrefined grains, vegetables, nuts, legumes, and fruits—an important component of a healthy diet.

Fibrosis

An abnormal formation of scar or other fibrous tissue.

Fibula

The outer and thinner of the two bones of the human leg extending from the knee to the ankle.

Fitness

There's no standard definition of physical fitness. Fitness is relative to a given activity or purpose. For example, someone who's fit for playing as a goalkeeper in soccer may not necessarily be fit for playing in the outfield, and fitness for running doesn't translate to fitness for swimming. This book promotes a broad definition of total fitness, comprised of five components:

1. Strength and lean muscular development
2. Cardiovascular conditioning
3. Flexibility

4. General activity

5. Non-exercise factors including healthy nutrition, no drug abuse, sufficient quantity and quality of sleep, moderate exposure to sunshine (but don't get burned), good posture, healthy relationships, and satisfying work.

For sportsmen and sportswomen, the additional component of skills specific to the given sport would be necessary in order to be totally fit for that activity.

All five components need to be well supplied before an individual can be said to be fit and healthy. It's possible, for example, to be strong and well-developed but physically unfit. It's also possible to be extremely fit physically and yet not be healthy. Although it's highly desirable to be physically fit, there's much more to total fitness (and good health) than that.

Flexibility

Suppleness of muscle masses. Adequate flexibility is a requisite for exercising with correct, safe technique through a full or at least large range of motion. Tight muscles restrict joint movement, and general mobility.

Flexion

Movement that *decreases* the angle between two bones. When you raise your hand through bending at your elbow, you're flexing your elbow. Flexion is the opposite of *extension*.

Food supplements

Food concentrates in tablets, capsules, powders, or liquid, used to enrich a diet or compensate for nutritional deficiencies. They include vitamins, minerals, and protein powders.

Footprint

The amount of floor space taken up by an exercise apparatus.

Forced reps

Use of assistance to permit additional reps to be performed beyond the point at which the trainee concerned can perform them under his or her own efforts. Suppose you're pressing a weight overhead, and it gets stuck half way. If a helper was to give the bar a push, you would be able to perform the full rep. That assisted rep is a *forced* rep. Forced reps are often called *assisted reps*.

Form

Another term for *exercise technique*—the manner of exercise execution.

Fracture

A break or rupture in a bone.

Freehand exercise

Calisthenic exercise performed without equipment, such as the push-up.

Free-weights

Barbells, dumbbells, plates, and related movable or "free" equipment, as opposed to machines.

Full-body routine

Method of working the entire body in one routine that's performed at a single workout, as distinct from a split or divided program that targets particular bodyparts or exercises each session. A full-body routine is also called a *whole-body* routine.

G

Gastrointestinal tract

The part of the digestive system that includes the stomach and intestines.

Gear

Training clothing and equipment used for athletic training. *Gear* is also slang for bodybuilding drugs.

Genetics

The inherited instructions, or genes, that determine much of how you look and function in general, and how you respond to training.

An exercise that may work well for a short, stocky man with legs and thighs that are short relative to his torso, may be dangerous for a lanky man who has long legs and thighs in proportion to his torso. A system of training that may work well for a thickly boned, athletic, and naturally muscular man may be useless for a man with a light bone structure and no athletic inclination.

Although beginners may need to individualize a given program to a degree, at least in some cases, this is a lesser concern than it may be at a later stage of training. Through experience and knowledge, you'll learn how your individuality affects your training.

Genetic factors affect much more than external body structure, and exercise selection. They also affect potential muscular hypertrophy (growth), and responsiveness to training. Some trainees can get very strong but without getting big—elite, lightweight powerlifters and Olympic weightlifters, for instance—whereas some trainees can develop big muscles without developing great levels of strength. Furthermore, some trainees can respond well to a volume and frequency of training that's overkill for most trainees, even when the latter are well conditioned to exercise.

Finding genetic advantages, marrying them with an activity or sport that exploits them, training diligently, consistently, and with passion, is how elite performers are produced. Most people don't discover their natural genetic advantages—provided they have some—or they discover them too late to make the most of them, or never marry them with the right activity to exploit them fully. But elite performers like Michael Jordan (basketball), Lance Armstrong (cycling), and Zinedine Zidane (soccer), found at an early age activities that they were genetically extraordinarily suited to, and trained with great dedication and commitment to exploit their natural advantages. But it's highly unlikely that Jordan would ever have become an elite soccer player had he chosen soccer rather than basketball. Jordan failed at baseball after he temporarily retired from basketball. It's also highly unlikely that Armstrong would have become an elite basketball player had he chosen basketball over cycling, or that Zidane would have become an elite cyclist had he chosen cycling over soccer. Furthermore, while strength training has potential value to all three of these men, it's highly unlikely that they have the genetic requirements for elite achievement in the bodybuilding or strength fields.

Similar things can be said for responsiveness to cardiovascular training. A few people are phenomenally responsive, a few have very poor responsiveness, whereas most are somewhere in between. A few have phenomenal cardio fitness potential—the Lance Armstrongs of the world—whereas the great majority of people have average potential.

The best that each of us can do, is the best that each of us can do. That's why it's important that you compete with yourself, rather than others. Keep bettering yourself, again and again and again, and over a period of years you'll go as far as your genetics will allow, or at least get close, and that may constitute an astonishing transformation relative to where you are now.

The entries for *Easy gainer, Hard gainer* and *Muscle bellies* have additional information on how genetics affect muscle-building.

Gland

Any organ that secretes a substance that's used elsewhere in the body.

Glutes

Abbreviation for the three hip or buttock muscles—gluteus maximus, gluteus medius, and gluteus minimus.

Glycemic index (GI)

A rating system for carbohydrates that indicates how quickly sugar enters the bloodstream from the digestive tract, and the extent of the following insulin response.

Glycogen

Primary storage form for carbohydrates in the liver and muscle tissue.

Grips

The various ways that bars are held, which affect musculature involvement, safety, and amount of weight that can be held. See *False grip, Parallel grip, Pronated grip, Reverse grip*, and *Supinated grip*.

Ground-based exercises

Exercises that are performed while standing on the floor. For example, the squat is a ground-based thigh exercise, but the leg press isn't, and the standing overhead press is a ground-based exercise, but the bench press isn't.

Guns

Slang for biceps, or biceps and triceps together.

GXP

Graded exercise protocol, a prescriptive form of hard cardio work taking just 12 to 15 minutes two times a week, which produces substantial benefits out of proportion to its time investment. The GXP was first developed by Dr. Robert Otto, and then adapted and studied by Drs. Ralph N. Carpinelli, Lesley D. Fox, Richard A. Winett, and Janet R. Wojcik.

Gym

A location for exercising in. Although most people may think of specialist gyms such as a Gold's Gym, gyms can also be found at health clubs, YMCAs, schools, colleges, universities, and leisure centers. There are also home gyms. Although gyms vary in their sizes and facilities, anywhere that houses exercise equipment can be considered a gym.

H

Hams

Abbreviation for the hamstring muscles (rear of the thighs).

Hand off

Assistance in getting a weight to a starting position for an exercise; also called a *lift off*.

Hard gainer

Opposite of *easy gainer*. A hard gainer is the genetically average or disadvantaged drug-free person, usually male, that typifies most trainees. Hard gainers are usually naturally thin, although there are fat hard gainers. Hard gainers respond poorly, or not at all, to conventional training methods, and vary in their degree of "hardgainingness."

Although the term *hard gainer* is common in the bodybuilding world, it's a misnomer. Because hard gainers are the majority, it would be more accurate to call them *normal gainers*. As it is, the term hard gainer implies a condition that's abnormal.

Heart rate monitor

Two-part device that provides instant, accurate feedback on heart rate. There's the heart sensor that's strapped around the chest to register the electric pulses of the heart, and the receiver—a special wrist watch—that provides the visual indication of heart rate. The sensor may need to be damp where it touches the skin, in order to work properly.

Heart rate reserve

The difference between maximum heart rate and resting heart rate.

Heavy weights, and light weights

These terms are used in a confusing way, and often their use has to be interpreted by the context. Some trainees use *heavy* to mean a weight that can be handled for fewer than five reps, whereas others use it to refer to a weight that's the *maximum* that can be handled regardless of whether it's for five, ten, or another number of reps. Some trainees use *light* to mean a weight that enables a lot of reps to be performed, even if performed until exhaustion. Such "light" work is tough.

Others use *light* to mean any weight that's substantially less than what could be used for the rep count under consideration. For example, if a trainee is capable of using 250 pounds for ten reps, and performs ten reps with 200 pounds, the 200 pounds would be considered light.

Some trainees refer to the light weights a weaker person uses even if that person is training with maximum intensity and with weights that are heavy for him—in such cases, *heavy* and *light* are relative terms.

In this book a light weight means that the set's rep target can be met easily, with little or no strain. A heavy weight is one that demands much effort to complete the set's rep target regardless of how many reps that is. For example, if a beginner can just manage ten reps with 100 pounds in the squat, that would be a heavy weight for him; and if an experienced man can just manage ten reps with 500 pounds, then 250 pounds for ten reps would be light for him.

Hernia

An abnormal protrusion of an organ, or part of an organ or other bodily structure, through the wall of the body cavity in which it's normally contained, especially in the abdominal region.

Herniated disk

Herniation or protrusion of the intervertebral disk of the spine, which may impinge on spinal nerve roots.

hGH

Human growth hormone.

HIT

Acronym for *high-intensity training*, which means different things to different trainees. It's often interpreted as meaning single work sets, one for each exercise, typically of rep counts other than low reps, each work set taken to the point of momentary muscular failure, with minimal rest between exercises and in some cases only sufficient time to move from one piece of equipment to another. Full-body routines are the norm, repeated two or three times per week. Within this basic format there's a moderate interpretation where there's only one full-body, high-intensity workout per week. The other one or two workouts would comprise of sets a few reps short of maximum effort, to try to prevent exceeding the body's recuperative abilities. Three or even two full-body, high-intensity workouts per week are excessive for many trainees.

The phrase *high-intensity training* is also used, generally, to mean hard work, although just how hard *hard* is, varies. Some bodybuilders who use high-volume routines boast of training in a high-intensity way. It's not possible to train hard *and* long. High-intensity training and high-volume training are incompatible—each precludes the other.

High-intensity training is sometimes used to refer to a given percentage of one's absolute best lift for a single rep, for a given number of reps, such as 65% of one's max, for six reps. Above a certain percentage is deemed to be high intensity, by some coaches. But this can be misleading. For example, 65% of one's maximum, worked until failure, requires far more effort and is much more intensive than 85% of one's maximum for just two reps.

Home gym

A gym at one's home—perhaps in a garage—as against a commercial or institutional gym. Institutional gyms are found in colleges, and YMCAs.

Hormone

A regulatory substance produced in a gland or other organ that's carried in the blood to another part of the body, where it stimulates specific responses.

HR

Heart rate.

HRmax

Maximum heart rate.

HR reserve

Heart rate reserve.
See *Heart rate reserve*.

HRrest

Heart rate at rest.

Humerus

Bone of the arm (above the elbow).

Hyperextension

Overextension of a limb or other bodypart.

Hyperglycemia

Abnormally high level of glucose in the blood, often associated with diabetes.

Hypermobility

Excessive movement in a joint.

Hyperplasia

Abnormal multiplication of cells; enlargement of a part because of an abnormal, numerical increase of its cells, such as muscle fibers, which doesn't appear to take place in humans.

Hypertension

High blood pressure.

Hypertrophy

Increase in size of a tissue (usually muscle), or organ—opposite of atrophy.

Hypoglycemia

An abnormally low concentration of glucose in the blood, usually resulting from excess production of insulin, or inadequate intake of food.

I

IFBB

International Federation of Bodybuilders, the organization founded by brothers Joe and Ben Weider, in the 1940s, to organize bodybuilding competitions.

Indirect effect

The belief that when a given muscle grows in response to training, the whole musculature of the body grows, although to a much lesser degree. There have been reports, for example, that training one arm has reduced the atrophy in the musculature of the other arm, which was in a cast. The greater the muscle mass directly involved in an exercise, the greater the musculature that's indirectly affected by that exercise.

Inferior

Directional term meaning lower in place or location, or toward the feet—opposite of *superior*.

Inflammation

Localized, protective response produced by destruction or injury of tissues—characterized by redness, swelling, pain, tenderness, heat, and disturbed function of an area of the body.

Inguinal

Of, pertaining to, or situated in the groin—for example, an inguinal injury.

Insertion, of a muscle

The point of attachment of a skeletal muscle that *moves* when that muscle contracts—opposite of the *origin* point. For example, the insertion of the calf or gastrocnemius is the calcaneus or heel bone.

Insomnia

A condition where one is unable to fall asleep, or where one awakens prematurely and is often unable to return to sleep.

Insulin

A hormone produced by the pancreas that enables cells to take in glucose, among many other effects.

Intensifiers

Exercise intensifiers are methods of intensifying a set beyond the point at which a trainee has completed the maximum number of reps under his or her own efforts, with a constant weight. The intensifiers include drop sets, forced reps, and negative-only reps. They have no place in a beginner's program. Other trainees may find intensifiers helpful, but only if they are used sparingly. They are commonly misused, with negative consequences.

Intensity

In this book, intensity is the *relative* degree of effort put into training. High-intensity exercise is hard training, whereas low-intensity exercise involves a much reduced effort level. Sufficient intensity of effort is required to stimulate muscular growth, although the precise degree of effort required is unknown.

Many coaches and organizations, however, define intensity in terms of a given percentage of one's single-rep maximum (1RM) for a specific exercise. For example, six reps at 75% of 1RM involves a higher intensity level than six reps at 65% of one's 1RM. Although this interpretation of intensity can be applied to all trainees, it requires knowledge of individual 1RMs. Testing for a 1RM in any given exercise is fraught with a high chance of injury, and should be avoided by all beginners. It's not even necessary for non-beginners to test for 1RMs, unless they are competitive lifters. It's possible, however, using conversion tables, to calculate 1RMs based on multiple-rep achievements. This is a much safer way to discover 1RMs.

Intervertebral disk

A cartilaginous disk that lies between vertebrae.

Intestine

The part of the digestive tract that extends from the stomach to the anus, consisting of the small and large intestines.

Involuntary muscle

Muscle that's not subject to voluntary control, such as in the digestive tract.

Iron Game

Umbrella term to include all forms of activities that focus on strength training, weight training, or weight lifting in some form. The principle activities are bodybuilding, Olympic weightlifting, and powerlifting.

Isokinetic exercise

Isokinetic exercise is an attempt at providing accommodating resistance, that is, resistance that, in theory, changes over the course of an individual rep of an exercise in line with the strength curve of the exercise—more resistance is provided where the muscle is strongest. In isokinetic exercise the accommodating resistance aims to keep the speed of movement constant for a given machine. The bar will move only at a certain speed regardless of how hard it's pushed or pulled. The greater the force exerted by the user, the greater the force that the apparatus exerts in response. Even a small effort will move the bar, which makes it easy not to work hard. You can reduce your effort and yet the bar will still move to completion. Progression can't be controlled like with plate-loaded or weight-stack equipment. Isokinetic exercise never took off, at least in part because of the theoretical value not working in practice.

Nautilus machines aren't isokinetic.

Isolation exercises

As noted earlier, exercises are commonly categorized into two basic types: isolation (*single*-joint), or compound (*multi*-joint). Isolation exercises are often tagged as *small*, *little* and *minor* ones, or the *supplementary*, *auxiliary* and *accessory* movements, whereas the compound exercises are often tagged as *big*, *major* or *core* movements. This is, however, an oversimplification, and some of its shortcomings were noted under *Compound exercises*.

Isolation exercises are often thought of as being inferior to compound exercises. Isolation exercises can be valuable if used properly, but some are more valuable than others. Some are essential for a balanced exercise program.

Also see *Compound exercises*.

Isometric exercise

Muscular contraction without movement—the muscles and joints don't move. Pushing against the jambs of a doorway is an example.

Isotonic exercise

Muscular action where the length of the muscle changes during exercise, while the resistance or weight stays constant. Normal weight training is an example.

J

Joint capsule

The sac-like envelope that encloses the cavity of a synovial joint, for strength and protection of the joint. It consists of a fibrous membrane, and a synovial membrane. The capsule adheres firmly to the outer layer of the articulating bones.

Juice

Slang term for *anabolic steroids*.

K

Ketogenesis

The production of ketone bodies in the body, as in diabetes mellitus, or low-carbohydrate weight-loss diets.

Ketogenic diet

A diet involving the restriction of carbohydrates to the point of inducing significant levels of ketones in the bloodstream.

Also see *CKD* (cyclical ketogenic diet).

Kilocalories (kcals)

The amount of heat required to raise one kilogram of water from 14.5 degrees C to 15.5 degrees C, equal to 1,000 calories. The calories referred to in nutrition are actually kilocalories.

Kinesiology

The study of muscular and skeletal mechanics of body movement.

Knee wraps

Thick, elastic-like bandages used to wrap around the knee in an effort to provide support for the joint. Wraps are commonly used by powerlifters, to boost their performances artificially. They are used by some trainees as crutches, or to mask a joint problem. Avoid wraps.

Knurling

Crosshatched grooves on barbells, dumbbells, and other training bars, to roughen the surface to help maintain a firm grip on the bar. Your grip will last longer, and be more secure, on a knurled bar than a smooth one.

Kyphosis

Abnormally increased convex or rearward curvature of the thoracic spine, when seen in the side view. A hunch-back deformity is an example of hyperkyphosis.

L

Lactic acid

An acid produced by muscle cells during intensive exercise in the absence or deficiency of oxygen, when oxygen is used faster than it can be delivered, leading to intense discomfort, and cessation of exertion. It's sometimes known as *lactate*.

Lactose intolerance

An inability to digest lactose (milk sugar), resulting from insufficient production of the enzyme lactase.

Lateral

Directional term meaning to the side of the body or bodypart, away from the central plane.

Lat machine

Piece of exercise equipment that typically has one or two pulleys, and enables a bar to be pulled from overhead to the upper chest, with the resistance suspended from a cable that runs over the pulley(s). The older models are invariably plate-loaded, whereas the more recent models may have built-in weight stacks. The major muscles worked by this machine include the latissimus dorsi, hence the name of the apparatus.

Lats

Abbreviation for the latissimus dorsi muscles (on the back, beneath the armpits).

Layoff

Extended rest period from training, which may be planned, or enforced.

Lean body mass or weight

This refers to everything in the body except fat, including bone, organs, skin, muscle, and connective tissue.

Lifter

Anyone who lifts weights.

Lifting belt

Belt made out of leather or synthetic material, usually four to six inches wide at the back and sometimes less at the front, usually with a buckle. Lifting belts are heavily used by powerlifters, but are usually crutches for other trainees. The best lifting belt is a strong, well-developed corset of midsection musculature. Not wearing a belt helps your body to strengthen its core musculature.

Lift off

Assistance in getting a weight to a starting position for an exercise. It's also called a *hand off*.

Ligament

A band of strong tissue, usually white and fibrous, serving to connect bones (at joints), and support muscles, organs, and fascia.

Light weights

See *Heavy weights, and light weights*.

Lipid

Fat.

Little discs

Weight plates or discs lighter than the smallest ones typically available in most gyms. Commonly, 2.5 pounds or 1.25 kilos are the smallest plates available. The little discs, or *microloads,* are plates that weigh, for example, 0.5 and 1.0 pound, and 0.1, 0.25, and 0.5 kilo. Instead of progressing from 150 pounds to 155 in one jump (using two 2.5-pound plates), for example, use the little gems to progress by one pound at a time. This can be invaluable for ensuring steady, gradual, safe, and consistent progress. Little plates can be placed on adjustable barbells, and adjustable dumbbells. They can also be pinned onto weight stacks.

Large washers, available from some hardware stores, are a reduced-cost alternative to specially made little gems. Find how many washers are needed to produce one pound, then slip that number on a barbell for an increment of one pound, or half as many for half a pound. Another alternative, also available from some hardware stores or ironmongers, is chain. Have lengths of chain cut to the weight you want—for instance, half a pound per length. The chains can be jammed between plates on a barbell, or hung from a weight belt for some exercises.

Lockout

The final few inches of an exercise before the joints are fully extended, or locked out.

Logbook

A written record of the weights, sets, and reps performed at each workout, to provide, among other things, a statement of what needs to be surpassed next time in order to register a progressive workout. A logbook is also called a *training log* or *training diary*.

Lordosis

There is, confusingly, variation with how lordosis is interpreted.

If you stand upright with your head, buttocks, and heels against a wall, there should be sufficient space between your lower back and the wall to fit your hand through. This is a normal and desired concave or inward (toward the navel) curvature of the lower spine provided it can be maintained as your natural posture as you move around. When the degree of curvature is exaggerated, it's termed *lordosis*; and when it's highly exaggerated, it's termed *hyperlordosis* or *sway back,* where the butt sticks out substantially and the belly protrudes in a pronounced way. When there's no curvature in the lower back, posture is poor, and usually accompanied by rounded or slouched shoulders (or kyphosis).

Although lordosis is often used to signify a defect—namely, excessive curvature of the lower spine—sometimes it's used to describe the normal, healthy curvature. Some chiropractors use the term *normal lordosis*, whereas most medical people may use *lordosis* as a standalone term to indicate an *increased* concave curvature of the lower back. The exact rendering of the usage of the word aside, the key point is that a moderate inward curvature of the lower spine is normal and desirable, whereas increases aren't.

During most weight-bearing exercises it's important to maintain the normal, concave curvature of the lower spine, and simultaneously pull your shoulders to the rear, in order to isometrically tense your spinal erectors and put the vertebral ligaments in a strong position. If you round your lower back so that the curvature is outward or convex, or exaggerate the inward degree of curvature, you'll expose your lower back to increased risk of injury.

Lumbar vertebrae

The lumbar vertebrae are numbered L1 through L5, and are directly beneath the twelfth thoracic vertebra.

Lymph

A clear, yellowish, slightly alkaline, coagulable fluid, containing white blood cells in a liquid resembling blood plasma, derived from the tissues of the body and conveyed to the bloodstream by the lymphatic vessels of the lymphatic system. The lymph bathes the tissues, maintains fluid balance, and removes bacteria from tissues.

Machines

See *Equipment*.

Macronutrients

The food substances needed in large quantities—primarily protein, fat, and carbohydrates, but a few minerals, such as calcium, are sometimes included in this category because they are needed in big quantities relative to true micronutrients, albeit small quantities relative to the major macronutrients.

Magnetic plates

Some small weight plates are magnetic, to make it easy to attach them to barbells, dumbbells, and weight stacks.

Malalignment

Malpositioning, that is, displacement out of line, especially of posture and joint position.

Manual resistance

Resistance that's applied manually, either by a training partner or spotter, or by the trainee. If you put your hands on your forehead, and push your head against the resistance provided by your hands, that would be neck work against self-administered, manual resistance.

Max

Maximum effort for one single rep of an exercise, or where an individual goes to the limit over a series of consecutive reps.

Maximum heart rate (MHR)

Also called the *age-adjusted maximum heart rate*. The MHR typically used in the exercise world is only an estimation, using the simple computation of 220 minus age. For example, if you're 35 years old, your estimated MHR would be 185 (220 minus 35). Although this computation may be accurate for some people, it's inaccurate for many, sometimes substantially so—perhaps out by about 15 beats one way or the other. For example, fit people can safely maintain a higher heart rate than unfit people of the same age. Fit people may need to work at a higher heart rate than the estimated MHR computes for them, to produce a training effect.

As an illustration, 80% of estimated MHR is supposed to translate to a number eight on a scale of one to ten where ten is the limit—total exhaustion. If, when working at 80% of your estimated MHR, it feels like number eight on the scale of one to ten, it's right for you. If it feels more like seven, you're probably fit and have a higher MHR than the computation of 220 minus age, indicates. But if the 80% estimation makes you feel like you're close to collapsing, the formula has overestimated your MHR. Never should an unconditioned person work at 80% or more of his or her estimated MHR.

Medial

Directional term meaning toward the central plane of the body or bodypart, or closer to the mid-line than some other structure.

Medline

See *PubMed*.

Mesomorph

See *Bodytype*.

Metabolic rate

The amount of energy used by the body in a specific period of time.

Metabolism

The sum of the chemical and physical processes in the body by which its material substance is produced, maintained, and destroyed.

Microloading

Use of small weight plates or discs—microloads, or little discs—to apply small weight increases to exercises. Adding one pound is an example.

Microloads

See *Little discs*.

Micronutrients

The food substances needed in tiny amounts—vitamins and most minerals.

Midsection

Musculature of the abdominal area.

Mitochondria

A microscopic constituent of muscle cells where ATP (a source of energy) is produced.

Momentum

The quantity of motion, force, or speed of movement.

Monitor

See *Heart rate monitor.*

Movement arm

The "arm" that extends from an exercise machine, often with padding over or around the end part of it. It's against this movement arm that force from a trainee's limbs or other bodypart, depending on the machine, is applied, to produce movement. When the force is applied, the resistance moves.

Multi-poundage sets

See *Descending sets.*

Muscle

A type of tissue consisting of cells capable of contracting, and producing movement. Additional to skeletal or voluntary muscle, there's smooth or involuntary muscle such as that involved in the digestive tract, and cardiac or heart muscle.

Muscle bellies

The muscle belly is the meaty part of a muscle, as distinct from the non-meaty tendons at the ends of the muscle.

Muscle control

The static contraction and relaxation of muscle groups, and the isolation of certain muscle groups. This includes the voluntary ability to make a given muscle shiver, wobble, and shake, without necessarily any flexion at any joints.

Muscle fibers

The contractile elements of muscle tissue, made up of subunits called *myofibrils.*

Muscle head

Someone whose life is dominated by bodybuilding.

Muscle memory

When a muscle has been well developed, then even after a long layoff and reduction in size, that muscle may be built up again with less difficulty and time. This phenomenon is termed *muscle memory*.

Muscle spasm

A sudden, involuntary (without intention) contraction of a muscle.

Muscle tone

Condition in which a muscle appears firm and in good condition.

Muscularity

Commonly considered to be the condition whereby the muscles are covered with little fat, so that the lines of the muscles show. There's ambivalence with this term. A 5-9 tall man of 150 pounds and minimal bodyfat has a different version of muscularity to a man of 5-9 and 190 pounds but with the same bodyfat percentage. Muscularity is the combination of hypertrophy and a low bodyfat percentage.

N

Natural, and naturally

Drug-free, as in *training naturally*.

Nautilus

Famous brand name of exercise machinery founded by Arthur Jones. Jones, born in 1926, has been designing and building exercise machinery since the 1940s. He transformed exercise equipment by being the first to involve cams in its construction. A cam is a spiral-shaped wheel or pulley mounted on a rotating shaft. The first commercial sale of a Nautilus machine—a plate-loading pullover machine—was in late 1970, and Nautilus Sports/Medical Industries, Inc., was established in the same year. (Jones sold Nautilus in 1986, but Nautilus continued under new direction.) Jones' innovatory work spawned other exercise equipment companies.

Nautilus training principles developed along with Nautilus machinery, based primarily on hard and brief training, using a controlled rep speed free of sudden, jerky movements. The principles applied to any type of exercise equipment, but Jones believed that only when they were applied to Nautilus machinery would they produce the best results.

Nautilus double machines combined two specifically related exercises so that the trainee could apply the pre-exhaustion principle without changing machines or equipment. The pre-exhaustion technique was important in Nautilus training, and is a method of training whereby a single-joint exercise is used to fatigue a given muscle and then, immediately afterward, a multi-joint exercise is performed for the same muscle.

The cam attempted to eliminate or minimize the effects of leverage through varying the resistance over the range of motion. It automatically reduces or increases the resistance during the exercise to approximate the changing strength of the user over the course of each rep—increased resistance during the strong part of a rep, and reduced resistance during the weak part. Different cams were used for different machines. Although the user puts a fixed weight on a given Nautilus machine, the cam increases and decreases the effective resistance over the course of a rep.

Free-weights, and most other equipment, typically yield exercises that have easy and hard phases, with the hard points being called the *sticking points*. In these exercises you're limited in the weight you can use by what you can handle through the sticking point. In each Nautilus exercise the weight feels comparable throughout the start, middle, and end phases of a rep—the sticking points are eliminated, or substantially reduced.

The cams were developed to best match the average strength curves of the involved muscles. The cams for some exercises were more successful than for others, and some Nautilus machines were more successful than others. There are different generations of Nautilus machinery, with variations in design and performance. Although the cam is probably the most important feature of Jones' original innovations, there are other distinctive qualities of Nautilus machinery.

Whether the theoretical advantages of Nautilus machinery were delivered in practice, is another matter. There may not be any significant difference between the potential results from machines without variable resistance cams, and machines with variable resistance cams, and free-weights may be more effective than machine manufacturers prefer us to believe. But because Nautilus satisfies most of the features of good machinery (noted under *Equipment*), it comprises one of the best lines.

Also see *Equipment,* and *Pre-exhaustion.*

Negative rep

The negative is the eccentric or lowering phase of a rep, when a muscle lengthens. Negative reps are abbreviated to *negatives,* and often called *eccentrics.*

A generally advanced form of training specializes on the negative part of the rep. For example, with the assistance of helpers, a weight in excess of what you can lift by yourself would be raised to the top position of an exercise, and then you would slowly lower the weight under your own control. The helpers would enable you to return the resistance through the concentric or positive phase, so that you can perform the next negative rep by yourself. The set typically continues until you can no longer control the descent to a speed slower than about four seconds.

Neutral spine

The alignment of the spine that tolerates mechanical forces most efficiently, which can vary from person to person. It means holding yourself in a natural, upright position with the spine retaining its natural curves. Rounding the back, and arching it in an exaggerated way, distort the neutral spine. A neutral spine is related to good posture.

For some exercises, there are specific techniques necessary for safety that modify the neutral spine. For example, when setting up to lift a weight from the floor, it's important to pull the shoulders back and tense the spinal erectors. This flattens the thoracic curve, to put the back in a more robust position.

Also see *Posture.*

NSAID

Non-steroidal, anti-inflammatory drug or agent—for example, aspirin, ibuprofen, naprosyn, and ketoprofen.

Nutrition

The act of nourishing or of being nourished; the process by which organisms take in and utilize food material.

O

Olympic lifts

The two movements of Olympic weightlifting—the snatch, and the clean and jerk. There used to be a third lift: the standing press.

Olympic plates

Weight plates with holes large enough to fit onto the ends or sleeves of an Olympic bar, as opposed to exercise plates that have smaller holes just large enough to fit onto an exercise bar.

Olympic set

Barbell set with a revolving sleeve at each end of the bar, where the plates are placed, on a bar of total length of about seven feet. The sleeves are about two inches in diameter, and the central length of the bar is a little more than an inch in diameter. Olympic sets are commonplace in gyms today. An Olympic barbell without outer collars weighs 45 pounds or 20 kilos.

Origin, of a muscle

The point of attachment of a skeletal muscle that remains stationary (or moves the least) when that muscle contracts—opposite of *insertion* point. For example, the origin of the calf or gastrocnemius is the femur or thighbone.

Osteopathy

A system of medicine originally based on the premise that manipulation of the muscles and bones, to promote structural integrity, could restore or preserve health. One who practices osteopathy is an osteopath. The training and expertise of osteopaths varies. In the US, osteopaths are doctors, and some are surgeons, too. But in the UK, osteopaths aren't entitled to call themselves doctors, and don't practice invasive medicine. Thus there's a greater similarity to conventional medicine in the US, and a more traditional, manipulative approach in the UK.

Overcompensation

The response by the body to a given stimulus—not just training—that develops a little bit of reserve to cope with the possibility of increased demands. Muscle-building occurs from repeated overcompensation. Stimulate growth through hard and brief exercise, allow sufficient time for recuperation, and the body will recover from the demands of the exercise and build a tiny amount of extra muscle tissue. The tiny bit extra is the overcompensation. But the stimulus has to be sufficient, and the period of recuperation adequate.

There are, however, other adaptations and compensations, to do with neurology and other internal mechanisms.

Overload

The principle of applying ever-greater resistance than normal, to stimulate an improvement in strength, muscular size, or other physical component.

Overtraining

Training beyond the body's current recuperative abilities, typically in the form of excessive training frequency, volume, or intensity. Symptoms of overtraining include stagnant training weights, reduced enthusiasm for training, lethargy, sleeping difficulties, resident aches and pains, reduced appetite, picking up colds easily and often, and diminished endurance. Increased attention to the components of recuperation—sleep, rest in general, and nutrition—can increase individual tolerance of exercise, and the rate of progress; but any more training than what can be currently coped with, is an excess. The body is tremendously capable of adapting to exercise provided it's given time to adjust, the workload is increased gradually, and the training is started from a modest beginning.

P

Palpitations

An abnormal throbbing or fluttering of the heart.

Parallel grip

A grip that has the palms parallel with each other—also called a *neutral grip*.

Partial rep

Performance of only part of a given rep—for example, the top few inches. Also see *Range of motion*, and *Burns*.

Patella

Kneecap.

Peak contraction

Working of a muscle using shortened movements, until the muscle cramps.

Pecs

Abbreviation for the pectoralis *major* muscles (chest).

Pelvis

Portion of the trunk of the body bounded by the sacrum, coccyx, and two hip bones—also called the *pelvic girdle*.

Perceived exertion

The *perception* of exertion level from exercise.

Periodization

A sequence of individual training cycles, or periods, that attempts to vary workload, intensity, and other variables, to meet a long-term goal of building greater strength or muscular development.

Personal record

Best, personal achievement in a given exercise or activity, typically abbreviated to *PR*. It's also sometimes called a *personal best*.

Personal trainer

A hired trainer or coach who, through teaching, assisting, and encouraging, provides one-on-one training, taking an individual through his entire workout with constant attention and monitoring. Personal trainers vary greatly in their competence. They may or may not have any formal qualification or certification, and even if they do, the qualifications or certifications may be of dubious worth. A list of letters after an trainer's name isn't necessarily an indication of competence.

Although the personal trainer needs to have had a lot of personal training experience, and experience of training others, he or she doesn't have to have an outstanding physique in order to be a competent coach. Good coaches are usually past their physique prime, and often spent many of their youthful years learning through experience about what *doesn't* work.

Ironically, some of the worst coaches have the best physiques. Young men with super physiques, and young women with outstanding bodies (which, in most cases, they had before they took up systematic exercising), are unable to understand the lot of genetically typical trainees.

Also see *Certification*.

PHA

Peripheral heart action, a system of training whereby you move from one exercise to another, with little or no rest in between. PHA is a variation of circuit training. PHA tends to use multiple, short sequences of exercises— several mini circuits—whereas circuit training is more likely to use a single, longer sequence of exercises. How well PHA trains the various components of muscular development, strength, and cardiorespiratory conditioning, depends on how the reps, sets, and exercise sequences are arranged.

Physiology

The study of the processes and functions of the body.

Physiotherapy

The treatment or management of physical disability, malfunction, or pain, by exercise, massage, hydrotherapy, therapeutic electrical current, and so forth, without the use of medicines, surgery, or radiation. It's also called *physical therapy*. One who practices physiotherapy is a physiotherapist, or physical therapist.

Pinch grip

A grip that uses the fingers and thumbs only, without the palms making contact with the object.

Pins

The long, strong, metal rods that are placed horizontally through the slots or holes in the uprights of a power rack, to prevent the barbell from moving below or above that point, depending on the relative position of the barbell at the start of the exercise. Pins, properly positioned, are used for safety, to avoid being crushed under a weight, or to avoid lowering a weight too far.

Placebo

An inactive substance given to a patient who's under the impression that it's a drug with therapeutic properties.

Plantar

Pertaining to the bottom surface of the foot.

Plate-loaded

When plates are loaded manually onto a device used for resistance training. For example, modern barbells are plate-loaded, unlike the old-fashioned globe barbells. Some dumbbells are plate-loaded, but others are single-piece weights.

Plates

The weights that are put onto the ends of barbells and dumbbells, and plate-loaded machines. They come in various sizes, including 45-pounders, 25-pounders, 10-pounders, and 5-pounders. For metric plates, they include 20-kilo plates, 15s, 10s, and 5s. There are also small discs, for making small changes in resistance. The stacks of weights on certain machines are another form of plates.

Plyometric exercise

Usually abbreviated to *plyometrics*, which is a system of applying loads in an explosive manner—for example, jumping off a bench and quickly rebounding to another bench. This is a specialized type of training that carries a high risk, even for elite athletes, and is best avoided.

PNF stretching

Proprioceptive neuromuscular facilitation stretching—which usually involves a partner, and is forceful and higher-risk relative to the static stretching promoted in this book.

Podiatry

The care of the human foot, especially the diagnosis and treatment of foot disorders. It's also called *chiropody*. One who practices podiatry is a podiatrist. Some specialist podiatrists have expertise in sports-biomechanical assessment and correction.

Positive rep

A positive rep is when a muscle shortens. For example, when you raise your hand through bending your elbow, your biceps contracts in a positive way. Positive reps are usually abbreviated to *positives*, and are also called *concentrics*.

Posterior

Directional term referring to the rear or dorsal surface of the body, or referring to something located to the rear of an organ or structure.

Posture

The position or bearing of the body, which refers to the overall alignment of the various bodyparts to each other when a person is standing in a relaxed stance. The ideal posture is assumed to be when the earlobe, tip of the shoulder, hip joint, and outside bump of the ankle line up vertically. This arrangement indicates that an individual's overall structure is in good, mechanical balance. Variations from this ideal indicate areas of the body that don't permit the full mechanical ability for which they are designed. Restoration of the mechanical abilities leads to improved posture.

Good posture is important, not just for general health and well-being, but for safe weight training. Variations in posture away from the ideal can greatly affect the impact of weight training on the body. Good posture and correct exercise technique are needed if weight training is to yield good results without injury or irritation.

Poor posture may prevent the implementation of correct exercise technique, especially in standing, multi-joint exercises. This leads to distortion of the stresses on the body, and can produce irritation and injury, even with light weights. Poor posture usually can't be immediately corrected, as it's ingrained physically and mentally.

For help with improving your posture, consult a chiropractor, osteopath, physical therapist, or provider of Active Release Techniques, the Alexander technique, or Feldenkrais method.

Also see *Kyphosis, Lordosis, Neutral spine,* and *Scoliosis.*

Poundage

Another word for *weight*, to refer to the resistance used in an exercise.

Powerlifting

The sport that consists of three lifts: squat, bench press, and deadlift. Powerlifting isn't an Olympic sport, and has multiple organizations that try to govern it. Most competitive powerlifting has become a high-tech activity because of the use of special suits, shirts, underwear, lifting belts, and joint wraps, all of which artificially increase the weights that can be elevated. The difference between these assisted lifts, and "raw" lifts, can be considerable. Drug use is rampant in powerlifting, which further inflates performances relative to natural, unassisted lifting.

Powerlifts

The three lifts used in powerlifting competition: squat, bench press, and deadlift. They are excellent, muscle-building exercises when used properly.

Power rack

Large four-post structure with cross members to hold the uprights in position. There's a series of holes in each post, through which bars (called *pins*) can be placed, to provide range-of-motion limitation for appropriate barbell exercises. Properly used, a power rack ensures you can never be pinned or crushed by a weight even if you train alone. A power rack is sometimes called a *power cage*.

Pre-exhaustion

Specialized method of training, not for beginners, whereby a single-joint exercise is used to fatigue a given muscle and then, immediately afterward, a multi-joint exercise is performed for the same muscle. The theory is that the single-joint exercise exhausts the target muscle, and then the multi-joint exercise takes the target muscle to a deeper state of exhaustion. In practice, what often happens is that effort is held back on the single-joint work in order to save oneself for the multi-joint work; or, if one is exhausted by the single-joint work, not enough effort is put into the multi-joint work to take the target muscle into a deeper state of fatigue. But properly used, and when appropriate, pre-exhaustion can be a valuable technique.

Prime mover

A muscle or group of muscles whose contraction produces the movement in an exercise.

Program

The total package of one or more training routines. For example, it could be two, different strength-training routines (which are alternated from workout to workout), a cardio routine, and a flexibility routine. Some trainees use *program* synonymously with *routine*.

Progressive resistance

System of training whereby the weight or resistance is incrementally increased as the muscles progress in strength and conditioning. Progressive resistance is at the heart of muscle-building, and weight training in general. The body is capable of tremendous achievement and adaptation provided that the resistance is increased in a gradual way, from an easy starting level. This applies to all sorts of physical stress, not just weight training. Doing too much too soon is one of the classic mistakes of all types of physical training, and one of the key explanations for frustration, injury, and giving up.

Pronated grip

One of the most popular grips, used in many exercises. When your hands are at your sides, a pronated grip has your knuckles facing to the *front*, and palms facing to the rear. When your hands are overhead, the pronated grip has your knuckles facing to the *rear*, and palms to the front.

Pronation

Pronation of your right hand involves a counterclockwise rotation of your forearm—opposite of *supination*.

Proprioceptive

Pertaining to *proprioceptors*, the stimuli acting on them, and the nerve impulses initiated by them.

Proprioceptor

Sensory nerve terminals that give information concerning movements and position of the body, found mainly in the muscles, tendons, and brain. Proprioceptors enable the brain to be aware of spatial relationships of bodyparts without having to look at them.

Proximal

Directional term referring to portions of limbs or bones relatively *nearer* their point of origin or attachment. For instance, the elbow is proximal to the hand, and the knee is proximal to the foot. Proximal is opposite of *distal*.

PubMed

A service of the National Library of Medicine, providing free, online access to more than 12 million Medline citations going back to the mid-1960s, and additional life science journals. PubMed includes links to many websites, providing full text articles and other related resources. Found at www.ncbi.nlm.nih.gov/PubMed/

Pump

The tight, blood-congested feeling in a muscle after it has been engorged or *pumped* with blood as a result of exercise.

Pumping

A method of training where the priority is pumping blood into the muscles through exercising—usually medium or high reps, many sets, and short rest periods between sets. Progressive resistance and getting stronger aren't important concerns here, if concerns at all. Some genetically gifted bodybuilders—drug-assisted, too, in most cases—built impressive physiques from pumping, but it's not a method that works for typical trainees.

Pumping iron

Lifting weights.

Pyramid training

Advanced system of training that starts with a set of higher reps using a light weight, and progresses through sets of increasingly lower reps with increasingly heavier weights—for example, 100 pounds for 12 reps, 125 for 8, 150 for 5, 165 for 3, and 175 for 1. Alternatively, following warm-up work, the pyramid could be reversed, and start with the heaviest weight and lowest reps. This is sometimes called a *descending pyramid*. An extreme interpretation uses the regular form of pyramid training followed immediately by the descending form.

Q

Quads

Abbreviation for the quadriceps muscles (front of the thighs).

Quality training

In one sense this refers to training of high quality, where effort, focus, and progression are staples. In another sense it refers to the training that competitive bodybuilders may engage in prior to competition, where intervals between sets are severely reduced in an effort to enhance muscle density and quality.

R

RACE Method of Training

The method promoted in this book: responsible, abbreviated, conservative, and effective. In order for training to be *responsible* and *effective* for most trainees, it needs to be *abbreviated* and *conservative*.

Rack

Three meanings: A rack is used for storing barbells or dumbbells; a rack is an abbreviation for a power rack; and rack is a verb that means to return a bar to its holders in a rack or any sort of stand that holds a barbell—"rack the bar," the opposite of *unrack*.

Radius

The bone of the forearm on the thumb side.

Range of motion

The range of motion of an exercise, often abbreviated to *ROM*. Exercises can be done with a full or partial range of motion. Usually, full-range reps are performed—all the way up, and all the way down—but the "full range" of a few exercises is actually not full. For example, few trainees squat to where their rear thighs touch their calves. To squat to a position of full knee flexion, with a weight that's heavy for the lifter concerned, can be injurious, usually because most trainees can't maintain the right back positioning at that depth.

Reps of just a few inches of motion are used in some programs of intermediate and advanced trainees. These are called *partial reps*, or *partials*. A partial rep could start at the beginning, middle, or end point of an exercise, or specifically from or to the *sticking point*. Partials can be done by themselves, in stand-alone sets, or immediately after a set of full-range reps. The latter partials are *burns*.

Recumbent

Reclining. For instance, on a recumbent bike the exercise is done in a seated position with the legs out in front, instead of below as in the vertical model.

Recuperation

The process of recovering from training. The major components of recuperation are nutrition, rest (during the day), and sleep.

Rep

Abbreviation for *repetition*.

Rep cadence

The rhythm of rep performance. Although rep cadence is often used interchangeably with rep speed, they aren't the same. Rep speed refers to the speed of individual reps in a given set, whereas rep cadence refers to the rhythm of the reps in the whole set.

Repetition

One complete, up-and-down (positive and negative) movement of an exercise—a single unit of the sequence of reps that comprises a set.

Rep out

Performance of as many reps as possible.

Rep speed

Reps can be done slowly, quickly, or somewhere in between. But one person's *slow* can be another's *fast*. More than one rep speed can be effective, at least for some trainees, but fast, explosive training commonly carries a high risk of injury, although in some lifts—such as the Olympic weightlifting movements—explosive speed is a necessity.

This book focuses on a controlled speed, and exercises where speed is not a necessity. This means lowering the weight under control, and then pushing or pulling the bar smoothly and with correct technique. There should be no explosiveness, throwing, bouncing, yanking, or jerking.

Resistance

The resistance that's used in an exercise, including weight plates. In manual resistance—for example, some neck work—weight plates aren't used for resistance. Instead, it's applied by another person, or by the trainee.

Resistance training

A broader term than *weight training* because resistance can be provided not just by weights but by rubber bands, manual resistance, or any other method that resists the movement of the exerciser.

Rest interval

The rest period between sets—be it between sets of the same exercise, or between a set of one exercise and a set of another exercise.

Rest intervals can be almost non-existent (the few seconds it takes to move from one exercise to another, provided that the back-to-back exercises are set up beforehand), short (one minute maximum), moderate (two to five minutes), or long (more than five minutes). The rest interval varies according to the type of training, individual preference, and practicalities of training in a busy gym.

Rest intervals are also called *rest periods.*

Sometimes a rest interval may refer to the brief pause between reps, although the between-*sets* rest period is the common definition.

Rest pause

The short pause between reps, usually for just a second, or a few seconds. Sometimes there's no rest pause between reps because they are performed in a continuous manner. In **The Program**, there's a brief pause between reps of each exercise, to set yourself for the next rep, and to help with bar control, and technique. This pause is often used to take a quick breath or two.

Rest-pause training

Training method whereby an exaggerated pause is taken between individual reps, of 10 to 20 seconds or, in extreme cases, even longer.

Reverse grip

A grip where a bar is held with one hand pronated and the other supinated, to increase grip power relative to an exclusively pronated or supinated grip. It's a specialized grip used for a small number of exercises, where gripping strength is often a limitation, such as the deadlift, and the shrug. It's also called an *alternating grip*, or *mixed grip.*

Revolving sleeve

Some exercise barbells (not Olympic sets) and dumbbells have a metal tube over the length between the inside collars, which rotates in the user's hands when the item is lifted. This makes the resistance easier to handle, in some respects, than a dead weight. Olympic barbells have revolving sleeves at the ends (where the plates are loaded), for easiest handling. An exercise barbell with a revolving sleeve between the inside collars is a compromise solution between the plain exercise barbell, and the more expensive Olympic bar.

RICE

Acronym for the four-stage response to many types of acute injuries: rest, ice, compression, and elevation.

Ripped

Extreme definition, cuts or muscularity, to the point where there's no visible fat.

'Roids

Slang for anabolic steroids

Rosin

An alternative to chalk, used for grip support, especially in back exercises, upper-body pressing movements, and grip work. Also called *resin*.

Rotator cuff

The area where the tendons of four small muscles on the upper back and shoulder area—supraspinatus, infraspinatus, subscapularis, and teres minor—fuse with the tissues of the shoulder joint, to rotate the humerus.

Rounding (of the back)

When the upper back is rounded, the shoulders slump forward, and the lower back is flattened whereby the natural inward curve of the lower back is lost. In some exercises, such as the squat and the deadlift, if the lower back is rounded this especially increases the risk of injury. This is because the back is put in a weak, disadvantaged position for bearing and lifting weights.

Routine

A list of exercises, sets, and reps used in one training session. There can be strength-training routines, cardio routines, and flexibility routines. A routine is also called a *schedule*, and sometimes a *program*.

S

Sacrum

The fusion of five sacral vertebrae numbered S1 through S5, directly beneath the fifth lumbar vertebra.

Safety bars

Bars—adjustable or fixed—designed to catch a barbell if control is lost. The pins of a power rack are safety bars. Some squat stands or racks have safety bars built into the structure, which may or may not be adjustable to meet individual needs for height.

SAID principle

Acronym for specific adaptation to imposed demands. See *Specificity of exercise*.

Scapula

The large, flat triangular bone that forms the back part of the shoulder or pectoral girdle, also called the *shoulder blade*.

Sciatica

Pain in the lower-back, buttock, thigh, and leg, usually resulting from compression of the sciatic nerve.

Sciatic nerve

Largest diameter nerve in the body, formed by nerve roots that exit the intervertebral levels L4, L5, S1, S2, and S3. The sciatic nerve travels through the rear of the pelvis, and down the back of the thigh, and has many branches throughout these areas.

Scoliosis

A deformity of the spine in which the vertebral column curves laterally (side to side) in an exaggerated way. From the side view of the body, the spine should be naturally curved in an elongated S shape, but in scoliosis, an S shape is seen from the rear view.

Set

A sequence of reps. A set can consist of one rep (*a single*), low reps (2 to 4), medium reps (5 to 12), high reps (13 to 25), or very high reps (25+). Different trainees may have different definitions of rep counts. **The Program** employs sets of between 6 and 12 reps for most exercises. At times, higher reps are used for some lower-body exercises. Once beyond the beginner stage, some degree of trial and error is needed to find what works best for the individual for a given exercise and goal.

Training tradition and many publications claim that low-rep sets build strength but not much muscular size, whereas medium reps (and sometimes higher) build more size for a comparable degree of strength. Powerlifters and Olympic weight-lifters, who focus on strength, usually favor low-rep sets. The differences in the effects of the different reps may not be as pronounced as tradition suggests, and may vary among different trainees and different exercises.

There are warm-up sets, and work sets. Warm-up sets are done with weights lighter than those to be used for the work sets. Warm-up sets prepare you for the demanding work sets, which are the ones that have the potential to stimulate strength increase and muscle growth.

Set system

The most common form of weight training. The system whereby a specific number of sets is performed for a given exercise before moving onto the next exercise. Warm-up work is done first for a particular exercise—one or more sets—and then the work sets are performed for that same exercise, prior to moving to warm-ups and work sets for the next exercise.

Shrug bar

A hexagonal bar commonly used for the deadlift, and the shrug. It's a variation on the *trap bar*. The shrug bar permits more foot and leg room.

Single progression

The method of maintaining a constant rep number for a given exercise, and progressively increasing resistance as time goes by. For example, 100 pounds for 8 reps this week, 101 pounds for 8 reps next week, 102 for 8 reps the following week, and so forth. Another type of single progression is to maintain a fixed weight, and keep adding reps.

Also see *Double progression.*

Singles

The performance of sets of just *one* rep each. Singles may or may not be maximum efforts. A one-rep maximum (1RM) effort is called a *maximum single.*

Six-pack

Well developed and defined rectus abdominis (abs), named after some resemblance to a six-pack of soda viewed from above A six-pack is also called a *washboard.*

Skeleton

Bones of the skeletal system can be divided into several groups according to various criteria such as flat bones, long bones, and irregular bones. There are 206 bones in the human skeleton. See Chapter 23.

Sliced

Alternative term for *cut* or *ripped*, the condition that exists when all visible fat has been dieted away.

Slow-twitch fibers

Muscle fibers that contract less quickly than fast-twitch fibers, and are resistant to fatigue. They are heavily employed in endurance activities.

Small discs

See *Little discs.*

Smith machine

A piece of exercise equipment that has a barbell fixed onto vertical or near-vertical bars, and which is moved up and down on smooth tracks. It's commonly used for a number of exercises, including the squat, bench press, incline press, and overhead press. It gives an illusion of safety because it simplifies technique in some exercises, removes the need for weight stands and racks, and reduces the chance of an accident relative to free-weights. It's the rigidity of bar pathway that's the serious shortcoming of the Smith machine, because it forces you to follow the bar path dictated by the machine, but the path of the bar should be dictated by the body. The Smith machine is overrated. Don't squat or perform any type of pressing movement in it.

Snatch

One of the two highly skilled, Olympic weightlifting lifts, where the weight is lifted from the floor to overhead, in one motion.

Spasm

A sudden, involuntary tightening of one or more muscles.

Specialization

Short-term focus on a specific exercise, muscle, or muscle group, typically with increased training volume, intensity, and perhaps frequency.

Specificity of exercise

It's impossible to be a master of all components of fitness and physical well-being, including muscular development, strength, cardiorespiratory conditioning, flexibility, and low levels of bodyfat. What you get is what you *specifically* train for. This is the SAID principle—specific adaptation to imposed demands. Some components of fitness are incompatible when a high level of achievement is required in one component. For example, a marathon runner can't develop big, strong muscles; and a big, powerful bodybuilder won't make a good marathon runner.

Spinal cord

Portion of the central nervous system that extends through the vertebral canal.

Spinal erectors

See *Erectors*.

Spine

The spinal or vertebral column, or backbone, which consists of the 33 or 34 vertebrae and their associated intervertebral disks and ligaments. In adults it measures about 28 inches (70 centimeters) in length. (There are 33 or 34 vertebrae in a child, but because of fusions that occur in the lower part of the spine, there are usually just 26 separate bones in the adult spinal column.) Ribs and muscles attach to the vertebral column, and contraction of these muscles permits the spine to bend in several directions. Most vertebrae are separated from one another by oval, shock-absorbing, intervertebral disks. These disks form the cartilaginous joints between vertebrae. The spine is divided into five distinct regions—from top to bottom, the cervical vertebrae, thoracic vertebrae, lumbar vertebrae, sacrum, and coccyx.

Split routine (or split program)

Method of dividing the body into two or more groups of bodyparts, training each group with a different routine, and alternating or rotating the routines over successive workouts. For example, exercises for the thighs, buttocks, back, and biceps may be grouped together, with the rest of the body in another group of exercises, to produce two routines that are alternated from workout to workout. Although a divided program also spreads the total list of exercises over two or more workouts, there may not be the stress on bodypart training that there is in the split routine. Furthermore, split-routine training usually involves more exercises and sets. The special split routine used in **The Program** isn't typical of conventional split routines.

Spondylosis

Immobility and fusion of vertebral joints.

Spot

Assistance for someone performing an exercise.

Spot reduction

The myth that fat can be removed from a specific spot on the body through localized exercise—typically the waist on a man, and thighs and hips on a woman. This has led, for example, to trainees doing high reps and many sets for their abs in the mistaken belief that it will lead to fat reduction on the waist.

It's possible to have a well-defined waistline without having done any direct waist exercise, and it's possible to have a flabby waistline while having done daily, high-rep ab work for years. Bodyfat needs to be reduced over the whole body to produce fat reduction in any specific area. Although there are many dietary interpretations of how to achieve the result of drawing on fat reserves, the basic principle of producing a sustained, caloric deficit is the same.

Genetic factors are often involved in accounting for uneven bodyfat distribution. Some women will always have lower bodies that are, proportionately, larger and fatter than their upper bodies no matter how much dieting and exercise they do.

Spotter

Someone who stands by and closely watches a trainee, to provide help—or a *spot*—when needed.

Sprain

To overstrain or wrench the ligaments of an ankle, wrist, or other joint, so as to injure without fracture or dislocation.

Stands

Moveable or fixed uprights that support a barbell when it's not being used.

Stabilizer

Muscle that assists in the performance of an exercise through steadying or stabilizing the joint or limb being moved, but without increasing the force being applied.

Standard plate

A weight plate designed to be loaded on a bar of about one-inch diameter. A standard plate is also called an *exercise plate*.

Static

Not moving.

Static hold

An advanced technique of holding a rep, typically at the mid point, for a predetermined number of seconds. Some trainees hold until failure—to the point where the weight returns to the starting point despite the best efforts of the trainees to prevent gravity winning—irrespective of how long it takes.

Sternum

Multi-part, narrow bone that extends along the middle line of the chest, connected with the clavicles and the true ribs—*breastbone*.

Steroids

Abbreviation for *anabolic steroids*—synthetic hormones that stimulate anabolism.

Sticking point

This has at least two meanings. It's the most difficult point in the range of motion of an exercise—the point at which the weight seems its heaviest. Most exercises have a point, often about halfway up, where the resistance seems to get heavier. This is the point where the resistance seems to stutter, or even get stuck if you're at your hilt of effort, hence the term *sticking point*. If you make it through the sticking point, the rest of the rep should be easy (but the sticking point could be at the end of the rep). A sticking point can also mean a *plateau* in overall progress.

Straight sets

A set, a designated rest interval, another set, another rest interval, and so on, without any forced or assisted reps, negatives, super-setting, or other method of trying to increase intensity, or prolong the duration of the sets. Straight sets are the mainstay of muscle-building, and the most common form of sets.

Strain

To injure a muscle or tendon because of overstretching or overexertion.

Straps

Strong lengths of material that are sometimes used to attach the hands to a bar for exercises where grip failure is common—for instance, the shrug, and the deadlift.

Strength training

This term has several interpretations.

Some people use *strength training* synonymously with *bodybuilding*, while some others use strength training to try to refer to muscle-building without an association with the bodybuilding world. (Some people also use *strength training* interchangeably with the broad terms of *weight training, weight lifting,* and *resistance training*.) Training to increase strength is, however, commonly part of bodybuilding, and muscle-building in general. This is especially the case for beginning and intermediate trainees. Advanced bodybuilders often focus on matters other than increasing their strength, including muscular hypertrophy without any strength gain, increased definition, overall muscular balance, and contest preparation.

Strength training is sometimes used for building strength when visible muscular hypertrophy is secondary, or even unwanted. In injury rehabilitation, for example, strength gain and functional improvement are the primary goals; and for some athletes, strength gain is desired but without significant muscular hypertrophy, because additional bodyweight may hinder their athletic performance, or alter their weight class. There are, however, some footballers and rugby players, for example, who are dedicated to strength training but who often require hypertrophy and bodyweight gain, to help overpower opponents.

In this book, progressive resistance is a cornerstone of the weight-training routines. This is a form of strength training. At what pace, and to what degree it will produce strength improvements or muscular hypertrophy, depends on the quality and consistency of training, and how well the components of recuperation are satisfied, and the gender, age and genetic potential for muscular growth of the individual. This form of strength training can also be called *bodybuilding*, and *muscle-building*.

The specific terminology used to describe the resistance training isn't important. What's important is that you train safely and effectively.

Stretch marks

Tears and slight scars in the skin usually produced when increases in fat and muscle mass take place faster than the skin can accommodate. These marks may be caused or encouraged by nutritional shortcomings. Stretch marks in the area where the biceps, pectorals, and deltoids come together can be produced by an exaggerated range of motion in some chest exercises.

Striations

The grooves or ridge marks seen under the skin on a ripped physique.

Stroke volume

The volume of blood pumped from a ventricle as it contracts.

Superior

Directional term meaning higher in place or location, or toward the head— opposite of *inferior*.

Super set

The alternating between two exercises, done with little or no rest between sets.

When two exercises that work different musculature are alternated (which some trainees interpret as *compound* training, rather than super-set training), one set of muscles gets rested to a degree while another set is worked. This is a method of speeding up workout time, but there may be a reduction in intensity, a reduction of weights used, and a reduction in the effectiveness of the training, depending on how precisely it's done.

Super sets are, however, often thought of as being the alternating of two exercises for the *same* bodypart.

Super slow

A method of training that uses a very slow rep speed, typically ten seconds for the lifting phase, and five seconds for the lowering phase, plus, in some cases, additional seconds for the turnaround from one phase of the rep to the next.

Supinated grip

Another of the most popular grips, used in many exercises. When your hands are at your sides, a supinated grip has your knuckles facing to the rear, and palms facing to the front. When your hands are overhead, the supinated grip has your knuckles facing to the front, and palms to the rear.

Supination

Supination of your right hand involves a clockwise rotation of your forearm. Supination is the opposite of *pronation*.

Supine

Body position where one lies on one's back.

Supplements

See *Food supplements*.

Support gear

Artificial aids including lifting belts, wrist straps, knee wraps, bench press shirts, special underwear, and squatting suits, that inflate strength demonstration. Heavily used by powerlifters who compete in contests that permit support gear, but not required by anyone else. Rather than help to reduce injuries, the use of support gear can cause injuries.

Sweats

Clothing used during training, to keep the body covered and warm.

Synovial fluid

A slippery fluid that lubricates synovial joints, to permit smooth, easy movement of the cartilage at the ends of the bones that contact one another.

Synovial joint

A type of joint that contains synovial fluid, in which the bones are moveable, limited only by associated ligaments, tendons, and other tissues—for example, the knee, ankle, and finger joints. There are several groups of synovial joints, each characterized by appearance or type of movement permitted.

Systemic

Affecting the entire body, as contrasted with something that's localized.

Systolic blood pressure

The hydrodynamic pressure of the blood in the arteries that results from contraction of the lower chambers of the heart. The systolic blood pressure is the first and higher of the two numbers that indicate blood pressure, such as 120/80.

Synergist

A muscle that assists in the performance of an exercise through adding to the force required to execute the movement.

T

Target heart rate (THR)

A percentage of your maximum heart rate to be sustained for a given period during cardio exercise. THR can typically be anywhere from 60% to 90% of your maximum heart rate (MHR).

Tendinitis

Inflammation of tendons and tendon-muscle attachments.

Tendon

Each individual skeletal muscle fiber is surrounded by connective tissue. Then each bundle of muscle fibers is surrounded by connective tissue. The body of the muscle is made up of a collection of these bundles of muscle fibers, and is surrounded by tough, connective tissue. All these connective tissues, which run the length of the muscle, merge to form the tendon or sinew at each end, which attaches the muscle to a bone.

Testosterone

The male sex hormone that promotes tissue growth. Its other effects include the development of a deep voice, and body hair. Women produce far less testosterone than men, which in part accounts for the great external differences between the two genders.

Thick bar

Any bar that has a diameter greater than the usual thickness of between one and 1-1/4 inch.

Thoracic vertebrae

The 12 vertebrae of the chest region directly below the cervical or neck vertebrae. They are numbered T1 through T12, with the first thoracic vertebra (T1) being directly below C7.

Thorax

The part of the trunk between the neck and the abdomen, containing the chest cavity in which the heart and lungs are situated.

Tibia

The inner and thicker of the two bones of the human leg extending from the knee to the ankle—the shinbone.

Trainee

Anyone who lifts weights. Confusingly, some people use train*er* when they mean train*ee*. The coach is the trainer, as in *personal trainer*, for example, and the person being coached is the trainee. Trainees are commonly called *lifters*.

Training cycle

See *Cycles*.

Training diary

See *Logbook*.

Training frequency

How often you train. There's strength-training frequency, stretching frequency, and cardio work frequency. All three components may or may not be combined in a single training session, depending on individual needs and preferences.

Training partner

A person who works out along with you, largely if not wholly duplicating your routine, typically through alternating sets, albeit with different weights. A training partner also functions as a spotter.

Training to failure

See *Failure (training to)*.

Trap bar

A rhombus-shaped bar designed by Al Gerard, commonly used for two exercises—the deadlift, and the shrug—and the precursor of the shrug bar. As with the shrug bar, the trap bar deadlift employs a parallel grip.

Traps

Abbreviation for the trapezius muscle—the large, kite-shaped muscle of the upper back and rear neck.

Trimming down

The losing of bodyfat in order to produce a lean physique.

Tri-set

The sequencing of three exercises, performed with little or no rest between sets.

Trunk

The chest and abdominal portions of the body.

TUL

Time under load, the length of time a given sequence of reps loads the involved musculature. TUL may be just a few seconds for a single rep, or 30 seconds for a sequence of five reps, or another time period. The number of reps, the speed of each, and any pause between reps, determine the overall TUL.

Turnaround

The point at which the upward phase of a rep transitions into the downward phase, and the downward phase transitions into the upward phase—the *turning around* points.

TUT

Time under tension, which excludes the pauses between reps from TUL, to produce the time period of a set that puts the muscle(s) under tension.

U

Ulna

The bone of the forearm on the side opposite to the thumb.

Universal

Brand name of exercise machinery. From the 1950s it was the first mass-produced equipment that permitted a number of trainees to exercise at the same time, each using a different station from a *multi-gym*. Weight stacks are built into the machine to make the apparatus self-contained and ideal for locations where theft or loss of plates and other free-weights equipment are problems, space is at a premium, and little or no supervision is available. Universal also makes individual machine units that aren't parts of a multi-gym.

Unrack

Verb that means removing a bar from the bar holders in a rack, or any sort of stand that holds a barbell. Unrack is the opposite of *rack*.

V

Vascularity

Visible veins.

Vegetarian

A person who doesn't eat meat, fish, fowl, or, in some cases, any food derived from animals, including eggs and dairy products. The latter is the strict interpretation of vegetarianism, and is also called *veganism*. A lacto-ovo vegetarian includes dairy products and eggs, but no flesh products; a lactovegetarian includes dairy products but no eggs or flesh products; and an ovo-vegetarian includes eggs but no dairy or flesh products.

Vein

A vessel that carries blood from various parts of the body *to* the heart.

Vertebral column

See *Spine*.

Vitamin

Any of a group of organic substances, mostly supplied by food, that are involved in chemical reactions, thus helping to regulate metabolism.

Voluntary muscle

Another name for skeletal muscle, because it's largely under voluntary control.

VO_2 max

Also called *aerobic capacity*, and *maximal oxygen uptake*. A measure of aerobic fitness, considered to be one of the most critical factors in predicting an individual's ability to perform in activities that last more than several consecutive minutes. It's the largest volume of oxygen that the body can use per minute during exercise. This varies among individuals relative to physical conditioning, and genetic inheritance. It's measured in milliliters of oxygen per kilogram of bodyweight per minute of exercise (ml/kg/min).

Generally, the higher your VO_2 max, the better your overall fitness. A typical, sedentary, young adult has a VO_2 max of about 35, an elite endurance athlete is at the 70+ mark, and an endurance phenomenon would be at the 90+ mark. Exertion that would exhaust someone who has a VO_2 max of around 40 ml/kg/min would be a leisurely effort for someone with a VO_2 max of 70+. VO_2 max is strongly associated with age, and strongly determined by genetic factors.

VO_2 is a major part of why racehorses run, over distance, much faster than elite, human, endurance athletes. A racehorse's VO_2 max is around 140 ml/kg/min.

V-taper

Wide shoulders and broad back, together with a small waist.

W

Warm-ups

A general warm-up for five to ten minutes—on a stationary cycle, ski machine, or rower, for example—should precede each weights workout, and should break you into a sweat before you touch a barbell. Thereafter, specific warm-up *sets* are performed for each exercise, to prime your muscles for the work sets that follow. Warm-up work should also precede other types of exercise.

Weight

Synonym for *poundage* and, often, for *resistance*, too.

Weightlifting

Specialized weightlifting as performed in the Olympic Games (or *Olympic-style lifting*, or *Olympic-style weightlifting*), as distinct from bodybuilding, powerlifting, strength training, or any other form of lifting weights. Olympic weightlifting consists of two events: the snatch, and the clean and jerk. Training for Olympic weightlifting also involves a number of assistance exercises. Some people, however, use weightlifting or weight lifting in a general sense, for any form of lifting weights.

Weights

Barbell plates. These are used for barbells, dumbbells, and plate-loaded machines. Weights may also be used, in a broader sense, to refer to plates *and* any equipment that employs weight plates.

Weight stack

Many machines—selectorized ones—have built-in plates in the form of a stack, akin to a vertical pile of thin bricks. This is a weight stack. A small pin is slotted in at the appropriate height to select the required weight. Weight stacks usually have increments such as 10 or 15 pounds per level. To produce gradual progression, small plates may be fixed onto the weight stack by putting the loading pin through the small plates prior to the pin going into the stack.

Weight training

An umbrella term used to include all types of training that involve the use of weights, with each type having its own goals and methods, but all forms having much in common.

Here's most of the entry on *Weight training* in the ENCYCLOPAEDIA BRITANNICA:

> Weight training is a system of physical conditioning using such weights as barbells and dumbbells and other devices, including Nautilus machines. It is a training system rather than a competitive sport such as weight lifting or power lifting.

> Weight training is used both for physical rehabilitation and for athletic and general conditioning. Athletes use it to improve their performance by increasing strength and endurance. It is used extensively by track-and-field athletes, swimmers, football players, and soccer players, as well as by other sportsmen for whom basic strength is important to their training program.

> Weight training also is used to promote general physical fitness and conditioning and to develop the musculature for physique and body-building contests.

> Generally, the type and number of exercises vary with the practitioner's objectives, age, sex, weight, and experience. Because of this, weight training is best performed under the direction of an experienced coach or physical therapist.

Weight tree

Apparatus to store weight plates on while they aren't in use.

Wheels

Slang for the *lower limbs*, also sometimes called *pins*.

Working in

Cooperatively working with a fellow trainee on a given exercise, typically through alternating sets. "Can I work in with you?" is a common gym refrain.

Workout

A bodybuilding, strength-training, cardio, or flexibility session.

Work sets

The demanding sets of a given exercise, as distinct from warm-up sets. Work sets have the potential to stimulate muscular growth and strength increase.

Y

Yoga

Many people consider the development of flexibility alone to be yoga, but the postures that promote suppleness are only a *part* of yoga. Hatha yoga is the main branch of yoga known in the West. Hatha yoga is an umbrella term for physical yoga, which emphasizes postures that develop suppleness, and yield health benefits. It also uses other physical practices including breath control, and possibly gestures and cleansing practices, according to the particular style. Hatha yoga styles include Ashtanga, Bikram, Iyengar, Kripalu, Satyananda, and Sivananda.

Yoga is a school of philosophy and holistic health—not religion—that originated in India over 5,000 years ago. It prescribes a course of physical and mental disciplines for attaining liberation from the material world and union of the self with the Supreme Being or ultimate principle. Hatha yoga, or asana, is one of the eight branches of yoga. The branches vary in the relative attention they give to physical and non-physical practices.

Westerners usually practice yoga techniques, especially postures, divorced from yoga's traditional background. Yoga postures can maintain and even restore one's physical health, but the full power of yoga is much greater.

Here's most of the entry on *Hatha Yoga* in the ENCYCLOPAEDIA BRITANNICA:

> (Sanskrit: "Union of Force"), a school of Indian philosophy that stresses mastery of the body as a way of attaining spiritual perfection. It is an outgrowth of the Yoga school of Indian philosophy.
>
> Hatha Yoga places great importance on purificatory processes, regulation of breathing (pranayama), and the adoption of bodily postures called asanas.
>
> Hatha Yoga has grown in popularity in the West as a form of exercise and relaxation. Western physiologists and psychologists have also become interested in it and in related forms of Yoga that focus on the control of bodily processes. Adept Yoga practitioners have shown

remarkable abilities to lower their own blood pressure and to regulate body temperature and respiration rate.

And here's most of the entry on *Yoga* in the ENCYCLOPAEDIA BRITANNICA:

(Sanskrit: "Yoking," or "Union"), one of the six orthodox systems (darshans) of Indian philosophy. Its influence has been widespread among many other schools of Indian thought. Its basic text is the *Yoga-Sutras* by Patanjali.

The *Yoga-Sutras* seems to span several centuries, the first three volumes apparently written in the 2nd century BC and the last book in the 5th century AD. Authorities tend to credit more than one author writing under this name, although there is wide variance in opinion. There is a possibility that many men used this name, as it was used by the authors of a number of other works on such diverse subjects as medicine, metrics, music, and alchemy. Patanjali itself is a pseudonym, because it denotes no caste and implies divine descent from the Great Serpent, Sesa.

Generally, the Yoga process is described in eight stages (astanga-yoga, "eight-membered Yoga"). The first two stages are ethical preparations. They are yama ("restraint"), which denotes abstinence from injury (ahimsa), falsehood, stealing, lust, and avarice; and niyama ("observance"), which denotes cleanliness of body, contentment, austerity, study, and devotion to God.

The next two stages are physical preparations. Asana ("seat"), a series of exercises in physical posture, is intended to condition the aspirant's body and make it supple, flexible, and healthy. Mastery of the asanas is reckoned by one's ability to hold one of the prescribed postures for an extended period of time without involuntary movement or physical distractions. Pranayama ("breath control") is a series of exercises intended to stabilize the rhythm of breathing in order to encourage complete respiratory relaxation.

The fifth stage, pratyahara ("withdrawal"), involves control of the senses, or the ability to withdraw the attention of the senses from outward objects to the mind.

The first five stages are called external aids to Yoga; the remaining three are purely mental or internal aids. Dharana ("holding on") is the ability to hold and confine awareness of externals to one object for a long period of time (a common exercise is fixing the mind on an object of meditation, such as the tip of the nose or an image of the deity). Dhyana ("concentrated meditation") is the uninterrupted contemplation of the object of meditation, beyond any memory of ego. Samadhi ("self-collectedness") is the final stage and is a precondition of attaining release from the cycle of rebirth. In this stage the meditator perceives or experiences the object of his meditation and himself as one.

In the course of time, certain stages of Yoga became ends in themselves, notably, the breathing exercises and sitting postures, as in the Yoga school of Hatha Yoga. Patanjali's Yoga is sometimes known as Raja ("Royal") Yoga, to distinguish it from the other schools.

In the 20th century, the philosophy and practice of Yoga became increasingly popular in the West.

Your input, please

All books have room for improvement. Please provide feedback to help improve this book in a future edition. Let me know of any typos and errors you may find, and feel free to make any suggestions on how to improve the book.

Stuart McRobert
CS Publishing Ltd.
P.O. Box 20390
CY-2151 Nicosia
Cyprus

cspubltd@spidernet.com.cy

About the author

I was born in 1958 in Stockton-on-Tees, England. I started resistance training at age 14, when I got a set of chest expanders. In 1973 I started weight training, in a gym at a local community center. That became the focus of my life until, in 1978, I went to college in Liverpool, England, where my single-minded dedication to bodybuilding continued. This included working out at a bodybuilding gym where one of Europe's leading physiques trained. We often worked out at the same time.

This man helped me to learn a major lesson. He was on bodybuilding drugs and, generally, was a genetic phenomenon for bodybuilding. But I had better calf development even though I was drug-free and had been training for far fewer years. He even asked me for advice on how he could improve his calves. *The explanation for the difference in our calf development was solely in our heredity.* I had better genetics for calf development, but he was much better off in all other bodyparts. *I trained my calves like I trained my arms, chest, and shoulders, but my calves were much more responsive than those other muscle groups.* And he hadn't neglected his calves. He knew they were his weakness.

Muscles were more important than everything else in my life. I craved to be a professional bodybuilder. School work, social activities, and sport were neglected in my quest to build a great physique.

Despite 100% commitment to bodybuilding, my initial gains were only modest. After getting even more "serious" about my training—increasing its volume, frequency, and intensity—progress came to a halt. Then started my appreciation of "hard gaining."

I learned that there was much more to account for bodybuilding success than effort and dedication. As well as the critical role of heredity, I also learned about the need to use training routines appropriate to the individual, and not to imitate the training methods used by people who have great genetic advantages for bodybuilding. Then, instead of further years of stagnation and frustration, I had years of training progress, and satisfaction.

I was motivated to share these lessons with others. I wrote my first article while at college, and had it published by Peary Rader in the June-July 1981 issue of IRON MAN, an American magazine. In addition to writing many further articles for IRON MAN, I started writing for a number of US- and UK-published bodybuilding magazines.

I graduated in 1982 but was unable to find a teaching post in England. I sought employment overseas, and in January 1983 I started teaching at an international school on the Mediterranean island of Cyprus.

In 1989 I founded CS Publishing, and started my own magazine called THE HARDGAINER (later changed to HARDGAINER). During 1991 I finished writing BRAWN. In 1993 I gave up school teaching and worked solely for CS Publishing. Over the next seven years I wrote THE INSIDER'S TELL-ALL HANDBOOK ON WEIGHT-TRAINING TECHNIQUE, THE MUSCLE AND MIGHT TRAINING TRACKER, BEYOND BRAWN, and FURTHER BRAWN.

In 2001 I started BUILD MUSCLE, LOSE FAT, LOOK GREAT, and completed it in late 2005. In early 2004 I retired HARDGAINER. Then I had the time required to maintain book production yet broaden my interests and activities beyond training, including becoming a provider of Active Release Techniques®.

And since starting in 1981 I've continued to write articles on a regular basis for international training magazines.

I had wanted to be a professional bodybuilder, but it was an unattainable goal because my heredity didn't provide me with the potential to build huge muscles. Furthermore, I was unwilling to take bodybuilding drugs. But the lessons I learned did, nevertheless, enable me to transform my body.

I didn't become a professional bodybuilder, but I did make a career out of my passion for training, and physique transformation. And the lessons I learned, which are detailed in this book, can enable you to transform your body.

I continue to live in Cyprus with my wife and our two daughters.

– *Stuart McRobert*

Personal consultations with Stuart

I wrote BUILD MUSCLE, LOSE FAT, LOOK GREAT to teach you how to become your own expert personal trainer. That's why the book is thorough. But if you believe you still require additional help with your training, you may contact me regarding a telephone or MSN Messenger consultation. I'm here for you if needed. You may access my knowledge directly, and have it tailored to suit you specifically.

A single one-hour consultation could accelerate your progress, and help you to reach your goals sooner. Periodic follow-up consultations, perhaps of a shorter duration, would help to keep you on track, and uncover other improvements to further your progress.

> *"One-to-one consultations with Stuart were essential for getting my training back on track after years of little progress. They were extremely effective, and covered all aspects of training, nutrition, and recovery. And they personalized instruction and information to make everything 100% tailored to me. I recommend these consultations for any serious trainee."*
> – Paul Pedge, Leicester, England

> *"Stuart's specific, detailed advice on how to customize strength training and cardio work to suit my lifestyle and goals, was spot on target. It rejuvenated my training, even after 38 years of working out."*
> – David Sedunary, Broken Hill, Australia

> *"Stuart's books and personal guidance have been invaluable. Without his advice, my recovery from a serious racquetball injury wouldn't have happened. The advice I got from a consultation was especially helpful, because it wasn't available from any book, and was personalized for me."*
> – Al Asherman, Manteca, California, USA

Stuart McRobert
P.O. Box 20390
CY-2151 Nicosia
Cyprus
tel +357-2233-3069   email cspubltd@spidernet.com.cy

Active Release Techniques® in Europe

I'm a certified provider of ART (see Chapter 6). If you're interested in combining a holiday in sunny Cyprus with ART treatment for injuries, and perhaps together with personal training, too, please contact me.

Visit www.hardgainer.com for further details of both services.

Resources

Bars, plates, and other training equipment

IronMind® Enterprises, Inc., P.O. Box 1228, Nevada City, CA 95959, USA (530-265-6725), www.ironmind.com

Ivanko Barbell Co., P.O. Box 6224, Reno, NV 89513, USA (775-624-0177), www.ivanko.com

Watson Gym Equipment, Unit 8 Washington Road, West Wiltshire Trading Estate, Wiltshire BA13 4JP, England (01373 859617), www.gymequipment.uk.com

York® Barbell Co., 3300 Board Road, York, PA 17402, USA, www.yorkbarbell.com

Hip belt

IronMind® Enterprises, Inc. (see above)

Little discs

PDA, 104 Bangor Street, Mauldin, SC, 29662, USA (864-963-5640), www.fractionalplates.com

Watson Gym Equipment (see above)

Magnetic little discs

PlateMates®, Benoit Built, Inc., 12 Factory Cove Road, Boothbay Harbor, ME 04538, USA (207-633-5912, 800-877-3322), www.theplatemate.com

Shrug bar (trap bar alternative)

In the UK, contact Watson Gym Equipment (see above)

In the US, contact PDA (see above)

Torsion-spring grippers

Handgrippers UK, www.handgrippers.co.uk (0551 143 5731)
This British company supplies an extensive range of grippers. The grippers start at a lower resistance than is typical, and they provide a gradual progression in resistance from one gripper to the next.

IronMind® Enterprises, Inc. (see above)

Ivanko super gripper

Ivanko Barbell Co. (see above)

PDA (see above) also supplies the Ivanko super gripper, and with the option of round, knurled grips for increased user comfort and a more secure grip.

See pages 46, 47, 80, 93, 120, and 121 for more resources, and further reading.

Stuart's other publications

BUILD MUSCLE, LOSE FAT, LOOK GREAT was preceded by six publications. They are packed with instruction for bodybuilders, strength trainees, powerlifters, and general fitness trainees.

1. HARDGAINER magazine

2. BRAWN

3. THE INSIDER'S TELL-ALL HANDBOOK ON WEIGHT-TRAINING TECHNIQUE

4. BEYOND BRAWN

5. THE MUSCLE AND MIGHT TRAINING TRACKER

6. FURTHER BRAWN

The content of THE INSIDER'S TELL-ALL HANDBOOK ON WEIGHT-TRAINING TECHNIQUE has been incorporated in BUILD MUSCLE, LOSE FAT, LOOK GREAT—fully revised, updated, and expanded.

Each of the other five publications has unique value to supplement what BUILD MUSCLE, LOSE FAT, LOOK GREAT teaches. Once you've studied and applied what this book teaches, you may want to read some of the other publications, for additional information.

The following pages outline what each publication has to offer.

HARDGAINER magazine

From July 1989 until its retirement in early 2004 there were 89 issues of HARDGAINER. It provided more result-producing advice for drug-free bodybuilders and strength trainees than was available in any other magazine. It was free of mainstream hokum, but crammed with practical advice, and wisdom.

It spoke to the hard-gaining typical individual. But average potential doesn't have to mean average achievements. In fact, an impressive physique and a terrific level of strength are well within your reach. They key, though, is in the right approach. That's what HARDGAINER was about. Fresh information, and the expertise and experiences of a range of contributors can be found in each issue. And there's plenty of grassroots material, to show you the ins and outs of the practical reality of applying abbreviated training.

The content of HARDGAINER doesn't date. The back issues represent a wealth of experience and advice. HARDGAINER includes such features as:

1. How-to articles about specific exercises—for instance, a seven-page article on deadlifting technique, including 15 photographs.

2. Inspirational pieces on developing the right training philosophy for you.

3. Sample workouts.

4. Advice for new, intermediate, and advanced trainees.

5. Questions and answers.

6. "From the Grassroots" articles, and readers' letters.

And Stuart edited each issue, and contributed to every one, too.

While most of the first 44 issues are in photocopy format, all the others are in original format although some of them will be in that format for a limited period only. All the back issues are available, however. The contents of each issue are listed at www.hardgainer.com.

Each magazine originally cost US $5.50 (or £3.50, in the UK), inclusive of postage and handling. Order six or more copies at a time, directly from Cyprus, and get them for just US $3.00 each (or £1.75, in the UK).

Specially reduced prices for HARDGAINER.

BRAWN

BRAWN is the classic book that started a training revolution, first published in 1991. BRAWN focuses on genetic realities, appropriate role models, and most of the ins and outs of successful drug-free training. It's especially strong in the philosophical underpinning behind rational training. It also details how the genetically blessed are gifted, and shows why conventional training is so unproductive for typical people.

BRAWN is now in a 230-page, second edition, from 2000.

"BRAWN bowled me over. It's an exceptional nuts and bolts compilation of productive training practices; so exceptional, in fact, that it's avant-garde."
– Jan Dellinger
York Barbell Company

"Are you tired of all the look-alike bodybuilding books? Are you tired of buying little more than a collection of photos of bodybuilding superstars and a pile of routines that will never work for the average person? Here's something different.

"If you thought Arnold Schwarzenegger put Graz, Austria on the bodybuilding map, how about Stuart McRobert and Nicosia, Cyprus? Imagine, one man, on a Mediterranean island, who has the audacity to directly challenge most contemporary bodybuilding advice. Instead of being yet another me-too bodybuilding book, McRobert's BRAWN is unique: Its tone is serious, its manner evangelical, but most important, its focus is on things that actually work for the average trainee. 'Drugs are evil and the scourge of bodybuilding,' says McRobert, in effect, 'and forget about Mr. O-type training—it just won't work for most people. I'll tell you about some things that do work.'

"BRAWN has most bodybuilding books beaten hands down in the depth department, but its biggest contribution just might be its breadth: BRAWN introduces you to 90-some percent of the factors that will determine your ultimate success in the gym. This is a very useful book, which can help a lot of people make tremendous bodybuilding progress."
– Randall J. Strossen, Ph.D.
Publisher of MILO

"BRAWN has no hype, no bull, and no commercial messages. It's the real thing and genuinely needed in this field."
– Dr. Ken E. Leistner
Co-founder of Iron Island Gym, New York

BRAWN costs $19.95 (or £11.95, in the UK), plus $5.00 (or £3.00) for postage and handling.

BEYOND BRAWN

BEYOND BRAWN is 512 pages of information about every facet of bodybuilding, and weight training in general.

This book is not just for novices. It can save you years of wasted toil regardless of your level of training experience. It will propel you into the detailed, practical know-how needed to turn you into an expertly informed bodybuilder or strength trainee. You can learn all of this from just a few weeks of serious study. Then apply what you learn and you'll develop a degree of muscle and might that will make a mockery of what you would have achieved had you stayed with other training methods.

BEYOND BRAWN will take you right "inside" weight training, to study the practical reality of applying knowledge. It's not a theoretical treatise, or a pack of pseudo-scientific hokum.

> *"For bodybuilding instruction, BEYOND BRAWN is par excellence, featuring an unprecedented depth of practical, relevant and readily applicable training information. Even more than that, the book is a training partner, companion, friend, and labor of love. A truly exceptional book!"*
> – Jan Dellinger
> York Barbell Company

> *"BEYOND BRAWN is the most comprehensive, helpful and honest book on natural strength training today. With great care and in extraordinary detail this book covers every training-related topic you can imagine, and without any hype."*
> – Bob Whelan, MS, MS, CSCS.
> President, Whelan Strength Training

> *"BEYOND BRAWN is the book we all wish we had years ago. It's a must read."*
> – Richard A. Winett, Ph.D.
> Publisher, MASTER TRAINER

> *"BEYOND BRAWN is the bible of rational strength training . . . Page after page is jam-packed with practical, real-world training information that you just cannot find anywhere else . . . This book has my highest endorsement—it's without a doubt the very best book on strength training I've ever read."*
> – Kevin R. Fontaine, Ph.D.
> Assistant Professor of Medicine
> Johns Hopkins University School of Medicine

BEYOND BRAWN costs $29.95 (or £18.95, in the UK), plus $5.00 (or £3.00) for postage and handling.

THE MUSCLE & MIGHT TRAINING TRACKER

This 136-page workbook contains everything you need to track your progress—day by day, week by week, month by month, year by year.

A training journal is indispensible for keeping you on track for training success. No matter where you are now—180-pound squat or 500, 13-inch arms or 17, 135-pound bench press or 350—the systematic organization and focus upon achieving goals that a training journal enforces, will help you to improve your physique steadily and consistently. While most trainees are aware of the potential value of a training log, few actually keep one; and that's one of the major reasons why they make minimal or no progress.

There are sample filled-out log pages, and then many detailed blank log pages. The log pages track not only the specifics of your weight training— exercises, set-up details, sets and reps, poundages, and a comments area for each workout—but also nutrition, sleep, and body composition.

As simple as it is to use a training log, don't underestimate the critical role it can play in helping you to maximize your training productivity.

One training log will track your progress for at least 24 months—that's a cost of just $1.00 per month. And this log is built for the job it's designed to do. For example, its robust paper provides the strength to withstand heavy use, and the spiral binding enables the book to open flat for ease of use when entering data. This is no ordinary training diary.

THE MUSCLE AND MIGHT TRAINING TRACKER costs $19.95 (or £11.95, in the UK), plus $5.00 (or £3.00) for postage and handling.

FURTHER BRAWN

This 320-page book gives answers to over 230 questions on how to build muscle and might. The other books tried to give readers all the information they need to achieve life-long bodybuilding success. But over time we found there were questions that had slipped through unanswered. This book has answers to fill in the gaps, and provide further information and wisdom.

Here are just eight of the 230 questions answered in FURTHER BRAWN:

- ❏ *"I've read about a number of different ways to train in an abbreviated way, and I'm confused. How do I make sense of all the variation?"*

- ❏ *"After heavy 20-rep squatting, my heart rate is very high. Does this have the same effect on my cardio system that hard aerobic work would?"*

- ❏ *"How much protein can I assimilate at a given meal?"*

- ❏ *"How can I increase hamstrings involvement in the stiff-legged deadlift?"*

❑ *"Is muscular soreness a good indicator that I've had a good workout?"*

❑ *"Which are the best supplements for fat loss?"*

❑ *"I've heard reports of some people having heart attacks when engaged in intensive exercise, with a few of them dying. Is this for real?"*

❑ *"Who influenced you most in the Iron Game, and how?"*

FURTHER BRAWN *costs $24.95 (or £15.95, in the UK), plus $5.00 (or £3.00) for postage and handling.*

ORDER FORM

HARDGAINER
❑ Order six or more copies at a time directly from Cyprus for just US $3.00 each (or £1.75, in the UK). Please specify which of the 89 issues you want:

_____

BRAWN
❑ $19.95 US, or £11.95 UK

BEYOND BRAWN
❑ $29.95 US, or £18.95 UK

THE MUSCLE AND MIGHT TRAINING TRACKER
❑ $19.95 US, or £11.95 UK

FURTHER BRAWN
❑ $24.95 US, or £15.95 UK

For a single book, please add $5.00 or £3.00, for p&h.
Order any two books and there's no charge for p&h.

Name _____

Address _____

_____ State & zip/code _____ Country _____

CS Publishing Ltd., P.O. Box 20390, CY-2151 Nicosia, Cyprus
email: cspubltd@spidernet.com.cy   tel: +357-2233-3069
Please allow 3–5 weeks for delivery upon receipt of order in Cyprus.

In the US, please pay by check or money order. Checks need to clear. No US or Canadian Postal Money Orders. In the UK, please pay by cheque or postal order.

Money-back guarantee

If you're not fully satisfied with our publications, return within 60 days what you bought and you'll receive a full refund.

Online ordering at www.hardgainer.com

Index

Boxes are indicated by b following the page numbers—for example, 86b—and illustrations by i. Page numbers for glossary definitions are in **boldface**. *See* directs the reader from a term not used in the index to the synonym where the information will be found. *See also* indicates that additional information is available under a related subject.

A

Abdomen, **544**
Abdominal muscles (abs), **544**
Abdominal work, 243b, 412–415
Abduction, **544**
Abductor, **544**
Achilles tendon, 535, **544**
Active Release Techniques®, 17, 105, 110–111, **544**
  benefits, 113b
  practitioners, 119b
Acute, **544**
Adaptation
  injury prevention and, 174
  The Program and, 452
  workout effectiveness and, 410
Adduction, **544**
Adductors, 538, **544**
Adenosine triphosphate (ATP), **544**
Adhesion, **544**
Adipose tissue, **544**. *See also* Bodyfat
Advertisements, misleading, 523

Aerobic exercise, **137**, **545**. *See also* Cardiovascular training
  for beginners, 20
  cardiovascular training vs., 159
  graded exercise protocol, 166
  limited role of, 160b
Aerobics, **545**
Age-adjusted maximum heart rate, **137**, **545**
Aging, 71–73, 73b, 106b
Agonist, **545**
Alcohol drinking, 79, 89–90
Alimentary canal, **545**
All-round lifting, **545**
AMDR (adult minimum daily requirements), **545**
Amino acids (aminos), **545**
Anabolic steroids, **545**, **576**
Anabolism, **545**
Anaerobic exercise, **138**, **546**
Anaerobic threshold, **546**
Anatomy, 531–541, **546**
  muscles, 534–541, 536i–537i

skeletal system, 531, 532i–533i, 534
    terminology, 19b, 199b
Androgens, 520, **546**
Antagonist, **546**
Anterior, **546**
Anthropometry, **546**
Anticatabolic, **546**
Arm, 19b, 199b
    development, 479
Armstrong, Lance, 5, **569**, **570**
ART. *See* Active Release Techniques®
Artery, **546**
Arthritis, **546**
Articular, **546**
Articulation, **547**
Assisted reps, **547**
Asymmetry, **547**
ATP (adenosine triphosphate), **544**
Atrophy, **547**
Axial, **547**
Axis, **547**

B

Back. *See also* Back extension
    flat, 257b, 357b
    injuries, sore back and, 179
    lower
        exercise selection, 436–437
        leg press and, 301, 302b
        recovery time, 438
    rounding, **595**
    stretching, 42
Backdown set, **547**
Back extension, 202–207, 475
    apparatus improvisation, 204, 204i
    basic, 203, 203i
    floor, technique, 23–24
    45-degree, 205, 205i
    machine, 206–207, 206i
    progression in, 207b
    spinal extension, 205, 205i
Ball-and-socket joint, **547**
Ballistic movement, **547**
Barbell, **138**, **548**
    handling, 405
    Olympic set, **149**, **585**
    regular-diameter vs. two-inch
            diameter, 398i
    symmetrical lifting, 175–176
Bars
    bench press, cambered, **552**
    chinning, **554**

exercise, **143**, **566**
    EZ-curl, 251i, **566**
    shrug, **596**
    squat, cambered, **552**
    thick, **603**
    trap, **604**
Basal metabolic rate (BMR), **138**, **548**
Basic exercises, **138**, **548**
Belts, **138**, **548**. *See also* Weight belts
    dipping, **561**
    lifting, 184–185, 268b, **578**
Benches, **138–139**, 249b, **548**
Bench press, 208–229
    barbell, 208–214
        bench-and-weight-stands unit, 209i
        errors, 213i
        grip, 210–211, 210i
        incline, 224–227
        performance, 211–212, 212i
        positioning on bench, 209–210, 210i
        set-up, 208
        spotting, 214, 214i
        tips for, 213–214, 213i
    close-grip, 220–222
    dumbbell, 216–219
        adding weight, 219
        description, 216
        incline, 228–229, 229i
        performance, 216–219, 217i, 218i
        spotting, 219
    technique rehearsal, 54
Bench press bar, cambered, **552**
Biceps brachii, **541**
Biocranial therapy, 110
Biofeedback, **548**
Biomechanics, **548**
Blood, **548**
Blood pressure, **548**
    diastolic, **561**
    high, dangers of 182–183, 184
    systolic, **603**
BMR (basal metabolic rate), **138**, **548**
Bodybuilding, **549**
    conventional training, 515–516
    deceptions in, 519
    drug-free, 520b
    extreme achievements, 516
    genetics and, 191b, 516–517, 521b
    motivation, 529
    physique changes and drugs, 519–520
    reality check, 521b
    resistance training and, 4
    self shame and, 527–528

striving for unattainable, 528
success, 498, 525b
"train like a champion," 517–518
Bodyfat, **549–550**
adipose tissue, **544**
aging and, 72
fast weight gains and, 81
measurement of, 81–82, 100
reduction
abdominal, 412–413
body composition and, 103
caloric deficits and, 98–99
discipline in, 101
energy consumption and, 99–100
exercise benefits, 103
fat loss rate, 102
foundation of, 98–100
muscle development and, 81–82,
96, 98
spot reducing, 413, 415b, **599**
with steady weight at beginning,
101–102
weight loss vs., 97
storage patterns, genetics and, 5
Body mass, lean, **578**
Bodypart, **139**, **550**
Bodytype, **550**
Bodyweight measurement, 81
Boyd, Robert, 110
Breakdowns. *See* Descending sets
Breakfast, 87b
Breathing
exercise technique guidelines, 200
preventing breath holding, 456b
safe training and, 182–184
in specific exercises
crunch, 241b
hand-gripper work, 288
pullover, 332–333, 333i
squat, 372–373
stretching, 32b
Buffed, **550**
Bulking up, **550**
Bumper plate, **551**
Burn and burns, **551**
Bursa, **551**
Bursitis, **551**
Buttocks, 37, 538, **570**

C

Cables, **551**
Caffeine, 63

Calcaneus, **551**
Calf muscles, 31, 534–535
Calf raise, 230–235
benefits, 231b
range of motion, 231, 235b
set-up and positioning, 230–231
standing
one-legged, 234, 235i
two-legged, 232, 233i
Calibrated weights, **551**
Calipers, **552**
Calisthenics, **552**
for beginners, 20
chair chin-up, technique, 26–27
crunch, modified, 20
floor back extension, technique, 23–24
freehand squat, technique, 24–25
push-up, technique, 25–26
in The Program, 450, 472
Caloric intake
bodyfat loss and deficits in, 98–99
dietary fats, 84–87
maintenance needs estimation, 82
for muscle building without bodyfat
gain, 82–84, 103b
requirements, 81, 101
sources of, 81
Calories, **139**, **552**
Capillary, **552**
Carbs (carbohydrates), **552**
Cardiorespiratory training, **552–553**
Cardiovascular training, **139**, 159–171,
553. *See also* Aerobic exercise
advanced, muscle building and, 171
aerobic exercise vs., 159
benefits, 159, 163b
cardio program, 160–163
fitness and, 168, 170–171
genetics and, 5
graded exercise protocol, 166
harder but shorter, 165–166
heart rate measurement, 166–167
heart rate monitoring, 167–169
individual responsiveness to, 171
muscle strengthening and, 163b
rate of progress, 164b
steady-state, 8
target maximum heart rate, **155**, 161,
603
treadmill for, 163–164
variations in, 507
Cardio work. *See* Cardiovascular
training

Carotene, **553**
Carpinelli, Ralph N., 166, 446b
Cartilage, **553**
Cartilaginous joint, **553**
Catabolism, **553**
Central nervous system, **553**
Certification, **553–554**
Cervical vertebrae, **554**
Chalk, 213i, **554**
    for barbell bench press, 213
    for deadlift, 265
    as grip aid, 410–411, 411b
Cheating, **140**, **554**
Checklists, 200, 400b
Cheese, 88b, 89
Chest, stretching, 40
Chest expanders, **551**
Chi, normalizing, 108
Chinning bar, **554**
Chin-up, 236–239
    chair, technique, 26–27
    description, 236
    parallel grip, 145i, 238i
    performance, 237–238
    setup and positioning, 236–237
    spotting, 238
    supinated grip, 145i, 237i
    tips for, 238
    weight belts for, 238, 239i
Chiropractic, **554**
    abuses, 115b
    exercise fitness evaluation, 17, 105
    goals, 114
    limitations, 116
    symptoms requiring, 115
Cholesterol, **554**
Chondromalacia, 36b, **554**
Chronic, **555**
Circuit training, **555**
CKD (cyclical ketogenic diet), **555**
Clavicle (collar bone), **555**
Clean, **555**
Clean and jerk, **555**
Close-grip bench press, 220–222, 221i
Clothing, 355b
    back squat, 371
    bench shirt, **548**
    front squat, 378
    sweats, **602**
Coaches, 196b, **587**
Coccyx, **555**
Cod liver oil, 86b, 92
Colitis, spastic, 92b

Collagen, **556**
Collar bone (clavicle), **555**
Collars, **140**, **556**
Compound exercises, **140**, **556–557**
Compound training, **557**
Concentration, 186
Concentric contraction, **140–141**, **557**
Connective tissue, 46b, **557**
Consistency, 66
Continuous tension, **557**
Contraction, **558**
    concentric, **140–141**, **557**
    peak, **586**
Conversion tables, **558–559**
Cool down, **141**, **559**
Cooper, Kenneth, 160b
Core exercises, **141**, **559**
Cortisol, **559**
Cramp, **559**
Creatine, **559**
Cross-training, **559**
Crunch, 240–249
    basic, 242–243, 242i, 243i
    bench, 249i
    breathing and, 241b
    description, 240
    machine, 245, 245i
    modified, 20, 244, 244i
    preparatory movement, 241, 241i
    reverse, 246, 246b–247b
    safety issues, 244i, 249b
    sit-ups vs., 244b
    technique rehearsal, 61
    twisting, 248, 248i
    with straight knees, 245b
Curl bar, EZ, 251i, **566**
Curls, 250–255
    barbell, 254, 254i
    description, 250
    dumbbell
        incline, 253, 253i
        seated, 60, 252, 252i
    grip, 250, 251i
    hammer, 255, 255i
    leg, 294–297
    spotting, 250
    straight vs. EZ-curl bars, 251i
Cutting up, **559**
Cycles, **141**, **560**
Cyclical ketogenic diet (CKD), **555**
Cycling, **560**

D

Dairy products, 88–89, 88b
Deadlift, 256–283
  basic (conventional), 260–269, 261i
    ascent, 263–264
    common errors, 266i–267i
    descent with bar, 264–265
    grip, 262, 263i
    set-up, 260
    spotting for, 268
    stance, 260–261
    start, 261i, 262–263
    tips for, 265, 267–268, 269b
  for beginners, 424
  dumbbell, 426
  flat back in, 257b
  forms of, 256
  good ability, components of, 258b
  leverages, 424–425
  lifting belts, 268b
  maximum forward lean, 259b
  parallel-grip, 270–277, 271i, 426–429
    advantages, 427–428
    common errors, 274, 274i
    correct back set, 272i
    description, 270
    disadvantages, 427b
    dumbbells, 275
    elevated handles and, 277b
    equipment, 270, 270i, 426, 427b,
      428–429
    grip, 273, 273i
    performance, 273–276, 275i
    range of motion, 275, 275i, 276i
    set-up, 271
    stance, 271–272
    as substitute for squat, 426, 427–429
    as substitute for straight-bar
      deadlift, 434
  partial, 278–280
    as conventional deadlift
      substitute, 433–435
    performance, 278–279, 279i, 280i
  physical structure and, 424–425,
    425b
  problems with, 433–435
  in The Program, 437
  rest interval, 484
  risk ratings, 435
  stiff-legged, 278, 281b, 281i, 434
  stretches for, 454
  sumo, 282–283, 283i, 433

technique rehearsal, 55–56
trap bar, 426
Decelerate, **560**
Decorum, gym, 129–131
Dedication, 497–498
Definition, **560**
Degeneration, **560**
Dehydration, **560**
Delayed-onset muscle soreness
    (DOMS), **561**
Deltoid muscles (delts), 541, **560**
Dement, William C., 76, 80, 90
Density, **560**
Descending sets, **560**
Diaphragm, **561**
Diarrhea, 92b
Diastolic blood pressure, **561**
Diet. *See* Nutrition
Dietary fats, 84–87
Dietary fiber, 87, **567**
Digestion, **561**
Digestive tract disorders, 92–93, 92b
Dipping belt, **561**
Dirty training, 418, 471
Discipline
  in bodyfat reduction, 101
  injury prevention and, 174
  training success and, 497–498
Disk herniation, **572**
Distal, **561**
Divided program, **561**
DOMS (delayed-onset muscle
    soreness), **561**
Dorsal, **561**
Dorsiflexion, **561**
Double progression, **141–142**, **562**
Double-split routine, **562**
Drop sets. *See* Descending sets
Drugs, bodybuilding
  androgenic, women and, 520
  cycling, **560**
  dangers from, 13–14, 518, 520
  physique changes and, 519–520
Dumbbell, **142**, **561**
  exercises
    deadlift, 426
    incline curl, 253, 253i
    one-arm row, 338–339, 339i
    press, progress report, 469
    seated curl, 60, 252, 252i
    upper-body, 200b
  handling of, 406
  small weight increments, 463–464

E

Easy gainer, **142, 561**
Eccentric action, **142, 561**
Ectomorph (bodytype), **550**
EFA (essential fatty acids), 84–85, **563**
Electrocardiogram (ECG, EKG), **563**
Electrolytes, **563**
Electronic muscle stimulation, 415
Electro pressure regeneration therapy
    (EPRT), 110
Elliptical machine, **563**
Endocrine system, **563**
Endomorph (bodytype), **550**
Endorphin, **563**
Endurance, **142**, 171, **563**
Enzyme, **563**
Epithelium, **563**
EPRT (electro pressure regeneration
    therapy), 110
Equipment, 142–143, **564–565**. *See also*
        Machines, exercise
    exercise technique and, 197
    safety issues, 177–178
Erasmus, Udo, 85
Erectors (erector spinae), 538, **565**
Ergogenic aid, **565**
Ergometer, **565**
Essential fatty acids (EFAs), 84–85, **563**
Estrogen, **565**
Etiquette, gym, 129–131
Exercise and exercises, **566**. *See also*
        Exercise technique
    aging and, 71–73, 73b, 106b
    benefits, 14–15
    clothing, 355b
    conservative approach, 1–3, 16
    dangers of, 13
    freehand, **568**
    general activity and fitness, 8, 450b
    individuality in, 437b
    intensifiers, 506b, **575**
    joy of, 15b
    optimizing selection of, 423–439
    overlap, **566**
    overview for beginners, 20
    physical restrictions (*See* Physical
        restrictions on exercise)
    priorities, 8b, 424
    risk rating, 435
    specificity, **598**
    types of
        anaerobic, **138, 546**
        basic, **138, 548**

compound, **140, 556–557**
cool down, **559**
core, **559**
ground-based, **570**
isokinetic, **576**
isolation, **147, 576**
isometric, **147, 576**
isotonic, **147, 576**
plyometric, **588**
units of measurement, 21b, 201b
variation in, 480b, 503–504
volume, variations in, 507
Exercise balls, **565–566**
Exercise bar, **143, 566**
Exercise-related products, 412
Exercise technique
    breathing guidelines, 200
    checklists, 200, 400b
    compromises and, 471, 479b
    consistency in, 337b
    descriptions, 331b
    equipment and, 197
    fundamentals, 401b
    individuality in, 195b
    mastering, 193–200, 194b, 453
    overtraining, 223b
    personal coaches and, 195b
    practice, 475b
    progressive resistance and, 418
    rehearsal, 20, 48–49
        bench press, 54
        crunch, 61
        deadlift, 55–56
        dumbbell curl, seated, 60
        dumbbell shrug, 59
        pulldown, 58
        seated dumbbell press, 57
        sets and reps, 61
        squat, 50–52
        standing calf raise, 53
    rep speed control, 418, 420b
    video recordings of, 215b, 268b
Exercise weight plates, **566**
Exertion, perceived, **587**
Extension, **143, 566**
    back (*See* Back extension)
    finger (*See* Finger extension)
    hyperextension, 202, **573**
    spinal, 38, 205, 205i
    triceps, 334
Extensor, **566**
Eye exercises, 10b
EZ-curl bar, 251i, **566**

F

Failure, training to, **566–567**
False grip, **567**
Fascia, **567**
Fast foods, healthy, 89
Fast-twitch fibers, **567**
Fatigue, safe training and, 179
Fats, dietary, 84–87
Fatty acids, essential, 84–85, **563**
FDA (US Food and Drug
       Administration), **567**
Femur, **567**
Fiber, dietary, 87, **567**
Fibrosis, **567**
Fibula, **567**
Finger extension, 284–285, 484
   band resistance, 285, 285i
   GripSaver Plus, 285b
   manual resistance, 284–285, 284i, 285i
Fish, 85
Fitness, **567–568**
   cardiovascular training and, 168,
      170–171
   components of, 7
   exercise and, 8b, 15
   general activity and, 8, 450b
   health vs., 7
   muscle-building and, 7–8
Flat back, 257b, 357b
Flaxseed oil, 85–86, 92
Flex, 19b, 199b
Flexibility, **144**, **568**
   injury avoidance and, 174
   knee, test for, 43
   loss of, 47b
   stretching and, 28
Flexion, 105, **144**, **568**
Floor exercises
   back extension, 23–24
   push-up, 25–26
Food. *See* Nutrition
Food supplements, 91, 517–519, **568**
Footprint, **568**
Foot problems, 105, 116–117
Footwear, 117, 185–186
Forced reps, **568**
Forearm, 19b, 199b, 541
Form, **144**, **568**. *See also* Exercise
      technique
Fox, Lesley D., 166
Fracture, **568**
Freehand exercise, **144**, **568**
Freehand squat, 24–25

Free-weights, **144**, 197, **569**
Full-body routine, **144**, **569**

G

Gastrocnemius, 534–535
Gastrointestinal tract, **569**
Gear, **144**, **569**
Genetics, **145**, 191b, 434b, **569–570**
   muscle-building and, 5–6, 5b, 516–517
   recuperation and, 94
   training limitations, 502–503
Gerard, Al, 426
Gland, **570**
Gluteus muscles (glutes), **570**. *See also*
      Buttocks
Glycemic index (GI), **570**
Glycogen, **570**
Goals, realistic, 6b
Graded exercise protocol (GXP), 166,
     170, **571**
Grip, **145**, **145i**, **570**. *See also* Hand-
      gripper work
   aids, 410–411
   for specific exercises
     back squat, 363
     barbell bench press, 210–211, 210i
     cable row, 343i
     chin-up and pull-up, 236–237
     curls, 251
     deadlift, 262, 263i
     incline barbell bench press, 225–
       226, 225i
     parallel-grip deadlift, 273, 273i
     pulldown, 324–325, 325i
     shrug, 346–347
   staying power, 411
   types of
     false, 210i, **567**
     parallel, 145i, **586**
     pinch, **588**
     pronated, 145i, **591**
     reverse, 145i, **594**
     supinated, 145i, **602**
GripSaver Plus, 285b
Groin muscles, stretching, 32
Ground-based exercises, **570**
Growth hormones, 93, **572**
Guns, **571**
GXP (graded exercise protocol), 166,
     170, **571**
Gyms, 123–133, **146**, **571**
   decorum (etiquette), 129–131

equipment, 125, 126b, 453b
first workouts, 128, 128b
home gym, 146, 507–509, **573**
locating and evaluating, 124–126
safety equipment, 132
tips for success, 127–128
trial workout, 126–127

H

Hackenschmidt, George, 438
Hack squat machines, 303, 438–439
Hammer curl, 255, 255i
Hamstrings (hams), 35–36, 297b, 535, **571**
Hand-gripper work, 286–291, 492b
   breathing and, 288
   description, 286
   grippers, comparison of, 289i
   Ivanko super gripper, 289–291, 290i,
      291b, 488b
   technique, 494b
   torsion-spring gripper, 287–288, 287i,
      288i
   as training option, 488b
Hand off, **146**, **571**
Hanson, David J., 90
Hard gainer, **146**, **571**
Harvey, Nathan, 397b
Hatha yoga, 47b, 112, **608–609**
Health, 7, 13–15
Heart rate (HR), **573**. *See also*
      Maximum heart rate (MHR)
   monitors, 168–169, 169b, **571**
   reserve, **571**
Heavy weights, **572**
Heel bone (calcaneus), **551**
Heel elevation
   squat and danger of, 369b, 370i
Heel raise, 230
Hernia, **572**
Herniated disk, **572**
High-intensity training (HIT), **572–573**
Hip
   exercise selection, 436–437
   flexors, 33–34, 243b
Hip-belt squat, 392–397
   description, 392
   loading pin, plate handling, 406–407,
      407i
   performance, 394–397
   set-up and positioning, 392–394,
      393i–395i
HIT (high-intensity training), **572–573**

Home gym, **146**, 507–509, **573**
Hormone, **573**
HR (heart rate), **573**
HRmax. *See* Maximum heart rate (MHR)
HRrest, **573**
Human growth hormone (hGH), **572**
Humerus, **573**
Hyperextension, 202, **573**
Hyperglycemia, **573**
Hypermobility, **573**
Hyperplasia, **574**
Hypertension, **574**
Hypertrophy, **146**, **574**
Hypoglycemia, **574**

I

Iliacus muscle, 33
Iliopsoas muscles, 538
Illness, workout and, 412
Incline barbell bench press, 224–227
   equipment, 224i
   grip, and bar placement, 225–226, 225i
   injury prevention, 227
   performance, 226, 226i
   set-up, 224–227
   spotting, 227
Incline dumbbell bench press, 228–229,
      229i
Indirect effect, **574**
Individuality, 195b
Inferior, **574**
Inflammation, **574**
Infomercial scams, 412
Inguinal, **574**
Injuries. *See also* Safe training
   avoiding, recommendations for,
      173–187
   bench press errors, 213i
   foolish mistakes, 185
   incorrect exercise technique, 194
   paramount safety concerns, 187
   rep speed and, 187b
Insertion, muscle, **574**
Insomnia, 77, **575**
Insulin, **575**
Intensifiers, 506b, **575**
Intensity, **146–147**, **575**
International Federation of
      Bodybuilders (IFBB), **574**
Intervertebral disk, **575**
Intestine, **575**
Involuntary muscle, **575**

Iron Game, **147**, **575**
Irritable bowel syndrome, 87, 92b
Isokinetic exercise, **576**
Isolation exercises, **147**, **576**
Isometric exercise, **147**, **576**

J

Jogging, 163, 164. *See also* Running
Joint
    ball-and-socket, **547**
    cartilaginous, **553**
    synovial, **602**
Joint capsule, **576**
Joint wraps, avoiding, 184
Jones, Arthur, **565**, **583**, **584**
Juice (slang), **576**
Junk foods, avoiding, 62

K

Kefir, 88b, 89
Ketogenesis, **577**
Ketogenic diet, **555**, **577**
Kiernan, James, 108–109, 111, 121b
Kilocalories (kcals), **577**
Kinesiology, **577**
Knee, 43, 358b–359b
Kneecap (patella), 36b, **586**
Kneeling, precautions, 36b
Knee wraps, **577**
Knurling, **577**
Komoszewski, Ed, 397b
Kyphosis, **577**

L

Lactic acid, **577**
Lactose intolerance, **577**
Lateral, **578**
Lateral raise
    dumbbell, 292–293, 292i, 293i
    machine, 293, 293i
Latissimus dorsi (lats), 540, **578**
Lat machine, **147**, **578**
Layoff, **578**
Leahy, P. Michael, 111, 119b
Lean body mass, **578**
Leg, 19b, 199b
Leg curl, 294–297
    adding weight, 297
    machine options, 296–297
    performance, 295–296

seated, 297i
set-up, 294–295, 295i
Leg press, 298–303, 429–430
    description, 298
    hip-belt squat vs., 437
    lower back and, 301, 302b
    machines, 298, 430
    performance, 301
    set-up and positioning, 298, 299i,
        300–301
    unilateral, 302–303, 302i, 303i
    use of, 429
Leverages, 424–425
L-fly, 304–307
    cable, standing, 306i
    description, 304
    muscle strength imbalance and, 307b
    performance, 304–305, 305i
    pulley, kneeling, 307i
Lifestyle, healthy, 14
Lifter, **578**
Lifting
    all-round, **545**
    considerations for, 407b
    symmetrical, 175–176
    weightlifting, 4, **585**, **607**
Lifting belts, 184–185, 268b, **578**
Lift off, **578**
Ligament, **578**
Light weights, **572**
Lipids, **578**
Little discs, **148**, **579**
Loading pin, 406–407, 407i. *See also*
          Hip-belt squat
Lockout, **148**, **579**
Logbook, **148**, 456, 457i, **579**
Lordosis, 105, **579–580**
Lower body, stretching, 43
Lumbar vertebrae, **580**

M

Machines, exercise. *See also* Equipment
    crunch, 245i
    hack squat, 303, 438–439
    leg curl, 296–297
    leg press, 298, 430
    lumbar-extension, 206
    movement arm, **582**
    neck machine, four-way, 310–311
    Smith machine, 376, 377i, **597**
    squat, 233i, 438–439
    variation in, 197

Macronutrients, 580
Magnetic plates, 580
Malalignment, 580
Manual resistance, 580
Maurice, Dave, 98
Max, 580
Maximum heart rate (MHR), 148, 580
    accurate measurement, 166–167
    age-adjusted, 137, 545
    continual monitoring, 167–168
    estimated vs. actual, 169–170
    perceived exertion and, 167
    talk test, 167
    target, 155, 161, 603
McGarey, Kevin, 107–108
Measurement, units of, 21b, 201b
Medial, 580
Medline, 591
Mental preparation for workout, 458b
Mesomorph (bodytype), 550
Metabolic rate, 98, 148, 581
Metabolism, 148, 581
MHR. See Maximum heart rate (MHR)
Microloading, 149, 581
Micronutrients, 581
Midsection, 582
Military press, 316
Milk, 88–89
Minerals, 92
Mitochondria, 582
Mixed grip. See Reverse grip
Momentum, 582
Monitor. See Heart rate (HR), monitors
Movement arm, 149, 582
Multifidii, 538
Multi-poundage sets. See Descending sets
Muscle bellies, 582
Muscle-building. See Muscular
            development
Muscle head, 582
Muscle memory, 583
Muscles, 582. See also Muscular
            development
    aging and loss of mass, 72
    anatomy, 534–541, 536i–537i
    control of, 582
    cramp, 559
    electronic stimulation, 415
    fibers, 582
        fast-twitch, 567
        slow-twitch, 597
    stretching and, 46b
    insertion, 574

involuntary, 575
    origin, 585
    soreness, 66, 178–179, 561
    spasm, 583
    tone, 583
    voluntary, 606
Muscular development
    balance and injury prevention, 181
    bodyfat loss and, 96, 98
    factors in, 82b
    fitness and, 7–8
    genetics and, 5–6, 191b, 516–517
    metabolic rate and, 98
    motivation for, 529
    muscle weight gain, fundamentals, 82
    overcompensation and, 75
    reality check, 521b
    size vs. strength, 419
    striving for unattainable, 528
    success in, 497–498
    terminology, 543
    timing of visible increase, 421b
Muscularity, 583
Myofascial therapy, 110–111, 113, 114.
            See also Active Release
            Techniques®; Soft-tissue
            restrictions

N

Natural (naturally), 583
Nautilus (brand name), 583–584
Neck work, 308–311
    four-way neck machine, 310–311,
            310i, 311i
    manual resistance, 309–310, 309i
    speed of movement, 308b
    stretching, 42
Negative rep, 149, 584
Nerves, stretching and, 46b
Neutral spine, 584
Non-steroidal anti-inflammatory drug
            (NSAID), 585
"No pain, no gain," 66, 173, 479
Nutrition, 62–64, 81–93, 585
    adult minimum daily requirements
            (AMDR), 545
    alcohol drinking, 89–90
    breakfast, 87b, 95
    caloric intake, 81–83
    dairy products, 88–89, 88b
    dietary fats, 84–87
    dietary fiber, 87, 567

foods, healthy, 63–64, 89
foods to avoid, 62–63
food supplements, 90b, 91–93
frequency of meals, 62, 83
grains, digestibility of, 87
growth hormones, 93
incremental changes in, 65
meal planning, 83–84
post-training, 91
pre-workout, 90–91
vegetarian diet, 62, 86–87
water and, 64, 88
weight-gain products, 92–93
Nuts, 85b

O

Obliques
anatomy, 539
development of, 415
stretching, 40b, 41
Olive oil, 86
Olympic lifts, 4, **585**
Olympic plates, **149, 585**
Olympic set, **149, 585**
Omega-3 fatty acids, 85
Omega-6 fatty acids, 85
"Open" rack, 133i
Origin, muscle, **585**
Osteopathy, 585
Otto, Robert, 166, 446b
Overcompensation, 75, 150, **585–586**
Overhead press. *See* Press
Overload, **150, 586**
Overtraining, **150, 586**

P

Pain killers, avoiding, 184
Palpitations, **586**
Parallel bar dip, 312–315
adding weight, 314–315, 315i
dangerous practices, 315b
performance, 314
positioning, 313–314
set-up, 312, 313i
tips for, 314–315
Parallel grip, 145i, **150, 586**
Partial rep, **586**
Patella (kneecap), 36b, **586**
Peak contraction, **586**
Pectoralis major (pecs), 215b, 539, **586**
Pectoralis minor, 215b, 540

Pelvis, **586**
tilted, 105, 107–108
Perceived exertion, **587**
Periodization, **587**
Peripheral heart action (PHA), **587**
Personal record, **587**
Personal trainers, 196b, **587**
certification, **553–554**
PHA (peripheral heart action), **587**
Physical examination, 15, 17
Physical fitness. *See* Fitness
Physical restrictions on exercise
aging and, 106b
chiropractic examination, 114–116
diagnosis, importance of, 116b
disorders causing, 105
injury avoidance and, 174
mistakes concerning, 107
non-invasive therapy, 107–108
nutrition and, 114b
podiatry and, 116–117
pre-exercise evaluation, 105–106
resources, 121
selection of practitioners, 106, 121b
soft-tissue therapy, 108–113
treatment recommendations, 119, 120b
Physiology, **587**
Physiotherapy, **587–588**
Pinch grip, **588**
Pins, **588**
Placebo, **588**
Plantar, **588**
Plate-loaded, **150, 588**
Plates, **150, 588**. *See also* Weight plates
handling of, 403–405, 404i–405i
small, 463–464, 463i, 464i
Plyometric exercise, **588**
PNF (proprioceptive neuromuscular
facilitation) stretching, **588**
Podiatry, 116–117, **589**
Positive rep, **151, 589**
Posterior, **589**
Posture, **589**
defects and exercise limitations, 105
importance of, 118b
strength training and, 73
Poundage, 151, 472b, **589**
Power cage. *See* Power rack
Powerlifting, 419, **589–590**
Powerlifts, **590**
Power rack, **151, 590**
for chinning, 237
four-post, with accessories, 132i

how to use, 131b, 356b
safety bar and locking pin, 131i
Pre-exhaustion, **590**
Press, 316–323
    barbell, seated, 316–319
        back support height, 319
        cautions for, 319, 319b
        performance, 318–319
        positioning, 317, 318i
        set-up, 316–317, 317i
    dumbbell, seated, 320–323
        cautions for, 323
        performance, 322, 323i
        positioning dumbbells, 320, 321i,
            322
    technique rehearsal, 57
Pressdown, 334
Prime mover, **590**
Program, **151**, **590**
    cardio, 160–163
    divided, **561**
The Program, 441–495. *See also*
        Strength training
    bench press in, 468b
    dedication and, 497–498
    exercise fundamentals, 441–442, 453
    exercise selection, 437–438
    for experienced trainees, 442b
    gradual approach, 451b
    lack of progress, dealing with, 481,
            484, 493, 502
    learning curve, 444
    phases, 9
    preparatory month
        calisthenics, 22–27
        exercises, 20–21
        nutrition, 62–64
        overview, 18–19
        sleep and recuperation, 65
        stretching, 28–47
        technique rehearsal, 48–61
        training schedule, 66
    program design, 444b–448b
        exercise variety, 445b–446b
        number of reps, 448b
        number of sets, 446b–447b
        rest intervals, 448b
        strength-training routines, 445b
        training requirements, 444b–445b
    RACE Method of Training, 3, 442–
            448, 495, **592**
    Seven-Point Plan, 443–444
    specialization routines, 509b

training schedule, 449–450, 449b
variation in, 501–507
Progressive resistance, 151, 417–421, **590**
    adding weight, rules for, 461–462
    consistent increase, 478
    correct technique and rep speed
            control, 418–419, 420b
    detrimental effects, 417–418
    incremental increases, 179–180, 467b
    poundage progression vs. rep
            progression, 472b
    progress and, 420, 471
    with little plates, 463–464, 463i, 464i
    without little plates, 465–466
THE PROMISE OF SLEEP (Dement), 76
Pronated grip, 145i, **151–152**, **591**
Pronation, **591**
Proprioceptive neuromuscular
            facilitation (PNF) stretching, **588**
Proprioceptors, **591**
Protein supplements, 92–93
Proximal, **591**
Psoas muscles, 33
PubMed, **591**
Pulldown, 324–327
    adding weight, 327
    common errors, 326i, 327b
    grip, 324–325, 325i
    performance, 325–326
    set-up, 324
    technique rehearsal, 58
Pullover, 328–333
    breathing, 332–333, 333i
    machine, 328–331
        adding weight, 331
        description, 328
        performance, 330–331
        safe range of motion, 329, 330i
        set-up and positioning, 328–330,
                329i
Pull-up, 236, 237i
Pump, **591**
Pumping iron, **591**
Pushdown, 334–335, 335i, 479b
Push-up, 25–26
Pyramid training, **591**

Q

Quadratus lumborum, 539
Quadriceps femoris, 535
Quadriceps (quads), 39, **592**
Quality training, **592**

R

RACE Method of Training, 3, 442–448, 495, **592**
Rack, **152**, **592**
Radcliffe, Paula, 5–6
Radius, **592**
Range of motion (ROM), **152**, **592–593**
  aging and, 71
  injury prevention and, 175
  in specific exercises
    calf raise, 231, 235b
    machine pullover, 329, 330i
    parallel-grip deadlift, 275, 275i, 276i
    squat, 358b
  stretching and, 46b
Recovery time, 75, 438
Rectus abdominis, 240, 414, 539
Recumbent, **593**
Recuperation, **152**, **593**
  fatigue and safe training, 179
  genetics and, 94
  importance of, 75
  nutrition and, 81–93
  optimizing, 75–95
  physical conditioning and, 94
  recovery time, 75, 438
  sleep and, 76–80
  tips for optimizing, 94–95
Rep cadence, **593**
Repetition (rep), **152**, **593**
  assisted, **547**
  conversion tables, 558–559
  discipline and injury prevention, 174
  forced, **568**
  negative, **149**, **584**
  partial, **586**
  positive, **151**, **589**
  poundage progression vs., 472b
  in The Program, 448b
  1RM, 544
  singles and low-rep work, 178
  speed control, 418, 420b
  speed vs. safety, 187b
  variation in, 505–506
Rep out, **152**, **593**
Rep speed, **593**
Research, interpreting, 523–525
Resistance, 4, **153**, **593**. *See also*
    Poundage; Progressive resistance
  manual, **580**
  training, **594**
Rest. *See* Sleep
Rest interval, **153**, 448b, 468, **594**

Rest pause, **153**, **594**
Rest-pause training, **594**
Reverse grip, 145i, **153**, **594**
Revolving sleeve, **594**
Rhomboids, 540
Rib cage work, 477
RICE (injury response), **594**
Ripped, **595**
1RM, 544
'Roids (slang), **595**
ROM. *See* Range of motion (ROM)
Romanian deadlift. *See* Deadlift, partial
Rope jumping, 452
Rosin, 411, **595**
Rotary torso, 336–337, 337i
Rotator cuff, 540, **595**
Rounding, back, **595**
Routine, **153**, **595**
Row, 338–345
  cable
    adding weight, 343
    grip, 343i
    performance, 342
    set-up and positioning, 340–341, 341i
    spotting, 342–343
  dangerous forms of, 338
  dumbbell
    one-arm, 338–339, 339i
    prone low-incline, 345, 345i
    machine, seated, 344–345, 345i
Rudin, Donald, 85
Running
  jogging, 163, 164
  safety concerns, 117, 119, 164–165
  on treadmill, 163
Rydin, Rich, 98

S

Sacrum, **595**
Safe training, 173–187
  accurate weights, 180–181
  avoiding pain killers, 184
  breathing and, 182–184
  choice of exercises, 176
  concentration and, 186
  equipment set-up, 177
  fallacy of "no pain, no gain," 66, 173, 479
  fatigue and, 179
  foolish mistakes, 185, 194
  footwear, 185–186

head and eye control, 176
joint wraps and, 184
lifting belts and, 184–185
paramount concerns, 187
preparation for sets, 182
range of motion and, 175
rep technique and, 178
resistance, incremental increases in,
    179–180
risk rating of exercises, 435
soreness and, 178–179
for specific exercises
    deadlift, 259b, 265, 267–268
    incline barbell bench press, 227
    seated barbell press, 319, 319b
    seated dumbbell press, 323
    squat, 358b–359b, 387b
    stiff-legged deadlift, 281b, 281i
symmetrical lifting, 175–176
training surface, 182
treadmills and, 163–165
warm-up and, 181
Safety bars, **595**
SAID principle, **595**
Sartorius, 535
Saturated fats, 86
Scapula, **595**
Schwarzenegger, Arnold, 1
Sciatica, **596**
Sciatic nerve, **596**
Scientific studies, interpreting, 523–525
Scoliosis, 105, 107–108, **596**
Sedentary lifestyle, 450b
Self-competition, 6
Self shame, 527–528
Serratus anterior, 539
Sets, **154**, 446b–447b, **596**
    backdown, **547**
    descending, **560**
    preparation and injury prevention,
        182
    straight, **600**
    super, **601–602**
    technique rehearsal, 61
    tri-set, **604**
    work, **157**, **608**
Set system, **154**, **596**
Seven-Point Plan, 443–444
Shirt, bench, 548
Shoes, 117, 185–186
Shoulders, 40
Shrug, 346–349
    calf machine, danger of, 349b

caution for, 347–348
dumbbell
    seated incline, 348, 348i
    technique rehearsal, 59
grip, 346–347
set-up and performance, 346, 347i
Shrug bar, **596**
Sickness, workout and, 412
Side bend, 350–354
    description, 350
    dumbbell
        seated, 352i
        standing, 351i
    pulley, 353, 353i
    tips for, 354
Single progression, **154**, **596–597**
Singles, 178, **597**
Sit-ups, with straight knees, 244b–245b
Six-pack, **597**
Skeleton, 531, 532i–533i, 534, **597**
Skin, diet and, 86
Skinfold thickness, 81–82, 100
Skipping, 452
Sleep
    deficits, 79, 79b
    disorders of, 80
        insomnia, **575**
        sleep apnea, 77
        smoking and, 78
    importance of, 76
    tips for improving, 77–79
    varying need for, 79–80
Sliced, **597**
Slow-twitch fibers, **597**
Small discs, **148**, **597**
Smith, Charles A., 12
Smith machine, 376, 377i, **597**
Smoking, 78
Snatch, **597**
Snoring, 77, 80
Soft-tissue restrictions
    effects of, 112
    therapy, 108–113
        methods, 110–111
        practitioners, 113
Somatotype (bodytype), **550**
Spasm, **598**
Spastic colon, 92b
Specialization, 509b, **598**
Specificity of exercise, **598**
Spinal cord, **598**
Spinal extension, 38, 205, 205i
Spine, **598**. *See also* Vertebrae

erectors, 538, **565**
muscles, stretching, 40b, 41
neutral, **584**
post-workout stretch, 44–45
Split routine, 485–487, **561**, **598**
Spondylosis, 17, 105, **599**
Spot reduction, **599**
Spotters and spotting, **154**, **599**
  injury prevention and, 182
  for specific exercises
    back squat, 373–374, 374i
    barbell bench press, 214, 214i
    cable row, 342–343
    chin-up, 238
    close-grip bench press, 222
    curls, 250
    deadlift, 268
    dumbbell bench press, 219
    incline barbell bench press, 227
    incline dumbbell bench press,
      228–229, 229i
    parallel bar dip, 314–315
    pulldown, 326
    seated barbell press, 319
    seated dumbbell press, 323
  tips for, 183b
Sprain, **599**
Squat, 356
  back squat, 360–377, 437
    ascent, 368–370, 368i, 369i
    bar positioning, 362, 363i
    breathing, 372–373
    depth of descent, 367–368
    descent, 366–367, 367i
    front squat vs., 383i, 431
    good form, 372i
    grip, 363
    heel elevation, danger of, 369b, 370i
    patience in training, 374b
    performance, 365–366
    racking the bar, 371
    sequence, 361i
    set-up, 360–362
    spotting, 373–374, 374i
    stance, 363–365, 364i, 365i
    standing between reps, 370, 371i
    tips for, 371–373
  ball squat, 388–391
    advantages of, 432
    performance, 388–390, 389i
    set-up and positioning, 388
    tips for, 391
  for beginners, 424

cambered squat bar, 360, 360i, **552**
  flat back in, 357b
  freehand, 24–25
  front squat, 378–386, 430–432
    ascent, 383–384
    back squat vs., 383i, 431
    bar positioning, 378–379, 379i
    bar tipping, 381b
    descent, 382
    disadvantages, 431
    gym equipment, 431b
    performance, 380–381
    racking bar, 384
    set-up, 378
    stance, 379–380
    standing between reps, 384
    tips for, 385–386
  hip-belt squat, 392–397
    advantages of, 432–433
    description, 392
    leg press vs., 437
    performance, 394–397
    set-up and positioning, 392–394,
      393i–395i
  improving ability for, 375b
  leverages, 424–425
  minimizing forward travel of knees,
    358b–359b
  parallel-grip deadlift as substitute
    for, 426, 427–429
  physical structure and, 424–425, 425b
  power rack for, 356b
  progress report, 469
  rest interval, 484
  risk ratings, 435
  safe range of motion, 358b
  safety reminders, 387b
  Smith machine, 376, 377i
  stretches for, 454
  technique rehearsal, 50–52
  twenty-rep, 510b–511b
Squat bar, cambered, 360, 360i, **552**
Squat rack, 133i
Stabilizer, **599**
Stair climbing, 163b
Standard plate, **599**
Standing calf raise, 53
Stands, **599**
Stark, Steven, 163
Static, **599**
Static hold, **600**
Sternocleidomastoid muscle, 540–541
Sternum, **600**

Steroids, **600**
  anabolic, **545**, **576**
  dangers from, 518, 520
Sticking point, **154–155**, **600**
Stiff-legged deadlift, 278, 281b, 281i, 434
Straight sets, **600**
Strain, **600**
Straps, **600**
Strength training, 4, **155**, **600–601**
  aging and, 72–73
  benefits of, 7–8, 7b, 72–73
  calisthenics and, 472
  cardio work and, 8
  Consistent Progression in, 470, 478
  exercises, 198–199
    intensifiers, 506b
    technique guidelines, 453
  fitness and, 7
  hydration and, 467
  mental preparation, 458b, 471b
  progress reports, 469–479
  range of motion and, 46b
  rest intervals, between-set, 468, 476
  rib cage work, 477
  routines, 445b
    week 1, 454–458
    week 2, 459
    week 3, 460
    weeks 4–12, 460–473
    month 4, 474–477
    month 5, 478
    month 6, 480
    month 7, 482–483
    month 8, 485–487
    month 9, 489
    month 10, 490–492
    month 11, 493–494
    month 12, 495
    split-routine options, 485–487
  strength vs. muscle size, 419
  success in, 525b
  training frequency and, 489b
  ultra-abbreviated, 505b
  variation in, 503–507
  warm-up sets, 467, 476, 478, 491–492
  weight progression
    in early weeks of training, 461–462
    with small plates, 463i, 464i, 467b
    status report at 12 weeks, 471–472
    technique compromise and, 471
    without small plates, 465–466
Stretching, 28–47, 450
  for beginners, 20
  benefits of, 28
  breathing and, 32b
  difficulties in, 37b
  flexibility and, 28
  how to stretch, 29–30
  implementing routine, 46
  introductory guidelines, 28–29
  physiology, 46b
  PNF (proprioceptive neuromuscular
    facilitation), **588**
  for specific areas
    back, 42
    buttocks, 37
    calves, 31
    chest, 40
    groin muscles, 32
    hamstrings, 35–36
    hip flexors, 33–34
    lower body, 43
    neck, 42
    obliques, 40b, 41
    quadriceps, 39
    shoulders, 40
    spine, 38, 40b, 41, 44–45
  for squat and deadlift, 454
  variations in, 507
Stretch marks, **601**
Striations, **601**
Stroke volume, **601**
Sumo deadlift, 282–283, 283i, 433
Superior, **601**
Super set, **601–602**
Super slow, **602**
Supinated grip, 145i, **155**, **602**
Supination, **602**
Supine, **602**
Supplements. *See* Food supplements
Support gear, **602**
Sweating, 97
Sweats (clothing), **602**
Symmetrical lifting, 175–176
Synergist, **603**
Synovial fluid, **602**
Synovial joint, **602**
Systemic, **155**, **602**
Systolic blood pressure, **603**

T

Talk test, 167
Target heart rate (THR), **155**, 161, **603**
T-bar row, danger of, 338
Tendinitis, **603**

Tendon, **603**
Tension, continuous, **557**
Testosterone, 93, **603**
Thick bar, **603**
Thigh
  adductors, 32
  exercise selection, 199b, 436–437
  recovery time, 438
  terminology, 19b, 199b
Thompson, Mike, 107
Thoracic vertebrae, **603**
Thorax, **603**
Tibia, **604**
Timed hold, 398–399, 399i
Time under load (TUL), **605**
Time under tension (TUT), **605**
Tobias, Jeffrey, 89
Toe raise, 230
Trainee, **155**, **604**
Training cycle, **141**, **560**
Training diary. *See* Logbook
Training frequency, **156**, 489b, 504–505,
      604
Training log. *See* Logbook
Training partner, **156**, 418b, 473b, **604**
Training schedule
  aging and, 71
  consistency and, 66, 71
  inviolable nature of, 458b
  in The Program, 444b–445b, 449–450,
     449b
  timing of training, 409
Training surface, 182
Training to failure, **566–567**
Transversus abdominis, 539
Trap bar, **604**
Trap-bar deadlift, 426
Trapezius muscle (traps), 540, **604**
Treadmill, 163–164
Triceps brachii, 541
Triceps extension, 334
Trimming down, **604**
Tri-set, **604**
Trunk, **605**
TUL (time under load), **605**
Turnaround, **605**
TUT (time under tension), **605**

U

Ulna, **605**
Units of measurement, 21b, 201b
Universal (brand name), **605**

Unrack, **156**, **605**
US Food and Drug Administration
    (FDA), **567**

V

Vascularity, **605**
Veganism, 62, 86, **605**
Vegetarianism, 62, 86–87, **605–606**
Veins, **606**
Vertebrae. *See also* Spine
  cervical, **554**
  lumbar, **580**
  thoracic, **603**
Video recordings, 215b, 268b, 459b,
    492b
Vitamins, 92, **606**
Voluntary muscles, **606**
VO$_2$ max, **606**
V-taper, **606**

W

Waist girth, 81
Wall squat, 388, 432
Warm-ups, **156**, **606**
  benefits of, 449–450, 467–468
  consistency in, 449
  injury prevention and, 181
  weight for, 476, 478, 491–492
Water, 64, 88
Weight, **607**. *See also* Poundage;
      Resistance
Weight belts
  for chin-up, 238, 239i
  dipping, **561**
  for parallel bar dip, 314–315, 315i
Weight-gain products, 92–93
Weightlifting, 4, **585**, **607**
Weight loss. *See also* Bodyfat,
      reduction
  bodyfat loss vs., 97
  caloric deficits in, 98–99
  scams, 100b
Weight plates
  exercise, **143**, **566**
  magnetic, **580**
  Olympic, **149**, **585**
  small, 463–464, 463i, 464i
  standard, **599**
Weights, **157**, **607**
  adding small weight increments,
     463–464, 463i, 464i, 467b

calibration, 180–181, **551**
free-weights, **144**, 197, **569**
handling of, 403–407
heavy vs. light, **572**
Weight stack, **157**, **607**
Weight training, **607**
  conservative approach to, 1–3
  conventional training methods, 515–
    516
  mistakes in, 1–2, 2b
  RACE Method, 3, 442–448, 495, **592**
  terminology, 4, 543
Weight tree, **608**
Wendell, Keith, 110
Wheels (slang), **608**
Winett, Richard, 165, 166, 167, 170
Wojcik, Janet R., 166
Women
  androgenic drugs and, 520
  dislike of big muscles, 529

Working in, **608**
Workout, **157**, **608**
  adaptation and, 410
  grip aids, 410–411
  grip staying power, 411
  length of, 477b, 484b
  mental preparation for, 458b
  sickness and, 412
  timing of training, 409
Work sets, **157**, **608**

Y

Yoga, **608–609**
Yogurt, 88b, 89

I wrote BUILD MUSCLE, LOSE FAT, LOOK GREAT to teach you how to become your own expert personal trainer. That's why the book is thorough. But if you believe you still require additional help with your training, you may contact me regarding a telephone or MSN Messenger consultation. I'm here for you if needed. Please see page 613.

If you need further help through the printed word, please see page 615.